IN EVERY PLACE

Habbaniya - 2nd May 1941. (Painting by Stuart Brown. Reproduced by kind permission of the artist and the RAF Regiment © 2012)

IN EVERY PLACE

The RAF Armoured Cars
in the Middle East
1921-1953

NIGEL W. M. WARWICK

First published in Great Britain in 2014 by

Forces & Corporate Publishing Ltd
Hamblin House
Hamblin Court
Rushden
Northamptonshire NN10 0RU

Copyright © Nigel W. M. Warwick 2014

ISBN 978-0-9574725-2-5

The right of Nigel W. M. Warwick to be identified as author of this work has been asserted to him in accordance with the Copyright, Designs and Patents Act 1988

A CIP catalogue record for this book is available from the British Library

All rights reserved. No part of this book may be reproduced or transmitted in any form or by any means, electronic or mechanical including photocopying, recording or by any information storage and retrieval system without permission from the publisher in writing.

Typeset in Sabon by
Forces & Corporate Publishing Ltd

Printed and Bound in England by CPI UK

Contents

Foreword		x
Appreciation		xi
Preface and Acknowledgements		xii
Prologue		xv
Chapter 1	The Royal Air Force Scheme of Control	1
Chapter 2	The Formation of the Companies	11
Chapter 3	Transjordan 1922-1924 'Amman's Sure Shield'	27
Chapter 4	Troubles in Kurdistan 1922-1924	47
Chapter 5	Iraq 1925-1929	78
Chapter 6	War in the Southern Desert 1923-1928	96
Chapter 7	War in the Southern Desert 1929-1930	128
Chapter 8	Transjordan 1925-1932 Policing the Tribes	142
Chapter 9	Iraq 1930-1939	163
Chapter 10	The Palestine Riots 1929	192
Chapter 11	The Palestine Disturbances 1936 'In Aid of the Civil Power'	208
Chapter 12	Operation Compass 'Wavell's Eyes and Ears'	243
Chapter 13	Habbaniya 1941 'Steadiness Under Fire'	269
Chapter 14	Syria 1941 '… A Long and Difficult Business'	313
Chapter 15	Operation Crusader	335
Chapter 16	The Msus Stakes	356
Chapter 17	Gazala and the Retreat to El Alamein 'Yeoman Service'	376
Chapter 18	El Alamein	403
Chapter 19	The Road to Tunis	416
Chapter 20	Here, There and Everywhere…The War Moves On 1943-1945	452
Chapter 21	Palestine 1945-1948 An Insurgency Re-Ignited and Transition to the RAF Regiment	474
Chapter 22	Aden 1928-1950	515
Chapter 23	Farewell to Armour	551
Epilogue		595
Appendix 1	Commanding Officers	604
Appendix 2	Armoured Fighting Vehicles	608
Appendix 3	Establishments	614
Appendix 4	Badges and Battle Honours	616
Appendix 5	Car Names	618
Appendix 6	The RAF Armoured Cars Association	620
Bibliography		622
Index		631

MAPS

Map 1	Palestine and Transjordan 1921-1923	15
Map 2	Iraq	24
Map 3	Transjordan	29
Map 4	Suweilah 16 September 1923	32
Map 5	Ziza 14 August 1924	41
Map 6	Northern and Central Iraq	51
Map 7	Kirkuk-Chamchamal-Sulaimaniya	66
Map 8	Mosul and Zakho	73
Map 9	The early Southern Desert raids	97
Map 10	Southern Desert 1924-1925	102
Map 11	Southern Desert - Renewal of raiding November 1927-January 1928	108
Map 12	Nuqrat Sulman	115
Map 13	Busaiyah Fort	116
Map 14	Southern Desert February-April 1928	121
Map 15	Southern Desert December 1928-February 1930	135
Map 16	'Souforce' Operations June-September 1932	158
Map 17	Operations against Sheikh Mahmud November 1930-May 1931	177
Map 18	Palestine and Transjordan 1929-1939	193
Map 19	Sidi Barrani October-December 1940	249
Map 20	Operation Compass October 1940-February 1941	253
Map 21	Iraqi Army dispositions RAF Habbaniya 1 May 1941	276
Map 22	The attack on Falluja 18/19 May 1941	297
Map 23	The advance on Baghdad 23-30 May 1941	300
Map 24	The advance into Syria June-July 1941	317
Map 25	Palmyra 21 June-3 July 1941	323
Map 26	Operation Crusader and the Retreat to Gazala	341
Map 27	Gazala 27 May 1942	384
Map 28	Gazala evening 15 June 1942	388
Map 29	The Delta and Western Desert of Egypt July-November 1942	395
Map 30	El Agheila to Mareth December 1942-March 1943	425
Map 31	The Left Hook at Mareth	434
Map 32	Tunisia - Gabes to Tunis	440
Map 33	Palestine and Transjordan 1945-1948	488
Map 34	Jerusalem 1945	495
Map 35	Aden Colony and Western Aden Protectorate	517
Map 36	British and Italian Somaliland 'Operation Appearance'	527
Map 37	The Trucial States and Buraimi Oasis	575

"Fi Kull Makáan - In Every Place"
The motto of the Armoured Cars in Iraq

Squadron Leader G. Elliot Godsave
OC No 4 Armoured Car Company
and Deputy Commander Armoured Car Wing,
The Tales of the Tin Trams,
Unpublished manuscript

Dedicated to the men who served on 'The Cars'

GLOSSARY

2 i/c	Second-in-Command
AFV	armoured fighting vehicle
AOC	Air Officer Commanding
AOC-in-C	Air Officer Commanding-in-Chief
APL	Aden Protectorate Levies
bedouin	the Arabs who live a nomadic life in the desert
chatta	Party of Turkish irregulars
CIGS	Chief of the Imperial General Staff
C-in-C	Commander-in-Chief
fellaheen	settled village-dwelling Arabs
FTS	Flying Training School
GOC	General Officer Commanding
HMAC	His Majesty's Armoured Car
LAA	light anti-aircraft
LAD	Light Aid Detachment
LG	Landing Ground
LMG	light machine-gun
LST	landing ship, tank
MT	Motor Transport or Mechanical Transport
NAAFI	Navy Army and Air Force Institutes
NCO	Non-Commissioned Officer
OC	Officer Commanding
ORB	Operations Record Book - RAF Form 540
OTU	Operational Training Unit
pdr	pounder e.g. 2-pdr anti-tank gun
POW	prisoner of war
R/T	radio telephony
RA	Royal Artillery
RAAF	Royal Australian Air Force
RAOC	Royal Army Ordnance Corps
RASC	Royal Army Service Corps
RE	Royal Engineers
RFC	Royal Flying Corps
RNAS	Royal Naval Air Service
RRAC	Rolls-Royce Armoured Car
RRWT	Rolls-Royce Wireless Tender
SSO	Special Service Officer
TJFF	Transjordan Frontier Force
vilayet	Ottoman province
W/T	wireless telegraphy

RAF Ranks

Airmen

AC2	Aircraftman 2nd Class.	*Entry level rank for airmen*
AC1	Aircraftman 1st Class	
LAC	Leading Aircraftman	

Corporal
Sergeant
Flight Sergeant
Warrant Officer

Officers

Pilot Officer *The lowest commissioned rank and equivalent to Second Lieutenant in the Army*

Flying Officer
Flight Lieutenant
Squadron Leader
Wing Commander
Group Captain
Air Commodore
Air Vice-Marshal
Air Marshal
Air Chief Marshal
Marshal of the Royal Air Force

FOREWORD

by
Air Chief Marshal Sir Stephen Dalton
GCB ADC LLD(Hon) DSc(Hon) BSc FRAeS CCMI RAF
(Chief of the Air Staff 2009–2013)
Honorary Air Commodore, Royal Air Force Regiment

Captain Somerset de Chair, an Army Intelligence Officer, recorded that the men of No 2 Armoured Car Company RAF "...were all rogues, God bless them, for whom the War had come as an eleventh hour reprieve. They were the sort of men to whom legend clung like the cloak of Mephistopheles." Such was the description of the Company in 1941, as it prepared to lead the 'Habforce' relief column from Palestine to lift the epic siege of RAF Habbaniya in Iraq. Here the beleaguered Station was being defended by, amongst others, their compatriots of No 1 Company, outnumbered ten to one by a brigade of the rebel Iraqi Army. This one account, from countless stirring tales of the RAF Armoured Car Companies that make for remarkable reading in their own right, also provide much from which the Royal Air Force continues to draw lessons for today's and tomorrow's operations.

Since the Royal Naval Air Service conceived of the idea of air power operating in conjunction with its own armoured cars on the Western Front in 1914 and the subsequent birth of the first Royal Air Force Armoured Car Companies in 1921 – both initiatives sponsored by no less than Winston Churchill, 100 years of near-continuous operations have both shaped and inspired the actions and deeds of their successors in The Royal Air Force Regiment.

Today, four key lessons endure across the intervening Century. Firstly, there is an absolute imperative to gain and maintain control of the air as an essential prerequisite for the success of any military endeavour. Secondly, control of the air requires the ability to dominate and, if necessary, fight on the ground to secure the airfields/helicopter landing sites so critical to the operational centre-of-gravity – just as at Habbaniya in 1941, and as continues around Bastion today. Thirdly, air power provides smarter options for our political leaders in delivering precise and timely effects by exploiting our grasp of technology whilst minimising the risk to our Nation's Armed Forces and interests – such capability was demonstrated effectively whilst enacting Churchill's doctrine of air control over British mandates and protectorates in the Middle East in the 1920s and from the skies over Libya in the 2011 Campaign. Finally, seamless air-land integration is critical to mission success – vivid examples here would be the pivotal role of Flight Lieutenant 'Dickie' Skellon of No 2 Armoured Car Company, who was literally and physically in the last line of defence forward of the desert airbase at Gambut in 1942, protecting the open road to Egypt and beyond, when he called in devastating airstrikes by Hurricane 'Tank Buster' aircraft of No 6 Squadron Royal Air Force to block the seemingly unstoppable armour of Rommel's Afrika Korps. More recently, there was the professional and measured performance of Flight Lieutenant Matt Carter of today's Royal Air Force Regiment, who won the Military Cross in Afghanistan for his calm and accurate actions in calling-in battle-winning air support against Taliban fighters who were threatening to overrun beleaguered British soldiers in Helmand Province in 2006.

The canvas upon which the history of the Royal Air Force Armoured Car Companies is painted, provides an evocative backdrop for *'Boys Own'* tales of rogues, heroes, Rolls-Royces and *esprit de corps*. Their stage comprised the ancient cities of Heliopolis, Jerusalem, Damascus and Baghdad; the deserts of Libya, Iraq, Palestine, Jordan and Trucial Oman; and the mountains of Kurdistan and Aden. But the names of these places still resonate across the sands of time, as scenes of action and valour both then and now. Today, and in recent military operations, from Shaibah to Basra, from Falluja to Baghdad and from Benghazi to Tripoli, not to forget Kandahar, Kabul and Camp Bastion, Royal Air Force Regiment Gunners continue to reflect in their actions the courage, ethos, professionalism and comradeship of their predecessors of those Armoured Car Companies.

This gripping official history of the Royal Air Force Armoured Car Companies, long overdue in the telling, provides a treasure trove of inspiration for those serving in the Royal Air Force Regiment today; they are the guardians of a rich and proud heritage. In 1682, in response to popular acclaim for his extraordinary scientific achievements, Sir Isaac Newton said: 'If I have seen further than other men, it is because I have stood on the shoulders of giants!' We salute those 'giants' of the Royal Air Force Armoured Car Companies upon whose shoulders the Gunners of today's Royal Air Force Regiment are proud to stand.

APPRECIATION

The history and stories of the men of the RAF Armoured Car Companies and Squadrons has never been so fully unveiled and told as in this book. Nigel Warwick has done true justice to these little known 'Sons of the Desert', with their exploits and achievements being brought to life and given the publicity that was much talked of but has never been told before.

This is a fitting history of the birth of the Companies through to the amalgamation into the Squadrons, and a brilliant testimony to their deeds and exploits which has been laid down in the genes of the RAF Regiment.

The members of the RAF Armoured Cars Association congratulate Nigel for telling their story.

We thank the RAF Regiment for their support of this book and our Association.

Mr John Rolph
Secretary RAF Armoured Cars Association (RAFACA)

PREFACE and ACKNOWLEDGEMENTS

On 19 December 2011, 1 Squadron RAF Regiment celebrated the 90th Anniversary of the formation of No 1 Armoured Car Company at RAF Heliopolis. The Royal Air Force Armoured Cars, however, are only fleetingly referred to in a few books and articles on the RAF operations in the Middle East. Their story is therefore long overdue in the telling.

As a 14-year old schoolboy, I recall finding Glubb Pasha's book, *The War in the Desert: An RAF Frontier Campaign*, in my local public library, and avidly read of the exploits of the RAF in the southern deserts of Iraq. I later read of Squadron Leader 'Cass' Casano's significant role in 'Kingcol' during the Iraq Revolt and in Syria, in Somerset De Chair's, *The Golden Carpet*. I was struck, however, by the paucity of detail on the RAF Armoured Cars in the literature on the RAF and also the large portions of mythology that had grown up around their operations. The intention of *In Every Place* is to set down the story of the RAF Armoured Cars using official operations record books, Air Ministry reports and documents and the personal reminiscences of the officers and airmen who served in the RAF Armoured Cars. This book therefore, presents the story not only from the political, strategic and tactical context, but also from the point of view of the men in the turret and driver's and wireless-operator's seats. I have long held an interest in the RAF in the Middle East between the Wars and also in the Mediterranean campaigns of the Second World War and I have been able to combine both these interests and in particular focus attention on the RAF Regiment and its predecessors, and their vital role in air-land integration, force protection and ground defence of air assets.

This book covers 30 years of RAF operations in the Middle East, during which 'The Cars' were ubiquitous. The history of the RAF Armoured Cars is the history of the RAF in these countries. The RAF, in applying the Scheme of Air Control in the newly-mandated territories and protectorates had to operate with considerable dexterity. Each venture inevitably involved understanding a new foe within a complex political and strategic context. The RAF armoured crews most often had to deal with age-old ethnic, cultural and religious conflicts in operations ranging from the relatively benign civil control, to insurgency and tribal warfare, and to total war.

This book could not have been written without the help of a number of people to whom I owe a great deal of gratitude. I would firstly like to thank my good friend, Mr John Rolph, the Secretary of the RAF Armoured Cars Association (RAFACA), ably supported by his wife, Ann. He has proven constant in his support, enthusiasm and encouragement in the writing of this book. I have enjoyed our collaboration and it was a great honour to have been made an Honorary Member of the RAFACA in 2011. John has provided photographs and documents from his late father, Arthur Rolph, and Vic Brandon's collections, as well as others from the Association archives. These have made a major contribution to the completion of the book. He has also been immensely helpful in interviewing and arranging contacts with the men who served in the RAF Armoured Cars or their relatives.

I especially wish to thank Air Commodore Russ La Forte CBE, former Officer Commanding 1 Squadron RAF Regiment (1994-1996), Commandant General RAF

Regiment (2010-2011), and currently Commander British Forces South Atlantic Islands, for his dedication and interest in this project. He has read through the drafts of the chapters in detail and has made many helpful comments and suggested useful improvements. I particularly thank him for directing me to the material on the early years of the RNAS armoured car squadrons and in helping with contacts at the Air and Naval Historical Branches and the Imperial War Museum.

Wing Commander Martin Hooker MBE RAF Regiment (Retd), the Regimental Secretary of the RAF Regiment, has, as always, been a cheerful, constant and loyal support, and has dealt with my varied requests with great equanimity. I thank him, the Station Commanders, and officers and NCOs at RAF Honington who have always been welcoming and enthusiastic during my numerous visits to Honington to delve into the RAF Regiment Museum Archives. I am grateful for permission given to reproduce photographs from the RAF Regiment Museum and II Squadron History Room. My gratitude also goes to successive Commandant Generals of the RAF Regiment who have been strongly supportive of my efforts.

The greatest pleasure and privilege has been meeting the men, some of whom have since passed away, who served in the RAF Armoured Cars and have willingly allowed me to record their reminiscences and have provided photographs. I thank Air Vice-Marshal E.L. 'Ted' Frith RAF (Retd), Wing Commander W. 'Bill' Foulsham MC OBE RAF (Retd), Wing Commander P.D. 'Pat' Lee RAF Regiment (Retd), Wing Commander Richard Skellon RAF (Retd), and Messrs Vic Morte, Eric Armitage, Dick Lock, Ray Ferguson, Dennis 'Harry' Hawkins, Len King, George Moyes (via Paul Cormack), Geoff Tindale, Alan 'Lofty' Hodge, Bert Bayliss, Fred Morris, Donald Price, Ron Fairweather, Ray Hill, Jon Jordinson, 'Nick' Nixon and Barry Walker.

The children and grandchildren of those who served in the RAF Armoured Cars have been extremely helpful in providing documents and photographs and my sincere thanks go to Mrs Patricia Bradley (daughter of Patrick 'John' Wyatt), Ms Anne Prentice, Messrs Richard Beaney, Steve Chester, Ivan Childs, Jim Elliot, David Petrie, Alan Spybey, Jonathan Secter and Commander Peter Stone RN (Retd).

I also thank John and Janine Lloyd at the Household Cavalry Regiment Museum Archive at Combermere Barracks, and Lieutenant-General Sir Barney White-Spunner KCB CBE, in assisting me in making contact with Mr Xan Smiley. My thanks go to him for allowing me to reproduce his father, David Smiley's, photographs from the Iraq Revolt and Syrian campaign. My thanks also go to Lady Juliet Tadgell for permission to quote from her late husband, Somerset de Chair's book, *The Golden Carpet*.

I wish to thank Dr Chris Morris and Mr Peter Burlton of the RAF Habbaniya Association for useful discussions and also provision of photographs. My thanks also go to the late Group Captain Kingsley Oliver RAF Regiment (Retd) for alerting me to the manuscript by Elliot Godsave and to Air Commodore Marcus Witherow RAF Regiment (Retd) for valuable discussions on the Trucial Oman States and Aden.

The Operations Record Books of the relevant Companies, Squadrons, Sections and Flights along with numerous Air Ministry Reports held in The National Archives of the United Kingdom, are a treasured and pivotal resource, and have provided the essential detail and context to support the reminiscences of the participants. All material is subject to Crown copyright and I am grateful for permission to quote from it. I thank the Australian War Memorial in Canberra and Peter Elliott, Senior Keeper at the RAF Museum Hendon, for permission to reproduce photographs held in their collections, as well as the Trustees of the Imperial War Museum for granting permission to reproduce photographs and quote from relevant documents and sound recordings. I also thank the Air Historical Branch for assistance in obtaining relevant Air Ministry documents.

I would like to express my great appreciation to my publisher, Ron Pearson and Forces & Corporate Publishing, who have been a pleasure to work with, and have fashioned a high quality production. I am also grateful to the RAF Regiment Fund Management Committee for provision of funding and wider support in bringing the book to publication.

My gratitude goes to Air Chief Marshal Sir Stephen Dalton, Chief of Air Staff (2009-2013) and Honorary Air Commodore to the RAF Regiment, for writing the Foreword.

Finally, but most importantly, I wish to express my deepest thanks to my wife Caroline, and my daughters Elinor and Clare, for their encouragement, advice, good humour and patience, and for allowing me to dedicate so much of my time of the past few years in researching and writing this book.

Dr Nigel W.M. Warwick
New South Wales, Australia

PROLOGUE

'Instilling a Holy Terror' Air Power and the Armoured Car

"CARS FOR ATTENDING ON MACHINES.... 'Most important to proceed'"
Winston Spencer Churchill, First Lord of the Admiralty, 1914[1]

On 25 August 1914, only three weeks after Great Britain had declared war on Germany, Commander Charles Rumney Samson of the Royal Naval Air Service (RNAS) was ordered by the Admiralty to take his highly-trained Eastchurch (Mobile) Air Squadron to Ostend in Belgium, where it was to establish an advanced air base.[2] The task was three-fold: to patrol the Channel for German submarines while the convoys carrying the British Expeditionary Force crossed to France; the interdiction of Zeppelins threatening London; and aerial reconnaissance in support of a brigade of Royal Marines. The Squadron was initially recalled to England in the face of the rapid German advance towards Paris, but once the German offensive stalled at the First Battle of the Marne, Samson's squadron was re-established at Dunkirk from where it operated in support of the French Army.[3]

Commander Samson realised that he needed to provide a forward and aggressive ground defence to support his air operations and to protect his airfields, so he had begun experimenting with the use of 'armed motor cars' fitted with Maxim machine-guns. Their roles were to recover downed pilots and their aircraft, conduct offensive patrols against German troop dispositions in the countryside surrounding the air station, and along with the Squadron's aircraft, 'deny the use of territory within a hundred miles of Dunkirk to German Zeppelins.'[4] The cars, which were soon fitted with steel-plate to protect their crews, operated in close cooperation with these aircraft which flew ahead to report on German military movements. This was pursued with considerable panache and piratical flair, with successful operations to Bruges, Ghent and Lille.[5] Samson and his cars were soon gathering up to half-a-dozen prisoners a day, preventing German cavalry from carrying out effective reconnaissance and had 'instilled a holy terror' into their opponents.[6] These were the first such operations by British aircraft and armoured vehicles. An Admiralty telegram sent to General Bidon, the local French Army commander, on 1 September, had elaborated on this strategy:

> With your permission, the Admiralty wish to take all necessary measures to maintain aerial command of this region. The Admiralty proposes therefore, to place 30 or 40 naval aeroplanes at Dunkirk or other convenient coast points. In order that these may have a good radius of action they must be able to establish temporary bases 40 to 50 miles inland.
>
> The Admiralty desires to reinforce officer commanding aeroplanes with 50 to 60 armed motor-cars and 200 to 300 men. This small force will operate in conformity with the wishes of the French military authorities, but we hope it may be accorded a free initiative. The immunity of Portsmouth, Chatham and London from dangerous aerial attack is clearly involved.[7]

It was under the guidance of the Admiralty and particularly the First Lord of the Admiralty, Winston Churchill, that the 'armed motor car' was to be further developed into the 'armoured car'.[8] Churchill had shown considerable enthusiasm for this concept, as was clearly demonstrated in an Admiralty minute written at the time. Under the heading, 'CARS FOR ATTENDING ON MACHINES', it noted:

> These should be armed with a light gun. They would assist in forming temporary bases for the machines so as to enable the aeroplanes to extend their flights to greater distance. About 50 will be required.[9]

An annotation by Churchill in the margin of this report said: 'Most important to proceed, reporting scheme in detail.' Furthermore, he altered the figure of 50 into 100. Churchill's approval of this paper led to the creation of the RNAS Armoured Car Force.[10]

Samson continued his operations with some success until March the following year when his air squadron was redeployed to the Mediterranean to take part in the Dardanelles Campaign. By his time however, the RNAS Armoured Car Force had been raised to 15 squadrons, to form a Division, with units that would operate in almost every operational theatre of the Great War - the Home Front, the Western Front, Gallipoli, East Africa and even Russia (both before and after the 1917 Revolution). A number of makes of chassis had been trialled, but it was the armoured car based on the Rolls-Royce that was found to be the most successful. Unfortunately, the development of the Armoured Car Force was not to be nurtured by the Royal Navy. The stalemate of trench warfare in France and Gallipoli had hamstrung the inherent mobile role of the armoured cars. The gradual dissolution of the Force began in May 1915, when their principal advocate, Churchill, was removed as First Lord of the Admiralty following the failures at Gallipoli. From 1915, the cars were gradually handed over to the Army (where they saw service with the Machine-Gun Corps[11]). By 1918, only the Squadron in Russia and an experimental unit in the UK remained under RNAS control.

Yet the seed of an idea had been sown - the concept of air/ground integration and the crucial requirement for ground defence of air assets had been established. It was to be with the fledgling RAF, the World's first independent air arm, that this seed was to flourish into full life in the arid wastes of Britain's post-War Mandates and Protectorates in the Middle East - and once again, Winston Churchill would foster its development.

Notes

1. M. Sueter, *The Evolution of the Tank*, (Hutchinson & Co: London, 1937), p. 29.
2. Later Air Commodore Charles Rumney Samson CMG DSO & Bar AFC RNAS and RAF (1883-1931). His exploits were recorded in detail in his autobiographical account, C.R. Samson, *Fights and Flights* (London: Ernest Benn, 1930).
3. M. Sueter, *The Evolution of the Tank*, p. 28.
4. W. Raleigh, *The War in the Air: Being the Part Played in the Great War by the Royal Air Force, Vol I* (Oxford: Clarendon Press, 1922), pp. 375.
5. *Ibid*, pp. 371-379.
6. M. Sueter, *The Evolution of the Tank*, p. 35-36 and H.St.G. Saunders, *Per Ardua: The Rise of British Air Power 1911-1939* (London: Oxford University Press, 1944), pp. 45-48.
7. W. Raleigh, *The War in the Air*, p.376.
8. Later the Right Honourable Sir Winston Churchill KG OM CH TD DL FRS Hon RA (1874–1965).
9. M. Sueter, *The Evolution of the Tank*, p. 29.
10. *Ibid*, p. 29. The Naval Airman's Armoured Car Force as it was first known was created and formed at the *Daily Mail* airship shed at Wormwood Scrubs.
11. D. Fletcher, *War Cars: British Armoured Cars in the First World War* (HMSO: London, 1987), pp. 91-92.

CHAPTER ONE

The Royal Air Force Scheme of Control

"I must remind Honourable members that we still have an Empire to defend. Odd as it may seem on the morrow of unheard-of victories, we still have all those dependencies and possessions in our hands which existed before the war, and in addition we have large promises of new responsibilities to be placed upon us. The first duty of the Royal Air Force is to garrison the British Empire."
                        Winston Spencer Churchill, Secretary of State for War and Air, 1919[1]

On 1 October 1922 the Royal Air Force assumed responsibility for military operations and civil control over the vast territories of Palestine, Transjordan and Mesopotamia (Iraq). With the end of the First World War, Great Britain and France had been given responsibility for large parts of the old Turkish Ottoman Empire under a mandate from the League of Nations. Ottoman power had been waning for some years and there followed a release of many tribal, ethnic, religious, nationalist and political tensions. Subsequently there were moves in some of these territories to rise up against their new overlords. The British government was faced with the resolution of the many difficulties that would arise from newly or as yet undrawn international boundaries.

At the same time, however, with the end of the Great War, there was substantial pressure on the British Exchequer to make savings in defence expenditure. The monetary cost of controlling these territories would be one of the key determinants of the methods and forces that would be employed. The post-war government of Lloyd George had committed itself to the principle that Great Britain would not have to fight a major war for the next decade. This principle came to be known as the 'Ten Year Rule'. The three ministries, the Admiralty controlling the Royal Navy, the War Office controlling the Army and the Air Ministry, the Royal Air Force, would therefore face severe financial stringencies and increased inter-service rivalries as the Treasury applied pressure to the three services. The view held by the War Office was that the new responsibilities in the mandated territories would require a large and costly deployment of conventional military forces – unwelcome news in the prevailing atmosphere of financial austerity.

The Royal Air Force had only been established as an independent service on 1 April 1918. With the end of the Great War this independence was already under threat. The senior services, the Navy and Army were determined to protect their own finances and numbers, and wanted the RAF to be absorbed back into their respective force structures. The Chief of the Air Staff, Air Marshal Sir Hugh Trenchard, had fought to establish an independent RAF and was determined that it would remain so.² The Smuts Report of 1917 had strongly commended the efficiency and effectiveness of combining the RNAS and the Royal Flying Corps to form the RAF, and that it should exist as an independent entity administered by an Air Ministry under the Secretary of State for Air, run separately from the War Office and the Admiralty.

By late 1918, Trenchard was overseeing drastic cuts to aircraft and personnel as the end of the War and the financial savings implicit in the 'Ten Year Rule' were applied, requiring him to demobilise large parts of the wartime RAF and re-establish it on a peace-time basis.³ He was required to severely prune the number of squadrons, close numerous airfields, sell land and equipment assets, and scrap large numbers of aircraft. The threat to the continued existence of the RAF was real. Yet, Trenchard was determined that it would play a significant role in the defence of the United Kingdom and the Empire. With a limited budget he set about building the foundations for the RAF at home with a large proportion of the expenditure earmarked for development, training and education of the officers and airmen.

Winston Churchill had been appointed Secretary of State for War and Air in early 1919 and in this role gave considerable support to the maintenance and sustenance of the RAF, despite the considerable pressure from the other services. His tenure was to have positive repercussions for the RAF when in April 1921 he assumed the role of Secretary of State for the Colonies. In this capacity he had the task of organising the British Government's plans for internal security in the newly-acquired mandated territories.

Eighty battalions of British and Imperial troops were stationed across the Middle

Air Marshal Sir Hugh Montague Trenchard Bt KCB DSO, Chief of the Air Staff, inspects apprentices at RAF Halton in 1922. He saw the armoured cars as integral to the Air Force Scheme of Control (© Crown Copyright, RAF Museum).

East. Some politicians felt these large concentrations of troops acted more as an incitement to dissent by local populations than in pacifying them. The Chief of the Imperial General Staff, General Sir Henry Wilson, still believed that the old-fashioned and time-honoured methods of punitive expeditions, and static garrisons located at strategic points could be used to restore order, and that the circumstances militating against a successful control of the early stages of the insurrection then developing in Iraq were lack of transport and the long distances involved.[4]

In 1921, an insurrection broke out in Iraq, and the annual cost rose to £32 million, causing consternation back in London.[5] Although not fully under control, the insurrection had quietened down by February 1921, and operations into early 1922 were limited to dealing with isolated outbreaks using a combination of air and ground forces. The significance of this period for the RAF was that it brought home to the British Government the expense involved in maintaining a large Army garrison in Iraq.

Churchill was keen to find a more effective method of control. Considerable costs savings had to be extracted from the Defence budget and therefore policies which were effective, but perhaps more importantly were of low cost, would be viewed favourably. Arising from his previous experience with the Air Ministry, Churchill approached Trenchard and asked him to submit a proposal from the RAF for the management of internal security of Iraq. Trenchard submitted that the RAF had the aircraft and personnel required to police these territories, and more importantly, it could do this at a significantly lower outlay than the War Office estimates. The RAF would operate a system of imperial policing using a combination of flying squadrons, fast moving ground forces made up of armoured car companies, and levies raised from local populations.

The RAF proposal had been aided fortuitously by recent events in British Somaliland. A dissident tribal leader, Mohammed ibn Abdulla Hassan, known at the time as the 'Mad Mullah', had risen against British rule, taken control of half the country, and pursued a policy of looting, kidnapping and torture. The 'Mullah' had been causing considerable trouble for more than two decades and his activities had become a source of great anxiety. The problem had become such that a more vigorous form of intervention was required. The CIGS informed the Colonial Office that the task required five or more battalions of African and Indian troops and three squadrons of aircraft. The operation would take up to a year to conclude ground operations, and a railway would need to be constructed to support and supply the forces required to police the recaptured territory.

As luck would have it, Trenchard was consulted as to his opinions on the problem by Churchill's predecessor as Colonial Secretary, Lord Milner. Seizing the moment and realising that he must submit a lower bid, Trenchard said, "Why not leave the whole thing to us? This is exactly the type of operation which the RAF can tackle on its own."[6] No extra ground troops would be required as there were sufficient for the purpose already in Somaliland. He offered to do the job with a single bomber squadron, a battalion of the King's African Rifles and the local Camel Corps.[7]

Given the go-ahead, the campaign proper lasted only three weeks, despite the CIGS expressing the view that the campaign would fail and that the War Office would later have to furnish troops to retrieve the situation.[8] In January 1920, the RAF despatched 'Z' Unit with 12 De Havilland DH9 bombers to British Somaliland.[9] The aircraft attacked the tribesmen in their camps and forts and then harried them as they moved into the open. In the space of three weeks, the Mullah was bombed and harassed from the air as he sought refuge from the onslaught. Finally, he fled to neighbouring Abyssinia where he died of natural causes a few months later. The cost of the air campaign came in under £70,000 and the total for both and air and land operations came out to £150,000.[10] Imperial casualties had amounted to three killed and nine wounded. A later Colonial Secretary, Leo Amery, famously described it as "the cheapest war in history."[11] However, the success was not purely due to air control. Considerable ground work had been done by the Army prior to the successful conclusion of the campaign and the 'Mullah' had made mistakes in moving from unconventional to conventional warfare by occupying fortified positions. Nevertheless, the RAF was able to claim a considerable portion of credit for its role in the successful conclusion to the campaign.

Royal Air Force operations were also being effectively carried out on the North-West Frontier of India and both these successes provided Trenchard with considerable justification for his plans for what came to be known as 'Air Control'. Technological developments in aviation would also aid the already strong case for the RAF playing a significant role in the Middle East and Mesopotamia. The RAF had another important task which only it could provide. Following the First World War, aircraft had become rapid and effective movers of people, products and mail. Imperial air routes were being developed. The quickest routes to the farthest parts of the Empire, to India, the Far East, Australia and New Zealand, lay across the trackless deserts of the Middle East. The RAF could develop the air routes, the landing grounds, the navigation methods and the support facilities.

Winston Churchill, now Colonial Secretary, had responsibility for Palestine, Transjordan and Iraq. Substantial political intrigue and ferment existed in these countries. The French and British governments now sought to introduce new administrative and political structures for their respective protectorates, whereby they could be ruled, and in some instances prepare them for eventual self-government.

In March 1921, Churchill convened the Cairo Conference. This brought together the mostly British civil, political and military figures with a stake in the mandates. The conference had the difficult task of resolving the often conflicting economic and political interests of Britain and France, the rise of Arab nationalism, Zionism and Jewish immigration to Palestine, the bringing together of the Kurds, the Arabs and the Assyrians to make the new state of Iraq, the territorial ambitions of a resurgent Turkey, and last but not least, Imperial defence. Pre-armed, the RAF had drawn up plans for air-substitution of ground forces for the control of these territories. The conference thus played a key role in securing the RAF as an independent force.[12] The Air Staff's recommendation, should internal security be maintained under Army control and assuming no external aggression or serious internal uprising, was:

2 British battalions
10 Indian battalions
1 British artillery battery
2 Indian pack batteries
6 squadrons RAF + armoured car companies
1 cavalry regiment
2 companies of sappers and miners
local troops, mainly Levies.

The clarity of the financial attractiveness of the RAF scheme can be seen in the force proposed to the conference should the RAF assume control:

1 British battalion
3 Indian battalions
8 RAF flying squadrons
4 to 6 RAF armoured car companies
4 RAF river gunboats
local troops, mainly Levies, should be raised to the number of 15,000.

Though it appeared unusual that the Air Staff were making estimates of ground force requirements, it should be remembered that the majority of RAF officers had started their military careers in the Army prior to joining the Royal Flying Corps. Trenchard, for instance, had served as an infantry officer in the Royal Scots Fusiliers during the Boer War and then in the Southern Nigeria Regiment for several years before he learned to fly. The CIGS, General Wilson, however, derided the Iraq scheme of the RAF. He believed that it was an experiment that would have no result and only lead to humiliation and reverses. In a letter to General Rawlinson, the C-in-C India he wrote, "I do not believe in Winston's ardent hopes of being able to govern Mesopotamia with hot air, aeroplanes and Arabs."[13]

Despite the misgivings of some, the relevant committee at the Conference endorsed Trenchard's plans after some iterations, and a few months later so did the British Cabinet. Realising that the scheme had a strong element of risk, a proviso was added that the Army battalions would not be sent home until the air scheme had been tested. The British and Indian army units would be gradually reduced after the RAF assumed responsibility. The Air Staff had not planned to completely replace ground forces with aircraft. The air element of the proposal was the key to the Trenchard scheme. A no less essential ingredient, however, was the use of fast light armoured forces and the locally-raised levies. Air stations and landing grounds and other vulnerable points would need ground protection and a land force would be a necessity in closing with the enemy. The near exclusion of the Army from the scheme, however, dealt a severe blow to its pride. Trenchard's proposal of 5 August 1921 outlined his plans for the armoured car companies that belonged to the Army and that were then stationed in Iraq:

> There are at present three armoured car companies in Iraq and I understand the GOC Iraq recommends that two of them should be replaced by tanks. I am, however, of the opinion that the armoured cars should be retained pending the production of a light tropical tank ... as soon as the new tanks become available, one of the armoured car companies should be replaced by tanks, and later on, if the tanks make good, a second car company should be similarly replaced.
>
> To immediate needs, however, the armoured car will be of great value. The armoured car and tank companies will require personnel.... It is clear in the first instance that it will be convenient for the necessary personnel to be supplied by the War Office, but I propose that the Army personnel should be replaced unit by unit according as Air Force personnel can be trained for this purpose.
>
> It must be clearly understood that the provision of armoured car and tank companies is an integral part of the Air Force Scheme of Control.[14]

The military theorist Basil Liddell Hart correctly described the plans as more 'Air-and-Armour-Control'. Furthermore, he explained the new concept thus:

> It substituted mobile control by a combination of fast-moving air and ground units for static control by infantry - a concentrated power of quick intervention replacing a widely spread garrison. The RAF could not fulfil its new police function without the help of units on the ground....[15]

Trenchard had adequate funds for armoured vehicles but the issue became complicated due to intransigence by the War Office. General Wilson was irritated that they had not been consulted as to the tactical worth of light armoured forces. The Air Ministry's initial approach to the War Office was as to whether they could supply such units. The War Office stated that the RAF would have to do without armoured cars since they were not empowered to help them. Furthermore, that their armoured cars were fully committed in Ireland and fast light tanks which were more suited to the desert were not yet in production. The Army also planned to withdraw two of the three armoured car companies from Iraq to India. Any suggestion that the Army would also provide the personnel for the armoured car companies were exemplified by a blunt statement from GOC Iraq to the War Office, "... OC Armoured Cars here informs me that, in the event of the Armoured Car Companies becoming units of the RAF, none of his officers and men are likely to transfer to that force."[16]

The availability of Rolls-Royce chassis, which were proven ideal for armoured cars, had become an issue in recent years. The Army had to rebuild its stocks of Rolls-Royce armoured cars following the end of the Great War. Most had been built using the pre-war model and they were wearing out. The demand for military use led the War Office to issue a press statement asking for understanding from those members of the public who were awaiting their new Silver Ghost:

> ... the Government are buying Rolls-Royce cars, and ... the Rolls-Royce Company is asking private purchasers to agree to postponement of delivery because the Government wanted cars. In order to remove misapprehension, it should be pointed out that the purchase of Rolls-Royce chassis is necessitated by circumstances in Mesopotamia, where through age and heavy wear and tear our armoured cars are being rapidly worn out. The existing cars there require immediate replacement, and as the Rolls-Royce chassis is of a type which experience has shown can carry the necessary weight of armour and give satisfaction in all circumstances of climate and terrain, it was necessary, to make urgent arrangements to supply replacement chassis. In view of the situation in Mesopotamia and the protection there of our detachments and women and children, it is thought that prospective buyers of Rolls-Royce cars would not object to a very short postponement of delivery in order to promote the safety of those mentioned above.[17]

The final straw came when Trenchard was informed that the Secretary of State for War had decided not to release *any* armoured car companies nor could the RAF order any army weapons without consulting the War Office as to their tactical worth. The consequence of this ruling being that the Air Force would have to manage without armoured cars. Trenchard famously asked one of his Air Ministry officials to contact the Financial Secretary of the War Office and to, "Tell him to pass it on to

The essential materiel. The chassis of the Rolls-Royce Silver Ghost (above) and the engine (right). The brass parts and fittings were often polished to a high gleam (© Crown Copyright. RAF Regiment Museum/RAFACA).

his masters that we shan't need their precious armoured cars. We'll build our own."[18]

The Army had no monopoly on armoured car construction or use. Indeed, they had first been deployed by the RNAS of the Admiralty in 1914, for the protection of their advanced landing grounds. The RNAS armoured vehicles were handed over to the Army and were formed into the Light Armoured Motor Batteries. The LAMBs, as they were known, had served in Turkey, Palestine, Egypt, the Western Front in France and Belgium and East Africa as part of the Machine-Gun Corps. Following the end

The armoured car crewman's view. Spade grips and trigger for the Vickers 0.303-inch medium machine-gun (upper) and the driving compartment of the Rolls-Royce armoured car with the front visor down (lower). To the right are the ammunition belts for the Vickers (© Crown copyright. RAF Regiment Museum/RAFACA).

of the First World War and the disbandment of that Corps, they were reorganised as armoured car companies within the Tank Corps and were stationed in Mesopotamia, Egypt Palestine and India.[19]

As a contingency in case of War Office obstruction, Trenchard had drawn up plans for the RAF to construct its own armoured cars. His caution had proven correct and he ordered Air Force workshops in England and Egypt to set about converting Rolls-Royce's car chassis into armoured vehicles. That the Air Force should be equipping itself with armoured cars was seen by Trenchard as an appropriate arrangement. The RAF already had drivers, mechanics, armourers and vehicle workshops and there were shared technical features between armoured cars and aircraft. The first batch of Rolls-Royce armoured cars were ready for dispatch before Christmas, 1921. The Air Ministry also purchased Lancia armoured cars which had been used during the Irish uprising. These were now surplus to requirements, following the ceasefire and eventual creation of the Irish Free State. They were, however, open-topped with upright armoured sides and more like armoured trucks or armoured personnel carriers than armoured cars.

By late 1921, the handover for Palestine, Transjordan and Iraq was being mapped out. Correspondence was flowing between the Air Ministry and the War Office as to the timetable for full assumption of responsibility by the RAF. One instance of the differences that arose during this period concerned the northern Iraq vilayet (or province of the former Ottoman Empire) of Mosul. The GOC Iraq wished to withdraw the major portion of the British army garrison by May 1922. This included the withdrawal of a Tank Corps armoured car company which was providing the ground defence component for No 55 Squadron, the resident RAF flying squadron, and the only RAF presence in northern Iraq.

The Officer Commanding RAF Iraq Group, Group Captain Amyas 'Biffy' Borton, was concerned that this would necessitate the withdrawal of the squadron to Baghdad.[20] Trenchard wrote to the Colonial Office requesting that it put pressure on the War Office to keep the company there until the RAF could send its own armoured cars. The RAF considered it essential that routine patrols and flights to outposts be maintained lest this should send the wrong signals to those in the north of Iraq, and in Turkey, as to the resolve of the British administration. It was feared that any withdrawal of outward signs of authority would inevitably lead to a local uprising. Fiscal matters were uppermost in the minds of the War Office and it was pointed out that the Army estimates had not accounted for the garrisoning of Mosul beyond the end of June. The matter was resolved when the Colonial Office agreed to provide the funds for the maintenance of these forces until the RAF could assume responsibility.[21]

All was being readied for the RAF to set in train the Air Force Scheme of Control. The flying squadrons were in place or moving to take up their roles. The second major component of the scheme, the Armoured Car Companies, had now to be established. The orders for the formation of the Armoured Car Companies were issued in late 1921 with the intention that the RAF would assume control of Palestine on 1 April 1922:

> Arrangements are also in hand to procure the armoured cars necessary for the two companies included in the garrison, and I am to request that every endeavour may be made to expedite the training of the RAF personnel now under instruction in Egypt, so they would be ready to form the two companies in March next.[22]

Notes

1. Churchill in A. Boyle, *Trenchard: Man of Vision* (London: Collins, 1962), p. 354. Address to The House of Commons, 15 December 1919.
2. Later Marshal of the RAF Viscount Trenchard of Wolfeton GCB OM GCVO DSO (1873-1956). Trenchard was Chief of the Air Staff in 1918, and then again from 1919 to 1930.
3. Boyle, *Trenchard*, pp. 354-355. From the wartime strength of 188 squadrons, only 25½ were retained – 19 were to be based overseas: eight in India, seven in Egypt and three in Mesopotamia and one for naval base defence.
4. I.M. Phillpott, *The Royal Air Force: An Encyclopaedia of the Inter-War Years, Vol. I* (Barnsley, Yorks.: Pen & Sword, 2005), p. 47.
5. P. Sluglett, *Britain in Iraq 1914-1932* (London: Ithaca Press, 1976), p. 259.
6. Boyle, *Trenchard*, p. 366.
7. *Ibid.*, pp. 366-367.
8. D. Omissi, *Air Power and Colonial Control: The Royal Air Force 1919-1939* (Manchester: Manchester University Press, 1990), p. 14.
9. F.A. Skoulding, 'With Z Unit in Somaliland', *RAF Quarterly*, 2 (1931), pp. 387-396. The DH9s were shipped to Berbera on HMS *Ark Royal*. The air component played a key role, though the operation was a coordinated air and ground campaign.
10. Omissi, *Air Power and Colonial Control*, p. 15.
11. Leo Amery, in Boyle, *Trenchard*, p. 369.
12. Phillpott, *The Royal Air Force, Vol. I*. p. 46
13. Wilson, in Omissi, *Air Power and Colonial Control*, p. 18.
14. AIR 5/477 *Memoranda on RAF scheme of control Iraq (Mesopotamia) 1921*.
15. B.H. Liddell Hart, *The Tanks: The History of the Royal Tank Regiment and its predecessors Heavy Branch Machine-Gun Corps, Tank Corps and Royal Tank Corps, 1914-1945, Vol. I* (London: Cassell, 1959), pp. 208-209. Credit should be given to the Tank Corps for the pioneering work they had done in developing the use of the armoured cars in Iraq. The reports of Lieutenant-Colonel G.M. Lindsay commanding No 1 Tank Group present a similar vision for the combined use of air and armour.
16. AIR 5/189 *Transition of control in, and withdrawal of, troops from Iraq, January 1922-December 1923*. Correspondence: GOC Iraq to War Office, 7 March 1922.
17. 'Armoured Cars for Mesopotamia', *The Times*, 24 September 1920, p. 10.
18. Boyle, *Trenchard*, p. 388 and G. Tindale, '50 Years On', *Centurion*, 1997, No 3, p. 26. Trenchard was proud of the Companies and held them in high regard. Pilot Officer Geoffrey Tindale served for nine months in Palestine in 1948, while on a 12-month short-service commission; he then left the RAF to take up a place at Durham University and after graduating, applied for a position with Unilever. At the final interview he discovered that the Chairman of Unilever, none other than Lord Trenchard, would be conducting the interviews. It was a group interview and Trenchard's ploy was to go round the table asking each applicant for details of their Service career. The first few he passed over quickly, until he came to Tindale. On learning that he had been in the RAF, the great man probed more deeply. When he learned that Tindale had served with No 2 Armoured Car Squadron, the interviewing was forgotten. For the next 20 minutes they were all treated to a graphic account of the events leading up to, and subsequent to, the formation of the RAF armoured cars. Trenchard then fixed him with a penetrating stare and asked the question: 'I did the right thing, didn't I Tindale?' The reply must have been satisfactory, as three weeks later he was on a BOAC airliner en route for Nigeria.
19. D. Fletcher, *War Cars: British Armoured Cars in the First World War* (HMSO: London, 1987), pp. 91-92.
20. Group Captain Amyas E. Borton CB CMG DSO AFC (1886-1969), OC HQ RAF Mesopotamian/Iraq Group, 1921-1922.
21. AIR 5/189, Correspondence from Under Secretary of State, Colonial Office, 21 March 1921.
22. AIR 5/188 *Proposed assumption by RAF of military command of Palestine, January 1921-December 1923*.

CHAPTER TWO

The Formation of the Companies

"My word the troops were good.... Am not shooting a line when I say they were easily the best drilled and smartest unit I have ever seen in the RAF...."
Wing Commander Tom Kinna[1]

RAF Heliopolis, one of the four main airfields of Egyptian Group, was located a few miles to the north-east of the bustling city of Cairo, on the Old Suez Road (Map 29, p. 395). In January 1922, a contingent of 50 airmen gathered to train for service in an RAF Armoured Car Company; a formation previously absent from the order of battle of the Royal Air Force. The officers had yet to arrive, so the responsibility for training and discipline was assigned to some from the administrative units and flying squadrons on the airfield. These airmen were earmarked for service in Palestine and Transjordan and were to form the nucleus of Nos 1 and 2 Armoured Car Companies. Eventually, 220 men were assigned to No 216 Squadron for administrative purposes, and given a temporary CO, Flight Lieutenant Henry Hanmer, who was a Training Officer on the Middle East Command Air Staff, one Flying Officer as Armament Instructor and another, Gilbert Martyn from No 216 Squadron, as the Technical Instructor. Flying Officer Martyn described the rudimentary steps taken to train the airmen for their new role:

> We were given instructions by Headquarters, Middle East to train these men as Rolls-Royce armoured car drivers fit for desert duties, and able to use Vickers and Lewis guns. This was to be accomplished by April.
>
> The men appeared to be newly-recruited to the RAF. None could drive a car. We were given two brand new Rolls-Royce cars on which to teach them, but early on decided to adopt other methods. Incidentally, the excellent Flying Officer S... [sic], by means known only to himself, converted these recruits into well disciplined, smart airmen during the few days which we spent in organizing their training.[2]
>
> We acquired from the Depot disposal scrapheap six aged Crossleys. These veterans were in such a sad state that each had to be conveyed to Heliopolis on a trailer. If one could have credited them with sentience, how they must have laughed at returning to the RAF in the hey-day of their retirement. Like many another old 'dug-out', they embarked on a new life crowded with indignity and usefulness.

The men were divided into six parties, each allotted to a car, and tools were issued. Then a blackboard lecture was given in the hangar about a particular unit of the car, and the men would thereupon strip it from their car. So each chassis was reduced to its lowest terms and so each was rebuilt. The men had no further assistance than that given at these lectures; therefore every car when finished was a liberal education to them when they learnt to drive. My time only permitted me to teach the two brightest members of each crew to drive and they taught the rest.

The deserted Suez Road had seen excitement in the old days of the Indian Mail but for amusement it had to wait until the year 1922 when it provided the kindergarten for the Royal Air Force armoured cars.

It will be realised that these cars were in no sense reliable, and when men had walked back a few miles for tools or breakdown gear once, they never left camp without all the tools they could lay their hands upon.[3]

Tom Kinna was a senior NCO in the group and responsible for drilling the men, he commented on matters from the airmen's perspective:

Numbers 1 and 2 Armoured Car Companies were very much my babies in the old days. Rather a one man band until I received 'Harthur' Chambers, the fitter armourer from 47 Squadron. He was really the cat's whiskers in instructing, but am afraid his 'H's' used to fly everywhere. However, 'Harthur' was a good scout during training hours. After which, he disappeared to married quarters with his wife and kiddie. I lived very much on my own in a tent on the edge of the desert.

...Later in the proceedings a number of ex-Naval 138ers, pilots and observers arrived. They hadn't the faintest idea of drill etc., but the majority turned out nice chaps. They insisted on awarding Naval punishment like 'so many days 10A etc.'[4] until I had 'em trained. Am afraid the officers were more trouble to me at the start than the airmen.

I used to train the troops to 'stand at ease' from the present ... then we had a posh parade. My word the troops were good. I must say in the end

Airmen of the newly established RAF armoured car companies at Heliopolis with one of the Crossley tenders (© Crown copyright. RAF Regiment Museum).

turned out quite good.... Am not shooting a line when I say they were easily the best drilled and smartest unit I have ever seen in the RAF. Yes I have seen a few at Uxbridge, Cranwell and Cardington but never to touch No 1 Armoured Car Company.[5]

While many of the officers had previously served in the Royal Flying Corps, there was a group who hailed from the RNAS and some indeed who held naval decorations such as the Distinguished Service Cross. Observer Officer Lorenzo Kerry, was one example. He would receive an award for gallantry two years later while serving with the armoured cars in Kurdistan. As the men became more proficient with their driving and mechanical skills more ambitious expeditions were planned. Flying Officer Martyn continues:

Later, when all could drive properly, Flying Officer S... [sic] and myself would lead a convoy some miles out into the desert and camp for the night. S... would give the men firing practice with the machine guns and teach them outpost duties, meanwhile I adjusted each car so that it was sure to break down on the homeward trip. The men learnt how to look after themselves at night, cook and generally get friendly with the desert. Next morning S... and myself would return on the Rolls and the rest used to get back later - much later. The first crew to arrive would receive instruction on a Rolls-Royce next day. Training terminated by practice in fast driving in the bazaars and thick traffic of Cairo. This was necessary, but very terrifying to the instructor.

In April we were able to hand over a reliable, and resourceful, collection of gunner-drivers.

Number 1 Armoured Car Company was formally established on 19 December 1921.[6] Operations, training, and discipline of the company were directly under the control of Headquarters, Egyptian Group. On 1 February 1922 it was raised from 'flight' to 'squadron' status and became self-accounting with 176 men, seven Crossley tenders and one Rolls-Royce armoured car.[7] Eventually ten 1914- and two

A group photo taken soon after the formation of No 1 Armoured Car Company (© Crown copyright. RAF Regiment Museum).

1920-pattern 'Type A' Rolls-Royces were on strength.[8] For the first few months they were led by Flight-Lieutenant Frank Fernihough MC who came over from No 14 Squadron in Palestine. Squadron Leader Alfred J. Currie, who had served with the RNAS during the Great War, arrived from Great Britain and assumed permanent command on 7 April 1922. A month later No 1 Company and the three sections received orders to move north to come under command of Palestine Wing. The Company HQ and one section were sent to Jerusalem, with a section each at Jenin and Semakh in northern Palestine (Map 1, p. 15).[9]

The train carrying No 1 Armoured Car Company personnel and the Lancias from Egypt to Palestine (RAFACA).

On 7 April 1922 the remaining airmen were formed into No 2 Armoured Car Company, under the command of Squadron Leader Martin Copeman.[10] The Company would initially consist of a Headquarters but only two sections and, by May, one of the latter had been despatched to Amman in Transjordan to work with RAF Trans-Jordania. A section of the No 2 Armoured Car Company would be permanently based in the Transjordanian capital for the next two decades and would play a crucial role in the defence of what would become the Hashemite Kingdom of Jordan. Number 2 Company spent another year at RAF Heliopolis before the Company HQ and the remaining section were also ordered to Palestine. By May 1923, the Company, completely equipped with Rolls-Royce armoured cars, had formed a third section. The HQ and one section were stationed at Jerusalem, with another based at Jenin, having taken over from the section from No 1 Company, with the third remaining at Amman.

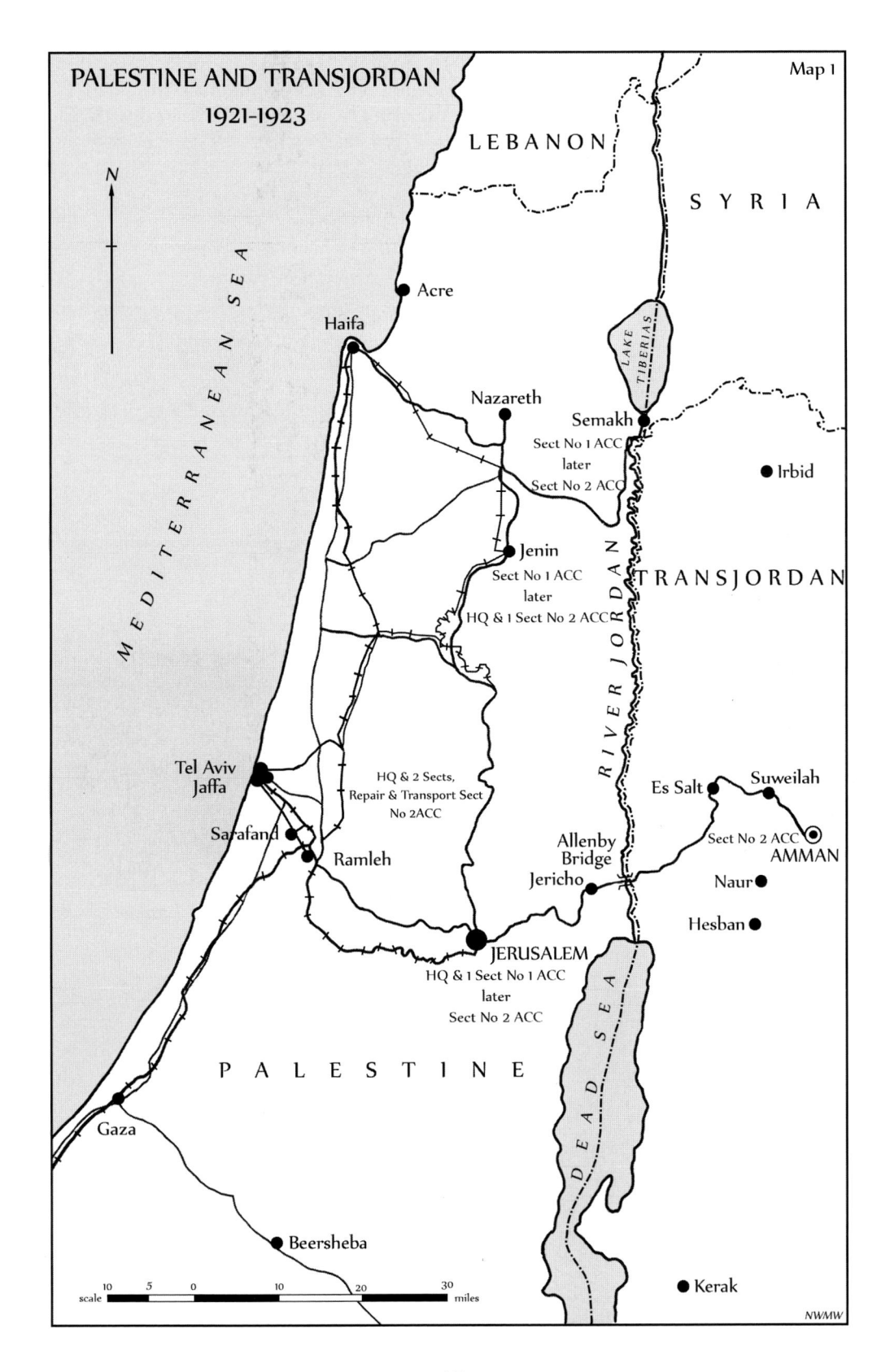

PALESTINE AND TRANSJORDAN
1921-1923

Map 1

LEBANON

SYRIA

MEDITERRANEAN SEA

Acre

Haifa

LAKE TIBERIAS

Nazareth

Semakh
Sect No 1 ACC
later
Sect No 2 ACC

Irbid

Jenin
Sect No 1 ACC
later
HQ & 1 Sect No 2 ACC

TRANSJORDAN

RIVER JORDAN

Tel Aviv
Jaffa

HQ & 2 Sects,
Repair & Transport Sect
No 2ACC

Es Salt

Suweilah

Sect No 2 ACC

AMMAN

Sarafand

Ramleh

Allenby
Bridge
Jericho

Naur

Hesban

JERUSALEM
HQ & 1 Sect No 1 ACC
later
Sect No 2 ACC

DEAD SEA

PALESTINE

Gaza

Beersheba

Kerak

scale — miles

NWMW

A parade and inspection of No 1 Armoured Car Company with their Lancia armoured trucks at Jerusalem, 1923 (© Crown copyright. RAF Regiment Museum).

Headquarters and 'A' Section of No 2 Armoured Car Company parade at Sarafand, October 1923 (© Crown copyright. RAF Regiment Museum).

Two Rolls-Royces of 'A' Section, No 2 Armoured Car Company, 1923. The leading vehicle bears the name Eagle and the winged roundel. This may have been the precursor to the 'winged wheel' which was used later on the badge of No 2 Company. (© Crown copyright. RAF Regiment Museum).

'B' Section of No 2 Armoured Car Company and a Bristol Fighter at Jenin in 1923. The Rolls-Royces still bear their Army registration numbers (© Crown copyright. RAF Regiment Museum).

Flight-Lieutenant Philip Yorke Moore, another ex-RNAS officer, had been one of the founding officers of No 2 Armoured Car Company. He arrived in Amman in March 1923 to take command of 'C' Section. He prepared a detailed report on his command soon after arrival. The crews had received their preliminary training at Heliopolis but some had a distance to go to reach a satisfactory state. While not a ringing endorsement of the abilities of some of the members of the Section, he did identify potential. Of one of his drivers, Middleton, he wrote:

> This airman is a fair driver, but he seems to have a very rough idea of how to look after a car and to keep the engine in proper running order. However, he seems to have taken notice of some points to remember, which I told him

Two Lancias near the River Jordan. In a reference, perhaps, to the RNAS lineage of some of the officers and airmen of the Companies, the vehicles bear the names of First Sea Lords, Wilson and Beatty. These may have been the Lancias from No 1 Company that became 'D' Section of No 2 Company in 1924 (© Crown copyright. RAF Museum).

about, and is keen to learn as much as possible. He now has a copy of the Rolls-Royce Handbook and should show considerable improvement in the up-keep of his car.

Up to the present I have him giving all the cars a good oiling and greasing of chassis, and overhauling of brake-rods....

He is now also receiving instruction in the handling of revolvers, dismantling and reassembling of same, Semaphore and Morse codes, otherwise he knows nothing more than his own particular trade of Fitter, Driver Petrol.[11]

The Section NCO, Corporal Lee, impressed Yorke Moore. He was the right man for the job, as he had a good knowledge of the Section armaments having been an armament instructor on another Station and had completed a four-month course. Lee had reported to his Section commander that the armourers, Aircraftmen Anderson, Phillips and Greenfield, seemed to have a good knowledge of the trade, but they needed rifle and bayonet drill. Yorke Moore decided to employ Lee in providing training in rifle, revolver and machine gun drill and musketry. Further training was given in: moving in extended order, grouping and application firing with the rifle, and if possible, the machine gun on the range, how to bring machine guns into action from the cars, and with the tripod on the ground. This was followed by a short course on Semaphore and Morse, bonds and hitches, knots and splices. The latter no doubt strongly influenced by Yorke Moore's naval background.

'B' and 'C' Sections of No 2 Armoured Car Company with their 1914 (left) and 'Standard Type A' cars (right) (© Crown copyright. RAF Regiment Museum).

The condition of the armoured cars, however, left something to be desired. The turrets were in poor working order and he ordered thorough cleaning of the outsides of the cars and engines. He concluded his report on a positive note:

... a satisfactory start has been made and the men are showing great keenness to learn things and in carrying out any work I have put them onto.... I should like bring to your notice the very great keenness and zeal shown by the Corporal in everything he does...I shall hope to have the cars and crews ready, and good enough, for an urgent call, after a fortnight with them? They will not, however, be very proficient after such short training for this particular work, but they should be good enough to deal with a real emergency.[12]

By late 1923, it had been decided that only one armoured car company was required in Palestine and Transjordan. For reasons that are unclear, No 1 Company was chosen for disbandment. The Repair and Transport Sections at Sarafand and the 'D' (Lancia) section stationed in Jerusalem were spared and were transferred to No 2 Company. The remaining officers and men were dispersed to other tasks in Palestine and Egypt or returned to the United Kingdom.[13] No 1 Company had served for more than a year and a half in Palestine.[14] Tom Kinna described the disappointment:

> The last sad thing about it all was [that] we were selected to form a large Guard of Honour at the opening of the War Graves Cemetery in Syria. We were subjected to parade after parade in which every Senior Officer flew up from Egypt to attend. The troops voluntarily arranged with Accounts for pay to be held back for the time. We all looked forward and lived for the wild parties to come. Then out of the blue we were disbanded.[15]

Sirius, a Lancia of No 1 Armoured Car Company on a patrol in Palestine (© Crown copyright. RAF Museum).

While Middle East Command had been preparing the Heliopolis armoured car contingent for service in Palestine and Transjordan, another group of officers and airmen were gathering in the United Kingdom in preparation for service in Iraq. At RAF Uxbridge in early 1922, a cadre of NCOs and airmen were selected to go out to Iraq to deal with the handover of the armoured car duties from the Tank Corps.[16] LAC William Edwards was in this party and continues:

> We went out on a private liner. There were 60 of us on the boat. Had a very nice time going over. Landed us at Bombay. Then we went up by rail to

Deolali ... for 6 weeks. We caught the train again from Deolali to Karachi. Picked up another boat there and went to Basra. It was the first of June we landed, and we then got the train to Baghdad and went straight to the Tank Corps. We were attached to them as the advanced party to get used to the 'armoureds' before the main body came out in early November.[17]

The main echelon of the Armoured Car Details or, as they later became known, the First Armoured Car Detachment, was gathering from late May 1922 at the School of Technical Training (Men) at RAF Manston in Kent. Under the command of Wing Commander W. Harold Primrose DFC, with about 15 officers, the Detachment was to be readied for service in Iraq and consequently an Armoured Car Crew Training Course had been instigated.[18]

RAF Manston, Kent, home of the School of Technical Training (Men), where the armoured car detachment for Iraq was assembled (© Crown copyright. Cox, RAF Regiment Museum).

Some of the airmen had just received their basic training at RAF Uxbridge where they were introduced to military discipline, saluting, first aid and personal hygiene, physical training, foot and rifle drill and firing. They were also required to be proficient with the Lewis and Vickers machine-guns, pistols, Stokes mortars and Mills grenades. Walter Brett joined up in December 1921 at White Hart Road in Portsmouth. After completing a medical examination and an educational test and having "an extremely long talk by the officer in charge", he and the two others took the Oath of Allegiance.[19] The next day an RAF Corporal took them to Uxbridge where they had another medical, were given the appropriate forms to fill out and hence became *bona fide* airmen. He continues:

The scale of kit was half Khaki, which was used for normal working, and Best Blue, which was used for walking out and ceremonial.

I became a member of 68 Squad, which was 30-strong and began our foot drill, rifle drill and ceremonial parades. Christmas was spent at Uxbridge and in early 1922 the whole squad was moved to the Isle of Grain on detachment to continue basic training, and after a further two months returned to Uxbridge to pass out parade. I was now posted to another unit at Uxbridge together with the other lads and now named by the Depot Warrant Officer as 'Machine-Gunners for Iraq.' One did not know much about the future at the time, but we continued to grow in strength, and we were divided into two sections, and commenced training, one on Vickers guns and the other on the Lewis gun. I was with a Vickers gun section.[20]

After three months, they all moved to RAF Manston for the Armoured Car Crew Course. Here they qualified for the trades of 'Driver Petrol', 'Fitter, Driver Petrol' or 'Fitter, Armourer'. By the end of the course they would have an intimate knowledge of the internal combustion engine, brakes, carburettors, oils and ignition systems. They were also given some Arabic lessons and trained in semaphore and Morse signalling to six-words per minute with an Aldis lamp.

The other men who made up the first drafts of the Armoured Car Companies came from a range of backgrounds. A few, such as Edward Middleton, had joined the RAF in 1919 as a Boy Mechanic and had just completed their time at the School of Technical Training (Boys) at RAF Halton. Mesopotamia would be their first posting. Many were ex-RFC and RNAS fitters, drivers and armourers who had re-enlisted in the new RAF, some ex-Army gunners and infantrymen, while others were aircraft hands who had been remustered to armoured car crew.[21] One group had arrived following the creation of the Irish Free State. With the British withdrawal from the southern counties of Ireland, the Government had a large contingent of demobilised men who had served in the Royal Irish Constabulary and the reserve units, the 'Black and Tans' and 'Auxiliaries'. Unsurprisingly, many them were in a hurry to leave Ireland given the changed circumstances. When the first Lancias arrived, a party of them drove up to London where they had a wild night until the Military Police rounded them up. Other airmen were content to take the more sedate trip to nearby Ramsgate, or Margate and the seaside amusement park known as 'Dreamland'.[22]

Many of the airmen already had military service but had returned from civilian life because the peacetime economy was still in depression. Jobs were in short supply as many ex-servicemen were looking for work at that time. The prospect of being paid to learn a trade and receiving three square meals a day made Service life an attractive proposition for many of these young men, as it would for much of the 1920s and 30s.

One young airman was James Cox. He had enlisted in the RNAS in 1916 and had been stationed in England for the duration of the war. He was transferred to the RAF on its formation and, following the Armistice, had been sent to Germany for two years. By June 1921 he had returned to the Transport Depot at RAF Uxbridge. On 30 August 1922, he was promoted to Corporal and joined the First Detachment of Armoured Cars at Manston, whose task he said was, "… to proceed to Iraq, otherwise Mesopotamia, for the purpose of policing the desert and opening up new lines of communication."[23]

The men would get experience on the detachment's Lancia armoured cars

Corporal James Cox at Baghdad, in late 1922 (© Crown copyright. Cox, RAF Regiment Museum).

and Crossley tenders, but not Rolls-Royces, though some fitters were sent off to Derby to attend a course at the Rolls-Royce Works.[24] That would have to wait until they reached Iraq. Cox described the preparations for the move, and some of the frustrations for the men who had already had seen service in the military:

> From this date until the morning of 13 September most of our time was spent in sorting of overseas kit … and a fair amount of squad drill, which was not digested with favourableness by the men … which resulted in the purchase of a large box of soldiers and [this was] sent to Flying Officer Norrington with a note enclosed – NOW B….R THESE ABOUT.[25]

At 0430 hours on 14 September 1922, the Detachment, organised now as two companies, marched off from RAF Manston in pouring rain to the strains of the band. By the time they reached Margate station two miles away they were feeling rather miserable. Here, however, they were met by a large crowd that had gathered to see them off, despite the early hour. To hearty cheers they boarded the train and travelled to Southampton Docks. Here they joined the remainder of the RAF Iraq contingent of 1000 airmen, 18 warrant officers, 81 officers and 10 nursing sisters, under the command of Group Captain, the Honourable, J.D. Boyle CBE DSO and embarked on the RAF troopship the SS *Braemar Castle*. Also loaded on board were 14 of the Lancias. The event was unique in that it was the first time the RAF had chartered a ship exclusively for a draft of troops. The *Daily Echo* described the departure:

> The troops were in a merry mood as they embarked and 'Here we are, then' and other songs of a light vein were sung with hearty enthusiasm.... Five hundred are for duty with the RAF armoured car and armoured train detachments. Most of the men have done at least two years' service, while quite 70 per cent were in the air service during the Great War.... The Manston men consisted of Nos 3 and 4 Companies, the first being under command of Squadron Leader Guard CMG DSO and the second under that of Squadron Leader Willock and Flying Officer Goring DSO MC.
> ... I have just come from Mesopotamia, the officer [Flying Officer Goring] went on, 'where I have been four years. We are going to be out for two years. We have been preparing for this for about six months. The idea is to police the country and cut down expenses by withdrawing troops and substituting a mechanical force of aeroplanes and armoured cars'.[26]

The *Braemar Castle* set sail at 1530 hours that afternoon and anchored off Lee-on-Solent, a stop made all the more exciting when a flying boat crashed into the side of the ship, as it cruised alongside. The following morning at 0630 hours the ship weighed anchor. James Cox wrote with some solemnity, "Can just see Isle of Wight away in the distance from our stern quarters. Good Bye dear Old England, who knows if we shall ever return."[27]

After crossing the Bay of Biscay through a heavy swell, squalls and fog, the ship passed through the Straits of Gibraltar, four days later. In the meantime, their intended destination of Iraq had been suddenly altered to Constantinople, due to deteriorating international relations between Britain and Turkey, in what became known as the Chanak Crisis.[28]

The first President of Turkey, Kemal Atatürk, had decided in September 1922 to repudiate the post-First World War Treaty of Sèvres, which had been signed with the Allied Powers two years earlier. This had guaranteed access by the Allies' to the Straits of the Dardanelles, Bosphorus, Black Sea and other strategic points, and use of telegraph and wireless communications. A stand-off had arisen when Turkish forces had come into close contact with British and French positions entrenched at Chanak on the eastern side of the Dardanelles Strait. If these positions were occupied, the Turks could set up gun positions that would control the Straits. Lloyd George, then British Prime Minister, ordered the troops to stand firm and despatched British air, ground and naval units to Constantinople.

The airmen of the Armoured Car Detachment could clearly see gunfire on the rocky shore as they sailed through the Dardanelles on 26 September. After passing under the guns of HMS *Revenge* and HMS *Centurion* their ship was held off Chanak where they were issued with helmets and made ready for a landing. Fortunately, no action was required and the *Braemar Castle* was ordered to sail for Constantinople, which was reached two days later. Here they disembarked, were issued with marching order equipment, rifles and bayonets, and in a show of force were marched through the city led by the Fife and Drum Band of the Irish Guards. For the next fortnight, they pounded the cobbled roads 'showing the flag'. The 'stag' lasted 14 days, with their task being to safeguard strategic points such as armouries, barracks, aerodromes and docks and as escorts to military supplies, until they were ordered to re-embark on the *Braemar Castle*. The whole incident was a very welcome break after two weeks at sea. Cox noted that this exercise had not been without gain as many airmen returned to the ship with an extensive collection of rifles and pistols which had been 'liberated' from the Turkish Armoury. The War Office had diverted the ship despite Trenchard arguing that these airmen were required urgently in Iraq to face their own Turkish problem. Fortunately the Chanak dispute was resolved peacefully and the detachment resumed their voyage.[29]

Port Said was reached by mid-October, and the ship passed through the Suez Canal and headed into the Red Sea. Hammocks were slung on deck as the heat below decks became unbearable. This was ameliorated to some extent as a high sea ran for the next few days. On reaching the Arabian Sea the ship was ordered to slow to 5 knots as a conference on Mesopotamia was in session and the troops could not land until matters were resolved.

The four armoured car companies, Nos 3, 4, 5 and 6 were formed up on the ship prior to disembarking. Aircraftman Walter Brett was posted to 'C' Section of No 6 Armoured Car Company, while Corporal Cox was pleased with the news that he would be attached to HQ of No 4 Armoured Car Company. Once the *Braemar Castle* had reached the Shatt el Arab waterway, the sand banks and unpredictable water depth meant they had to be transferred to the SS *Varela* with its shallower draft. At 0800 hours on Friday 3 November 1922, the men of the First Armoured Car Detachment alighted onto the Anglo-Persian Oil Company wharf at Basra (Map 2, p. 24). This first day in 'Mespot' was noted almost hour-by-hour by Corporal Cox:

0930	All ashore now for a four mile march to the rest camp at Camp Makina
1130	Arrived rest camp and detailed to tents. Sand, sand, sand.
1400	Issue of rations half a pint of tea and a small loaf of dry bread to each man. What a country? Miles of sand, wherever you look.
2145	Turn in for the night. One blanket to lay upon, one for cover. Flies by the millions.[30]

By Sunday, the initial excitement of life in the Camp was wearing thin, particularly following breakfast of only two slices of bread, tea and one rasher of bacon. "Not enough to keep a fly alive", commented Corporal Cox.[31] One of his fellow NCOs, Corporal Early, accidentally shot himself in the leg while trying to break a revolver procured from the Turkish Armoury. This led to an immediate general inspection of kit for the contraband weapons. After four days in camp, the officers and airmen of No 4 Company boarded a train, each man being allocated one wooden seat and two blankets, and they set off on the 270 mile journey to Baghdad, a day's ride away.

Notes

1. Wing Commander T.J. Kinna MBE, late No 1 Armoured Car Company. Correspondence: 26 January 1961 to OC 1 Squadron RAF Regiment.
2. This could possibly be Flying Officer Gilbert F. Smylie DSC, No 216 Squadron RAF.
3. AIR 1/2391/228/11/146 *An account by course students of service experiences: F/Lt. G. Martyn, 1914-1922.* These were Crossley tenders which were standard issue transport vehicles in the RAF.
4. '138ers' were Royal Navy (RNAS) personnel who had transferred to the newly-formed RAF under Air Ministry Weekly Order 138 while those who had transferred from the Army were covered by AMWO 139. '10A punishment' required the recalcitrant rating to turn out an hour before all other hands, eat meals on the exposed part of the deck if on board ship, periods standing facing the bulkhead and varying degrees of limitation on the rum ration.
5. Kinna, *Correspondence.*
6. AMWO 48 *No 1 Armoured Car Company: Formation, 19 January 1922* and AMWO 86 *No 1 Armoured Car Company: Administration, 26 January 1922.*
7. AIR 5/1239 *HQ RAF Middle East: monthly summaries Vol. I, 1921-1924.*
8. B. Robertson, *Wheels of the RAF* (Cambridge: Patrick Stephens, 1983), p. 41.
9. AMWO 477 *Movement of No 1 Armoured Car Company to Palestine, 15 June 1922.*
10. AMWO 288 *No 2 Armoured Car Company: Formation, 6 April 1922.*
11. Yorke Moore papers, RAF Regiment Museum Archives.
12. *Ibid.*
13. AMWO 55 *Reorganisation of Armoured Car Companies in Palestine, 24 January 1924.* Squadron Leader Currie went to the Aircraft Depot in Egypt and later to HQ Palestine Command. Flight Lieutenant G.E. Gibbs and Observer Officer Lorenzo Kerry went to No 2 Company. The remaining officers returned to the RAF Depot in the United Kingdom.
14. Sadly, no Form 540s seem to have been kept for the period that No 1 Armoured Car Company was stationed in Palestine from 1922 and 1923.

15 Kinna, *Correspondence*.
16 B.H. Liddell Hart, *The Tanks: The History of the Royal Tank Regiment and its predecessors Heavy Branch Machine-Gun Corps, Tank Corps and Royal Tank Corps, 1914-1945, Vol. I* (London: Cassell, 1959), pp. 472-473. Tank Corps armoured car units in the Middle East were distributed as follows:
Mesopotamia (Iraq and Persia): 1 and 2 Armoured Car Companies (June 1920-Dec 1923), 6 Armoured Car Company (January 1920-December 1921); Egypt: 3 Armoured Car Company (1920-1929); Palestine: 4 Armoured Car Company (September 1920-May 1922) and Liddell Hart, pp. 208-209, noted that the loss of this role by the Tank Corps Armoured Car Companies was "unfortunate for the future of the forces that the armoured arm did not have the possibility of breaking away from the cramping grip of old-fashioned hands as the air arm had done. Although the RAF long-suffered from being the youngest sister of the Services, the Tank Corps suffered much worse from being the most junior combatant corps of the Army. Its story was to be that of a Cinderella without a fairy godmother."
17 William H. Edwards, *Interview 4824* (London: IWM Sound Archive, 1981).
18 Air Commodore W. Harold Primrose CBE DFC (1884-1957). Primrose served in the Argyll and Sutherland Highlanders from 1903 to 1909. He re-enlisted at the outbreak of the Great War and transferred to the RFC a year later. He retired in 1944 after having been AOC of No 38 Wing and RAF Northern Ireland.
19 AC85/6 *The Erk and his Armoured Cars: Flight Lieutenant Riggs* (RAF Museum, Hendon: Unpublished manuscript, n.d.). Walter H. Brett retired from the RAF as a Squadron Leader in 1953 after 32 years' service.
20 AC85/6 *The Erk and his Armoured Cars*.
21 Edward Middleton, Correspondence, 24 August 1978. RAF Regiment Museum Archives.
22 AIR 5/188 *Proposed assumption by RAF of military command of Palestine, 1922*, and Robertson, *Wheels of the RAF*, p. 41.
23 J.A.S. Cox, RNAS/RAF, *Photographic Album and Diary*. RAF Regiment Museum Archives.
24 AC85/6 *The Erk and his Armoured Cars*.
25 *Ibid*.
26 'Airmen for Mespot,' *The Daily Echo*, Southampton, 14 September 1922. Flying Officer Charles Hubert Goring DSO MC had begun the First World War as a Lance Corporal in the 20th Hussars before being commissioned in the Royal Fusiliers. He was later attached to the Motor Machine-Gun Corps. He was then seconded for service with the RAF where he was gazetted as a Flying Officer in the RAF armoured cars. He was awarded his MC while serving with the Machine-Gun Corps and the DSO for gallantry during a convoy ambush in Mesopotamia in 1920 while in No 1 Armoured Car Company, Tank Corps. During the Second World War he served with the Special Operations Executive.
27 Cox, *Photographic Album and Diary*.
28 Constantinople became known as Istanbul following the creation of the Republic of Turkey in 1923.
29 J. Laffin, *Swifter than Eagles* (Edinburgh: William Blackwood & Sons, 1964), p. 165.
30 Cox, *Photographic Album and Diary*.
31 *Ibid*.

CHAPTER THREE

Transjordan 1922-1924 'Amman's Sure Shield'

"... I want to send you my very hearty congratulations on the result of your battle and on the highly successful manner in which the armoured cars justified the title of Amman's Sure Shield. I am so glad you have had an opportunity at last of proving the high efficiency of your training and the excellence of your personnel."
                                        Wing Commander Thomas Hubbard, Palestine Wing[1]

The end of the Great War had not led to peace in the Middle East. There had been a rebellion in Iraq in 1920 which had required some 20,000 British and Indian troops to quell. The French had assumed control of Lebanon and Syria but after disagreements with King Feisal they occupied Damascus in 1919 and drove him into exile. This had outraged the Arab world and led to great concern that Britain and France would not keep their wartime promises. Palestine was to be administered by a British High Commissioner in Jerusalem. There was suspicion, however, from Arab leaders arising from the Balfour Declaration of 1917, by which Britain had agreed to support a Jewish homeland in Palestine.

With so much unease and discontent by Arab leaders, the British administration decided to create a state under Arab administration in the wild and unwanted mountains and deserts east of the River Jordan. The area known as Transjordan, had been specifically excluded from the provisions of the Balfour declaration. It had been ruled in a limited way from Damascus but, following the expulsion of Feisal, there was a return to the *status quo* that had operated during Ottoman times, whereby Transjordan had not existed as an identifiable political entity.

Transjordan was to be ruled as an Emirate under Abdullah ibn al-Hussein, the brother of King Feisal of Iraq and second son of the King Hussein ibn Ali of the Hedjaz, Sharif of Mecca and King of the Arabs. The Amir Abdullah was a soldier, scholar and a diplomat possessing great personal charm. He had played an important role in the negotiations with the British which had led to the Arab Revolt against the Ottoman Empire and commanded an Arab army in the war that followed. In early 1921, Abdullah moved north with a 5000 strong force with which he intended to fight to regain the Syrian throne for his brother Feisal from the French. Churchill, keen to avoid confrontation with the French, had agreed to meet with him in Jerusalem during March 1921. On arrival by train in Amman, Abdullah had been received with a tumultuous welcome from the local citizenry and had been invited to remain there and take the Emirate of Transjordan (Map 3, p. 29).[2]

Abdullah's first administration was formed in April 1921 and Transjordan was proclaimed as an independent state under British tutelage on 25 May 1923, following confirmation by the League of Nations. The capital of Transjordan was established at Amman, which, despite its high status in the ancient Roman Empire, was now only a small village of only 2000 people, a third of which were Circassians who had been driven from Central Asia by the Russians some 50 years earlier. The new state had a population of 230,000, with many village dwellers, the *fellaheen*, who were settled and cultivated the land, while more than 55,000 were *bedouin*, who dwelled in the desert with their camels, sheep and goats. Much of the country was desert and lacked revenue sources. The collapse of the Ottoman Empire had left the settled inhabitants without any form of government, while the bedouin roamed the deserts as warring tribes.[3]

Abdullah requested that he be given British officers, funds and some form of 'aerial support' to assist with the establishment of the new kingdom. While not garrisoned by large numbers of British troops, the RAF would construct airfields, provide aircraft and detachments of armoured cars, and establish the air routes from Cairo to the border with Iraq. This heralded the beginning of a long, close and fruitful relationship between Transjordan, later the Hashemite Kingdom of Jordan, and the RAF, which would last through the Second World War and up to the departure of the British military from the Middle East in 1956.

An aerial view of RAF Amman (© Crown copyright. RAF Regiment Museum).

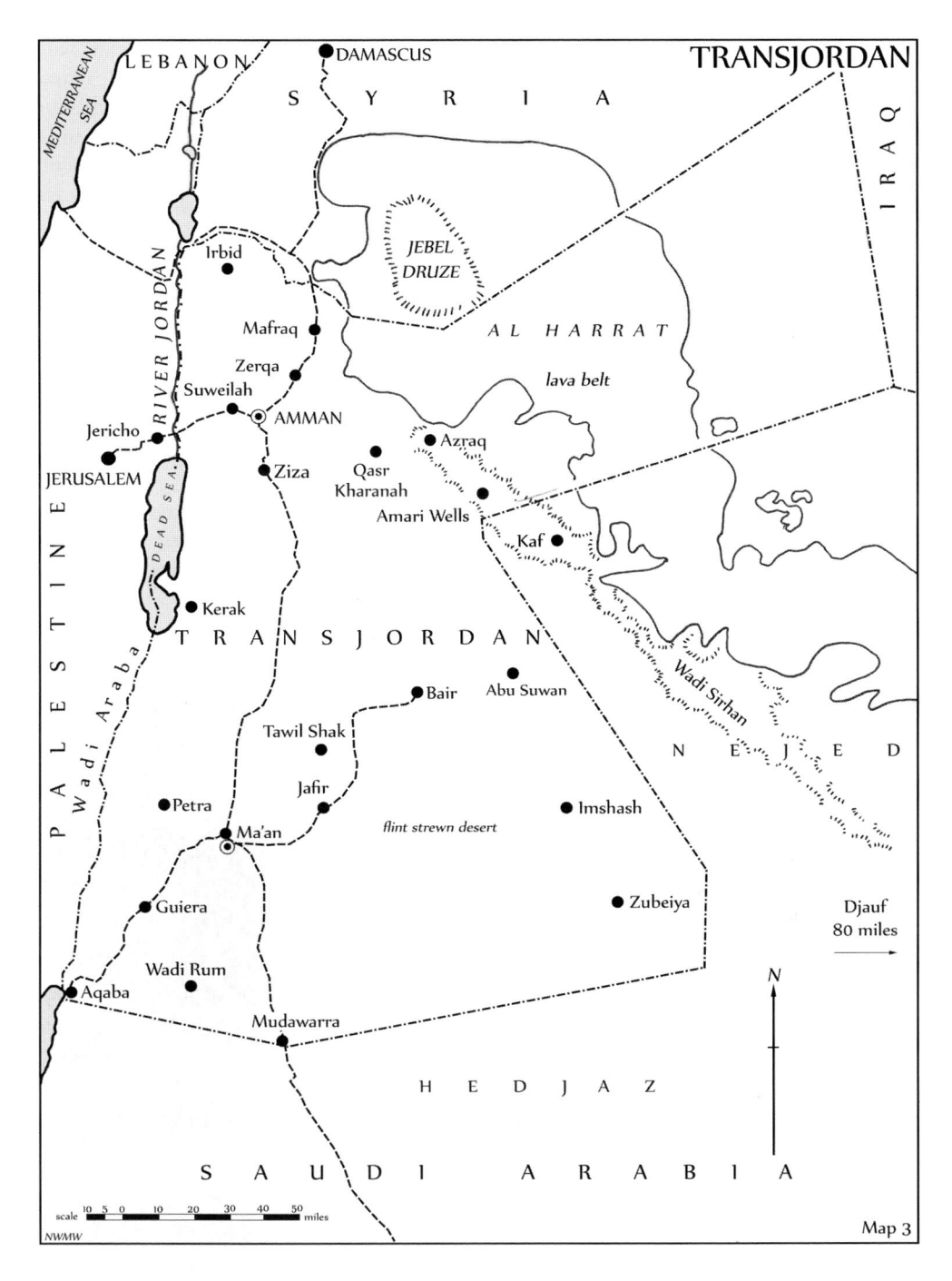

There were a number of political and inter-tribal intrigues still to be dealt with in the fledgling state. The national boundaries were ill-defined and Abdullah's throne was by no means secure, and one of his first actions was to form a police and military force. Given the budgetary restrictions, funds were only sufficient to maintain order in the capital and the provincial towns of Irbid, Salt and Kerak. The military force was composed predominantly of men who had served in the Ottoman army before transferring their allegiance to the Arab banner on the march to Damascus in 1917. Abdullah named this force, Jeysh al Arabi, or the Arab Army.[4] In British circles, this was considered too grand and it was referred to as the Arab Legion. The commander was Captain F.G. Peake, who became known as 'Peake' Pasha, a British officer who had served during the Arab Revolt as commander of the Egyptian Camel Corps. By 1921, the Arab Legion was composed of two infantry companies, two squadrons of cavalry, a troop of artillery and a signals section. A subsidy was provided by the British Government to support the Legion and police force.

A small RAF contingent known as RAF Trans-Jordania was established in June 1922, and an airfield was built on the eastern outskirts of Amman. Under the command of Group Captain Robert Gordon CB CMG DSO, it comprised a flying section of No 14 (Bomber) Squadron, equipped with the Great War vintage Bristol Fighter, one section of No 2 Armoured Car Company, and a meteorological station. The RAF camp and aerodrome were situated on a small natural plateau among the hills to the east of the town. The western edge of the aerodrome had a precipitous drop into a wide wadi[5], which became infamous for those pilots with too heavy a load or too short a run when taking off in that direction, or for those who overshot when landing.

Amir Abdullah's task was a complex one. Many of his people had previously looked to Damascus or Jerusalem for their markets; the society was highly tribal and he had to deal with political advisors with either Arab or British perspectives, and balance their often conflicting expectations. With the Emirate having only been in existence for a few months, there were many difficulties already being encountered in public administration. Many of the public officials had come from Syria following the expulsion of Feisal from Damascus. This had excluded Jordanians from many of these positions and tax collection tended to favour some tribes and ethnic groups over others. There were also extravagances, which meant the limited revenues were being wasted. This led to agitation for changes in the administration and it was no surprise when more serious threats arose to the Amir's position.

Airmen of Yorke Moore's Section stop for a meal (© Crown copyright. RAF Regiment Museum).

From the time of the stationing of the RAF armoured car detachment in Amman there developed a spirit of close cooperation with the Arab Legion. The cars would often be called out to assist a Legion detachment dealing with recalcitrant local tribes. The Adwan, a settled tribe occupying the country to the north-west of Amman, were particularly stirred to action in late August 1923. A dispute over excessive taxation, and poorly administered watering rights, which favoured the Beni Sakhr tribe over the Adwan, had resulted in bloodshed. This led to their Sultan asking for an audience with Abdullah. Although prepared to hear their case, little was done after the meeting to resolve the problem. Dissatisfied, in mid-September they moved *en masse* towards Amman, demanding a resolution. The Amir Abdullah agreed to meet them to hear their grievances. Their leader, Sultan ibn Adwan, arrived with 500 men armed with rifles, some with swords drawn. Despite meeting with the Amir, they departed in an unhappy mood and further trouble was expected.

An inspection of Flight Lieutenant Yorke Moore's 'C' Section, of No 2 Armoured Car Company, by Group Captain N.D.K. McEwen CMG DSO Officer Commanding RAF Transjordania (© Crown copyright. RAF Regiment Museum).

By 13 September, events had taken an unfortunate turn. The Adwan and their associated tribe, the Ajarmi, were reported to be harassing travellers on the Amman to Jericho road. They had captured two Arab Legion posts, while some 300 tents were observed at Hesban close to Amman and later they picqueted the hills to the north of Amman. An ultimatum was sent to Sultan Adwan asking for his surrender. Failing this, the Arab Legion, with the assistance of the RAF, would move against him. At the same time, preparations were made for the defence of Amman railway station, the Amir's camp, the Arab Legion camp and the RAF airfield. To add further to the tension, the Adwan then captured another Legion post at Suweilah, cut the telephone and telegraph wire to Es Salt, and blocked the Suweilah to Amman road. The ultimatum had not expired but it was considered necessary to act.

RAF Amman had been placed on full alert the previous night with machine-gun teams and riflemen being placed in defence posts. At 0500 hours on 16 September, two aircraft of No 14 Squadron, the lead aircraft piloted by Flight Lieutenant Magrath, took off from Amman aerodrome to locate the Adwan. He failed to observe any unusual activity, although this wasn't helped by the presence of heavy ground mist. A second sortie an hour later, however, found Suweilah town full of bedouin horsemen (Map 4, p. 32).[6]

'C' Section of No 2 Armoured Car Company, under the command of Flight-Lieutenant Philip Yorke Moore, had patrolled to Hesban on 15 September and then spent the night 'standing-by' at the Amir's camp as an attack was expected

Map 4

SUWEILAH
16 September 1923

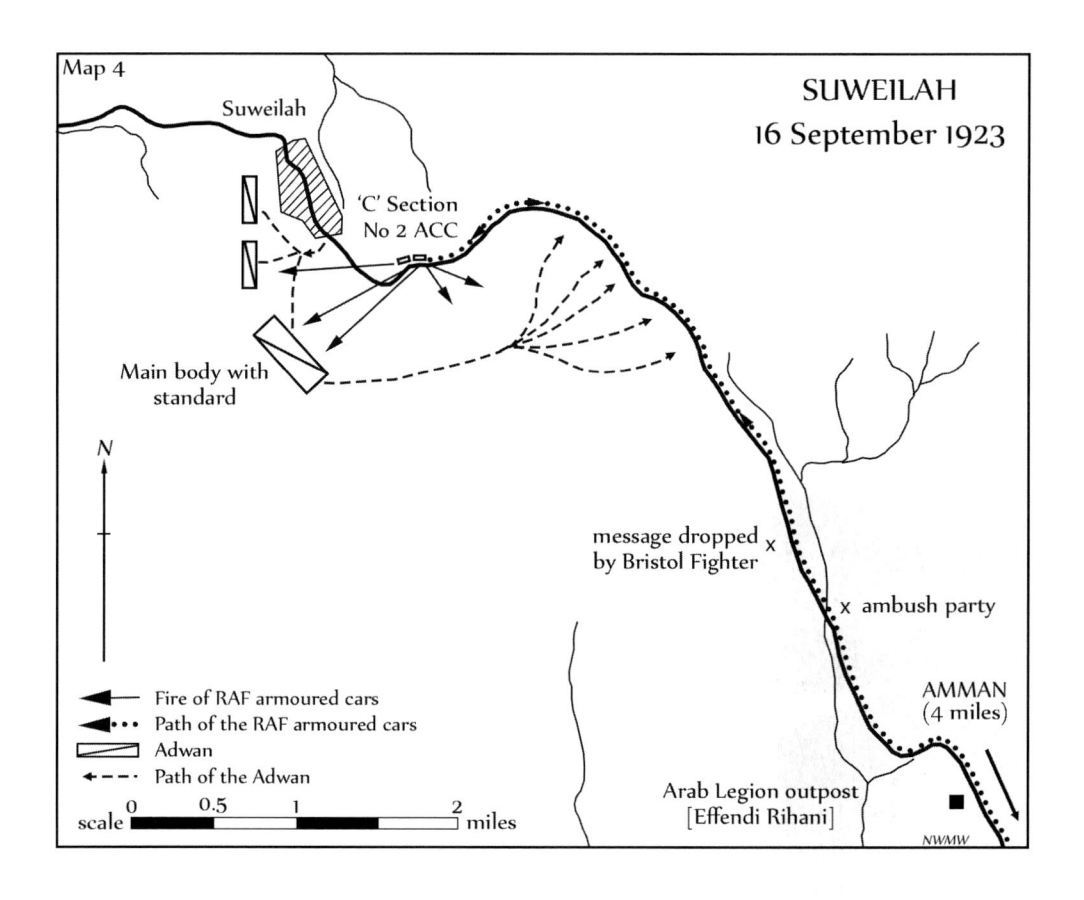

- Suweilah
- 'C' Section No 2 ACC
- Main body with standard
- message dropped by Bristol Fighter
- x ambush party
- AMMAN (4 miles)
- Arab Legion outpost [Effendi Rihani]

Legend:
- Fire of RAF armoured cars
- Path of the RAF armoured cars
- Adwan
- Path of the Adwan

scale: 0 – 0.5 – 1 – 2 miles

NWMW

Flight Lieutenant Philip Yorke Moore stands in front of a spoke-wheeled 1914 pattern Rolls-Royce armoured car still bearing Army markings (© Crown copyright. RAF Regiment Museum).

at daybreak. Early the following morning, a message was dropped from Magrath's aircraft. The large body of Adwan that had been seen in the vicinity of Suweilah were advancing on Amman. Leaving Rolls-Royce Armoured Car No 2 to protect the Amir's camp, Yorke Moore in Car No 1 and Sergeant Kenney in No 4, moved off at 0630 hours to reconnoitre and report on the situation. They were accompanied in the cars by Alec Kirkbride, the Second Assistant to the Chief British Resident, who would act as interpreter and provide political advice. The Arab Legion had also been alerted, and 3½ miles out of Amman they passed a cavalry patrol under the command of El Mulasim Awal Abdullah Effendi Rihani. While Yorke Moore in No 1 had moved rapidly past Effendi, he was able to flag down Sergeant Kenney's car and warn him of an ambush further up the road. Yorke Moore forged ahead with the

The road to Suweilah (© Crown copyright. RAF Regiment Museum).

cars proceeding up the road to a point 2½ miles east of Suweilah.[7]

Flight Lieutenant Magrath, meanwhile, had flown north and could now see that the cars were heading for a large concentration of Adwan who had dismounted and taken up positions on the hills overlooking the road south of the town. Yorke Moore's cars were moving straight towards them. Magrath fired Very lights and then dropped a message informing them that most of the party had moved into camp, but 50 horsemen were moving in from Suweilah. Car No 1 had just halted to pick up the message when Yorke Moore spotted a body of six men, about 200 yards to his rear, partially concealed in a culvert and acting suspiciously. Reversing the car up to the culvert, the men then began to walk away to the hills to the south of the road.

With a Lewis gun covering him, Yorke Moore dismounted and moved towards the six men, twice calling out 'Ta Al'. At this greeting they began to run and the Lewis gunner opened fire, and as Car No 4 arrived, it also joined in with its Vickers gun. Four of the men were killed, but the other two made their escape. Kenney then warned his section commander that he had seen another 12 men disappear behind a hill to the north once the Lewis gun had opened fire. He quickly recalled Kirkbride and the airman who had been sent to collect the air message. He then ordered Car No 4 to move to the north of the hill, while he remained on the road and attempted to cut off their escape.

The crew of Car No 1 of the Amman Section. This is the new 1920 pattern 'Type A' Rolls-Royce with deeper sides on the turret and disc wheels and double tyres at rear (© Crown copyright. RAF Regiment Museum).

As they approached the Suweilah they spotted a small party of horsemen. More surprisingly, some 1200 yards to the south of the cars, they saw three large parties, both on foot and horsed, with the central party gathered around a standard. Yorke Moore ordered the two cars to open fire on the central group, which they did with their two Vickers and two Lewis guns. The standard wavered and fell. The main body broke up and began moving southwards and eastwards along the hilltops, parallel with the road, on either side of the cars, and then began an advance under cover towards the two cars. The intention was to cut off the cars' path of retreat. Heavy fire poured in on them from the hill and the nearby village, and the Lewis gunner had to be called back into the turret.

Yorke Moore estimated that they were now facing a party of some 500. He decided, perhaps wisely, that his best option was a partial withdrawal. With fire coming in from three sides, the cars reversed half a mile down the Amman road until a place could be found to turn. Car No 4 had halted while Yorke Moore's car caught up. Car No 1 turned and headed down the road while No 4 tried to locate a point to turn. Looking back, Yorke Moore was disturbed to see that the car was now at an angle across the road. Car No 1 covered No 4 as it turned but, for Sergeant Kenney, matters were becoming more difficult as his front and rear tyres were now punctured, the Vickers had jammed and the Lewis gun had developed a bent feed arm and stopped firing after only a few rounds. Kenney fired off two red Very lights as a signal to his Section Commander that all was not well. Despite getting the Vickers working again he could now see seven men within 30 yards of his car and he and his crew had to fight them off with their revolvers.

Reversing Car No 1 up to Kenney's car, bullets began coming through the open doors at the rear of the turret where the Lewis gun had been set up. Further bad news was conveyed to Yorke Moore by Kenney. His radiator was holed and he feared that the engine would seize up at any moment. Yorke Moore ordered him to turn the car and get back to Amman as fast as possible. The car did not move off at once, and it was then that he realised that the engine had stopped. Yorke Moore describes what he saw next:

> As he did not drive off at once it was thought that possibly the orders had not been heard. It was then noticed that Aircraftman 2nd Class C.S. Booker was preparing to jump out of the car, which he did as soon as covering fire from the gun had commenced. Running to the front he started up the engine. I wish to bring to notice that this act was carried out under continuous fire, at short range and I strongly recommend that AC2 Booker should receive suitable recognition. Previously, the whole crew had volunteered, but AC2 Booker had been selected.[8]

What Yorke Moore fails to mention in his report is that he had carried out the very same act only 15 minutes earlier when Car No 4's engine had first stopped, and when the fire was no less intense. Rather disturbingly his and Booker's brave act was necessary because there was no electrical starter working in the car and the hand-starter mechanism had been removed as it impeded the working of the Vickers gun.

Booker succeeded in restarting the car and it was quickly turned and headed back down the road to Amman. Yorke Moore and the crew of No 1 watched it safely onto the road. Following in its tracks, No 1 now took most of the fire and in doing so received a bullet in the radiator. Moving under closer and heavier rifle fire, both cars were now running on their rims as many of the tyres had been punctured and were now shredded. Making only 10 miles per hour, two tasks were of utmost importance. First, to get as far away from the rebel party before the engines seized and second, to get news back to RAF Headquarters in Amman. Car No 4 was able to limp back to the outskirts of Amman, by which time it was running on the brake drum on one wheel. One man was sent on ahead with a local policeman, by Sergeant Kenney, to find a telephone station. He was to get Car No 2, located at the Amir's camp, to immediately move up to assist No 1, and with which Kenney had now lost touch.

The engine of No 1 had seized up but was safely away from the rifle fire of the rebels. Miraculously the engine coughed into life after cooling down and freeing itself. In the meantime, Kirkbride had decided he had no choice but to move on foot to the Amir's camp and arrived in there before Sergeant Kenney's message had been received. Yorke Moore, meanwhile, fitted a single wheel on the rear hub and, with the radiator leaking badly, was able to limp back into RAF Amman just over two hours after departing on the reconnaissance. In his final report he noted the following about 'C' Section:

> All personnel conducted themselves coolly and efficiently and in this connection it is noteworthy that only Sergeant Kenney and another airman had been under fire before. I was particularly impressed by the conduct of all crews and cannot speak too highly of their behaviour under fire, and the way they worked their guns.[9]

Unbeknown to Yorke Moore at the time they had been aided by the Arab Legion cavalry detachment. Rihani, the officer who had alerted Kenney to the ambush, had placed his men in a position to provide cover when he saw that the cars had run into trouble and while Car No 1 was worked on. He had kept his men so well concealed, that Yorke Moore was unaware of their presence when only 300-400 yards away.

Further support was given by a local Sheikh, Minwar ibn Hadid, and five others, who joined in the fray from positions in the hills to the north.

The sounds of the battle could be heard from the Amir's camp and an aircraft was sent up with orders to bomb or machine-gun the rebels should they show any hostility. They showed no such intention and after flying over them "the rebel forces were observed to be in full retreat with all the tracks to the south-west encumbered with flocks of sheep, goats, laden camel, women etc."[10] The aircraft contented themselves with keeping them under observation. An Arab Legion force of 220 cavalry, two guns and two machine-guns moved out from the Amir's camp to pursue the rebels, but the RAF armoured cars had had a demoralising effect on them. A few shots from the two Arab Legion guns only served to speed the retreat and it was decided to break off the action. Over the next few days, the Arab Legion pursued the rebels and drove them from their strongholds of Naur and Hesban to the west of Amman. On 19 September, following the delivery of an ultimatum, the Legion took the surrender of 12 rebel Sheikhs, while the Sultan and his sons fled to Syria.

It was surprising that despite the intensity of rebel fire and the state of the cars, there were only minor injuries to the airmen. Three received scratches from bullet splash entering the turret, while losses on the opposing side during the operation were far greater, with some 73 dead, of which 30 were due to the fire of the armoured cars, along with many wounded. The remaining losses were attributed to the Arab Legion.[11]

When the cars were examined following the battle, there were some 58 hits on the body and chassis of No 1 and 75 on No 4. Car No 1 had three tyres punctured, while No 4 had lost seven of the eight fitted on the vehicle. The bonnets of the cars had also not been fitted with proper armour due to difficulties with the radiator filler

Whitewash circles indicate the bullet scars on the armour and woodwork of Car No 4 of Sergeant Kenney after the action at Suweilah (upper and lower left) and the wheel and suspension of Yorke Moore's Car No 1 (lower right) (© Crown copyright. RAF Regiment Museum).

caps and the engine covers had therefore been temporary fittings made of wood. At a tactical level it had been clear that lessons had been learned; most importantly, that the Section should operate with no fewer than three cars. Furthermore, the force of RAF Armoured Cars and Arab Legion should have coordinated their actions more closely. The crews of Nos 1 and 4 cars of 'C' Section could count themselves lucky as the situation could have easily turned for the worse. [12]

There was obviously some criticism of Yorke Moore's actions, as he felt the need to note in his report that he had been given orders, the first of which had been given personally by the Amir that he was to open fire on any large body of tribesmen found outside their villages, and from Group Captain MacEwen, OC RAF Transjordania, that he should use his discretion as to whether to open fire or do so if fired upon.[13] Flight Lieutenant Yorke Moore, Sergeant Kenney and AC2 Booker all received mention by MacEwen in his final report, as did four of the Arab Legionnaires. Harry St. J. Philby, the Chief British Resident, wrote in his report to the High Commissioner, Palestine, "The action of the armoured cars ... was decisive and Flight Lieutenant Moore who was accompanied by Mr Kirkbride deserves the greatest credit for the manner in which he conducted this brisk little operation."[14]

Abdullah's standing among the people of Transjordan was enhanced and, indeed among the half of the Adwan who had not rebelled. Despite the success of the action, there was serious disquiet in the Colonial Office that this situation should have arisen and led to questions as to the suitability of Abdullah as ruler of Transjordan. There was sympathy expressed for the case of maladministration put forward by Sultan Adwan and his Sheikhs and it was a strongly held belief, by those in command in Transjordan, that, had the Adwan revolt been allowed to escalate further, it might have led to a widespread and successful rebellion. The Amir was, however, in a difficult situation. He had to balance the many competing interests, Arab bureaucrats, the fellaheen, the bedouin, and British officials, in the fledgling state. Added to this was the relative poverty of the state purse which had meant that at one point Peake had found it necessary to send half the Arab Legion on leave.

Despite these internal difficulties, much more serious external threats remained. At the same time that Amir Abdullah had emerged as the leader of Transjordan, another central political figure, who would later become the founder and first King of Saudi Arabia, was building up his own political standing in Central Arabia. He was Abd al Aziz ibn Saud, Amir of Nejed.[15] There had been considerable rivalry between the Hashemite and the Saudi families and after post-war struggles the Saudis held sway over much of Central Arabia, known as the Nejed, and the region inland from the Red Sea, known as the Hedjaz.

The deserts of Arabia were in considerable turmoil following the Great War. Firstly, the break-up of the Ottoman Empire had led to an administrative vacuum and, secondly, there had been increased access to modern weapons. These had been widely distributed during the war against the Turks. Ibn Saud aspired to be the King of the bedouin and was able to skilfully obtain the backing of the tribes that followed the strict teachings of Mohammed ibn Abd al Wahhab.[16] His followers were known as the Wahhabis or Al-Ikhwan (the Brotherhood). Ibn Saud would make use of them to expand his rule over much of Central Arabia. This militant religious sect had re-emerged in the deserts to the south-east of Transjordan and they were determined to convert their Transjordanian neighbours, who they considered lax and unorthodox, to stricter religious principles - if necessary by the sword.

Bedouin warfare underwent a major transformation following the Great War. It had been fought under a number of conventions for centuries, mostly with spears and rusty muzzle-loading rifles, and had, as the primary aim, the acquisition of camels and other livestock. With this limited weaponry there were few casualties, but this changed with the advent of the modern rifle and the machine gun. There was also the rise of the Ikhwan; they had swept the raiding 'conventions' aside and now inspired terror wherever the tribes watered and grazed their flocks and herds. Their aggression was not limited to the usual livestock raids, but was escalating into wanton slaughter of those in the villages or encampments that lay in their path, and who they felt had moved from the true path of Islam. They had begun moving up from Central Arabia in 1920 and were seen as a serious threat by the inhabitants of the Transjordan to their way of life, and indeed the existence of the newly-established state. In a later chapter we will also see that their influence extended to the southern deserts of Iraq. Their *modus operandi* was the same as that used by the first conquering Muslim armies of the seventh century and was described as follows:

> Their aim was to confuse and then to terrify. Assembling a thousand men or more together with their camels took time and could not be concealed. However, their objective was invariably secret and known only to a handful of their leaders. Rumours preceded their advance and led to a wholesale panic among those who supposed themselves to be the target. Then, in one swift move, generally overnight they would cover 70 miles or more on their camels before transferring to horses for the final charge. Usually this was just about dawn when they would come screaming out of the desert ... butchering every male in their path by sword, lance and dagger. No quarter was given or asked because every Wahhabi killed in battle was assured of paradise.[17]

Amir Abdullah of Transjordan, later King Abdullah I of Jordan (Library of Congress, Prints & Photographs Division [LC-M32-9709]).

The first involvement of the RAF with the Ikhwan came during August 1922 when a messenger reported to Peake Pasha, the head of the Arab Legion, that a large party of Ikhwan raiders were attacking the village of Umm el Amad only 9 miles from Amman. An aircraft was sent out immediately and the RAF armoured cars were ordered to prepare for action. On the return of the aircraft, it reported that there was a concentration of camels at Yadude. Group Captain Gordon decided to investigate on the ground, so he and Peake Pasha moved out with the section of armoured cars.[18] At midday they passed through the Tuneib where they were told the village had been raided at early that morning by 700 Ikhwan. They were shown the corpses of some 30 men and women of the Beni Sakhr scattered about the village and another half a dozen at the next, although the terrified villagers were reluctant to provide much information.[19]

Fortunately, the activities of the Ikhwan were brought to a halt when the only functioning RAF aircraft in Transjordan flew over the next village while they were involved in further plunder. The pilot failed to notice their activities but the mere passing caused panic amongst the raiders and they moved off. Various attempts were made to pursue them and plans were made to bring them to battle. Group Captain Gordon had only one serviceable Ninak, of the other two, one was unserviceable, and the other had crashed a few weeks earlier. An aerial pursuit was not therefore possible.[20] The Bristol Fighters could not be used as they had only a limited range and the raiders would soon be too far into the desert. This proved to be the case when a flight was made the following morning. Peake and Gordon attempted a ground pursuit in the armoured cars to 'teach them a lesson' but had no success even after reaching Azraq, as their flight had been so rapid.

A section from No 1 Armoured Car Company came over from Jenin as reinforcement but no further action occurred. The raiders successfully made their escape down the Wadi Sirhan to the Hedjaz, whence they had come. The Beni Sakhr bravely followed the party and were able to extract some revenge, claiming to have killed about one hundred and capturing a Wahhabi banner. It was later learned the raiding party intended to wipe out the Beni Sakhr south of Amman and then move on to Amman and kill the Amir Abdullah. The outcome of the action, however, was relatively inconclusive, but the next incursion by the Ikhwan would not be.[21]

The most serious threat by the Ikhwan to Transjordan and the Hashemite crown came exactly two years later.[22] At 0500 hours on 14 August 1924, an RAF lorry departed from Amman on a routine petrol and oil run to Ziza landing ground, located 20 miles to the south.[23] Just over the crest of hills to the south they came across small groups of Arabs. The size and numbers increased and many appeared to be fleeing in panic. The driver was soon hailed by some who passed their finger across their throat. They were warned that Ziza and Yadude had been raided by the Ikhwan. Sensibly, the driver and his companion returned to the RAF camp at Amman and reported the raid (Map 5, p. 41).

Following the incursions of the previous years, the Arab Legion had established an outpost at Kaf in the Nejed, then in the no-man's-land between Transjordan and the northern part of what is now Saudi Arabia. It was later learned that this post had seen the Ikhwan cross the frontier. Although safe behind the ramparts of their fort, they were powerless to warn anyone in Amman of the approach of thousands of Ikhwan as the authorities had refused to equip them with a wireless set due to the cost![24] Shortly after passing Kaf, the Wahhabis had encountered a supply party taking rations to the frontier post and all 18 members of the Arab Legion and 40 of

DH9As of No 14 (B) Squadron RAF drawn up with 'C' Section of No 2 Armoured Car Company at RAF Amman (© Crown copyright. RAF Regiment Museum).

the Beni Sakhr, who were travelling with them, were killed. The raiders then rested overnight and prepared for their assault on the Amman[25]

The onslaught had not been accepted passively by the Transjordanians. The villages and encampments put up strong resistance to the massed charge of the columns. The Beni Sakhr were forced back as the size of the raiding party became apparent. They then rallied support from relatives, followers and neighbouring tribes and held off the enemy for some two hours while the RAF prepared their counterattack.

A Ninak from No 14 Squadron was sent out at 0655 hours, and on its return corroborated the driver's report. The crew had been greeted by the awe-inspiring sight of a mass of camel riders and horsemen, three or four miles wide, bearing their unfurled green *Baraiq* or war banners, advancing across the plain of Ziza and towards Amman. Pillars of smoke and dust rose from overwhelmed villages.

Three Rolls-Royce armoured cars of 'C' Section of No 2 Armoured Car Company were ordered out towards Yadude to reconnoitre. The cars were under the command of Flying Officer Henry Thornton who had been on the Company since its formation.[26] Meanwhile, with further corroboration from a second reconnaissance flight, the DH9As were bombed up and the Lewis guns armed. At the rate they were moving, the raiders would soon be on the outskirts of Amman and the aircraft and armoured cars would not be able to operate with advantage.

At 0823 hours, word was received from Palestine Command giving permission to take action and just over half an hour later three DH9As took off. The lead aircraft was piloted by Squadron Leader John D'Albiac.[27] Accompanying him was the civil servant, Alec Kirkbride. Arriving over the raiders seven minutes later, Kirkbride confirmed immediately that they were Wahhabis. The raiders were now dispersed across a number of villages and encampments and were engaged in sacking and looting, and the gathering of sheep, camels and horses. An attack was launched with bombs and Lewis guns. At the first bomb blast, the mass of camels and horsemen ceased their advance and began to retreat. This had one positive effect in that it drew the parties that were widespread across the plain back into one large mass as they rallied to their banners. Faced with the modern weapons of bombs and machine-guns this was the worst action that could have been taken.

D'Albiac, having dropped all his bombs, flew back to locate the armoured cars. He found them a mile north-west of Tuneib and was gratified to see the rapidly moving columns of dust as the armoured cars roared towards the advancing host. Dropping a message, he ordered Thornton to take action and pursue the enemy towards Ziza. At 0930 hours the armoured cars sighted the raiders. Thornton takes up the story:

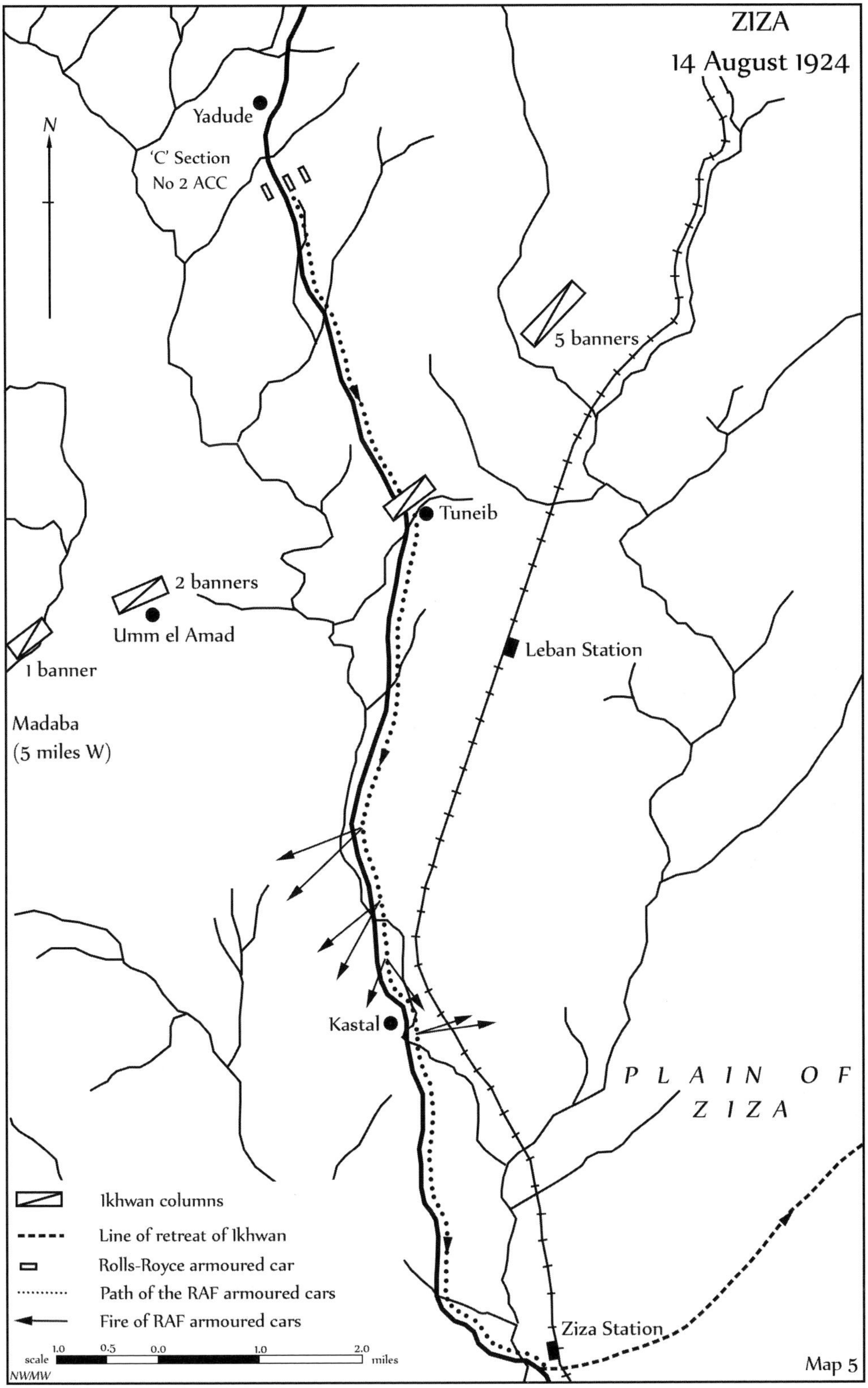
ZIZA
14 August 1924
Yadude
'C' Section
No 2 ACC
N
5 banners
Tuneib
2 banners
Umm el Amad
1 banner
Leban Station
Madaba
(5 miles W)
Kastal
P L A I N O F
Z I Z A
Ikhwan columns
Line of retreat of Ikhwan
Rolls-Royce armoured car
Path of the RAF armoured cars
Fire of RAF armoured cars
Ziza Station
scale 1.0 0.5 0.0 1.0 2.0 miles
NWMW
Map 5

On arriving at Yadude I was told by the inhabitants that they had been attacked that morning by Wahhabi who were present four miles east. I therefore proceeded along the track in the direction of Tuneib until on a rise about one and half miles from Yadude. I was in a position to observe the raiders disposition which was as follows: Their main body was dismounted on top of a hill about one mile north of Tuneib. I counted five green standards with them. They appeared to be resting and no action was taking place. Tuneib they also occupied but I saw no banners. Umm el Amad was in their hands. This party with two standards were evacuating and making their way to join the main body. Further south I observed a party with one banner also coming in to the main body from the direction of Madaba.

I at once proceeded to get into communication with Amman and to do so had to go back to Kasr, where I could tap the telegraph line. While doing so I saw three 9As take off from Amman so returned immediately to Yadude as I reasoned that the machines would discover the situation for themselves and if I was visible in the vicinity would give me orders. On arriving at Yadude and making enquiries, I was told that bombs had been dropped. Reasoning that action was thus authorised I proceeded in the direction of the raiders, and about one mile north-west of Tuneib a message was dropped ordering me to follow enemy and attack.

I passed through Tuneib just as they had evacuated. The various bodies I have mentioned before were now converging and retiring in an easterly direction. I remained on the track which runs practically south and advanced until a large party of the enemy were crossing my front from right to left (they were accompanied by several long strings of camels which I presumed were loot...).

I opened fire here at 0930 hours with three guns at 900 yards range, and inflicted visible casualties. A running action was kept on until all the enemy were east of the track. I then took up a position on Kastal hill and engaged the enemy there until I was unable to observe the effect of my fire.

From here I proceeded to Ziza in order to cross the railway. Arranging the section in line I then re-advanced on the enemy who were now in a mass formation covering an area of about one and a half miles by half mile and whose strength I estimated to be about 5000. They were now being followed by local tribesmen so to avoid confusion I ran along their right flank and, when opposite their centre, turned in, halted, and opened fire at 600 yards.[28] The target was so excellent that I saw no reason to approach closer and take unnecessary risk. I carried out these tactics of following them and engaging them from two miles east of the railway to 12 miles east of the railway, bringing the three Lewis guns into action as well as the Vickers...

Visible casualties were inflicted on all occasions, and I estimate about 500 dead or badly wounded were left behind.

At this point the enemy were travelling fast, at about eight to 10 miles per hour and no resistance was offered. They replied to our fire, but very wildly and probably owing to the distance I kept only three hits were registered on the cars.[29]

The Section had been fighting for two hours, 6000 rounds had been expended,

The Plain of Ziza (© Crown copyright. RAF Regiment Museum).

and it was lack of ammunition that forced the cars to cease firing. No let-up was allowed, however, as five minutes after their withdrawal the three DH9As, re-armed and bombed up, returned to cause more destruction in the retreating mass. Thornton maintained a watch on the raiders until D'Albiac landed beside him and he was ordered back to Ziza. Here he rendezvoused with two Bristol Fighters carrying the OC RAF Transjordania, Group Captain MacEwen and Peake Pasha of the Arab Legion. They had made an inspection of the field of battle and now considered it safe for the cars to return to Amman. As reinforcements, a flight of Bristol Fighters and a section of armoured cars were despatched from Palestine. John Bagot Glubb who later assumed command of the Arab Legion, described the action at Ziza thus:

> It was first time the Ikhwan had encountered modern weapons efficiently handled. They did the worst thing they could have done - they rallied around their war banners. The [more compact] the mass of men, camels and horses, the easier the target for the spitting machine-guns. Soon men and animals were falling over one and another in inextricable confusion...
>
> The war banners wavered, contradictory cries broke out, the machine-guns rattled, at last the great host broke, the banners fell and a stream of scattered camelmen raced for the hills and safety. The bravery of a world that was gone was broken by lead and steel. There was no pursuit. The plain was strewn with dead and dying men and animals. The RAF were sick with killing.[30]

The Beni Sakhr had been the first target but once the Wahhabis had been turned they pursued their attackers and cut off the stragglers. The Arab Legion cavalry followed up, dealing with isolated parties that showed resistance and rounding up prisoners. A Ninak and four Bristol Fighters of No 14 Squadron went out in mid-afternoon to harry the retreating Wahhabis with machine-guns. The action was not all one sided with all the machines being hit by rifle fire and an officer and an airman wounded. A reconnaissance was made by two DH9As the following morning over the Wadi Sirhan and watering places but they could find no trace of the raiders. One of them developed engine trouble and was forced to land. At a time like this No 14 Squadron were grateful for the assistance of the RAF armoured cars:

The airmen of No 14 (B) Squadron and No 2 Armoured Car Company with the captured Wahhabi banners (© Crown copyright. RAF Regiment Museum).

... the Wahhabis were known to be on the border, intent on raiding, a machine went down not 20 miles from the border and needed a new engine. Within one hour of the news reaching Amman - yes, one hour - a Leyland lorry, with a spare engine on board, escorted by an armoured car, had left, and, journeying through the night, accomplished the 100-odd miles in under 12 hours, which, considering the nature of the country and the fact that most of the trip was done during the hours of darkness, was a truly marvellous performance. With a new engine required three armoured cars were ordered to proceed without delay from Amman to the Amari Wells and the aircraft and crew given protection until the new engine could be fitted.[31]

There was little doubt that the primary objective of the Wahhabis had been Amman. It was concluded that, prior to the first bombing, the parties had been organised into two columns which were to converge on Amman for this purpose.[32] The attack from the air was unexpected, created panic, and prompted the retreat. It appeared the moral effect of the air attack was a significant factor, though the local tribes had caused some of the columns to fall back due to their own firm resistance. Prisoners stated, however, that while they did not mind rifle fire and would have advanced against the armoured cars, they were terrified of bombs, which they did not understand. The raiders also made the mistake of moving onto the Ziza Plain which is flat and smooth for several miles. Had they retreated into broken country the pursuit by the armoured cars would have been made extremely difficult and limited their mobility. To a certain extent, the effect of the bombing on morale can be accepted, however, it should be noted that there was a period of two hours when the three Rolls-Royce armoured cars were the only force in contact with the 5000-strong raiding party and that, at any time, they could have turned and attempted to overwhelm Thornton's section. That they didn't can be attributed to his astute handling of his cars and the extraordinary firepower that they were able to apply.

Seven of the Wahhabi standards were retrieved from the field of battle along with 600 camels and 1000 rifles. The significance of the victory was not lost on Amir Abdullah who presented one of the banners to Peake Pasha, another to RAF

Transjordania HQ and the third and fourth to No 14 Squadron and No 2 Armoured Car Company.[33]

The human cost was heavy for the attackers with around 500 killed and 300 captured. The Arab Legion lost 62 men killed. Around 115 Transjordanians were dead in the encampments and villages south of Amman, but this toll would have been much higher had the Wahhabis reached the heavily-populated areas around Amman. In his final report Group Captain MacEwen noted:

> ... the excellent manoeuvring of the section of armoured cars by Flying Officer H.N. Thornton reflects upon him the highest credit, as it does on Flight Lieutenant T.P. Yorke Moore, OC, Section, who, although not present, has been responsible for the training of the armoured car personnel to such a high state of efficiency.[34]

Notes

1. Yorke Moore papers, RAF Regiment Museum Archives. Correspondence: Flight Lieutenant Philip Yorke Moore from Wing Commander Thomas O'B. Hubbard MC AFC, OC Palestine Wing, Bir Salem, Palestine, 20 September 1923. Hubbard had previously served with RAF Transjordania
2. J. Lunt, *The Arab Legion 1923-1957* (London: Constable, 1999), pp. 18-19. Abdullah I ibn Hussein, King of Jordan (1882-1951). He ruled Transjordan as Amir from 1921 until 1946 when he was crowned King of Jordan, and reigned until his assassination on 20 July 1951. On 30 November 1940, he was appointed to the honorary rank of Air Commodore in the RAF.
3. *Ibid.*, pp. 12, 15.
4. The Arab Legion would acquire great renown as a professional and efficient military force. The current Jordanian Army has a direct lineage with Arab Legion and is considered one of the most efficient and effective military forces in the Middle East.
5. A sharply-defined depression or valley in the desert. Usually the dry bed of a stream that only runs during heavy downpours of rain.
6. AIR 5/1243 *Operations: Palestine, Vol. I, Chapter 1 to 14, 1920-1930*. The group was estimated to have 300 men on horses and 500 moving on foot.
7. Yorke Moore papers, Correspondence: Yorke Moore to Group Captain MacEwen, Report on Armoured Car Action near Suweilah on the 16.9.23 against rebellious tribes, 17 September, 1923.
8. Yorke Moore papers.
9. *Ibid.* The crews of the cars were as follows: No 1 Car - Flight Lieutenant Yorke Moore (OC and Car Commander), Mr Kirkbride (Interpreter), AC1 Piper and AC2 Westbrook (gunners), AC1 Harvatt (driver); No 4 Car - Sergeant Kenney (Car Commander), LAC Ramsay (driver), AC1 Mahon and AC2 Booker (gunners).
10. AIR 5/1243.
11. M. Abu Nowar, *The History of the Hashemite Kingdom of Jordan, Vol. 1* (Oxford: The Middle East Centre, 1989), p. 109.
12. Yorke Moore papers. Among the more unusual but practical recommendations from Flight Lieutenant Yorke Moore was that plasticine should be provided as standard in the tool kit so that bullet holes and other damage to radiators could be plugged to prevent engine seizure.
13. Yorke Moore papers, Correspondence: 7 December 1978. Group Captain Norman D.K. MacEwen CMG DSO had assumed command in April 1923.
14. AIR 5/1243 *Operations: Palestine Vol. I*.
15. King Abd al Aziz ibn Saud (1902-1953), King of the Hedjaz, Sultan of the Nejed and King of Saudi Arabia.

16 Mohammed ibn Abd al Wahhab (1703–1792).
17 J. Lunt, *The Arab Legion*, p. 29.
18 Group Captain Robert Gordon had commanded 'Z' Unit in the successful campaign in Somaliland of 1920.
19 C.S. Jarvis, *Arab Command* (Hutchinson & Co.: London, 1946), pp. 100-102.
20 The 'Ninak' or DH9A was the standard RAF biplane light bomber from 1918 to 1931. It served in both the United Kingdom and overseas.
21 Jarvis, *Arab Command*.
22 Abu Nowar, *The History of the Hashemite Kingdom of Jordan*, pp. 138-143. They were led by Sheikh Awad al Dhuwaibi of the Harb and Sheikh Nahdi ibn Nuhair of the Shammar, both from the Nejed.
23 Ziza is now known as Al Jiza or Zizya and is the location of Queen Alia International Airport. Ziza airfield had been established by 1924 as the first airfield on the trans-desert air mail route from Cairo to Baghdad.
24 The raiders were thought to have set out from Qasom north of Riyadh and had ridden up through the Wadi Sirhan. According to Jarvis, the alarm was also reportedly raised by Peake Pasha, the OC of the Arab Legion, who happened to be out riding before breakfast that morning and was passed by women crying 'Ikhwan, Ikhwan'. He stopped them to enquire what they were running from. He then galloped over to the RAF camp at Amman, alerting the Arab Legion on the way. He asked for all assistance that the aircraft and armoured cars could provide.
25 Abu Nowar, *The History of the Hashemite Kingdom of Jordan*, p. 139. The Beni Sakhr had been alerted to their presence the night before and evacuated their women and children to relative safety west of the railway line.
26 'Service Aviation: Appointments,' *Flight*, 14 June 1945, p. 649. Flying Officer Henry N. Thornton had originally served in the 9th Battalion Northumberland Fusiliers as a private soldier from 1914 before transferring to the Royal Flying Corps in 1917 where he was commissioned. He was awarded a short-service commission in the RAF in 1921. He ended his career as Air Vice-Marshal H.N. Thornton CBE in 1947.
27 Later Air Marshal Sir John D'Albiac KCVO KBE CB DSO (1894-1963). D'Albiac would later become AOC Palestine and Transjordan from August 1939 to October 1940, AOC British Forces in the ill-fated Greek campaign from November 1940 until April 1941 and then AOC British Forces in Iraq during the Iraq Crisis of April to May 1941.
28 Abu Nowar, *The History of the Hashemite Kingdom of Jordan*, p. 142. There had been some casualties to the local tribesmen during this and the previous bombing as they had become mixed up with the Wahhabis in their pursuit.
29 AIR 5/1243 *Operations: Palestine, Vol. I*. Report by Flying Officer H.N. Thornton to Group Captain MacEwen, 16 August 1924.
30 Lieutenant-General Sir John Bagot Glubb KCB, CMG, DSO, OBE, MC (1897-1986). J.B. Glubb, *The Story of the Arab Legion* (London: Hodder & Stoughton, 1948), p. 63.
31 'No 14 (Bomber) Squadron', W.A. Cooke, *Flight*, January 18 1934, p. 52.
32 V. Orange and Lord Deramore, *Winged Promises: A History of No 14 Squadron RAF 1915-1945* (Fairford: RAF Benevolent Fund, 1998), p. 49. According to the No 14 Squadron ORB the Wahhabi commander had orders that 'no aeroplanes, cars or English were to be attacked; old men, women, and children to be spared, young men to be killed'.
33 *Ibid.*, p. 49. The banners were placed in the mess at RAF Amman and were always commented on by the Amir when he attended dining nights. During the Second World War they were transferred to the Officers' Mess at RAF Akrotiri where, sadly, they were lost in a fire in 1963.
34 AIR 5/1243 *Operations: Palestine, Vol. I*. Report, Group Captain MacEwen to AOC Palestine, Major-General Henry H. Tudor, 16 August 1924.

Chapter Four

Troubles in Kurdistan 1922-1924

"The Lines of Communication by which the two Columns would concentrate in this event, and of which no recent information was available, were at once reconnoitred by Armoured Cars. A post was also speedily established by Armoured Cars at the river bridges at Altun Kupri..."
Air Vice-Marshal Sir J.M. Salmond, Commander British Forces in Iraq[1]

*"The Turks up at Mosul say we've no business here,
But England declared we'll stay here four years,
The taxpayer at home's having awful nightmares,
Over the deserts of Mesopotamia"*
Corporal James Cox, No 4 Armoured Car Company[2]

Great Britain had first become involved in Mesopotamia in 1914, following the outbreak of the Great War. An Indian Expeditionary Force had landed at Basra in November 1914, and had early successes against the Turkish forces. Regrettably this soon turned to disaster in April 1916, when the 6th Indian Division was forced to surrender after being besieged at the town of Kut Al Amara. After replacement with competent commanders, and improvements in logistics and command structures, Baghdad was captured in 1917. By October 1918, when an armistice with Turkey was implemented, two Indian Corps' were nearing Mosul. By this time there were two RAF flying squadrons for air support, while armoured support was provided by the Rolls-Royce armoured cars of the British Army-manned Light Armoured Motor Batteries. The campaign had been a blend of disaster and triumph, but overall, it was severely criticised for being run by a military command ill-informed as to conditions, with poor intelligence, and lacking a clearly thought-out plan for operations.

The Ottoman Empire had governed Mesopotamia as three provinces, or vilayets; Mosul in the north, Baghdad in the centre and Basra in the south. These vilayets had not been combined previously as a unified state and the peoples of each vilayet were from very different religious, cultural and ethnic backgrounds. Mosul had close connections with Syria and southern Turkey and consisted of Kurds, Assyrians (Aramaic-speaking Christians) with some Armenians and Turcomans. Mosul had considerable oil wealth, much of it as yet undeveloped, and this was essential to the viability of the new state. Both Baghdad and Basra were primarily Arab but included a sizeable Jewish population. The people of the lower provinces had close relationships with neighbouring Persia, the Gulf and India. Culturally those who populated the areas outside the large cities had social structures based around the tribe and village, and looked neither to Baghdad nor Basra. The Ottoman Empire had not exerted strong control outside the cities and, therefore, power was strongly placed in the hands of various local tribal leaders. This was particularly so around Mosul and in the marsh areas of the south. The nomadic bedouin of the deserts had no recognition of formal international frontiers and roamed freely back-and-forth across them.

The state of Iraq, a country of over 207,000 square miles, came into being in August 1921. Derived from the Arabic term 'al-Iraq' meaning an 'area abounding a great river'. In fact, it encompassed the two great rivers, the Euphrates and the Tigris, along which the bulk of the population live. Iraq comprised high peaked mountains and deep ravines in the north and east, fertile alluvial plains down the major rivers, and deserts to the west and south. The flat plain from Baghdad to Basra follows a gradual fall of only 100 feet in 350 miles (Map 2, p. 24).

Following the Armistice of 1918, the British Government was given responsibility for implementing the League of Nations mandate for the creation of the new state. This was established, following a two year period of negotiations, as a monarchy ruled by King Feisal. The government consisted of a council of ministers operating under the direction of the British High Commissioner. Britain's long involvement with Iraq continued up to the departure of the Royal Air Force from Habbaniya in 1955. The objectives of Great Britain in Iraq were four-fold:

1. To protect her own interests and Imperial communications,
2. To defend Iraq against invasion,
3. To maintain internal peace and security,
4. To achieve the first three aims as cheaply as possible.[3]

The British Army established garrisons at strategic centres of population. Military manpower was run down following the cessation of hostilities in 1918 and, by early 1920, the military garrison consisted of only 60,000 troops, including three Tank Corps armoured car companies and two RAF flying Squadrons.[4] Matters were initially calm, but as steps were taken to negotiate the creation of the new Arab state, a number of disaffected groups began to exert themselves. Attempts to stamp out local blood-feuds also led to resentment and there was no shortage of weapons and ammunition left over from the Great War to equip the insurgents. Loyalty to the central government had to be left to the persuasive powers of the British colonial and police officials. While the Mandate process was designed to lead to eventual self-government, many saw this simply as the replacement of rule by Turkey for that by the British. By July 1920, the total British and Indian forces had to be increased to around 120,000

There had been sporadic outbreaks of trouble in both the north and central regions from 1918 onwards. The most significant, however, was from June to October 1920, when large numbers of British Army reinforcements were required, as an insurrection broke out in the lower Euphrates bringing with it a complete breakdown of civil order. Troubles arose due to the loss of autonomy that tribal chiefs had enjoyed under the relatively inefficient Ottoman rule, and the introduction of far more effective tax collection methods. Despite the reinforcements, the troops were spread thinly across the country. Whilst the relief Columns were successful in some instances, in others it was apparent that more troops were required. The troops were often besieged in outlying posts and found it difficult to fight the insurrection due to the long distances involved, lack of transport and poor, vulnerable communications. A most serious setback came in July 1920, when a column consisting predominantly of the 2nd Battalion of the Manchester Regiment was virtually wiped out in an Arab ambush north of Baghdad, losing 400 killed.[5] The insurrection cost the security forces 2269 casualties, against more than 8450 suffered by the local populace.[6]

The financial cost was such that there were long periods when the British government considered leaving Iraq before completing the Mandate. Indeed, even in October 1922, the future of the RAF was still not secured, despite being given responsibility for Iraq. Then Prime Minister Bonar Law, who served in office for only seven months, thought an independent air force to be too expensive. He offered the Air Ministry post to Sir Samuel Hoare at the very time the RAF were taking responsibility for Iraq, but with the understanding that 'the post may be abolished in a few weeks'.[7]

Despite these uncertainties, RAF Iraq Command was formally established on 1 October 1922. The AOC was Air Vice-Marshal Sir John Salmond and his headquarters was located in Baghdad city.[8] For the first time in service history an RAF commander would have Army troops serving under his command.[9] The majority of the eight flying squadrons were eventually located at the huge air station and cantonment which was being constructed at Hinaidi, 10 miles south-east of the city, on the east bank of the Tigris. There were four principal air bases in Iraq: Hinaidi and Shaibah - 350 miles

RAF Hinaidi. The armoured car lines are in the area beyond the far hangars. Baghdad and the Tigris River are in the far distance (RAF Habbaniya Assn).

to the south - and Kirkuk and Mosul - 150 and 250 miles to the north, respectively. Large numbers of emergency and contingency landing grounds would, however, be developed over the next few years. Salmond's tasks were two-fold: the first was to 'inaugurate and maintain the first scheme for the control of a semi-civilised country by means primarily of Air Forces.' However, underlying this was the requirement to, at the same time, 'effect those reductions in the total garrison of the country of which air control would admit and which had been envisaged at the Cairo Conference.'[10]

The Army presence had been wound back by degrees and by the time the RAF took control, the Imperial garrison consisted of eight British and Indian battalions, two artillery batteries, along with a company of Indian sappers and miners, and a pioneer battalion. RAF Iraq Command was now composed of 3000 airmen distributed across eight flying squadrons, four river gunboats, and the four armoured car companies that were in the process of forming.[11] The Iraq Government had also begun to raise a small separate Army, predominantly from the Arab population, which consisted of three cavalry regiments, two pack batteries and three infantry battalions.[12]

Most importantly, Salmond could now also call on a locally-raised force paid from Imperial funds. These were the Iraq Levies, and they would play a key role over the next two decades in the defence and security of Iraq, providing staunch support to the British military, and particularly the RAF. The Levies, under the control of British officers, with native officers and NCOs, had been formed in 1915 with just 40 mounted Arabs recruited from local tribes in southern Iraq. The force had been gradually enlarged until, by 1922, it numbered 6155 and was a force of all arms, consisting of three cavalry regiments, a pack battery and four infantry battalions. It was spread down the length of the country, but was particularly concentrated in the northern regions.[13] The role of the Levies as specifically defined by the British Cabinet, following the Cairo Conference, was:

> ... to relieve British and Indian Troops in Iraq, take-over outposts in Mosul vilayet and in Kurdistan, previously held by the Imperial Garrison, and generally fill the gap until such time as the Iraq National Army is trained to undertake these duties.[14]

The personnel were initially Arabs, Kurds, Assyrians, Turcomans and Yezidis. With the creation of the Iraqi state, and under financial constraints, the numbers had to be reduced. The Arab battalions and regiments were gradually absorbed into the Iraq Army, while Arab recruits were prevented from enlisting in the Levies.

A major element in the Levies were the Assyrians, Nestorian Christians, who hailed originally from the mountainous region of Hakkiari in Turkey. At the instigation of Tsarist Russia, they had risen against the Turks in 1916, only to see the Russians withdraw. The Turkish Army had then moved in and dealt severely with this small minority of about 100,000. The only option was for the entire community, including families, to stage a fighting withdrawal into Persia. The support from Russia faded with the Bolshevik Revolution and by 1918 some 40,000 had sought refuge in Mesopotamia, and were located in a large camp at Baqubah, to the north of Baghdad. The Assyrians had demonstrated their fighting qualities as they fought their way out of Turkey, later in the Assyrian repatriation camp near Mosul in 1919 when greatly outnumbered, and again during the 1920 rebellion when local Arabs attacked their camp at Baqubah. The Assyrians were considered to be excellent fighting men,

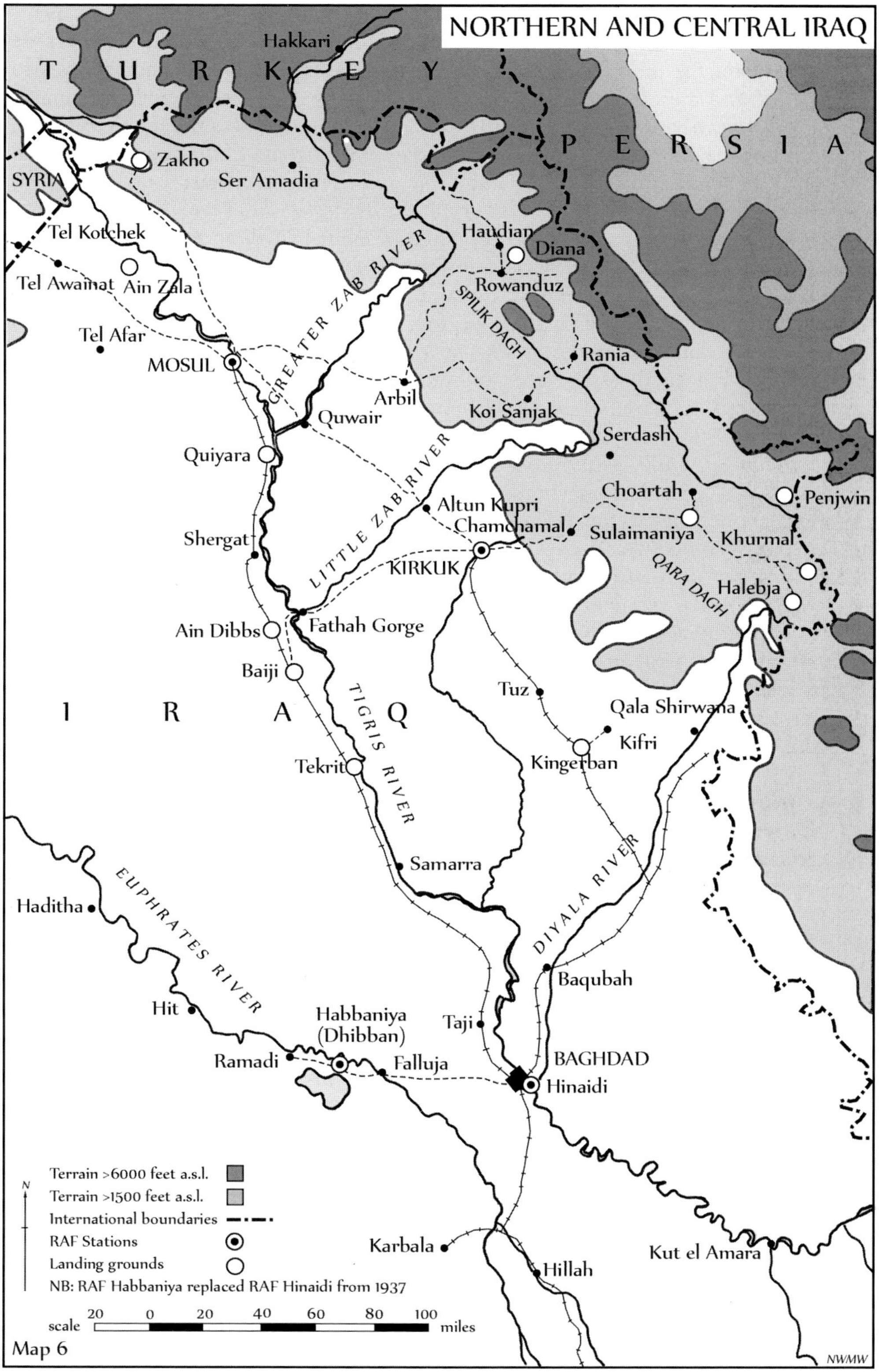

NORTHERN AND CENTRAL IRAQ
TURKEY
PERSIA
SYRIA
IRAQ
Hakkari
Zakho
Ser Amadia
Tel Kotchek
Tel Awainat
Ain Zala
Tel Afar
MOSUL
GREATER ZAB RIVER
Haudian
Diana
Rowanduz
SPILIK DAGH
Rania
Arbil
Quwair
Koi Sanjak
Serdash
Quiyara
LITTLE ZAB RIVER
Choartah
Penjwin
Altun Kupri
Chamchamal
Sulaimaniya
Khurmal
Shergat
KIRKUK
QARA DAGH
Halebja
Ain Dibbs
Fathah Gorge
Baiji
TIGRIS RIVER
Tuz
Qala Shirwana
Kifri
Kingerban
Tekrit
Samarra
DIYALA RIVER
Haditha
EUPHRATES RIVER
Baqubah
Hit
Habbaniya
(Dhibban)
Taji
Ramadi
Falluja
BAGHDAD
Hinaidi
Karbala
Hillah
Kut el Amara
Terrain >6000 feet a.s.l.
Terrain >1500 feet a.s.l.
International boundaries
RAF Stations
Landing grounds
NB: RAF Habbaniya replaced RAF Hinaidi from 1937
N
scale 20 0 20 40 60 80 100 miles
Map 6
NWMW

loyal and tough, and quick to learn. Therefore, in August 1921, it was decided to enlist Assyrians in the Levies. They would eventually become the dominant ethnic group in this force.[15]

Air Vice-Marshal Sir John Salmond's task was a daunting one. Since the RAF had been given responsibility for Iraq, a number of events had changed the assumptions upon which the Air Force Scheme of Control had been formulated. Salmond faced not only having to deal with internal insurrection, but also external threats not envisaged only six months earlier. Turkey had recovered rapidly since the Armistice and, with Kemal Atatürk as its new leader, had reorganised its military and revived a strong nationalist spirit. It set about regaining some of the possessions that had been lost as part of the Treaty of Sèvres. It had already regained occupied territory from France and Italy, and inflicted a crushing defeat on the Greek Army in Anatolia. This had led to the Chanak crisis, in which the Armoured Car Detachment had become caught up in the voyage out to Iraq. The Treaty had not formally defined the boundaries of southern Turkey and northern Iraq. New boundary negotiations opened in Lausanne in Switzerland in November 1922, and each side was determined to maintain the *status quo* or expand the territory they held before the new treaty was signed. In particular, Turkey demanded the restoration of the Mosul vilayet on historical, ethical, economic and ethnic grounds (Map 6, p. 51).[16]

For the last five months of 1922, the Turkish Army had been massing troops on the frontier, only 90 miles from Mosul. Bands of Turkish irregulars and Iraqi supporters, known as *chattas*, and under the command of a Turkish officer, Euz Demir (which literally translates as 'Iron Shoulder'), had occupied major towns in the mountainous frontier areas to the east. Demir's mission was to stir up a revolt in the tribes around Rowanduz through development of pan-Islamic sympathies and the provision of ammunition and supplies. By January 1923, it was estimated that a force of 8000 infantry, 2000 cavalry and 33 guns was within six to 20 days march of Mosul. Furthermore, it was estimated that within five weeks of the outbreak of a war, the Turkish Army could concentrate 18 divisions for an advance on Mosul. In a striking contrast, Iraq Command had a force numbering some 15,000, but this was required to maintain order across the entire country. With the fiscal constraints imposed on the military by the Treasury, Salmond was told, however, that he could not expect any reinforcements. If they had wished to do so, the Turkish Army could easily have marched in and taken Mosul.[17]

The feeling among the pro-Turkish agitators in Iraq was that the British would not defend Mosul. Salmond first had to convince the Iraqi populace, and Turkey, that he was not going to give up the vilayet easily, while at the same time it was thought he lacked the force with which to defend it. Nor could Salmond withdraw his force from Mosul, as this would be perceived as weakness and would undoubtedly lead to an uprising by the local tribes. It was thought with the loss of British prestige, the position in Iraq would collapse, and he would have to make a fighting withdrawal the length of the country, through a hostile population.[18] Salmond noted on his arrival:

> ... I could find no operational plan or any indication that it was intended to do otherwise than leave the enemy a free passage to his objective.
> At what point that free passage would stop was a matter of conjecture, but one thing was quite clear, should the Mosul vilayet fall, the whole country would be against us, and we should have had the utmost difficulty, if it were possible at all to clear out of Basra.[19]

Not only was there anxiety about the external threat, but the Turks had formed an alliance with nationalists in Kurdistan. Turkey, through Euz Demir, was using propaganda, provision of arms and ammunition, and the penetration of irregulars into the border districts, to enhance her impression of strength and prestige. In late February 1923, it was discovered that the Governor of Sulaimaniya in Southern Kurdistan, Sheikh Mahmud Barzinji, was planning to occupy Kirkuk and raise a rebellion, in conjunction with moves by the Turkish frontier commander.[20]

A view of the rugged terrain of Kurdistan with the hills of Persia in the distance (Rolph, RAFACA).

Despite being in control for only a few months, operations under the new RAF Iraq Command were reaching a high tempo. Matters had not been going well in the months prior to the takeover. At the end of August 1922, a column of Imperial troops and levies, known as 'Ranicol', had been sent to deal with an internal uprising near Rania, but had been met with strong resistance from the Pishder tribe and suffered casualties, the loss of equipment, and the parts of two artillery pieces. The Turkish strategy had proceeded better than envisaged and the situation for Iraq Command was precarious.

With the limited means available, Salmond was determined to use mobile ground forces, air observation and reconnaissance, and direct air action to adopt an aggressive posture in Kurdistan, known as his 'Forward Offensive Policy'. He was fortunate to get the support of Trenchard, though the politicians were unenthusiastic, as they feared this might incite the Turks to move on Mosul. Early in January 1923, tensions increased with Turkey and the negotiations over the Treaty of Lausanne broke up. Despite demands for the incorporation of Mosul into Turkey becoming more strident, little direction to Iraq Command came from London. After notifying Trenchard, Salmond decided to act and ordered his forces north to demonstrate the British determination to maintain the current borders of Iraq.[21] As a first step two companies of the 14th Sikhs moved from Baghdad by rail to Kingerban and, given the poor state of the roads, were flown to Kirkuk. This was the first such large scale movement of troops by air by the RAF.[22]

Airmen of No 6 Armoured Car Company on a 'recco', February 1925 (© Crown copyright. Cox, RAF Regiment Museum).

Squadron Leader R.P. Willock, Officer Commanding No 4 Armoured Car Company (first from left), Air Vice-Marshal J.F.A. Higgins, AOC Iraq (1924-1926) (second from left), and Wing Commander W.H. Primrose DFC, Officer Commanding Armoured Car Wing (first on right) watch an armoured car exercise (© Crown copyright. Cox, RAF Regiment Museum).

For the RAF Armoured Car crews, the last months of 1922 had been spent in organising, equipping and training the Companies. With only a short time available before operations began, they busied themselves with preparing the vehicles they had brought from Great Britain and the Rolls-Royces they had inherited from the Tank Corps. The overall coordination and control of the companies was to be carried out by Armoured Car Wing, under the command of Wing Commander Harold Primrose, and was located at South Gate in Baghdad. Number 3 Armoured Car Company was stationed at Makina, in Basra, under the command of Squadron Leader Frederick Guard. This Company had responsibility for the towns, villages and tribes of southern Iraq, particularly the Southern Desert, which contained the tribal grazing areas that bordered the Nejed. Numbers 4, 5 and 6 Companies were under the command of Squadron Leaders 'Robin' Willock, Douglas Harries DFC and Jasper Cruikshank OBE, respectively, and would deal with operations in northern and central Iraq. Number 5 Armoured Car Company had immediately moved north to Mosul, soon after arrival where it joined No 55 (Bomber) Squadron RAF, and the military garrison of a few battalions.[23]

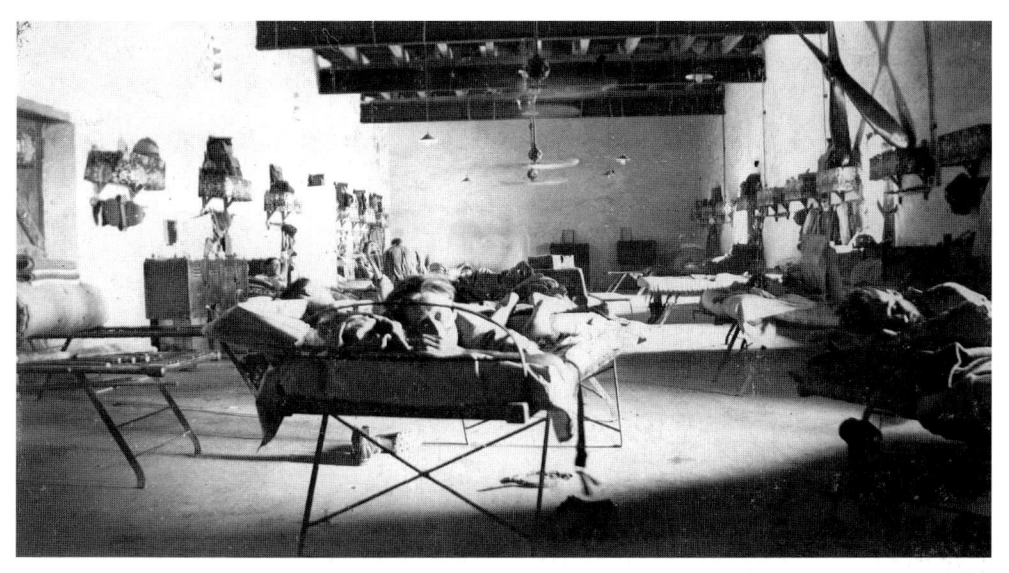

Interior of the Headquarters Hut, No 4 Armoured Car Company, at RAF Hinaidi (© Crown copyright. Cox, RAF Regiment Museum).

The first task of the armoured car crews was to familiarise themselves with the routes and terrain, and the problems of travel with a 4-ton Rolls-Royce armoured car across a largely unmapped country of sand, rock and marshes, with few tracks, rudimentary roads and primitive river crossings. Therefore, on 11 November 1922, after only a few weeks at Baghdad, one Section of No 4 Company set off up the road north to Mosul, for their first long distance run. By the end of the first day 'out in the blue' they had travelled 50 miles from Baghdad.

Corporal James Cox was with the Section, and noted that the weather had become unpleasant, with cool temperatures and plenty of wind, which blew up drifts of sand. By 13 November they were nearing Samarra, but travel soon became difficult as heavy rain had started falling, and dried-up river beds were soon in flood. By the

The first day out, 50 miles from Baghdad. Number 4 Armoured Car Company pose in front of a Rolls-Royce fitted with a frame aerial. The wireless set occupied a large amount of space within the car and as a consequence the sets were eventually placed in separate wireless tenders (© Crown copyright. Cox, RAF Regiment Museum).

fourth day after departure they were 280 miles from Baghdad. At each halt they set up the 30-foot telescopic mast to make contact with base to test the reliability of wireless communication with Baghdad. A local water course provided the opportunity for his first wash for five days. For the next two days they followed the left bank of the River Tigris, passing through Baiji, and then on to Shergat, the site of the ancient Assyrian city of Ashur. Shergat was the terminus of the railway line from Baghdad. After another 80 miles they reached Mosul, where the Section moved to the airfield and joined their comrades of No 5 Armoured Car Company.[24]

Rolls-Royce armoured cars and Lancias near Samarra. Heavy rain made progress difficult and the dry river beds began to flood (© Crown copyright. Cox, RAF Regiment Museum).

While the flying squadrons had been in minor actions for many months against the Turkish irregulars and Kurdish 'rebels', operations were now set to intensify. The 'Forward Offensive' plan was to be implemented on 2 February 1923. The larger part of the ground forces in Iraq, including the British and Indian infantry battalions, were moved to northern Iraq by rail, and then force-marched to Mosul.[25] This would leave the rest of the country virtually undefended, but Salmond considered the risk worthwhile. In preparation for this, No 4 Armoured Car Company had been ordered to proceed to northern Iraq to reinforce No 5 Company. 'A' Section, accompanied by Squadron Leader Willock, went to Mosul and began a number of reconnaissances to the south-east; to Kingerban via Quwair North, Arbil and Kirkuk. This was to determine the best routes to bring supplies to Arbil, where 'C' Section was now located. They had been occupied with preparation of route reports, and protection and repair of bridges. Meanwhile, 'B' Section had joined the garrison at the vital railhead at Shergat, which they shared with some Indian pioneers, and a battalion of the Iraq Army. All supplies for the military operations now planned around Mosul were transferred here to camel caravans or motorised convoys. As well as defence of the railhead, the Section also had the task of identifying potential landing ground sites to the south towards Baiji (Map 6, p. 51; Map 8, p. 73).

'Out in the blue.' Sending out a message, 280 miles from Baghdad with the 30-foot telescopic aerial (© Crown copyright. Cox, RAF Regiment Museum).

Salmond was concerned about the build-up of Turkish forces on the Mosul front. In conjunction with air reconnaissance, No 5 Company patrolled continuously out to the north and north-west in preparation for a possible move by the Turkish across the Nisibin Plain. Should the Turkish Army attack from this direction, it would be the two sections of armoured cars, two regiments of Iraqi cavalry and the RAF Bristol Fighters, Sopwith Snipes and Ninaks that would have to stop them. The plain was, however, ideal for the rapid movement of the cavalry and armoured cars. In preparation for this eventuality, the Company carried out tactical exercises and battle practice on the desert up to the hills of Sheikh Ibrahim to the west of the town. Should he face an overwhelming advance on Mosul, Salmond also prepared plans for a concentration of all his forces at a point further south. However, there was no information on the lines of communications by which his infantry columns would move. 'C' Section of No 4 Armoured Company was at once ordered to reconnoitre the route. The river bridges at Altun Kupri were identified as vulnerable points and the armoured cars speedily despatched to establish posts for their protection.[26]

Sheikh Mahmud would prove to be an unvarying thorn in the side of the RAF and Iraq government for the next decade. The Sheikh had first come into conflict with British forces in 1915, when fighting alongside the Turkish Army to repel the foreign invaders of Mesopotamia. He had great influence throughout the villages south of the Greater Zab River. As a consequence, following the 1918 Armistice, he was appointed by the British administration as head of an autonomous Kurdish province, but this had proven a failure. This was further exacerbated when he ordered the internment of the local British political officer. He was defeated during a short military operation in 1921, captured, and deported to India for imprisonment, but by 1922 had been released to live in Kuwait. The Sheikh was soon, however, reinstated as Governor by the British Prime Minister, Bonar Law, in an attempt to placate Turkish calls for a Kurdish uprising. Assurances were, however, sought from the Sheikh that he would resist political advances by Turkish operatives.[27]

Extreme concern was generated in March when a Turkish general and his staff were reported to have arrived at Jezireh ibn Omar, only a few miles from the Iraq border town of Zakho.[28] Sheikh Mahmud was making political overtures to groups in central Iraq with the aim of launching a general insurrection. He had also made contact with Euz Demur, the leader of the Turkish chattas. The Sheikh was therefore summoned to Baghdad by Sir Percy Cox, the British High Commissioner, to explain his position; however, he refused to attend. Turkish Irregulars had been occupying Rowanduz for two years. The town was located 30 miles within the Iraq frontier and was of great strategic significance, as the narrow pass was the major bottleneck for the roads leading into Turkey and Persia. The chattas were also scheming with the Sheikh to occupy Koi Sanjak. Hostile forces were threatening to move against Kirkuk and Arbil, while another group threatened Ser Amadia, and smaller detachments were moving on Rania and Sulaimaniya.

By early March 1923, Iraq Command was ready to act. A proclamation was dropped on Sulaimaniya to warn Sheikh Mahmud and the populace that the town would be bombed if he did not comply with the summons to Baghdad. To emphasise the intent of the RAF, delayed action bombs were dropped outside the town limits. In response to this, the Sheikh resigned as Governor. Consulting his political officers in Kirkuk and Arbil in early March, Salmond was satisfied that Mosul was not threatened and that he could transfer most of his forces to the east, as he was determined to restore the situation in the mountains of Kurdistan. Salmond planned a combined ground and air operation, to be launched immediately. Two columns were formed, 'Koicol' and 'Frontiercol'.[29] The former would move from Mosul, cross the Greater Zab River, at Quwair, thence to Arbil, and on to Koi Sanjak. This Column would hold down the Pishder tribe, an ally of the Sheikh Mahmud, and any attempts by Euz Demir and his Irregulars to attack Kirkuk. It would also drive a wedge between the Sheikh and the Turkish chattas. 'Frontiercol' was concentrated at Arbil, and would move on Rowanduz and further threaten the chattas.

The RAF presence at Mosul, Kirkuk and Arbil was considerably reinforced. The flying squadrons closely cooperated with the two Columns, as well as carrying out independent action against the insurgent strongholds. Mosul Wing, consisting of Nos

1, 30 and 55 Squadrons RAF, was formed under the command of Wing Commander C.R.S. Bradley OBE, and. In addition, No 6 Squadron, located at Kirkuk, began harassing Sheikh Mahmud and his supporters, and took over the air support of 'Koicol' as it moved east.

'Koicol' departed from Mosul on 18 March and 'Frontiercol' eight days later. The Columns moved into difficult mountainous country, with rudimentary roads and bridges, and poor communications. The campaign suffered a major setback right at the start when the only bridge in Mosul was damaged by a severe flood. At the same time the only lorry-bearing bridge in Baghdad was swept away, along with the bridge over the Diyala River at Qaraghan. This severed the main line of communications between Baghdad and Kirkuk. An alternative route had to be found as soon as possible. Number 4 Armoured Car Company was ordered out to reconnoitre the route across the desert from Kirkuk, westwards to the Fathah Gorge, on the Tigris. They clearly defined the route, and installed directional arrows, and then escorted the Chief Engineering Officer on an inspection of the route from Fathah to Kirkuk, and on to Kingerban. Supplies were now diverted to the Kingerban to Kirkuk road. The remainder were moved to Baiji by rail, and were then sent across the Fathah Gorge and over the desert route to Kirkuk.[30]

The operations by the two Columns had progressed well and they were in position by the first week of April. 'Koicol' had concentrated at Koi Sanjak, and advanced on Rowanduz from the south. 'Frontiercol' assembled at Arbil, advancing from the west via the Spilik Dagh. Numbers 30 and 55 Squadrons, with Ninaks, covered their progress by machine-gunning groups of rebels, either independently or when requested by the RAF wireless-telegraphy party attached to each Column. The advance of 'Frontiercol' was held up for a time at Spilik Dagh by a strong force of Euz Demir's followers and local tribesmen. The pass was too difficult to take by frontal attack and, in a brilliant tactical move, the AOC mustered the Levies in view of the pass, called in the RAF to bomb the defenders and then, with their attention fixed, deftly ordered 'Koicol' to outflank the position from the south. Air attacks by the RAF, along with the threat posed by 'Koicol' to the enemy rear, forced the enemy to withdraw and 'Frontiercol' was able to occupy the Spilik Dagh. Marching rapidly, the Column moved on to attack Rowanduz. It was then discovered, however, that Euz Demir and the Turkish chattas had fled across the Persian border, where they were disarmed and interned, and the town was captured unopposed. Fortuitously, the restoration of Iraqi administration in the town coincided with the resumption of the Treaty talks in Lausanne, and this aided considerably in establishing the British case for maintenance of the *status quo* for the northern boundaries of Iraq.[31]

'Koicol', having assisted 'Frontiercol', was then ordered back to Kirkuk where it was refreshed with three new battalions. There had been an outbreak of dysentery during early May, and the harsh weather had taken a toll on the ground troops. The new advance had been planned, but the concentration of reinforcements could not be delayed. A draft of the 1/13th (Coke's Rifles) Frontier Force Rifles did not arrive in time for the departure of 'Koicol', and they were rushed forward with the armoured cars of No 4 Company, catching up with the Column that same evening.[32] Two armoured car crewmen were also flown to Kirkuk for duty with 'Koicol' as Lewis gunners. 'Koicol' was successful in moving rapidly along the Kirkuk to Sulaimaniya road and prevented Sheikh Mahmud organising a holding position at the Baziyan Pass. Sulaimaniya fell on 16 May and the Column pursued the Sheikh up the valley to Serdash, to the north-west. With the insurrection having failed, Sheikh Mahmud,

Coke's Rifles of 'Koicol' fording a stream to the east of Kirkuk (© Crown copyright. Cox, RAF Regiment Museum).

and those tribal chiefs who had rallied to his cause, took refuge across the frontier in Persia.

'B' Section of No 4 Company had spent May marking out and preparing new landing grounds at Ain Dibbs, Baiji and Tikrit. 'C' Section, under the command of Flying Officer Charles Goring, had also taken on a heavy work-load, doing 29 operational runs during May, many in support of the Sulaimaniya garrison. These included escort duty, conveyance of troops, rations, weapons and ammunition to 'Koicol', carriage of bombs for the flying squadrons, and provision of assistance to force-landed aircraft. In one instance, two Lancias transported 20 sick and wounded from Altun Kupri back to the railhead at Shergat. By month's end this section had covered some 3732 miles of the 6680 of the total mileage for the Company.

Salmond was still determined to ensure the Turkish forces across the frontier were aware of the resolve of Iraq Command to hold the north. During early May,

A section of Rolls-Royces and Lancias of No 4 Armoured Car Company (© Crown copyright. RAF Regiment Museum).

No 5 Company, with the commanding officer, Squadron Leader Harries, and all 12 of the Rolls-Royce armoured cars, was placed under orders of the Mosul Field Force and moved to the Zakho Pass on the Turkish frontier. The gunners were exercised in taking up correct firing positions within the Pass, carried out machine-gun training, and the use of dismounted guns on rough ground.

With the recapture of Sulaimaniya, the focus of operations now shifted away from Mosul and towards Kirkuk. Number 4 Company which had been operating at high tempo since March was gradually withdrawn, section-by-section, back to Baghdad, where they were to move into the newly-constructed Armoured Car Quarters at RAF Hinaidi. Flying Officer Goring and 'C' Section remained, but had moved on to Kirkuk to keep open the lines of communications. The road from here through Chamchamal and the Baziyan Pass was the tenuous supply line for the troops at Sulaimaniya. With three Rolls-Royce armoured cars and three Lancias, many runs were made along this road. Their main task was to provide escort to vital supply convoys, but also to various notables, including six vehicles assigned to escort the AOC, Air Vice-Marshal Salmond, on his tours of inspection following the recent successes. In another operation, a Lancia transported the entire replacement main wing of a Vickers Vernon, weighing 1¾ tons, from Baiji, over the difficult and mountainous terrain, to a damaged aircraft at Sulaimaniya, in just two days.

'Koicol' had remained at Sulaimaniya for three weeks while the civil administration was re-established. With the weather deteriorating, and matters improving, orders were issued for the return of the troops to Kirkuk and thence to their normal stations in the south. Number 4 Company's, HMAC *Drake*, a Rolls-Royce Armoured Car fitted with W/T, and a Lancia, were assigned to monitor and report on the progress of the Column as it moved from Kirkuk across the desert road to the ferry at Fathah Gorge. By the first week of July they could report that

The Baziyan Pass on the road between Kirkuk and Sulaimaniya (Rolph, RAFACA).

the last echelon had crossed the Tigris and had reached the railway station at Baiji. The hard-working 'C' Section remained for a few weeks to carry out instructional reconnaissances for their replacement, No 6 Armoured Car Company, but they were safely back at Hinaidi by mid-July. The total mileage for No 4 Company operations in June had reached 4495 miles.[33]

It was now the turn of No 6 Armoured Car Company to operate in the north. During May, a section had been sent to Kingerban, which was the terminus of the railway line from Baghdad and on the road to Kirkuk. The remainder of the Company moved a few weeks later and set up Headquarters at Kirkuk airfield. For the airmen, the living conditions and accommodation in the old Turkish barracks were pretty primitive. Malaria and infectious diseases were commonplace, and medical treatment for those so-afflicted required evacuation to the RAF Hospital in Baghdad. LAC William Edwards recalls the time when he contracted malaria and sandfly fever:

> Well, they used to give us quinine every evening. But that didn't seem to do a lot.., because I contracted malaria and sandfly fever. I got sent down by 'armoured' to Kingerban, where the aerodrome was. Put on a stretcher, strapped on the wing, and flew to Baghdad. A distance of about 300 miles. The aircraft was only a two-seater ... a Bristol Fighter in them days, and ... I was strapped right up tight to the fuselage.
>
> It was very breezy! I remember having a Balaclava helmet on, about five or six blankets, and strapped well into this.... Of course they only flew about 90 mile an hour in them days, so it wasn't all that much.[34]

The pace of military operations had slowed and, therefore, No 6 Company's main tasks for the next five months concentrated on work with the local police and political authorities dealing with 'small bands of armed malcontents' who were causing trouble on the roads around Kirkuk. In one instance they were given permission to purchase native clothing and a car so as to create a decoy to lure out the road thieves. A Lewis gun was hidden in the vehicle driven by a disguised crew. Unfortunately no thieves were tempted, however, but perhaps due to this ruse, the level of activity declined.

Number 5 Company was kept busy from July until the end of October 1923 assisting the authorities with minor civil disturbances in Mosul town. Those events arose mainly between the Assyrians and the local Moslem population. The arrival of large numbers of Assyrians in 1918 had created problems. The town and plain dwellers of Iraq disliked and indeed feared the mountaineers from Hakkiari, and the feelings were reciprocated. There was also the natural antipathy between the two groups due to religious differences. Feelings were particularly inflamed in August 1923 when troubles occurred in the local meat market and this led to the death of two Assyrian children. The Company provided routine armoured car patrols through the town, and a permanent post was established outside the Police Barracks until late November when matters had settled down.

The operational demands on No 5 Company at Mosul had lessened, however, and they were able to dedicate more time to training. In one exercise, when given the signal, the crews of four Rolls-Royce armoured cars had their Vickers machine-guns ready for dismounted action within 85 seconds. Squadron Leader Jasper Cruikshank was able to write with confidence that '... the formation of highly efficient machine-gun units from armoured car crews is rapidly approaching maturity.'[35] During early

The armoured cars escort King Feisal I of Iraq on a tour of the villages (© Crown copyright. RAF Regiment Museum).

October the Company carried out a co-operative 'shoot' between No 55 Squadron and 43 Battery Royal Field Artillery and later, 120 (Ambala) Pack Battery, Indian Artillery with the Company's W/T car being used as the link between the aircraft and batteries. Other tasks included provisions of escorts to the local political officers when visiting local sheikhs, to King Feisal and the High Commissioner on tours of the Mosul district, and assisting the police with the arrests of groups carrying unauthorised weapons.

By August 1923, the successes of Iraq Command in the north had borne fruit. Turkey had signed the Treaty at Lausanne in July, and had agreed that a frontier be 'laid down in friendly arrangement ... between Turkey and Great Britain within nine months'.[36] The Turkey-Iraq frontier was quiet for the early part of 1924, but Air Headquarters were still concerned with Turkish intentions. On 6 March, the AOC and Wing Commander Primrose arrived in Mosul from Shergat, under armoured car escort for a special conference, held in the Armoured Car Officers' Mess at RAF Mosul, with RAF, Levy and Iraq Army field officers. The outcome of this was that the Company, now under the command of Squadron Leader Denis Mulholland AFC, were ordered to reconnoitre the front from Tel Awainat to the Golat Pass. They were to ascertain the possibilities for armoured car action against Turkish chattas, should they try and make any aggressive moves across the Syria-Iraq border. It was decided that a line of protection would be established from Tel Abu Dahir to Tel Awainat. The Company were also tasked with clearing and defining tracks across the waterless Nisibin Plain to Golat Pass. Following heavy flooding on the Tigris River, they also reported on the damage to the ferry crossings further south at Shergat and Quwair. A section of No 6 Company working out of Kingerban was similarly engaged on the roads to Kirkuk, Altun Kupri, Fathah and Quwair.[37]

While Salmond's success in Kurdistan had temporarily removed the threat from Sheikh Mahmud, he had not been defeated and, not unexpectedly, by late 1923 he had returned from Persia. His attitude, not surprisingly, was even more pro-Turkish than before. The Government had detached many of the surrounding administrative districts around Sulaimaniya to decrease his influence. It was, however, accepted that if he returned he would become the *de facto* ruler of Sulaimaniya, and that it would become an 'un-administered' tract of Iraq. The High Commissioner sent a message to the Sheikh indicating that as long he remained within a defined area, and did not participate in intrigues in opposition to the government, or move into adjacent districts, then no action would be taken against him. However, it was not long before he had violated these conditions. By December, however, having consolidated his forces, he renewed his activities and was again interfering in the affairs of surrounding districts, spreading anti-British propaganda, and intriguing with the Turkish military on the frontier. Sulaimaniya was bombed again and matters quietened down for a few more months.[38]

Having come to the end of his tenure as AOC Iraq, Air Vice-Marshal Sir John Salmond returned home during March, and his place was taken by Air Vice-Marshal Sir John Higgins CB DSO AFC.[39] By April 1924, Iraq Command had decided that strong action again needed to be taken against Sheikh Mahmud and his followers. He had been enlisting men for his own force, and collecting taxes illegally from local villages. During March, an aircraft of No 30 Squadron on a raid on one of the Sheikh's villages was engaged by ground fire and made a forced-landing.

The ground force for operations against Sulaimaniya, composed of Levies and Iraq Army units, gathered during April at Kirkuk. The 2nd Battalion, Iraq Levies, was made up of Assyrians, and had been stationed at Kirkuk for the last six months. As operations were being planned against Sulaimaniya, the families and followers of the Battalion had set up a camp in Kirkuk and at Chamchamal, 40 miles to the east. Many of the local populace were in sympathy with the Sheikh and with the larger part of the Battalion having departed on operations, some of the Kirkuk townsfolk had begun making threats against the Assyrian families (Map 7, p. 66).

On 4 May, two Assyrian soldiers became involved in a serious argument with a Kurdish shopkeeper in the bazaar at Kirkuk. Personal, and more seriously, religious insults were exchanged. This led to physical violence, and with tempers inflamed, the wounded Assyrians returned to camp. News of the argument spread quickly through the ranks of the Levies, and attempts were made by the officers to mollify the outrage, but this proved unsuccessful. The Companies were paraded, and assurances given by their officers that the shopkeeper who had caused the trouble would be dealt with by the police. Unfortunately, tempers were further inflamed when insults were exchanged with the Levies from a nearby coffee shop. The Levy officers vainly tried to calm their men, and attempted to disarm those men who were seeking retribution. Shots were fired from the direction of the town, and soon the Assyrians were returning fire. One small armed party moved on into the town and took up position overlooking the bazaar. A riot broke out and the bazaar was soon in flames. By the day's end, 50 of the town's inhabitants were dead, as were five Levies, along with seven wounded. In retaliation, the following day a group of rioters from the town looted Christian shops and killed nine more and about one-hundred Christians sought refuge in the town fort.[40]

With the situation moving towards a complete breakdown of civil, and indeed, military order, the Administrative Inspector of Kirkuk sent an urgent message to Baghdad. Two platoons of the 1st Battalion, Royal Inniskilling Fusiliers, were flown in from Hinaidi late in the afternoon, on the Vickers Vernons and a Victoria belonging to Nos 45 and 70 Squadrons.[41] Realising that the Royal Inniskilling Fusiliers would

A street scene in Kirkuk (Rutter, RAFACA).

take a few hours to arrive, the Administrator of Kirkuk requested immediate assistance from the armoured cars at Kingerban. Flying Officer George Richardson of 'A' Section, No 6 Company, at Kingerban, was ordered to move in three Rolls-Royce armoured cars as fast as possible to Kirkuk, and to report to Colonel-Commandant Dobbin of the Iraq Levies. They were followed later in the day by two Lancias with Flying Officer Gerald Elliot. Flight Lieutenant Sturley Simpson and Observer Officer Lorenzo Kerry, with five Rolls-Royces and a Lancia, were to be despatched from Baghdad to take over responsibility at Kingerban. Two more platoons of the Royal Inniskilling Fusiliers were requested but they could not be flown out of Baghdad in time, so Kerry and his Rolls-Royces quickly moved on to Kirkuk the next day as reinforcement. A day later, Flight Lieutenant Charles Wardle and the remaining five Lancias, a Rolls-Royce and a Crossley tender of the Company had departed from Hinaidi for Kingerban. With no prior notice given, the section was ready to move, fully equipped, within 1½ hours, despite many of the airmen being away on sporting activities and other tasks. Number 6 Company was now fully committed in Southern Kurdistan.

Flying Officer Richardson of 'A' Section had immediately implemented continuous day and night patrols of Kirkuk town in cooperation with the Royal Inniskilling Fusiliers and by nightfall the situation in the town had stabilised. Though the cars had arrived first and possessed considerable firepower it was essential that they had this infantry support. The many narrow streets in the town limited the cars' manoeuvrability, and with only a small number of vehicles they would have been hard-pressed to guard all the important buildings in the town.

Flying Officer Elliot, with a detachment of three Lancias, was assigned to guard the aerodrome, where the Royal Inniskilling Fusiliers were being flown in. Most importantly, it was essential that the Levies and their families be evacuated, as bitter feelings were now held in the town and threats were being made against them by the townsfolk. The following evening, with an armoured car escort, the Assyrians formed up and marched out, to a campsite a few miles from the town. On the morning of 6 May, the column, consisting of two Levy companies, and 600 women, children and old men, under the command of Lieutenant-Colonel Sorel-Cameron, set off for the main camp of the 2nd Battalion at Chamchamal. Rumours had been circulating that the local Kurds intended to attack the column and Flight Lieutenant Richardson and Flying Officer Elliot and their section were assigned for its protection.

The column had halted that evening at Qara Anjir. At 1830 hours, Captain Fry of the 2nd Battalion of the Levies was inspecting his picquets on the north side of the camp, while Colonel Cameron inspected those on the south. Fry noticed a party of about 15 Kurds advancing on one of the picquets. He reported this to Flying Officer Elliot, who immediately moved off with two Rolls-Royce armoured cars, HMACs *Explorer* and *Avenger*, taking Captain Fry and a guide with them. Passing through the picquet line, they succeeded in bringing the cars behind the attackers without their knowledge. Unfortunately, one of the cars became stuck, and it immediately came under heavy fire. Flying Officer Elliot continues:

> A piece of embankment gave way and the leading car, HMAC *Avenger*, stuck for about three minutes, here we were first fired upon. HMAC *Avenger* was pulled out of the rut by HMAC *Explorer*. Corporal Ashcroft jumped out of his car, and thus exposing himself to the fire of the Kurds, helped to place a tow rope on to the *Avenger* [Elliot did not mention that he had aided Ashcroft in this task].[42]

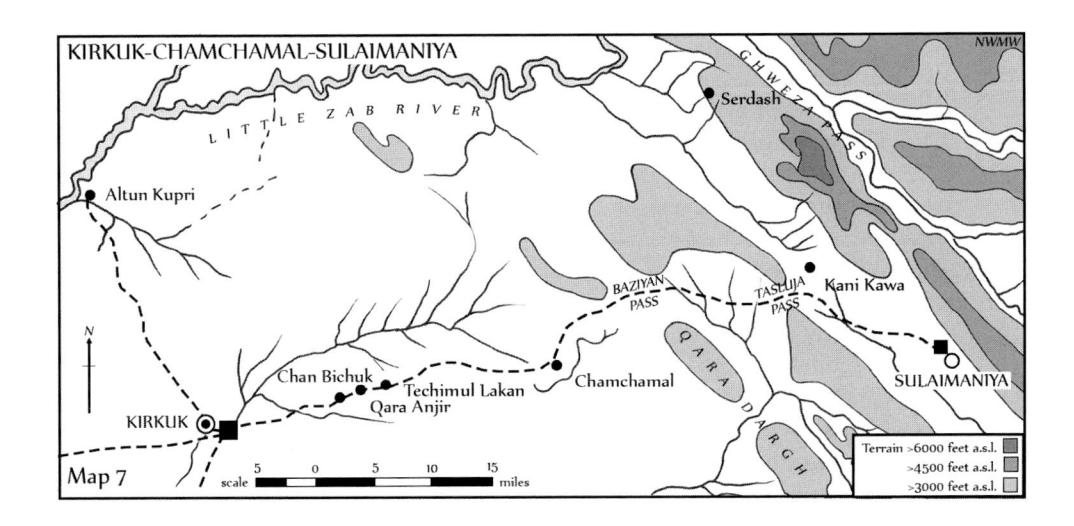

The cars moved off again, however, owing to the steepness of the hill, further progress became difficult, and Flying Officer Elliot ordered Corporal Lewis, the gunner on *Avenger*, and his number two, Aircraftman Osborne, to prepare for dismounted action. While Captain Fry covered them with a single rifle, the three ran to place the gun in a position from where they could put down cross fire on their assailants; Fry managed to shoot one of the Kurds in the process. Lewis, carrying his Vickers gun, reached a position some 20 feet above the road. Elliot continues:

> Our machine-gun then came into action and replied to the [Kurds] fire by spraying the top of the hill with short bursts.... During this period *Avenger* and *Explorer* had turned ready for a retreat, and it being very nearly dark, this I decided to do.[43]
>
> Captain Fry and myself covered with rifle fire the withdrawal of the machine-gun and then retreated to the cars, which returned car-by-car in distances of about 200 yards. Each car covering the other car's withdrawal by machine-gun fire, and got back to camp about five minutes before dark.
>
> ... Corporal Lewis and AC2 Osborne both displayed absolute disregard of fear while under fire. Not once hesitating to get and maintain their car in action.[44]

Captain Fry wrote a few days later:

> Owing to the initiative of the Armoured Car Commander and conduct of the crew the Kurds never again approached within firing distance of the camp and sniping was effectually arrested.

The enemy party had consisted of about 45 men on horseback, under the control of Sayed Mohammed Jabbari, an ally of Sheikh Mahmud. He had been injured in the fighting in the town on 4 May and this was largely why the people from his village had attacked the column. He was watching events from a nearby hillside, and on hearing the sounds of the firing had moved to watch the attack on HMAC *Avenger*. His group came under fire from the cars, killing one man, as well as Jabbari's prize mare. This was a valuable animal, and it was rumoured that he was particularly incensed at the loss.[45]

Despite the success of this counterattack, the column was still seriously threatened. Observer Officer Lorenzo Kerry had returned after completing an overnight run to Chamchamal and at about 0700 hours on 8 May, he was requested by Colonel Cameron to attach his two Rolls-Royces to the column. Kerry then took the lead with his car, HMAC *Busrah*. An hour-and-a-half later, the Kurds attacked the column from all sides, and maintained fire until three miles from Chamchamal. The Assyrian Levies did not accept this meekly, and at one point they closed with the Kurds and inflicted heavy casualties.[46] Surprisingly, the column lost only one man killed and one missing. Kerry continues:

> Heavy rifle fire was exchanged between the Levy outposts and hill men from the moment the column moved off. [On] my arrival at Techimul Lakan, 2 miles from the Chamchamal side of Qara Anjir, I surprised an ambush of approximately 50 horsemen, and a similar number of un-mounted men, all apparently armed, who were lying in wait for the column in a swamp. A very excellent position which commands the junction of the higher and lower roads leading to Chamchamal.
>
> I immediately issued orders for the Vickers gun to be trained on them, but that no firing was to take place. They allowed me to pass by in the first instance without them firing on me, but when I turned again in the direction

No 4 Company were sent from RAF Hinaidi with vehicles and crews from 'A' and 'B' Sections to reinforce No 6 Company at Kirkuk.[54]

A note was then sent to Sheikh Mahmud asking him to come in and surrender before 25 May. If he did so, his headquarters in Sulaimaniya would not be bombed. The Sheikh had communicated earlier that he did not wish to surrender to the Assyrian Levies and Primrose, therefore sent a message saying that he would send an armoured car detachment forward to ensure he could surrender to British troops. Wing Commander Primrose, and the Company commander, Squadron Leader Cruikshank, travelled from Kirkuk with Flight Lieutenant Simpson and his armoured cars to Chamchamal. Here the Simpson awaited orders to move, should a positive response be received from the Sheikh, however, no reply came.

On 27 and 28 May, 14 raids were carried out on Sulaimaniya, and 28 tons of bombs dropped. There were no casualties as the inhabitants had abandoned the town in response to the proclamations. Sheikh Mahmud and his followers had also departed and watched the bombing from the caves high on the Qara Dagh, where they had taken refuge. Having made a demonstration against the town, the flying squadrons were withdrawn to their bases. Number 6 Company remained at the advanced landing ground at Chamchamal until early June, and continued to provide escorts for the supply runs to the Levy camp. The Sheikh's prestige had, however, been lowered and his hold over his people reduced by the bombing. On his return to Sulaimaniya, in early June, he was met with distinct hostility by the local townspeople.

In early July, Air Headquarters Iraq had decided it was time to re-open the road to Sulaimaniya and reoccupy the town to deny the Sheikh influence and sources of revenue. A column, known as 'Sulcol', with two cavalry regiments of the Iraq Army and 100 Iraq Police moved on Sulaimaniya, with the support of Nos 1 and 30 Squadrons. The armoured cars of No 6 Company were ordered to assist the advance and their first task was to escort the ground party of No 1 Squadron, consisting of officers, airmen and NCOs, including nine 'followers' and 9000 lb of stores and spares, from the rail terminus at Kingerban to Kirkuk.

An RAF W/T pack set came under command of Squadron Leader Cruikshank to provide signals communications to 'Sulcol'. Air reconnaissance had shown the road to be in poor condition, and the cars moved well ahead of the column to effect repairs. On 15 July, Squadron Leader Cruikshank, with eight Rolls-Royces, five auxiliary vehicles and three ambulances, moved from Kirkuk to Chamchamal, and hence to the Baziyan Pass. With the heights having been picqueted by the 2nd Battalion, Iraq Levies, they moved east, transporting an officer and 30 men of the Levies, who carried out essential road repair work under the cover of their guns. Six miles of culverts and bridges were made passable for motor transport by the end of the day. By the evening of the next day they had reached Tasluja Pass, the gateway to Sulaimaniya. On 18 July, following an aerial reconnaissance, the cars proceeded to the foot of the pass and awaited the arrival of 'Sulcol', which had yet to arrive on foot and horseback.

Once the column had arrived, the armoured cars moved through the pass in single order. This task was made difficult by generally appalling road conditions and the two mile-long steep gradient, along a boulder-strewn track, at the entrance to the Pass. The cars required a large amount of manhandling, and conditions were so severe that one car suffered a badly-cracked chassis. Once on the eastern side of the pass, the cars were quickly went in pursuit of a party of 12 Kurdish horsemen.

They had been observed by the Levies from their picquets, but the cars had to halt the chase, as the Kurds fled across broken ground.[55] The Company and column had a disturbed night camped at Kani Kawa, with intermittent sniping, and just after midnight, an enemy party set fire to the surrounding scrub and the rest of the night was spent on 'stand-to'. Fortunately, the flames moved away from the encampment.

Early on 19 July, 'Sulcol' with the armoured car escort entered Sulaimaniya, unopposed. Four of the cars were sent off to guard the northern approach to the town, while the other three cars moved at once to the aerodrome, held it until the troops arrived, and were able to welcome the Sopwith Snipes of No 1 Squadron as they flew in. The crews spent another uncomfortable night subjected to sniping, but the following day they were assigned to defensive positions around the southern side of the aerodrome, carried out patrols and acted as mobile pillboxes.

Two days later, Sheikh Mahmud was located at the Ghweza Pass to the north of the town. A company of the Iraq Army was then given orders to take the position held by his followers at the summit of the Ghweza Pass. In cooperation with aircraft of No 30 Squadron, three armoured cars were detailed to cover the advance and on reaching the foot of the Pass the Section dismounted their Lewis guns and crews provided fire support and the advance to the summit was a success.

The No 6 Company cars remained at Sulaimaniya until relieved in late July, but they would still provide weekly escorts to convoys transporting supplies from Kirkuk to Sulaimaniya for the remainder of 1924 and into 1925. With the inauguration of these escorts, the adherents of the Sheikh made no further attempts to interfere with or block the passage of the supply convoys.

During the winter periods, the roads became waterlogged and the Rolls-Royces and Lancias found the going difficult. The light Ford Model T cars, used as Section runabouts and to move over tracks and terrain impassable to the armoured vehicles were, therefore, modified with extra armour to use as escort vehicles for the Sulaimaniya convoys beyond the Tasluja Pass, where road conditions were the harshest.[56]

Despite the signing of the Treaty of Lausanne, the frontiers with Turkey had, as yet, not been clearly defined and further trouble was expected north of Mosul. It came as no surprise when, during the first week of September 1924, Turkish regulars troops and chattas were again reported to be concentrating ten miles north of Zakho. Furthermore, they intended to cross into Iraqi territory to seize the town. Despite warnings from the High Commissioner, the enemy parties advanced on 13 September, and at dawn the following day, Bristol Fighters of No 6 Squadron successfully dispersed a 300-strong force of armed tribesman and a few Turkish regulars with animal pack transport, crossing the Hezil Suyu [River], only five miles from the frontier town. For the next two days air action was taken against this, and another force, crossing by a more easterly route (Map 8, p. 73).

The AOC Iraq, Air Vice-Marshal Higgins, was confident he could hold the advance by air action, however, he also ordered Colonel Commandant Dobbin of the Iraq Levies to establish a force at Mosul.[57] In response to this threat, a section of No 5 Armoured Car Company, under command of Flight Lieutenant Garret O'Brien, was immediately ordered to proceed to the Zakho Pass, in company with a troop of Iraqi cavalry. The Company was to undertake ground defence duties in the event of a hostile advance south of the Khabur River. They were to reinforce the resident Iraqi infantry battalion guarding the Zakho Pass and to afford protection to the aircraft operating from the advanced aerodrome at Zakho.

'A' Section, No 5 Armoured Car Company in 1924, with Rolls-Royce armoured car and Lancia, at RAF Mosul (© Crown copyright. RAF Regiment Museum).

An advanced operational headquarters, 'Aerowing', under the command of Wing Commander Primrose, with Flight Lieutenant Robert Jope-Slade DSC as the sole staff officer, was established at Mosul a few days later.[58] It consisted of No 5 Armoured Car Company, and Nos 6 (Army Co-operation) and 55 (Bombing) Squadrons, based at Zakho and Mosul, respectively. Wing Commander Primrose continues:

> No 5 Armoured Car Company... continued in spite of darkness, to successfully negotiate the Zakho Pass by night, and in doing so reassured the panic-stricken inhabitants who were evacuating Zakho.... [The Company] continued ... guarding the aerodrome throughout the period of operations. They also successfully undertook escorting the transport of all supplies to Zakho, in such an efficient manner, that in spite of all road difficulties and the reported impossibility for armoured cars of the road though the Zakho Pass, the squadron at Zakho was never once short of any necessary supplies or munitions.
>
> Whilst doing this they also undertook the transporting and escorting of all urgently-required supplies from railhead at Shergat to Mosul. This work was first carried out with the Company's own transport, and the old Fiat lorries of the Shergat convoy. With these vehicles 120 tons of supplies were carried 1700 miles in 12 days.
>
> Later all the RAF transport in Mosul was placed under the control of No 5 Armoured Car Company who continued to carry out all the many and difficult duties involved in a most efficient and creditable manner.[59]

The flying squadrons took immediate and decisive action against bodies of Turkish troops and tribesman which had crossed the frontier, and then moved to attacks on the Turkish supply lines over the frontier. By mid-October, the offensive by 'Aerowing' had been so effective it had become near impossible to find targets. The wearing effect of repeated and unpredictable bombing and strafing had sapped

MOSUL AND ZAKHO — Map 8

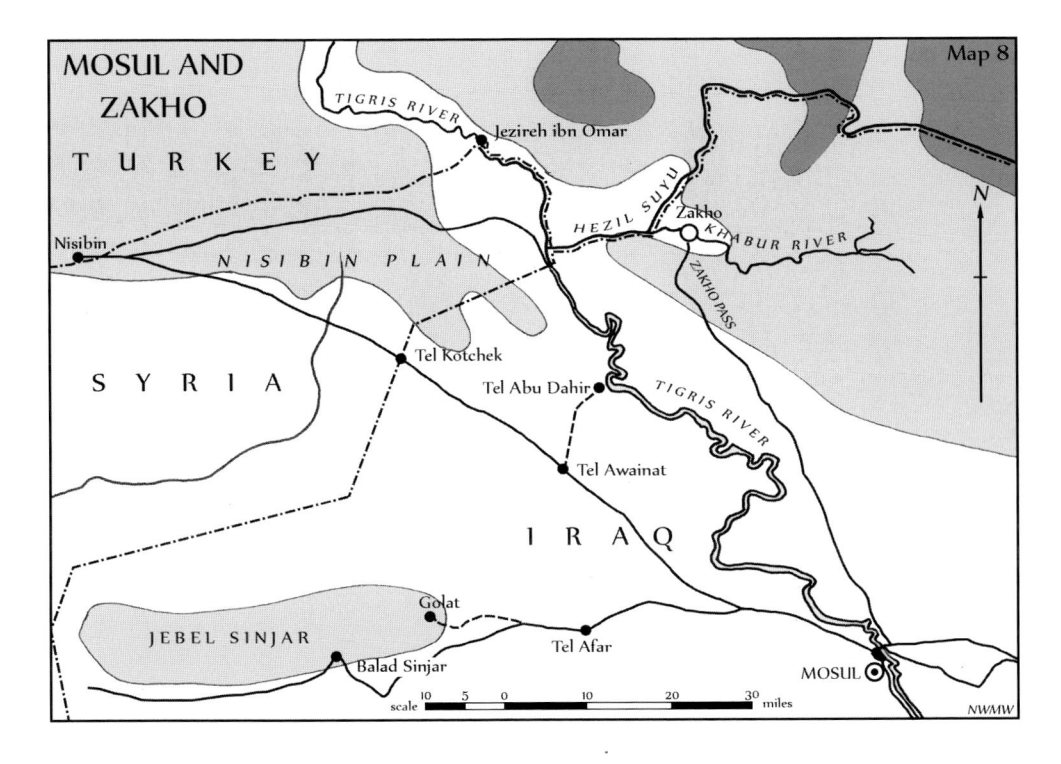

the morale of the attackers and caused local tribes to waver in their support. The Turks withdrew their troops and consequently on 4 November 1924, 'Aerowing' was disbanded, as the threat to the north had receded.

On 15 November, agreement was reached in Brussels on the provisional boundary between Iraq and Turkey, and both parties settled on the current boundaries of the Mosul vilayet, until the League of Nations Commission made a final decision. Zakho was no longer required as a forward landing ground, and as a consequence the RAF units were withdrawn, and escorted back to Mosul by No 5 Armoured Car Company. The threat from Turkey had been held, and the northern frontiers of Iraq were confirmed.[60]

The inherent speed, flexibility and effectiveness of air power had been clearly demonstrated in northern Iraq. The success of the Kurdistan campaign of 1923 was greeted with great acclaim in London and, indeed, it was one of the major factors that ensured the survival of the fledgling RAF as an independent Service. At the command level, Salmond had been able to closely coordinate the movements of his ground columns by flying in to meet with and discuss his plans with the column commanders. Air attacks on Sheikh Mahmud had also dissuaded other tribes from joining the insurrection. Each column had been provided with an RAF liaison officer and W/T pack set, which allowed close contact to be kept with Air Headquarters and to request air support. The flying squadrons carried out long distance reconnaissance for the columns, and dropped messages indicating difficulties ahead, or provided close air patrols to protect the columns when negotiating narrow passes. Finally, considerable savings were made in the number of troops required for the protection of the lines of communications and by the use of air evacuation for hundreds of sick and wounded personnel. Furthermore, there was the reduced suffering for those afflicted, by not having to be moved back along poor roads and tracks over many days. The lessons that had been learned in 1923 were re-applied and improved upon in the operations in the following year.

In monetary terms, the Air Control policy in Iraq had maintained the British presence, influence and prestige for a smaller outlay than for a conventional Army garrison. Henry Dobbs, the High Commissioner, had stated in early 1924 that, 'Air Control had been so brilliantly, magnificently successful that it had far outstripped the expectations of the Cairo Conference of 1921'.[61]

The remit given to the AOC Iraq had not only been to deal with the various problems in Iraq, but also to do so cheaply. In spite of the campaigns being fought, there had also been a gradual reduction in the garrison in the two years of intensive military operations command. Salmond had engineered a reduction in the Imperial Army units within two years, from nine battalions to four, and the Levies from eight battalions and cavalry regiments to six.[62]

The RAF Armoured Cars had not been involved in any direct armed action during the Kurdistan campaign of 1923, as the primitive roads and limited mobility of the cars in the mountains, and off the roads, prevented their deployment. They had, however, performed an important role in aerodrome defence, maintenance of civil order, convoy protection and reconnaissance. This had been developed further during the operations in 1924 against the Turks near Zakho, and Sheikh Mahmud and his followers at Sulaimaniya. The supply lines were tenuous, not only because of their primitive nature, but also because of the threat posed by the local populace, many of whom did not agree with the presence of the British military or the conception of the State of Iraq.

The speed of movement, range and capacity of the armoured cars to defend themselves meant that small detachments of just one or two Rolls-Royces or Lancias could be despatched by the AOC on vital tasks at short notice, and with little logistical complication. A marching military column would not have had this flexibility or speed. In one particular instance, that of the Kirkuk disturbances, their presence had clearly been a key factor in preventing a more serious uprising. Furthermore, operating in cooperation with the Levies forestalled the possible slaughter of a vulnerable column of Assyrian old men, women and children. Despite limitations imposed by climate and terrain, the RAF Armoured Cars had demonstrated a deterrent effect. Their presence had also been crucial in many instances due to the intricate ethnic, religious and cultural differences which underpinned the various military forces employed in the Air Control of Iraq.

Notes
1. Air Vice-Marshal Sir J.M. Salmond, Despatches, 15 February to 30 April 1923, Supplement to *The London Gazette*, 11 June, 1924, p. 4655.
2. J.A.S. Cox RNAS/RAF, *Photographic Album and Diary*, RAF Regiment Museum Archives, Verse entitled 'To be carried by all officers and airmen on leave on arrival in England from Mesopotamia, 1922'.
3. P. Sluglett, *Britain in Iraq 1914-1932* (London: Ithaca Press, 1976), p. 259.
4. C. Bowyer, *RAF Operations 1918-1938* (London: William Kimber, 1988), p. 67. Numbers 6 and 30 Squadrons. Their operational capability was, however, limited. In July-August 1920 the average availability of aircraft was 11 for No 6 and five for No 30 Squadron, and seven of the aircraft were old RE8s of World War One vintage.
5. D. Omissi, *Air Power and Colonial Control: The Royal Air Force 1919-1939* (Manchester: Manchester University Press, 1990), p. 22.

6 AIR 10/1367 *RAF Operations in the Middle East and India from 1920 to 1924*. By March 1921 the military garrison of Iraq consisted of the following British and Indian Army units: 33 battalions, 6 cavalry regiments, 16 artillery batteries, 6 supply and maintenance companies, 3 RTC armoured car companies and 4 RAF flying squadrons.

7 In J. Cox, 'A Splendid Training Ground: The Importance to the Royal Air Force of its Role in Iraq, 1919-32'. *Journal of Imperial and Commonwealth History*, 13 (1985), p. 166.

8 Later Marshal of the RAF Sir John Salmond GCB CMG CVO DSO (1881-1968), AOC Iraq 1923-1924.

9 A. Boyle, *Trenchard: Man of Vision* (London: Collins, 1962), p. 395.

10 AIR 5/1253 *Operations: Iraq, Chapters 1 to 13*. Iraq Command Report, October 1922 to April 1924, Air Publication 1105, p. 3 and, Sluglett, British expenditures on Iraq defence had to decrease from £32 million in 1920-1921 to £4 million in 1926-1927.

11 In preparation for the implementation of Air Control in Iraq No 1 (Fighter) Squadron was moved from India and Nos 8 (Bomber), 45 (Bomber-Transport) and 70 (Bomber-Transport) Squadrons from Egypt. Number 6 (Fighter) and Nos 8, 30, 55 and 84 (Bomber) Squadrons were already in the country. Number 55 Squadron would continue with the work at Mosul and No 84 Squadron at Shaibah.

12 AIR 5/1253 *Operations: Iraq, Chapters 1 to 13* and J. Lunt, *Imperial Sunset*, (London: MacDonald, 1981), pp. 28-29. A pack battery transported the mountain guns by mule.

13 J.G. Browne, *The Iraq Levies 1915-1932* (London: Royal United Service Institute, 1932), pp. 30-31. The Iraq Levies at October 1922 were under the command of Colonel-Commandant H.T. Dobbin DSO, and were composed as follows: the 1st and 3rd Cavalry Regiments were made up of Kurds and Turcomans, the 2nd Cavalry Regiment was composed of Kurds and Assyrians, and the pack battery was Assyrian. Of the four battalions the 1st Battalion was made up of Marsh Arabs, the 2nd and 3rd Battalions were composed of Assyrians while the 4th were Kurds, with one company mounted.

14 *Ibid.*, p. 14.

15 Lunt, *Imperial Sunset*, pp. 30-31; Browne, *The Iraq Levies* and D. Omissi, 'Britain, the Assyrians and the Iraq Levies, 1919-1932', *Journal of Imperial and Commonwealth History*, 17 (1989), pp. 301-322.

16 The Treaty of Sèvres was signed between Great Britain and France and Turkey in 1920.

17 A.O. Pollard, *Royal Air Force: A Concise History* (London: Hutchinson, 1934), p. 218.

18 *Ibid*.

19 J. Salmond, 'The Air Force in Iraq', *Journal of the Royal United Service* Institute, LXX (1925), p. 486.

20 Sheikh Mahmud Barzinji (1878-1956). He had been a leading figure in the Iraq revolt of 1920 and had proclaimed himself King of Kurdistan in November 1922. His aim, in all of the campaigns in which he fought, was to form an independent Kurdish nation.

21 J. Laffin, *Swifter than Eagles* (London: Blackwoods, 1964), pp. 176-177.

22 AIR 5/1287 *Iraq Command: monthly operational summaries, Vol. I January 1921-December 1923*. The airlift was carried out on 21-23 February 1923, when two companies of the 14th Sikhs (later 1/11th Sikhs); composed of 2 British officers and 320 Indian other ranks, 13 supply and W/T personnel, plus ammunition and equipment and three bearers, were flown to Kingerban to Kirkuk in ten lifts. Five Vickers Vernons of No 45 Squadron and five of No 70 Squadron completed the lift.

23 AIR 5/1287 *Iraq Command*. One Indian battalion and pack battery, a Levy cavalry regiment with one-and a half Levy battalions and a Levy pack battery

24 Cox, 'A Splendid Training Ground'.

25 AIR 5/1287, A Field Force or 'Mobile Striking Force' was formed under the command of Colonel Commandant B. Vincent CB CMG and was composed of a company of sappers & miners, a signal section, an RAF W/T mobile pack set CW, two batteries, an Indian pioneer battalion, two British battalions, three Indian battalions, a Field Ambulance, an Indian mobile veterinary section, a Levy pack battery, Levy cavalry regiment and a Levy battalion, an Iraq Army pack battery and two cavalry regiments with No 5 Armoured Car

Company and five flying squadrons. A 'Frontier Force' was formed to protect the right flank under the command of Colonel Commandant H.T. Dobbin DSO and composed of No 55 (Bomber) Squadron, No 4 Armoured Car Company less 'B' Section, an RAF W/T mobile pack set, two Levy cavalry regiments and two Levy battalions.

26 *Ibid.*
27 AIR 10/1845 *Report on Operations in Southern Kurdistan against Shaikh Mahmud, October 1930-May 1931,* pp. 40-42.
28 Browne, *The Iraq Levies,* p. 31 and J.L. Cox, 'A Splendid Training Ground: The Importance to the Royal Air Force of its role in Iraq, 1919-1932', pp. 168-169.
29 Salmond, Despatches, pp. 4654-4655. 'Koicol' was under the command of Colonel-Commandant B. Vincent, CB, CMG, and was composed of:
    A Headquarters, with a Political Officer and a RAF Liaison Officer attached, Brigade Signal Section, RAF Mobile W/T (CW) Pack Set, 120 (Ambala) Pack Battery, 63rd Company QVO Madras Sappers and Miners, 2nd West Yorkshire Regiment, 2nd Cameronians (Scottish Rifles), 2/11th Sikh Regiment, 40th Combined Field Ambulance (less 2 Indian Sections), 7th Indian Mobile Veterinary Section, Pack Transport Train and a troop of thirty Mounted Police;
    'Frontiercol' was under the command of Colonel-Commandant H.T. Dobbin, DSO and was composed of:
    Headquarters, with a Political Officer, a Military Officer expert in mountain warfare, and an RAF Liaison Officer attached, an RAF Mobile W/T (CW) Pack Set, a section Iraq Levy Pack Battery, 2nd, 3rd and 4th Battalions Iraq Levies, one Machine Gun Company Iraq Levies and a troop of 30 Mounted Police.
30 *Ibid.*
31 D. Omissi, 'Britain, the Assyrians and the Iraq Levies, 1919-1932', p. 32. The Treaty talks in Lausanne resumed about this time.
32 Salmond, Despatches.
33 The Commanding Officer of No 4 Armoured Car Company, Squadron Leader R.P. Willock, was mentioned in despatches for the operations in Kurdistan, 15 February to 19 June 1923.
34 William H. Edwards, *Interview 4824* (London: IWM Sound Archive, 1981).
35 AIR 5/1287 *Iraq Command.*
36 'Treaty of Peace with Turkey, Signed at Lausanne, July 24, 1923', in, L. Martin, *The Treaties of Peace 1919-1923, Vol. II* (New York: Carnegie Endowment for International Peace, 1924).
37 AIR 23/544 *Mosul Operations, February-August 1924.* The forces at Tel Awainat consisted of: One flight No 6 Squadron, No 5 Armoured Car Company, one squadron of 1st Levy Cavalry Regiment and a Wireless Station, with 3rd Iraq Cavalry Regiment at Tel Abu Dahir, less one squadron, with one troop at Golat.
38 AIR 23/565, *Operations and Intelligence: Kirkuk and Sulaimaniya, 4 June 1923.*
39 Air Vice-Marshal Sir John F. A. Higgins CB DSO AFC (1875-1948). His nickname was 'Bum and Eyeglass'.
40 Air 23/562 *Disturbances in Kirkuk, May-September 1924.* A Court of Inquiry suggested that troubles had not been reported before, and may have been intentionally inflamed by elements acting on behalf of Sheikh Mahmud.
41 AIR 5/1288 *Iraq Command: Monthly Operational Summary, Vol. II January-December 1924.* This was the first large scale movement of British troops by air in any theatre of operations. The troops arrived within eight hours of the troubles beginning. The alternative would have entailed a 12 hour rail journey to Kingerban and a four day march to Kirkuk. A second detachment of 79 officers and men was flown in on 6 May to make the total number up to 145. The first airlift of Imperial troops was the move of 14th Sikhs during February 1923.
42 *Ibid.*
43 *Ibid.* Report from Flight Lieutenant G.A. Elliot to Officer Commanding No 6 Armoured

Car Company (Squadron Leader J.W. Cruikshank OBE), 8 May 1924.
44 *Ibid*.
45 Air 23/562 *Disturbances in Kirkuk*.
46 Browne, *The Iraq Levies*, p. 36. The 15 that were killed were taken back to Kirkuk.
47 AIR 23/562 *Disturbances in Kirkuk*. Correspondence: Observer Officer L.T. Kerry to Officer Commanding No 6 Armoured Car Company, 9 May 1924.
48 AIR 23/562 *Disturbances in Kirkuk*. Report from Flight Lieutenant G.A. Elliot to Officer Commanding No 6 Armoured Car Company (Squadron Leader J.W. Cruikshank OBE), Chamchamal, 9 May 1924. Two Rolls-Royce armoured cars - HMAC *Avenger* with Flying Officer Elliot, Corporal Lewis and Aircraftmen Osborne and Kendal; HMAC *Explorer* with Corporal Ashcroft and Aircraftmen Porter and Morris; and a Lancia, HMAC *Canada*, with Corporal Ward, Aircraftmen Sunter, Hopton and Reed, the Wireless-Telegraphy operator.
49 AIR 23/562 *Disturbances in Kirkuk*. Captain Chapman received reports that three men were killed by Elliot's guns.
50 *Ibid*.
51 *Ibid*., Correspondence: Officer Commanding 2nd Battalion, Iraq Levies to Headquarters, Iraq Levies, 13 May 1924.
52 Captain Oliff Fry 2nd Royal West Kent Regiment and 2nd Battalion Iraq Levies was also awarded the Military Cross for the actions of May 1924.
53 Nos 8, 30, 45 and 55 Squadrons were given the bombing task, while No 6 Squadron, with Bristol Fighters, was given the job of rescue of aircrew who had forced landed.
54 Vehicles employed were three Rolls-Royce armoured cars, three Lancias, a Rolls-Royce tender and a Ford van
55 AIR 5/1288 *Iraq Command*.
56 In recognition of valuable and distinguished services rendered in connection with operations in Kurdistan during July to October 1924 Flight Lieutenant Sturley Simpson was awarded the Military Cross.
57 'Frontier Force' consisted of a garrison at Mosul: 1/2nd Bombay Pioneers, 113 Dardoni Pack Battery, 116th Animal Transport Company, one squadron 1st Levy Cavalry Regiment, 1 company 3rd Levy Battalion, Headquarters Iraqi Mosul Brigade, 3rd Iraq Cavalry Regiment (less one squadron), 3rd Iraq Infantry Battalion (less one platoon), 1st Iraq Pack Battery, 1st Iraq Transport Company; Tel Afar: one squadron 3rd Iraq Cavalry Regiment; Zakho Pass: 4th Iraq Infantry Battalion; Ser Amadia: 1 company each of the 3rd and 4th Levy Battalions.
58 AIR 23/543 'Aerowing': *Mosul operations September-November 1924*. In his report Wing Commander Primrose noted the heavy work load placed on his one Staff officer for the first week of operations. Jope-Slade worked 12 to 16 hours per day with great dedication, ability and efficiency. He not only had responsibility for collecting and recording intelligence information concerning reconnaissance reports, and keeping track of troop movements, but undertook all clerical work; typing, filing and registering. Primrose and Jope-Slade were eventually allocated a clerk to assist their work. Later Group Captain Jope-Slade OBE DSC (1896-1941). He was awarded the DSC for gallantry in air operations over the coast of Flanders in 1915 while flying with the 'Naval 5' Squadron of the RNAS.
59 *Ibid*.
60 *Ibid*.
61 Dobbs, in D. Omissi, *Air Power and Colonial Control*, p. 35.
62 AIR 5/1287 *Iraq Command*.

Chapter Five

Iraq 1925-1929

"...the crews... took their vehicles into the uncharted wastes of the northern Arabian deserts, and... carried out their duty under conditions of hardship, and in the face of great difficulties, in these desolate places. However wearisome the task, great the challenge or trying the conditions, they were a cheerful band of willing workers who contributed their share towards opening the roads and into the unexplored deserts."
  Squadron Leader Elliot Godsave, Deputy Commander Armoured Car Wing,
  RAF Hinaidi[1]

The decision by the British Government to implement Air Control in Iraq had more than justified itself operationally for the RAF, and financially for the Exchequer. In the first fiscal year of operation, 1921-1922, expenditure in Iraq totalled £23 million; this fell to around £8 million in the first year of RAF air control, 1922-1923, and by 1926-1927 less than £4 million.[2] As the Iraq Army was built up and gained in strength and experience it was planned that the contribution to the garrison by the RAF, the British and Indian infantry battalions and the Iraq Levies was to be correspondingly reduced. The number of British and Indian Army battalions was decreased from four to two in 1926, with all of them having departed by 1929.[3] Over the same period, the number of RAF flying squadrons in Iraq was reduced from eight to four. The RAF was to concentrate at Hinaidi, with flying stations at Mosul and Shaibah; however, it would still play a key role in supporting the operations of the Iraqi Army for a few more years when required.[4]

For the Levies, there had also been changes. In early 1926, a general reduction in size of the Iraq Levies had begun and several Levy cavalry, infantry and artillery units were disbanded, amalgamated or transferred to the Iraq Army. On 1 July 1928, the Iraq Levies passed from the control of the Colonial Office to the RAF. Two Companies of the Levies took over guard duties at Hinaidi cantonment, as the last Army battalions departed, and three companies were moved to garrison Sulaimaniya. The Levy regiments and battalions had originally been a broad mix of the various cultural and ethnic groups of Iraq; however, by early 1928 only two predominantly Assyrian Battalions remained.[5]

The operations in the Southern Desert against the Ikhwan occupied most of the sections of the RAF armoured cars during the latter half of the 1920s until the successful conclusion of the campaign in 1930. The northern and western provinces of Iraq, although quiet for periods, were not however, completely settled and there was still plenty of work for the cars in these regions. There were regular incursions by the bedouin from Syria and Transjordan intent on the age-old pursuit of camel and

The Rolls-Royces of No 4 Armoured Car Company parade for King Feisal in Baghdad, 1925 (© Crown copyright. Godsave, RAF Regiment Museum).

livestock raiding. Moreover, in Kurdistan the Iraqi Government had yet to resolve the nationalist aspirations of the Kurds. The official report by the AOC Iraq at the time described the situation thus:

> The inhabitants are Kurds, whose independent spirit and lawless ways have proved a source of trouble to the Turks from time immemorial, and to ourselves since the occupation of Iraq. Moreover, the Kurd is distinctly antipathetic to the Arab and viewed with dismay the establishment of a government which he disliked and mistrusted.
>
> Thus the topography of the country, the character of its inhabitants… presented a picture of considerable military difficulty.[6]

One difficulty facing the air and land commanders was that they were operating over an area of roughly 30,000 square miles, with a ground force of only two battalions and two cavalry regiments. They were searching for rebel bands varying in size from around 2000 to often less than 40, who were received favourably by much of the local populace. The Kurds knew their country well and were tough and determined hill fighters.

In contrast to the open and dusty deserts of the south and west of Iraq, Kurdistan was a place of rugged and precipitous snow-clad mountains rising up 6000 feet, narrow scrubby valleys and with few suitable locations for landing grounds. The summers were warm but the winters bitterly cold, with torrential rain and driving snow. The main area of operations was defined to the north-east, by the Iraq-Persian frontier and to the south-west by the stretch of the main Kirkuk-Baghdad road, from Kifri to Kirkuk. The roads, if they existed, were rudimentary in many places and posed considerable problems in supplying garrisons, the movements of convoys and deployment of RAF flying squadrons. The main route into southern Kurdistan was via the 'motor road' through Chamchamal, the Baziyan Pass of the formidable Qara Dagh mountains, on through the Tasluja Pass and on to the major town of Sulaimaniya (Map 6, p. 51).

Despite setbacks during the campaigns of 1923 and 1924, Sheikh Mahmud had been determined to continue his struggle to establish the Kingdom of Kurdistan and rid his country of control from Baghdad. The campaign which began in 1925 would follow a similar pattern for the next three years, with summer operations against the rebels to force them back into Persia, followed by a winter lull. Severe weather conditions limited the activity of the rebels from late 1924 and into 1925; however, during the spring of 1925, Mahmud had returned from his Persian exile and set about stirring up a revolt. He instigated an active programme of propaganda and enlistment of followers from both sides of the frontier. As the weather cleared, he had appeared in force near Sulaimaniya and had resumed collecting taxes.

The Iraq Government in response was determined not to bring him to battle but to gradually establish a chain of police posts and garrisons in the area to erode his influence. During May 1925, a Levy cavalry column, ironically composed of a large number of Kurds, was attacked by his followers as they moved on Halebja where there had been tribal disturbances. A flight of Sopwith Snipes from No 1 Squadron, stationed at Sulaimaniya, joined battle with the Sheikh's followers, a large party of which were caught in the open, and after repeated RAF strafing attacks, suffered heavy casualties. This attrition allowed the Levy force to occupy Halebja the following day with some ease.

In early June 1925, British troops had occupied Choartah, to the north of Sulaimaniya, located in the centre of a region where the Sheikh's influence was undisputed. There was a strong reaction and he launched an all-out ground attack on the town. Again, with assistance this time from No 6 Squadron in their Bristol Fighters, the rebels were heavily defeated and forced back across the Persian frontier. Due to the nature of the terrain, the RAF armoured cars were confined to the primitive, tenuous roads and tracks. Nevertheless, the major task for the Kirkuk-based No 6 Armoured Car Company during 1925 and 1926 was provision of vehicles and armed escorts for the convoys of ammunition, supplies and mail travelling along the Kirkuk-Chamchamal-Sulaimaniya road. These convoys supported the detachments of the Iraq Levies and Iraq Army which were operating against the Sheikh and his followers in the villages and mountains surrounding Sulaimaniya. The convoys were operated weekly during quiet periods but increased to as many as 20 per month during the campaigning, with total mileage for the Company reaching 15,000 to 20,000 miles during these months.

Whilst the quickest runs to Sulaimaniya could take just under five hours, inclement weather, difficult track conditions or mechanical problems could extend the journey to a day or more (Map 7, p. 66). The Chamchamal to Sulaimaniya section of the road posed the greatest problems for the Rolls-Royce armoured cars in the descent and ascent of the many hills. The primitive road was heavy-going and littered with rocks which threw the cars about. Long periods travelling in low gear could lead to abnormally high fuel consumption, stripped gears, smashed sumps, wrecked axles and suspension, and damaged engines. Vehicles had to be manhandled over difficult stretches, and in some instances lorries arrived with shredded tyres. During winter, the weather could change quickly, with high winds and snow drifts forming around the passes at Baziyan and Tasluja. Heavy snow could completely obliterate the path, and on a few occasions the airmen were forced to spend the nights in freezing conditions. They then had to excavate their cars from the snow the next morning before they could move off. As the snows melted from the mountains and torrential rains fell, tracks could be carved away by rushing torrents, while bridges could be washed away or collapse under the weight of the armoured cars. Floods caused devastation and even loss of life in towns such as Chamchamal. During the winter months, the lighter Armed Fords were used instead of the heavier Rolls-Royce armoured cars as the use of the latter on this road had proved futile. Despite these difficulties, the convoys always got through on all but a few occasions, primarily through the outstanding initiative and mechanical skills of the car crews.

A Rolls-Royce armoured car caught in snow in the mountains of Kurdistan (© Crown copyright. RAF Regiment Museum).

There were few attacks made on the RAF-escorted convoys during these operations; however, in September 1925, only 15 miles from Kirkuk, an Iraq Army camel convoy escorted by the Iraqi Police was confronted by local tribesmen from the village of Qara Anjir. This village was located close to the road and the temptation of so much loot, so lightly guarded, seems to have been irresistible. News of the attack reached No 6 Company at Kirkuk the next day, and a section was sent out. However, by the time they arrived, the assailants had disappeared. Later searching by the Iraq Police recovered much of the stolen supplies. Following this incident, the Armed Fords were assigned as escorts to the camel convoys through as far as Chamchamal.

A month later, a column commanded by Wing Commander Ernest Norton DSC, the OC Troops Kirkuk and No 6 Company, with eight Armed Fords, a Rolls chassis, the 2nd Iraq Levy Cavalry Regiment and two platoons of the 2nd Battalion, Bedfordshire and Hertfordshire Regiment were sent to support Iraq Police operations against Qara Anjir and the neighbouring village of Chan Bichuk in retribution for a spate of road robberies and attacks on the convoys. The Administrative Officer Kirkuk and Inspecting Officer of Police accompanied the column, which the following morning

An Armed Ford comes to grief on the rudimentary tracks found in many parts of Iraq. The Lewis machine-gun was mounted on a Scarff ring taken from scrapped aircraft and allowed full traverse. The Fords were given names such as HMAF Sleaford, Stamford and Tugford (© Crown copyright. RAF Regiment Museum).

surrounded Chan Bichuk. Having found that the inhabitants had fled and that they had failed to comply with the instruction of the local civil officials, the village was burned. A detachment of Armed Fords escorted the Administrative Inspector further on to Qara Anjir which suffered a similar fate, with the buildings being completely destroyed.

The composition of the convoys going through to Sulaimaniya could be unusual at times. In one instance, the convoy consisted of 24 Ford taxis which were paid to transport rifles for the Iraq Army. Needless to say, many of the taxis found the trip a challenge and the column was forced to halt repeatedly due to mechanical breakdowns. Three camel convoys were run in November 1925, and ranged in number from 200 to 2000 beasts. The latter case gave rise to great difficulty for the airmen in watching over a 6-mile long column, with front and rear cars being unable to maintain communications, while placing a car in the middle of the column caused the camels to stampede. Flight Lieutenant Andrew Ward had a particular challenge when he was placed in charge of a camel convoy returning a load of RAF bombs to Kirkuk from the stocks of No 1 Squadron at Sulaimaniya.

A long quiet period ensued during the winter of 1925-1926, but Sheikh Mahmud was determined to return, and in the New Year his men began to infiltrate back into the border villages. By March, despite appalling weather, Levy and Iraqi Army units were launched into the Qara Dagh in an attempt to deter a party of Kurds that had been tax-collecting and to support the villagers against whom the taxes were being levied. While returning from this operation, it was reported that a large rebel party led by one of the Sheikh's staunchest lieutenants, Karim Fettah Beg, was now moving into the Qara Dagh mountains. Two columns were immediately despatched. Moving with the main column, 'Camcol', under Colonel Sorel-Cameron, were two Armed Fords of No 6 Armoured Car Company. Equipped with a wireless, they were to afford radio contact with the other column, 'Grimcol', under Captain Grimwood. It had been hoped that with the Tanjero River having risen, the rebels would be trapped and unable to escape back into Persia. Despite bringing the Kurds to battle, Grimwood was unable to surround the party. The river level fell before they could close the trap and they made their escape. The columns returned to Sulaimaniya without their prey; however, they had succeeded in thwarting the tax-raising efforts of the rebels.[7]

With the poor weather clearing during June 1926, columns again went out from Sulaimaniya. This time they were supported by two flights of No 1 Squadron and one from No 30 Squadron. Intensive operations were resumed to protect the nomadic tribes, such as the Jaf, from whom the Sheikh often exacted taxes for their grazing rights, and against villages with rebel sympathies. These villages were bombed, but only after adequate opportunity had been given for the evacuation of the inhabitants and their livestock. The military operations by the Iraq Army, Levies and RAF had taken their toll on Sheikh Mahmud. Deprived of reserves to pay his followers, he again withdrew to the safety of Persia, taking with him a force of more than 2000 men. The Iraq Government attempted to negotiate with the Persian Government to take joint action against Sheikh Mahmud, but this met with little success.

A decision in July 1926 to station a flight of No 1 Squadron at Sulaimaniya, and alterations to the military posts located there, led to an increase in convoys with RAF and Army stores. Five times during August 1926, trips were made with the Armed Fords and the Rolls-Royce armoured cars escorting Crossley tenders and Leyland lorries to Sulaimaniya. On one occasion while at Sulaimaniya, a reconnaissance was conducted towards Serao to test the suitability for travel over a road had never previously been covered by the cars. Two Rolls-Royce armoured cars and a Rolls-Royce wireless tender reached Serao successfully despite the three-hour journey. The journey was necessarily long as each of the numerous bridges had to be inspected to ensure they could take the weight of the Rolls-Royce armoured cars before they could be crossed.

As the weather worsened and the campaigning season drew to a close, the RAF armoured cars then had the responsibility of escorting parties of No 1 (Fighter) Squadron RAF back to Kirkuk. It had been decided that a fighter squadron was of little use in Iraq, as the Sopwith Snipes were considered to have too short a range and they were not needed for their primary role as air interceptors. The Squadron was therefore disbanded and reformed in the United Kingdom with the Snipes being burnt before the departure of the Squadron from Sulaimaniya.

Number 6 Armoured Company was kept constantly busy on other tasks as well as the Sulaimaniya convoys. Apprehension that Sheikh Mahmud was moving to the south against Kifri led to the despatch of a section of armoured cars to the area and the establishment of daily patrols. Other tasks included escorting the Administrative Inspector from Kirkuk on tours around villages in the province, routine patrols north along the Mosul road from Kirkuk to the ferry crossing on the Little Zab River at Altun Kupri, and occasional work escorting officials from the Turkish Petroleum Company.[8]

The cars also escorted the Commanding Officer of No 30 Squadron along the Kirkuk to Sulaimaniya road establishing the locations for five emergency landing grounds. Aircraft were often forced to land in inhospitable terrain due to engine troubles or after being hit by rifle fire from rebels or local inhabitants. It was the job of the RAF armoured cars to stand by the aircraft until new engines or the spare parts could be delivered so they could be flown out. In one instance, an aircraft repair was not possible and the decision made to return the aeroplane by road. During June

1926, Flying Officer Elliot MC with two Rolls-Royce armoured cars and a Rolls-Royce wireless tender departed Kirkuk to patrol the Kirkuk-Chamchamal Road. As the convoy was about to leave, news was received that a machine of No 30 Squadron had forced-landed at Qara Anjir. The convoy proceeded there immediately, taking with them Flight Lieutenant Jenkins of No 30 Squadron. On arrival, Flight Lieutenant Jenkins with two Lewis guns and crews and one Rolls-Royce W/T tender were left to guard the machine, while Elliot took the Rolls armoured cars to patrol further towards Chamchamal. Fortunately there was no sign of hostile tribesmen so Elliot returned to the machine and the decision was made to tow the machine in to Kirkuk. All proceeded quite well until only 10 miles from Kirkuk, where the DH9a turned over crossing a ditch, injuring the two airmen. The machine was too badly damaged and was ultimately burned.[9] The aircrews would often reciprocate and drop spare parts to armoured car detachments that had suffered breakdowns. In one instance in the Northern Desert, a new gearbox was delivered by air and fitted to a Rolls-Royce armoured car in 14 hours, despite a daytime shade temperature of 45 °C.[10]

During the operations of June 1926, Sheikh Mahmud had captured the crew of a Ninak of No 30 Squadron that had forced-landed, and had taken them back over the mountainous frontier into Persia. They were treated well, but after living under the harsh conditions in the mountains, their health began to deteriorate. Support for the insurrection had again faded and Sheikh Mahmud was persuaded to return the two airmen without harm a few months later. This also gave rise to the opportunity to encourage him to consider his plight, and he began negotiations with the British and Iraq Governments. However, he was to make one more effort before he could be brought to terms.

In March 1927, it was decided to strike a decisive blow to Sheikh Mahmud. Penjwin, only four miles from the Persian border, had always been a safe haven for him as it had neither been occupied for a long period by the British and Iraqi forces, nor had it experienced any civil authority from Baghdad. The winter months of 1927 in Kurdistan were again severe with heavy snows and rain, however, by April a flight of No 30 Squadron had been moved to Sulaimaniya, with two more operating from Kirkuk. Two columns, from the Levies and Iraqi Army were sent to occupy Penjwin and to bring Sheikh Mahmud to battle, and in doing so inflict a severe defeat. By July

A detachment of the RAF armoured cars head off into the desert (© Crown copyright. RAF Regiment Museum).

1927, as a consequence of the sustained military activity, Sheikh Mahmud had found it impossible to maintain the guerrilla struggle. He therefore submitted to the Iraqi Government and made a solemn undertaking that he would reside outside Iraq and would not attempt to return to the country or interfere in its internal affairs. He then retired to Persia and for the next three years would not be a problem.

Many of the deserts of Iraq were unexplored and unbroken by the wheels of motor cars prior to 1925. Elliot Godsave was appointed as the Iraq Command Navigation Officer in 1924, having spent the previous seven years on the staff of the Admiralty Compass Department. In 1925, he became Officer Commanding No 4 Armoured Car Company and then finally as Deputy Commander of the Armoured Car Wing. He was to successfully command the Car Reserve Column in the war against the Ikhwan in 1928-1929. Subsequently, prior to his retirement from the RAF in 1935, he was responsible in large part for the preparation of the RAF Armoured Car Manual.[11]

While at the Admiralty, Godsave had worked on the Type '0.2' magnetic compass which was designed to function in armoured vehicles. The Arabian deserts were unsurveyed and unmapped and the only aid to navigation for aircraft flying Cairo to Baghdad, on the air route from England to India, was a ploughed furrow which ran from Amman through Rutbah on to Ramadi (Map 2, p. 24).[12] This was found to be unreliable and often obscured by dust storms or the movement of tribesmen with their flocks. Consequently, the AOC Iraq, Air Vice-Marshal Sir John Higgins, ordered

Flight Lieutenant (later Squadron Leader) Elliot Godsave, 1925 (© Crown copyright. Godsave, RAF Regiment Museum).

his navigation staff to examine ways to survey and map the desert. Godsave thus adapted his '0.2' compass and mounted it in a Rolls-Royce armoured car and found this to be a feasible method of survey. He also designed a special light mobile desert vehicle, HMRC *Rapid*, based on a Rolls-Royce chassis fitted with wooden platform at the rear for petrol, kit, (and his loyal dog) and a mounting for a Vickers machine-gun. *Rapid* enabled him to travel quickly and with fewer encumbrances over country that the Rolls-Royce armoured cars would have otherwise found difficult. He covered some 2000 miles in HMRC *Rapid* from Basra, Baghdad, Rutbah and Amman, many on solo reconnaissances. During his time with the Armoured Cars, he led a number of expeditions through Iraq, Syria, Kuwait, Palestine and Transjordan which provided the details for the 1:1,000,000 and 1:250,000 maps. After his retirement from the RAF, he returned to Baghdad and became, for a time, the manager of the Baghdad office of the Nairn Transport Company.[13]

Specially modified Rolls-Royce HMRC Rapid, with Squadron Leader Elliot Godsave at the wheel (© Crown copyright. Godsave, RAF Regiment Museum).

At the end of the Great War, two New Zealand-born brothers, Gerald and Norman Nairn, had seen the potential of motor car travel across the desert. They had both served in the New Zealand forces in the Middle East and had stayed on after hostilities had ceased. In 1922 they had established a successful passenger route, running from Damascus through to Baghdad. Their business, known as the Nairn Transport Company, grew as they obtained the contract to transport the mail from Haifa and Beirut to Baghdad and on to India and Persia, as well as to carry personnel from the Anglo-Persian Oil Company. Starting with a fleet of Buick and Cadillac cars, each with a capacity of five, with the mail and baggage ingeniously fastened on the wings and running boards, they travelled across the rudimentary desert tracks and flooded rivers in all weathers. By the 1930s, they had purchased a larger four-wheel bus and later a 36-seater articulated Pullman coach pulled by a Marmon-Herrington tractor. The latter was complete with air conditioning, buffet, adjustable seats and toilet. It was at one time described as the largest bus in the world.[14]

In September 1925, however, the Nairn convoy was attacked by a band of brigands near Damascus, the driver was killed and some passengers were wounded. The considerable unrest in Syria due to the Druze uprising had led to the formation of groups of brigands hoping to benefit from the disturbances by robbing passing

The Overland Mail of the Nairn Bus Company meets a car of No 4 Armoured Car Company in the desert west of Rutbah ((© Crown copyright. Godsave, RAF Regiment Museum).

travellers. It was therefore decided for safety reasons that the Overland Mail Convoy, as it was known, should travel from Haifa, via Jerusalem and Amman to Baghdad. The RAF armoured cars from Transjordan and Iraq were ordered to patrol the track, escort the Nairn bus and endeavour to apprehend the brigands if they made further attacks on the convoy. Consequently, Squadron Leader Elliot Godsave of No 4 Armoured Car Company was assigned to this task (Map 3, p. 29).

The cars were to go out week after week and it is of great credit to their crews and those in the workshops that they remained serviceable. On 26 September 1925 the first escort column of five cars, *Orion*, *Cleopatra*, *Terror*, the Rolls-Royce armoureds, and *Ranger* and *Rutbah*, the Rolls-Royce tenders, left Baghdad to patrol the track to Amman, with orders to ensure the safe passage of the Nairn bus. The first journey was punctuated by a sandstorm of great violence that assailed the airmen with a wall of blinding driving sand and flashes of blue lightning. There was an encounter with potentially hostile Shammar tribesmen but these were peaceful as the presence of the

On a survey west of Ramadi. The Iraqi Desert Police pose with an officer of No 4 Armoured Car Company in front of Kenilworth. The Lancias of this Company were named after the novels of Sir Walter Scott, including HMAC Ivanhoe and HMAC Waverley. These vehicles were found to be unsuitable and were not used on operations from 1925 onwards (© Crown copyright. Godsave, RAF Regiment Museum).

Desert repair workshop. The crews had to be proficient at keeping their vehicles running while on patrol. Spare parts were often delivered by the supply aircraft (© Crown copyright. RAF Regiment Museum).

Vickers machine-guns tempered any threat to the convoy.

Progress was painfully slow across the eastern edge of the lava belt or Al Harrat which was marked with the large black boulders which played havoc with the tyres. Once through this country the pace increased for a time as they reached the well-defined tracks that had been made by No 2 Armoured Car Company in their frequent journeys from Amman. There was then a ten-mile section of terrain taken to avoid the flooded mud-flats of Azraq. Here there were hard mounds of sand that had accumulated around the roots of desert shrubs. It was impossible to sit the cars on the level and the cars were reduced to walking pace as they lurched and wallowed. The wheels were wrenched from side-to-side, throwing the crews inside against the hard faces and sharp edges of the armoured shell. On reaching the far side of the marshland, respite from the jolting was finally provided as the fort of Qasr al Kharanah could be seen on a distant crest. Despite the many trials all the vehicles reached their destination. Godsave described the arrival of the cars at Amman after their first journey as follows:[15]

> Eventually the leading car crept round the final hairpin and the cliffs parted to expose a picture of white houses, studded with olives and poplars, shining in the moonlight on the far side of the valley. This was Amman.
>
> The cars forded the stream at the bottom of the hill, squeezed through a crumbling Roman Arch and passed along the deserted streets and joined the main track – which we had missed in the dark – to the RAF camp on the hill which we reached at 0200 hours... Here we were greeted by the officers and men of No 14 Squadron and No 2 Armoured Car Company who did not allow the unconventional hour to diminish the lavish hospitality - for which we were exceedingly thankful.[16]

Godsave and the car crews of No 4 Company had opened the 450 mile route over which the Mail Convoy was to pass for the next five months. There was, however, little time for rest. He continues:

> After two days of hard work on the cars, we set out again for Baghdad with the east bound mail convoy, and reached our destination three days later after an uneventful journey.

Al Harrat – 'the lava belt'. The sharp rocks were treacherous to motor vehicles and a road was eventually built through the lava belt (RAFACA).

This was the first of the escort columns that pioneered the way for the weekly patrol which was carried out with unbroken regularity throughout the whole of the winter, though there were adjustments made

> By the end of October the strain of the weekly convoys was beginning to take its toll on the armoured cars, and it was decided to establish an advanced base at Rutbah and thus reduce the extent to the patrol from Baghdad to Amman to Rutbah-Amman, almost half the distance. We were to accompany the westbound mail as far as Landing Ground 'D' where the cars of No 2 Company would take over the convoy from us while we took over the eastbound convoy from them for the return trip to Rutbah.[17]

The patrols continued until February 1926, but were fraught with difficulties arising from the weather and terrain, though the convoy was never again attacked by brigands. Unusually heavy rains turned the desert tracks to inland seas; the armoured cars and Nairn convoy were stranded at times, and in some instances the aircraft of No 45 Squadron had to fly out food and supplies until the track became passable again. Godsave's light vehicle HMRC *Rapid* came into its own in these conditions. In March 1926, however, with the Druze Revolt in Syria still in full spate, the Nairn Transport Company decided that a more northerly route from Beirut through Homs to Palmyra and on to Rutbah was more satisfactory than the difficult route through Amman to Rutbah, and the convoy escorts ended.[18]

The primary area of responsibility for the officers and airmen of No 5 Armoured Car Company stationed at Mosul was the northern border with Turkey and the

An escort from No 4 Armoured Car Company hands over the 'Nairn' to No 2 Company on the road to Amman (© Crown copyright. Godsave, RAF Regiment Museum).

deserts to the west. The RAF Station at Mosul was self-contained with a wired perimeter and was located beside the River Tigris, to the south of the predominantly Kurdish town. While the dispute over location of the international boundary had been resolved, routine patrols were made of the roads to Zakho and surrounds. Another important patrol was that along the road to the south towards the railhead at Shergat. Track marking in the desert areas was a regular task along with a survey of the Iraq-Syria border from River Euphrates to the Jebel Sinjar and by 1928, a network of petrol dumps for aircraft and armoured cars had been established at Arbil, Shergat and Zakho landing grounds and Ain Ghazal. With the settlement of the line of the frontier with Turkey, a chain of Iraqi Police posts had been established on the northern border, and these were regularly checked by both the Bristol Fighters of No 6 Squadron and the armoured cars operating from Mosul (Map 6, p. 51; Map 8, p. 73).

The Kurdish rebellion had been dealt with by aircraft, cooperating with the cavalry and infantry of the Iraqi Army or Levies whereas the actions against the bedouin raiders of the deserts of the north and west of Iraq was purely a coordinated effort between aircraft and the RAF armoured cars. The story of what had happened to the Ikhwan in Transjordan in 1924 in the face of the guns of No 2 Armoured Car Company still had great currency in the desert tribes and any trouble was more often resolved without bloodshed.

In 1925, Flight Lieutenant Arthur Lee had been sent to No 5 Armoured Car Company and had been somewhat disappointed at no longer being on a flying squadron. He did, however, find the work interesting as the cars had "a free hand to go wherever we pleased north of Baghdad, and so were able to see the country and people at close quarters."[19] Lee recalled participating in a patrol by two armoured car sections across the steppe-like desert near Abu Kemal south-west of Mosul. After sighting a raiding party of the Huweitat from Syria, clearly intent on causing trouble, the eight cars formed into a Vee-formation on the flag signals of the detachment commander, Flight Lieutenant Bill Fenwick. They swept across the level and hard ground at 60 mph and moved to head off the party. After encouraging the 200 cameleers to turn back, the Rolls-Royces proceeded on for a few miles trailing the raiding party to ensure they maintained their path towards the Syrian border.

On their return journey, the two sections of RAF armoured cars came across hundreds of camels, sheep and goats and the low black-tented encampment of the local Iraqi Shammar tribe who were probably the target for the raiders. A feast was ordered by their Sheikh and leaving the airmen to guard the cars, Fenwick, Lee, his interpreter and two others were received with great ceremony and traditional bedouin hospitality; strong coffee and then a mound of steaming rice mixed with mutton, including the innards, and topped with the grinning skull of the unfortunate animal. Both officers were presented with the delicacy of the meal, an eyeball each from the sheep's head, which they diplomatically ingested, though with some nauseous reluctance. Flight Lieutenant Bill Fenwick was an experienced armoured car officer who had a trick for which he was well-known by his armoured car crewmen. He had lost an eye and so he carefully removed his own glass eye and proffered it to the shocked, but surprisingly composed, Sheikh. He politely touched it as protocol required, as a sign of acceptance, and then motioned to Fenwick to return it to the appropriate place. With the meal over, and to evade any other dubious delights that might be offered should they sleep in the camp, the airmen tactfully withdrew with the cars to a few miles from the encampment, and slept the night under the stars in the silence of the desert.[20]

By March 1926, a further problem was building in the western desert of Iraq. A feud had broken out between the followers of Daham el Hadi, Chief of the Syrian Shammar Jarba and Aijal el Yawar, Chief of the Iraqi Shammar Jarba. As a consequence, six Armed Fords from No 5 Armoured Car Company were despatched from Mosul to Aijal's camp to assist in maintaining peace on the border with Syria. Their instructions were rather complex. Should Aijal's camp be attacked, they were to assist in its defence; however, they were also to prevent Aijal's men from crossing the Syrian border to attack Daham el Hadi. Constant reconnaissance flights were made by No 6 Squadron to locate Daham and to make it clear that his every move was being watched, and that the balance of power favoured Aijal el Yawar.

A section of Rolls-Royce armoured cars and W/T tenders cross a small river in the mountains east of Mosul (© Crown copyright. RAF Regiment Museum).

The Rolls-Royce armoured cars and tenders and Armed Fords (at rear) of No 5 Armoured Car Company at Mosul in 1925. (© Crown copyright. RAF Regiment Museum).

Matters simmered for a few weeks, but in late-March, raiding parties of Daham's men were noticed closing in on the Aijal's encampment. Consequently, a section from No 5 Company was despatched to bolster his defences. Early on the morning of 2 April, a patrol of Rolls-Royce armoured cars and Armed Fords came under fire from 300 of Daham's men, mostly horsemen, while patrolling on the Iraqi side of the frontier. The cars returned fire and as instructed, withdrew in good order and took up defensive positions as Daham el Hadi's men followed swiftly in pursuit.

The Lewis guns were dismounted from the Fords while the three Rolls-Royces closed down and launched forays towards the attackers. The fighting continued throughout the morning with the RAF armoured cars closing at times to within 50 yards of the enemy, assisted by Aijal's horsemen watching the flanks. They succeeded in driving off two attacks by Daham el Hadi's followers, by now estimated at 2000 men on horse and on foot. By mid-morning, Daham's men had been driven back more than a mile, but had taken up strong entrenched defensive positions still inside Iraqi territory from which they could not be dislodged. The RAF armoured crews began to fear that Aijal's men might waiver, and if so the cars would be in serious danger. Shortly after midday however, the enemy were seen to scatter as a flight of Bristol Fighters of No 6 Squadron swept in to save the situation. They proceeded to bomb and machine-gun Daham el Hadi's positions; within minutes, his followers had broken and were fleeing towards the frontier, leaving 50 dead and many wounded. Both the RAF aircraft and armoured cars had strict instructions not to pursue them across the Syrian border, but a subsequent aerial reconnaissance the following morning failed to find any sign of their tents on either side of the frontier.[21]

The formation of the Armoured Car Wing HQ at RAF Hinaidi during April 1927 led to the disbandment of Nos 4, 5 and 6 Companies in April 1927 and a reduction to eight sections. Four armoured car sections (Nos 2-5) were located at Hinaidi, No 1 was at Basra, Kirkuk was garrisoned with Nos 6 and 7 Sections, while Mosul was the sole responsibility of No 8 Section.[22]

In June 1927, Air Headquarters Iraq received reports that a raiding party of the Huweitat and Beni Sakhr, about 250 to 300 strong, had stolen 250 camels from the Fad'an and Saba tribe. Although the tribes were Syrian, the Fad'an and Saba had been legitimately grazing in Iraq territory, some 65 miles south-east of Abu Khemal.

In conditions of considerable heat, Flight Lieutenant Norman Saward and Flying Officer Frank Kingham with No 4 Section from Hinaidi were ordered to proceed to Ramadi to intercept the raiders. A flight of No 55 Squadron was also sent to join them. Later that day, Squadron Leader Arthur Peck DSO MC and bar, OC of the Armoured Car Wing, departed Hinaidi with a Rolls Royce armoured car and a Rolls

Royce wireless tender. Travelling with him was Flight Lieutenant Frederick Benstead, to replace Saward, who had become medically unfit to continue, possibly due to the heat. Squadron Leader Peck was to take command of the column of cars, but was to await orders and only move to Rutbah if news was received that the Huweitat were moving towards the Wadi Miyah wells near the Transjordan frontier (Map 2, p. 24).

An aerial reconnaissance by the Ninaks of No 55 Squadron that evening failed to locate the raiders. Notwithstanding the lack of information on the raiders' location, Peck and his column, known as 'Comcol', and consisting of four Rolls-Royce armoured cars and a Rolls-Royce wireless tender, set off that evening towards Rutbah at 2020 hours, arriving at 1600 hours the following day. For the 20-hour journey, he had been out of radio communication with Air Headquarters in Baghdad due to faulty W/T.

Three Ninaks then flew to Rutbah with the Administrative Inspector from Ramadi. They located raiders near Bir Melussa, proceeding in a westerly direction. However, the Administrative Inspector forbade any firing at the Arabs; instead the pilots were told to drop messages ordering them to return over the Syrian frontier. This would have meant the loss of the camels which had been stolen from the Fad'an and Saba. Fortunately, none of the raiding party could read and consequently the message was ignored.

Meanwhile, Peck had received a report that the raiders were at Wadi Melussa and after only a night's stay at Rutbah, he moved off early on 9 June towards the wells at Wadi Miyah. The RAF armoured cars and Fords were concealed in a depression and remained there until sunset, awaiting reports on the aerial reconnaissances by No 55 Squadron. With no information from the aircraft, he withdrew his force into the Wadi Miyah and placed the cars and Lewis guns posts in positions covering the wells and wadi.

After an uneventful night, 'Comcol' departed at 0300 hours and set off along Palmyra-Rutbah track. After three hours journey they sighted the raiders, strung out over about two miles on the frontier side of Palmyra road and about four miles ahead of the column. The ORB continues:

> Squadron Leader Peck with three Rolls-Royce armoured cars went into action, leaving one Rolls-Royce armoured car and one Wireless Tender in the rear with instructions to keep in touch, but keep out of effective range. The Special Service Officer, Flying Officer N.A. West and three Camel Policemen, accompanied the cars into action. The cars closed down and approached the head of the camel column at 40 mph. The leading camels were seen to swing back and the party bunched together. A burst of fire was directed at two of the raiders who attempted to break away and immediately a white flag was hoisted from the main body of the raiders.
>
> The cars were placed in position covering the raiders, who were warned by the Special Service Officer that any attempt at resistance would be met by machine-gun fire without further warning. All rifles, revolvers, knives and ammunition were taken from the raiders and burnt in a pile in front of them. 200 rifles, knives and belts; and about 13,000 rounds of ammunition destroyed.
>
> The captured raiding party consisted of 205 men under Abu Teyah and Ibn Jazzi and were in possession of 220 raided camels. The two leaders were detained and the remainder given half an hour to be out of sight in the

direction of the frontier. The Special Service Officer ascertained from Abu Teyah that a smaller party of 55 raiders, with 40 looted camels, had broken off from the main party and had taken a northerly direction.[23]

As the cars were running short of petrol and this party had probably crossed the frontier, it was not considered advisable to follow them.[24] The looted camels were driven into Rutbah by the camel police and the two leaders handed over to the Administrative Officer at Rutbah and 'Comcol' returned to Hinaidi.

Peck was criticised in the report on the action by the AOC Iraq, Air Vice-Marshal Sir Edward Ellington, for losing radio contact with Baghdad and the other Company vehicles. He had moved off to intercept the raiding party and had taken a Rolls-Royce wireless tender with him, but the W/T failed and the searching aircraft failed to locate his force and he was therefore out of contact with the rest of his command. Furthermore, there had been poor cooperation between aircraft and cars, while the new Ford lorries bringing the reserve petrol had suffered from overheated engines and had failed to arrive in time, and there had been misunderstandings between RAF officers of the column and the local Administrative Inspector.

Despite these criticisms, Squadron Leader Peck's actions had borne fruit, with the operation a clear success. Arthur Peck was undoubtedly a man of action. He was a fighter ace and had been awarded an MC and bar, as well as the DSO. These had been won in the skies over the Western Front while taking on superior numbers of German aircraft. Despite the criticism due to the failed W/T, Ellington did concede:

> Though as Officer Commanding the RAF forces during this operation, Squadron Leader Peck made mistakes, I consider that he acted with energy throughout the operation and that his conduct when the armoured cars made contact with the raiders on the 11th, is deserving of praise.[25]

Notes
1. G.E. Godsave, *Fi Kull Makáan*, ed. K. Oliver (RAF Regiment Museum Archives: Unpublished manuscript, 1969), p. 23.
2. D. Omissi, *Air Power and Colonial Control: The Royal Air Force 1919-1939* (Manchester: Manchester University Press, 1990), p. 38.
3. I.M. Phillpott, *The Royal Air Force: An Encyclopaedia of the Inter-War Years, Vol. I* (Barnsley, Yorks.: Pen & Sword, 2005), p. 51.
4. By 1929, No 30 Squadron was stationed at Mosul, Nos 55 and 70 Squadrons at Hinaidi and No 84 Squadron at Shaibah. Number 1 Squadron had been disbanded in late 1926 and reformed in the United Kingdom while Nos 6 and 45 Squadrons had been moved to Egypt and No 8 Squadron to Aden.
5. J.G. Browne, *The Iraq Levies 1915-1932* (London: Royal United Service Institute, 1932), pp.65-77.
6. AIR 5/1254 *Operations in Iraq: Chapters 14 to 25 January 1924-December 1928, Iraq Command Report April 1924 to November 1926*, p. 5.
7. The columns of Levies and Iraqi Army units were accompanied by the RAF personnel with W/T pack sets as the main means of communication.
8. 'RAF Flying Accident', *Flight,* July 29, 1926, p. 465 and C.G. Jefford, *The Flying Camels* (High Wycombe, Bucks.: Privately published by the author, 1995), pp. 89-90. During this period, No 6 Armoured Car Company was to have some misfortune with its commanding officers. In February 1925, Squadron Leader Jasper Cruikshank died after contracting typhoid. Then in July of the following year, Squadron Leader Eric Pollard was killed in an

air accident. He and six other RAF personnel lost their lives when a Vickers Vernon of No 45 Squadron, on the routine mail run to Kirkuk and in which he was a passenger, suffered engine failure on take-off from Hinaidi and crashed.

9 AIR 5/1290 *Iraq Command monthly operational summary, Vol. IV January-December 1926.* Flying Officer Gerald Elliot MC served in No 6 Armoured Car Company for the four-and-a-half years of its existence.

10 G.E. Godsave, 'Armoured Cars in Desert Warfare', *Journal of the Royal United Service Institute,* LXX (1925), pp. 401-402.

11 *The Royal Air Force Armoured Car Manual, Air Ministry Publication 1418* (London: Air Ministry, 1931). The RAF Armoured Car manual arose from a meeting of RAF armoured car officers in Baghdad held on 28 February 1929.

12 B.H. Liddell Hart, *The Tanks: The History of the Royal Tank Regiment and its predecessors Heavy Branch Machine-Gun Corps, Tank Corps and Royal Tank Corps, 1914-1945, Vol. I* (London: Cassell, 1959), p. 213. The furrow was actually a combination of partly ploughed furrow and predominantly wheel tracks, and had first been marked out in June 1921 by a detachment of three officers and ten men of the RAF and a section of one officer and 8 men from No 4 Armoured Car Company of the Royal Tank Corps equipped with three Rolls-Royce tenders. AIR 5/1253 *Operations: Iraq, Chapters 1 to 13.* In February 1923, A column lead by Major Holt of the Royal Engineers and Flying Officer Wynne with nine Crossley tenders and two Fords remarked the furrow and landing grounds.

13 George Elliot Godsave was born on 11 September 1894 and educated at Alleyn's School in Dulwich. He enlisted in the 14th London Regiment in August 1914 and was commissioned in 1915. He was seconded to the RFC as an observer in 1916. Badly gassed in January 1917 he became unfit for further flying, but was awarded a permanent commission in the Technical Branch of the RAF where he specialised in Navigation Instruction. He died at Luton on 13 June 1965.

14 J.M. Munro, *The Nairn Way* (New York: Delmar, 1980) and J.S. Tullett, *Nairn Bus to Baghdad* (Wellington: AH & AW Reed, 1968).

15 G.E. Godsave, *The Tales of the Tin Trams* (RAF Regiment Museum Archives: Unpublished manuscript).

16 G.E. Godsave, *Fi Kull Makáan,* pp. 14-15.

17 *Ibid.*

18 Tullett, *Nairn Bus to Baghdad,* pp. 78-80

19 Later Air Vice-Marshal Arthur Lee MC (1894-1974). A. Lee, *Fly Past: Highlights from a Flyers Life* (London: Jarrolds, 1974), p. 54.

20 A. Lee, *Fly Past,* pp. 54-57. Lee comments on the generosity of the bedouin. "I could not but reflect on the way these nomads lived, with the heat and vermin and hardships, yet with a fine code of hospitality and good manners that could put some of us westerners to shame."

21 AIR 5/1254 *Operations in Iraq.*

22 From June 1926 both HQs and two sections each of No 4 and 5 Armoured Car Companies were at Hinaidi with only one section at Mosul. HQ and two sections of No 6 Company were at Kirkuk with one section permanently at Hinaidi. By October 1927, No 7 Section had also been disbanded

23 AIR 29/50 *No 1 Armoured Car Company, Habbaniya: before 1 April 1930 Armoured Car Wing, Hinaidi; from 3 October 1946 No 1 ACC incorporated in RAF Regiment, redesignated No 2701 Squadron.*

24 Petrol was being conveyed to Rutbah in Victorias by No 70 Squadron RAF but could not reach it that day while a convoy of Ford tonners were also dispatched. The armoured car crews tried to obtain petrol from Imperial Airways at Rutbah but their stocks were low. As a consequence it was decided to establish a reserve of fuel at this location for future RAF operations.

25 AIR 5/1254 *Operations in Iraq.* Correspondence: The Secretary, Air Ministry, 2 July 1927.

Chapter Six

War in the Southern Desert 1923-1928

"I cannot help feeling, therefore, that these events, far from being hushed up, deserve wider publicity, for they provide an example of an intervention by British forces, which rendered signal service to both Nejed and Iraq"
Lieutenant-General Sir John Bagot Glubb[1]

"The elegant 'Silver Ghosts' played their part in desert warfare as grim determined knights in armour, known to their great hearted and gallant crews as 'The Old Tin Trams.' They were indeed modern ships of the desert, each with its name, its individuality, its crew and its own battle honours of years of faithful service in every place."
Squadron Leader G. Elliot Godsave[2]

It would seem that the fighting in Kurdistan and along the northern frontiers, and policing the deserts west and north-west of Baghdad, alone could have fully occupied the senior RAF commanders and civil officials in Iraq for much of the time that the Air Force Scheme of Control had been in operation. Iraq Command had, however, not only been dealing with a number of internal outbreaks of trouble from various tribes in the districts surrounding Baghdad and the two rivers, but had since 1924, also been aware of an escalating threat in the Southern Desert from raiding parties of the Ikhwan from the Nejed.

In the south of Iraq, the initial operational activities for No 3 Armoured Car Company had been limited to reconnaissances of the areas surrounding Basra (Map 2, p. 24; Map 9, p. 97). By May 1923, its cars had travelled to Nasiriyah and the country south of Hammar Lake, Fao and south to Jebel Sanam and the border with Kuwait, to determine the suitability of the country for armoured car operations. In the first year of operations, the Company had carried out intensive ground training with Vickers and Hotchkiss machine-guns, and had provided a Guard of Honour for King Feisal, and then the armed escort of five Rolls-Royces and four Lancias for his visit to Zubair. To gain access to the river-bound areas to the north and east of Basra, successful experiments were carried out in trans-shipping the Rolls-Royces and Lancias across the Shatt al Arab using steel barges and a steam tug. Special recces were requested to Umm Qasr and Safwan, in co-operation with No 84 Squadron,

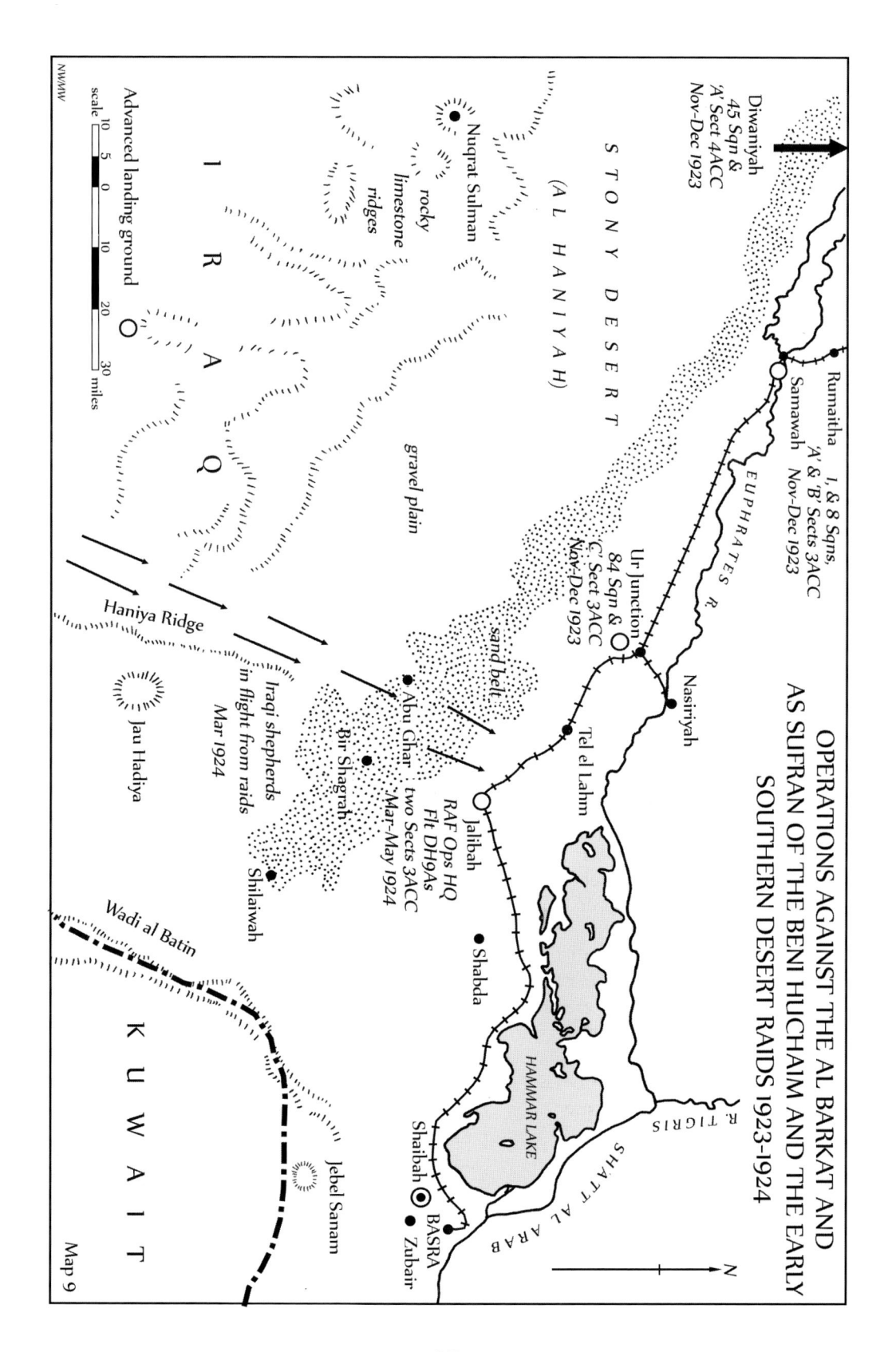

Map 9: Operations against the Al Barkat and As Sufran of the Beni Huchaim and the Early Southern Desert Raids 1923-1924

which had a marked pacifying effect on a restless local population. On one occasion, they deployed to Basra Gaol with six armoured cars and successfully quelled a minor prison riot. Later they assisted Customs officials in an operation to intercept gun-runners working around Basra.³

Internal troubles had arisen frequently in central and southern Iraq from 1922 onwards, as the Government sought to impose a much stricter regime of tax collection, and administrative contact with the citizenry, than their erstwhile Ottoman rulers. Problems arose in one incident involving the tribes of the riverine plain south-east of Baghdad. The area lay 160 miles from Baghdad, between the towns of Rumaithah and Samawah, on the Hillah branch of the Euphrates and had been a constant source of problems during Ottoman times; it was to prove the same under the new Iraq administration. The local tribesmen were well armed with modern rifles and had a history of successful resistance to the Government. Since 1920, little effort had been made by civil officials to deal with or enter the area. Tax collectors and police officers were fired on and driven off when they approached encampments and villages. The area was bereft of roads and largely inaccessible to motor vehicles, due to the large number of irrigation channels, canals and drainage ditches criss-crossing the marshy plain. Importantly, the Baghdad to Basra railway line passed through the region, and though relatively unmolested by the local population it had been torn up in parts during 1920, and in a later instance, the track pins were made into daggers to continue inter-tribal struggles. A military column had attempted to enter in 1920 but had been driven off and this had lowered the standing of the Government in the eyes of the assailants. The Iraq Army in late 1923, had not reached a state where it

HMACs Orion, Harvester, Terror and an unidentified Rolls-Royce sit in the sun outside the bays at RAF Hinaidi, 1927. On the far left is a Dragon Artillery Tractor Mark I fitted with a Rolls-Royce 'Type A' turret and was still present during the siege of 1941 (© Crown copyright. Godsave, RAF Regiment Museum).

could be used effectively, and the small force of Levies available was inadequate for operations.[4]

In November 1923, for matters of prestige, and to protect the only supply line with the Persian Gulf, Air Vice-Marshal Salmond resolved that decisive action needed to be taken against the tribes around Samawah. He therefore planned a period of operations under the command of Group Captain Arthur Longmore DSO, which had to be completed before the onset of the inclement winter conditions, as the next period of favourable weather would not be until the following April. After consultation with officials and Special Service Officers (SSO), 42 sheikhs were summoned to the Government Headquarters at Samawah.[5] Only four took up the offer, and only one of those would agree to placate his people. A further offer was made to the sheikhs, to avoid the need for action, but again the conference did not happen.[6]

Therefore, on 29 November, armoured car detachments, and the necessary stores for air action were transported by rail to three advanced landing grounds that had been established along the railway line. 'A' Section of No 4 Armoured Car Company, with three Rolls-Royces and three Lancias, drove south to Diwaniyah where they were joined by a train carrying stores to support a flight of No 45 Squadron. Here the section patrolled between the railway and aerodrome; cars were utilised in the carriage of bombs and stores and the pilot of a forced-landed aircraft was rescued. They also formed a defensive position against northern movement by the tribes should the disaffection spread. HMAC *Drake*, the Company W/T armoured car was the mobile wireless vehicle for the operation. A small group of Levies was assigned to guard two of the important bridges on the Baghdad-Basra railway line.[7]

Meanwhile, 'A' and 'B' Sections of No 3 Armoured Car Company moved north-west by train to Samawah, with stores for Nos 1 and 8 Squadrons. 'C' Section was railed to Ur Junction, where they protected a flight of No 84 Squadron that

His Majesty's Armoured Car Drake of No 4 Armoured Car Company. The gazelle was shot with the Vickers machine-gun (© Crown copyright. Cox, RAF Regiment Museum).

had flown in from Shaibah. The responsibility of the armoured cars was, however, predominantly aerodrome defence, as the riverine terrain was entirely unsuitable for their deployment in offensive action.[8]

Intensive bombing was carried out against the villages of the Al Barkat and As Sufran tribes, whose headmen and sheikhs had failed to attend the conference. After two days, the majority had surrendered, and the neighbouring tribes had offered to submit to all the requirements of the Iraq Government. Mounted police and RAF SSOs then entered the area under the cover of the Sopwith Snipes of No 1 Squadron and matters calmed down. Group Captain Longmore recalled the conclusion of the operation:

> I remember riding into Samawah, attended by my staff and with an escort of Iraq Cavalry to accept the surrender of the sheikhs. Lieutenant-Colonel Ronnie MacLean of the Iraq Army and Squadron Leader Freddie Guard of the armoured cars were two of my chief supporters on that occasion. We had used overwhelming force at the right place at the right time, a combination desirable in dealing with any trouble...[9]

Most of the armoured car sections from Nos 3 and 4 Companies had returned to base by mid-December. However, 'C' Section of No 3 Company, with three cars, was back at Ur on 17 December, while a further air raid was made by No 1 Squadron on the As Sufran to enforce compliance. A few weeks later, the weather conditions deteriorated and the roads around Basra became impassable. The Company moved back to the Makina, and spent time on much-needed maintenance. The last section of No 4 Company was back in Baghdad by mid-January.[10]

The most serious threat to the stability and development of government in southern Iraq, however, came from the Ikhwan tribes (the Mutair, Harab, and Ajman), who dwelt across the borders in the barren deserts of the Nejed. With the stabilisation of the more populated areas of Iraq, and the establishment of proper government structures, it was then possible to consider moving the policing and administration further out from the riverine regions of Iraq. In the large tracts of desert to the west and south-west of the Euphrates River lived the nomadic tribes who, for centuries, had drawn their livelihood from breeding and husbandry of sheep, goats, donkeys, and most importantly, camels. These tribes (the Dhafeer, Zayyad and Budoor), were heavily dependent upon the growth of the desert pastures and thus were slaves to the changes and unpredictability of the seasons, and would move in rhythm with the rains. They travelled out into the desert during winter, sometimes as far as 200 miles, as the dry and barren desert was carpeted with grasses, wild flowers and sprouting desert shrubs. As the summer heat withered the pasturage, and the runnels and pools dried up, the animals would begin to suffer, and they moved closer to the Euphrates. Several important caravan routes also crossed these deserts in this region, and as a consequence, raiding was a tempting prospect for the Ikhwan tribes located across the frontier.

The Ottoman Empire had never attempted to extend its influence more than a few miles from the Euphrates. The struggles in the Southern Desert for the next eight years, in which the RAF armoured cars would play a part, stemmed from two main causes; the fanaticism of the Ikhwan, and the rivalry and mistrust between King Abd al Aziz ibn Saud of the Nejed and the Hashemite ruler of Iraq, King Feisal. The British Government encouraged treaty negotiations between the two, as it wished to see a general pacification of Arabia. International boundaries had, however, been unknown in Arabia before this time, and any attempt to draw them was treated with suspicion by the Saud family. Ibn Saud also saw himself as surrounded by his enemies, with Transjordan, Iraq and the Hedjaz ruled by the Hashemites.

Two agreements were signed in 1922. In May, the Muhammerah Treaty was limited to defining the allegiances of the tribes in the cross-border area, while the agreements signed in December, known as the Uqair Protocols, defined the location of the borders. The High Commissioner, Sir Percy Cox, was able to obtain agreement on a frontier 120 miles south of the Euphrates. This solution was not as easy as it appeared, as poor or unpredictable rains in the Nejed meant that the only choice for these tribes was to move north into Iraq for better grazing. A diamond-shaped area of desert, of 2700 square miles, was defined between the two countries as the Neutral Zone. Both countries agreed to allow use of water supplies by the bedouin in the area, but not to build any dwellings or installations. Ibn Saud also continued to extract taxes from the Iraqi tribes when the opportunity presented itself, and the Ikhwan still remained a serious threat.[11]

The Southern Desert covered 45,000 square miles, and there were great difficulties in predicting the size, location and timing of an Ikhwan raid. The major problem facing the RAF was the speed with which the raiding parties could be assembled and the pace at which they could move. The raiders would concentrate on the Nejed side of the frontier and then move rapidly at dawn. They would make their raid, and then, just as quickly, move back across the frontier, before the RAF and Iraqi authorities could react. A further complexity to the Ikhwan problem was the presence of a large number of Ikhwan refugees who had incurred the displeasure of Ibn Saud and had sought safety in Iraq. They had then proceeded to use their safe haven to carry out small raids back into the Nejed against their fellow countrymen.

The sand and gravel of the vast and unending desert (© Crown copyright. Godsave, RAF Regiment Museum).

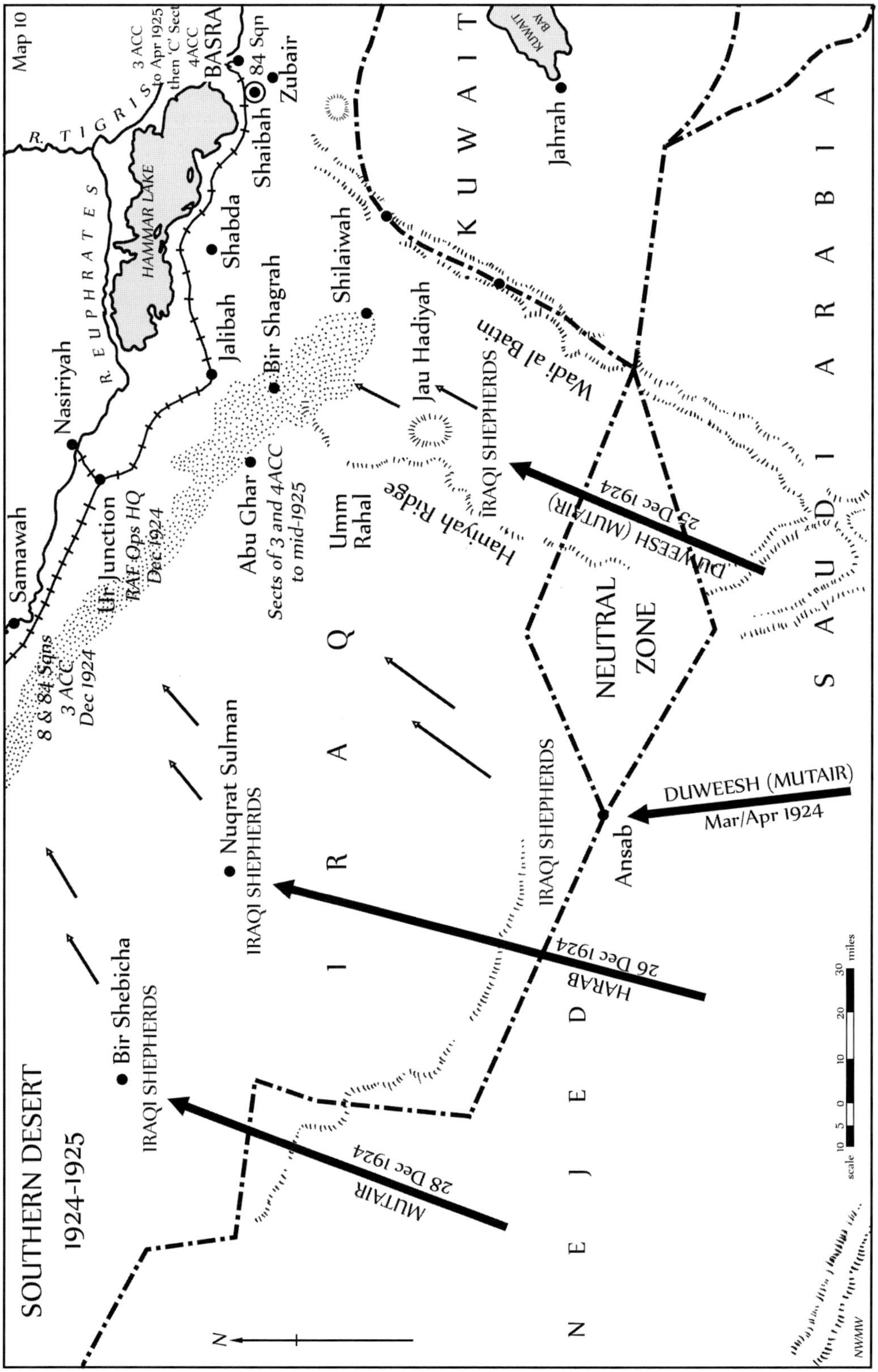

Map 10
SOUTHERN DESERT
1924-1925
R. TIGRIS
R. EUPHRATES
HAMMAR LAKE
BASRA
3 ACC to Apr 1925 then 'C' Sect 4ACC
84 Sqn
Shaibah
Zubair
Shabda
Jalibah
Nasiriyah
Samawah
Ur Junction
RAF Ops HQ Dec 1924
8 & 84 Sqns 3 ACC Dec 1924
Abu Ghar
Sects of 3 and 4ACC to mid-1925
Bir Shagrah
Shilaiwah
Umm Rahal
Jau Hadiyah
Haniyah Ridge
Wadi al Batin
Jahrah
KUWAIT BAY
KUWAIT
IRAQI SHEPHERDS
DUWEESH (MUTAIR) 25 Dec 1924
NEUTRAL ZONE
DUWEESH (MUTAIR) Mar/Apr 1924
Ansab
Nuqrat Sulman
IRAQI SHEPHERDS
HARAB 26 Dec 1924
Bir Shebicha
IRAQI SHEPHERDS
MUTAIR 28 Dec 1924
IRAQ
NEJED
SAUDI ARABIA
N
scale 10 5 0 10 20 30 miles
NWMW

This gave the Ikhwan a further excuse to carry out incursions into Iraq.

The first efforts of the RAF armoured cars in the Southern Desert had been made by No 3 Armoured Car Company. The Company had spent a large part of September 1923 determining the feasibility of armoured car operations in the area, demonstrating their mobility and ubiquity, and reporting on those routes passable to the cars. They had, however, been preoccupied with the operations against the Beni Huchaim nearer the river during November and December. January 1924 had been particularly wet, and the cars could not travel more than a few miles from Basra, making further exploration impossible until the weather had cleared and the tracks became passable. The weather was so severe that the barracks leaked badly and the crews had to be accommodated in the wings of the RAF hospital.[12]

During March and April 1924, raids by Ikhwan led by Feisal al Duweesh, the chief of the Mutair tribe, delivered a massive blow to the Iraqi shepherd tribes located at Ansab, on the west edge of the Neutral Zone. This resulted in 146 deaths, the loss of 30,000 animals, and the looting of tents and property. The reports of the raids only reached the Euphrates a week later, when the victims straggled in from the desert. The RAF and Iraqi authorities failed completely to halt the raiders, or attack them, despite daily aircraft patrols. It had become apparent that more would have to be done to protect the tribes, and the RAF agreed to operate up to the Nejed frontier. Aircraft patrols alone, over many thousands of miles of desert could not hope to locate the raiders; better intelligence was needed, together with an armed presence on the ground close to the threatened tribes (Map 10, p. 102).

The major impediment to vehicular travel out into the Southern Desert was a long belt of sand, located some 20 miles from the Baghdad-Basra railway line, which formed a barrier to vehicular movement into the Southern Desert. The sand belt paralleled the railway for 80 miles, from just south of Samawah, to a point about 20 miles from the Wadi al Batin, on the border with Kuwait.

During March 1924, Group Captain Longmore established a temporary headquarters in the railway siding at Jalibah, on the Baghdad-Basra railway, with a detachment of Ninaks and a company of armoured cars under his command. Number 3 Company moved two sections by rail and then sent out patrols north-west to Ur Junction, east to Shabda, and then into the sand belt to Abu Ghar and Bir Shagrah. They also visited the local Dhafeer and other grazing tribes and gathered information for the local SSO back at Jalibah. Rumours of raids were frequent, and panic was being spread by Ikhwan fifth columnists. Some alarm was caused when two of the tribal groups approached the aerodrome and seemed intent on passing right through the camp. The cars were placed on 'stand-to', but, fortunately the tribes moved away. Jalibah was the main operating base for the next three months until, as there had been no raids by the Ikhwan, they were ordered back to Basra. During this period, another section had been rushed back to Shaibah, and then sent out to deal with the threat of another raid, but again turned up nothing.

No let-up was allowed in operations; this time the Company was ordered in its entirety to Baghdad to assist No 4 Company deal with any civil strife that might arise from a meeting of the delegates to the Iraqi Assembly. The remainder of 1924 was spent on minor civil control operations in Basra, an unsuccessful search around Jalibah for two airmen of No 84 Squadron whose Ninak had come to grief, and then a recovery operation on a downed aircraft. Sporting activities were prominent by October, when the Company won the Basra Group Boxing Championship Challenge, defeating the Stores Depot, in bouts described as 'keen and clean throughout'. The

Company then went on to take the Group Cricket League Cup, winning all but the first match of the six games of the season.[13]

The Ikhwan problem did not arise again until the last two months of the year. Coinciding with increased tribal activity was the arrival of the first replacement drafts for the armoured car companies. Flying Officer Horace Bowen and 55 airmen of No 3 Company departed for the United Kingdom, and 40 replacements arrived in their place. The new draft was not as well trained as hoped; they were soon being put through their paces on the firing range and were readied to begin a three-month intensive training course for armoured car crews.

In the last week of December 1924, the Mutair and Harab tribes, in three separate raids, attacked Bir Shebicha, Nuqrat Sulman and Jau Hadiya (Map 10, p. 102). Unfortunately, with the good rains the Iraqi tribes had moved further out into the desert, and thus were easy prey. The males were slaughtered in cold blood, while the women and children fled in terror in the face of the charging camelmen. Captain John Glubb, the SSO, described the state of the tribes people as they fled to the safety of Jalibah and the railway line:[14]

> The desert around the station buildings was now crowded by a mass of tents, flocks, donkeys, and shepherds who had fled back in alarm to the fancied security of the railway. On the station platform sat huddled groups of women and children, many half-naked, exhausted and weak from lack of food. They were the women survivors of the... camps that had been raided. All their male relatives had been killed. They maintained day and night a continuous and nerve-wracking sound of wailing and sobbing... A week ago they had been mothers, wives and sisters in contented little shepherd families. Now they were orphaned widowed, half-naked and utterly destitute.[15]

The news of the raids took a day to reach the Euphrates and then snow and rain prevented pursuit for a day. Ninaks were eventually sent out from Shaibah to investigate and were able to bomb the raiders for two days running. Disappointingly, no protection was offered to the shepherds by the RAF or Iraq Army, only retaliation against their attackers. A further raid on the last day of 1924, 70 miles south of Samawah, exacted a heavy toll on the Iraq tribes. Number 8 Squadron, however, caught the raiders on 7 January 1925, as they had proceeded in a leisurely retreat with their livestock back to the Nejed. They were bombed for the next four days with the loss of some 53 men and 76 animals.

The heightened fear of attack meant the shepherds chose to camp closer to the railway, creating heavy competition for the more restricted grazing. The only way to resolve this was to ensure the shepherds felt more secure and to provide adequate warning of the approach of raiders. The AOC Iraq, Air Vice-Marshal Sir John Higgins, sent Major Bovill of the Iraq Army, and Captain Glubb, now designated 'SSO Ikhwan Defence', on an extended reconnaissance of the desert in early December 1924 to determine suitable sites for advanced bases.[16] On the recommendation of Glubb, the authorities established a landing ground and an Iraq Army post at Abu Ghar, 30 miles out from the railway, with a direct W/T link to Air Headquarters.[17] At the same time, No 8 (Bomber) Squadron was moved to Samawah in readiness for operations in the Southern Desert. The post would have to be supplied with fuel and rations; therefore the armoured car companies were charged with reporting on route conditions and the 'going'. Comprehensive recces by Nos 3 and 4 Companies were

Near Kut, on a road survey between Baghdad and Basra, 26 February 1925. Flt Lt Robert Jope-Slade DSC bags some duck for dinner. Jope-Slade had a long association with Iraq, serving on No 4 Company, the Armoured Car Wing, and Air Staff (Armoured Cars) at Air HQ Iraq from 1923 to 1925. He returned to Iraq from 1927 to 1929, working on the Air Staff as an Intelligence Officer, and was mentioned in despatches and later awarded the OBE for services rendered in the operations in the Southern Desert against the Ikhwan. By 1938, he was back on Intelligence duties at Air HQ Iraq and was killed on 5 May 1941, when the Vickers Vincent in which he was a passenger went down in the Persian Gulf (© Crown copyright. Godsave, RAF Regiment Museum).

therefore planned.

The task was to push the operational area of the RAF armoured cars out to the edge of the sand belt, thus providing a larger zone for the tribes for safe grazing, but as yet, there was little knowledge of the 'going'. Three Rolls-Royce armoured cars, six Lancias and auxiliary transport of No 3 Company left Camp Makina, by rail for Samawah during December, tasked to determine the routes through the sand belt. The first recce, in cooperation with No 4 Company, was to the north and found a route from Najaf to Samawah, where the cultivated area meets the desert. Ninaks of Nos 8 and 84 Squadrons assisted the operation, reporting the ground ahead of the cars, and making regular deliveries of food and rations. At one point, a Ninak had to force-land, and an armoured car remained with the crew and aircraft to protect it until a new engine could be brought out with another armoured car. Number 4 Company visited Bir Lussuf, Bir Shebicha and Nuqrat Sulman. A second recce by No 3 Company was more ambitious and the cars moved from Samawah to Abu Ghar and across the Haniyah Ridge with the aim of reaching Shaibah. Menacing weather and numerous belts of sand prevented any movement beyond Shilaiwah, and the cars were forced to return to Samawah.

A few weeks later, another attempt was made to reach Shilaiwah, this time from Shaibah, but using the lighter Armed Fords. With the help of Ninaks from No 84 Squadron they soon found the old car tracks from the December recce and successfully completed the circuit. Meanwhile, Fords of No 4 Company, under the command of Flight Lieutenant Charles Goring, had managed to travel through from Jalibah to Abu Ghar, and on to Bir Shagrah, with the journey only taking two and a quarter hours. The first ten miles from Jalibah was flat desert covered in gravel and dotted with small desert shrubs. Then a long line of dunes would appear, stretching endlessly from left to right, and it was here the path became difficult. Two Rolls-Royces of No 3 Company were despatched by rail to Jalibah to test the track with the heavier car and, with some struggle, were also able to reach Bir Shagrah. However, the soft sand and light crusting along the track easily gave way, and made the journey difficult for the heavy armoured cars.

If the RAF was to carry out effective desert air and ground patrols, it would need accurate maps, but even by 1925, most were grossly inaccurate or incomplete. Using a combination of air and ground surveys, the maps, covering some 30,000 square miles, were improved considerably. The tracks along the sand belt needed further development so that Abu Ghar could be established as an advanced base by the next winter. Therefore, two detachments of Armed Fords of Nos 3 and 4 Companies carried out recces to find passable routes from Jalibah to the outpost. They then ran a number of supply convoys to the advanced base over the next three months, whilst some of the cars accompanied Captain Glubb on recces further to the south. The presence of the sections was vital, as rumours circulated that Feisal al Duweesh of the Mutair had sworn to exterminate the post at Abu Ghar.

Meanwhile, in a successful effort to survey the south-eastern route from Basra, another three Armed Fords of No 4 Company, under the command of Flight Lieutenant Maurice Ballard and an officer of the Chief Engineer's Staff, departed Makina camp, and travelled out into the Southern Desert, moving via Shilaiwah, Umm Rahal, then up to Abu Ghar and to Jalibah. Trenches were dug at various points in the shapes of letters and noted on the maps to guide pilots on desert recces. After a refit at Jalibah, they moved to Samawah and then out to the area south of Najaf. The Desert Survey Party returned to Hinaidi on 11 April, after two months continuous work, having covered 4156 miles between Basra and Najaf. The sandy and rocky terrain was such that each Ford virtually required rebuilding during the journey; this was done without workshops and spoke volumes of the initiative and skill of Ballard and airmen of the survey party.

Only successful negotiation with Ibn Saud would provide a long-term solution to the problem of raiding, but these had broken down and the new AOC Iraq, Air Vice-Marshal Sir John Higgins, was ordered to meet the incursions with force. Constant air patrols were carried out during the grazing season for the first four months of 1925, no interference was reported from the Ikhwan. This was only partly due to the threat posed by the RAF patrols, as it transpired that Ibn Saud, King of the Nejed, had ordered that raiding was to cease for the time being. Furthermore, many of the Ikhwan were away fighting with Ibn Saud, as he pursued the ultimately successful campaign to gain control of the Hedjaz from King Hussein ibn Ali of the Hedjaz, Sharif of Mecca. In mid-1925, therefore, with the summer heat increasing, the Iraqi tribes moved back to the Euphrates and away from the post at Abu Ghar. The No 4 Company detachment at Abu Ghar, having travelled 25,033 miles in the last few months of operations, was withdrawn and the outpost was closed down.

However, there was still a problem with the Ikhwan refugees, now resident in Iraq, and their retaliatory raiding against tribes in the Nejed. This was dealt with in June and July by the SSO, Flight Lieutenant G. M. Moore MC, who successfully negotiated the movement of these tribes from close proximity to the Nejed border. Not all tribal leaders were amenable to the move and 'C' Section of No 4 Company sent a detachment to arrest three leaders who had disobeyed orders and had refused to come in. The situation was resolved peacefully and the cars returned to Zubair with the prisoners and their looted camels.

Overlying the intensive pace of operations was the ever-present requirement for the reduction of Iraq garrison, so as to meet the financial stringencies of the British Treasury. As a consequence in 1925, Iraq Command had ordered the transfer of a regiment of Levy Cavalry to the Iraq Army, whilst two flying squadrons, a pack battery and transport company departed from Iraq.[18] Only three British and Indian battalions now remained, but the Iraq Army was growing in size. On 1 April 1925, 'C' Section of No 4 Company had taken up permanent residence at Basra, as it had been decided that No 3 Armoured Car Company was to be disbanded. The Officer Commanding No 3 Company, Squadron Leader Frederick Guard, however, remained in Basra, where he took command of Iraq's Inland Water Transport organisation. Sadly, a few months later he contracted pneumonia, complicated by malaria, and died back in the United Kingdom as a consequence in June 1927.[19] The Armoured Car Wing HQ was also disbanded in December 1924. Wing Commander Primrose, who had performed a sterling task, returned to the United Kingdom, and was replaced by Wing Commander Sidney Smith DSO AFC, who was appointed Air Staff (Armoured Cars), and operated out of Iraq Command Headquarters in Baghdad. Smith was in turn replaced in July 1925 by Wing Commander Gilbert Cooke DSC AFC, who had previously commanded No 4 Armoured Car Company.

In October 1925, the Bahra Agreement, signed with Ibn Saud, further resolved the fraught frontier relations between the Iraq and Nejed Governments. Both agreed to do all in their power to prevent raids. The shepherds, with renewed confidence, moved out into the desert for grazing and moved right up to the border with the Nejed. Furthermore, a warning system was established to give alarm should a raiding party cross the frontier. As it happened, the end of 1925 and early 1926 were free from raiding by the Ikhwan.

During October 1926, to exemplify the complexity of the tribal animosities in Iraq, a 200-strong party of the Shammar Abdah tribe had swept down from Syria into Kuwait, to Jahrah, and had returned through Iraq with 1100 looted camels. Iraq Command was determined that this raid, though it did not concern the Ikhwan, could not be allowed to go unpunished. The Shammar were located by aircraft and when they refused to move to Abu Ghar, were attacked by aircraft of Nos 8 and 84 Squadron as they returned north. This caused the party to splinter into smaller groups and they were then intercepted successfully by aircraft of a flight of No 55 Squadron and a section of armoured cars of No 4 Company.

This raid further convinced the authorities that permanent posts needed to be established in the deserts to police the tribes. An Iraqi tribe had raided across into the friendly state of Kuwait; Abu Ghar, only 40 miles from the railway, was too far back to be effective. In February 1927, the construction of a police post was approved at Busaiyah, in the centre of the Stony Desert (or Al Haniyah) (Map 11, p. 108). Captain Glubb had recommended this as an ideal location for an intelligence centre, a location to more effectively control the winter migration, and from which to intercept raiding parties moving to and from the Nejed, into Iraq and Kuwait. Busaiyah had a number of wells and was therefore an important watering place for raiding parties, as there were no other watering points north of this that did not already have a police post. However, the Uqair Protocols had forbidden the construction of forts and the stationing of troops near the Nejed border. To Ibn Saud this was a clear contravention of the Protocols. However, the Iraq Government

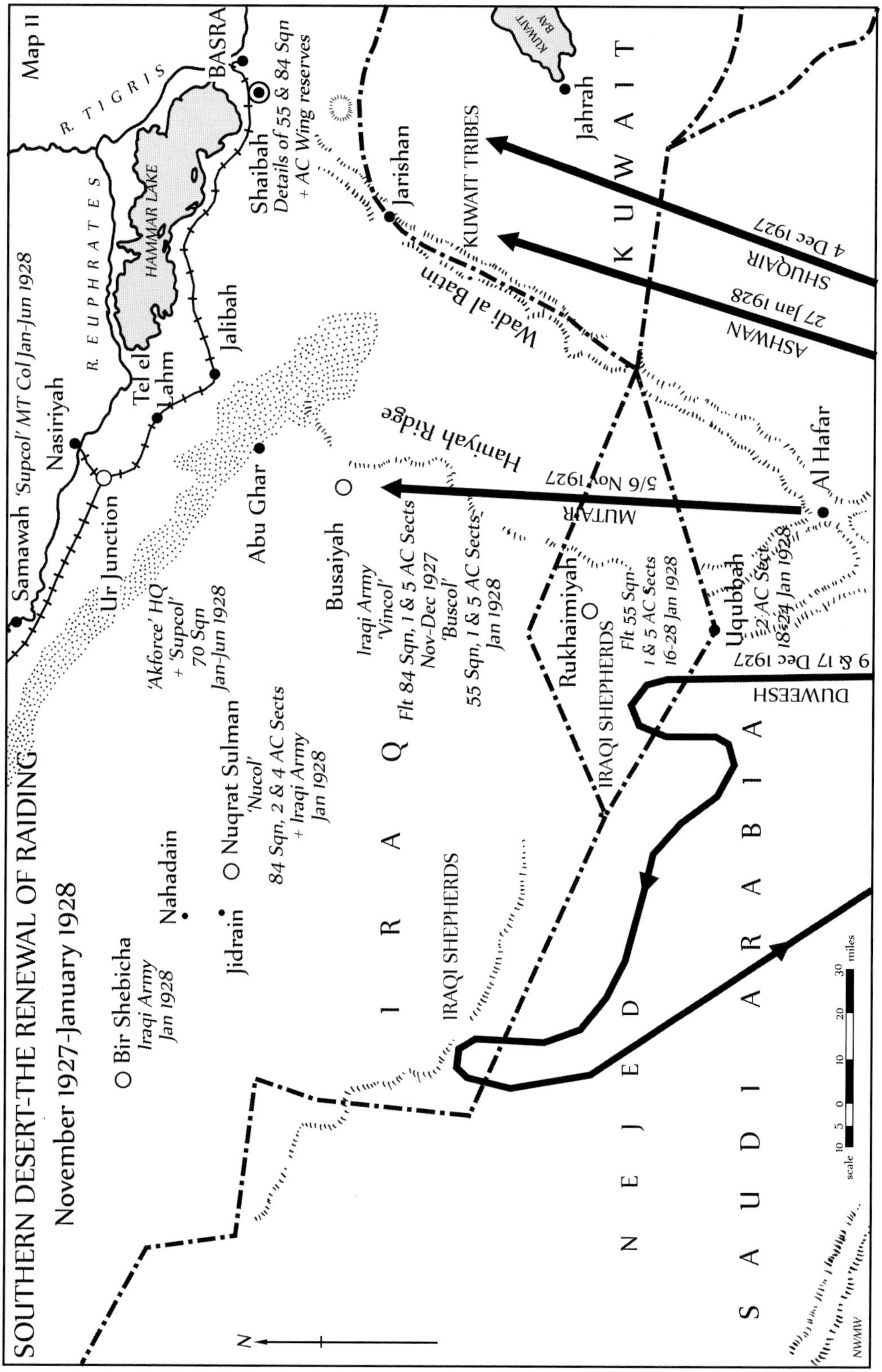

SOUTHERN DESERT-THE RENEWAL OF RAIDING
November 1927-January 1928
Map 11
R. TIGRIS
R. EUPHRATES
HAMMAR LAKE
BASRA
Shaibah
Details of 55 & 84 Sqn
+ AC Wing reserves
Samawah 'Supcol' MT Col Jan-Jun 1928
Nasiriyah
Tel el Lahm
Jalibah
Ur Junction
'Akforce' HQ
+ 'Supcol'
70 Sqn
Jan-Jun 1928
Abu Ghar
Busaiyah
Iraqi Army
'Vincol'
Flt 84 Sqn, 1 & 5 AC Sects
Nov-Dec 1927
'Buscol'
55 Sqn, 1 & 5 AC Sects
Jan 1928
Nuqrat Sulman
'Nucol'
84 Sqn, 2 & 4 AC Sects
+ Iraqi Army
Jan 1928
Jidrain
Nahadain
Bir Shebicha
Iraqi Army
Jan 1928
I R A Q
IRAQI SHEPHERDS
Rukhaimiyah
IRAQI SHEPHERDS
Flt 55 Sqn
1 & 5 AC Sects
16-28 Jan 1928
Uqubbah
2 AC Sect
18-24 Jan 1928
Al Hafar
Haniyah Ridge
MUTAIR
5/6 Nov 1927
Wadi al Batin
Jarishan
KUWAIT TRIBES
Jahrah
KUWAIT BAY
K U W A I T
SHUQAIR
4 Dec 1927
ASHWAN
27 Jan 1928
DUWEESH
9 & 17 Dec 1927
N E J D
S A U D I A R A B I A
scale 10 5 0 10 20 30 miles
N
NWMW

saw it as entirely acceptable within the terms of the agreement. To them, this was a 'police' post, not a military fort, and the location was not 'in the vicinity' of the frontier, as the Protocol stated, but 80 miles from it. Ibn Saud's arguments were also quite plausible, as no distinction was made between the Police and the Army in the Nejed. Maps were also fairly unused or unavailable at that time, and to Ibn Saud the exact location seemed much closer to his capital, Riyadh, than it in fact was, and was therefore a threat to his State. Negotiation might have resolved these issues but at the time they were not entered into. False rumours were rife, such as the large size of the fort and that the Iraq Government planned to construct a branch railway to the outpost. Feisal el Duweesh of the Mutair saw this move as threatening the security of the Ikhwan faith and a further encroachment of Western civilisation.

By the end of 1927, the RAF units in Iraq Command consisted of five flying squadrons and seven sections of armoured cars. The sections had been formed from the conversion of the nine sections in the three armoured car companies, which had been disbanded on 1 April 1927. One of the armoured car sections, No 6 at Kirkuk, was earmarked for disbandment by the end of March. The overall control of the armoured car sections was again in the hands of the Armoured Car Wing HQ. This had been reconstituted on 1 April 1927, under the command of Squadron Leader Alfred Morris OBE, but by mid-year he had handed over to Squadron Leader Arthur Peck DSO MC. The sections were stationed at Basra, Kirkuk and Mosul - Nos 1, 7 and 8, respectively - and the remainder, Nos 2, 3, 4 and 5, at Hinaidi. Iraq was, in general at this time, relatively quiet, although trouble was expected in the Barzan district about 70 miles north-east of Mosul. The forces at Mosul therefore, could not be used in the south should the Ikhwan resume their activities.

Unfortunately, the warning system that had been set up in 1924 and 1925 to warn of the Ikhwan, had been dismantled after the signing of the Bahra Agreement. By this time, the Ikhwan had returned from their successful campaign against King Hussein in the Hedjaz and were full of confidence and seeking fresh conquests. The Iraq Government was determined that the construction at Busaiyah should continue. In September 1927, a party of 12 workmen accompanied by ten camel policemen, armed only with rifles, arrived at Busaiyah to construct the police post. Construction proceeded slowly, and was watched and reported on by the spies of Feisal al Duweesh, the leader of the Mutair tribe. Once completed, the post would be a considerable thorn in his side, as it would restrict the freedom of movement the Ikhwan had enjoyed previously. On the night of 5/6 November, the post was attacked by a Mutair party of about 50, and all the inhabitants, apart from one policeman, were massacred. The police, camped outside in tents, had foolishly left their rifles inside the fort. One policeman was seriously wounded but saved himself by feigning death. He escaped the slaughter, crawled into the nearby wadi, and then ran as fast as humanly possible, reaching the post at Abu Ghar some 28 miles to the north. The alarm was raised and aircraft of No 84 Squadron were summoned by wireless, but by the time they arrived, the Mutair had moved back across the border that by international agreement with Ibn Saud, the RAF was not authorised to cross.[20]

At the same time, on the morning of 7 November, No 1 Section, Armoured Car Wing, stationed at Basra, and under the command of Flying Officer 'Henry' Ford, was ordered to proceed with a wireless tender and six Armed Fords to Shaibah, travelling via Zubair. The track conditions were appalling, owing to recent rains, and they arrived having taken five hours to cover the 18 miles. Newly-arrived Pilot Officer 'Jack' Stone had remained at Basra with the three Rolls-Royce armoured

The fort and landing ground at Busaiyah from the air (Webb, RAF Habbaniya Assn).

cars.[21] Only two were serviceable and he received orders to take these cars to Shaibah by rail the next morning. He arrived at midday, and joined the remainder of the Section. Though initial orders were to proceed with haste, these were countermanded and they then waited for six days for further instructions.

At dawn on 14 November, No 1 Section left Shaibah and moved to Busaiyah, which was reached at 1700 hours. Unaware of what the situation might hold, Stone ordered the leading Rolls-Royce to drop its battle flaps and proceed ahead ready for action. Fortunately, the fort was unoccupied and showed no signs of life. He immediately prepared Lewis and Vickers gun posts and instituted a 'two hours on, four hours off', duty during the night. The Section orders were to move on to Abu Ghar, which they did the following morning 'after a rough feed', and where they remained for four more days, until joined by No 5 Section, which had travelled down from Hinaidi. One flight of No 84 Squadron, the two armoured car sections and two Victorias of No 70 Squadron were then placed under command of Squadron Leader F.J. Vincent DFC, forming a force to be known as 'Vincol'.[22]

On 18 November, with Major Corry of the Iraqi Police, and Forster, an Engineer of the Iraq Government, Stone and No 1 Section returned to Busaiyah. The first grisly task was to rebury the bodies of the policemen who had been killed in the massacre, as the jackals had scrabbled them from their shallow graves. A party of 'coolies' were flown in by Victorias to begin work on the building, while the armoured car crews set about constructing barbed-wire entanglements around the fort. Over the next few days, various important visitors arrived for inspection tours; Air Commodore Thomas Higgins, the Chief Staff Officer for Iraq Command, and a few days later Air Vice-Marshal Sir Edward Ellington, the new AOC, Iraq, accompanied by Major-General Locke of the Iraq Army, was flown-in.[23]

For the next few days, the routine for the cars was one of collecting drinking water from Abu Ghar (the Busaiyah water was nearly undrinkable, having the odour of camels, and a slimy taste, best disguised by strong tea) and provision of escorts to

An Armed Ford of No 1 Section, Armoured Car Wing operating in the Southern Desert. The Fords were useful vehicles in both the desert and mountains as their light weight meant that they could move easily and rapidly across terrain that the Rolls-Royce armoured cars found difficult (© Crown copyright. Stone, RAF Museum, Hendon).

the workers at the nearby quarry. Pilot Officer Stone was also called on to deal with the tensions arising between the workmen. He describes as follows:

> On Wednesday a 'coolie' and a bricklayer entered into a somewhat heated discussion and eventually the bricklayer dealt the 'coolie' a blow on the head with a brick. This annoyed the 'coolie' and a noisy fight commenced. Hearing the noise, I went out and intervened and distributed numerous 'coup-de-pieds' amongst the 'coolies' and bricklayers and they fled like hunted foxes back to their various jobs. The interpreter told them that if they did not work more quickly, the Armoured Cars would go away and leave them to the mercy of the Ikhwan. This made them work frantically hard and they then sang a song of praise to the Sahib (c'est moi; 'Henry' and Bill had gone out shooting) and his Armoured Cars for protecting them, and a song of curse and hate for the Ikhwan. Rations, mail etc. were flown out to us by 84 Squadron and machines (Victorias) attached to 84 about five times a week [24]

A practice stand-to alarm was held that Friday at 2300 hours. Stone continues:

> We...let off a few rounds from all the Lewis and Vickers. Unfortunately, the native police patrols out in the desert had not been warned and one patrol was within earshot. Hearing about 20 Lewis and Vickers banging away, they immediately imagined that the Ikhwan had succeeded in launching a surprise attack. The three men fled for their lives to a tribe about 30 or 40 miles north of Busaiyah, and reported the Ikhwan were attacking. The report drifted through to Abu Ghar, but we had already wirelessed Abu Ghar about the practice. The police were informed of the fallacy of their report and they returned to Busaiyah two days later, and were placed under

close arrest for fleeing (as they thought) in the face of the enemy. Finally, they received two months imprisonment.[25]

The fort soon boasted high whitewashed walls. It rose on a small gravel eminence where, from the sentries' post on the four corners of the roof, one could see for many miles across the gravel wilderness in all directions. The room allotted as an office and mess to the RAF officers of the flight or section that was in residence, was ill-lit, stuffy and full of flies, although it was protected from the constant shimmering haze of the desert. Life at Busaiyah was made tolerable by games of dice or hunting trips, as the crews awaited the order to move off into 'the blue' to pursue a Mutair raiding party.

The following Sunday, 20 'coolies' were discharged as the fort neared completion. This coincided with the news that a 300-strong party of Mutair had raided into Kuwait and the country's ruler, Sheikh Ahmad Al Jaber Al Sabah, had repulsed the attack with an army of horsemen and commandeered cars. At his request, the RAF began reconnaissance flights over Kuwait territory.[26] Rumours also continued to come in of raiding parties moving north from the Nejed and Flying Officer 'Henry' Ford and Flight Lieutenant Bill Fenwick went out with the Armed Fords to investigate, but found nothing.

Four days later, three Ninaks, out on a reconnaissance, were fired on in the Neutral Zone, near Rukhaimiyah, by a tribe with about 100 camels and 50 tents. The aircraft returned fire and one machine was badly riddled with bullets, while the W/T operator in another was shot through the leg. 'Jack' Stone wrote in his diary:

Perhaps there is a chance for a scrap for us now. Awaiting orders.

Meanwhile, Fenwick and Ford had taken all the Rolls-Royce armoured cars and had gone on a recce down to Rukhaimiyah, leaving Stone as 'OC Fort'. He continues:

At 1600 hours two bedouin came to Busaiyah and reported an attack on their tribe at 0700 hours yesterday... near Rukhaimiyah. Many killed and attackers believed to be Ikhwan. There was great grief among the remaining 'coolies' as they had many near relatives in the tribe. I wired information out and prepared extra gun posts. The Rolls Armoureds returned after dark... having discovered no trace of raiders this side of the border.[27]

Three days later, dozens of refugees of the Ghalidh shepherds began drifting in, in dreadful condition and were a pitiful sight. They had been attacked by a large Ikhwan raiding party and had walked from Rukhaimiyah, across the desert, for three to four days. Many were footsore and some were wounded. Again, as the raid had occurred so close to the frontier, by the time news had arrived, the raiders were back in the Nejed. Two days later, a platoon of the Iraq Army was flown in, and with orders to hand over to them, the two Sections returned to Basra.[28] Stone describes the return journey on 19 December:

Both sections left at the crack of dawn...Ground not too solid - in fact very soft - so progress was very slow. Considerable engine trouble on the Fords retarded us. En route column was about four miles long. Six Rolls Armoureds, two Rolls W/T Tenders and ten Armed Fords. Arrived at Shaibah 1600 hours. Stopped and had some food and continued at 1730 hours. Arrived Basra at 1815 hours. Had a good tub and change and sheets to sleep between. First night for six weeks that I have been able to go to sleep without a loaded rifle and revolver beside my bed.

Finally, he noted presciently:

Feisal al Duweesh and his followers are still giving trouble with various small raids across the border and it is not easy to foresee the results of this continued raiding. It is quite possible a great deal of fighting is [likely] in the near future and that the RAF will be called upon to deal definitely and finally with these raiders.[29]

The Headquarters camp of 'Akforce' at Ur Junction. Vickers Victoria transport aircraft in the middle distance (Webb, RAF Habbaniya Assn).

Following the renewed attacks, the Iraqi tribes had been warned to withdraw towards the Euphrates behind Busaiyah to avoid raiders. However, with the pastures near the frontier providing good grazing for their animals, they were reluctant to move. Pamphlets were dropped on the tribes telling them that they must move within ten days, or be assumed to be hostile. There was a significant failing in this system as it assumed that the tribesmen could read and that they had all received the warning in the pamphlet. It was also now apparent that Ibn Saud could no longer guarantee the control of his tribes, and the Iraq Government had to do all it could to protect its own citizens.

On 14 December, permission had been received from the British Government that the RAF could pursue any Ikhwan parties across the frontier, if they were known to have carried out a raid. Ibn Saud was informed of the intention of the RAF to take direct air action against the tribes beyond the Nejed border and that the main object was to help him control Feisal al Duweesh.

On 8 January 1928, an advanced headquarters, known as 'Akforce' was set up at Ur Junction, close to Abraham's old city, Ur of the Chaldees, under Air Commodore Thomas Higgins, the Chief Staff Officer for Iraq Command (Map 11, p. 108). His force was distributed in four groups:

> 'Buscol' at Busaiyah, under the command of Squadron Leader H.A. Whistler DSO AFC, with nine aircraft of No 55 Squadron, and two sections of Armoured Car Wing;
> 'Nucol' at Sulman, under the command of Squadron Leader F.J. Vincent DFC, with nine aircraft of No 84 Squadron, and two sections of Armoured Car Wing;
> A Supply Column called 'Supcol', under the command of Wing Commander H.R. Nicholl OBE, with No 70 Squadron at Ur and an MT column at Samawah.
> Shaibah Details, under the command of Squadron Leader A.H. Peck DSO MC, the remainders of Nos 55 and 84 Squadrons, with the reserves for the Armoured Car Wing at Basra.[30]

The operation was planned in three phases. The first phase, the warning and driving back of the tribes from the Iraq-Nejed border and Kuwait, would be followed by the second phase, operations against the raiding parties, and finally, the third phase in February would be to watch and ward, up to and including the period of the Jeddah conference, where negotiations were continuing between King Abd al Aziz Ibn Saud and the British Government as to how to manage the problems on the Nejed border.[31]

The plan was to operate the aircraft and armoured cars from advanced operating bases in the desert at Busaiyah and Sulman, 100 miles to the west of Ur. Temporary operating bases would be pushed out further and used for a few days, subject to supply of potable water, and the unpredictable and inclement weather conditions. Once the armoured cars reached the outposts, the aircraft would be sent out. The forward posts would be supplied by the aircraft of No 70 Squadron. Squadron Leader Godsave, Officer Commanding No 4 Armoured Car Company and later Second-in-Command of Armoured Car Wing described their work as follows:

> To another Squadron, No 70 (Bombing) Squadron was due our very existence. Our food, our fuel, and sometimes our water, was transported in the big 'Victoria' troop-carrying aircraft, and the tale of their efficiency is told in the fact that wherever we were in the desert, they always found us and in all the years the wanderers in the wilderness never went short of so much as a bottle of beer.
>   Did we need a new gear box for a car, did an aeroplane desire a new engine; or rations or our mail from home, had we a man injured or sick, were we sitting in a wadi on the frontier, a speck in the open plains, we had but to ask, and 'Seventy' would come to aid us...[32]

The RAF could also rely on the additional support of the Iraq Army, though still in its embryonic stages, and a few camel police who operated under the civil authorities, but were an essential part of the intelligence gathering apparatus.

Map 12

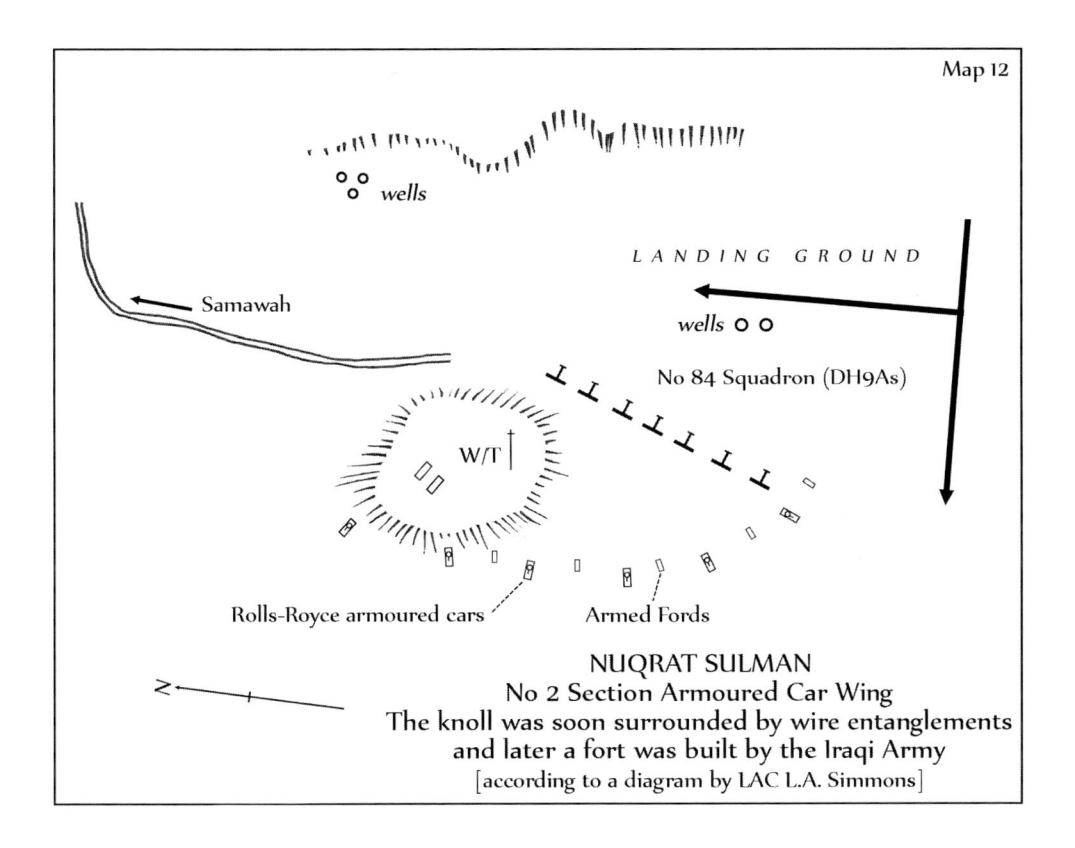

NUQRAT SULMAN
No 2 Section Armoured Car Wing
The knoll was soon surrounded by wire entanglements
and later a fort was built by the Iraqi Army
[according to a diagram by LAC L.A. Simmons]

The operations began with high winds and heavy rain showers. The armoured car component of 'Nucol' was made up with Nos 2 and 4 Sections. The two sections were stationed at Hinaidi, and on 7 January, were ordered to load their vehicles onto a train at Baghdad West Station. LAC L.A. Simmons was a driver with No 2 Section and had no idea where the train was headed or what was going to happen.

Rolls-Royce armoured cars and tenders stand watch over the fort at Nuqrat Sulman (© Crown copyright. Godsave, RAF Regiment Museum).

The airmen arrived in a frozen state early the next morning at Ur Junction, having spent all night with the cars on the open rail trucks. Here they met the convoy of about 20 Ford one-tonners, from the RAF MT pool at Baghdad, that were loaded up with petrol, and the Sections were ordered to escort them to Nuqrat Sulman. The column escort was composed of six Rolls-Royce armoured cars, two Rolls-Royce W/T tenders and eight Armed Fords. They also had a Hucks Starter travelling with them from No 55 Squadron, for use by the squadrons 'in the blue'.[33] The Sections were divided among the lengthy convoy. The first part of the journey was across salt marsh, and then a belt of soft sand 15-18 miles in depth, with the latter parts being traversed in low or second gear. Sulman was reached the next day, where they found the Ninaks of No 84 Squadron had already landed. Camp was pitched on the site where, a few months later, a fort was to be built. The petrol was unloaded and the Fords set off back to Samawah (Map 12, p. 115).

On 18 January, some of the armoured cars went out to Uqubbah on the Nejed border. This was a halting place for large caravans en route to Mecca. Simmons describes events after four days there:

> ...while on a local reconnaissance, we came to the edge of a long valley in which we sighted tents and many head of camel. Number 84 Squadron were immediately informed by our W/T and two DH9As were sent to bomb. It was impossible to get the cars into the valley owing to the soft sand and the range was too long for our Vickers...

On 24 January, we returned to Sulman, the opinion apparently being

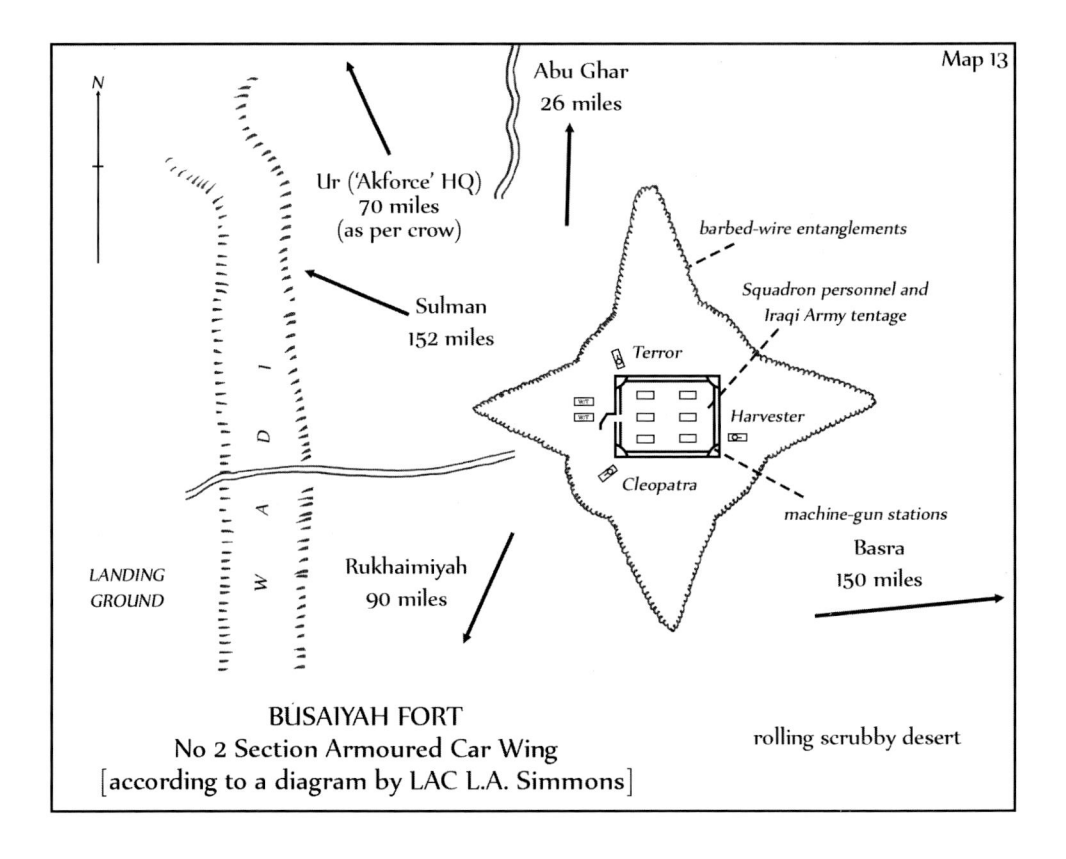

BUSAIYAH FORT
No 2 Section Armoured Car Wing
[according to a diagram by LAC L.A. Simmons]

that we were of insufficient strength to remain in this advanced position. The chief danger lay in being attacked at night. During this time, and all the previous weeks, daily seven hour recces were being performed by the aircraft... Many hundreds of rounds begin expended, and bombs being dropped, chiefly as a warning to tribes, who had been given notice to move south by means of pamphlets dropped from planes...[34]

Following their return to Sulman, the Iraq Army began to arrive and they set up barbed-wire entanglements and laid the foundation for the new fort. While the cars were carrying out reconnaissances, the Camel Police were also going out daily into the desert, bringing in Ikhwan spies who proved very useful. The landing ground gave No 84 Squadron some hard times, due to the soft sand and the many mounds and wells scattered around it, with eight Ninaks being written off in two months. Simmons continues:

During the latter end of January and beginning of February, we had much rain and squally weather. On one occasion, we in the Armoureds, woke to find the gun pits flooded and their crews, with their kits, in fact everything, under water. Fortunately, the following few days were fine so the blankets could be dried. We got our warmth and cooking by means of four gallon tins of petrol, 'aviation', at that. A certain amount of wood was flown out each day in Vickers Victorias and Vernons. But this didn't go far. There was rum ration issued as well but this, at first anyway, tasted like coach varnish and no one cared for it (except a few!).[35]

During early February, the cars went out to investigate the water sources near Nahadain and Jidrain, but these were dry, and the sites were deemed unsuitable as advanced landing grounds. On 20 February, No 2 Section was ordered to move down to Busaiyah while No 4 Section was sent to Shebicha, north-west of Sulman, where another landing ground had been established and there were plans for another fort.

At Busaiyah, No 2 Section relieved Nos 1 and 5 Sections, as they had orders to move south into the Neutral Zone (Map 13, p. 116). Number 2 Section formed a camp on the opposite side of the wadi to the fort, each car having its own Lewis gun emplacement. The camp provided close protection to the aircraft on the landing ground, particularly against night attack. Friendly tribes had also moved in under the protection of the fort and thousands of animals had to be watered each day. The cars continued their reconnaissance and surveyed large tracts of hitherto unmapped desert. Conditions were difficult and cars were often caught in soft sand and had to be dug out or manhandled by all men available.

The Iraq Army, now in residence at Busaiyah, fully manned the machine-gun posts on the fort. Very lights were fired as warning of raids and inevitably there were false alarms. Simmons continues:

Several false alarms came about, which every time came off as per schedule. The one snag being the rifle grenades [of the Iraq Army] which either failed to explode or just trickled from the rifles over the fort walls! The Armoureds [HMACs *Terror*, *Harvester* and *Cleopatra*] were outside [under the walls] and one never knew whether one was going to sit down beside me!!!

In the last few weeks we had been hoping for a section to come and relieve us. The clothing on all ranks was starting to show signs of falling off their backs, and very few had any seats in their pants! On 22 March [one and half months since leaving Hinaidi] a Sergeant who had been sent to Baghdad to get certain men's kits returned and we got something to wear.[36]

No 1 Section had spent a 'jolly and enjoyable' Christmas and New Year at Basra, with No 5 Section as guests. On 5 January 1928 however, they received orders for both sections to proceed to Shaibah and await further orders, as the Mutair continued their raiding (Map 11, p. 108). Squadron Leader Elliot Godsave, described the journey of the armoured cars to Busaiyah:

A supply column of 140 assorted vehicles assembled to move 2000 gallons of fuel from Basra to Busaiyah (© Crown copyright. Godsave, RAF Regiment Museum).

Busaiyah lies 140 miles west of Basra in the stony gravel wastes of Al Haniyah. The armoured car route runs south west from Basra to the walled town of Zubair which stands on the ruins of ancient Bussorah, once the home of Sinbad [the] Sailor. Today Zubair is a desert staging post from where the caravans depart for Kuwait, as Shamiyah and the Nejed. From here the track drops down through the cultivation and date plantations... to Shaibah... From the edge of the cultivation the track runs like a ribbon into the open desert on a heading of 225°. Away to the left rises the Jebel Sanam, a curious hump of limestone which is visible for nearly 50 miles and marks the frontier with Kuwait.

The monotony of the open plain is broken by clumps of sidr bush where the Wadi Hulaibah runs across the track, but thereafter the desert reverts to its featureless state until the delta of the Wadi al Batin is reached. The little rounded hill, Jarishan, marks the western bank of the Batin and is the junction for the armoured car tracks: west for Busaiyah and south for al Batin and the frontier with the Nejed (here, at Jarishan, was an arrow, and writing in the sand, for all who travelled to read: on one side of the arrow 'BUSAIYAH', and on the other 'THIS WAY TO THE WAR'.) From Jarishan to Busaiyah the undulating scrubby desert of Al Haniyah was unbroken until six miles from the fort where a sharp descent of 50 feet led the track into the wadi from where the fort could be seen on the far side of the valley.[37]

On 10 January, the two Sections were joined at Busaiyah by the Ninaks of No 55 Squadron, thus completing 'Buscol'. Pilot Officer Stone was in charge of rationing the entire column and catering for the Officers' Mess. The tents had taken three days to arrive. They were desperately needed as the high winds and heavy rains were proving troublesome. Busaiyah was now garrisoned by half a company of Iraq Army, who lived in tents in the courtyard of the fort, while a squadron of the Desert Camel Police dwelt in camel hair tents alongside their camels outside the walls. Busaiyah was now a base for the armoured cars and an aerodrome and refuelling point for the aircraft that went out before dawn each day and spent five to seven hours scouring the waterholes and wadis of the Shamiyah Desert for raiding parties.

On 18 January, both sections were ordered down to Rukhaimiyah, in the Neutral Zone. 'Jack' Stone followed with an escort of two armed Fords for the Hucks Starter. He completed the journey in four-and-three-quarter hours, despite having to fit a new spring to one of the Fords, which broke just after leaving Busaiyah. On 21 January, after three days heavy rain the Ninaks carried out bombing raids and machine-gunning over the Nejed. On 24 January, they were ordered back to Busaiyah, with the cars remaining another day to protect a flight of Ninaks suffering engine problems. Ten days later, Stone was made Officer Commanding No 1 Section as Flying Officer 'Henry' Ford was admitted to Basra hospital with a severe case of 'Baghdad boils'.[38] He continues:

On 11 February, 2i/c of 5 Section and I took out four Armed Fords to reconnoitre for a better track to Rukhaimiyah and returned the same day having found better ground for about 50 miles.

Six days later, with offensive operations again planned from Rukhaimiyah, No 1 Section was ordered south. Accompanying them was Squadron Leader Godsave who described the early morning departure of the cars:

A white fort, a glittering canopy of stars, a cool and gentle breeze. The

The Rolls-Royce tender, HMRC Relentless, carried supplies, the radio and the important prisoners from the coming battle (© Crown copyright. Godsave, RAF Regiment Museum).

sentries yawn, and peer across the sands, down into the wadi, where bushes seem to move, and a little stretch of the imagination conjures up fantastic figures of creeping raiders. A camel in the lines grumbles, and shuffles in the sand, - a man snores and turns in restless sleep, - a lizard scuffles on the mud wall, - slight sounds which break the desert silence, and set the sentries peering forth anew into the waste.

Three o'clock. In half an hour the camp will be astir. The sentries pace around the walls noting a glimmer in the Eastern sky, - a short half hour more: the watch is finished, and the native bugler sends the crisp clear call of Reveille ringing down the wadi, and sets the fort into activity. In an incredibly short time there is a mutter then a roar, which dies into a gentle throb: the acrid smell of the exhaust fumes of engines taints the morning air: the crews are starting up their engines.

The kits are loaded up and the cars pull out into the line ahead, standing at the wire gate of the entanglements, engines throbbing, awaiting the signal to go forth into the Great Shamiyah and by moral effect, or bullet, counter the murderous schemes of the Mutair, and drive them empty handed into Nejed again.

The camels of the police are astir, for they too will be out in the desert hunting for spies and isolated parties of marauders, and visiting the grazing tribes for news, for the information which sends the columns hot foot upon a trail, comes through a network of agents, and the camel police glean much by their daily visits to the nomads' tents.

The troopers come over to look at the cars, and stand in silence, their cloaks drawn close around them for the morning air is chill. They stiffen and raise a hand in salutation, murmuring the conventional "As-salamu alaykum" - peace be upon thee - as the Commander of the column passes down the line inspecting each car, on his way to mount in the leading car. Four armoured cars, *Tigris, Eagle, Shark* and *Panther,* and two Tenders, *Rapid* and *Relentless*, all Rolls-Royces, are drawn up, and as the Commander climbs up into the turret of *Tigris*, two native troopers fling

The Ninaks of No 55 (B) Squadron and RAF armoured cars await action at the forward landing ground at Rukhaimiyah in the Neutral Zone (© Crown copyright. Godsave, RAF Regiment Museum).

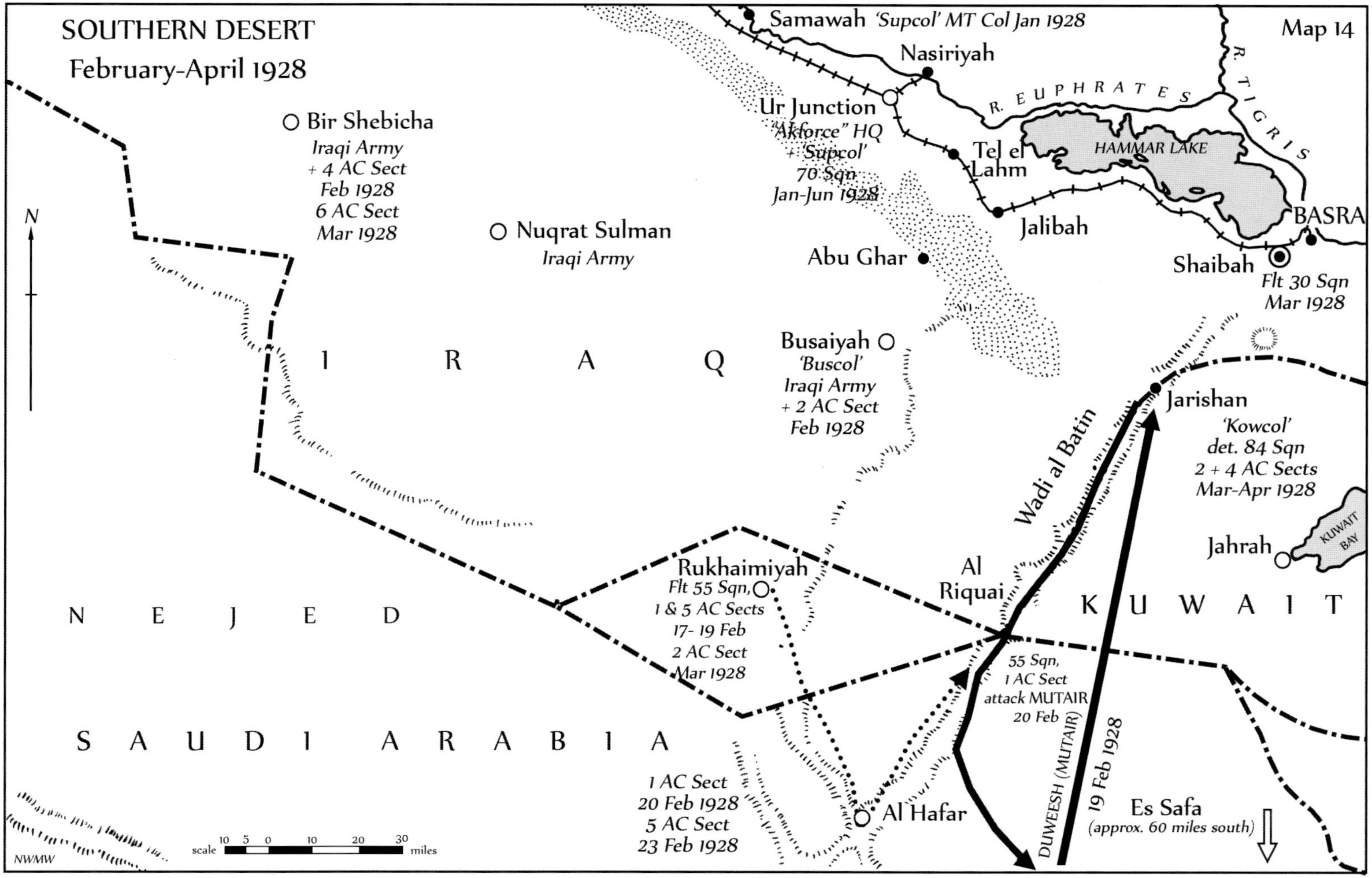
SOUTHERN DESERT
February-April 1928
Map 14
N
Bir Shebicha
Iraqi Army
+ 4 AC Sect
Feb 1928
6 AC Sect
Mar 1928
Nuqrat Sulman
Iraqi Army
Samawah 'Supcol' MT Col Jan 1928
Nasiriyah
Ur Junction
"Akforce" HQ
+ 'Supcol'
70 Sqn
Jan-Jun 1928
Tel el Lahm
Jalibah
Abu Ghar
R. EUPHRATES
R. TIGRIS
HAMMAR LAKE
BASRA
Shaibah
Flt 30 Sqn
Mar 1928
I R A Q
Busaiyah
'Buscol'
Iraqi Army
+ 2 AC Sect
Feb 1928
Jarishan
'Kowcol'
det. 84 Sqn
2 + 4 AC Sects
Mar-Apr 1928
Wadi al Batin
Jahrah
KUWAIT BAY
Rukhaimiyah
Flt 55 Sqn,
1 & 5 AC Sects
17- 19 Feb
2 AC Sect
Mar 1928
Al Riquai
K U W A I T
N E J E D
S A U D I A R A B I A
55 Sqn,
1 AC Sect
attack MUTAIR
20 Feb
DUWEESH (MUTAIR)
19 Feb 1928
Es Safa
(approx. 60 miles south)
1 AC Sect
20 Feb 1928
5 AC Sect
23 Feb 1928
Al Hafar
scale 10 5 0 10 20 30 miles
NWMW

wide the gate, and the "Go Ahead" flag breaks from the hand of the waiting Section Commander.

"All ready, Sir."

"Yes, please. Go ahead."

The flag drops and the Section Commander passes the order to the driver: each engine gives a full throated roar, for the sand at the wadi crossing is soft, and it must be rushed at a good speed in low gear, and in a tremendous cloud of dust the column moves off heading South for a well called Rukhaimiyah, the appointed rendezvous with the aircraft.[39]

After checking that Rukhaimiyah was not held by the Ikhwan, the cars had moved in, taking the opportunity to vary the usual diet of bully beef and tinned stew, by picking off a few bustards that were the only avian inhabitants around the wells (Map 14, p. 121). Three DH9As had soon arrived overhead, and landed on the plateau above the sandy basin in which the wells lay. Twelve DH9As and three Victorias were soon concentrated there in readiness for operations to the south. Meanwhile, the column commander and section leader stood on the turret of a Rolls-Royce armoured cars and scoured the desert through their glasses for signs of life or movement. Within an hour, the Ninaks refuelled and had taken off to do a sweep to the south.

Rukhaimiyah was now set up with barbed-wire entanglements and trenches, and a large aviation fuel and bomb dump. The wreckage of two DH9As provided a land mark for both pilots and car crews. While the engines had been salved and flown back to Ur in a Victoria, the fuselages remained, and these soon provided a source of firewood on the freezing desert nights. Stone describes the conditions:

Very windy weather prevailed and about three inches below the surface, the sand was just like powder. So what with no washing because of the scarcity of the water, food, lungs, ears, eyes and heads full of sand we were not exactly enjoying the heart of luxury and comfort.[40]

On 19 February, Flying Officer Ford returned from Hospital. On the same day, serious news came through that the Mutair had carried out a big raid on the Juwareen shepherds and had reached Jarishan on the Wadi al Batin, only 40 miles from Shaibah. The Ninaks went out and bombed them for three days running, and Flight Lieutenant Fenwick of No 5 Section, Flying Officer Ford and Pilot Officer Stone of No 1 Section, left with five Rolls Armoureds, a Rolls W/T tender and two Armed Fords for Al Riquai in the Nejed. Their intention was to intercept the raiders as they made their way down the Wadi Al Batin and watered at Al Riquai. The country was quite new to them, as the Armoured Cars had never crossed the border into the Nejed.

While camping at Al Hafar, they were informed that the raiders were at Al Riquai. A four-hour delay in a refuelling delivery by a Victoria, delayed their move and by the time it had arrived, darkness forced the cars to halt short of their objective. It was here they received the sad news, by W/T message, that Flying Officer Rolf Jackson of No 55 Squadron had been compelled to force land over the raiders while on a bombing run. He had successfully landed and burnt his machine and then attempted to 'beat it'. Unfortunately, he was too near the raiding party and he was shot through the head and heart. His body was recovered during a later aerial reconnaissance and returned to Basra.

The next day, the cars were alerted by the pilot of a Ninak that had landed near the column that the raiders were only 10 to 15 miles north. The Section was ordered to proceed to the north, and prepare for immediate action. Stone continues:

> About 20 minutes later one of the Armed Fords petered out so I had to remain behind with my Armoured and the other Armed Ford while repairs were effected, the remainder of the column continuing at all possible speed. Repairs were completed (carburettor trouble) in about 15 minutes and I moved off...I was sitting outside on the battle flap and told the driver to make all possible speed...to catch up the rest of the convoy before dark as the sun was now setting.

As the leading armoured cars approached they had sighted 30 camels and riders. The 'enemy in sight' flag was raised and almost immediately, 'action stations-line ahead' was signalled from the column commander's turret. Turrets were shut down, leaving just the head of the car commanders looking out to control their cars. The section leader halted with his wireless tenders, and the aerial was raised and the information passed to the aircraft.[41]

Meanwhile, HMACs *Tigris*, *Eagle* and *Shark* formed line-abreast and moved to outflank the Mutair raiders. They drove down into the wadi separating them from the camel raiders, increased speed and swept over the crest of the hill. The Mutair brought their rifles to the ready and fired. At 300 yards range, the Vickers from *Tigris* fired three short bursts, into the ground, to the left of the enemy. *Eagle* and *Shark* then joined in. The camels stampeded at the rattle of the machine guns and the roar of the engines. The raiders returned fire where they could. Suddenly, to the noise was added the roar of aero-engines and the Ninaks came roaring down out of the blue sky. Bullets spurted up dust around the panic-stricken animals. 'Jack' Stone, meanwhile, had managed to catch up with the other cars:

> After about three or four miles, I suddenly heard reports and almost immediately bullets sputtered around me on the turret. I have never before leapt off the battle flap into the turret so quickly. It was just absolute fate that it was not me being hit, but the turret both sides of me. I called both Ford drivers to abandon their Fords (they had no guns aboard for this reason) and come into the Armoured which they did with amazing celerity. We crammed five of us into the car, dropped the battle flap and speeded for action.
>
> About 500 yards ahead of us we saw the remainder of the cars in action and a few men and camels scurrying over the skyline. The ground was very bad for cars, and the sun was beginning to set, and as there is hardly any twilight in this part of the world, night clouds were quickly gathering. We succeeded in killing one man and wounding another. Neither of these two had any ammunition left and had expended all their rounds on us, the only damage being a shattered Rolls side lamp, my Rolls turret scratched a bit, several holes in both Fords and three holes in the W/T tender just near the driver's head, but no casualties.[42]

The larger part of the Mutair had fled, driven on by the aircraft. The cars made for the group surrounding their leader; their brave chieftain saw no option but to surrender. Very few of the Ikhwan had been killed or wounded, but the overwhelming firepower made it clear that further resistance would be futile. The car commander flew the 'cease fire' signal and halted his Rolls near the Sheikh. After a period of negotiation, the leader of the party and his two lieutenants were taken back as prisoners in HMRC *Relentless* to Busaiyah, escorted by HMAC *Panther*. HMACs *Shark*, *Eagle* and *Tigris*, and the aircraft, were ordered to herd the rest of the party the 20 miles to the Nejed border. Pilot Officer Stone had remained near the battlefield:

> We searched the dead Ikhwan and the wounded one for any rounds or knives... I then took the drivers in my Armoured to collect the two Fords we had to abandon, and on reaching the spot we were highly amused to discover the engine of one of the Fords still running.[43]

Returning to the other cars, they formed camp as, with the approach of darkness, pursuit was not possible over bad ground and in poor light. They refilled petrol tanks, replaced empty ammunition belts, and cleaned their guns, while the signals reporting the action were sent to Headquarters at Ur. Stone continues:

> [A] wounded man asked to be brought in near the cars, as he was afraid of being eaten by the jackals if left alone on the desert. If we complied with his request he promised us some information, so we bandaged up his wounds and brought him in near my car. He told us, that the main body was coming down south about two or three hours behind him and that they numbered about 2000 Mutair.
>
> We posted sentries, erected W/T and commenced to prepare some food. It was now quite dark and about 1830 hours. Before food was ready, one of the sentries called me out to him and asked if I could hear anything peculiar, so I went down on the ground and listened and could hear singing and shouting in the distance, which he confirmed. I immediately reported to Flight Lieutenant Fenwick and he at once silenced the camp and extinguished all lights and we 'stood to', with Lewis guns dismounted and the Vickers in the cars. The shouting came nearer and nearer, but we were compelled to adopt the defensive, as any offensive action on our part was impossible, because of the bad ground, darkness and our ignorance of Nejed country.
>
> I was on the ground with a Lewis gun near the man we had taken prisoner and I had with me a bayonet. The prisoner was told that if he made any noise or any suspicious movement, I should immediately run the bayonet through his throat and he had sense enough to remain like a corpse till daylight. Eventually the shouting appeared to be within 2 or 3 miles of us and then it began to fade away. We 'stood to', from 1845 hours till dawn the next morning but our position was not discovered and evidently about 1500 to 2000 Ikhwan had passed us during the night. We numbered 21.
>
> Next morning we effected W/T communications with Base HQ and we were ordered to remain where we were and await further orders, thus losing the chance of chasing down south after any straggling raiders. At 1200 hours we were ordered to proceed south. In the meantime we had gleaned considerable useful information from our prisoner, so we fed him well, so well in fact that he said if he had known how well the English would treat

him, he would never have fired on us (large pinch of salt?).[44]

The prisoner had told them that the raiders would reach Es Safa in three days' time and share out their loot. Es Safa was surrounded by a sand belt and thus the cars would not be able to reach it but the aircraft could. The cars moved south and were met by a Victoria which delivered rations, petrol, water and last week's mail. They handed over their wounded prisoner, who was flown back to HQ at Ur.

Three days later, on the morning of 24 February, 12 Ninaks, with one 112-lb bomb and eight 20-lb bombs on each machine, and three Victorias with 520-lb and 20-lb bombs passed over them en route for Es Safa. Should it be needed, a refuelling base for the aircraft was established at Al Hafar on 23 February, and No 5 Section was sent to guard it. The aircraft had concentrated the previous day at Rukhaimiyah under the protection of No 2 Section. At 1300 hours they returned, and the W/T soon reported that despite strong winds, they had successfully located the raiders and bombed two concentrations of the tribes. Half the formation had dealt with a group of camels and men located around the mud fort and wells at Es Safa, while the remainder hit another target 20 miles north. After eight days out the column returned to Busaiyah and the crews cleaned themselves up. Two days later, Nos 1 and 5 Sections were ordered to return to Basra where they formed the Armoured Car Reserve.

After two-and-a-half months in the desert, LAC Simmons and No 2 Section had also been told they could move to Basra once the relieving section arrived. After scanning the horizon their wishes were realised and the section arrived late in the day; the next morning, No 2 Section departed from Busaiyah. Considerably cheered, they were looking forward to a period of rest and many had already planned what they would do when they got back to civilisation. To their chagrin, the stay in Basra would be short-lived.[45]

Notes

1. J.B. Glubb, *War in the Desert: An RAF Frontier Campaign* (London: Hodder & Stoughton, 1956), p. 10.
2. G.E. Godsave, *Tales of the Tin Trams* (RAF Regiment Museum Archives: Unpublished manuscript).
3. AIR 5/838 *Monthly War Diary for No 3 Armoured Car Company, January 1923-December 1924*.
4. AIR 5/1254 *Operations: Iraq Chapters 14 to 25 January 1924-December 1928, Iraq Command Report, April 1924-November 1926*.
5. When the RAF had assumed responsibility for Iraq, a number of Special Service Officers, known as SSOs, had been appointed. Each one had to learn Arabic and was assigned a different portion of the country and, should an uprising occur in his area, it was his responsibility to familiarise himself with the situation and conditions operating on the ground. He reported to Air Staff Intelligence staff in Baghdad. It was the SSO's job to lead in the aircraft, and point out to the pilots the village or encampment which had caused the trouble, and identify friendly villages.
6. Air Chief Marshal Sir Arthur Murray Longmore GCB DSO (b. Australia, 1885–1970). Later AOC Middle East 1940-1941.
7. AIR 5/839 *Monthly War Diary for No 4 Armoured Car Company, January 1923-December 1924*.
8. AIR 5/838 *Monthly War Diary for No 3 Armoured Car Company*.

9 A. Longmore, *From Sea to Sky: Memoirs 1910-1945* (London: Geoffrey Bles, 1946), p. 120.
10 AIR 5/839 *Monthly War Diary for No 4 Armoured Car Company*.
11 Glubb, *War in the Desert*, pp. 62-63.
12 AIR 5/838 *Monthly War Diary for No 3 Armoured Car Company*.
13 *Ibid*.
14 Although most of the Special Service Officers were from the RAF, the one who gained notoriety in the Middle East was Captain John Bagot Glubb MC, late Royal Engineers. He would go on to great fame as the commander of the Iraq Southern Desert Patrol, and then the leader of the Arab Legion of Jordan as Glubb Pasha.
15 J.B. Glubb, *Arabian Adventures: Ten Years of Joyful Service* (London: Cassell, 1978), pp. 137-138. Glubb spent two days arranging the evacuation of the women and female children by train to Nasiriyah and Samawah. Here they were taken in among the settled villages and fed. Glubb wrote 'The ever-tender Arab humanity will always take pity on the poor and the destitute, and admit them without question or hesitation into their tents and houses.
16 AIR 5/1254 *Operations: Iraq*.
17 Glubb, *Arabian Adventures*, pp. 33. In December 1923, Captain John Glubb was appointed as the SSO for the Muntifiq Division, which covered a large part of the Southern Desert and the Lower Euphrates.
18 In 1927 No 8 Squadron was sent to Aden and No 45 Squadron moved to Egypt.
19 J.A.S. Cox RNAS/RAF, *Photographic Album and Diary*, RAF Regiment Museum Archives, WO 372/8/171926 *Medal Card*, F.H.W. Guard and personal correspondence. Squadron Leader Guard's life had been, to say the least, eventful and diverse. Born in 1889, he had travelled to Canada as a young man and been a fruit grower and the manager of a refrigeration company. Returning to the United Kingdom he worked for *The Times* but fell in with bad company. He then found employment with the Sierra Leone Railways and on the outbreak of the Great War obtained a commission in the West African Field Force. Invalided home from West Africa he then served as Commanding Officer of 15th Battalion, Royal Scots on the Western Front where he earned a DSO, and was gassed. In one action he personally prevented the rout of his battalion, using appeals and threats, when they were shelled by their own guns, thus preventing a break in the Division line. In early 1918 he went to North Russia, and fought against the Bolsheviks, where he commanded 'Force A' on the Vologda Railway, on one occasion enlisted the assistance of a detachment of Cossacks. He was subsequently awarded the CMG, but again invalided home. His departure was considered a great loss for a 'born guerrilla leader'. In October 1920 he became a Company Commander in the Auxiliary Division of the Royal Irish Constabulary and rose to become second-in-command of the Division. On the formation of the Irish Free State he transferred to the RAF, and in 1922 assumed command of No 3 Armoured Car Company. While serving in Iraq he also qualified for his 'Wings' on Bristol Fighters, and was recommended for advanced flying training. Following his death, Air Marshal Sir John Salmond wrote in a letter of condolence, 'He did great work in the East with his Armoured Car Company, which he infused with his own fine spirit and energy'. A newsprint photograph of Frederick Guard is present in the Diary of Corporal Cox with the simple inscription 'one of the best'.
20 R.J. Stone, *Trouble with the Akhwan Tribes in 1927* (Short manuscript written 22 March 1928). In their attack the Mutair had also killed the wife of one of the policemen who had been visiting her husband, bringing with her their baby. The sleeping baby had been spared, or overlooked during the massacre, and it was with some surprise that it was found alive. Being trained in matters aeronautical and not in child-rearing the two pilots of No 84 Squadron nearly succeeded in killing the baby. The baby was crying, so one of the pilots, deciding it must be hungry, produced a tin of condensed milk and with the baby held by the other pilot, poured the contents of the tin down the child's throat. Luckily the doctor noticed this in time and accused the pilots of attempted homicide for using such

concentrated stuff on a baby. The officer administering the milk, then proceeded to pour water down the child's throat with the intention of diluting the concentrated milk. The child survived this episode and Squadron Leader Vincent, the Squadron Commanding Officer, flew the baby back to Shaibah in his Ninak. It was then sent up to Nasiriyah to relatives. The wounded policeman was strapped to the wing of one of the Ninaks after receiving medical attention at Abu Ghar and was flown back to Shaibah for surgical treatment and later returned to normal health and strength.

21 Pilot Officer Reginald J. Stone, *Trouble with the Akhwan Tribes in 1927*, document provided by P. Stone. Stone had qualified as a pilot, but shortly after had a nasty motorbike accident and was concussed badly. He was told he could not continue a flying career and so went to RAF armoured cars for the rest of his initial engagement. He met his wife-to-be in Basra, where she was a Nursing Sister in the Hospital. He resigned his commission in 1930, but returned to the RAF during the Second World War, when he was stationed in the Orkneys, various other parts of the United Kingdom and in Naples. His final posting was as Commanding Officer of RAF Kenley, before his 'demob' at the end of the war.
22 R.J. Stone, *Trouble with the Akhwan Tribes*.
23 Air Commodore Thomas C.R. Higgins CB CMG (1880-1953). Higgins served in the RAF Regiment during the Second World War.
24 R.J. Stone, *Trouble with the Akhwan Tribes*.
25 *Ibid.*
26 Sheikh Ahmad al Jaber al Sabah KCIE KCSI (1885–1950). AIR 5/1254 *Operations: Iraq. Report on situation on Iraq-Nejd borders, November 1927-May 1928*.
27 R.J. Stone, *Trouble with the Akhwan Tribes*.
28 AIR 10/1839 *Operations carried out in the Southern Desert in connection with the Iraq-Najd Borders, November 1927-May 1928*. With the establishment of the post at Busaiyah, that at Abu Ghar was closed down. The fort was in a bad state of repair and considered no longer necessary.
29 R.J. Stone, *Trouble with the Akhwan Tribes*.
30 AIR 10/1839 *Operations carried out in the Southern Desert*, p. 8.
31 *Ibid.*, pp. 9-17.
32 G.E. Godsave, *Tales of the Tin Trams*.
33 The Hucks Starter was a light truck that had a motor-driven starter to be used to start piston engine aircraft, thus replacing the need for ground crew to spin the propeller by hand.
34 L.A. Simmons, *Private Papers 7284* (London: IWM Document Archive, n.d.).
35 *Ibid.*
36 *Ibid.*
37 G.E. Godsave, *Tales of the Tin Trams*.
38 'Baghdad Boils' or Leishmaniasis is a skin disease with symptoms of eruptions on the skin caused by infection with a parasite that lives in the gut of sand flies. Although not painful, the lesions, about 30 mm across, can eventually leave permanent, burn-like scarring.
39 G.E. Godsave, *Tales of the Tin Trams*.
40 R.J. Stone, *Trouble with the Akhwan Tribes*.
41 *Ibid.*
42 *Ibid.*
43 *Ibid.*
44 *Ibid.*
45 L.A. Simmons, *Private Papers 7284*.

Chapter Seven

War in the Southern Desert 1929-1930

"When aircraft were operating from temporary advanced bases in the desert, the only protection it was possible to provide for them was that given by the armoured car sections, plus what they could provide for themselves"
Air Vice-Marshal Sir Edward Ellington, AOC Iraq[1]

During the last week of February 1928, Ibn Saud had sent a message to the Sheikh of Kuwait, to the effect that Feisal al Duweesh and his Mutair tribe were completely out of control. Many of the Ikhwan were now joining him in a holy war against all non-Ikhwan. This had the potential to create a force of up to 50,000 men and had implications not only for the Southern Desert, but western Iraq and eastern Transjordan. A Flight of No 30 Squadron was sent down from Kirkuk to Shaibah and No 6 Section at Kirkuk moved to Basra. A new section of cars was formed at Hinaidi from the reserve vehicles and was ready by early March. In late March, No 6 Section was sent out to Lussuf and Shebicha to protect and stabilise the tribespeople of the Amarat of Mahrut Beg, who had shown great loyalty to the Government.[2]

Furthermore, with the threat posed by the Ikhwan to Kuwait, it had been decided to send a detachment of RAF armoured cars and aircraft to assist in repelling the Ikhwan raiders. The Sheikh of Kuwait had done exceptionally well in repelling the invaders, with a combination of a camel-mounted force and by mustering every taxi and automobile he could find. He went out and fought the Ikhwan in the open desert, though this cost him heavily, including the loss of one of his sons in the action. He appealed for assistance from the British Government, and thus it was that two sections of armoured cars and a flight of Ninaks were despatched to Kuwait under the name of 'Kowcol'. The Royal Navy had also become involved. The light cruiser, HMS *Emerald*, and the sloops, HMS *Crocus* and HMS *Lupin* were anchored offshore in Kuwait Bay, and had landed Royal Marines and Naval parties to defend the town.

LAC Simmons and his section, No 2, had enjoyed their rest for only three days before it was quickly terminated and they were ordered to move to Kuwait, to reinforce No 4 Section and Ninaks of No 84 Squadron. Reports from the Camel

The RAF armoured cars move south to Kuwait (© Crown copyright. Godsave, RAF Regiment Museum).

Police placed the Ikhwan at Al Hafar on the Wadi al Batin (Map 14, p. 121 and Map 15, p. 135). The day after their arrival, the two sections were despatched on a reconnaissance of the Al Hafar-Hadiqa area. LAC Simmons describes the move to Kuwait and the problems being faced with constant operational demands:

> Certain cars needed repairs - in fact all cars needed attention and that put the tin hat on any leave that they would have given us. The various jobs were rushed through and on March 30 we went to Kuwait. The five Armed Fords went in the afternoon accompanied by W/T Tender *Rover* and the armoureds left at sunset. During the night, HMAC *Terror* broke a spring bracket and could not proceed until another one had been obtained from Basra. W/T was quickly put up and communication established... a new bracket was brought out, reaching the stranded car at 0400 hours the next morning. Meanwhile, the rest of the column reached Kuwait at 2200 hours.
>
> Here again we expected at least a day to get settled, but not so. As soon as *Terror* arrived and had filled up with petrol and oil we left for Al Hafar.
>
> This day proved to be one of the hardest during the whole time I was out. Before striking inland, we had to follow the Basra track for a matter of ten miles. The road - it could hardly be called that - lay across a salt marsh along the coast. Last night by sheer luck we came along it without getting bogged, but today we were not at all lucky [and one of the Rolls was bogged and had to be dug out].
>
> After an hour and ten minutes of real hard work, we got moving again, during which time another car had tried to get me out and had gone in herself. This was quite a mild affair compared with what was to come later.
>
> Presently, we came to the walled village of Jahrah which stands at the foot of the range of hills that go inland. We stopped to have a short break, principally to form convoy again as we had been broken up during the passage of the salt marsh. Here our troubles began for there is a sand belt,

approximately 10 miles in depth, and as the surrounding country had not been surveyed for a route to cross this, there was nothing to do but try it. We carried rolls of close-mesh wire-netting to use on the soft patches but even these failed to save the armoured sinking in.

By five in the evening we had only covered 14 miles but had just come to hard country again and it was decided to camp for the night. It had been usual in ordinary circumstances to make camp in 'star' formation, but now that we had news that the Ikhwan was in the vicinity, a camp of a different nature had to be made so as to present a stronger front in case of night attack (the section was drawn up so that they could move off immediately in case of necessity with the W/T tenders in the centre).

During the night, the heaviest thunderstorm came up, that I had experienced (of course the wireless was useless and gave the wireless operator time off). It necessitated moving the cars from their close order in case of being struck and the heavy rain made it all beastly uncomfortable for the crews (each car carried a large tarpaulin so we did not get a wetting). However, it lasted a short time and we were able to get settled again to sleep before moving at 'crack o dawn'.[3]

The cars reached Al Riquai on 1 April and prepared a landing ground for the Ninaks of Nos 55 and 84 Squadron. Although the enemy were known to be about, a series of reconnaissances had failed to locate them as the Ikhwan had moved far south to prepare for the attack on Kuwait. The Section therefore, returned to Kuwait City to find it being fortified with Vickers machine-gun posts and Pom-Pom emplacements and barbed wire, with HMS *Lupin* lying offshore to provide heavy support. Despite the preparations, and perhaps because of them, the enemy never came.

During May, the hot weather began and the wells dried up and the lack of water supplies made movement across the desert by both sides more difficult. The Ikhwan returned south of the border to more favourable country. All Government forces were withdrawn from Busaiyah, Sulman and Kuwait, Ur was closed down and, on 3 June, 'Akforce' ceased to exist. A decisive blow had not been struck, but the RAF had held off the raiders until the Jeddah conference could address the Ikhwan problem. In late April, Ibn Saud had agreed to do his best to restrain the tribes from further raiding; however, a new complexity had arisen. The Ikhwan had been the spearhead of Ibn Saud's army, but with their recent successes in the Hedjaz they were now threatening his own throne. Ibn Saud did not want to fight Britain, but the repeated incursions by the Ikhwan increased this possibility. He therefore had a delicate balance between bringing the Ikhwan to heel, while avoiding a civil war.

As the winter approached in late 1928, heavy rains fell and the pasture grew. The Iraq shepherds moved out into the desert and the spectre of the Ikhwan began to reassert itself. The problem had still not been resolved at a political level, and the winter of 1928/29 was a period of unrelenting activity for the Armoured Car sections. The Ninaks would go up in search of raiders and the forward posts in the desert - Busaiyah, Sulman and Shebicha - were re-established as landing grounds, while the Iraq Army detachments at the outposts were reinforced. To assist with this deployment, the RAF armoured car crews helped train a Motor Machine-Gun Company of the Iraq Army that would strengthen one of the outposts. One or more of the platoons from this Iraqi Company was out with the tribes from November 1928 until April 1929. Captain Glubb was given permission to form the Southern

Desert Camel Corps, partly on camels, partly on motor vehicles armed with machine-guns. They patrolled out in front of the tribes and if attacked, concentrated to drive off the aggressors.

By November 1928, the Mutair, Ataiba and Ajman rebel tribes of the Ikhwan had declared their intention to resume raiding, despite the request of Ibn Saud not to do so. As the rumour of raids spread in late December, No 1 Section went off down the Wadi al Batin to investigate, while No 2 Section was sent off to Busaiyah. Meanwhile, No 3 Section was ordered out to the north-west, to Lussuf and Nukhaib, to reinforce No 4 Section. This latter section had been sent to reassure the Amarat tribe and to establish an advanced base for operations by No 55 Squadron. The leader of the Amarat, Mahrut Beg, though leading a numerically superior force, was concerned as to how his tribesmen would fare against the Ikhwan. Furthermore, these incursions could threaten the Trans-Desert Route from Baghdad to Amman.

On 3 January, the AOC, Iraq, Air Vice-Marshal Sir Edward Ellington KCB CMG CBE, was given sole responsibility for civil and military forces in the 'Desert Area', as defined by a line drawn south and west through Rutbah-Karbala-Basra.[4] To complicate matters, the British Government, in a concession to Ibn Saud, decreed that RAF aircraft could not patrol closer than 20 miles from the frontier. Although appearing sound at the political level, this decision complicated matters for those in the air and on the ground.[5]

A front, some 600 miles in length from Western Iraq to the Persian Gulf, was threatened by Ikhwan raids. However, only on one occasion, on 19 December 1928, did an Ikhwan party from the Mutair of Ibn Ali Ashwan violate the Iraqi territory. They were immediately attacked from the air and fled before any damage was done, although the raiders lost a few camelmen, including the nephew of their leader. This had an immediate and positive deterrent effect, as two other raiding parties that were moving separately towards the frontier turned and headed back on hearing of the fate of the others.

On 4 January 1929, No 5 Section at Mosul was moved south where it relieved No 4 Section at the Iraqi Army post at Nukhaib. For the next five months, Nos 3, 4 and 5 Sections, together with No 30 Squadron, dealt with matters around Karbala and Nukhaib, while further south, Nos 1, 2 and 6 Sections and Nos 55 and 84 Squadrons operated from Busaiyah and Sulman.

From early-on in the campaign, Captain Glubb was critical of the performance of the RAF senior command. Glubb put this down to the unfamiliarity of the RAF with the desert and that the command of operations was exercised from an 'office chair in Baghdad'.[6] He spoke highly of the RAF pilots with whom he had frequent contact, and indeed flew with them on a regular basis. He, however, conceded that he should have spent more time in Baghdad establishing closer working relationships with the RAF staff officers. In his memoirs he was also highly critical of the role played by the RAF Armoured Cars in the struggle against the Ikhwan, and in particular, in the fighting around Busaiyah in 1927. His case is made using an anecdote from 1924; some six years before the Ikhwan were defeated. He wrote:

> At the same time, in December 1924, a detachment of RAF armoured cars was sent to carry out a reconnaissance in the desert. This operation might have been useful as a training exercise in desert driving, but it was not linked in any way with the general defensive situation. The cars nowhere approached within 70 miles of the frontier. That is to say they did not

approach within the danger area. In the middle of December they returned to Baghdad in order to be back in their barracks in time for Christmas.

Moreover the use of British armoured cars in the desert was rendered difficult by the high standard of physical comfort to which the men were considered to be entitled. The whole column, for example, had to make a long halt at midday in order to cook a hot meat meal. At the same time, the necessity for the daily issue of fresh meat and bread required the supply of rations by air, involving a prohibitive amount of flying.

The raiding season was about to begin and the Iraqi shepherds were already far out in the desert. Aircraft, even if they could ever overtake raiders, could only inflict light casualties on the scattered camel riders. But if armoured cars could overtake them on the ground they might inflict on them a defeat which could cure them of raiding forever. Armoured cars were, therefore, the answer to our problem but to me in my enthusiasm they appeared only half-hearted in their operations.[7]

It is indeed true that there were a relatively limited number of occasions when the RAF armoured cars closed with the Ikhwan. A number of factors led to these criticisms, which require a response. Although able to move rapidly across desert with good 'going', the deserts of Iraq were not all hard sand, but could be covered with rock, salt marsh or drifts of soft sand and rapid travel was often difficult. Glubb himself noted in his memoirs, that: 'The armoured cars from Busaiyah would probably not have arrived for four or five hours, the heavy vehicles moving slowly in the soft shrub covered desert... but had we won or lost, the RAF aircraft certainly, and the armoured cars possibly, would have overtaken the Ikhwan and inflicted casualties.'[8] Considerable use was made of the lighter Armed Fords to seek out the best paths for the heavier armoured cars. The tactical direction of the cars onto the raiding parties was difficult given these problems, the cars and crews were, and of course dependent on supplies of petrol, parts, water and rations to keep them going.

It is somewhat harsh and perhaps partisan (albeit unsurprising from such a junior, yet influential, officer), that Glubb chose to use a training reconnaissance from December 1924 as an example of the relative inefficiency of the armoured cars, when he was to be involved with them for nearly six years. This example belittled the sterling efforts of the RAF armoured cars on numerous occasions when they had sallied forth to deal with incursions by the raiders. The date corresponds to the arrival of first replacement crews from the United Kingdom, following the completion of the first two-year tour in Iraq. The operation Glubb refers in 1924 was a familiarisation reconnaissance for new car crews and should not have been taken as typical. This indeed serves to denigrate the hundreds of thousands of miles covered by the cars in Southern Desert over the six-year campaign. It is clear from reading the accounts of the RAF armoured car crews that their life was certainly not one of 'luxury and roast dinners at lunchtime'. The car crews would have been dealt with in a similar fashion to the pilots and aircrew, with regard to rationing and supplies, and of whom Glubb speaks with great admiration.

The RAF armoured cars had a number of roles, of which offensive operations was one. They also had responsibility for defence of the aerodromes and advanced landing grounds where they provided a safe haven for the aircraft, what the RAF Iraq Command considered their primary striking force. On the matter of closing with the enemy, although possessing great firepower, this would be virtually useless at night

An armoured car crew have a brew-up at the end of the day (© Crown copyright. Godsave, RAF Regiment Museum).

if attacked in the open by a raiding party of any large size. Any attack on a raiding party had to be closely coordinated with air action and in those situations when the cars did close with the enemy, the results were clearly decisive.

Air Headquarters Iraq had noted the important role that the RAF armoured cars played during the operations in the Southern Desert:

> In view of the necessity of armoured car personnel becoming acquainted with the Southern Desert in case of Ikhwan raids, armoured car route reconnaissances were despatched from Basra in December and February. Much useful information regarding terrain was obtained and opportunities were afforded for carrying out co-operation between aircraft of No 84 (B) Squadron and the armoured cars. The lessons learnt on these reconnaissances were to become extremely valuable later.[9]

Glubb's account of the raiding season of 1927 and 1928 also understates the part played by the RAF armoured cars. His only reference to them being that 'In January 1928, RAF armoured cars were sent to Busaiyah, as static guard for workmen building the post.' This, of course, unfairly discounts the work carried out by Nos 1, 2, 4 and 5 Sections against the Ikhwan incursions at that time, as described in the memoirs of Godsave and Stone.[10] The cars were not 'static' at that time, but moved south and into the Nejed when they were ordered to do so, and engaged the enemy whenever possible. They provided the safe haven of Rukhaimiyah from which the Ninaks and Victorias flew off to bomb the Mutair. The geographical limitations on movement imposed on the armoured cars, and the aircraft, in the following raiding season would be due to a stricter application of the Uqair Protocols, which meant that the RAF were unable to intervene in a similar manner to that in the previous year. This was a wholly political, rather than a military, decision.

Even after Glubb's Southern Desert Camel Corps had fought successful skirmishes with the raiders, he wrote. 'Yet, on the whole, the success of the operations was due to the moral effect of the presence of the RAF behind us.' Furthermore, he quotes Feisal al Duweesh, the most famous of the Ikhwan leaders, who, in giving the order for retreat said; 'We must pass Uqubbah before daylight, or the armoured cars may come.'[11]

What is not in question is Glubb's deep commitment, skill, and guile in the resolution of the Ikhwan problem, and his unparalleled understanding of, and ability to form close bonds with, the bedouin. His frustrations with RAF senior commanders are arguably justified, as they had differing views on how the problem should be resolved, particularly given the emphasis on resolution by the use of air power. However, Glubb does admit in his memoirs that he could have dealt with this differently, and then he might have had more success in obtaining the resources he required. He wrote:

> Operations against the Ikhwan were to last for six years, but I was never able to secure the co-operation of the armoured cars. I was too inexperienced to appreciate the value of talking things over. I should have gone to Baghdad, made friends on the staff and discussed the whole problem with them.[12]

Despite the criticisms by Glubb, the armoured cars were held in high regard by the RAF commanders. Air Marshal Sir Robert Brooke-Popham, who was AOC, Iraq from November 1928 until October 1930, at the height of the Ikhwan raids, commented:

> When I was commanding in Iraq recently I was struck by the extraordinary reliability of the armoured car sections out there. One gave orders to an armoured car section, perhaps by wireless late one evening, that by 3 o'clock on the next afternoon, it was to be at some place 100 or 150 miles away. One never worried about it anymore, because one was always sure that it would be at the given spot at the given time.[13]

In January 1929, it was reported that the Ikhwan planned to attack Sulman and the tribes in the Neutral Zone. A small raid was made into the Neutral Zone on 10 January but, in an encouraging sign, this was beaten off by the Iraqi shepherds. A few days later, Captain Glubb had requested that the section of RAF armoured cars at Busaiyah move further forward, but this was refused as it would contravene the Uqair Protocols. Disappointingly, an immense amount of firepower could have been brought to bear; however, diplomatic niceties prohibited their use forward of Busaiyah. Fortunately, the Ikhwan were intimidated enough by the small force assembled by Captain Glubb at Al Abtiyyah, a few miles north of the frontier; four machine-guns from the Iraq Army Motor Machine-Gun Company, the Southern Desert Camel Corps, 70-strong, with a few vehicles and machine-guns, in concert with the three tribes, the Zayyad and Budoor shepherds and the Dhafeer bedouin drew themselves up for battle. They waited for four days, knowing that if the Ikhwan attacked and won, they would all be slaughtered. In the event, the Mutair did not come; they had intended to attack, but their spies had returned with the news that not only were the tribes waiting for them, but four aircraft had also been seen near

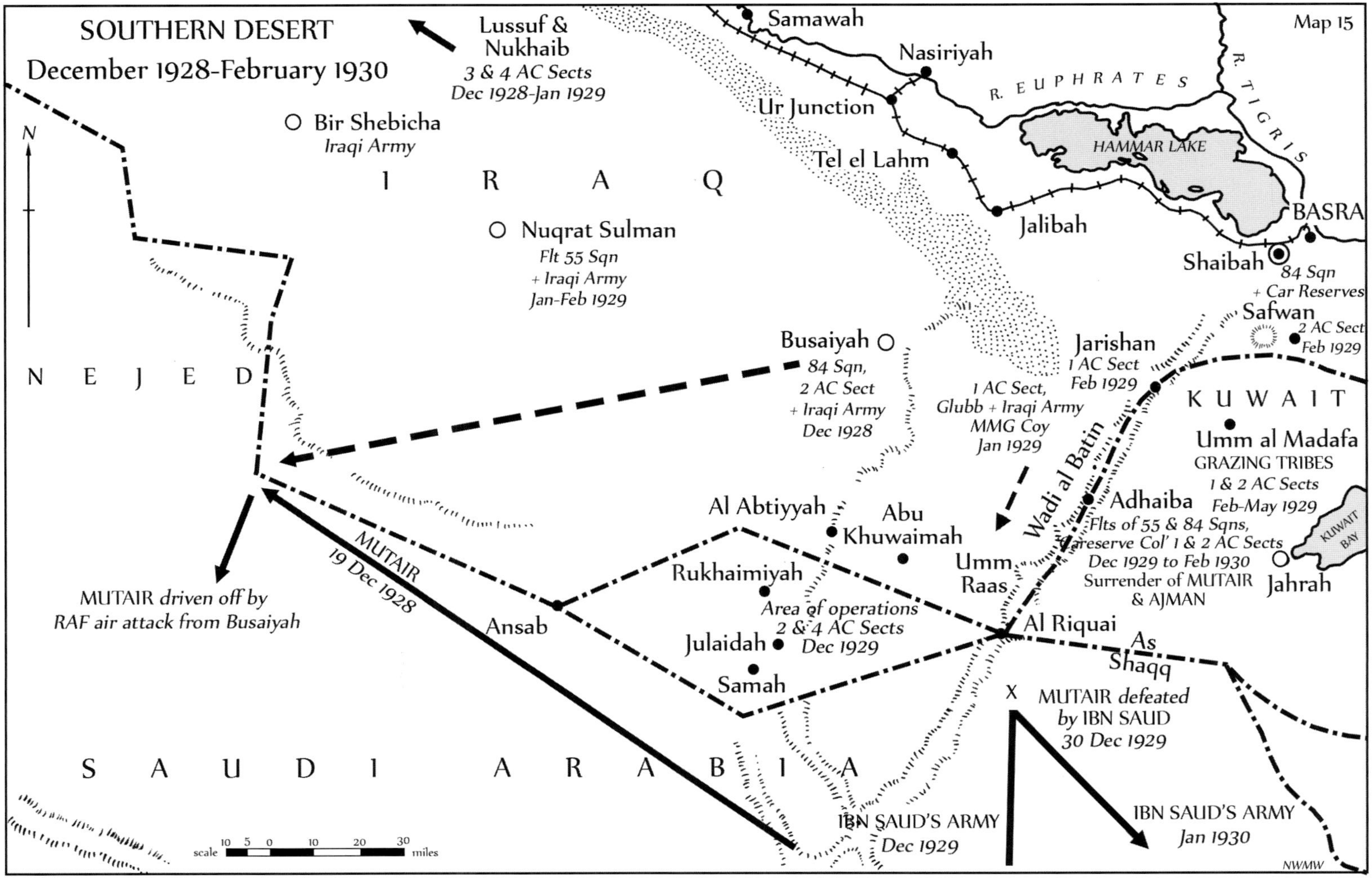

SOUTHERN DESERT
December 1928-February 1930
Map 15
Lussuf &
Nukhaib
3 & 4 AC Sects
Dec 1928-Jan 1929
Bir Shebicha
Iraqi Army
I R A Q
Nuqrat Sulman
Flt 55 Sqn
+ Iraqi Army
Jan-Feb 1929
N
N E J E D
Samawah
Nasiriyah
R. EUPHRATES
R. TIGRIS
Ur Junction
Tel el Lahm
HAMMAR LAKE
Jalibah
BASRA
Shaibah
84 Sqn
+ Car Reserves
Safwan
2 AC Sect
Feb 1929
Busaiyah
84 Sqn,
2 AC Sect
+ Iraqi Army
Dec 1928
Jarishan
1 AC Sect
Feb 1929
1 AC Sect,
Glubb + Iraqi Army
MMG Coy
Jan 1929
K U W A I T
Umm al Madafa
GRAZING TRIBES
1 & 2 AC Sects
Feb-May 1929
KUWAIT BAY
Wadi al Batin
Adhaiba
Flts of 55 & 84 Sqns,
'Reserve Col' 1 & 2 AC Sects
Dec 1929 to Feb 1930
Surrender of MUTAIR
& AJMAN
Jahrah
Al Abtiyyah
Abu
Khuwaimah
Umm
Raas
Rukhaimiyah
Area of operations
2 & 4 AC Sects
Dec 1929
Julaidah
Samah
Al Riquai
As
Shaqq
MUTAIR driven off by
RAF air attack from Busaiyah
MUTAIR
19 Dec 1928
Ansab
X
MUTAIR defeated
by IBN SAUD
30 Dec 1929
S A U D I A R A B I A
IBN SAUD'S ARMY
Dec 1929
IBN SAUD'S ARMY
Jan 1930
scale 10 5 0 10 20 30 miles
NWMW

the encampment. Glubb described this moment as the turning point in the war in the Southern Desert. They had demonstrated that the Iraqis themselves were prepared to stand against the Ikhwan.

With the Iraqi tribes looking a difficult prize, additional parties of Ikhwan were then reported, by late January, to be moving up the Wadi al Batin and into Kuwait. This was confirmed when two groups of motorists were attacked on the Kuwait to Basra road and an American civilian was killed. An armoured car section, each, had been moved to Jarishan, and Safwan, in anticipation of raiding into Kuwait. On 23 January, half of No 1 Section and a detachment of the Iraqi Motor Machine-Gun Company, along with Captain Glubb, chased an Ajman raiding party retreating down the Wadi al Batin to Umm Raas, but they made good their escape as the cars were held up by soft sand. The raiders also had a five hour head-start and therefore, reached the Nejed frontier before they could be run down.

Whereas the RAF had restrictions placed on patrols over the Iraq-Nejed frontier, they had no such limits on flights and armoured car patrols over in Kuwait, and if necessary had permission to establish an advanced base. In pursuit of better grazing, Captain Glubb convinced the tribes to move into Kuwait to take advantage of the lush pastures. Therefore, during February, and with the agreement of the Sheikh of Kuwait, the Iraqi tribes moved eastwards to Umm al Madafa. The Sheikh was however, opposed to Iraqi Army units entering his country, so a section of RAF armoured cars was assigned to Glubb, to substitute for the Iraq Army Motor Machine-Gun Company. In a rather bizarre ruling, Captain Glubb, as a servant of the Iraqi Government, was allowed to enter Kuwaiti territory, but not sleep there. A compromise was later reached, and the Desert Police were allowed to enter and make camp, but not the Army. His strong opinions against the RAF armoured cars seem to have been mollified by this time. He continues:

> But what was even better, we were given a section [No 2, and later No 1 Section] of RAF Armoured Cars to accompany us.[14]
>
> At Umm al Madafa...the Nejed-Kuwait frontier lay 50 miles to the south of us. We arranged to picket it with tribal horse and camelmen and to patrol it with police cars from dawn to dark. We were moreover only 50 miles from Shaibah, where our good friends 84 Squadron were ready for action. Having a section of RAF armoured cars with us would enable us to communicate direct with the squadron if we were attacked... With the frontier well covered by our pickets and patrols and the RAF close at hand we could reap the reward of our past labours and anxieties.[15]

From late February, one Section had formed the rallying point for the tribal concentration at Umm al Madafa, and kept watch over the tribes as their animals grazed on the knee-high grass. Once this had fattened the camels and sheep, and the April heat began to dry the grass off, the tribes needed to move on. The Section then patrolled out to the southern flank of the bedouin with their herds and flocks, and provided a reassuring presence, as they were convinced to move north to Safwan and the Euphrates to find better pasturage.

By May 1929, matters were again calming down, but the RAF armoured cars had covered great distances. Over the first five months of the year, the total mileage for the Armoured Car Wing had totalled between 37,000 and 65,000 miles per month. However, the Ikhwan problem had still not been resolved; neither the RAF nor the Iraqi Army had been able to strike the decisive blow against them. Due to both the efforts of Captain Glubb with the bedouin and the threat posed by the RAF however, the serious raiding of previous years had subsided.

The Ikhwan, notably, had also changed their target. In late February, frustrated at not being able to raid any 'infidel' Iraqi tribes, Ibn Humaid of the Ataiba, had attacked the Shammar tribe, and the caravans of Nejedi merchants, all subjects of Ibn Saud, and within Nejed territory. The merchants were massacred to a man. This rapidly changed the perceptions of the townspeople and the bedouin tribes of Arabia. They rallied to Ibn Saud, a civil war ensued, and the Ikhwan faced opponents on two fronts. This was not an unintentional action on the Ikhwan leader's part, as the rebel chiefs had already discussed the carve up of Ibn Saud's dominions, The rebels were however, defeated at Sibilla, 90 miles north of Riyadh on 29 March 1929 by the army of Ibn Saud. Feisal al Duweesh, thought to be mortally wounded, was allowed to return to his base to die in peace, while Ibn Humaid and the Ataiba refused surrender, and retired to their lands on the other side of Arabia.

By the middle of 1929, the changes arising from the defeat of the Ikhwan by Ibn Saud had begun to be felt. The tables had now turned, and the tribes that had caused such terror for many years were now themselves pursued by a ruthless opponent. Ibn Humaid finally surrendered to Ibn Saud, was imprisoned and died soon after; his tribe, the Ataiba, pledged their allegiance to Ibn Saud. Only the Mutair and Ajman now remained a problem. Matters worsened for the Ikhwan when during September, a Mutair party of 500 men, under the eldest son of Feisal al Duweesh, were met and defeated in battle by an army led by one of Ibn Saud's lieutenants.

As winter approached, Iraq Command expected another season of raiding. The plight of the Ikhwan rebels was now difficult however, as Ibn Saud's army and his loyal tribes were gathering their strength and would soon be camped only a few miles away from the frontier. The Ajman and Mutair feared the inevitable and merciless retribution from Ibn Saud and, therefore, moved up close to the border and sent out emissaries to seek asylum in Iraq. It was still unclear to Iraq Command as to what exactly was happening, but they were determined that the Ajman and Mutair would not enter Iraq, as had been decreed by the British and Iraqi Governments. The Sheikh of Kuwait, Ibn Sabah, was now somewhat sympathetic to the plight of the Ikhwan; however, the Kuwait Government was equally determined that they would not find refuge in their territory, as Ibn Saud had threatened to follow them if they were given sanctuary.

At one point, Feisal al Duweesh approached Ibn Sabah and the Political Adviser in Kuwait, Colonel Dickson, to ask for protection for his wife and children, while he returned to fight Ibn Saud in the Nejed. Not surprisingly, this request was received unsympathetically by the British Government.

In the first week of December 1929 therefore, Nos 1 and 2 Sections, organised as 'Careserve Column', were ordered to proceed to Jahra in Kuwait (Map 15, p. 135).[16] Here they were joined from Basra by Squadron Leader John Woodhouse DSO MC, the Officer Commanding Armoured Car Reserve and the Political Adviser Kuwait and the SSO. They then proceeded on a reconnaissance to the Iraq-Kuwait frontier. The task of 'Careserve Column' was to show the flag and convince the Kuwait tribes that the RAF were doing their utmost to keep the Nejed tribes out, as well as to drive off any small parties of rebels they might encounter, but only after giving adequate warning. At Ash Shaqq they found the remains of large camps, covering several square miles that had belonged to the Ajman of Ibn Hithlain. They also found a few small, scattered Ajman camps still occupied, while other groups were found moving towards the frontier. At this point they were told the reason for the flight of the tribes by the Sheikh of Kuwait's representative. He had unfortunately warned Ibn Hithlain the previous day that they would be attacked by 'British Armoured Cars' if they did not move. This caused considerable annoyance to Squadron Leader Woodhouse and Colonel Dickson, the Political Adviser, as the official had exceeded his authority and should have awaited the car column's arrival. With Ibn Hithlain having fled, 'Careserve Column' returned to Basra.

A bedouin encampment (© Crown copyright. Godsave, RAF Regiment Museum).

To enforce the Iraq Government's requirement that no Ikhwan could enter their country, three sections of 'Careserve Column', were sent down the Wadi al Batin, this time from the Iraqi side of the border, to Adhaibah. They were to investigate the concentrations of Ajman tribe found by aircraft of No 84 Squadron, and hasten their movement out of Iraq. The armoured cars were also instructed not to become embroiled in any action with Ibn Saud's forces, which were known to be in the area. Numbers 2 and 4 Sections reached Abtiyyah where they received an urgent request for help from the Police Post at Julaidah in the Neutral Zone. This turned out to be a false alarm; however, as the Sections returned to Adhaibah, they came across the tents of Ferhan al Ibn Mashur and 200 followers at Abu Khuwaimah. A defensive camp was formed and Ibn Mashur was ordered to leave Iraq.

On 23 December, a Flight each of Nos 55 and 84 Squadrons rendezvoused with 'Careserve Column'. A Vickers Victoria was placed on stand-by to assist. Also joining 'Careserve Column' was Air Commodore Charles Burnett, the Chief Staff Officer, Iraq Command, who arrived from Baghdad on 22 December and took charge of operations.[17] He was joined two days later by Captain Glubb. Glubb and Burnett worked well together and this ensured the closest co-operation between the RAF and the civil authorities. Glubb then instructed Ibn Mashur and his followers to leave Iraq, via Rukhaimiyah and Ansab. They were told that if they were found north of a line Ansab-Samah-Al Riquai after daylight on 24 December they would be attacked. Ibn Mashur was reluctant to leave and according to Glubb said that 'if he had to die, he begged the government to order the armoured cars to shoot down his followers and himself at once.'[18] With Ibn Mashur's failure to comply with the order to move, his camp was visited by armoured cars and aircraft on the morning of the deadline, and with his followers, he formally surrendered to Air Commodore Burnett as Commander of Operations. The rebels were disarmed and they and their leader were sent off to Busaiyah under police escort.

But for the terrible weather, the cars also very nearly caught the Duweesh:

> The armoured cars were working under conditions of considerable discomfort; the demands of mobility rendered the transportation of tents impracticable and weather conditions added considerably to the difficulties to be overcome... when the capture of Al Duweesh appeared imminent, No 2 Section who were keeping in touch with him, were badly bogged and unable to move.[19]

The relief of Feisal al Duweesh at having evaded the cars was only short-lived as he now faced retribution from Ibn Saud. On 30 December, Feisal al Duweesh and the Mutair, who had returned to the Nejed, were surprised and attacked by Ibn Saud's forces. The Mutair fled in panic back into the Wadi al Batin, losing 500 camels and all their tents, and then across into Kuwait (Map 15, p. 135).

Burnett and the 'Careserve Column' had carried on to Adhaibah following the capture of Ibn Mashur. On 5 January 1930, with rumours spreading that Ibn Saud and nearly 8000 men were moving to Al Riquai on the frontier. Burnett, Glubb and the 'Careserve Column' now pursued the tribes as they moved into Kuwait, until the main body of the Mutair were overtaken at dawn on the following morning, when some 20 miles from Jahrah. The cars then occupied themselves with rounding up the fugitives.

Although an agreement had been made with Ibn Saud that the Mutair would not be allowed to enter Iraq or Kuwait, Air Commodore Burnett could not possibly order the cars to shoot down the crowds of men, women, children and camels that now gathered in large groups in Kuwait territory. Rather, Burnett flew to Baghdad and quickly obtained permission to offer terms to the Ikhwan. Furthermore, Burnett was facing many thousand Ikhwan with only the four sections of RAF armoured cars. A request to allow the Iraq Police and the Iraqi Army Motor Machine Gun Company to enter Kuwait to assist was refused by the Iraqi Government. Ibn Saud was also becoming impatient that the tribes had not been evicted and he had suggested that the RAF stand aside and let him enter Kuwait and 'finish the affair in the quickest possible time'.[20] The AOC had also, therefore, to consider at this time the possibility of an invasion of Kuwait by Ibn Saud.

The tribes had to be kept together, lest they break up into small uncontrollable parties and escape into Iraq or Kuwait, and this could only be done with constant aerial patrols and maintenance of close contact by the RAF armoured cars. During the first week of January, 'Careserve Column' made touch with Feisal al Duweesh of the Mutair, and Ibn Hithlain of the Ajman at a camp two miles east of Al Riquai. Air Commodore Burnett met with them, and demanded their unconditional surrender, and that their tribes move to Jarishan where they would be disarmed. The rebel leaders were given permission to consider the offer, but had to give their reply the following morning. Feisal al Duweesh refused the terms and headed south.

Three days later, Ibn Hithlain surrendered and was flown to Shaibah. He spent the night in a small tent pitched for him in front of the guard room.[21] This was followed the next day by the surrender of Feisal al Duweesh. On 9 January, the Ajman and Mutair were ordered by the RAF to move to Jarishan to be disarmed, and to stay there until their fate could be determined. The armoured cars shepherded them, but the task was made all the more difficult because the poor condition of the flocks, lack of grazing and poor water supply. At one point, a group attempted to break away from the main group to head north-eastwards, but a few bombs were dropped in their path, and though no casualties were caused the group then headed back to the main body. No large breakaway could be allowed as Ibn Saud would then find an excuse to nullify the agreement.

A few of the tribesmen managed to flee into Kuwait, fearing retribution from Ibn Saud, and sought refuge with the Kuwaiti tribes. Other groups of rebels attempted to flee back to the Nejed, were intercepted by Ibn Saud's army and killed to a man. Duweesh and Ibn Hithlain, along with another captured leader, Ibn Lami, were transferred to the Royal Indian Marine Ship *Patrick Stewart* anchored in the Shatt al Arab. A week later they were transferred to HMS *Lupin*, which then transported them down to the Bay of Kuwait.

Following negotiations between the British Resident in the Persian Gulf, Air Commodore Burnett and Ibn Saud, agreement was reached on the fate of the Ikhwan rebels and their leaders. On 28 January, the three captured leaders, Feisal al Duweesh, Naif Ibn Hithlain and Jasir Ibn Lami were flown from Kuwait to the camp of Ibn Saud and handed over; with the promise their lives would be spared.[22] They were imprisoned in Riyadh and are believed to have died shortly afterwards. Ibn Saud undertook to prevent any future raids into Iraq, which he duly observed.[23] The agreement also specified that all the rebel tribes had to be returned to Ibn Saud with their flocks and herds. On 8 February, the last of the Mutair and Ajman crossed the Kuwait-Nejed frontier.

By mid-February, the four armoured car sections had been withdrawn from the Southern Desert, having covered a total of 32,085 miles during the last three months. The Victorias of No 70 Squadron flew back to Hinaidi, while the Flights of Nos 55 and 84 Squadrons returned to Hinaidi and Shaibah.

On the evening of 21 February 1930, a conference was convened on board HMS *Lupin*, anchored in the Persian Gulf and out of sight of land. Attending were King Abd al Aziz ibn Saud and King Feisal I of Iraq, together with officials from the Iraqi and Nejed Governments. With the diplomatic effort on the part of the British Government, an agreement of *Bon Voisinage* was signed that led to a permanent peace on the frontier.

The official report on the events of December 1929 to February 1930 emphasised the benefits of the combined operation of RAF aircraft and armoured cars:

> Throughout this period of operations it is interesting to note the moral effect resulting from the use of aircraft and armoured cars. The constant harassing by armoured cars both day and night and the frequent presence of aircraft overhead, culminating in the dropping of very few bombs (actually only 25 bombs were dropped) proved sufficient.[24]

The RAF armoured cars were given the task of escorting the Ikhwan tribes back from Jarishan to the Nejed frontier. Rather surprisingly, on 5 February, the Officer Commanding the Armoured Cars received a letter from King Ibn Saud congratulating him on the action taken to expel the tribes. The tribes of the Nejed-Iraq frontier never raided one another again. It was the closing of an important chapter in the history of the RAF Armoured Car Companies.

Notes

1. AIR 5/1254 *Operations: Iraq Chapters 14 to 25 January 1924-December 1928. Report on situation on Iraq-Nejd borders, November 1927-May 1928*.
2. AIR 5/1291 *Iraq Command: monthly operation summaries, Vol. V, 1927-1929*.
3. L.A. Simmons, *Private Papers 7284* (London: IWM Document Archive, n.d.).
4. Air Vice-Marshal, later Marshal of the RAF Sir Edward L. Ellington GCB CMG CBE psc (1877-1967). AOC Iraq Command, from November 1926 to October 1928 and Chief of the Air Staff 1933-1937.
5. J.B. Glubb, *Arabian Adventures: Ten Years of Joyful Service* (London: Cassell, 1978), p. 179.
6. *Ibid.*, p. 187.
7. *Ibid.*, pp. 134-135.
8. J.B. Glubb, *War in the Desert: An RAF Frontier Campaign* (London: Hodder & Stoughton, 1956), p. 271.
9. AIR 5/1254 *Operations: Iraq Chapters 14 to 25 January 1924-December 1928. Command Report – Iraq, November 1926-November 1928*.
10. Glubb, *War in the Desert*, pp. 290-291. Glubb states, when referring to a skirmish of his Southern Desert Camel Corps as 'the first occasion in which the Ikhwan had come into contact on the Iraq frontier with vehicles mounting automatic weapons'. In fact, the action near Es Safa by the RAF armoured cars in early 1928 predates this skirmish.
11. *Ibid.*, p. 270.
12. Glubb, *Arabian Adventures*, pp. 134-135.
13. In G.E. Godsave, 'Armoured Cars in Desert Warfare', *Journal of the Royal United Services Institute*, LXX, (1925), pp. 404. Later Air Chief Marshal Sir Robert Brooke-Popham (1878-1953).
14. Glubb, *Arabian Adventures*, p. 186.
15. Glubb, *War in the Desert*, p. 276.
16. AIR 23/624 *Southern Desert operations: south-east area, November 1929-January 1931*. Numbers 1 and 2 Sections consisted of HMACs *Terror*, *Cleopatra*, *Fox*, *Euphrates* and *Eagle*; HMWTs *Boadicea* and *Panther*; HMSTs (Morris Six-Wheeler) *Mortlake*, *Morwell*; and HMAF (Armed Fords) *Tugford*, *Henford* and *Stoneford*. The Column included Flight Lieutenant Charles Toogood and Flying Officer Oswald Williams, along with newly-promoted, Flying Officer, 'Jack' Stone.
17. Air Commodore Charles S. Burnett CB CBE DSO, Chief Staff Officer Iraq Command. Later Air Chief Marshal Sir Charles S. Burnett KCB CBE DSO (b. USA, 1882-1945).
18. Glubb, *War in the Desert*, p. 324.
19. AIR 23/624 *Southern Desert operations*.
20. *Ibid.*
21. Glubb, *War in the Desert*, p. 341.
22. Ibn Mashur was a Syrian subject and was, therefore, not covered by Ibn Saud's request to return all the tribal leaders and was not handed over.
23. Glubb, *War in the Desert*, p. 341.
24. AIR 23/624 *Southern Desert operations*.

Chapter Eight

Transjordan 1925-1932 Policing the Tribes

"The force seemed inadequate and I arranged with the ever-willing Royal Air Force for a section of their armoured cars to accompany us."
Lieutenant-General John Bagot Glubb[1]

Transjordan had common frontiers with Palestine, Syria, Iraq, the Nejed and Hedjaz, and from 1928 to 1932 the operations of the RAF would be primarily focused on dealing with both benign and unfriendly incursions across them.[2] The drawing of the northern frontiers of Transjordan with Syria was uncontroversial, though internal problems arose soon after the French had arrived in Syria to take up their portion of the Sykes-Picot Agreement. By 1920, the French had expelled King Feisal from Syria and many of his supporters had been forced to flee to Transjordan.[3] The Syrians had not welcomed the French Mandate, as they considered themselves to be an independent people, with a sound government administration already in place. A strong Syrian armed resistance developed quickly following the arrival of the French military force, which whilst ostensibly employed on 'policing' duties, undertook a bitter campaign of pacification in the mountains and deserts (Map 3, p. 29).

While matters in Syria had settled in most parts by 1925, the Druze, a Muslim minority in the mountains of the Jebel Druze just over the border from Mafraq in Transjordan, had risen up against the French colonial power. This was largely the outcome of poor or devious decisions by the newly-appointed French High Commissioner.[4] He had a group of Druze chieftains who had travelled to Damascus merely to discuss problems with local civil matters thrown in gaol.[5] With nationalism thereby reawakened, the uprising by Druze and other Syrians who joined with them was initially successful and France had to send thousands of troops from its African colonies to quell the unrest.[6]

British and French policy on the League of Nations Mandate differed significantly and this led to a deepening mistrust and suspicion between the two powers in the region. In addition, Transjordanians were sympathetic to the Druze cause and wished to assist with their struggle, while the Syrian tribes located near the Transjordan frontier saw this as a path of escape and avoidance from attacks by the columns of the French military. The small command of RAF Transjordan, with a flight of No 14 Squadron and one section of No 2 Armoured Car Company had therefore to deal with the consequences of the conflict.

The uprising in the Jebel Druze began in September 1925; the armoured cars of No 2 Armoured Car Company and aircraft of No 14 Squadron RAF were asked to carry out aerial and road patrols and reconnaissances to assist in preventing Transjordanian and Palestinian supporters moving across the Syrian frontier to support their Druze brothers. As the French Army regained the upper hand in Syria in 1926, they pushed the rebels back into the Jebel Druze, and as a consequence the families of the fighting men sought refuge in Transjordan. The Druze chieftains approached Amir Abdullah of Transjordan for permission to camp at the oasis town of Azraq, some 50 miles east of Amman, and the only permanent source of water in 12,000 square miles of desert. The Amir agreed, but on the proviso that the camp was to be only for the use of the Druze dependants, women, children and old people. They were instructed that it could not accommodate armed Druze fighters other than a few guards, and that they deal in good faith with the Transjordanian inhabitants. This worked for a few months; however, it became apparent by late 1926 that the camp was being used as a base for the main Druze leaders, both as a permanent habitation and as a safe haven from the fighting in Syria.

The question of which force should police the deserts of Transjordan was made more complicated during 1926, when the recently-arrived British High Commissioner, Field Marshal Lord Plumer, had concluded that the Arab Legion, which was subject to the orders of the Amir of Transjordan and not the British High Commissioner, did not have the requisite capabilities to operate as a military force. This was a short-sighted decision primarily made due to pressure for fiscal restraint. Despite the bitter opposition of Amir Abdullah and the Legion's commander, Peake Pasha, the Legion was converted to a gendarmerie, reduced in size to only 1000 men and its area of responsibility restricted to the settled districts.[7]

The military responsibilities of the Arab Legion were assumed by the Transjordan Frontier Force (TJFF) which was organised along very different lines. Working in cooperation with the RAF, the TJFF was charged with providing military aid to the civil power and ensuring the security of Transjordan's borders. The Headquarters was established at Zerqa, 15 miles to the north-east of Amman. The TJFF was structured as a typical 'colonial' force much like the Indian Army, with British officers in all executive positions and Arabs in subordinate appointments. The area of greatest weakness was however, that it was recruited entirely from the settled town Arabs, the fellaheen (albeit from a mix of Moslem, Christian and many ethnic groups found in the Middle East) who were unfamiliar with life in the desert. The force was instructed to maintain law and order west of the Hedjaz railway and operate against raiders and tribes within a 15-mile strip of desert east of the railway. It soon became apparent that merely preventing the tribes from raiding the settled areas would not resolve the problem, and more ambitious thinking would be required.

Marking out the newly-agreed international borders was one of the tasks given to the Amman section of No 2 Armoured Car Company. It also completed many extensive 'reccos' of the surrounding area to ascertain the suitability for armoured car movement. Serving with the Company at this time was Flight Lieutenant Stanley F. Vincent who had flown in the Royal Flying Corps in the Great War and would later fly in the Battle of Britain. He described this routine work:

> During 1926, I had to go with my section of cars for two months 'out in the blue' with a company of Levy mounted infantry [Transjordan Frontier Force] under a [Major] Yard-Buller. Here we guarded our frontier which I

had also to delineate. We spent days and nights sleeping by the cars, marking the undefined frontier on the north. This we did after consulting maps and compass, by building cairns of stones on the highest bits of the undulating country and painting them white so that each was visible from those on each side. One such spot appears on later Survey maps as 'Vincent's Cairn'![8]

In April 1927, a force with the name of 'Azrakcol', consisting of three sections of No 2 Armoured Car Company and three companies of the TJFF (450 men and their horses), under command of Group Captain L.W.B. Rees VC MC, and acting in conjunction with No 14 Squadron, moved to occupy Azraq to proclaim martial law. Their role was to enforce the neutrality of the camp, eject all armed Druze and prevent their return.[9] A section of armoured cars formed the advance party of the column and convoyed ammunition, defence stores and rations to the proposed campsite. Their approach had been anticipated and many of the Druze chiefs and their men had already departed. Some 650 had left with their leader, Sultan Atrash, in late March, while another 800 departed on 15 April. On the arrival of the armoured cars however, the area was searched and any armed Druze men were interned.

The oasis at Azraq, where the Druze sought refuge (Hodge).

A pass system was introduced and rifles issued to 100 Druze men to act as guards for the refugees, while a census of the Azraq population was initiated. In order to avoid complaints, the old men were ordered to remain in their houses, while great care was to be taken in those houses where there were women present. Only 20 men were found to be without passes. At the same time, a Medical Officer examined all children with a view to prevention of malaria, the season for which was fast approaching. By 10 May, the situation had quietened such that only small patrols were required and the garrison received a visit from the Amir who witnessed a march past by 'Azrakcol' and was then entertained to lunch. The operation had been successfully completed without the need for offensive activity while the 'Druze Committees' were now in regular contact to ensure the smooth running of the camp.

Other than the usual patrolling, a rather more strenuous duty for the RAF armoured car crews at Azraq was track making. The first track was constructed so that a new engine could be delivered to a downed No 14 Squadron aircraft, and the next to allow the passage of the Rolls-Royce armoured cars and the lorries of the TJFF so that they could move tactically behind the inhabited areas of the Druze camp should the need arise. The Zerqa to Azraq road was also considerably improved, and this would allow rapid movement of the RAF armoured cars should any more trouble erupt at the camp. In the last week of April, an aircraft returning to Amman from Azraq went missing; however, its position was soon reported by a passing bedou tribesman. Unfortunately there was no track through the basalt boulders of the lava country where it had landed. Flight Lieutenant Vincent was with 'Azrakcol':

> When we were under canvas 'out in the blue' at Azraq, one of the Squadron's Flight Commanders, Horace Wigglesworth, had a forced landing out in the lava country, and for some reason, no one from his squadron went out to him for two whole days. Feeling sorry for him I commandeered one of their visiting DH9As at our landing-ground, and with another armoured car officer, Evans-Evans, in the back seat, took out a load of cigarettes, books, blankets and other provisions. We found his aeroplane on a strip cleared of lava rocks and marked out. When I landed and he saw who it was, he flung his cap on the ground in fury, 'Well I'm ...! Two armoured car officers - no one from my own squadron!' He was justifiably annoyed but also grateful to us for finding out what was needed to get him airborne again, and for the comforts meantime.

A track had to be constructed to Wigglesworth's aircraft, along the 15 miles of what became known as the 'Brighton Road' using paid local volunteers. After three days' work the new engine was delivered to the stranded aircraft on a tender of No 2 Armoured Car Company.

Azraq, being a sizeable oasis, with large bodies of water, could provide some simple pleasures at the end of a hot day, though not without its problems. The oasis sits at the northern end of the Wadi Sirhan and controls movement between Transjordan, Syria, Iraq and Saudi Arabia. It had been a Roman settlement and still retained Roman and Byzantine structures. The blue lakes and wetlands were teeming with wildlife including waterfowl and it was not long before the RAF officers at Amman had built a lodge for weekend shoots during the season, at first under the watchful eyes of the Arab Legion located in their newly-constructed fort. Stanley Vincent recalled one of the 'delights' of the oasis:

> ... there were two 'lakes' in which it was nearly pleasant to bathe at the end of a hot, sticky day - the qualification 'nearly' being caused by the mosquitoes! We had our camp about half a mile away for this reason; to bathe we would put on our trunks in our tents, get in a Rolls tender and drive to the water's edge - run and dive in. Even then much splashing was necessary before putting one's head out! After ten minutes or so of good cooling, one of us would say 'All out - Go!' Whereupon a rush would be made to the bank and so to the Rolls tender and away as quickly as possible, in a heap, without pausing to dry.[10]

In early July, a French delegation from Syria attended a conference with the

Chief British Representative, Lieutenant-Colonel Henry Cox, and Druze leaders to offer terms to the refugees.[11] None availed themselves of the offer and as a result of negotiations the Druze, still expressing their determination to fight the French as soon as it was convenient, were ordered to move further south a few miles over the Transjordanian frontier into Nejed territory. Their food requirements were determined, and a convoy organised to their new location. The RAF armoured cars and aircraft were then ordered to carry out regular patrols to ensure Druze raiding parties were not moving towards the Syrian border from their new refuge. Vincent continues:

> During this period some interesting months were spent, as it were, on the French-Druze war in Syria. The Druze, an attractive tribe, didn't approve of the French sent by the League of Nations, in their country and did what they could to annoy. The French came to visit us in our camp at Azraq, where they couldn't believe their eyes when they saw we did not have any native women there! They told us that the Druze were in the habit of crossing over the border from Syria into Transjordan going round in a semi-circle and re-crossing to attack the French supply lines and rear positions and could we please do something to stop it.
>
> On several occasions we intercepted large bands of armed Druze raiding parties and bid them retrace their steps. They treated it as a big joke and duly returned without argument, acknowledging they had been caught out - and also appreciating that four armoured cars with Vickers guns trained on them are not things with which to trifle.[12]

By July, all the Druze had departed Transjordanian territory and 'Azrakcol' was disbanded and its units returned to Amman. This operation had been handled with extreme and commendable sensitivity by the RAF and TJFF. In the early stages, events could easily have taken an unfavourable turn; however, it was terminated without any offensive action being necessary.

On 20 February 1928, Transjordan signed a treaty with Great Britain and thereby became an independent state, although still under strong guidance and financial control of the Chief British Resident. The British Government however, retained responsibility for the external defence of Transjordan. The bedouin remained a problem, and the RAF and TJFF had been ordered further east into the desert, charged with putting an end to inter-tribal and cross-frontier raiding, particularly on the border with Saudi Arabia, because of the implications for international relations.

The eastern boundaries of Transjordan were redrawn following treaty negotiations with the Saudis. Kaf, an outpost originally manned by the Arab Legion, was ceded to the Nejed region of Saudi Arabia. However, this gave Ibn Saud control over the largest part of the Wadi Sirhan which had been the main path of entry of the Ikhwan raiders of 1924. It led therefore, to a situation where there were watering places on the Saudi Arabian side of the frontier while those on the Transjordan side were some distance away. This meant that raiders from Central Arabia could water their camels and horses and then move rapidly across the border and attack Transjordan. Furthermore, the international boundaries, having been only slowly and recently drawn, had closed off access by the Transjordanian bedouin to a large area of watering and pasturage that they had used for many centuries and this was to exacerbate problems, with cross-border excursions by the tribes (Map 3, p. 29).

The early attacks by the Ikhwan had demonstrated that Transjordan could be easily and quickly reached by raiding parties from Central Arabia. However, with their resounding defeat at the hands of the RAF and Arab Legion at Ziza in 1924, the Emirate would not have to face such a large-scale invasion again.[13] Incursions from the south and east were to continue however, on a smaller scale for another six years. The authorities not only had to deal with Saudi Arabian tribesmen moving north from the Hedjaz into Transjordan, but also had to prevent the bedouin of Transjordan from crossing the frontiers to the south to do their own raiding, or to retaliate for raids on their own people (such was the traditional nomadic lifestyle of the bedouin).

The signing of the border agreement with King Ibn Saud in 1927, made matters more complex for the RAF. Incursions by Transjordan tribes across the Hedjaz frontier were soon met with complaints by the Saudis, sent through diplomatic channels in London. These found their way through the Foreign Office and on to the Colonial Office, thence to Amman, where the responsible RAF commander was queried as to why no action had been taken against the raiders. For the latter half of the 1920s, the major task for the RAF in Transjordan was to assist the authorities in the prevention and suppression of bedouin raiding for both local and more intricate geo-political reasons.

Prior to 1926, the RAF presence at Amman had consisted of only a single flight of No 14 Squadron, with their Bristol Fighters, and one section of No 2 Armoured Car Company. The years 1928 to 1930 were however, very difficult for the inhabitants of Transjordan's deserts, with numerous raids between tribes both inside the country and across the borders with Saudi Arabia, Iraq and Syria. As a consequence, Government operations against the bedouin raiders were intensified in the south of the country during the summer months, when raiders were most active. Consequently, the balance of No 14 Squadron and No 2 Armoured Car Company moved in their entirety to Amman from Palestine. The cars then spent a large part of their time on track marking, mapping and reconnaissances in preparation for these operations. Apart from the three-month period from August 1929, when the armoured cars were recalled to Ramleh to deal with the outbreak of the disturbances in Palestine between the Arabs and Jews, the major focus of operations for one, and sometimes two sections, of the armoured cars became the deserts of Transjordan.

Amir Abdullah of Transjordan had ordered the desert tribes to desist from raiding, not only because of the internal implications for civil order in the new state, but also due to the potential to create difficulties in foreign relations with neighbouring Saudi Arabia. In the latter half of 1928, the Beni Sakhr tribe, led by Fahad Ibn Zebn, had been caught in direct defiance of the Amir's order and the Police had attempted to collect a fine measured in a number of camels. The Beni Sakhr tribe however, had no fear of the relatively impotent Police and were indifferent to their requests. Consequently, it was decided to send a military force of adequate size to surround Ibn Zebn's encampment and extract the fine.

Under the command of the AOC Transjordan, Group Captain P.H.L. Playfair MC, two sections of No 2 Armoured Car Company, along with the Company Commander, Squadron Leader Leslie Forbes MC, and a mechanised detachment of the TJFF of four officers and 78 other ranks departed from Amman before sunrise on 29 December 1928.[14] Ninak aircraft of No 14 Squadron had spotted the tribe some 30 miles north-east of Bair. The ground component of the Force aimed to strike rapidly and without notice. The TJFF were transported in eight Morris six-wheeled

The convoy halts while on the operation to exact a fine on the Beni Sakhr (© Crown copyright. RAF Regiment Museum).

tenders, but these were soon experiencing difficulty moving across the desert with two of the vehicles damaging their axles.[15] Number 14 Squadron came to the rescue and a Ninak flew out the required spare parts.

Having lost a day, the Force moved off at sunrise the next morning and camped in a Wadi, 15 miles from the last known camp of Ibn Zebn and the Beni Sakhr. Number 14 Squadron were contacted by wireless and asked to sweep the area for signs of the Beni Sakhr, and at the same time Amir Abdullah's cousin and ADC, Amir Shakir ibn Zeid, who had special responsibility for bedouin affairs, stopped and questioned a passing group of bedouin.[16] He learnt that the chieftain had moved off towards the Nejed, where he intended to sell some camels. Moving in the direction they had been given, the column soon drew up in full view of the encampment of the Beni Sakhr. Ibn Zebn could not be found but Amir Shakir went forward and took his son as a hostage, to be taken to Amman and only returned when his father presented himself to the Amir Abdullah. The camels constituting the fine were collected, but leaving enough to carry the tents and those with young children. A party of the TJFF accompanied by an RAF wireless tender from the Company along with the confiscated camels went back to Amman, a day's ride away, while the remainder of the force stayed in the area as a rearguard.

The operation had been completed with minimal casualties, although the Company Commander, Squadron Leader Forbes, was hit in the arm by a piece of flint which flew up in the propeller draught while standing beside a Ninak. This sliced an artery and he was evacuated back to Amman by air the following morning in a returning aircraft. From there he was immediately flown to Ramleh and then by road to the Palestine General Hospital. Discharged after only nine days, he was able to be present for the AOC Middle East Command's annual tour of inspection.

Not all these operations ended as peacefully. Only three months later, in March 1929, 'A' Section with three Rolls Royce armoured cars and three armed tenders under the command of Flight Lieutenant William Hurley was ordered north to counter a raid being launched across the Syrian frontier against the Beni Sakhr by the Sharafat, Huweitat and Mazzaid tribes. Three troops of the TJFF were also collected at Zerqa in RAF tenders provided by No 14 Squadron. The armoured cars encountered the raiders near Um el Jemal, three miles from Mafraq. The raiders opened fire immediately but were driven back by the combined efforts of the cars, Ninaks and TJFF. Unfortunately, the rough terrain restricted the movements of the cars, and the raiding party then split up into small groups and moved back into Syrian territory. The Ninaks were however, able to attack the raiders but as always had to cease their attacks once the bedouin had crossed the frontier. The action lasted for six-and-a-half hours with about 25 of the raiders being killed and only two airmen slightly wounded, while 350 head of looted stock were recovered.[17]

Two weeks later Hurley and his section received reports of a raid having been carried out at the Zubeiya Pass on the Nejed frontier. Surprisingly, this was launched by the Ikhwan, and was the largest raid by them on the Huweitat in Transjordan for some time. Tragically, the RAF armoured cars arrived too late to effect any action and found only the bodies of the Huweitat victims. A Ninak from No 14 Squadron flew in a Huweitat sheikh in order to identify and locate the bodies of his people so that they could be collected for burial. Despite patrolling to the eastern frontier of Transjordan they found the raiders had re-crossed the border. Later in the year, 'A' Section went out from Ma'an in response to reports of a raid from the Nejed on Abu Suwan. Again by the time they arrived, the raiders had gone back across the frontier and the locals had fled, although the cars were able to bring in two of the wounded who had been left behind.

A similar operation on the south-east frontier with Saudi Arabia occurred in late May 1929. The Amir had received intelligence that a large raid into the Nejed was being planned by the Huweitat and Beni Sakhr, and that they were gathering in the neighbourhood of Bair. The Amir Shakir was despatched by car to order them to return to their tents. However, were he to be unsuccessful in convincing the tribesmen to change their plans, he was instructed by his brother, Amir Abdullah, to request the assistance of the aircraft and armoured cars of the RAF.

The Sheikhs apprehended in the operations of May 1929 (© Crown copyright. RAF Regiment Museum).

The following morning, a patrolling Ninak of No 14 Squadron landed near the party of Amir Shakir and observed him remonstrating with a group of about 150 tribesmen. Shakir sent a return message with the pilot indicating that his mission was unlikely to succeed. Consequently, Flight Lieutenant Henry Walker MC DFC with two sections of armoured cars of No 2 Company was ordered to Bair in support of Lieutenant-Colonel Ernest Stafford, known as 'Stafford Bey', the 2 i/c of the Arab Legion. By the time the armoured cars arrived, the tribes had indeed dispersed. The seven Sheikhs were, however, still required by Amir Shakir to present themselves for punishment in Amman. Stafford Bey, accompanied by the armoured cars and aircraft, visited the camps of each of the tribes who had taken part in the concentration. The RAF armoured cars were of great assistance in this operation by taking up effective covering positions at each camp while Stafford Bey and the Arab Legion went in to make the arrests. Any reluctance to surrender was quickly changed by the arrival of the Rolls-Royce armoured cars. The Sheikhs were held imprisoned in Amman before they were brought to trial before the Bedouin Control Board, which had been formed that year to deal with such disputes. Again, the operation was successfully concluded without a shot being fired.[18]

The operations of the TJFF and RAF were suppressing raids by the Transjordan tribes to a limited extent, but their attempts to intercept the rapidly-moving raiding parties coming from neighbouring Nejed, Hedjaz and Syria were often unsuccessful. The TJFF were not seen by the Transjordanian bedouin as operating fairly and many believed that their own Government was acting disproportionately against them. By 1930, despite the best efforts of the TJFF supported by the RAF, the situation seemed intractable and the policing methods were leading to resentment, the imminent destitution and in some cases, starvation for many of the tribes. Moreover, they could see the Saudi tribes raiding with near immunity from sanction or military action.

The following month, operations were launched in response to reports that a force of 1000 camelmen and 200 horsemen from Saudi Arabia had attacked the Huweitat, killing more 30 and looting a couple of thousand camels and sheep, along with tents, bedding and belongings.

Flight Lieutenant Francis Ronksley MC and a half-section formed an advanced base at Bair from which the Fairey Gordon aircraft of No 14 Squadron could fly desert reconnaissances.[19] During March 1930, a flight of Bristol Fighters from No 6 Squadron RAF also became involved and flew over from Ramleh to Bair. Cooperation between the armoured cars, No 6 Squadron, the TJFF and Arab Legion led to the arrest of several sheikhs from tribes that had been raiding into the Nejed. At the same time, another column of armoured cars and TJFF, also working in cooperation with No 6 Squadron, arrested three more sheikhs in the Azraq area and organised their conveyance by air to Amman.

During May, further effective air-ground cooperation was achieved around Imshash between No 14 Squadron and 'B' and 'C' Sections of No 2 Company. The Fairey Gordons were able to find and direct the cars onto two parties of raiders and halt them with limited, but well-directed machine-gun fire, until the armoured cars were able to reach them. The leaders were arrested and fines (again, in camels) were agreed to, and arms and ammunition confiscated.

In the same month, the Rowalla tribe, who were on their annual northerly migration from the Nejed, were reported to be in possession of camels looted earlier from Transjordan tribes. A mobile column, 'Stracol', composed of 'B' Section of No 2 Company, assisted by No 14 Squadron, left Amman for Hamad with the objective of recovering the loot. A small party of 11 men of the TJFF were flown in on Vickers Victorias from No 216 Squadron as reinforcements, while half a section of armoured cars joined them from Azraq. After locating the Rowalla 170 miles east of Amman, more than 450 camels were impounded as security while further negotiations occurred. These were unsuccessful and the decision made to drive the recovered camels to Zerqa where they could be distributed by the civil authorities among the tribes who had suffered losses in recent raids. A Victoria was quickly despatched to bring in supplies of rations, petrol, oil, water and personnel but also ten bedouin to take charge of the camels.[20]

Despite the success of the preceding operations in apprehending the perpetrators, the raids were not decreasing in intensity and were prosecuted with the customary vigour. Furthermore, the view was growing within the British Government that the long-term placement of detachments of RAF armoured cars and the TJFF at points where trouble was expected or reported, and the large number of reconnaissance flights required to support this, was a misuse of the Imperial forces stationed in Transjordan. It was determined that this duty would be better dealt with by an arm of the Transjordan Government; the most suitable force being the Arab Legion.

Similar difficulties with the age-old tradition of raiding had been experienced in Iraq, but this had now been dealt with to a large extent. Searching for a more effective solution to the problem, in late 1930, the Amir Abdullah, with the support of the Chief British Resident, Alec Kirkbride, appointed a young British officer as second-in-command of the Arab Legion. Major John Bagot Glubb, Royal Engineers, later famous as 'Glubb Pasha', had recently played a key role as a Special Service Officer in the success of the operations in the Southern Desert of Iraq against the Ikhwan. He began work in Transjordan without delay, in close cooperation with Kirkbride

The hangars and airfield at Ma'an (Rolph, RAFACA).

and Amir Shakir. Taking a civilian car, and with only a driver, Glubb immediately departed on a three-month trip into the desert to visit the tribes. On his safe return, he successfully proposed, though not without some opposition, that the best means of ending desert raiding was to recruit the bedouin as part of an elite camel police of the Arab Legion, known as *Al Badia* or the 'Desert Patrol'. They would therefore police their own people. To carry out this task, he selected bedouin from all the desert tribes, without prejudice, and soon he had men from the noblest families serving in the Desert Patrol with great pride. In February 1931, the decision was made to withdraw the TJFF from the desert, leaving only a detachment at Ma'an, and two months later, responsibility for control of the bedouin was handed over to Glubb's Desert Patrol.

It was decided however, to establish a permanent RAF presence at Ma'an and a contract was issued for the erection of suitable accommodation for the RAF. Each section of No 2 Company would spend three months in residence and then return to Ramleh in Palestine. Despite the Arab Legion taking greater responsibility for the deserts, the RAF armoured cars remained in a support role as well as providing the area defence of Ma'an aerodrome, from where the cars were continually active., During December 1930 for example, 132 reconnaissances were carried out by No 2 Company, covering a total of 6089 miles with Rolls-Royce armoured cars and 7111 miles with Armed Morris Tenders.

Ma'an had been the location of a Turkish military flying school during the Great War and was located on a plateau 4000 feet above sea level, 120 miles south of Amman. The climate was one of unpleasant contrasts, with winters influenced by the cold winds from the north and east from Central Asia and the Caucasus Mountains. In summer, the air was so thin that aeroplanes had difficulty taking off around midday. The airfield boasted two hangars and a barracks for a company of the TJFF and normally a flight of No 14 Squadron and a section of No 2 Armoured Car Company. Despite Ma'an being located in a desert, the contrasts of the climate could make travel difficult. Mornington Wentworth, having served in Iraq had then moved on to Palestine and was now an NCO on No 2 Company. He continues:

> Headquarters of Armoured Cars in Palestine was at Ramleh, but there was always one section out at a village called Ma'an. The idea was security and the one thing we always did there was our annual firing practice, so we took all our ammunition up. The system was that one section completed three months at Ma'an. They left Ma'an at six o'clock in the morning, and the section that was relieving them left Ramleh at the same time, and you met at Allenby Bridge, the crossing over the River Jordan.
>
> Now it was pouring with rain on this particular morning. It was my section that was going from Ramleh to Ma'an. So we signalled Ma'an, "What was the weather like?" "Not too bad", they replied. They were leaving, so we left and it poured with rain, something terrible, till we got through Jerusalem. Then it stopped raining and right down through the Jordan Valley, past Jericho, and it was sultry, really sticky. Well we got to Allenby Bridge where we were supposed to meet and handover officially… but still no sign of the other section.
>
> Well we had our tiffin. We waited, and still no sign of them. We had a wireless tender loaded with ammunition and it was bit heavy, so we'd sent it on. Anyway, we went eventually as we weren't going to wait any longer.

I don't know how many miles, it was a way from Allenby Bridge, but not very far and we came across this wireless-tender in a snow drift. Three completely different climates in a country that is noted for its heat, and there was snow. Several of us bogged down and eventually we got moving and got to Amman because from Allenby Bridge to Amman we'd had a reasonably hard track.

And still no sign of the other section. We eventually saw them, five days later! The leading armoured car [of the section coming from Ma'an] had bogged in worse conditions than ours. They were coming through snow plus mud. The second car decided; well I'm not going to bog behind him so he carried on, and he didn't get more than a hundred yards and down he went. The third car did likewise, until the whole section was spread over a distance of about a mile. All bogged down to the axles and they just could not get out!

It was so cold that one chap lost two toes through frostbite. They dropped blankets and dry clothing, because they were in a shocking state, and until rations arrived they were living on chapattis supplied by local Arabs. They were a sorry mess when they arrived. Of course we had to wait three weeks before we could move on to Ma'an because of the conditions of the track.[21]

Hector Bolitho, the distinguished New Zealand author, wrote of his visit to Ma'an in the early 1930s and provided a vivid description of the RAF outpost:

About 8 o'clock we saw a dark form on the skyline; blacker than the night. "The Trees of Ma'an" said the driver. So we came to a little town, a clinging group of white buildings, isolated in the desert. There was a small hotel, with a verandah on which two silent and tipsy men dozed over their drinks. Then barracks, for the RAF and the Frontier Force, the incongruous plantation of trees, a few streets of rickety houses, so frail that they looked as if they might be tossed into the air at any time, on the whim of a storm...

Cars and a tender of 'C' Section depart on a patrol from Ma'an (© Crown copyright. RAF Regiment Museum).

At speed on the Ma'an mudflats (Skellon).

While I was there I lived in the RAF mess, which was apart from the rickety little Arab town. The bedrooms, in a long low building, led on to a verandah and then to the flower-beds which were the pride of the English officers. There they grew geraniums and spring onions, in paraded straight lines. The commanding officer, whose name was Ford and of course called 'Henry' by his friends, walked up and down the line of onions and geraniums each morning, and they seemed to straighten their stalks, at his glance.[22]

The hangars and garages were full of aircraft and armoured cars. This little core of power was planted in the desert, and protected by barbed-wire entanglements, and traps for wicked Arabs who might try to trespass. Every now and then an armoured car would become restive in its garage: it would snort, emerge into sunlight and hurtle off into the desert, to warn the bedouin of its power...

One was not aware of these savage intentions within the barbed-wire corral of the RAF. This was my first experience of the Service... And I trace my liking for the RAF to those days in Ma'an: I found a candour, a lack of introspection, and kindliness I have seldom known in a community of men. Perhaps their isolation, with their little group of aircraft and armoured cars, developed these virtues: the relationship between the few officers and the men was unselfconscious and delightful; the humour was frothy and spontaneous and the habits of life were as English as they could make them, within a world of Arabs and sand.

On his second night at Ma'an, after dinner in the Officers' Mess, Hector Bolitho was taken by two officers to visit the NCOs. He continues:

We drank beer; we told bawdy stories and we talked sentimentally about England. No more than that...but very funny when you are sitting in a smoke-filled room in Ma'an, a struggling speck of civilisation in the desert, with eight or ten young Britons who never heard of Hillel and to whom Muhammad is only a name, but who have learned to practise and live the best of their teaching.[23]

My liking for the RAF was greatly encouraged by the sessions of drinking beer in the NCOs' mess, to which the officers went most evenings after dinner. Perhaps they found that sergeants and corporals were less inhibited, for they shed their own slight stiffness the moment they entered the smoky room. Such phrases as *"esprit de corps,"* "morale" and "team spirit" were suspect with me until I lived in Ma'an. I thought they were the mottoes of jingoism. But there was more than this in the unsentimental comradeship, the mutual dependence and the good humour I enjoyed with the RAF.

The isolation forced them to create their own life, without the stimulus of girls and cinema. They had no amusements but those they made for themselves. Beyond the cluster of frail buildings in which they lived was nothing but the village at Ma'an and then the infinity of the desert...

Before daybreak I was on the verandah smelling the border of spring onions, and waiting for the armoured car. It drew up in front of me, with the precision of a London taxicab. I know nothing about motor-cars and less about warfare, so the gross, dangerous monster was an object of dark magic to me. I was shut into a case of metal, with a slim opening in front of me. In this, the desert was framed; a prospect of interminable dust, still grey and indefinite in the changing light. I clung to every available support as the car crashed forward. I was Jonah in a steel whale; a die in a box.

Next to me sat the corporal, excited, it seemed, at the sensation of driving. He said that speed thrilled him. We flew over the sand towards the yellowing horizon. Fifteen miles out into the desert, we stopped. Craning forward, we watched the golden rim of the sand. The light spread like liquid, mile upon mile, until lively shapes began to form upon it... Flame burst through the yellow light; the sun, big and red... It rose and in a second the desert woke up. Every grain of sand was lighted; every miserable tussock burst into flower; every slumbering, living thing stirred and rejoiced. I turned and looked at the airman next to me. He too seemed to be radiant with the sensations of the dawn. From living on the desert so long, he seemed to be part of it... He turned the car and we travelled back to the barracks.[24]

From Ma'an, the RAF armoured cars made regular reconnaissances to Gueira in the south, northwards to Tawil Shak, north-eastwards to Jafir and then Bair, with its wells, castle and favoured camping ground of the Huweitat tribe, and on to Bir Imshash, some 100 miles from Amman and as far as one could go before crossing the frontier into Saudi Arabia. A welcome break from the desert was a patrol down to Aqaba, where they could find time to swim and fish in the clear waters of the Red Sea.

Glubb's plan for the Desert Patrol was to build a series of forts, each manned by 10 to 20 men of the Arab Legion, and located near permanent wells or wherever the bedouin had to pass on their annual migrations to better pastures. In the first instance, he prepared for the arrival of the tribes from the Jebel Druze in Syria during summer and autumn of 1931. To enable vehicles to move to these places, he set about clearing and opening new tracks. Glubb continues:

Our idea was to move out before the tribes and plant ourselves exactly on

The loyal servants of the armoured cars. A Crossley six-wheeled tender has its water tanks replenished at Aqaba (© Crown copyright. RAF Regiment Museum).

the line of their migration. I had about 25 men available for this task, and we were going to place ourselves in the path of many thousand tribesmen, in country where vehicles could move only down our very narrow tracks at the pace of men walking on foot. The force seemed inadequate, and I consequently arranged with the ever-willing RAF for a section of their armoured cars to accompany us. We duly took up our position after some heavy work through a particularly dense field of lava, through which we literally moved yard by yard, levering enormous boulders out of the way with crowbars. But no sooner were we in position, than the heavens were opened, and it rained and rained. Our camp was soon a river and all the vehicles, especially the armoured cars, were completely bogged. Fortunately there were plenty of bushes available to keep a large fire going to warm and dry us. We lay thus bogged, and damped in spirits as well as in body, for five days, and no tribes appeared.[25]

On the sixth day the rain stopped, and camelmen were seen approaching. Glubb and his force provided a cordial welcome and great hospitality to the new arrivals. They were a party of the Sharafat tribe and their Sheikh arrived few days later. Following the reception accorded to this Sheikh and another of the same tribe, they both agreed to put an end to raiding. Glubb continues:

With affairs taking a favourable turn, we thanked the armoured cars for their support, and they returned, nothing loath, to Amman, in time for Christmas.[26]

Glubb and the Desert Patrol immediately had a positive effect on raiding and within a short time the desert was at peace. The last bedouin raid occurred during July 1932 when tribesmen from Saudi Arabia looted camels from the Huweitat while in Saudi territory. Glubb's great achievement was the suppression of raiding within two years of his arrival. This was not through repression and imprisonment, but by negotiation, financial subsidies, and by creating a force, the Desert Patrol of the Arab Legion, to which the bedouin flocked in great numbers. His success is further reinforced by noting that after 1932, the Rolls-Royce armoured cars of No 2 Company were never again required to deal with any troubles to do with bedouin raiding.

To the south-east of Transjordan, Amir Abdullah's father, King Hussein ibn Ali had been driven from the Hedjaz in 1925 by Ibn Saud and the Wahhabis, who as a consequence took control of the holy sites of Mecca and Medina. This also brought them much closer to the Transjordan frontier.[27] The boundary negotiations between the British Colonial Office and King Ibn Saud were resolved to a certain extent by 1927 with the southern boundary of Transjordan being a line drawn east from the port of Aqaba through Mudawarra. This gave Transjordan access to a port of considerable strategic value with an outlet to the Red Sea.

Notwithstanding the successes in suppressing raiding, there remained other matters of greater strategic significance to the region in which the RAF would play a role. In 1927, Ibn Saud had sent a punitive raid against the certain section of the tribes located in the Red Sea area near Aqaba. Many of their leaders were killed, but among the survivors was Hamid ibn Refada of the Billi tribe and he and his followers had fled to the Sinai desert in Egypt.

In April 1932, Ibn Refada began to collect a following and made clear his intention to raise an anti-Saudi insurrection in the northern Hedjaz (Map 16, p. 158). The civil authorities in Amman learnt of this in early May, but the threat was not made known to the RAF until the Special Service Officer at Ma'an reported the movement of 250 tribesmen from Aqaba on 21 May. To reach the Hedjaz, the rebels had to cross a small stretch of Palestine and Transjordan and this would give the Saudi government cause for complaint. Furthermore, as there was some sympathy for the rebels among Transjordan government officials, the local Arab Legion and police, their transit across Transjordan would not be blocked. There was also concern that the local bedouin might resume raiding or more seriously, rise up in support of this revolt, inflaming a broader conflict between Transjordan and Saudi Arabia. The British Government was however, anxious to maintain friendly relations with the Saudis, to provide proof of its neutrality and to show that no support was being given to Ibn Refada. The changing relationship between the British and Saudi Governments was clearly demonstrated in early January 1930 when the aircraft of No 14 Squadron and a section of No 2 Company had escorted a caravan travelling though Transjordan to supply a military force of King Ibn Saud's men at Djauf in the Nejed.

An Imperial force, designated 'Souforce', under the command of Group Captain Ivor Fowler AFC, the Officer Commanding RAF Amman, was therefore despatched to southern Transjordan to cooperate with, and bolster the Arab Legion posts. 'Souforce' consisted of two flights of No 14 Squadron, 'C' Section of No 2 Armoured Car Company (plus an additional section standing by at short notice at Ramleh), one bomber-transport aircraft No 216 Squadron, a detachment of the TJFF with two troops 'D' Company (Camels) and 'M' Company (Mechanised) and a Hotchkiss Machine-gun Troop. The Royal Navy at Aqaba provided HMS *Penzance* which was later replaced by HMS *Hastings*.

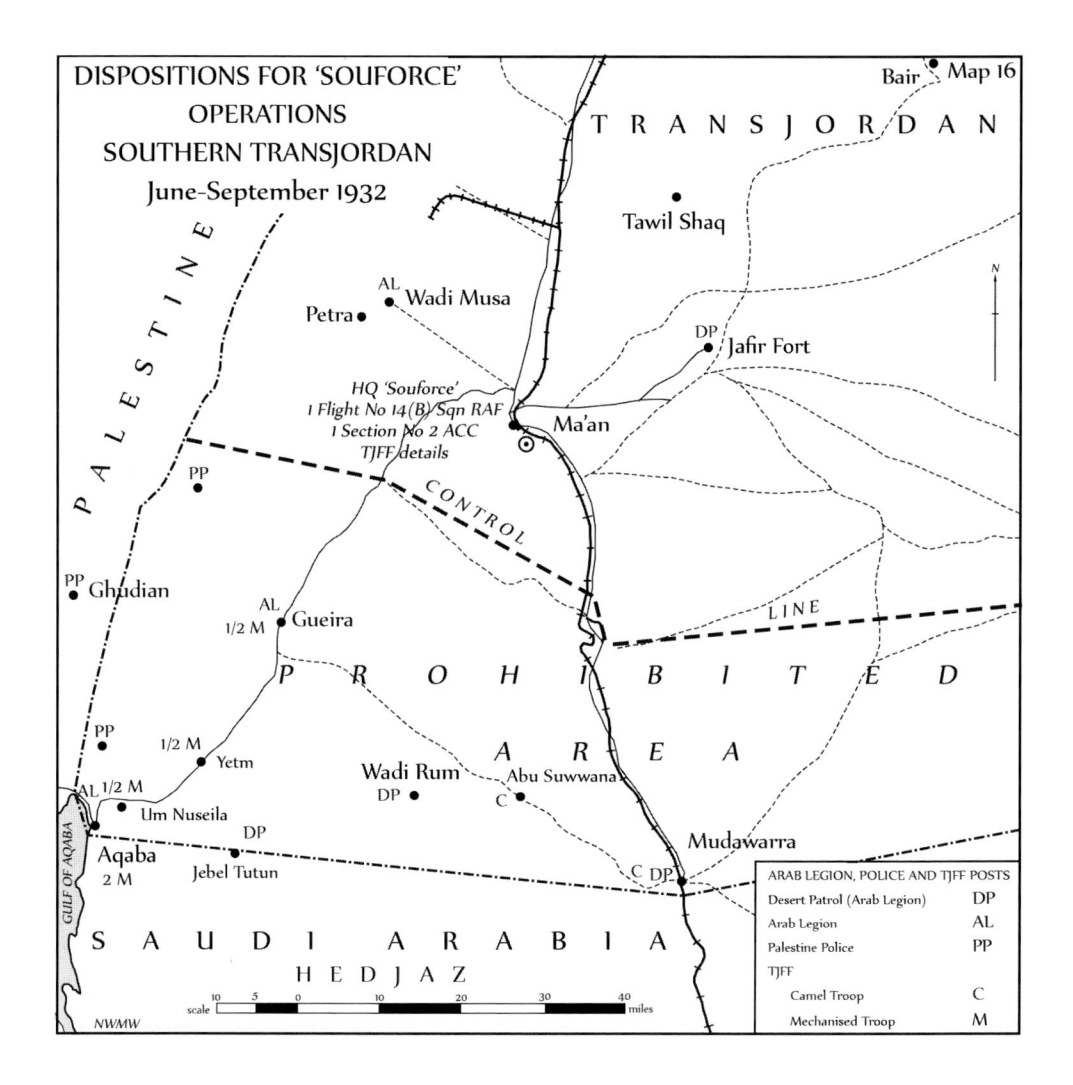

Operations lasted from 14 June to 2 September 1932. The border with Palestine and the Hedjaz of Saudi Arabia was watched closely for Ibn Refada and his followers, by the aircraft patrols of No 14 Squadron, the Mechanised and Camel Companies of the TJFF and the Arab Legion and Police posts that lay in the likely path of movement. The objectives of 'Souforce' were to prevent the passage of supplies or movement of reinforcements through Transjordan to the Ibn Refada's rebels. A prohibited zone was defined to the north by Ma'an and the south by Aqaba. It was made clear that every effort was to be made to turn the rebels back without opening fire and even then, should they ignore this request, their camels or vehicles were to be the targets. Firing on the tribesmen was to be a last resort.

The initial passage of the largest group of the rebels had occurred without hindrance and so in the event that they attempted to retreat through Transjordan, they were to be intercepted, disarmed and then handed over to the Transjordanian authorities. Furthermore, 'Souforce' were to repel any attempt by the Saudi forces or more particularly the Ikhwan, should they use this incursion as an excuse to sweep

The Wadi Rum, Transjordan (Rolph, RAFACA).

into Transjordan to capture Aqaba and Ma'an and threaten Amman. 'Souforce' had little to stop an invasion, other than a few machine-guns in the TJFF companies, the aeroplanes of No 14 Squadron and the Rolls-Royce armoured cars and tenders of the one section of No 2 Company.

By mid-July, Ibn Refada's force in the Hedjaz had grown in size to 800 men. However, with their supply lines cut and with no more hope of reinforcements reaching them from Transjordan due to the blockade by 'Souforce', discontent with their leaders and fear of being trapped began to take hold. On 30 July, the rebels were routed by a combined force of Saudi Government troops equipped with machine-guns and Ikhwan camelmen. Ibn Refada, along with 370 of his followers, was killed in battle. Henceforth, 'Souforce' concentrated on the interception and disarming of the retiring rebels and refugees, men, women and children, now fleeing the ruthless 'mopping up' operations being carried out by the Ikhwan against the rebels and suspected local sympathisers in the Hedjaz.

After nearly 12 weeks of great tedium, watching and patrolling by the armoured cars at the height of an extremely hot summer, operations came to a successful conclusion. The task had initially been complicated by the presence of groups of non-belligerent bedouin moving through the prohibited zone, with most being ignorant of the larger events at play. The Royal Navy sloop, HMS *Penzance*, intercepted a boat bringing arms and supplies across the Gulf of Aqaba, and on land, a few small rebel parties were sighted by the RAF armoured cars and the TJFF, and were handed over to the Arab Legion.

Experience had also been gained in the use of aircraft to supply the scattered detachments. The attachment of a single Vickers Victoria of No 216 Squadron altered and simplified the supply problem. The RAF armoured cars were supplied by air with

3   King Feisal had entered Damascus at the head of the Arab Army and not unreasonably had formed an Arab kingdom. This had not however been part of the plan for the Sykes-Picot agreement.
4   Général Maurice-Paul-Emmanuel Sarrail (1856–1929).
5   A. Geraghty, *March or Die* (London: Guild Publishing, 1986), pp. 165-168.
6   A. Clayton, *France, Soldiers and Africa* (London: Brassey's, 1988), pp. 111-112.
7   J. Lunt, *The Arab Legion 1923-1957* (London: Constable, 1999), p. 52.
8   S.F. Vincent, *Flying Fever* (London: Jarrolds, 1972), p. 70. Air Vice-Marshal S.F. Vincent CB DFC AFC DL would be the only man to have shot down enemy aircraft from single-seat fighters in both World Wars. He would later command 221 Group RAF in the Burma campaign with great success.
9   AIR 5/1243 *Operations: Palestine, Vol. I, Chapter 1 to 14, 1920-1930*.
10 Vincent, *Flying Fever*, pp. 68-69.
11 Lieutenant-Colonel (later Sir) Henry Cox replaced Philby in 1924 and remained as Chief British Resident until 1939.
12 Vincent, *Flying Fever*, p. 69.
13 Y. Gil-Har, 'Delimitation Boundaries: Transjordan and Saudi Arabia', *Middle Eastern Studies*, 28 (2000), pp. 374-384.
14 AIR 5/1243 *Operations: Palestine, Vol. I*. Under the command of Group Captain P.H.L. Playfair MC. The force was accompanied by Kirkbride, Amir Shakir and the ADC to the Amir.
15 *Ibid*. Interestingly, the RAF tenders had been used for the transport of the TJFF detachment as the usual procedure of hiring vehicles would have signalled the intention of the Government days before the operation. It was also thought unwise to use hired civilian drivers as the column was thought likely to come under fire and their behaviour would have been unpredictable, if not fatal for themselves or their passengers.
16 Amir Shakir ibn Zeid had fought alongside Amir Abdullah and T.E. Lawrence during the Arab Revolt of the First World War. His son, Field Marshal Shakir ibn Zeid, became the Commander-in-Chief of the Jordanian Armed Forces and then Prime Minister. J. Lunt, *Hussein of Jordan*, (London: MacMillan, 1989), p. xxv, and Glubb, *The Story of the Arab Legion*, p. 96.
17 AIR 29/54 *2 Armoured Car Company, Heliopolis (Egypt); formed 7 April 1922. Includes detachment at Amman (Trans-Jordan); moved to Ramleh (Palestine) 12 March 1923; moved to Amman 1 May 1928; moved to Ramleh 28 August 1928 with detachments at Amman and Ma'an; later detachments at Jerusalem and Haifa*. The wounded airmen were Corporal Cobden and LAC Upcraft.
18 AIR 5/1243 *Operations: Palestine, Vol. I*.
19 No 14 Squadron had handed in their Ninaks for Fairey Gordons.
20 AIR 29/56 *2 Armoured Car Company, appendices only; September 1923-July 1946*.
21 Mornington S. Wentworth, *Interview 4768* (London: IWM Sound Archive, 1980).
22 Possibly Flight Lieutenant Richard J.A. Ford No 2ACC, April 1931 to March 1933.
23 Hillel was a famous Jewish religious leader and scholar born in Babylon c. 110 BC. He is associated with the development of the Talmud, one of the central texts of Judaism.
24 H. Bolitho, *Angry Neighbours* (London: Arthur Barker, 1957), pp. 83-87. Bolitho joined the RAFVR at the outbreak of the Second World War and worked in intelligence, reaching the rank of Squadron Leader. He edited the *RAF Weekly Bulletin*, later the *RAF Journal*.
25 Glubb, *The Story of the Arab Legion*, p. 109.
26 *Ibid.*, p. 110.
27 Hussein took refuge in Aqaba with his remaining followers, where he stayed until offered exile by Great Britain in Cyprus.
28 'No 14 (Bomber) Squadron', W.A. Cooke, *Flight*, January 18 1934, p. 52.
29 J. Lunt, *The Arab Legion 1923-1957* (London: Constable, 1999), p. 44.

Chapter Nine

Iraq 1930-1939

"Orders were at once issued for No 3 Section, Armoured Cars, to close on Sulaimaniya in order to take up a fresh patrol line to the south-east, but although the Section Commander, Flight Lieutenant Noel Keeble DSC DFC moved promptly and with great energy, the rebels just won the race..."
Air Vice-Marshal Edgar Ludlow-Hewitt, AOC Iraq[1]

By early 1929, the number of RAF armoured car sections in Iraq had been further reduced from eight to six. The armoured cars had departed from Kirkuk in August 1928 after six years in residence. Only one section, No 5, remained in the north at RAF Mosul, with the remainder at Hinaidi and Basra. For months at a time during 1929 and 1930 however, the Mosul section was often located at Hinaidi, leaving no RAF armoured cars stationed in the north of Iraq for the first time since 1922. Additional demands were made on the Armoured Car Wing from outside Iraq in early September 1929 when No 3 Section was despatched to assist No 2 Armoured Car Company in Palestine, as the disturbances there intensified. At the same time, eight armoured car personnel from the Wing departed from Baghdad on the Nairn bus en route for RAF Aboukir in Egypt where they were to form a new armoured car section to serve as part of No 2 Company.

Further reductions in the armoured cars were required by April 1930. The Armoured Car Wing HQ was disbanded and No 1 Armoured Car Company, which had been disbanded in Palestine in December 1923, was re-established at Hinaidi and the six sections were reduced to four with the Headquarters, Workshops and Nos 2 and 3 Sections stationed at RAF Hinaidi and Nos 1 and 4 Sections at Mosul and Basra, respectively.[2]

The early months of 1930 were spent in reorganising No 1 Armoured Car Company into four sections, reallocating the vehicles and on general maintenance. The crews practised their gun and car drills, map reading and signalling. In early 1929, new Morris and Crossley six-wheeled tenders had arrived; however, efforts in the United Kingdom to develop a new armoured car were still faltering. The first of these, the Crossley six-wheeled armoured car, was collected in early March 1929 from Amman and brought to Baghdad for trials by the Company. A few weeks later, the Crossley armoured car broke down while being tested cross-country near Karbala and was returned to Hinaidi by train. Eighteen months later, a new experimental Crossley armoured car was collected from Haifa. It was noted pointedly that it arrived at Hinaidi with a badly bent front axle, whereas no troubles of any kind were experienced with the escorting Rolls-Royces.[3]

A card highlighting the supposed effects of service with the RAF in Iraq (Beaney, RAFACA).

"! My Relief—I hope !"

Iraq was not considered a plum posting in the RAF due to the adverse climate. The severe heat and high humidity at Basra and Shaibah was particularly unpleasant. The officers and airmen were only required to serve two of their five years of overseas service in either country. The officers could then opt for a home posting. The airmen could choose to sign on for a third year in Iraq, if medically fit, or more likely they would go on to Palestine, Transjordan, Egypt or India, the more pleasant climate and surroundings making the former location an attractive posting.[4]

The airmen who were coming to Iraq by the 1930s were too young to have served in the Great War. Some had joined the RAF to escape unemployment, some because their home situation was not happy or the family needed another income; others joined for the adventure. Arthur Rolph joined the RAF in 1929 when he was 19 years old. He had left school at 15 and already had a regular job as a driver for a company that made radio parts. His eldest brother had served in the Army in the Great War and was now in the Fire Service, and his elder brother was serving in the Royal Navy. The RAF was a modern and exciting service that particularly attracted those like Arthur with a mechanical bent. The other factor was the lure of overseas travel and a chance to see the world. Arthur went straight from training to the Armoured Cars, and arrived in Iraq in 1930, where he was posted to No 2 Section at RAF Hinaidi. One of his fellow airmen was Vic Brandon. He had arrived the previous year and had been sent to No 3 Section. Both would take part in the operations that would finally see the capture of Sheikh Mahmud.

Aircraftman Mornington Wentworth had started his RAF career at Uxbridge and then trained as a driver at Manston before being sent to RAF Digby for a few years. He had then volunteered for the Armoured Car Course at Eastchurch. There was the attraction of a higher pay rate, 22 rather than 16 shillings a week, and attendance at the course implied automatic volunteering for overseas service. Furthermore, there were other career benefits. If you passed a trade or educational exam while serving with the armoured cars, you were automatically reclassified or promoted, which didn't necessarily happen in other branches. He continues:

Aircraftman Vic Brandon of No 1 Armoured Car Company (Brandon, RAFACA).

You had to know far more on armoured cars than as an ordinary driver. There was a lot more to a Rolls-Royce engine than there was to the usual car engines. There were twin ignitions, a magneto on one side and a coil on the other. Each cylinder had two sparking plugs. It was a different carburettor from what we'd been used to. You had to be able to use Morse code with buzzers and Aldis lamps, and semaphore with flags and all at a certain speed.[5]

The main means of transport to the Middle East was still in one of His Majesty's Troopships, usually with 2000 troops on board. The airmen slept on hammocks hung from beams packed closely with the other airmen in poorly-ventilated mess decks. During inclement weather, the stench and mess due to sea-sickness made the situation even more unpleasant. Officers had more space with two to a two-berth cabin. The 'trooping season' was normally during the cooler months late in the year. The troopships travelled to India, disembarking troops at Egypt, Iraq and Aden. Those more fortunate came on passenger ships if travelling between trooping seasons.

Mornington Wentworth arrived in Basra in 1934 on his first overseas posting after three weeks on HMT *Dorsetshire*. None of the new arrivals had been told where in Iraq they were to be stationed. Upon disembarking, they were taken directly to Basra railway station to board the train to Baghdad. He continues:

The impression when I got on the train was not good, although we were to find worse. You were crammed in these tin cattle trucks. On Sunday they had arrived full of donkeys. They were swept out and bundles of blankets were put in and cases of tinned food. The smell was disgusting and the heat inside was terrible.

You had the tinned food you could help yourself to and periodically along the line they would stop and there would be some natives there with a fire going and they'd made you a cup of tea. I don't recall much variety in the food. I can always remember this Harris' and Maconochies tinned food and it looked good. There was a coloured label on the tin with nice pieces of meat and vegetables. It was foul and I never liked it. If I was going on a trip and I knew we were going to have this I would buy a tin of sardines rather than eat them.

Then we arrived at Baghdad and had a day at Hinaidi. We were then flown in Vickers Valentias to Mosul. The reception that we got was out of this world. There was a red carpet; always a humorous side to it. There were airmen there already that we had known at Manston and they were told that if they saw an airman they had known previously they were to take him to the NAAFI for a cup of tea. You were given an extra special dinner that night and a concert. It was really wonderful. You felt at home.

The happiest station I ever served on was Mosul. The comradeship was out of his world. You'd nothing outside mind; you had to make your own amusements. There was one chap, LAC Oliver Cromwell. If ever there was a Christian chap he was it, he would give his all for the airmen. He'd organise concerts, he'd spend night after night playing records for us in the NAAFI. And that lad would kneel by his bed every night and say his prayers and nobody jeered at him.[6]

Time for a brew-up and a smoke. Airmen stretch their legs while a troop train en route to Baghdad makes a short stop at Samawah (Brandon, RAFACA).

While on the Station, there were the daily inspections of the barrack rooms and kit by the NCOs and by the Section or Company commander each week. An airman could however, pay a local man to bring him tea twice a day in camp, do his washing, clean the barrack room, make up his bed, polish his buttons and clean his web equipment. The major events were the King's Birthday Parade and the inspection by the AOC which both involved a lot of drill and the cleaning and preparation of the cars.

Whilst RAF Hinaidi was in close proximity to Baghdad, there were few options for entertainment. For the officers there was a limited social world associated with the civil and military officials and their families, but much of the activity had to be created on the station itself. For three shillings, an airman could catch a taxi and spend Saturday night at the few hotels, where you could drink in an open-air courtyard. There were areas that were out of bounds such as the coffee shops and cabarets in the deeper parts of Baghdad where there was belly dancing and other entertainment. The RAF Police did their best to ensure that airmen didn't go out of bounds, but were not always successful in that task. Female company for the airmen was virtually non-existent as the only women at Hinaidi were the English nurses in the hospital. As Stan Eastmead, a fitter at the Armoured Car Workshops noted, if you wanted to see a white woman you had to get very ill.[7]

On Sundays, there were Church Parades for the officers and airmen. They could visit the bazaars in Baghdad to view the carpet and linen stalls, to watch the coppersmiths at work or peruse the souvenirs and other wares being purveyed by jostling crowds of shopkeepers. There were hordes of street urchins pouncing on the newly-arrived airmen, offering their services as guides or interpreters for a tour of the city's attractions. Further afield they could, on occasions, take an RAF tender and visit some of the famous archaeological sites such as Babylon, the Ukhaidr Palace and the Ctesiphon Arch (at that time the largest unsupported arch in the world).[8] Some of the officers would go off for a time on shoots for waterfowl in the marshes to the south. AC1 Vic Brandon described one such trip, to the west of Baghdad, in a letter to his sister, Lily:

> A party of us left Hinaidi for a place known as Notch Falls [sic Notchfall]. It actually consists of a huge lake with a waterfall, and a few Arab houses. We often take day trips to that place during the summer as it affords excellent swimming and just as good fishing.[9]

Sport was strongly encouraged as the main means of keeping fit and active. The armoured car sections often had their own football teams and there was a Company team that entered the Iraq Command competitions. Cricket, tennis, hockey, soccer and boxing were popular, while there was also a very large swimming pool where an airman could earn his RAF Swimming Certificate. The first three years of the decade had been quite successful for the Company, as it had excelled in a broad range of sports. In August 1931, the cricket team won the final round of the 'RAF Iraq Hard-hitting Cup' and a few weeks later the 'Open Cup'. The Featherweight Championship of the RAF Iraq Boxing Association Championship for Novices was won by LAC M.S. Moore, and the following March, the Company won the Hinaidi Association Football League Senior Division. Later triumphs included winning the Hinaidi Water Polo League.

There was also the opportunity for education, with the RAF Station employing a civilian school teacher who ran small evening classes for airmen and junior NCOs studying for the higher education certificates. Trade-training classes were run, with tests twice a year given by a travelling trade test board.

At night there was the NAAFI canteen, a camp cinema, table tennis, darts and games of cards were a very popular pastime. Every Friday night there was Housey-Housey[10] and, once a month, a sing-song. Number 1 Armoured Car Company had a concert party and shows were often put on. Vic Brandon wrote of the difficulties of keeping these entertainments going, with demands from operations and postings:

> I am pleased to say that I have got the "Fireman's Wedding" off pat by now and am just getting into a humorous song called "Football". Even now we are not certain yet whether the concert party will perform again as when I had to leave Hinaidi to join No 3 Section, two or three other members of the party had to leave, so the whole show was thrown in. Still I believe they are taking heart again and are going to make another valiant attempt to collect the talent, so the poor suffering audiences are not spared yet awhile.[11]

Another more mundane amusement was to keep the local predatory insects, such as scorpions, tarantulas and the 5 inch long centipedes, as pets or use them in fighting competitions, the arenas being large copper bowls.

There were the famous welcoming-in and farewell 'boat-dinners', held in October for those arriving or departing 'on the boat'. Officers had their own parties, dining-in nights and occasional visits for games of darts in the Sergeants' Mess, which also had its own rounds of functions. Vic Brandon continues:

> I don't know whether mother told you about our 'do' last Saturday when we held a dance and impromptu concert in the canteen. Anyway, it was

The 'Boat Dinner' of 1930 (Brandon, RAFACA).

to celebrate the arrival of the last boat from Blighty. So of course all our homemade songs and parodies were rendered, including 'Come and join us'. The dance went down okay although we only had a piano and drums as accompaniment....[12]

Christmas was the time that the celebrations really took off. The barrack rooms were stripped of their fittings and could be turned into dens, cocktail bars, Wild West saloons complete with swinging doors, or hunting lodges; whatever their designers' imaginations and ingenuity would allow. This would often take the form of a competition for the best decorated barrack room. The Commanding Officer's prize might be a crate of McEwans Red Label beer or rather disappointingly for the airmen in one year, a silver trophy.[13] Later on Christmas Day, for those still able to stand, there might be a comic football match before, as tradition demanded (as it still does today in the RAF), Christmas Dinner would be served to the airmen by the officers and senior NCOs. The Christmas break lasted for six days and those of more temperate habits found the drinking and consequent poor behaviour disagreeable.[14]

In 1930, it was decided to establish an RAF Summer Training Camp at Ser Amadia, 6000 feet up in the Kurdish mountains, 85 miles north-east of Mosul and close to the Persian frontier. Airmen were either driven or flown to Mosul and on to Simele where they transferred to trucks for a five-hour ride on the road up precipitous mountainous slopes. This trip could be hair-raising with sheer drops and sharp bends. The lorries often had to go round partially, then reverse, and then go straight again. For the last 2000 feet of the climb, the airmen transferred to mules to carry them up

The RAF summer training and rest camp at Ser Amadia. It was 85 miles north-east of Mosul, close to the Turkish frontier and 6000 feet up in the hills of Kurdistan (Rolph, RAFACA).

a mountain path to the camp. The camp was occupied by a Kurdish Company of the Levies who provided the local guard.

The camp, open from April to September each year, was set in beautiful and spectacular mountain scenery and allowed the officers and airmen to escape to the cool mountain air, away from the oppressive summer heat of the plains. While at Ser Amadia, usually for a fortnight, the airmen took their annual musketry course, but the main reason was for rest and relaxation, with opportunities for fishing, swimming in a specially-built pool, and hiking or mule riding to local villages.

Airmen look on with some trepidation as a dust storm approaches (© Crown copyright. RAF Regiment Museum).

The first visit for newly-arrived drafts at Hinaidi would be to sick quarters for a check-up and each airman would then be allocated to an armoured car crew. The first expedition off the station was usually an overnight practice 'recco' about 50 miles out into 'the blue'. This provided them experience on driving on rough tracks, extraction of the cars from sand, and driving prolonged distances in dusty conditions. At the day's end, they would learn the procedures for making camp; how to light a fire and start the cooking, the precautions to be taken in camp, organising guard patrols and how to be always ready for action. The training took up a large amount of time, particularly in the months following the arrival of 'the Boat'. Mornington Wentworth continues:

> Our main job was to keep tracks open, making ourselves familiar with the countryside, show a bit of strength in the villages and do a lot of training… Each section had seven armoured cars, six were out and the seventh was

always in the workshop. When that was overhauled you took another in and took the overhauled one out. The Rolls-Royce that I was using had been built in 1912 and I was still driving those cars as a Car Commander in 1943. Snags were broken half shafts and cracked sump plates. The sump was rather low and there were no roads and if there was load of rocks to go over, we went over them we didn't pick our way around.

It was a wonderful life and I enjoyed it to the full… We used to go out a fortnight at a time. If we were to camp for three or four days we would put up tents and toilets. Other than that we slept with the sky as a roof.

The cars were quite heavily laden. They carried two camel tanks as well as chargals full of water… Underneath the car running boards there were two ditching boards for getting out of sand. We had a large tow chain and spare spring on the back. There was a beautiful tool kit either side from Rolls-Royce, a spare sump plate and half shaft. Of course you put your rations in the tool box and they both acted as seat each for the gunner and the car commander. We carried eight signal flags. These flags used in various ways to give orders to the other cars. They meant stop or go or all car commanders report to leading car, form Vee-formation or line abreast. The armour was 3/8 inch thick steel plate but it was a two man job to lift off side plate to get at your engine.

The temperature inside during summer was terrific and I'd known it to get up to 55 °C inside the car. You couldn't do a thing to keep the temperature down other than any breeze you might get through the car. You had a view of about six inches, but if it was battened down for action it was about one inch. That was all you got to see out of. You had to take notice of what the car commander told you because you couldn't see back, that's for certain.[15]

The road and tracks could prove difficult for the tender drivers, particularly as they had to keep up with the swifter Rolls-Royces. Mornington Wentworth continues:

Two miles in 36 hours. The difficulties of desert travel across salt marsh and soft sand (Rolph, RAFACA).

I was involved in a road accident with a vehicle. It should never have gone out. I was having a rest from armoured cars and was driving a six-wheeler. I knew before I went that the brakes weren't working. We used to get a wriggle on mind you, because the armoured cars would be going up to 60 miles an hour; as heavy as they were. The lorries used to have to keep up with them. I went off the road and went down a concrete slip way and I couldn't get back and there was a bridge in front of me, and I just managed to get the front wheels up as I was approaching the bridge. There was a spare wheel on the outside and it caught that and it ripped the side of my vehicle out. It was a right old 'do', and I had to have a court of inquiry.[16]

Cooperation between RAF aircraft and armoured cars was essential. At this time however, there were no radios and the only means of communication with RAF aeroplanes was by message pick-up. Wentworth continues:

You put two poles up, with a string across the top, and you tied a message to it. The aircraft would come over and he lowered a hook from the underside of his aircraft. And he flew low and he picked up that piece of string with the message on it. It worked perfectly and we use to do this as practice back in camp.

Now I had a very nasty crash while I was there. This pal of mine had volunteered with me on armoured cars. We'd never left; I'd joined up with him. I was at Uxbridge with him, Manston, Digby, Eastchurch, and Mosul. We were really close pals. We'd been up on the firing range and there was only two armoured cars taken up there and I was driver of one of them.

The CO of our section came up and he came to see us started and then he took off in an aircraft. These Section commanders had been flying training instructors and had then been sent on to armoured cars; almost as a rest. They were really clued-up officers who even asked an LAC for advice if necessary. They had to do so many hours flying to keep them in touch. He'd told us he was just going to take off and visit somewhere close-by.

We'd been firing at 200 yards, and these two armoured cars were moving back from 200 to 300 firing range, and two chaps were dragging a tarpaulin; one at either corner. And one of them was my pal.

The CO came over in his aircraft; he'd done it dozens of times. He'd get into a dive and give us a dip and away he went and we'd know that was Flight Lieutenant Sandiford. For some reason or other he didn't pull out. My pal saw this aircraft wasn't going to pull out and he ran straight into it. He went the wrong way.

The plane hit the first armoured car and lost a wing, he came to mine and he lost another wing. If I hadn't been in an armoured car I would not be relating this story that is for sure. It was a Wapiti two-seater and it was going up in flames and all in bits. Out of this wreckage, and it's a miracle and we'll never understand how, this LAC walked out. He'd been taken up by the Flight Lieutenant as his air gunner. He must have picked his feet up to get out of the wreckage. How he got out I don't know. Anyway, we got him down and rolled him on the ground to put the fire out but he was shockingly burnt. Then we looked inside and we could see the pilot still sat in his seat, dead, still strapped in... and a third body. This was remarkable, a two-seater aircraft; we had one man out, we could see the second one and yet there was a third.

   We had the eerie experience of having to fall in and call the roll to find out who it was. And it was my pal. It really shook me. He was a marvellous cricketer, this lad. And this day we'd drawn the cricket gear out of store for his first game up at Mosul.[17]

Wentworth's pal was AC1 John Plevey and he was buried in the RAF cemetery at Hinaidi along with their Section Commander, Flight Lieutenant Henry Sandiford.[18] The aircraft gunner LAC Jack Rogers was badly burnt but survived, though badly scarred. Another LAC, Harold Keattch of No 1 Section, was fortunate to receive only slight injuries.

South Kurdistan had remained quiet for the last few years of the decade as Sheikh Mahmud had kept his pledge and remained in exile in Persia. In the first weeks of September 1930 however, there was an outbreak of civil unrest in Sulaimaniya as a consequence of the parliamentary elections (Map 6, p. 51)). A political rally had developed into a riot, and the crowd was fired upon by the Iraqi Army. Although matters quietened down, reports were soon received that Sheikh Mahmud had collected an armed tribal force on the Persian border and that he had subversive intent. Despite being sent warning letters from the High Commissioner and the Iraq Minister of the Interior, Mahmud crossed from Persia into Iraq on 17 September and made contact with the Pishder tribe north of Sulaimaniya in his third attempt to raise an insurrection. Two further ultimatums were sent during October but he failed to comply and the decision was made to take offensive action.

The newly-appointed AOC Iraq, Air Vice-Marshal Edgar Ludlow-Hewitt, had assumed command on 12 October and determined that the Iraqi Army should take the lead role in the operations under their own commanders.[19] He would retain oversight of the plans and general conduct of the campaign, but British officers would act only as advisers and only one relatively junior officer would accompany each Iraqi Army column. The Iraq Levies would remain at Sulaimaniya in reserve, charged with putting the derelict defences in order and to provide parties to load aeroplanes during operations. The Iraq Army force consisted of a cavalry regiment, three infantry battalions and an artillery battery.

Notwithstanding the experience that had been gained by the Iraqi Army over the last few months, there was still a necessity for an RAF component in the operations to conduct reconnaissance and demonstration flights over the villages of Kurdistan. Ludlow-Hewitt was determined that on no account should villages be bombed if they had an association with the rebels. He felt that while they were not hostile to the Sheikh, the inhabitants had neither the moral or physical means to prevent him establishing his force in their localities. Air action would only be taken against the rebels should the Iraqi Army be threatened and require assistance.

The RAF provided an independent force under the command of Wing Commander 'Paddy' Quinnell DFC.[20] On 25 October, a flight of four Wapitis of No 30 Squadron from Mosul was sent to Sulaimaniya. This was soon found to be inadequate, and on 1 November a further flight each of Nos 30 and 55 Squadrons, and No 2 Section of No 1 Armoured Car Company were sent to Kirkuk. The force, known as 'A Squadron', was commanded by Squadron Leader R.V. Goddard. The main tasks of the armoured cars were to patrol the Sulaimaniya road as far as Chamchamal, to maintain wireless contact with the RAF at Sulaimaniya, and reinforce the Iraqi cavalry at Chamchamal if necessary. During this time they escorted the Levy transport column and the Iraqi Army artillery battery as these columns moved to Sulaimaniya (Map 17, p. 177).

By late October, Sheikh Mahmud had moved back into Persia, where he unsuccessfully attempted to raise support from the local tribes. He then moved back across the frontier and began operating in the vicinity of Khurmal. In response, an Iraqi Army column departed from Sulaimaniya and reached Serao during the last week of October. Meanwhile, a second column moved towards Choartah as the Sheikh had moved north to that area, and by the end of November the Iraqi Army had occupied Penjwin. Sheikh Mahmud had continued to move from village to village levying taxes and demanding arms, but by late-November reliable information had been received that he was retiring to the Avroman mountains on the Persian frontier. Furthermore, with the onset of the winter rains, both military operations and rebel movements would be severely limited.

A small Iraqi Army garrison remained at Sulaimaniya, but after covering the withdrawal of the remaining Iraqi units to the railway station at Kirkuk, the RAF composite force was disbanded, and the units returned to their stations. The aircraft had cooperated in every move of the Iraqi Army columns and had been used in reconnaissance, patrolling police posts, and dropping orders and supplies to the columns. Their main benefit had been to provide confidence to the ground troops, or by intervening when the situation had become serious. They had only been used in limited bombing attacks on a few occasions, as Ludlow-Hewitt was determined not to ostracise the local inhabitants. In the instance of Penjwin, this approach resulted in the villagers helping to drive away rebel picquets.

With their tasks completed, No 2 Section departed for Hinaidi. During a month of operations, they had covered 5166 miles, albeit it had not been considered desirable for the cars to travel any further than the Chamchamal, as the country beyond was considered unsuitable for armoured car operations.[21]

Small skirmishes continued between the rebels and the Iraqi Army during the winter months, with the Sheikh suffering a temporary setback at Serdash. However, by early-January he had reappeared in the south near Halebja, where he overran two police posts and obtained a large supply of arms and ammunition. Air Vice-Marshal Ludlow-Hewitt visited the area and quickly implemented a plan for the Iraqi Army in co-operation with the RAF to sweep the Halebja Plain. These operations prevented the capture of Halebja, but unfortunately, lack of mobility of Army units, compounded by terrible weather as well as poor tactics and commitment by some Iraqi Army commanders enabled Sheikh Mahmud to evade capture. The RAF armoured cars did not participate as the road conditions made their use impracticable.

Whilst the Iraqi Army was gaining experience, Mahmud was no closer to being apprehended. Indeed, his activities not been curtailed and he was gaining in prestige. Ludlow-Hewitt therefore implemented some changes during a two-month lull in operations. To enhance mobility, a force of Iraqi police was formed from local men that could move as fast the rebels. At the same time, an Iraqi cavalry regiment was trained specifically for hill warfare. To support these mobile operations, a chain of supply dumps was established across the hills. The Iraqi Government also requested that the RAF relax its prohibition on bombing of villages that were known to be harbouring rebels. Permission was subsequently given for air attacks on villages, but only after efforts had been made to drive the rebels out, and that even if they remained, adequate warning was given of the intention to bomb. Where possible, the rebels were to be attacked in the open once they had departed the villages. To

A Westland Wapiti in the Kurdish mountains (Rolph, RAFACA).

improve coordination of air operations in South Kurdistan, Wing Commander Guy Garrod MC DFC was appointed the local RAF commander at Sulaimaniya.[22]

In early-March, Sheikh Mahmud scored a further success when he attacked and looted an Army supply convoy moving towards Khurmal. His stature was growing amongst the inhabitants of the region as he had been operating for five months with few setbacks. He could move rapidly, in small or large groups depending on his need, live off the country and had an intimate knowledge of every mountain path. He did not have it all his own way; for example, when No 55 Squadron aircraft caught the rebels in the open, attacked, and caused a few casualties. However, matters became more serious when he moved further west with 500 followers and crossed the Qara Dagh. Here he hoped to raise a rebellion amongst the Jaf and Shaikhan tribes, exploiting emerging unrest as the Iraqi Government began tax collecting (Map 17, p. 177).

There was serious concern in Baghdad that the situation was deteriorating (the Jaf tribe for example, had some 2500 armed men, and were in danger of allying with Mahmud) and that the rebellion might spread, with all of South Kurdistan breaking out into open revolt. Air Vice-Marshal Ludlow-Hewitt therefore, despatched an RAF intelligence officer, Squadron Leader V.D. O'Malley MC, to the Kifri area with a W/T set and half of No 2 Section of the armoured cars as his armed support.[23] He established himself at the Qala Shirwana police post, on the Sirwan River, and made contact with friendly sections of the Jaf to ascertain the attitude of hostile elements. Together they did excellent work keeping Ludlow-Hewitt in touch with the situation. The area was composed of sparse rock and limestone and there was a complete absence of level ground. It was predominantly uninhabited except when the Jaf were grazing their livestock during the winter and spring months. There were few villages

Number 2 Section of No 1 Armoured Car Company passes Qala Shirwana as it deploys to Kifri to support No 55 (B) Squadron at Kingerban landing ground in March 1931 (Rolph, RAFACA).

or tracks and it was devoid of trees. A landing strip was found nearby from which a flight of No 55 Squadron sent aircraft to observe tribal encampments and movements and to support O'Malley's work. The frequent overflights by these aircraft and visits by the RAF armoured cars to local villages over the next fortnight had a calming effect on the tribesmen and prevented the spread of disaffection.

Notwithstanding the good work of O'Malley's group with the Jaf, the efforts of Sheikh Mahmud were bearing fruit to the east of Kifri, on the east bank of the

Airmen of No 2 Section on operations against Sheikh Mahmud. LAC Arthur Rolph is first on the right. Note the signalling flags strapped to the turret roof. These were used to communicate between cars (Rolph, RAFACA).

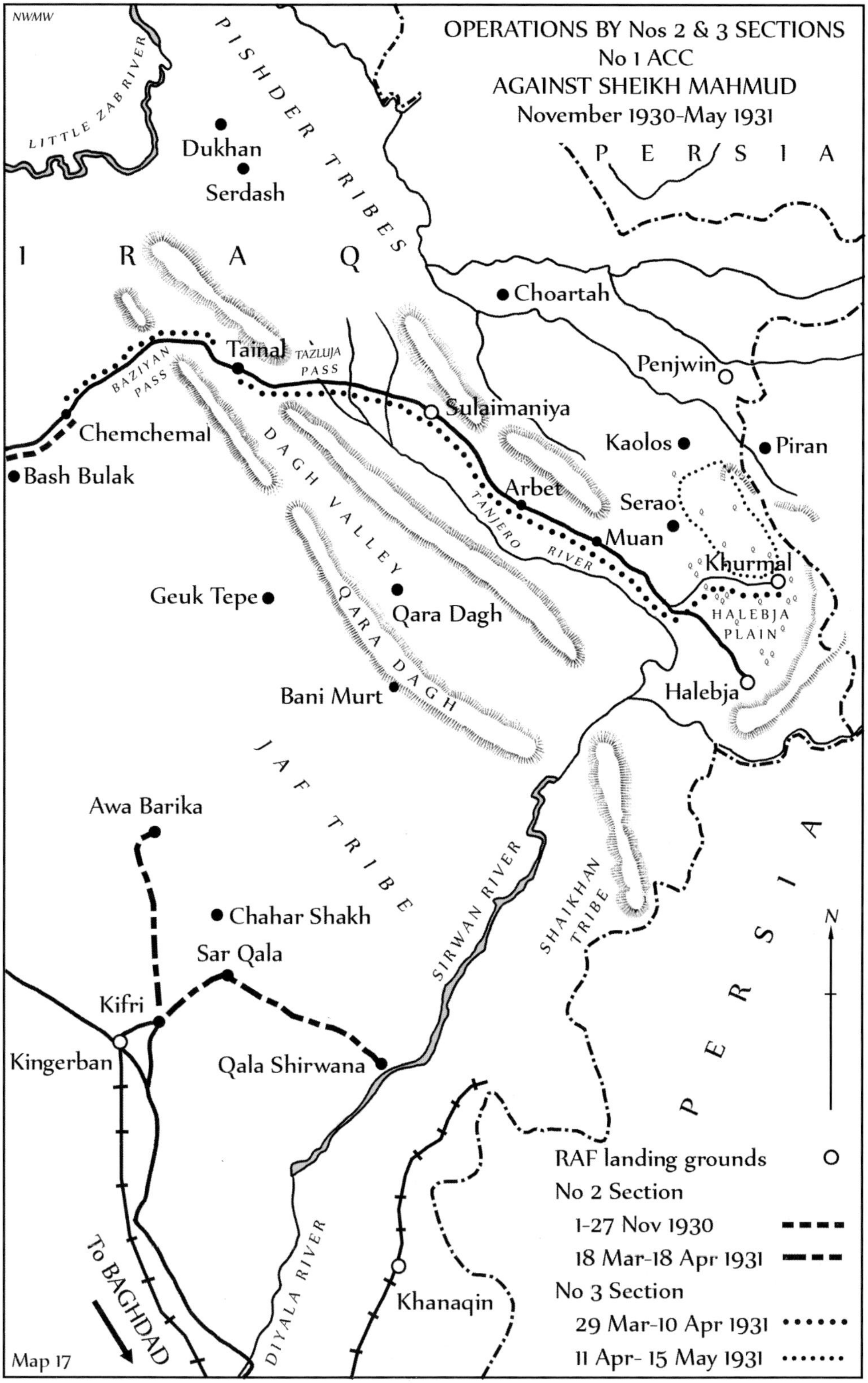
NWMW
OPERATIONS BY Nos 2 & 3 SECTIONS
No 1 ACC
AGAINST SHEIKH MAHMUD
November 1930-May 1931
PERSIA
IRAQ
LITTLE ZAB RIVER
PISHDER TRIBES
Dukhan
Serdash
Choartah
Penjwin
Tainal
TAZLUJA PASS
BAZIYAN PASS
Chemchemal
Bash Bulak
Sulaimaniya
Kaolos
Piran
DAGH VALLEY
Arbet
Serao
TANJERO RIVER
Muan
Khurmal
HALEBJA PLAIN
Halebja
Geuk Tepe
Qara Dagh
QARA DAGH
Bani Murt
JAF TRIBE
Awa Barika
Chahar Shakh
Sar Qala
Kifri
Kingerban
Qala Shirwana
SIRWAN RIVER
SHAIKHAN TRIBE
PERSIA
N
DIYALA RIVER
Khanaqin
To BAGHDAD
Map 17
RAF landing grounds
No 2 Section
1-27 Nov 1930
18 Mar-18 Apr 1931
No 3 Section
29 Mar-10 Apr 1931
11 Apr- 15 May 1931

Sirwan River, where the Shaikhan were showing signs of wavering. Police posts were being threatened and it was reported that parties of rebels were being given shelter. Prompt action was taken by Ludlow-Hewitt who sent a flight each of No 55 and 84 Squadrons to Khanaqin. After being given warnings, the villages sympathetic to Mahmud were bombed. The rebels quickly left the district and the local leaders affirmed their obedience to the Iraq Government.[24]

By 28 March 1931, all was ready for the main operation against Sheikh Mahmud. He had last been seen at the south-eastern end of the Dagh Valley. The plan to kill or capture him was implemented. Infantry posts were established to block the few mountain crossings over the steep, rugged and precipitous, Qara Dagh range, and also to block the southern exit from the Qara Dagh valley. Two mobile cavalry columns were to sweep down the valley from the north-west, combing out the villages as they progressed. A third column of mobile mounted police was to remain in readiness near Muan, from where it could strike at the rebels if they broke away from the Qara Dagh valley to the north-east. Finally, No 3 Section, RAF armoured cars was to patrol the Arbet-Muan-Khurmal road. Three RAF aircraft were held in readiness at Sulaimaniya for reconnaissance, and air attack, if required.[25]

Number 3 Section prepares for operations with the Iraqi Army against Sheikh Mahmud (© Crown copyright. RAF Regiment Museum).

Number 3 Section was commanded by Flight Lieutenant Noel Keeble DSC DFC,[26] who had flown with distinction with the RNAS during the Great War, receiving a permanent commission in the RAF in 1919. His Section departed from Hinaidi on 28 March and arrived late the following day at Sulaimaniya. Their orders were to report to Wing Commander Garrod, who arrived by air the same day.[27] Less than 24 hours after their 290-mile journey, they began night patrols on the road between Sulaimaniya and Khurmal, where there were many difficulties with 'bad ground, unmarked tracks and roads, and four very awkward water splashes'.[28]

Establishing themselves at Muan, Flight Lieutenant Keeble's command soon grew, when four Iraqi Army motor machine-gun vehicles (known as 'momags') and their crews were placed directly under his orders. A few days later, they moved north-west to the Baziyan Pass, where two Iraqi Army Morris six-wheelers were added

Flight Lieutenant Keeble's Section at the patrol base near Muan, on the road between Sulaimaniya and Halebja (Brandon, RAFACA).

to the column. Night patrols were made from Tainal to Chamchamal and 'reccos' between the Tasluja and Baziyan Passes. With another five 'momags' attached on 4 April, Keeble now had a column of nine RAF vehicles, nine 'momags' with Iraqi Army officers and crews, and a platoon of Iraqi infantry. Two days later a further company of Iraqi infantry with nine more Morris six-wheelers were added. Thus, the Officer Commanding No 3 Section, No 1 Armoured Car Company, had a force of 27 vehicles and 228 men under his orders.

It was however, soon established by the cavalry sweep of the valley that Mahmud had moved to the west of the Qara Dagh mountains. An aerial reconnaissance on 30 March found that Bani Mirt and the neighbouring villages were full of rebels. Whilst air action was launched against them, the commanding officer of the Iraqi cavalry regiment failed to exploit the situation with energy and enthusiasm as he considered his force too weak, thereby allowing Sheikh Mahmud and his followers to again escape.

Mahmud was then reported to be moving into Jaf territory, where he hoped to join with them and organise a concerted rebellion. Attention therefore shifted to the south-western boundary of the operational area. Squadron Leader O'Malley and the armoured cars of No 2 Section were ordered to move north the following day to Kifri where the nearby landing ground at Kingerban was inspected, cleared and reconditioned. The RAF armoured cars also went out and established contact with the Iraqi Army units at Qala Shirwana, Sar Qala and Chahar Shakh. With the RAF flight at Sulaimaniya now out of range for convenient observation of rebel movements, a flight of No 30 Squadron was flown in to Kingerban on 2 April to work closely with Squadron Leader O'Malley and No 2 Section.

By 4 April, a flying column of Iraqi cavalry and police had concentrated at Guek Tepe. Early on the morning of 5 April, Easter Sunday, the column marched some 18 miles to the south-west. Meanwhile, aircraft of Nos 30 and 55 Squadron had located about 100 rebels, including the Sheikh, near the village of Awa Barika. Leaving an aircraft to watch the rebels and their movements, he returned to refuel and re-arm. The aircraft then kept up a non-stop bombardment of the rebel positions for the rest of the day. Taken by surprise, the rebels had no option but to remain and establish defensive positions in the village. The Iraq Army column arrived in mid-afternoon, after a rapid 30-mile march, and found the village well-fortified and strongly held. Under cover of air bombardment, the Iraqi troops charged the rebel positions in a spirited attack but despite some success could not drive their enemy completely from the village. An encircling movement was attempted but this was also unsuccessful.

At 2240 hours of that day, a signal was received at Kifri ordering No 2 Section to proceed at once, with all available ammunition, to the village of Awa Barika. The message indicated that the Iraqi Army mobile column was in a determined fight with Sheikh Mahmud. For the first time since 1919, he and his followers had been drawn into a direct battle. Unfortunately, the message was not passed on to the Officer Commanding No 2 Section until 0530 hours the next morning. Two Rolls-Royce armoured cars and a Rolls-Royce wireless tender departed half-an-hour later with aircraft from Kifri maintaining contact as they moved. Although only 20 miles to the north of Kifri, the track conditions were not easy, and they reached Awa Barika after five-and-a-half hours. With the failure of the encircling move, the rebels had an escape route and the following morning the village was found to be deserted, the rebels having slipped away during the night.

The day after No 2 Section arrived at Awa Barika. Iraqi soldiers wounded in the fighting with Sheikh Mahmud and his followers (Rolph, RAFACA).

Proof of the seriousness of the defeat was evident. The Kurds had suffered 40 casualties and had left eight of their dead behind, with their rifles and ammunition; something which they never did as a point of honour. Unfortunately the RAF armoured cars of No 2 Section had arrived too late to influence the outcome of the battle, but the bullet marks and blood splashes on the buildings testified to the intensity and effectiveness of the air attacks. Further evidence of the ferocity of the encounter was the number of Iraqi soldiers having their wounds treated.

Despite having escaped again, Sheikh Mahmud had come close to being captured and he abandoned his efforts to win over the Jaf. He quickly moved north-eastwards, taking with him any men that he met so that no-one was left to reveal his movements to his pursuers. The mountain passes had been blocked as planned by Iraqi infantry, and the Sirwan River was in flood with all crossings guarded, preventing any attempt

HMAC Cheetah negotiates a ford on a water splash near Sulaimaniya in pursuit of Sheikh Mahmud (Brandon, RAFACA).

to escape to the south. To the north of the plain, the road from Chamchamal and Tainal was being patrolled by the RAF armoured cars of Keeble's No 3 Section. On the same day that Sheikh Mahmud's force had left Awa Barika, Keeble had also placed each of the Morris six-wheelers, with ten Iraqi infantrymen, at selected locations along the road, while machine-gun posts were located at Baziyan, Tasluja and Bash-Bulaq. The night patrols along this line were intended as a show of force to deter Sheikh Mahmud from attempting to break through to the north-east before fresh dispositions could be put in place to the south-east.

A veritable game of 'cat-and-mouse' now developed as Sheikh Mahmud endeavoured to evade the trap that had been set. On 7 April, Keeble was informed that Mahmud would attempt to break through further west of his current patrol route, between Baziyan and Chamchamal. He quickly gathered his infantry and re-deployed them in groups of three at half-mile intervals along the road west of Chamchamal. At midnight, he received a further 40 Iraqi infantry which had arrived to consolidate the line. It was hoped that the Sheikh would reveal himself and be caught between the patrol line and the Iraqi flying column that was in pursuit.

The next day however, new and disappointing intelligence was received concerning his location. Mahmud had crossed the Qara Dagh during the night. One of the passes had been left unguarded by the Iraqi infantry, and it was believed that he had been guided by a fire which had been lit as a signal to indicate the open pass. As soon as it was known that Sheikh Mahmud had crossed the Qara Dagh, No 3 Section, with its attached troops was given orders to proceed with all haste eastwards to Arbet in the Tanjero Valley. The troops and 'momags' were quickly collected along the line and the column was ready to move within an hour. Passing through Sulaimaniya, they reached at Arbet just before midnight. A patrol sent out the following morning made contact with the rebels, and shots were exchanged, with one of the rebels and a horse being killed. The cars had just missed the rebel party, including the Sheikh, who had crossed the Halebja Plain only a few hours earlier.

Despite the fact that he had avoided capture, Sheikh Mahmud had now experienced a number of narrow escapes. He had been brought to battle at Awa Barika and had suffered heavy casualties whilst expending valuable ammunition. Intelligence information reported that some of his men were deserting and that he was worn out. He was now located in caves to the north-east of Muan and so the Wapiti flight at Kingerban was ordered to withdraw to Hinaidi, as were the RAF armoured cars of No 2 Section, after having travelled a total of 8085 vehicle miles during the operation.

After only a few days, the Sheikh was on the move again and was being pursued by two columns of the Iraqi Army. After Awa Barika, he had avoided pitched battle but he was given no respite. On a number of occasions, the rebels were located and attacked from the air by the RAF. The Pishder tribe and Persian tribes failed to support him and his influence in the Sulaimaniya began to fade as the Iraqi Army re-established control in a region that had previously been regarded as his own.

Flight Lieutenant Keeble's command had grown even larger following the Sheikh's escape across the Halebja Plain. A further 100 Iraqi cavalrymen had arrived, bringing the size of his 'Carthree' command to 368. Patrols were maintained for the next seven days but there was no sign of the rebels. The attached Iraqi troops departed and the Section returned to Sulaimaniya. The remainder of April and early May was spent visiting more than 30 villages in the hills and mountains to the north and north-west of Halebja, assisting the local police in the search for arms and ammunition and arresting suspected rebels.

Flight Lieutenant Keeble and No 3 Section had covered over 20,000 miles during nearly two months of operations. The Rolls-Royce cars had 'behaved magnificently'.[29] Although they had come close but had not captured the Sheikh, their efforts were significant enough to receive a mention in Air Vice-Marshal Ludlow-Hewitt's official despatch on the campaign:

> Orders were at once issued for No 3 Section, Armoured Cars, to close on Sulaimaniya in order to take up a fresh patrol line to the south-east, but

Iraqi cavalrymen inspect the body of a dead rebel. These men formed a part of Keeble's rapidly-expanding 'Carthree' command (Rolph, RAFACA).

although the Section Commander, Flight Lieutenant Noel Keeble DSC DFC moved promptly and with great energy, the rebels just won the race and managed to get across the Halebja Plain shortly after midnight on 8/9 April, when the Armoured Car patrol had reached Serao.[30]

On 24 April, Sheikh Mahmud crossed the Persian frontier and arrived at Piran. Negotiations began between the Iraqi and Persian military to discuss cooperation in apprehending him, and on 2 May it was agreed to cooperate in their actions against the rebels. Sheikh Mahmud had by now realised that the rebellion was failing and he consequently wrote to Captain V. Holt, the Oriental Secretary to the High Commissioner in Baghdad. On the same day that a cooperative agreement was reached with the Persians, Sheikh Mahmud was given an ultimatum by Captain Holt. In return for his surrender, his life would be spared, he would be guaranteed an income from his estates and he would be permitted to live with his family in a location in Southern Iraq selected by the Iraqi Government. On 11 May, he arrived at Penjwin for a meeting with Captain Holt and the Governor of Sulaimaniya. After retiring to discuss the terms with his family, he returned on 13 May to Penjwin where he surrendered to a party of Iraqi Army and RAF officers. The official report on the operation made the following observation:

> It is interesting to note that at the first meeting at Penjwin, Sheikh Mahmud went up to a Royal Air Force officer who was present and pointing to the wings on his tunic said "You are the people that have broken my spirit."[31]

Sheikh Mahmud, his entourage and an Iraqi Army escort arrive at Kaolos following his surrender. Highly regarded by his people, local Kurdish villagers came out from their houses to bid him a sad farewell (Rolph, RAFACA).

On 14 May 1931, two RAF armoured cars, eight Iraqi 'momags' and a Morris six-wheeler proceeded to Kaolos to provide an escort for Sheikh Mahmud who had ridden over from Penjwin with his captors. From there they took him to Sulaimaniya, where he was flown to Ur on the Euphrates. He remained in exile in southern Iraq for 10 years, until allowed to return to his home village in Kurdistan in 1941.

The officers and airmen who served in this campaign against Sheikh Mahmud in Southern Kurdistan in 1930 and 1931 were awarded the Iraq Active Service Medal by His Majesty the King Feisal I of Iraq. King George V granted permission for RAF personnel to accept and wear the medal without restriction.[32]

The campaign of 1930 and 1931 in Kurdistan against Sheikh Mahmud represented a period of transition for Air Control in Iraq. The Iraqi Government was to take greater responsibility from the RAF for the defence of its frontiers and the maintenance of civil order. Nevertheless, despite the greater role played by the Iraqi Army and Police, the ultimate success of the campaign was due to the coordination of ground and air operations provided by the RAF at critical stages.

After two years in Iraq, many of the airmen could opt for the more pleasant climes of Palestine to complete their five year overseas tour. LAC Arthur Rolph transferred to No 2 Armoured Car Company at Ramleh at the end his tour. AC1 Vic Brandon did not. On 13 April 1932, he was admitted to RAF Hinaidi Hospital with typhoid and died eight days later. His commanding officer, Wing Commander Vivian Gaskell Blackburn, wrote the following to Brandon's father:

> His funeral took place on the morning of the 22nd of April, and was very impressive and well carried out. The coffin covered by a Union Jack was carried on a specially prepared Armoured Car with numerous floral wreaths. The funeral was attended by representative officers, warrant officers, non-commissioned officers and aircraftmen from all Units the cantonment, and was conducted with full military honours.[33]

The Iraqi Army, Police and flying units of the RAF were occupied in northern Kurdistan until 1932. With the defeat of Sheikh Mahmud the Iraq Government wanted to extend its control over the remaining areas of North Kurdistan and had therefore come into conflict with the local Kurdish leader, Sheikh Ahmed of Barzan. In conjunction with these operations, the RAF had established a flight of No 30 Squadron at Diana to support the Iraqi Army but the major portion of operations was now up to the Iraqis. The RAF armoured cars had been despatched for a short time during winter but the poor weather and track conditions prevented their use and they were returned to Hinaidi.

The British Mandate in Iraq ended in October 1932, following the entry of Iraq into the League of Nations. As a consequence of this, and the independence of the Iraqi Government, there were to be no further significant British contributions to Iraqi military operations for the remainder of the 1930s. Furthermore, with the reduction in the number of government advisers and limited military presence, there was a reduction in British influence. Indeed, there was little cooperation of any kind between the RAF and the Iraqi military, and by 1933-34 there were political disturbances and deepening anti-British sentiment.

The approaching end of the British Mandate aroused serious alarm among the Assyrian Levies. Their concern being that with transition to Arab rule they would be disbanded, losing both a source of employment and security. There was an understandable reluctance from the Assyrians to serve the Iraqi government in the Police or Army. They were determined to obtain some concession on land to which they could settle as their own area in Iraq. Though there were Arab and Kurdish Companies, the Assyrians were now the largest part of the force protecting the RAF stations and installations in Iraq, and the threat of disaffection had serious consequences. By June 1932, the leadership of the Assyrian Levies had threatened to withdraw their services. They would then march north with Levies, civilians and dependants, some 8000 people, and establish their own autonomous Assyrian enclave in Turkey. This movement would pass through Kurdish territory and because of past animosities there would be certain to inflame conflict and serious bloodshed. Furthermore, disturbances involving the Assyrians would lead to Iraq's application to join the League of Nations being postponed.[34]

In mid-June 1932, Nos 2 and 3 Sections were despatched to the Levy camps at Sulaimaniya, Kirkuk, Diana and Rowanduz (Map 6, p. 51). Concern was such that the 1st Battalion of the Northamptonshire Regiment was flown in to Baghdad from Egypt at the same time, with a company each deployed to Diana, Sulaimaniya and Mosul. For the last weeks of June and into early July, all RAF armoured car personnel at Hinaidi were ordered to stand by their vehicles by day and night and Rolls-Royce armoured cars and Armed Morris cars were deployed on various precautionary tasks on the crossroads leading from Levy lines and posts. Concern was so great that a section of armoured cars from No 2 Company were also brought over from Palestine.

By 12 July however, matters had calmed. The Assyrian officers and men gave assurances that they would not leave their posts and the Company returned to normal duties. As they returned south, the sections in the north transported the Levy arms and ammunition from Diana and Sulaimaniya to Hinaidi. The Treaty of Iraq laid down that the Levy force should be set at 1250 and a plan was effected to reach that number by April 1933.

The year 1933 was, however, a tragic one for the Assyrians in Iraq. In the spring and summer of that year there were clashes between the Iraqi Army, assisted by Kurdish tribesmen, which led to the massacre of several hundred Assyrians civilians in areas of the Mosul Vilayet.[35] In early August, aircraft of No 30 Squadron on aerial reconnaissance reported seeing burning villages. As a consequence, Air Headquarters Iraq placed No 1 Section at Mosul at the disposal of the commission of RAF and Iraq Levy officers that had been formed for the formulation of relief measures for the Assyrian Levy families. In this role also a Rolls-Royce wireless tender accompanied an RAF column from Hinaidi that was carrying members of the Commission and relief baggage to Mosul. Meanwhile, the Victorias of No 70 Squadron evacuated about 800 Assyrian old men, women and children from the disturbed areas. They were transported from Mosul to Baghdad, where they were housed in surplus buildings in and around the air cantonment at Hinaidi.

It had been intended that the Iraqi Army would eventually take over airfield protection duties. However, the inclination of the Iraqi Army officer corps to involve themselves in politics, including the dreadful events of 1933, and a bloody coup in 1936, raised concern in British circles and this proposal was not pursued. Meanwhile, the Assyrians were given no concessions in the newly-independent Iraq and they felt betrayed by the British. Many senior RAF officers however, saw themselves as unofficial protectors of the Assyrian people and as a consequence as many as possible were employed in the RAF Levies Iraq, which was formed for the protection of the British aerodromes. This was a task they were to perform with great devotion, loyalty and efficiency. Thus the Assyrians came to form the largest proportion of the Levies and in a few years would play a key role in the defence of RAF Habbaniya during Rashid Ali's anti-British coup.[36]

In April 1932, Armed Fords which had done sterling service since 1922, often taking the place of the heavily armoured Rolls-Royces when conditions made their use impractical, were replaced by Morris'. In November 1933, each section was increased from four to six Rolls-Royce armoured cars. The Rolls-Royces continued to perform superbly, but during October 1935, yet another experimental armoured car, this time a Straussler design, arrived from United Kingdom having travelled via Port Said and then overland to Iraq. By 1938 the Morris tenders and six-wheelers had been replaced by Albion and Fordson 2-ton tenders, but the Rolls-Royces were still going.[37]

In June 1930, the Governments of the United Kingdom and Iraq signed the Anglo-Iraq Treaty which promised full independence to Iraq in September 1932. The Iraqi Army would take over the majority of internal and external security responsibilities. Furthermore, it was agreed that the RAF would leave Hinaidi and Mosul but within five years of Iraqi independence, it would establish a new base at Dhibban on the Euphrates. Dhibban, which would be later renamed RAF Habbaniya, was 50 miles west of Baghdad, which was half an hour by air and two hours by road. Article 5 of the Treaty of Alliance specifically provided for the construction of 'an air base to be selected by His Britannic Majesty to the West of the Euphrates'. The site chosen was considered more strategically suitable than RAF Hinaidi. River crossings over the Euphrates at Ramadi and Falluja could be easily controlled and any bedouin attackers would have to cross open desert from all directions. Furthermore, the air base lay astride the main lines of communications to Transjordan and Palestine and the road ran through an area that was sparsely populated with friendly tribes in open

A hive of activity at the armoured car lines at Habbaniya as armoured car crews prepare to depart on a 'recco' (Rutter, RAFACA).

desert country that could be readily negotiated by motor transport.

The relative isolation of Dhibban was considered a strength. The alternative for instance, on the road between Baghdad and Basra was far less suitable as it was heavily populated with powerful tribes that had been active participants in past insurgencies in Iraq.[38] Furthermore, it was much healthier site, being free from malaria and other mosquito-borne diseases, as well as distant from the cholera and typhoid epidemics that were common in Baghdad. The site also afforded ample space for the provision of recreational and sporting facilities, including bathing and sailing at Lake Habbaniya.

In June 1934, No 4 Section had moved from Basra to Shaibah where it was permanently attached to No 84 Squadron. By 1934, the new RAF station at Dhibban was taking shape. As the buildings were developed along the 28 miles of roads and boulevards, it would take the form of a fair-sized city. The thoroughfares would be planted with palms, towering eucalyptus and English trees would shade the inhabitants from the desert sun. In preparation for the move, the armoured cars had already begun work in the areas surrounding the new base. Flight Lieutenant Alan Shipwright DFC carried out inspections of the route and compiled track reports in the Dhibban locality with No 2 Section. From late 1935 onwards the Company began developing a defence scheme for the new air base. The three Hinaidi sections now spent much of their time carrying out track reconnaissances in northern and western Iraq and to the frontiers with Transjordan and Syria.

Once the Mandate had ended, the RAF armoured cars and aircraft could no longer operate in Iraq at the behest of the High Commissioner. From 1932, Iraq had its own sovereignty, and permission for all RAF armoured car movements had to be obtained from the Iraqi authorities. One highly anticipated operation was the 'Northern Recco'. In July 1934, No 3 Section under the command of Flight Lieutenant

Crossing the Little Zab at Altun Kupri (Humphreys, RAFACA).

Watched over by the local constabulary, a detachment of No 1 Armoured Car Company refuels at a village pump while on a 'recco' (Rutter, RAFACA).

Hugh Constantine departed Hinaidi for North Kurdistan.[39] The RAF armoured cars travelled to Kirkuk, and then after taking 12 hours to ferry six cars across the Little Zab River at Altun Kupri they travelled to the ancient city of Arbil. They then headed into the mountains of Kurdistan, down into the spectacular Rowanduz Gorge and nearly to the Persian border at Rayat. From here, they returned south to the landing ground at Diana and then on to the Sulaimaniya. Travelling back north, they reached Dukhan and then west across to Kirkuk and completed the return journey to home at RAF Hinaidi. There was the wait outside Baghdad for permission to enter the city

Airmen on a 'recco' set up their gun pits before nightfall while on the annual manoeuvres at LG 5 in 1938 (Rutter, RAFACA).

from the government. The 'recco' was completed in nine days and covered some 800 miles.

This journey would not have been possible by road a decade earlier. The road from Arbil to Rayat, though the Rowanduz Gorge had been opened in 1932 after five years of construction. Interestingly it had been constructed through the period of considerable unrest in Kurdistan, with a workforce of Persians, Arabs, Kurds and Assyrians, but nonetheless had been completed with little interruption or bloodshed. It greatly improved the ability of the military to access the Kurdish areas that could previously only be reached by marching columns travelling on mountain tracks. The 'Northern Recco' was completed without incident and indication of the changed state of affairs since the beginning of the Mandate in 1922. It is still one of the most strategically important roads in the region,[40]

On 1 January 1937, RAF Mosul was closed down and the Iraqi Air Force moved in. Number 30 Squadron had already relocated to Dhibban, along with No 1 Section of the armoured cars and No 8 (Kurdish) Company of the Iraq Levies, who joined No 5 (Arab) Company, already in residence. The HQ and Nos 2 and 3 Sections of No 1 Company would be stationed at Hinaidi until November 1937 when three sections of the Company would be concentrated at Dhibban, along with the Vickers Vincents of No 55 Squadron, the Valentias of No 70 Squadron and No 4 (Assyrian) Company. Number 4 Section would remain at Shaibah. The RAF was now concentrated at Dhibban and Shaibah with a small flying boat station at Basra.[41] From 1 May 1938, RAF Dhibban was renamed and was henceforth known as Habbaniya (Map 1, p. 15).[42]

By the 1930s, the major operational focus of the RAF had shifted westward as the conflicts between the Arab and Jewish populations of Palestine deepened. As the disturbances intensified, No 1 Armoured Car Company would be called on to support

Weary airmen of No 1 Armoured Car Company returning from the 'Northern Recco' await permission from the Iraqi authorities to move through Baghdad (Rutter, RAFACA).

the work of No 2 Armoured Car Company. Whereas the deserts of Transjordan and Iraq had been their training ground they were now to face an insurgency which would severely test the concept of Air Control.

Notes

1. AIR 10/1845 *Report on Operations in Southern Kurdistan against Shaikh Mahmud, October 1930-May 1931*, pp. 33, 41-42.
2. Nos 1 and 2 Sections were disbanded and the Car Reserve ceased to exist from 1 April 1930. To preserve the numbering sequence, Nos 5 and 6 Sections were renumbered as Nos 1 and 2 Sections.
3. AIR 29/50 *No 1 Armoured Car Company, Habbaniya; before 1 Apr 1930 Armoured Car Wing, Hinaidi; from 3 Oct 1946 No 1 ACC incorporated in RAF Regiment, redesignated No 2701 Squadron*.
4. S.J. Carr, *You are not Sparrows* (London: Ian Allan, 1975), p. 60.
5. *Ibid*.
6. *Ibid*.
7. Stanley A. Eastmead, *Interview 4504* (London: IWM Sound Archive, 1979).
8. *Ibid*.
9. V. Brandon, Correspondence: 23 March 1932, RAF Armoured Cars Association.
10. Now called Bingo.
11. V. Brandon, Correspondence: 28 February 1930.
12. *Ibid*.
13. S. Eastmead, *Interview 4504*.
14. Mornington S. Wentworth, *Interview 4768* (London: IWM Sound Archive, 1980).
15. *Ibid*.
16. *Ibid*.
17. *Ibid*.
18. Now known as Ma'asker Al Raschid RAF Cemetery.
19. Later Air Chief Marshal Sir Edgar Ludlow-Hewitt GCB GBE CMG DSO MC DL (1886–1973), AOC Iraq 1930-1932.
20. On the Air Staff (Operations) HQ Iraq Command. Later Air Commodore John 'Paddy' Quinnell DFC (1891-1983).
21. AIR 5/1292 *Iraq Command: Monthly Operational Summaries, Vol. VI 1930-1932*.
22. Later Air Chief Marshal Sir Guy Garrod GBE KCB MC DFC (1891–1965).
23. The half section consisted of two Rolls-Royce armoured cars, a Rolls-Royce wireless tender, a Morris six-wheeler and two Armed Fords. LAC Arthur Rolph served in the half section of No 2 Section on this operation.
24. AIR 10/1845 *Report on Operations in Southern Kurdistan against Shaikh Mahmud*, pp. 22-26.
25. *Ibid*., p. 27.
26. Squadron Leader Noel Keeble DSC DFC (1891-date of death unknown) served in the No 1 Wing RNAS from 1915 before transferring to the RAF on its formation and serving on No 202 Squadron. He was credited with the downing of six German aircraft. He received a permanent commission in the RAF on August 1919 and retired in 1934. He spent a long period in Iraq during the 1920s All three of his sons joined the RAF. Two were killed while flying for the RAF during the Second World War and the third was invalided out in 1939 while in training. C. Shores, N. Franks and R. Guest, *Above the Trenches: a Complete Record of the Fighter Aces and Units of the British Empire Air Forces 1915-1920* (London: Grub Street, 1990), p. 220.
27. The Section consisted of four Rolls-Royce armoured cars, a Rolls-Royce W/T tenders and two Morris six-wheelers. LAC Vic Brandon was serving on this Section at the time.
28. AIR 29/50 *No 1 Armoured Car Company*.

29 *Ibid.*
30 AIR 10/1845 *Report on Operations in Southern Kurdistan against Shaikh Mahmud, October 1930-May 1931*, p. 33.
31 AIR 5/1292 *Iraq Command: Monthly Operational Summaries, Vol. VI.*
32 *London Gazette*, 23 September, 1932, p. 6018. LAC Arthur Rolph received this medal.
33 Correspondence, Wing Commander V. Gaskell Blackburn, Commanding, No 1 Armoured Car Company to W.C. Brandon Esq, 26 April 1932, and Record Office RAF Ruislip, 13 May 1932 to W.C Brandon Esq. The funeral was attended by the Adjutant, three Officers and 60 Warrant Officers, NCOs and Aircraftman of No 1 Armoured Car Company. A total of six officers and 120 airmen were present from No 70 (Bomber-Transport) and 55 (Bomber) Squadrons, Aircraft Depot and RAF General Hospital and Air Headquarters. The bearer and firing party were supplied from No 1 Armoured Car Company and the Band and Trumpeters from the Aircraft Depot. Some 15 wreaths were laid on the grave.
34 D. Omissi, 'Britain, the Assyrian Levies and the Iraq Levies 1919-1932', *Journal of Imperial and Commonwealth History*, 17 (1989), pp. 301-322.
35 A. Lee, *Fly Past. Highlights from a Flyers Life* (London: Jarrolds, 1974), p. 82.
36 J. Lunt, *Imperial Sunset* (London: MacDonald, 1981), pp. 40-41 and AIR 5/1293 *Iraq Command: monthly operation summaries, Vol. VII, 1933-1935*. By the mid-1930s the Iraq Levies consisted of five companies of Assyrians (Nos 1 to 5), two Arab companies (Nos 6 and 7) and one Kurdish company (No 8).
37 AIR 29/50 *No 1 Armoured Car Company*.
The vehicle strength of No 1 Armoured Car Company at 31 December 1938 was:

	Habbaniya Nos 1, 2 and 3 Sections	Shaibah No 4 Section (attached to No 84 Squadron)
Rolls-Royce armoured car	18	7
Rolls-Royce W/T tender	6	1
Fordson	6	2
Crossley	3	1
Hillman Hawk	1	-
Albion	4	2
Fordson W/T tender	1	-
Leyland	-	1

38 'The Air Estimates', *Flight*, 15 March 1934, p. 257. The distance of the new air base from Baghdad was the subject of criticism by some. However, as the Under-Secretary for State for Air, the Right Honourable Sir Philip Sassoon, MP, pointed out during the Air Estimates speech to the House of Commons, 'It is a good deal nearer, for instance, than my own constituency of Hythe is to Westminster.'
39 Later Air Chief Marshal Sir Hugh Constantine KBE CB DSO LLD (Hon) (1908-1992)
40 Archibald M. Hamilton, *Road through Kurdistan*, 2nd Ed (London: Faber & Faber, 1958). The road had been constructed under the supervision of the New Zealand-born engineer, A.M. Hamilton (1989-1972), of the Iraq Public Works Department. It was a major engineering feat having been built in the blazing heat of the summer and the freezing cold of winter. It traversed five mountain ranges and two gorges, the Rowanduz and the Beserini. In places the path had to be carved from solid rock.
41 There were three Rangoon flying boats from No 203 Squadron operating from Basra on the Shatt el Arab.
42 AIR 29/50 *No 1 Armoured Car Company*. Although the tempo of operations had decreased the Company still lost personnel during this period. On 12 December 1937, Pilot Officer G.W. Jones was by killed by 'natives' [sic] on the track to Lake Habbaniya, and LAC Frederick J.W. Edbrooke was killed on 18 January 1939 when his Fordson tender crashed while driving between Ramadi and Habbaniya.

Chapter Ten

The Palestine Riots 1929

"The deficiency in the shape of a suitable reinforcement for the police could not be entirely met with the resources at the disposal of the Government but to some extent it was alleviated by the untiring devotion to duty shown by all ranks. In particular the Armoured Car crews and the personnel who formed the ground parties, worked night and day without rest for four days on end. Nothing less could have prevented on the first three days a repetition of the Hebron massacre on a much larger scale in Jerusalem."

Group Captain P.H.L. Playfair, OC RAF Transjordan & Palestine[1]

Whereas the Air Control of Transjordan, Iraq and the Protectorate of Aden was primarily focussed on dispersed and dissident tribes, or ethnic groups living in sparsely-populated deserts and mountains, the policing and internal security of Palestine presented very different problems. The setting of the struggle in Palestine was complex, with the contrasts of the age-old architectural wonders of Jerusalem and the ancient city of Jaffa against the modern buildings of Tel Aviv, and between the deserts of Gaza and Beersheba, the barren hills of Judea, and the fertile coastal plains with their verdant orange groves (Map 18, p.193).

Palestine had long been ruled by the Ottoman Empire before it was conquered by the Army of General Allenby in 1917, and was densely-populated with many villages and towns. The primary focus of the British civil and military forces was dealing with the clashes arising from the territorial claims of the Zionists, and emerging Arab nationalism. In the latter stages of the Great War, the British Government had unwisely made conflicting promises to both the Zionists and the Arabs regarding the political and geographical division of Palestine and Transjordan. The Arabs feared that increasing Jewish immigration arising from the Balfour Declaration of 1917, where the British Government had agreed to look favourably on the formation of a Jewish homeland in Palestine, would lead to a loss of their land and subjugation to a Zionist state.[2]

Tensions between the Arab and Jewish communities had arisen as early as 1920 when there were attacks on Jews in Jerusalem. There were further riots in 1921 in Jaffa, leaving more than 80 Jews and Arabs dead. With the locally-established Police force relatively ineffectual in dealing with the outbreaks of violence, the British Government proceeded with a plan for a special British and Palestinian paramilitary Gendarmerie, supported by two RAF armoured car companies, a single bomber squadron and a British cavalry regiment. This arrangement was a tempting prospect, given the reduced cost compared with the maintenance of a large British regular ground force. The Gendarmerie was composed of 550 local Jews, Muslims and

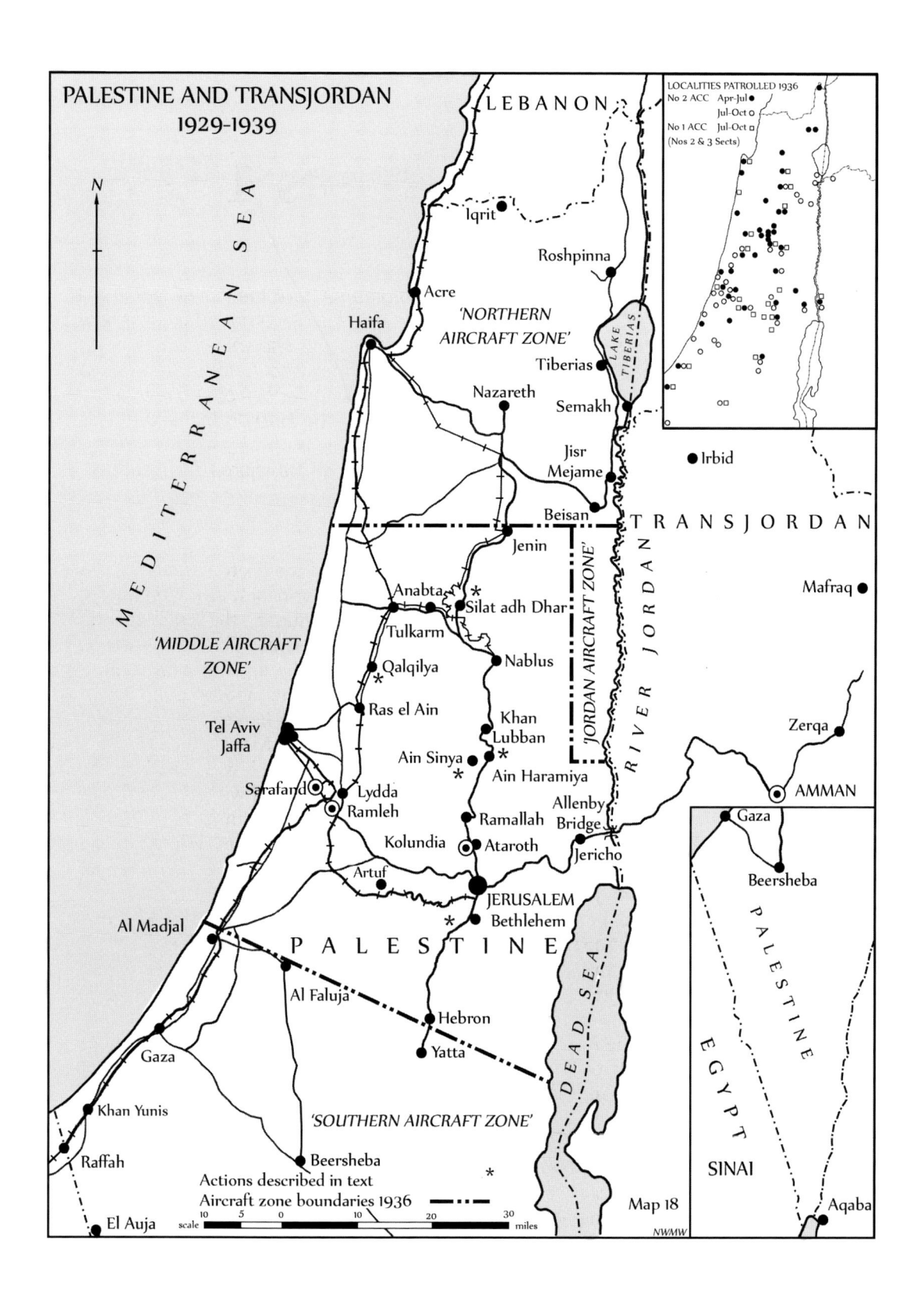

PALESTINE AND TRANSJORDAN 1929–1939

Map 18

Christians and 800 British personnel, many of the latter having been 'Black and Tans' who had been released recently from the newly-independent Republic of Ireland. The assumption by the British Government was that this force could deal satisfactorily with all matters of external and internal security.[3]

Having taken responsibility for Palestine in October 1922, the RAF could already point to successful instances of Air Control. In April 1920, a group of Arabs had held up a train and cut telegraph wires at Semakh while in May 1921 others had gathered to attack Jewish settlements. These had been dealt with by an RAF air attack, albeit in the first instance in collaboration with an Indian cavalry regiment.[4]

The British High Commissioner from 1920 to 1925, Sir Herbert Samuel, had expressed concern that the resources available would be terribly inadequate should there be a resurgence of trouble on a larger scale. Despite this, by early 1926, his replacement, Lord Plumer, held a different view and recommended that the Gendarmerie be disbanded and that the remaining British Army cavalry regiment, the 9th Queen's Royal Lancers, leave the country.[5] There was now only No 2 Armoured Car Company working across Palestine and Transjordan, No 1 Company having been disbanded by early 1924. There was no provision for ground troops, as there was in Iraq with the locally-raised Levies. The Transjordan Frontier Force (TJFF), composed of about 700 officers and men, had been formed in April 1926 for internal security in Palestine and Transjordan, had established its Headquarters at Zerqa in Transjordan and did not operate in the larger cities and towns of Palestine.[6]

By the mid-1920s, internal unrest in Palestine was considered to be on the wane and it was proposed to reduce the size of the Gendarmerie to only 200 men as recommended by Plumer. There was, however, to be a corresponding increase in the numbers of the Palestine Police to 1500.[7] Arab resentment remained, but tensions

RAF Ramleh. The home of No 2 Armoured Car Company from 1926 until 1948, for the greater part of its existence and the base for operations during the riots and disturbances (Rolph, RAFACA).

had decreased, albeit not disappeared altogether by 1927, as Arab population growth had more than exceeded the rate of Jewish immigration. The assumptions of a decline in unrest appeared well-founded with the attention of the TJFF and the RAF armoured cars and aircraft being on bedouin tribal movements and camel-raiding, and the incursions of the Ikhwan on the Transjordan frontier with Syria, Iraq and Saudi Arabia. Any civil order problems were left to the Palestine Police to deal with.

It was in Jerusalem in 1929 that the sectarian divisions would again lead to conflict. Of great significance to Muslims, Jews and Christians, it was in the Holy City that these three religions, as so often before, came to clash. In late 1928, an argument developed over the Western (Wailing) Wall, as Muslims and Jews had become increasingly bitterly entrenched over their respective access rights to the area. In mid-August 1929, there were Jewish protest marches followed by counter-protests by Muslim groups encouraged by the President of the Supreme Muslim Council, otherwise known as the Grand Mufti of Jerusalem, Haj Amin El-Husseini. These events would soon escalate into widespread civil disorder.

By this time, the entire RAF Palestine and Transjordan Command consisted of only 440 officers and airmen, with 12 aircraft and 12 armoured cars.[8] The majority of RAF personnel in Palestine were concentrated at Ramleh, with the armoured cars, and at nearby Sarafand with the Palestine General Hospital and Supply Depot. However, for most of the preceding year, No 2 Armoured Car Company Headquarters had been located at Amman alongside the RAF Transjordan and Palestine Command Headquarters. By the time of the outbreak of trouble on 17 August 1929, No 2 Armoured Car Company had only three sections with a total of ten Rolls-Royce armoured cars and ten tenders. With tensions rising, the civil authorities requested the swift return of 'C' Section to Ramleh to await further orders. On the morning of Friday 23 August, the Officer Commanding Palestine and Transjordan, Group Captain Patrick Playfair MC, was called urgently to Jerusalem by civil officials and he proceeded there accompanied by the OC of No 2 Company, Squadron Leader Leslie Forbes MC.

The same day, the situation exploded with a series of violent attacks made against Jews. 'C' Section was immediately deployed to Jerusalem from Ramleh, while 'B' Section departed from Amman that afternoon and arrived at Police Headquarters in Russian Buildings in the Holy City a couple of hours before midnight, only to be told that a large armed crowd was moving along the Ramallah road towards Jerusalem. The report continues:

> The Section accompanied by the British [Palestine] Police was promptly despatched with orders to turn back the crowd and disperse them. Two miles south of Ramallah a crowd about 800 strong with swords and sticks was encountered… [and] turned back to Ramallah and dispersed. The police reported that the Arabs intended to raid Ataroth, the Jewish settlement at Kolundia, so 'B' Section returned to Ataroth and patrolled the area… as well as the main Nablus road… Several parties of Arabs moving in cars towards Jerusalem were stopped on the road and turned back.[9]

There was a desperate need for more men on the ground to back up the Police and RAF armoured cars. This was partially dealt with by gathering up about 80 RAF technical and other base personnel who could be spared from Ramleh and Amman, and allocating ten or so each to a Morris tender. Police numbers were bolstered with 100 Special Constables who had been hastily enrolled from untrained British residents in Jerusalem. However, these were inadequate for the task and two days after the outbreak of violence, a company of the 1st South Wales Borderers was flown in from Egypt, with the remainder of the Battalion coming by train. The latter announced their arrival in a bold manner by marching from the station to the Police Headquarters led by their Band.

One of the Vickers Victorias that had flown in the troops had to spend the night at Kolundia airport near Jerusalem and two Rolls-Royce armoured cars were provided for its protection. The effectiveness of their presence was clearly demonstrated the following morning when a group of Arabs were spotted proceeding towards the Jewish settlement of Ataroth. The official report continues as follows:

> At Kolundia… there was a Vickers Victoria on the aerodrome, the Arabs advanced on Ataroth from the direction of Ramallah and in spite of the presence in the neighbourhood of two armoured cars and a detachment of infantry, opened fire and continued to move forward. As soon as the armoured cars came into action however, they beat a hasty retreat and except for spasmodic sniping throughout the night they made no further threat.[10]

Following an earlier attack, another armoured car had patrolled the Jewish settlement of Talpioth, from mid-morning until late afternoon. The report continues as follows:

> The situation had been clear… and consequently at 1700 hours, as a result of reported Arab movements towards Kolundia just before the troop carriers were due to land, the Armoured Car from Talpioth was withdrawn and sent to Kolundia. No sooner had the Armoured Car left Talpioth than Arabs began advancing…[11]

The only spare armoured car was unserviceable and it took some hours to repair. Group Captain Playfair and the Commandant of Police then accompanied the repaired armoured car in a touring car. They approached Talpioth without headlights, hoping to surprise the attackers but they had apparently departed. They were assured all was well by the Jewish inhabitants and set off back to Jerusalem. However, before they could reach the Police HQ, they received a report that the attack had broken out again. The armoured car returned but yet again the attackers had melted away and the situation calmed.

At Artuf, the armoured cars arrived to find the Jewish inhabitants imprisoned in one house, while their rest of the houses were being looted. Once the cars arrived, the looters dispersed but again they returned and burnt the village once the cars departed on other task. The Report continues:

> The colonists were evacuated by train; only because they had lived more than 50 years alongside the Arabs, giving the latter employment and medical attention, were they allowed to escape with their lives.[12]

The authorities were concerned that despite the early attacks being against Jews and their property, the violence would develop into open rebellion against the

Smoke rises from the Jewish settlement of Artuf (Library of Congress, Prints & Photographs Division [LC-M32-4122]).

Palestine Government. The trouble had initially been isolated to Jerusalem but as news inevitably leaked, there were soon outbreaks of violence, looting and arson across the country.

On morning of 24 August, two Armed Morris tenders of No 2 Company, with British police and 10 airmen, left for Hebron in response to reports that Arabs were attacking Jews. Their arrival was unfortunately delayed as they halted to disarm crowds of Arabs they met on the road, as well as deal with small parties which opened fire on them as they passed. On reaching Hebron after nearly four hours, they assisted in restoring order with continuous patrols and evacuating frightened and injured Jews from their houses and ensuring their safe transfer to the Police Station. The extent of the suffering was not known until a day later when it was found that more than 50 Jews had been killed and a similar number wounded.[13] The airmen were praised for their work and in particular in a letter of commendation from Colonel C.E. Hughes of the Imperial War Graves Commission who had observed them going about their tasks:

> They all did extremely well, but one man… LAC William Kittles of No 2 Armoured Car Company I noticed particularly. It did not matter if it was his turn for duty or not, he turned out. Food wanted, he found it, sick or wounded to be pacified, he did it, in fact any job going he was on the spot, cheery and tactful… I felt as an outside observer that I would like to let you know how his and all the RAF personnel conduct struck me at Hebron.[14]

The next threat emerged in the ancient Arab port and city of Jaffa, near the neighbouring modern Jewish city of Tel Aviv. The Arab and Jewish populations were

Airmen of No 2 Armoured Car Company called out to deal with a demonstration at Sarona, north-east of Tel Aviv (© Crown copyright. RAF Regiment Museum).

similar in size and it was feared that an all-out struggle could develop. 'B' Section, with the Company Commanding Officer, Squadron Leader Leslie Forbes MC, arrived the following day with orders to take charge of the situation. He had to control the crowds as they left the local mosque, preventing any attempt by the Arabs to move towards Tel Aviv. A mob had gathered that morning and Forbes ordered that Lewis machine-gun teams be deployed, but after Magistrates had warned that the teams would open fire, the crowd soon dispersed. Despite this brief respite, tension soon flared up again, and rioting erupted across Jaffa, albeit the presence of the armoured cars did prevent it spreading to Tel Aviv.

A handful of armoured cars from the two sections could not however, deal with the disturbances on their own. 'A' Section of the Company was still on a reconnaissance out from Ma'an on the plain north of Aqaba, and it was recalled to Palestine; although the message sent by W/T was so delayed and distorted by atmospheric interference that the Section Commander had to guess its importance. For the next few days, the armoured cars were despatched either singly or in pairs to assist the Police at various disturbances and were occupied continuously in stopping and disarming Arabs, protecting lives and property and covering the evacuation of civilian personnel from threatened areas. Incessant and urgent requests came for help from threatened settlements, and small detachments of one Roll-Royce and one or two Armed Morris tenders were despatched to troubled areas where available. Throughout this period, the RAF armoured cars visited nearly every town and Jewish settlement in Palestine, and were frequently involved in fighting with armed groups. Often their mere presence had a significant deterrent effect on the rioters, although with their departure, hostilities often resumed.

The arrival of the South Wales Borderers from Egypt and the frenetic work of the RAF armoured cars had calmed the situation in Jerusalem, Jaffa and Haifa but there was continued unrest and danger to the 135 Jewish settlements in the surrounding country. With calls for help coming from many of them, the British authorities now sought to protect them, albeit with insufficient military resources. Police detachments were hard-pressed, and on the second day of unrest at Nablus, some 2000 fellaheen had gathered with the intention of marching on Jerusalem. Two RAF armoured cars were sent to assist, while another pair escorted a column of 17 ambulances bringing out the wounded from the rioting and subsequent massacre in Hebron.[15]

Two more infantry battalions were quickly sent from the Cairo Brigade, joined by sailors and Royal Marines from HMS *Barham* and HMS *Sussex*, which had docked at Haifa and Jaffa, respectively. The senior RAF officer in Palestine was a Group Captain, and consequently with the presence of three British infantry battalions, the operational command was temporarily handed over to a more senior officer, Brigadier William Dobbie CMG DSO of the Cairo Brigade. This was a blow to Air Ministry claims that it could police Palestine with aircraft and armoured cars alone.

Following the arrival of the Army troops, the main task of the RAF armoured cars and aircraft changed to reconnaissance patrols to keep the authorities informed of any large movements of insurgents across the frontiers or within Palestine. Air support for the operations was initially provided by No 14 Squadron at Amman which flew patrols over threatened areas to disperse Arab mobs and on a number of occasions their action proved the salvation for the threatened communities.

By 7 September, the air component had been considerably strengthened with the arrival of Nos 208 (Air Cooperation), 216 (Bomber) and 45 (Bomber) Squadrons RAF at Ramleh. With the Malta-based HMS *Courageous* now anchored at Jaffa, the Royal Navy also contributed aircraft from the Fleet Air Arm which operated from

With RAF units in Palestine stretched to the limit British troops were sent as reinforcements from Egypt. A lorry loaded with British troops patrols the roads (Library of Congress, Prints & Photographs Division [LC-M33-4129]).

Gaza. Making a distinction between warring Jews and Arabs living in close proximity in urban areas and discerning violent intent and peaceful protest was difficult if not impossible from the cockpit of an aeroplane. The pilots were therefore ordered to only attack large identifiable groups of Arab insurgents.

While dealing with internal disturbances, the RAF was also concerned that the bedouin from Transjordan might decide to move into Palestine to support their town-dwelling fellaheen brothers. Two companies of the TJFF were consequently brought in to patrol the Jordan Valley to watch for any attempt by Arab gangs to infiltrate from Transjordan, and to protect Jewish settlements. The Arab Legion also played a vital role in persuading parties of Transjordanian Arabs moving towards the frontier to return to their villages.[16]

As the Army and Police took primary responsibility for internal control, the RAF armoured cars were gradually released by Brigadier Dobbie to concentrate on watching the frontiers. Their first concern was that the tribes in the south of Transjordan might move into Palestine, and the local Police Inspector threatened their leaders with air action if they continued on their path. As a consequence, a section of RAF armoured cars travelled to Beersheba from Gaza during the night of 28 August as a further disincentive to any move by the tribesmen. This had the desired effect and the Arabs returned to their pastures. The RAF armoured cars were relieved the following morning by a section of the 12th Royal Lancers (Prince of Wales's). Interestingly, the Lancers had terrible trouble with a bad batch of tyres, which were failing at a great rate. This had adverse consequences in one operation on 2 September when having captured some 1000 Arabs, the lack of tyres rendered the cars immobile and most of their captives escaped the following morning. In a clear demonstration of the use of air power they were quickly resupplied with replacements by air.

Despite matters having calmed down by the beginning of September, No 2 Company remained dispersed across Palestine and Transjordan at the strategic points of Amman, Irbid, Semakh and Beisan, Ramleh and Lydda. Further armoured car reinforcements were therefore sent in the form of No 3 Section, under Flight Lieutenant Maurice Ballard, from the Armoured Car Wing at RAF Hinaidi in Iraq.[17] They arrived at Amman on 6 September before moving to Ramleh a week later. On 21 September, this Section escorted the newly-appointed AOC Palestine and Transjordan, Air Vice-Marshal Hugh Dowding CB CMG, on a special reconnaissance of Northern Palestine and the Sea of Galilee, through Nablus, Jenin, Nazareth, Tiberias and Jisr Mejamie.[18] The Section moved a fortnight later to Haifa and took up twice-daily road patrols. A Rolls-Royce armoured car each stood by the Haifa Court and Governorate during trials for Jewish and Arab prisoners, escorting them to and from the gaol at Acre. The following week was spent on familiarisation reconnaissances of the Jewish colonies in their operational area. Other than the cool weather conditions requiring the despatch of a Victoria from Hinaidi with winter clothing for the armoured car crews, there were no other incidents, and in late November they received orders to return to Baghdad.

During the disturbances, the effectiveness of the Palestine Police had been seriously compromised, as personnel from different ethnic groups were often reluctant to protect other groups during instances of sectarian violence. On occasions some of the Arab police had 'melted away' under the stress of the confrontations, leaving the British section insufficient to cover all the calls for assistance.[19] There were also concerns with the effectiveness of the intelligence network that gave warning of any trouble.[20] A report on the disturbances had however, highlighted the important part by the RAF armoured cars:

> The deficiency in the shape of a suitable reinforcement for the police could not be entirely met with the resources at the disposal of the Government but to some extent it was alleviated by the untiring devotion to duty shown by all ranks. In particular the Armoured Car crews and the personnel who formed the ground parties worked night and day without rest for four days on end. Nothing less could have prevented on the first three days a repetition of the Hebron massacre on a much larger scale in Jerusalem.[21]

The limitations of the multi-ethnic, partisan Palestine Police had been clearly demonstrated when they had been powerless to control the riots which had led to the death of more than 133 Jews across Palestine. Some 116 Arabs were killed by the Army, RAF and TJFF in the subsequent responses to acts of violence, arson or theft.[22]

A review of the disturbances concluded that although overall command should remain with the Air Ministry, it was necessary to have two British infantry battalions stationed in Palestine. The Headquarters of RAF Palestine and Transjordan was moved permanently to Jerusalem from Amman in order to be alongside the High Commissioner. Meanwhile, No 6 Squadron arrived from Hinaidi with its Hawker Harts, and joined the Headquarters of No 2 Company which had moved back to Ramleh. It was also decided that a fourth section should be added to No 2 Company. Meanwhile, two sections were still required in Transjordan, with the remaining two needed in Palestine for aerodrome protection and urgent requests for aid to the civil power. On 4 October, the new 'D' Section was formed at Ramleh from armoured car crews relocated from Iraq, personnel collected at the Depot at Aboukir in Egypt and others who had been rapidly gathered together from units in the United Kingdom.[23]

In November 1929, there was an Arab demonstration in Jerusalem on the twelfth anniversary of the Balfour Declaration, but while the armoured cars were placed on stand-by, nothing untoward transpired. For the next few years, the activities of the bedouin in the deserts occupied the armoured cars and the TJFF. There were infrequent Arab protests in Palestine and there was concern each year during the week-long Palestinian Muslim religious festival of Nebi Musa, that trouble would erupt, but the armoured cars were not called upon. However, during October 1933 the level of violence increased. Leo Hetherington had arrived on No 2 Company after serving for a period in Egypt, and was an NCO in a section of armoured cars called out to assist the Palestine police in Jaffa, as he describes:

> Well, from Aboukir I was posted at very short notice to Palestine to No 2 Armoured Car Company at Ramleh. During my time with them I did experience riots and some small active service. There were quite fierce riots about 1933-1934 in Jaffa, which is hard by Tel Aviv and is the Arab section. It was very lively at times. We were housed in some police stables… The odd shot used to come through the corrugated fencing.
>
> On one occasion we went out thinking we were going out for a day and we came back three days later looking very dirty and tired. And that was quite a frightening affair – the Arabs were already beginning to realise the threat of the Jews to them, their land was being taken over and so on – legitimately – it was being paid for and purchased, but nevertheless the nomadic Arab

The Palestine Police take up position in anticipation of a riot (Skellon).

was inconvenienced and so they did have quite big demonstrations in Jaffa in the main square.

I remember on one occasion I saw it completely filled. I estimated 6000 and we were supposed to make a show of strength in our four armoured cars. I've never been more terrified in all my life when we went at about eight miles an hour through this lot, and the consequences not so much to us but to the Palestine Police... very brave men. But they certainly got a mauling from the Arabs on that occasion, I remember. It was protectorate in those days you see and it was necessary for Police to make a show of strength before the military could come in. So these poor devils formed their thin line and advanced with short batons and the Arabs had long poles and they were just hitting them in the face. I saw one lad carried by me that his own mother wouldn't have recognised.

With the conflict intensifying, the Palestine Police began using their service revolvers:

Well there was only one thing for it and they had to start shooting and it was very untidy thing altogether that. [Some of the Arabs were hit] but more policemen were hurt actually. Half-a-dozen police were stabbed, they went down alleyways – they were told not to, but they did, and were stabbed in the back. A few were shot. But mostly it was this long stick in the face business.

We were going at this snails-pace though the crowd, swinging our guns in a menacing way. But we ourselves never fired. The nearest I got to it was handing out reserve supplies of revolver ammunition to the police who had quickly exhausted their ammunition.

… It was from that time I think that we evolved a new technique as a result of that. They were banging away at the cars and that, and they were old Rolls-Royce cars, marvellous things. They'd been made in 1914 for the First World War and they were still going strong… We had a hand magneto that you could wind up and it was wired to the car itself so that anybody touching it from outside got an electric shock. That, I think, came from the experience of that very incident.

There were difficulties in communication when dealing with these large demonstrations as Leo Hetherington describes:

We were just told that on no account were we to fire until we were ordered. Each car carried an officer or a senior NCO, so we were pretty well controlled. Really there was no danger of anybody losing his head; there was nothing wild about it and we were ourselves were disciplined. But for actual instructions, it's difficult you know with four cars separated, and of course there wasn't any intercom. In the desert we communicated by flags. Just as the naval semaphore men did in those days. Tighten it in a town, where there was no communication, so each car was an entity… If it had come to the crunch we would have done what we were told to do.

The use of petrol bombs would have been devastating for the crew inside the cars but fortunately they were not used, although a more subtle form was attempted on one occasion, as Hetherington describes:

We thought it rather funny at the time. There was an instance of an Arab woman coming along with a pitcher on her head. You've seen them swaying gracefully. Naturally one concluded it was water, but as she went by a car she tipped this into the back, the open section of the car. It was petrol, a torch was thrown into this and this car was blazing in a matter of seconds. I think it was only then that they realised the danger of the floor being wooden planking. It ran throughout; even into the turret part which was supposed to be protected. And of course the floor boards being set alight on the outside, quickly spread to the inside as well.

That car a flaming wreck in a matter of seconds – the crew scrambled out. We onlookers thought this was funny at the time… I think the person responsible was hustled away… The vehicle was a write-off.

There was a clear likelihood of armed conflict developing between the Arabs and Jews, and that there would soon be serious bloodshed. Hetherington recalls one small incident:

I'd gone down on the Sunday just to check the cars, and last minute details, knowing full well that we were due out early on the Monday morning. I found a box of my ammunition missing, over a 1000 rounds in all had been stolen, and sold to the Jews, as it happened on this particular occasion. Both sides were more than ready to buy ammunition.

Despite the underlying tensions, the officers and airmen were still able to pursue a relatively peaceful life outside of Ramleh. The married accommodation for No 2 Armoured Car Company was in Ramleh, an Arab town, and whilst it was necessary to bring the families into the camp on occasions, the families generally remained in their town quarters. Furthermore, at Christmas, a 2-ton lorry load of Jaffa oranges, sent courtesy of some local Arabs, would arrive at the Guard Room at Ramleh. The airmen continued to socialise and play sport in Tel Aviv or go swimming at the beach in Jaffa without disturbance, as Hetherington recalls:

> We had the affairs such as I described with the Arabs in Jaffa. We had about three over a period of perhaps two years. Now this isn't to say that the whole country was restive or anything. We travelled around quite easily when we were off duty. I certainly did – I used to go to Tel Aviv and have an evening out and a carefree trip back. There was no real trouble at that time. It was well advertised when there was going to be a demonstration.[24]

At the domestic level, there was a serious outbreak of scarlet fever in mid-1932 with a large portion of the Company being admitted to the Palestine General Hospital at Sarafand. That November, an airman contracted diphtheria and a series of 'gargling parades' were instituted to prevent its spread. While there were no losses on operations there were accidents in training and routine patrols. Two airmen were killed in separate road accidents in late 1932. AC1 Arthur Rolph, who had transferred to the more beautiful climes of Palestine, after serving his time in Iraq, was with No 2 Company at Ramleh and in late-1934 endured a four-month stay in hospital at Sarafand, with a shattered left femur, after his armoured car rolled while training at Amman.

Meanwhile, the air routes of the Empire were developing, and in May 1932, Imperial Airways began flying in to Ramleh. The station underwent an extensive building programme with a new Guard Room and Barrack Block. As well as the

Number 2 Armoured Car Company at the King's Birthday Parade in Jerusalem 1933, along with the TJFF and the Seaforth Highlanders (Rolph, RAFACA).

routine rotation of a section to Amman and Ma'an every month, there was the annual AOC's inspection and the regular attendance alongside the TJFF and the resident British infantry battalion at the King's Birthday Parade in Jerusalem, in the presence of the High Commissioner, General Sir Arthur Grenfell Wauchope GCMG KCB CIE.

Pilot Officer Bill Foulsham arrived in February 1935 at Port Said on the SS *Ranpura*.[25] He had been on flying training in the United Kingdom, but had an air accident, after which it was determined that he had eye problems. He was therefore taken off flying after only a few solo flights and posted to No 2 Armoured Car Company. Now that the road from Amman into Iraq was opened up, there were opportunities for visits to RAF Hinaidi in Iraq. In May that year, Foulsham travelled with 'B' Section across to Baghdad for a fortnight long visit. On the return journey they stopped at the fort at Rutbah; now a police post, wireless station and the rest-house for Nairn Transport Company's travellers. One feature that Bill Foulsham recalled about Rutbah was that a bottle of beer cost about ten shillings (at the time a day's pay was about 14 shillings).[26]

An exchange trip to Ramleh was organised a few months later by No 2 Section of No 1 Company, when there was an opportunity for a cocktail party with the visiting officers. Ramleh was a station where the officers and airmen could have their families, and a schoolhouse was even built on the station. The Commanding Officer at this time was Squadron Leader Denis Mulholland AFC, and as Bill Foulsham recalled he was referred to as 'Muldoon' by many, and he and his wife, Félice, were both well-liked.[27] At Christmas, there was a pantomime and a children's party. There were also various dances organised by the RAF units at Ramleh and Sarafand with the pool of European female company being far greater in Palestine than in Iraq. One example was on Armistice Day 1935, when No 2 Company organised a dance in the main hangar at Ramleh in aid of the RAF Benevolent Fund.

The officers of the Armoured Car Companies were still predominantly pilots on 'ground tours'. To keep their flying hours up, they would often go up in RAF aircraft when the opportunity presented itself, such as on communication or ferrying duties. Flying Officer Bill Dennehy was a New Zealander who had been serving on the Company since early 1933 after volunteering for overseas service. Prior to being offered a commission in the RAF in 1930, he had served as a Lieutenant in the Machine-Gun Squadron of the 6th Wellington Mounted Rifles back in New Zealand. He had then completed his pilot training at Digby in Lincolnshire. On 18 June 1934, he was flying to Ma'an in an Avro Tutor, with LAC H. Leete from the Company as passenger, when the aeroplane began vibrating violently, which began working the wings loose. It was later learned that a rod and piston had disintegrated inside the engine. The aeroplane rapidly lost height and began to fall apart. Unable to find a suitable landing place amongst the ridges and hills the only option was to take to their parachutes. He ordered Leete to jump at about 2000 feet, who did so and landed safely. However, by the time Dennehy was ready to jump himself he was very low. As a consequence when he leapt backwards from the starboard sailplane he was only 500 feet from the ground and he landed heavily on a steep slope.

Flying Officer Dennehy spent two months recovering from his injuries in the RAF Hospital at Sarafand. Both he and Leete were made proud members of the Caterpillar Club; for those who had successfully bailed out of a disabled aircraft. As members they received a golden caterpillar badge with two bright ruby eyes from the parachute manufacturer and convenor of the club, the Irving Air Chute Company from Hertfordshire. The dangers of desert flying had been evident in Dennehy's case, as on a previous occasion he had forced-landed in the desert with a broken oil pipe. He was found after three days searching and flew his aircraft off a mudflat once it was repaired.

After serving as Company Adjutant, he returned to Wellington in New Zealand for four months leave to visit his family. He returned to the Company in April and was put in charge of 'A' Section. Sadly, on 26 September 1935, the Tutor aircraft that he was piloting with passenger and fellow Company officer, Flying Officer Theodore Sanders, stalled at the top of a loop and spun into the ground near Sarafand. Both were buried the following day at Ramleh War Cemetery.[28]

The Rolls-Royces continued to form the mainstay of the armoured car companies. Although by 1933 there was concern at the age of the vehicles, no suitable replacement had yet been created and new Rolls' continued to arrive from the RAF Stores Depot at Kidbrooke in London. Despite their age, they proved to be reliable mounts and their performance was considerably improved with the arrival of the more robust camel-tread tyres. The 3-ton six-wheeler Crossley tenders were replaced by lighter Commer 30-cwts and the Rolls-Royce W/T tenders were re-built at Aboukir with a better arrangement of equipment. The limitations of the heavier Crossleys were noticed in October 1934 when all four sections of No 2 Company had gathered at RAF Amman for the annual collective training. Each Section, consisting of four Rolls-Royce armoured cars, two Rolls-Royce W/T tenders and a Crossley six-wheeler, departed on a reliability run at half-hour intervals. They travelled via Zerqa to Azraq and then back to Qasr al Kharanah and onto Amman. All arrived back within the time specified averaging 14½ mph but it was noted that without the Crossley tenders the sections could easily have averaged 25 mph.[29]

While the first few years of the new decade had been relatively tranquil, by 1933 the rising tide of anti-Semitism in Poland and the persecution of Jews in Nazi Germany had resulted in the dribble of Jewish refugees rising to a flood. Between 1932 and 1933, arrivals doubled, and by 1936 the Jewish population in Palestine had reached nearly 400,000, approximately 30 per cent of the total population.[30] This dismayed the Palestinian Arab population who protested this influx in fear of their economic independence, their land and the sacred Islamic sites. Sir Arthur Wauchope, the High Commissioner, had attempted to set up a legislative council with an Arab majority but this had been rejected by Arabs, Jews and the British Government alike.[31] By 1936, the Arabs had declared a wish for independence to the Mandatory Government on a number of occasions, but they had become frustrated in trying to achieve their political aims.[32]

Notes

1. AIR 20/5996 *Report on Palestine Riots 23 August 1929-11 September 1929*, p. 33.
2. D. Omissi, *Air Power and Colonial Control: The Royal Air Force 1919-1939* (Manchester: Manchester University Press, 1990), pp. 43-44.
3. D. Omissi, 'Technology and Repression: Air Control in Palestine 1922-36', *Journal of Strategic Studies*, 13 (1990), pp. 44-45.
4. AIR 5/1243 *Operations in Palestine, Vol. I, Chapter 1 to 14 1920-1930*.
5. Omissi, 'Technology and Repression: Air Control in Palestine 1922-36', pp. 46-47
6. J. Lunt, *Imperial Sunset* (London: Macdonald, 1981), p. 52.
7. Omissi, 'Technology and Repression: Air Control in Palestine 1922-36', p. 46
8. AIR 20/5996 *Report on Palestine Riots*.
9. *Ibid.*

10 *Ibid.*
11 *Ibid.*
12 *Ibid.*
13 Omissi, 'Technology and Repression: Air Control in Palestine 1922-36', p. 48.
14 AIR 20/5996 *Report on Palestine Riots*. Two other airmen were mentioned in related documents: Flight Sergeant Eric V. Hibberd and LAC Frederick Hubert.
15 *Ibid.*
16 Lunt, *Imperial Sunset.*
17 In the last week of August, while the majority of No 2 Company was in Palestine, only one Rolls-Royce armoured car was available for operations in Transjordan.
18 V. Orange and Lord Deramore, *Winged Promises: A History of No 14 Squadron RAF 1915-1945* (Fairford: RAF Benevolent Fund, 1996), p. 60. Later Air Chief Marshal 1st Baron Dowding of Bentley Priory GCB GCVO CMG (1882-1970). With the appointment of Brigadier Dobbie in overall command the Air Ministry had quickly despatched Dowding from the United Kingdom. Outranking Dobbie, he then replaced him in command in Palestine on 11 September. By this time, however, most of the troubles were over.
19 Omissi, 'Technology and Repression: Air Control in Palestine 1922-36', pp. 47-48.
20 AIR 9/19 *Palestine and Transjordan 1921-1936.*
21 AIR 20/5996, *Report on Palestine Riots*, p. 33.
22 Orange, *Winged Promises*, p. 60.
23 AIR 9/19 *Palestine and Transjordan.*
24 Leo Hetherington, *Interview 4838* (London: IWM Sound Archive, 1981).
25 Later Wing Commander W. Foulsham OBE MC (1914-2012)
26 Wing Commander W. Foulsham RAF Retd, *Interview with the author*, 2008.
27 *Ibid*. Squadron Leader Mulholland had previously been OC No 5 Armoured Car Company at Mosul for the first two years of its existence in 1923 to 1924 during the operations on the Turkish frontier.
28 'Crash in the Wilds,' *Evening Post,* Wellington, NZ, 23 January 1935, p. 10, and 'Killed in Smash – NZ Airman,' *Evening Post,* Wellington, NZ, 27 September 1935, p. 9.
29 AIR 29/54 *2 Armoured Car Company, Heliopolis (Egypt); formed 7 April 1922. Includes detachment at Amman (Trans-Jordan); moved to Ramleh (Palestine) 12 March 1923; moved to Amman 1 May 1928; moved to Ramleh 28 August 1928 with detachments at Amman and Ma'an; later detachments at Jerusalem and Haifa.*
30 N. Stewart, *The Royal Navy and the Palestine Patrol* (London: Frank Cass, 2002), p. 7.
31 Orange, *Winged Promises*, p. 92.
32 D. Clarke, *The Eleventh at War* (London: Michael Joseph, 1952), p. 42.

CHAPTER ELEVEN

The Palestine Disturbances 1936 'In Aid of the Civil Power'

"My advice to all young commanders in all the Services is, whenever you see any prospect of being called out 'in aid of the civil power' in any part of the world, to get the hell out of there as quickly and as far as you can."
Marshal of the Royal Air Force Sir Arthur 'Bomber' Harris[1]

"Dealing with the rebellion was a very unsatisfactory and intangible business, and I don't think I produced any better answers than anyone else. But I think I kept within bounds and did as much as I could with the troops available."
Major-General Archibald Wavell, GOC Palestine & Transjordan[2]

Despite the deployment of British infantry battalions to the garrison following the riots in 1929, the responsibility for Palestine remained in the hands of the RAF, under the command of Air Vice-Marshal Richard Peirse CB DSO AFC, with No 14 Squadron, a flight of No 6 Squadron, No 2 Armoured Car Company and 900 officers and men of the Transjordan Frontier Force (TJFF). If there was a resurgence of trouble, he could now call upon 'British Troops in Palestine' commanded by Brigadier J.F. Evetts MC, comprising 1st Loyal (North Lancashire) Regiment at Haifa and 2nd Queen's Own Cameron Highlanders at Jerusalem, supported by No 14 Company RASC. This amounted to around 2000 men, with just under 3000 Palestinian policemen, of which half were Arab (Map 18, p. 193).

Arab resentment had not abated and in the mid-1930s there was to be a resurgence of violence and rioting. Dissent was further encouraged by the failure of Britain and the League of Nations to prevent the Italian invasion of Abyssinia in 1935, thereby lowering British prestige amongst the Arabs. They could also see that across their frontiers, Iraq and Transjordan were nearing independence, and that Syria and the Lebanon also appeared to be heading towards self-government. At a purely economic level, the discontent was further exacerbated by the failure of the tourist season in Palestine.

The Arab Higher National Committee was formed at Nablus in April 1936 in response to continued Jewish migration. The Committee declared that there would be a national strike in protest at the British policy under the Mandate. In Jerusalem on 25 April they demanded the cessation of Jewish immigration, prohibition of land sales to Jews and the establishment of a representative government. The first effects of the strike soon began to be felt, with a tax boycott and serious interruption to road and rail transport and the port of Jaffa. Thus began a seven-month insurgency that would severely test the capacity of the Mandatory Government and British military to maintain civil order, and lead to questioning of the effectiveness of Air Control and ultimately the ending of the Royal Air Force's sole responsibility for Palestine.

Whereas the troubles in 1929 had consisted predominantly of outbreaks of rioting, incendiarism and looting directed against Jewish interests, this was to become a more widespread and sustained insurgency aimed at the Mandatory Government and commerce. These disturbances of 1936 can be broken up into three phases. The initial phase consisted of rioting and civil disobedience, which after a month, developed into a regime of terrorism and sabotage, and finally reached its climax in July with a long period of guerrilla warfare fought by Arab bands from Palestine and others from Syria and Transjordan. During the latter period, groups of Arab guerrillas, some as small as three or four, others of 50 or more, began attacking the roads, railways and communications.

On 15 April 1936, robbers had halted a car on the road between Tulkarm and Nablus and murdered two Jews, while the following day the bodies of two Arab watchmen were found near the Jewish Settlement of Petah Tiqvah. Following the funeral for the Jews in Tel Aviv, serious violence broke out. These events fuelled the deep-seated antipathy between the two groups, and led to hostilities bursting out again on the morning of Sunday 19 April, in both Jaffa and on the Tel Aviv to Jerusalem road. Several Jews and Arabs were killed and policemen injured, civil control was lost, the violence became increasingly brutal, and unrest began spreading,

The crew of A105 from No 2 Armoured Car Company keeps watch over an Arab gathering (© Crown copyright. RAF Regiment Museum).

with the mood in Nablus particularly rebellious.[3]

The RAF armoured cars had been routinely holding exercises and conducting short operations with the resident British infantry battalions over the preceding years for the 'Internal Security Scheme'. In early-March 1936, No 2 Company initiated a planning exercise for these types of operations and organised a week-long 'cooperational course' involving the officers and senior NCOs of the Company and their counterparts from the 2nd Royal Berkshires. A series of lectures were given on the characteristics and uses of the two arms, culminating in an exercise for a motorised column of infantry with an armoured car escort under internal security conditions.[4]

The role that the RAF armoured cars performed in Palestine during 1929 and from 1936 was very different from that which they had been required to carry out in deserts of Transjordan and Iraq, where they had operated according to the RAF Armoured Car Manual. The internal security operations in Palestine however, necessitated close cooperation with motorised infantry in difficult country. This role had never been clearly laid down, nor did combined tactics for armoured cars and infantry exist in any of the three relevant service manuals – the War Office Cavalry Training and Armoured Car Training manuals, and the RAF Armoured Car Manual. The problem had therefore to be closely studied and many of the necessary tactics evolved on the forthcoming operations.[5]

In mid-afternoon of 19 April, the 'Internal Security Scheme' for Palestine was activated and the warning order to implement their part of the scheme was received by No 2 Armoured Car Company. They had continued with exercises during March, albeit the Ramleh Station soccer team had been allowed to travel north to Syria and played matches in Damascus and Beirut. Two officers flew from Ramleh to Damascus to watch the games and were well-received by the French Air Force; however, the outbreak of internal disorder in Palestine led to their immediate recall.

Personnel in Palestine were ordered to wear side-arms when leaving the camp and only go out in groups of two or more. 'C' Section of No 2 Company began immediate patrols around Ramleh, and in one instance helped the Palestine Police round up protestors who had been throwing rocks at a Jerusalem-bound train as it passed along the eastern boundary of the aerodrome. At the same time, 'B' and 'D' Sections were sent north to Nablus and Haifa where they made reconnaissances of northern Palestine, visiting local Jewish settlements that were subject to sniping, and Arab villages to show the flag and search for arms. On one occasion, the armoured cars of 'B' Section dispersed an Arab mob in Jenin with some speed and with a decisive show of force.

'A' Section had remained in Transjordan until early May when the worsening situation necessitated its return to Palestine. The Section Commander, Flight Lieutenant Shenton, received an unfriendly welcome as he and the Company Commander's cars passed through Ramleh on their way to Sarafand. A large rock was thrown by a rebellious local that hit him on the side of the face, causing severe bruising and knocking out four of his teeth.

On 23 May 1936, the AOC, Air Vice-Marshal Richard Peirse, and the Commander, British Troops Palestine, Brigadier Evetts from Nablus, were flying to Tulkarm to inspect a detachment of the 1st Seaforth Highlanders, when they came across a 200-strong party of Arabs armed with a variety of weapons. At this stage, the authorities had ordered that no offensive action was to be used against troublemakers by the military forces. He therefore dispersed the crowd by firing a Very light at the crowd and then diving at them.

After a short time at Nablus, Peirse decided to return by the same route, but this time by road, and set off with a Rolls-Royce armoured car and W/T tender as escort, under the command of Flying Officer Robert Yaxley. After travelling only a mile, they came upon the same crowd. As they approached, those with rifles ran for the cover of the hillside, while those with sticks, knives and other implements scattered. Fire was immediately opened on the riflemen from the single Rolls-Royce armoured car and they were subsequently captured, with their rifles. The remainder of the journey made difficult time due to the route being frequently blocked by boulders that had been rolled onto the road. The events of this day provided a clear illustration to Peirse that many of the Arab population of Palestine were in open, widespread revolt.[6]

That evening, while on patrol to Tulkarm, the same half-section were fired on near the cemetery and two of the attackers were killed. After three-quarters of an hour, the half-section set off to clear the Nablus to Tulkarm road near the prison. The cars returned fire once they were fired upon, and the Lewis guns were used in a dismounted action against snipers. The road was cleared successfully with the only casualty being a Seaforth Highlander who was slightly wounded in the left shoulder and evacuated in an RAF Commer tender to Nablus. The cars were however hit three times, one bullet penetrating a petrol drum.

Banditry on the roads, sniping, arson and crop destruction were becoming widespread, and the strike began to have a significant impact. Peirse realised he would have difficulty dealing with the insurgency with the forces that he possessed. For example, the vulnerable points such as the railway workshops in Haifa, oil depots, the powerhouse and the General Post Office in Jerusalem and broadcasting station at Ramallah all needed military guards. The 1st Royal Scots Fusiliers and 1st Seaforth Highlanders had been sent from Egypt during May, along with a company of the 6th Battalion, Royal Tank Corps, with their Vickers Mk III light tanks; at the same time, the RAF presence was bolstered by two flights of No 6 Squadron.[7]

'A' Section of No 2 Armoured Car Company and the Vickers Mark III light tanks of 6th Battalion Royal Tank Corps at the fort at Nablus (© Crown copyright. RAF Regiment Museum).

section would go in for maintenance while the other stood by in reserve for special purposes such as recovery or repair of stranded aircraft. The armoured cars were widely distributed and attached more or less permanently to the infantry battalions. This led to a close and intimate cooperation between junior officers of the infantry and RAF, and later the Royal Navy, as they lived for long periods of time with the infantrymen with whom they were working. The emergency was therefore very much a "Subaltern's War".

By June 1936, the cars of No 2 Company, and those of Nos 2 and 3 Sections of No 1 Company, were allocated across Palestine as follows: two sections were placed under the command of Northern Brigade and located at Haifa (half-section), Jenin (half-section) and Nablus (one section). One-and-a-half sections were allotted to Southern Brigade and were placed at Jerusalem (one section) and Gaza (half-section). One half-section remained at Amman in Transjordan, while two sections remained at Ramleh as Headquarters Reserve.

The experience gained on the night patrols showed that there was a need for increased firepower for the road patrols and convoy escorts, as well as the capability to illuminate the hillsides from whence the night-time fusillades of rifle fire were erupting. A 3-pdr gun of the Royal Artillery and five 2-pdr Pom-Pom guns from the ships of the 3rd Cruiser Squadron of the Royal Navy, moored at Haifa, were mounted on hired 5-ton heavy lorries crewed by naval ratings and driven by Jewish auxiliaries. Searchlights were also provided by the RAF and from the naval ships at Haifa. The gun crews were protected behind half-inch armour plating reinforced with protective mattresses. The Pom-Pom, which fired 40-mm high-explosive shells at a rate of fire of 200 rounds per minute, could be fearsome at close range against any attackers, and they proved to be a great success.[8]

Eight Rolls-Royce armoured cars of Nos 2 and 3 Sections of No 1 Armoured Car Company, under the command of Wing Commander R.S. Sugden AFC, arrived at Ramleh from Iraq in early May.[9] Within a few days, No 2 Section under Flight Lieutenant Alan Shipwright DFC was working out of Ramleh and Gaza, alongside the local Police, where they spent a large proportion of the next two months. They provided protection at the local airport and made regular patrols south to Khan Yhunis and along the railway north-east to Al Majdal, as well as escorts to Haifa. Meanwhile, No 3 Section under Flight Lieutenant Hugh Constantine was sent to

A Half Section of No 1 Armoured Car Company pose for a photograph with their supporting lorry-mounted Royal Navy Pom-Pom gun, November 1936 (© Crown copyright. Constantine, RAF Regiment Museum).

Officers of the Cameron Highlanders and No 1 Armoured Car Company discuss operations (© Crown copyright. Constantine, RAF Regiment Museum).

Talavera Barracks in Jerusalem to relieve 'B' Section of No 2 Company and was attached to the 2nd Battalion, Queen's Own Cameron Highlanders. Talavera Barracks was described as:

> A neat and tidy collection of wooden huts, with corrugated iron roofs – lay on the slope above the [railway] station. Although a temporary barracks, and primitive in many ways, it was not uncomfortable, nor inconvenient, except for the water shortage. Baths were rationed to once a week, and the water was carefully conserved afterwards for use in Government House garden. The messes were strictly utilitarian, but agreeable enough.[10]

Although, working in close cooperation with a Scottish regiment had its disadvantages as LAC Riggs describes:

> Most of our patrols were carried out at night, and we slept during the day, much to our disgust we were allotted a hut next to the regimental band, who spent most of their day at band practice. Imagine trying to sleep with bagpipes bashing away. After our Section Commander complained, we were given another hut.[11]

This section, along with 'B' Section of No 2 Company, was located here for most of the next three months carrying out patrols with the Camerons, who noted their close collaboration with the RAF armoured cars in their regimental history:

> A detachment of these quickly moved up to Jerusalem and were attached to

215

the Battalion. The armoured cars were Rolls-Royce of the 1914-1918 war and had seen service in the Western Desert. They remained a familiar sight on the square at Talavera Barracks and became part of the daily life of the Battalion from then on, taking part in most of the patrols and operations carried out by the Battalion.[12]

Much of the action over the next few months occurred after dark when the roads were patrolled by the mobile Pom-Pom guns travelling with armed escorts provided by the armoured cars. The main aim was to keep the roads clear of obstructions, mines or snipers in preparation for the morning convoy.[13] Flight Lieutenant Hugh Constantine recalled the frustrations of one particular roadblock operation:

> The attack, I think, was unique in that the three services were all on wheels, led by the RAF armoured cars. I was ordered to take 3 Section on a night patrol on the Jerusalem-Nablus road and deal with a band of Arabs who repeatedly blocked the road at Kilo 33 in a defile.
>
> Our armoured patrol consisted of me leading in HMAC *Jaguar*, next a Leyland lorry mounting a Naval Pom-Pom gun and manned by naval ratings – followed by another armoured car and two civilian buses with two platoons of Cameron Highlanders and a third armoured car bringing up the rear.
>
> As usual the road at Kilo 33 was blocked and we were fired on from the hills. The plan was to contain the shooting while the Cameron Highlanders de-bussed up the hill to try to surround the band. Not very successful I'm afraid! The first shell from the Pom-Pom nearly took my head off – an hour later the Camerons returned the worse for wear; three or four limping and one with a broken leg. The Arabs had disappeared!![14]

The close work with the Camerons continued over the next six months. On 19

Flight Lieutenant Hugh Constantine and HMAC Jaguar on operations in Palestine 1936 (© Crown copyright. Constantine, RAF Regiment Museum).

June, Pilot Officer Neville White was in charge of a half section of No 3 Section, accompanied by a dozen Cameron Highlanders under Captain Clarke in two lorries, on a patrol from Jerusalem to Khan Lubban. At 2230 hours they came across a barricade at Kilo 27 on the return journey and immediately came under fire. White continues:

> ... the patrol was fired upon from both sides of the road at ranges varying from 200 to 500 yards. Fire was returned with Vickers, Lewis and rifle. A green Very light was expended in order to see if there were any hostile forces near the barricade. There were none.
>
> According to a pre-arranged plan, Captain Clarke with ten men climbed the hillside in an endeavour to get behind the position from where most of the fire was coming. Upon seeing his pre-arranged signal of one red Very light the Patrol ceased fire on that side and concentrated their fire on the other. One Jewish driver becoming frightened had abandoned his vehicle and out of control it plunged off the road into the wadi on the western side, where it remained resting on one side ten feet below the level of the road. The Camerons in the Jewish truck fortunately escaped with minor injuries such as cuts or abrasions, and were quickly in action with two Lewis Guns on the western side of the road.
>
> Hostile fire was gradually silenced, and Captain Clarke returning to the road with his Patrol having found nothing. The barricade was removed by the Patrol and a punctured wheel caused by a bullet on the leading armoured car was changed. Attempts were then made to right the Jewish truck, but after the tow-ropes had broken was given up as impossible with the force at hand. Firing now recommenced from the eastern side of the road and was replied to by the Patrol.[15]

Having been unsuccessful in their attempts to right the Jewish truck, all useful gear was removed and it was abandoned. The patrol then moved on to Ramallah where first aid was given to the injured.

In another incident, two cars of No 2 Section and a platoon of the Camerons rapidly turned out to answer an emergency call from a party of police and their own troops. They had been ambushed at Kilo 32 on the Hebron Road, by a 50-strong armed band. The road was found to be blocked in three places and each obstruction had to be cleared before they could proceed. It took some two hours to reach Kilo 32 which was under heavy fire, and the cars were sniped the entire time. An RASC lorry had to be abandoned after it was holed in the petrol tank and an ambulance ditched, injuring the four occupants. The armoured cars and accompanying troops however, provided covering fire and the party was successfully evacuated.[16]

The RAF armoured car crews gradually improved their vehicles and weapons in light of their combat experience. Modifications were made to the Vickers machine-guns that added 8 degrees of elevation, thus allowing fire to be directed at the hill tops. To improve this further, the cars were sometimes driven on to ramps to obtain greater elevation. Spotlights were also mounted on the turret, while Lewis guns were mounted on the turret tops and on the cabs of the tenders in all-round traverse Scarff rings taken from the air gunners' position on obsolete biplanes. The addition of the Lewis allowed fire to be brought to bear from both sides of the car during close-in fighting. This had been further aided by the issue of rifle grenades as standard

A Rolls-Royce armoured car of No 3 Section of No 1 Armoured Car Company keeps watch from the top of the winding section of Seven Sisters road near Jerusalem (© Crown copyright. Constantine, RAF Regiment Museum).

equipment which provided considerable physical and moral effect when fired at rebels shooting from cover or houses. Good radio communications were a key component of the operations in Palestine, and as the RAF armoured car companies had their own Rolls-Royce W/T tenders, these were often attached to the Army command units such as brigade headquarters.[17]

On the good main roads of Palestine, the armoured cars were faster and quieter than the Vickers light tanks of the Royal Tank Corps and suffered less wear and tear. Although susceptible to ditching, the cars gave a commendable performance even on the rough tracks. They were however easy to trap, particularly in the labyrinthine streets of the ancient towns and villages, and being unarmoured underneath they were vulnerable to mines. It was therefore essential that they were accompanied by a platoon of motorised infantry to assist in removing roadblocks and for close protection.[18]

The vulnerability of the RAF armoured cars in urban areas was made clear during an incident at Gaza involving two Rolls-Royces of No 2 Section. Half the section was to guard the Imperial Airways airport, keeping watch during landings and take-offs. The cars had also been patrolling the town, the railway and surrounds and had come under fire on a number of occasions – often three or four times in one night. It had also become apparent over the preceding few days that the movements of the cars were being signalled by the inhabitants of the towns and villages they had passed through.

On 25 May, large crowds had gathered in Gaza and began to stone the police. An urgent request for reinforcements was made by the District Commissioner and two armoured cars of No 2 Section were quickly despatched from Ramleh. The cars drove down the main road into Gaza but were taken by surprise when they found that they had been completely blocked-in by hastily constructed barricades. The armoured car crews showed considerable resourcefulness and, after establishing a defensive position at the Railway Station, were able to extricate themselves by getting their cars onto the railway and driving down the line.

Meanwhile, the 6th Royal Tanks had been alerted and arrived to provide assistance. By this time, the mob had almost complete control of the town and had constructed a score of road blocks comprising large stones, furniture, telephone poles and steel girders. The tanks 'charged' and cleared the main street of barricades and rioters, and were able to make their way to the Police Station where they rescued the few European residents, the small Police contingent and an incomplete platoon of infantry who had been trapped. As a consequence of this episode, an order was made prohibiting the employment of tanks and armoured cars in the narrow twisting streets of the old towns and villages where they were likely to encounter resistance, of which Gaza was a prime example.[19]

By early June, Air Vice-Marshal Peirse found he had another problem. A political internment camp had been built at El Auja, in the desert on the Sinai frontier with Egypt; however, a proportion of the police guarding it had defected. The defence of the camp and police post was therefore assumed by 'B' Section of No 2 Company, as there was a fear that with the large numbers of bedouin camped in the deserts nearby, some might attempt to free their Arab brethren. An aircraft of No 6 Squadron was placed on standby at the disposal of the RAF armoured car officer at Auja should it be needed. To alleviate the problem, Peirse arranged for a new and more convenient camp to be set up at Sarafand and this was ready in three weeks. Movement of the Arab internees to the camp was however, temporarily disrupted when the inmates objected to be driven to the new location by Jewish drivers. The situation was resolved by the irregular but practical solution of permitting the internees to provide drivers from amongst themselves.[20]

Meanwhile, further north there was considerable action on the main roads around Nablus in Samaria. Some idea of the intensity of these operations can be gained by looking at a four-day period in early June, when 'A' Section of No 2 Company repeatedly dealt with hit-and-run attacks on the narrow winding roads. Just before midnight on 8 June, about two miles from Nablus, a patrol of three Rolls-Royce armoured cars with a detachment of Seaforth Highlanders, was hit by rounds fired from the nearby hills but also from only 300 yards away. The cars got quickly into position to return fire and using their spotlights and Very cartridges, attempted to locate the enemy. The cars replied with 400 rounds from their Vickers and Lewis guns, and the RSM and a Sergeant of the Seaforths replied with rifle grenades. The machine-gun registered on the ridge below which the enemy were seen taking cover. After ten minutes, the firing by the column ceased and they waited in silence for quarter-of-an-hour, but no more firing came. The column continued to Tulkarm and returned without further incident.[21]

Just after 2300 hours the following night, while two Rolls-Royce armoured cars patrolled the Nablus to Jenin road searching for mines and roadblocks, three other Rolls-Royces were assigned to camp defence. Snipers began firing from the surrounding hillsides at the Old Turkish Fort and the nearby tented military camp, and continued through the night. In response, the armoured cars fired scattered bursts at the muzzle flashes of the snipers. Little else could be done, but it was hoped this would at best eliminate the snipers, or at least dislodge them and put them to flight.[22]

With Lewis guns manned, a Half-Section of No 2 Company makes a halt on a Palestine road (© Crown copyright. II Squadron RAF Regiment History Room).

The Section Commander, Flight Lieutenant Harold Owen, was in action with his cars again the following day:

> About 1630 yesterday I left with two armoured cars to investigate along the Tulkarm road. At a point about one mile west of Anebta, fire was opened on me by two rifles on the South Hill Side. They were taking cover either in a house or in the trees in the garden. Fire was returned for about ten minutes and the enemy fire ceased. The cars proceeded for about another 200 yards and, on turning a corner, fire was opened on us from the top of the northern hills. Two separate firing points were noted.
>
> The cars were stopped and the fire returned. After about five or ten minutes, three aircraft appeared from the direction of Nablus. Fire was continued and seven Very Lights fired in the enemy direction to give the aircraft an indication of where they were located. Enemy fire ceased so cars were turned round and started back for Nablus. After we had covered about 400 yards one aircraft dropped a message to say that they had seen two Arabs disappearing into a cave.
>
> ... 259 rounds were fired during the engagement. No hits were registered on the cars or personnel and, so far as I know, no Arabs were hit.

The cars reached Nablus without further incident. However, just before midnight, two cars of the same section, under Flying Officer Robin Yaxley, set out from Nablus to patrol the Jenin road. Again they came under attack. The Operations Record Book continues:

> They were fired on by eight rifles at a point one mile from the District Commissioner's office in the Jenin direction. Six of the rifles were on the Western side and two on the East. Fire was returned with both Lewis and Vickers Guns and Rifle grenades. Seven grenades were fired, all of which exploded, and 351 rounds fired. The sniping ceased at 2355 hours.[23]

The matter of Air Cooperation was discussed between the Flight Commander of No 6 Squadron at Ramleh and Flight Lieutenant Owen, following his experience during the ambush at Anebta. This led to discussions at a higher level, and ultimately the creation of a scheme to facilitate rapid air support to ground forces. Cooperation with the aircraft was enabled by the RAF armoured car company W/T tenders or commercial lorries newly-fitted with wireless. These latter came to be known as *Rodex* vehicles and they travelled with each motorised column and convoy. Once resistance was encountered, a special code call of great simplicity was sent out. These messages were to be given priority over all other messages. A single letter denoted the main arterial road along which the convoy was passing, the number of the last kilometre post passed and the letters 'XX' for air support alone, or 'GG' for the intervention of the local ground-based 'Striking Force' as well. The latter usually consisted of a half section of armoured cars and a platoon of motorised infantry.

Palestine had first been divided into Northern and Southern Aircraft Zones, with the dividing line being drawn through Jenin. The Air Striking Force that was to respond to the 'XX' calls was composed of one flight of No 14 Squadron based at Jisr Mejamie for the northern zone and two flights of No 6 Squadron at Ramleh in the south. In mid-July, No 33 Squadron was also redeployed from Egypt to Gaza. The aircraft were held at high readiness and response times could sometimes be measured in minutes. By September, the rapidity with which aircraft could provide support was further improved by dividing Palestine into four aircraft zones: Northern, Middle, Jordan and Southern.[24]

The effectiveness of coordination between aircraft and armoured cars was further demonstrated on Wednesday 24 June 1936, at a location known as 'Windy Corner', approximately two miles north of Qalqilya. A patrol of the Royal Scots Fusiliers came under fire in a defile and suffered several casualties as the troops leapt from their lorries to take up firing positions. They were pinned down and unable to move from their positions until two Rolls-Royces of 'D' Section, under Flight Lieutenant Richard Shenton, along with the CO, Squadron Leader Mulholland, came to their assistance. They were supported by the Fairey Gordon aircraft of No 6 Squadron. Mulholland reported the events of the skirmish:

> The Royal Scots Fusiliers officer in charge stated that he had been fired upon from the hill about one-and-a-half miles east of the road. The Company Commander and Flight Lieutenant Shenton proceeded in two Rolls-Royce armoured cars across country being directed to the spot by an aircraft of No 6 Squadron. No enemy could be seen; but an Arab headdress was picked up at the position where the enemy had been firing at the convoy. This was carefully wrapped up in clean cloth and handed over to the Police for any action they wished to take.
>
> On the return journey to the road over heavily boulder strewn ground the sump plate of one of our cars was smashed. The second Rolls-Royce towed the unserviceable car back to the main road. Watchers were observed on several hills in the vicinity. As the repair of the sump plate was likely to take about 45 minutes, the officer in charge of the Royal Scots Fusiliers patrol decided to proceed on his way to Sarafand.

With the shooting having died down, the crew turned their attention to the task of repairing the car. However, it soon became apparent to Mulholland and Shenton that there were insurgents still in the area. Mulholland continues:

> During the period when a new sump plate was being fitted, heavy rifle and machine-gun fire was heard in the direction of Qalqilya. Flight Lieutenant Shenton was sent to investigate with instructions not to enter the town. He returned with the report that the firing appeared to come from the north-west direction of the town.
>
> After receiving a Situation Report, the Company Commander decided to proceed with one Rolls-Royce armoured car in a northerly direction along the railway line where enfilade fire could be brought to bear. The armoured cars got to a position about one mile north of the railway crossing where fire was brought to bear on a Wood and where a clear view could be had of the enemy's probable line of retreat. After a lapse of about 15 minutes, all hostile fire ceased on the north side of the main road [and] the armoured cars then returned to the railway crossing.
>
> Flight Lieutenant Shenton was ordered to proceed about two miles down the railway line to the south as firing was heard in that direction, and was followed by the Company Commander in the second armoured car. Most of the firing now appeared to come from an orange grove and parallel to the railway line. The orange grove was traversed by the [fire of] two Vickers guns supported by the Lewis guns in the new turret Scarff mounting. The new mounting was found to be of considerable value as the two armoured cars were able to keep four automatic rifles in action throughout the period of the ambush.

At this stage, the difficulties of fighting a battle from, and using as a thoroughfare, a working railway, became apparent to the armoured car crews and which could have had serious consequences for the armoured cars, the train and the Company Commander:

> A train proceeding from Ras el Ein to Qalqilya caused momentary consternation to the crew of the armoured cars. The leading armoured car was able to get off the permanent way but the second armoured car had to remain in position between the rails. Order was given to abandon car and to bring the Lewis gun for local protection. A series of red Very lights fired from the car was seen by the engine driver and the train came to a halt about 200 yards from the car.

All enemy fire had ceased by this time however, and the engagement was broken off after three hours in action and having expended around 1800 rounds of ammunition. Mulholland made a last comment in his report regarding the importance of air cooperation:

> Throughout the period of this engagement, aircraft were giving the utmost assistance, both by machine-gun fire and directing the armoured cars along the enemy's line of retreat.[25]

The armoured cars at Nablus and Jenin were worked particularly heavily. Resistance was encountered with monotonous regularity, and for the month of June the armoured cars were in action on no fewer than 22 occasions.

'B' Section, under the command of Flight Lieutenant Leslie Bennett, was operating from Jerusalem at this time. On his patrols he repeatedly found that the telegraph wires had been cut in many places by the rebels. On the last day of June, two Rolls-Royce armoured cars escorted a repair party from the Post & Telegraph Department along the Jerusalem to Jericho road. In the process, they arrested five Arabs who were found in possession of wire cutters and who were suspected of cutting the telegraph wires. Early the following morning, a patrol of the Jerusalem to Lydda railway line to Kilo 42 found that not only had a further 12 spans of telegraph lines been cut, but also that two rails had been lifted. Fortunately, they were able to halt a goods train before it reached the break and derailed. They did see individuals moving near the line and fired a short burst of Vickers fire to drive them off.

On 3 July, two cars patrolled the same stretch of road and found 29 spans of telegraph wires had been cut and another rail lifted. Five days later, No 3 Section escorted Post & Telegraph employees to repair more cut telegraph lines on the Nablus road to Haramiya. Using police dogs, the culprits were traced to the village of Ain Sinya where an arrest was made. Bennett became frustrated with the repeated damage to the line and on 9 July learned the wires had again been cut. This was the fourth instance of sabotage on the Jerusalem to Lydda railway line.

It was on occasions such as this that the difficulties and unpleasant nature of fighting an insurgency were to become apparent to the RAF armoured car crews. On the previous occasions where this type of damage had occurred, the Mukhtars of the villages had been collected together and warned that the cutting of wires was to cease. They were to inform the authorities of the identity of the perpetrators, who should be handed over. Then having failed demonstrably to comply with this previous request, Flight Lieutenant Bennett determined to take action against one of these villages. He continues:

> Upon arrival this morning, the Mukhtar was sent for and interrogated as to why my instructions had not been complied with. He was inclined to be sullen and uncommunicative. I warned him to clear the area and placed a cordon of armoured cars and Cameron personnel round it.
>
> I then fired two grenades into the pumping apparatus (consisting of an inclined drive and buckets driven by one donkey). Fairly extensive damage was done which will probably take a day to repair. Five dwelling houses were next cleared and grenades thrown into the living rooms of each doing little damage but causing considerable disorder. The last grenade was thrown into the village store causing a fair amount of damage and a conflagration which was extinguished after a short while in case the fire spread to other houses.
>
> Extreme care was exercised to avoid any damage to persons or livestock and any form of brutality. The Mukhtar admitted after the action that he knew who was doing the work but was too frightened to act as an informer in view of the intimidation. We parted on quite friendly terms and I despatched him to have a conference with the other villagers as to ways and means of stopping this tiresome practice.[26]

Only three days later, Bennett, with two Rolls-Royces, was on a night patrol with infantrymen of the Dorsets on the road to Nablus when they came under fire.

A detachment of British troops at Jenin. Note the civilian buses used for transport (© Crown copyright. RAF Regiment Museum).

been very carefully planned by the attackers, estimated to be about 30 strong, firing from positions 360° and using modern Mauser rifles and ammunition. Remarkably, the cars of No 3 Section were turned out less than two hours later to go and recover the abandoned truck, which they did without disturbance. Bennett was particularly pleased with the performance of the men in his Section:

> I would particularly like to mention LAC Ross who acted as runner for me during the whole engagement, apart from the great work he did with the searchlight and as driver of the truck. All Armoured Car Crews behaved in an exemplary manner, keeping their heads and going about their work systematically. Both Rolls-Royce drivers turned their Cars without the use of lights, and completely battened for action. This is no mean feat, when one takes into consideration that the road was of normal width without any turning point and that both cars were under heavy rifle fire at the time.[28]

This location had proved so troublesome that the Dorsets established a permanent picquet on the hills around it and no further trouble occurred. In all these encounters, despite the large volume of rounds exchanged, very few cars or personnel were hit and enemy casualties were rare or more often unknown, the only evidence being traces of blood on the rocks surrounding their sangars. These patrol actions began to assume a similar repeated pattern of being sniped at, the column halting and replying, expending large amounts of ammunition and an assault by the infantry covered by the armoured cars and Pom-Pom. The assailants were rarely detained as they had usually fled; however, the fire from the Pom-Pom was so effective that night ambushes soon became less frequent.

The motorised infantry were carried in a combination of Army 15-cwts and hired civilian lorries or buses. However, the occupants of any unarmoured vehicles ran a serious risk from mines or close-range bursts of fire from ambush positions. It also became clear that one reason that Bennett had received his wound was because the searchlight truck had insufficient protection for the crew. When coming under fire from both sides of the road, the searchlight operators could only bring the light to bear on one side and were then clearly silhouetted and therefore easy targets for the snipers. Subsequently, it was recommended that two of the Rolls-Royce armoured cars themselves be fitted with the large searchlights.

In early July, although some intelligence reports suggested that the rebellion was weakening, it was also learned that Arab ex-Ottoman Army officers from Iraq, Syria and Transjordan were now re-organising and retraining the Arab armed bands for further struggle. One of these officers was Fawzi el Qawukji, who had served in the post-war Saudi and Iraqi Army, had fought in the Druze uprising against the French in Syria, and was considerably anti-British. He had styled himself as the Commander-in-Chief of the Arab Revolutionary Army and was now leading organised bands of up to 2000 men of Iraqi, Syrian and Druze origin. He became well-known to the RAF armoured car companies who were to fight him in more than one conflict over the next few years.[29] By the first week of July, definite information was received from the Intelligence Service regarding the location of two of his guerrilla bands, each some 150 to 200 strong, which had been operating against the railway and roads between Nablus, Ramallah and Qalqilya. The locality was near trackless and inaccessible to motor transport, with many of the hill villages rarely visited by police or administrative officers since the beginning of the Mandate. On the night of 5 July, a 'drive' of the area was conducted with a force of four infantry battalions, the 8th Hussars, two flights of No 6 Squadron and five-and-a-half sections of both Armoured Car Companies.[30] The aircraft of No 14 and 33 Squadrons were to standby on immediate call. Operation 'X' as it was known was coordinated between the Northern and Southern Brigades with both Brigade Headquarters allocated an RAF W/T Tender from No 2 Company for radio communications.

The cordon and search operation lasted until the morning of 7 July. As the Southern Brigade troops had been preoccupied with operations in Jerusalem, the operation was delayed until 5 July. Secrecy was lost as the military were required to notify the District Commissioner and the plans for the operation were published in the *Palestine Post* on the day of the operation. The RAF armoured cars with the Southern Brigade formed a cordon from Huwara to Ain Sinya and patrolled the roads for the next 16 hours and assisted the infantry companies with searches, but other than some desultory fire on one occasion the operation was uneventful.

With the loss of surprise, and as became increasingly apparent, an inadequate number of troops on the ground, it was assumed that the weapons of the band had been quickly buried and that the rebels had dispersed. In an attempt to impress on the local villagers the resolve of the military, demonstrations were made of the effectiveness of mortar and 20-pound bombs. These were fired or dropped from aircraft in front of the gathered Arab men of the villages that had been searched, but this merely evinced applause and delight rather than awe. The operation ceased on the morning of 7 July with the troops thoroughly exhausted having covered large areas of very difficult trackless country. Despite the failure to find any major cache of arms or ammunition or bring the bands to battle, the drive was considered to have been a limited success in one respect, in that the district gave little further trouble.[31]

The following day however, the intensity of the workload and the increasing sophistication of the insurgents were further demonstrated. Number 2 Section had escorted the Colonel of the Seaforth Highlanders to a conference in Jenin that morning and returned to Nablus without incident in the early afternoon. The two half-sections then had to complete three night patrols of the Nablus to Silat adh Dhahr road, taking just under one hour for the round trip. Ten minutes after leaving Nablus at 2200 hours, the second patrol noticed a pile of stones to one side of the road, and the leading car, RRAC *Cathay*, pulled well over to the right to avoid them. Just as the front wheels of the vehicles had passed the stones, there was a loud explosion. On investigation it was found that a bomb made from a piece of drainpipe had exploded under the car. The striker had been tied down with cotton and then stretched across the road and this had then been broken by the car. Whilst the sump of the car had a large hole knocked in it rendering it unserviceable, the blast had not penetrated the car or injured anyone. A second bomb which was soon discovered had failed to explode. The third patrol had then departed at 2315 hours and were on full alert given this new development but experienced no trouble.[32]

Of the numerous patrols that were carried out by the sections and the accompanying infantry, there were very few where they were able to inflict casualties on their attackers. One of the few exceptions was on 12 July, when two cars of 'C' Section proceeded to Kilo 108 on the Jenin to Silat adh Dhahr road where they had received reports that an armed band was operating. On arrival, they found the road blocked. They were immediately fired on, and this was returned by the cars and the troops of the 1st York and Lancaster Regiment. The troops dismounted and gave chase to the snipers and were able to report that they had killed eight of the party.

A further small success occurred when 'A' Section was on a night curfew patrol with the Seaforth Highlanders:

> The road from the fort to the town takes a left hand turn, to go into Nablus, and facing this bend was a house, which had been giving us trouble, by housing snipers, who used to let off a few rounds at us when we passed, and hitting the sides of the armoured cars.

A drive-past of No 3 Section No 1 Armoured Car Company at a parade in Jerusalem in 1936 (© Crown copyright. Constantine, RAF Regiment Museum).

So it was decided the next patrol would open fire first as the cars took the bend…two armoured cars started their patrol and did open fire on the bend, into the first floor window.

Having passed the house it was decided to stop and investigate, and it was found that the guns had found their target, and in the upstairs room two Arabs were found, and very shot up. [Disturbingly], when the guns were examined, they were the same as ours, .303 Lee Enfield, and the ammunition was new and marked 1932, and we were still using 1922 vintage.[33]

Inflicting casualties on the attackers was extremely rare as they invariably had the advantage of surprise, often the cover of night, and a thorough knowledge of the local terrain. The common entry in the Operations Record Book following an enemy contact was 'No casualties, Enemy casualties unknown.' The overwhelming firepower of the Vickers or that from an aircraft was of use only on the rare occasions when the attackers were caught in the open. Invariably they slipped quickly away in the darkness, easily evading capture.

Operation 'X' had made it unmistakeably clear that more troops were required. Furthermore, the RAF armoured cars had been heavily committed but there were seldom enough to go around. After more than two months continuous activity, they required rest and refitting. They happily welcomed therefore, the arrival of the 11th (Prince Albert's Own) Hussars, also known by their regimental nickname 'The Cherry Pickers', also equipped with Rolls-Royce armoured cars, sent from Egypt in mid-July to aid them in their tasks. Number 2 Company were to have a close and friendly relationship with this fine regiment both in Palestine and during the early days of the coming World War. The 11th Hussars had been the first of two regular cavalry regiments to be equipped with armoured cars in 1928, the other being the 12th Lancers, who No 2 Company had met briefly during the disturbances of 1929. The 11th Hussars were allocated to the Northern Brigade and the RAF armoured cars the HQ Reserve to the Southern Brigade.[34]

A further cavalry regiment, the 8th King's Royal Irish Hussars had arrived from Egypt in early June. However, they were mounted in open 'soft-skinned' 15-cwt trucks, and were escorted from the Egyptian frontier to Jerusalem by No 2 Section of No 1 Company and an aircraft of No 6 Squadron. After a period in the north, it was found that the motorised cavalry of the 8th Hussars was better suited to the deserts around Gaza. They were assisted by September in this role by No 3 Section, which, having spent the majority of time since their arrival in and around Jerusalem, left their comrades of the Cameron Highlanders and moved south. Air support was provided by the Hawker Harts of No 33 Squadron. By this time, it was considered that only in this open desert area of Palestine could true Air Control be practised effectively.

The railway in the south was of particular importance as it was the major land link with the British garrison in Egypt. It had been the subject of numerous sabotage attempts and consequently, No 3 Section began patrolling twice daily to the railway station at Al Majdal, 20 miles north-east of Gaza and then another 20 miles across to Al Faluja. On an evening patrol, only a few days after their arrival, the station at Al Madjal was sniped, a pile of sleepers and a platelayers' hut were set on fire and a platelayer killed. An armoured car of the Section soon arrived and fired 500 rounds in reply, but again no casualties were identified.[35] On another occasion they came under heavy fire from an estimated 15 snipers, again replying with Vickers and Lewis guns with no result discernible.

By mid-July, a further two battalions were sent from Malta together with another cavalry regiment, while by late August a further battalion from the Malta Garrison and another brigade headquarters were needed. As the Arab resistance continued into September, a second division was despatched to Palestine and the British Cabinet decided to restore law and order by more drastic measures, ordering the imposition of martial law. The 5th Division was based at Haifa and took responsibility for northern Palestine, while the 1st Division operated from Jerusalem and dealt with the south.

Air Control in Palestine was considered to have failed for a second time since 1929 and as a consequence, the British Cabinet decided to move the primary responsibility from the Air Ministry to the War Office. With the largest part of the garrison by this time being Army units, it seemed logical that a senior Army officer should be placed in command. On 15 September, Lieutenant-General Sir John Dill CB CMG DSO took command of the British Forces in Palestine and Transjordan from Air Vice-Marshal Peirse and established his Corps Headquarters at the King David Hotel in Jerusalem. Dill, accompanied by Air Vice-Marshal Peirse, was escorted there by No 3 Section of No 1 Company on 18 September. Peirse remained in an advisory capacity for a further month, while Air Commodore Roderic Hill MC AFC assumed command of the RAF in Palestine and Transjordan.[36]

The role of the RAF in Palestine was gradually changing. It would no longer be the lead arm in the conflict as the demand for more troops on the ground became imperative. Aircraft still had an important role, but in close coordination with significant forces of ground troops. The RAF armoured cars continued to play a major role in dealing with the disturbances and the high regard in which they were held are exemplified by the letters received from senior Army commanders at the time. In a letter written to Squadron Leader Mulholland, Brigadier Archibald Beauman DSO, of the Northern Brigade, wrote of his appreciation of their work:

> Please convey to all ranks of RAF armoured cars who have been working under my command how sorry I am to lose them and how much I appreciate their gallantry on many occasions and zeal throughout.[37]

While the Commanding Officer, 1st Seaforth Highlanders, with whom they had seen much action, wrote:

> 'A' Section [of No 2 Armoured Car Company] left us today and we were very sorry to see them go, they know our ways and what we require and our liaison was excellent. During the time they have been here we have had many incidents and actions under fire, the Armoured Cars being sniped at during their night patrols on all occasions. I have nothing but praise for the officers and men who carried out their work and hope they will return again.[38]

The 11th Hussars returned to Egypt during October after three months of active service and the experience gained while serving alongside the RAF armoured cars was not forgotten, as their history recounts:

> Their partnership in Palestine marked the beginning of a close and valued association with the armoured car units of the Royal Air Force. Later on,

Pilot Officer William Foulsham MC (© Crown copyright. RAF Regiment Museum).

in the early days of the desert war, some of these were to serve under the tutelage of the 11th Hussars, but in 1936 the airmen had been able to teach a thing or two to the cavalry. It was the result of the experience of the RAF companies in Arab countries that the Eleventh installed Lewis guns in aircraft mountings to supplement the Vickers in the turrets of the Rolls-Royces, thereby adding considerably to their effective firepower.[39]

With the arrival of more Army units, some sections of RAF armoured cars were able to reduce their role in the more populated areas and concentrate on operations in the east of Palestine and in the Jordan Valley, where the armoured cars were more suited.

Particularly vulnerable was the Iraq Petroleum Company's oil pipeline that had been completed in January 1935, and which ran from Kirkuk through the northern hills near Nazareth, across difficult and rough going, to the refinery and storage tanks at Haifa. In the latter half of 1936, this became a major target of the Arab bands attempting regularly to disrupt the flow of crude oil.

With the departure of the 11th Hussars, a section of No 2 Company was assigned to the near-impossible task of patrolling the pipeline. The section routinely worked from Beisan, near the frontier with Transjordan. The insurgents continued to target the roads on which the cars travelled. A Rolls-Royce armoured car, A105, was rendered unserviceable when it was blown up on a mine near Beisan while returning from a patrol. The saboteurs' prime target however, was the pipeline itself. They would puncture the pipe with a single rifle bullet and then ignite the stream of fuel. This usually resulted in a satisfying eruption of flame, though it was not without its risks for the saboteur! Mornington Wentworth recalls the routine:

> We patrolled the pipeline from November 1936 to April 1938. The Arabs were smart in damaging the pipeline; mainly, in the time that it took them. We'd have a patrol car covering a distance of maybe a mile protecting pipeline, and then there would be another one taking the next mile. Now we'd go for one mile, and everything was okay. We'd go back but when we got down there, there was hole in the pipeline and they'd set it on fire. As quick as that! And it didn't take us long to cover a mile; only a matter of minutes.[40]

Despite a calming of the insurgency during August, it resumed with renewed ferocity the following month. Jerusalem and its surrounding roads were still a focus for civil disorder and insurgent activity and there were always two sections of cars, often one from each armoured car company, allocated to the Holy City. Pilot Officer Bill Foulsham of 'B' Section experienced a particularly intense period of activity on the road patrols from Jerusalem to Hebron. Having relieved 'C' Section on the morning of Thursday 17 September, they were in action by 2130 hours that night clearing roadblocks on the road to Hebron. There followed a series of engagements on 21 and 26 September, and 1, 7 and 8 October.

The 2nd Cameronians (Scottish Rifles) had arrived in the last week of September and were located at Bethlehem and Hebron as part of the heavy reinforcement of the Palestine Garrison by 1st Infantry Division. On the evening of 9 October, a company of Cameronians and Pilot Officer Bill Foulsham with two Rolls-Royce armoured cars from Jerusalem, were returning from a patrol to Yatta, south of Hebron, when

Major-General Archibald Wavell, GOC Palestine and Transjordan, presents the Military Cross to Flight Lieutenant L.V. Bennett in a ceremony at Ramleh on 26 October 1937 (© Crown copyright. RAF Museum).

they were fired on by about 50 snipers from the hills on either side of the road. Roadblocks had been set up over the next three miles and at one location, an Army lorry detonated a mine, igniting the petrol tank, causing casualties to four of the occupants and blocking the road. Returning fire, they were able to gradually silence their opponents with mortar, rifle and machine-gun fire and the roadblocks were eventually cleared after an encounter lasting several hours. Although Rolls-Royce A130 was hit twice, there were no casualties among the airmen. At least two of their assailants were known to have been hit, but local intelligence reports later indicated they had caused heavy casualties to their attackers. Two nights later, Foulsham was again in action, dealing with a roadblock and then later half-a-dozen snipers who began firing at his patrol and the billets in Hebron. Replies with both the Vickers and the accompanying Pom-Pom soon silenced them.[41]

The deployment of the overwhelming numbers of troops from two infantry divisions, the damaging effect of the strike on Arab enterprises, particularly the coming citrus exporting season, and the promise of a Royal Commission to investigate the Arabs' grievances, began to have an effect upon the insurgency. Only a few days later, on 12 October, the Arab Higher National Committee terminated the strike they had called in April, and ordered all resistance to cease. The activity of the Arab armed bands decreased, at least for the time being. The rebel leader, Fawzi el Qawukji, was pushed back across the Jordan River by the 1st Division and he withdrew to Baghdad, but told his men to bide their time until the call was again made. On 19 October 1936, with the insurgency having abated, the order was given that convoy escorts were to cease and be replaced only by road patrols. The uprising had cost the lives of 197 Palestinians (both Muslims and Christians) and 80 Jews, while the Police and military had lost 27 killed and 207 wounded.[42]

If the political climate had calmed in Palestine by the end of October, in Iraq there was renewed instability, with a successful *coup d'état* by the Iraqi military. The following day, after nearly six months of continuous and intensive operations, Nos 2 and 3 Sections of No 1 Armoured Car Company were ordered to prepare for their immediate return to Baghdad. Number 2 Section reunited with No 3 Section at Ramleh, having driven down from Jerusalem, where it had been operating for two months. The two sections departed from Ramleh at 0600 hours the following morning, in a convoy under the command of Squadron Leader Mulholland, the Officer Commanding No 2 Company. As they departed, they passed a guard of honour provided by his Company. The convoy halted outside Jerusalem to have breakfast, where they were met by the AOC Palestine and Transjordan, Air Commodore Roderic Hill, who bade them a further farewell and read out a message of congratulations from General Dill. The two sections arrived back at Hinaidi on 3 November, with their Company Commander, Wing Commander Sugden AFC, having driven out to meet them at Dhibban on the Euphrates.[43]

Following the end of the strike, No 2 Company resumed their work in Transjordan, with a section returning to Transjordan to operate from Amman and Ma'an. During November, No 2 Company received the news that Flight Lieutenants L.V. Bennett and A.H. Owen and Flying Officer R.G. Yaxley had each been awarded the Military Cross and LAC R.E. Ross, the Military Medal arising from the Palestine emergency operations of the previous seven months. A month later, further good news was received with the award of the Military Cross to Pilot Officer W. Foulsham. On 9 December 1936, Company paraded in front of GOC, General Dill and the AOC, Air Commodore Hill where they were presented with a new Company badge that had recently received Royal Approval.⁴⁴

In November 1936, the Royal Commission on Palestine began gathering information amidst widespread protests and boycotts by the Arabs. The Commission continued to take submissions and produced its report the following July, after seven months of work. It recommended that Palestine be divided into two major parts, with the Jews receiving most of the coastal plain and those parts that were predominantly Jewish, and the Arabs, the remaining two-thirds, including the hills of Judea. Certain enclaves that were of security or religious import, particularly the corridor from Jaffa through to Jerusalem, Nazareth and Bethlehem, were to be maintained under a British Mandate. The partition proposal was rejected by both the Arab and Jewish representatives, and by November 1938 the Palestine Partition Commission had declared that the plan could not be implemented.⁴⁵

The release of the Commission report in July 1937 ended the uneasy peace that had prevailed since the previous October and the negative reaction and a steady worsening of the internal security situation ensued. In September 1937, General Dill was replaced by Major-General Archibald Wavell CB CMG. On 26 September 1937, only a fortnight after Wavell's arrival, the Acting District Commissioner for Galilee, Lewis Andrews, was assassinated in Nazareth, as he left the Anglican Church following the morning service. The events of this day signalled an intensification of the disturbances. The military resources of the Mandate had been considerably reduced at the end of the strike from two infantry divisions to only two experienced but rather weary brigades.

The reaction of the British Government was immediate. The Arab Higher Committee was outlawed and those that had not escaped the country were arrested and flown to exile in the Seychelles. The Grand Mufti fled from Jerusalem, and eventually escaped to Damascus, from whence he could further direct operations. Emergency powers and regulations were expanded and strengthened, and a system of military courts introduced, with the power to award the death penalty for possession of arms and explosives. The Army and police intensified the 'cordon and search' operations. The Arab peasants and villagers suffered terribly; often trapped between the intimidation of the insurgents and retribution of the military. Arab property of suspect individuals and villages implicated in acts of violence were ransacked and crops and livestock confiscated. A policy of house levelling and village demolition was instituted, and in some instances, these actions went beyond those officially sanctioned.⁴⁶

Inevitably, the Arab insurgency resumed and a campaign of assassination, intimidation and sabotage was reinstituted against civil, police and military figures. The 14th and 16th Infantry Brigades which had remained in the country, though experienced, had already been fully-committed for some months. Air support was again provided by the stalwart No 6 Squadron. A retired Indian policeman, Sir Charles Tegart, was brought out to improve the efficiency of the Palestine Police and its intelligence service, of which it was sorely in need. Furthermore, he oversaw the building of a series of massive fortified police posts throughout Palestine, and the construction of a nine-foot high defensive wire system supported by a series of forts and pillboxes along the northern frontier with French-mandated Syria and Lebanon. The latter designed to keep out infiltrating Arab guerrilla bands.⁴⁷

The activities of the guerrillas had become more organised and to a certain degree, more coordinated, with increasingly sophisticated weaponry. The triangle of country enclosed by Nablus, Tulkarm and Jenin was particularly troublesome, as

Rolls-Royce A104 of 'D' Section of No 2 Armoured Car Company complete with Section pennant and the newly-approved Company badge on operations during the late 1930s (© Crown copyright. RAF Regiment Museum).

Mornington Wentworth recalls:

> We were up at a place called Nablus. There was a large hill that went up from Nablus fort and the Army were up there on lookout, looking all over the countryside. And early one morning two of the soldiers came down the hill with a bucket for tea. They never got back. By the time they'd got their tea and had gone halfway up that hill a bomb had been planted with a trip wire and it blew them both to smithereens. [The Arabs] were quick, there's no doubt about it.[48]

The roads and railways were once again subjected to regular disruption, but with the Army taking on the major role in Palestine, the Air Ministry reconsidered the establishment of the RAF armoured car companies. The Air Ministry made the suggestion that No 2 Armoured Car Company was no longer required in Palestine for internal security purposes, and that the Companies in both Iraq and Palestine could be reduced in size. It also made the questionable proposal that:

> In times of tension or disturbance… it is therefore reasonable to suppose that reductions in present strength could be made provided reinforcements could reach Iraq quickly if they were required.[49]

Where the reinforcements were to come from was not made clear. As the AOC Palestine and Transjordan, Air Commodore Roderic Hill, noted in correspondence with RAF Middle East Command during December 1937:

> ... until a decision is reached on the scope of Army and Royal Air Force responsibilities ... it seems as if any assumption that Royal Air Force armoured cars may no longer be required in Palestine for purely internal security purposes must inevitably be held in abeyance. The premise made in the Internal Security Scheme is that a portion of No 2 Armoured Car Company will form an integral part of the Palestine defence force.
>
> In the somewhat unlikely circumstances of the RAF armoured cars not being required by the Army in Palestine, it is still considered that they could be utilised and would indeed be an almost indispensable adjunct for protection of, and cooperation with, detached air units during times of tension and unrest, and for the rescue of personnel compelled to land away from their bases.
>
> Moreover, in the present disturbed condition of the country, the advantages of retaining a homogeneous unit, equipped with a vehicle of proven efficiency in this country, might with advantage be considered, until an opportunity occurred for complete re-equipment.[50]

Notwithstanding the increased contribution of troops by the War Office for internal security in Palestine, the RAF armoured cars continued to be used by the Army in this role. However, during periods of increased international tension, the armoured car units of the Army were often recalled to Egypt. Furthermore, retaining the Companies at their current establishments would also leave Palestine, Transjordan and Iraq with a dedicated RAF protection force highly experienced with the theatre of operations. Moreover, with the looming threat of war with Germany and Italy, there

Rolls-Royce armoured cars and a Fordson tender of Number 2 Armoured Car Company parked outside the YMCA in Jerusalem (Skellon).

would inevitably be large RAF convoys travelling from Iraq to reinforce Egypt that would need adequate protection. Fortunately, the proposals for the disbandment of the Companies were not implemented and No 2 Armoured Car Company remained an integral part of the Palestine defence forces under the provisions of the 'Internal Security Scheme'. In the coming war, both Companies would more than justify their continued existence.

Despite the damp chill of winter, the first months of 1938 were a busy time, with the three sections of armoured cars spread widely across Palestine. A section each was attached to 14th and 16th Infantry Brigades and served alongside regiments such as the Hampshires, West Kents and the Black Watch at Jerusalem, Haifa, Tiberias and Acre. The 16th Infantry Brigade inflicted heavy losses on the insurgents after launching operations in the Tulkarm-Jenin area. The Company vehicles cooperated in these operations over the course of the year, travelling between 20,000 and 43,000 miles, and firing 3000 to 20,000 rounds of .303 each month.

As well as supporting the infantry, the RAF armoured cars also provided escorts on a number of occasions to senior officials including General Wavell, Air Commodore Hill and the newly-appointed High Commissioner, Sir Harold MacMichael, as they moved about Palestine and Transjordan on various tours of inspection and to attend conferences. Changes in the higher command occurred when General Wavell returned to the United Kingdom in April 1938 to take up another appointment and he was replaced by Lieutenant-General Robert Haining CB DSO. In mid-June 1938, 'B' Section escorted Air Commodore Hill to Kolundia on his departure from Palestine. His replacement was Air Commodore Arthur Harris OBE AFC, who would earn fame as the AOC-in-C Bomber Command, and who later expressed strong opinions on the difficulty of the role the RAF and Army were performing in Palestine:

> My advice to all young commanders in all the Services is, whenever you see any prospect of being called out 'in aid of the civil power' in any part of the world, to get the hell out of there as quickly and as far as you can. If you fail by being too soft you will be sacked; if you succeed by being tough enough, you will certainly be told you were too tough, and you may be for it... There are two things you can get from aiding the civil power, and two things only – brickbats or blame.[51]

Harris did however continue to pursue the air cooperation with the Army, and considerable progress was made in the development of new methods, particularly among junior leaders. This was made more efficient and effective by a system of ground signals and more importantly mobile wireless vehicles, of which the Armoured Car Company W/T tenders were the prime example.

Despite a view that Air Control in Palestine had failed, the Army continued to make frequent requests for air support with considerable saving in effort and casualties.[52] Air Control, purely manifested by the bombing of villages, was not the panacea for an Arab uprising in Palestine, just as it had not been in Iraq. Notwithstanding the limitations of Air Control due to the dense population and the difficulties of telling friend from foe, close cooperation between land and air forces had been achieved, particularly in dropping supplies, in close-support and in cordon and search operations. By mid-1936, this had been developed to a high level of efficiency in Palestine with the development of W/T and the use of aircraft zones.[53]

The RAF armoured cars in Palestine from 1929 until 1939 also provided a well-

The aftermath of the attack on the Potash convoy (Skellon).

trained mobile force experienced in 'civil order' operations. Furthermore, the officers and airmen knew the ground over which they had to work and were able to rapidly respond to trouble and at least stabilise the situation until the ground troops could arrive. Indeed, the arrival of the RAF armoured cars in many instances was decisive to the successful conclusion of the action.

Half of 'B' Section spent part of that summer alongside the 2nd Royal Ulster Rifles in the high, rugged mountains of northern Galilee at Iqrit, on the Syrian frontier, guarding against infiltration by the insurgents. Their old friends, the 11th Hussars, returned from Egypt to assist in dealing with the renewed insurgent activity, and during the middle months of 1938 had a squadron stationed at Sarafand, sharing the patrolling duties with the section of No 2 Company stationed at Ramleh.

By late August, three sections were concentrated at Jerusalem as it was threatened by attack, and as a consequence were carrying out all-night boundary patrols. The Officer Commanding No 2 Company, Squadron Leader C.H. Stilwell, was appointed Town Commander of Jerusalem. He had a small force, consisting only of one company of the 2nd Battalion, Black Watch, and the three armoured car sections, with sole responsibility for defence of the entire city.[54]

On 13 September, 'B' Section was sent to Guweira to assist in the recovery of a crashed aircraft. En route, the section came across an Army column held up by a road block and under fire. Once cleared, they proceeded to Guweira and started the return journey with the salvaged parts from the crashed aircraft. They also evacuated the local police post and carried arms, equipment and personnel back to Jerusalem. While negotiating a blown bridge, the wireless tender overturned and had to be righted under fire.

The insurgency aimed to cripple the economy and social life of the country, targeting all the major industries and transport routes. The Palestine Potash Company had been established in 1930 on the shores of the Dead Sea and it was soon making

Purpose-built Alvis-Straussler armoured cars were used for a short time prior to the Second World War by No 2 Armoured Car Company and the Aden Section (Skellon).

a significant contribution to the export earnings from Palestine. This made it a target for the Arab insurgents. In one instance, on 16 September 1938, 'B' Section, while escorting the supply convoy to Amman, had to stop to assist the Potash convoy, which had been held up. Later that day, 'A' Section received an urgent call from the police to come to the assistance of another Potash convoy. They had been ambushed by an Arab band which had destroyed five lorries and killed three Arab drivers. 'A' Section departed immediately, and was sniped at for a large part of the journey. However, they arrived in time to fight off the attackers, and were able to save the lives the remaining five employees.

A month later, half of 'D' Section was returning from Allenby Bridge on the same road after completion of escort duty when they came under fire from both sides of the road at Kilo 27. Four airmen were wounded, two seriously. While most of the encounters since 1936 had seen few casualties to the armoured car crews this was the most serious casualty toll they had yet experienced.[55]

By late October 1938 however, there was an increasing threat from improvised land mines and this led to the fitting of metal plates underneath the Rolls-Royces. New Fordsons had also begun arriving to replace the Morris tenders, and to improve protection for the wireless operators, armour plate was fitted around the wireless gear.[56] The New Year also saw the arrival of two new Alvis Straussler armoured cars, which had been sent from the United Kingdom for trials. Following trials held in Iraq with an earlier model, the RAF had decided to purchase a limited number. However, only 27 of this type were ever built, with 12 being delivered to the RAF. Their arrival would have been greeted with some interest. With an angled-hull and dual-driving positions it was the first purpose-built armoured car considered for the RAF armoured car companies. The cars were tested on roads, rough ground and wet terrain but were found to overturn easily. On 9 June, Pilot Officer G.A. McWhinney and LAC F. Dawson were both killed when their Alvis-Straussler rolled when a tyre burst. The Rolls-Royces remained however, and by late 1939 there is no further record of the use of the Alvis-Straussler armoured cars on No 2 Armoured Car Company.[57]

By November 1938, events in Europe were again overshadowing the troubles in Palestine and the British Empire hovered on the brink of war with Germany and Italy. Adolf Hitler had ordered the annexation of Austria. It now appeared inevitable that there would be a war, but Prime Minister Chamberlain returned from Munich promising 'Peace in our Time'. Despite this false hope, it at least delayed the inevitable and allowed Great Britain breathing space to continue its rearmament for the coming conflict.

The unrest in Palestine continued into 1939, although the situation did ease somewhat as the pressure from the Army operations and the arrival of further reinforcements dislocated the organisation of the Arab bands and significantly reduced their effectiveness. However, although the symptoms of the rebellion had been suppressed militarily, the causes of it remained, and in the towns there were still terrorist attacks with bombings and shootings instigated by both Jewish and Arab groups, with subsequent retaliatory attacks. Many more landmines were being used and although the Army began to suffer casualties as a consequence, No 2 Armoured Car Company was fortunate not to be so afflicted.[58]

Meanwhile, Hitler ignored the Munich Agreement and the German Army marched into Czechoslovakia, while Mussolini followed suit and overran Albania. By Easter 1939, it had become clear that war with Germany and its ally, Italy, was unavoidable. On 1 September 1939, the German Army invaded Poland and Nos 1 and 2 Armoured Car Companies were warned to mobilise for war. Two days later, on Sunday 3 September, following Germany's refusal to withdraw from Poland, Great Britain and its Empire declared war.

At 0600 hours the following day, Rolls-Royce armoured car A103 and Fordson Tender A192, were assigned as an escort to an RAOC breakdown vehicle on the Hebron-Beersheba Road. At Kilo 40, A192 detonated a land mine and the front of the tender was blown apart. AC1 Lloyd was fortunate to be only slightly wounded, but LAC Geoffrey Slade was fatally injured. He was buried a few days later at the Ramleh War Cemetery. LAC Slade's death, although the result of the ongoing troubles in Palestine, made him the first fatal casualty for the Armoured Car Companies and RAF Middle East Command in the Second World War.

With war now declared, the primary threat to the British position in the Middle East came from Mussolini's Italian Army poised on the Egyptian frontier in Italian Libya. It was in this direction that the RAF armoured cars would first turn their focus.

Notes

1. A. Harris, *Bomber Offensive* (New York: MacMillan, 1947), p. 30-31. Marshal of the Royal Air Force Sir Arthur 'Bomber' Harris GCB OBE AFC (1892-1984), AOC Palestine & Transjordan, 1938-1939.
2. Quoted in, J. Connell, *Wavell. Scholar and Soldier* (London: Collins, 1964), p. 197.
3. AIR 5/1244 *Operations: Palestine, Vol. II, Chapter 15 to 25, 1930-1940*.
4. AIR 29/54 *2 Armoured Car Company, Heliopolis (Egypt); formed 7 April 1922. Includes detachment at Amman (Trans-Jordan); moved to Ramleh (Palestine) 12 March 1923; moved to Amman 1 May 1928; moved to Ramleh 28 August 1928 with detachments at Amman and Ma'an; later detachments at Jerusalem and Haifa*. On 22 April 1936, Acting Pilot Officer Michael Peter Casano arrived on posting to No 2 Armoured Car Company from No 4 Flying Training School in Egypt. Casano was to have a long and eventful service with No 2 Armoured Car Company, eventually leaving as Commanding Officer in February 1943.
5. *The Royal Air Force Armoured Car Manual, Air Ministry Publication 1418* (London: Air Ministry, 1931).
6. AIR 29/54 *2 Armoured Car Company* and Air Vice-Marshal R.E.C. Peirse, *Abridged Despatch - Disturbances in Palestine 19 April to 14 September 1936* (London: Air

Ministry, 1937), p. 24. Peirse wrote: 'The importance of this incident was that it proved to me conclusively that the fellaheen – in Samaria at any rate – were completely out of control.' Later Air Chief Marshal Sir Richard Peirse KCB DSO AFC (1892-1970).

7   B.H. Liddell Hart, *The Tanks: The History of the Royal Tank Regiment and its predecessors Heavy Branch Machine-Gun Corps, Tank Corps and Royal Tank Corps, 1914-1945, Vol. I* (London: Cassell, 1959), pp. 284-285. Sixth Battalion, Royal Tank Corps had been formed in Egypt in 1933 by amalgamating the 3rd and 5th Armoured Car Companies. They handed their Rolls-Royce armoured cars over to the 12th Lancers. The Royal Tank Corps became the Royal Tank Regiment in April 1939 and became part of the newly-formed Royal Armoured Corps.

8   Captain Compton P. Norman RN, *Imperial War Museum Interview 4629* (London: IWM Sound Archive, 1980) and N. Stewart, *The Royal Navy and the Palestine Patrol* (London: Frank Cass, 2002), p. 7.

9   Due to confusion in the use of numbered sections for No 1 Company and lettered sections for No 2 Company, it was decided that all sections should be lettered for the time being. Numbers 2 and 3 Sections therefore became 'X' and 'Y' Sections, respectively, for the period they were operating in Palestine.

10 G. Blight, *The History of the Royal Berkshire Regiment (Princess Charlotte of Wales's) 1920-1947* (London: Staples Press, 1953), p. 126.

11 AC85/6 *The Erk and his Armoured Cars: Flight Lieutenant Riggs* (RAF Museum, Hendon: Unpublished manuscript, n.d.).

12 *Historical Records of the Queen's Own Cameron Highlanders, 1932-1948, Vol. I* (Edinburgh/London: William Blackwood & Sons Ltd, 1952), p. 60.

13 AIR 5/1244 *Operations: Palestine, Vol. II*.

14 H.A. Constantine file, RAF Regiment Museum Archives.

15 AIR 28/663 *Air Ministry and Ministry of Defence: Operations Records Books, RAF Stations, Ramleh. Appendices May-July 1936*. Pilot Officer R.N.J. White, Report on Patrol on Route 'D' by 2nd half Section No 3 section 19 June 1936

16 AIR 29/50 *No 1 Armoured Car Company, Habbaniya; before 1 Apr 1930 Armoured Car Wing, Hinaidi; from 3 Oct 1946 No 1 ACC incorporated in RAF Regiment, redesignated No 2701 Squadron* and AIR 29/54 *2 Armoured Car Company*.

17 AIR 5/1244 *Operations: Palestine, Vol. II*.

18 *Ibid.*

19 *Ibid.*, AIR 29/50 *No 1 Armoured Car Company* and AIR 29/54 *2 Armoured Car Company*.

20 AIR 29/54 *2 Armoured Car Company*.

21 AIR 28/663 *Air Ministry and Ministry of Defence: Operations Records Books, RAF Stations, Ramleh. Appendices May-July 1936*.

22 *Ibid.*

23 *Ibid.*

24 AIR 5/1244 *Operations: Palestine, Vol. II* and AIR 28/661 *Air Ministry & Ministry of Defence Operations Record Books RAF Stations: Ramleh April 1933-July 1942, October 1942-December 1943*.

25 AIR 28/663 *Air Ministry and Ministry of Defence: Operations Records Books, RAF Stations, Ramleh. Appendices May-July 1936*.

26 *Ibid.*

27 *Ibid.*

28 *Ibid.*

29 Fawzi el Qawukji, *Memoirs, 1948, Part I, Journal of Palestine Studies*, 1 (1972), pp. 27-58.

30 All but half a section of the RAF armoured car force in Palestine.

31 AIR 5/1244 *Operations: Palestine, Vol. II*.

32 AIR 29/51 *1 Armoured Car Company, Habbaniya, Iraq: appendices only, May 1936-June 1943* and AIR 29/54 *2 Armoured Car Company*.

33 AC85/6 *The Erk*.

34 Peirse, *Abridged Despatch*. The other was the 12th Lancers.
35 AIR 23/633 *Disturbances in Palestine: weekly resumé of operations, August-November 1936*.
36 Later Air Chief Marshal Sir Roderic Hill KCB MC AFC and bar (1894-1954).
37 AIR 29/54 *2 Armoured Car Company*.
38 *Ibid*.
39 D. Clarke, *The Eleventh at War* (London: Michael Joseph, 1952), p. 59.
40 Mornington S. Wentworth, *Interview 4768* (London: IWM Sound Archive, 1980).
41 C.N. Barclay, *The History of the Cameronians (Scottish Rifles), Vol. III, 1933-1946* (London: Sifton Praed, 1948), p. 23.
42 Cited in M. Abu Nowar, *The History of the Hashemite Kingdom of Jordan, Vol II* (Oxford: Ithaca Press, 1989), p. 182.
43 AIR 29/50 *No 1 Armoured Car Company*. 15 December 1936. Two airmen, Sergeant P.J. Bains and Corporal W. Hall, from No 1 Armoured Car Company were mentioned in despatches by General Dill for their devotion to duty and outstanding work.
44 Peirse, *Abridged Despatch*. Flight Lieutenants H. Constantine and R.N.J. White of No 1 Company and Squadron Leader D. Mulholland AFC and Flying Officer G.N. Amison of No 2 Company and were mentioned in despatches, while Warrant Officer G.G. Meager of No 2 Company received the MBE. Bennett and Yaxley were presented with their Military Cross' at Ramleh on 26 October 1937 by General Wavell.
45 'Summary of the Report of the Palestine Royal Commission', *American Jewish Yearbook*, 1937-1938, pp. 503-556.
46 M. Hughes, 'The Banality of Brutality: British Armed Forces and the Repression of the Arab Revolt in Palestine, 1936–39', *English Historical Review* Vol. CXXIV, 507 (2009), pp. 313-354.
47 Connell, *Wavell*.
48 Wentworth, *Interview 4768*.
49 AIR 5/1212 *Armoured Cars Policy: Palestine, Transjordan and Iraq, 1933-1942*. Correspondence: Air Ministry to RAF Middle East, 25 November 1937.
50 AIR 5/1212 *Armoured Cars Policy*. Correspondence: Reply to RAF Middle East by Air Commodore Hill, 31 December 1937.
51 Harris, *Bomber Offensive*.
52 D. Omissi, 'Technology and Repression: Air Control in Palestine 1922-36', *Journal of Strategic Studies*, 13 (1990), pp. 42-63.
53 The armed bands had grown accustomed to the presence of aircraft and developed tactics whereby a guerrilla would lie prone, as if dead, on the ground as the aeroplane passed over. He would then roll over and fire up into the fuselage.
54 AIR 29/54 *2 Armoured Car Company*. Shenton was on leave in the United Kingdom.
55 *Ibid*. The wounded were Sergeant C. Mortimore, Corporals C. Field and J. Drayton, and LAC E. Fender.
56 *ibid*. 31 December 1938. Following personnel were brought to the attention of the GOC Palestine and Transjordan for their good work during the operations of 1938:
Squadron Leader R.F. Shenton, Flight Lieutenant N.C. Singer, Flying Officers W.O. Jones, M.P. Casano, Pilot Officers G.A. McWhinney and T.H. Stockdale; Flight Sergeants R. Sweetlove, D. McHaffie, Courtney; Sergeants P. Lynch and F. Peart; Corporals H. Robbins, A. Cook, D. Butler and W. Thorley and LACs T. Booth and L. Williams.
57 *Ibid*. 9 June 1939.
58 *Ibid*. Flight Lieutenant T.W.C. Fazan and Flight Sergeant F.C. Peart were mentioned in despatches for their distinguished service during the period of operations from 1 April to 30 July 1939.

Chapter Twelve

Operation Compass
'Wavell's Eyes and Ears'

"The Eleventh's old friends from the RAF in Palestine came down to help them.... Air Chief Marshal Sir Arthur Longmore offered them to General Wavell.... and for many weeks afterwards the airmen and the cavalry fought together side by side."

The Eleventh at War[1]

The primary activity of the RAF in the Middle East during the 1920s and 1930s had been the maintenance of internal peace and civil order in the mandated territories. The Middle East was however, of vital strategic value to the British Empire. Oil flowed from Persia and Iraq for transport and industry, and for the increasingly mechanised military forces. Palestine had been the focus of military activity for the last years of the decade. Egypt however, possessed the largest British military base outside of the United Kingdom, and the Suez Canal was the key to the shortest and surest transport routes from Great Britain to East Africa, India, Singapore, Australia and New Zealand.

The Italo-Abyssinian crisis of 1935 had raised the threat of an external war with a European power and had drawn Germany and Italy closer together. While no conflict occurred at the time, this did give the British Forces in Egypt some indication as to what a future war in the desert might require. The RAF, with nine squadrons, had moved west to Mersa Matruh and established an advanced headquarters in the desert. The difficulties of maintaining air operations in this environment became apparent; particularly the effect of dust on engines, aeroplanes, guns and bomb gear. The Army and RAF had also to face the problems of movement and coordination of large mechanised forces across the desert. The focus of the British Government was now fixed on dealing with the growing strength of Germany, and therefore the threat from Italy had a lower priority. However, it was clear that the Middle East could be used as a springboard for military action against the Italian Empire in Libya, Abyssinia and Italian Somaliland. While resources were limited, the RAF did set about constructing new airfields around Cairo and Alexandria, as well as in the Western Desert. The RAF had also begun to investigate more fluid methods of operation and control. Importantly it also possessed 'seasoned and experienced air and ground crews' and the 'training and experience gained in Egypt, Iraq, Sudan, India and Singapore was about to pay very full dividend.'[2]

The intention was to avoid war with Italy if possible, but by 1937 the neutrality of Italy had come into question, and it was clear it had hostile intentions. On 1

September 1939, Germany invaded Poland, Scandinavia in the spring of 1940, and then finally launched their *Blitzkrieg* on 10 May and moved into the Low Countries and France. By June, the British Expeditionary Force had been evacuated from Dunkirk, France had signed an armistice with Germany, and Britain and her Empire stood alone. Mussolini had met with Hitler in March of that year, and it was therefore no surprise when, on 10 June, Italy declared war on Great Britain and France. With a swift and total victory in the West imminent, Mussolini had decided to throw his lot in with Germany. Hostilities against France ceased on 25 June and her colonial forces in the eastern Mediterranean in Syria, Lebanon and in the west in Morocco, Algeria and Tunisia could no longer be used in a struggle against the Axis powers.

The North African campaign of 1940 to 1943 was fought in a theatre some 3000 miles long, stretching west from the Suez Canal, along the southern shores of the Mediterranean across Egypt, Libya and Tunisia. Although the Western Desert is technically confined to Egypt, it has very few water sources, and extends into Libya for 1000 miles south to the borders with Sudan and Chad and the Sahara. The area to the east of Benghazi, the mountain of the Jebel Akhdar, accommodated the only patch of green between Cairo and Tripoli, possessing fertile soils and encouraging high rainfall.

There were few inhabitants in the deserts, mostly bedouin, while the coast was punctuated by widely-spaced small towns, some possessing small harbours, only two of which, Alexandria in the east and Benghazi to the west, that could be used as major supply ports. The interior was composed of a vast sand sea, dotted with a few oases, that was difficult to cross with motor vehicles in large columns. This region would be used for the passage of Special Forces units, intent on reconnaissance and raiding missions behind the enemy lines.

Major landmarks were rare other than the odd cairn, well or wadi, and navigation during the day, and particularly at night, presented great difficulties. The impediments to movement of mechanised forces were areas of soft sand, salt pans, wadis, and the escarpments, which approached the coast at a few points, or for the most part, lay a few miles inland. Thus the campaign was fought in a thin coastal band, only 20 miles deep at the most, and ebbed and flowed along the coast for the next two and a half years. Much of the surface consisted of hard 'going' that allowed for rapid movement of mechanised forces. This only became difficult after heavy rain or during dry weather which produced almost unendurable dust storms; a thick hot fog of sand known as the *khamsin*. In all but one location, the southern extent of any coastal defensive line could be easily outflanked by an attacking force. Supply and transport was dependent on a single coast road, a railway that initially went only from Cairo to Mersa Matruh or inland on rudimentary desert tracks. The campaign in the Western Desert was one of the first to be fought between two fully mechanised armies, but as each side advanced, the supply lines and distance from their main bases lengthened, and they therefore became weaker. In contrast, the force that was withdrawing could fall back and gain in strength as their supply problems decreased.

The AOC-in-C Middle East and Mediterranean, Air Chief Marshal Sir Arthur Longmore KCB DSO, had assumed command on 13 May 1940 and inherited a huge area covering Egypt, the Sudan, Palestine and Transjordan, East Africa, Aden and Somaliland, Iraq and adjacent territories, Cyprus, Turkey, the Balkans, Malta, the Red Sea and Persian Gulf. His main focus however, was the defence of Egypt and the Suez Canal. In Egypt and Palestine, the RAF possessed only 205 aircraft, none of which were modern fighters or long-range bombers, while the Italian *Regia*

Aeronautica had 101 fighters, 140 bombers and 72 other types of aircraft to deploy in Libya and the Dodecanese.[3]

The British Army in Egypt was similarly disposed. The Commander-in-Chief was Lieutenant-General Sir Archibald Wavell with command of 36,000 men in Egypt. His troops were predominantly regulars of high quality, but equipment was in short supply, especially artillery, ammunition, transport and fighting vehicles. In Egypt, there was the 7th Armoured Division, 4th Indian Division and an incomplete New Zealand Division in the process of formation. In Palestine, there was the 1st Cavalry Division, a British Infantry Brigade, and the 6th Australian Division, the latter also in the process of formation. In striking contrast, Wavell's opponent, Marshal Radolfo Graziani, had under his command in the Libyan provinces of Cyrenaica and Tripolitania, 250,000 men with 200 tanks. With the defeat of France, and the removal of the threat from the French North African colonies, Graziani's forces could now be concentrated against the British in Egypt.

The British forces in Egypt had been anticipating an outbreak of hostilities with Italy and were alert and ready. Seventh Armoured Division assembled near Mersa Matruh, 200 miles from Alexandria, and the Support Group with two Royal Horse Artillery regiments and two motor battalions covered the area between Matruh and the frontier. Major-General Richard O'Connor arrived from Palestine and on 17 June assumed command of HQ Western Desert Force. General O'Connor proved to be a clever tactician, carefully marshalling his scarce resources and using them to greatest effect.[4] At the same time, Air Chief Marshal Longmore sent No 202 (Bomber) Group RAF, with four light bomber squadrons, one fighter squadron and one army co-operation squadron, to Maaten Bagush, a few miles to the east of Mersa Matruh, to prepare for offensive action. The squadrons were placed on airfields stretching back from Mersa Matruh to El Daba.[5] He appointed Air Commodore Raymond Collishaw to command the Group (Map 19, p. 249).[6]

In the early hours of 11 June 1940, every bomber and half the fighters that Longmore possessed took off from airfields across RAF Middle East Command, to attack the *Regia Aeronautica* and the supply dumps of the Italian army. Wavell's plan was to launch limited ground attacks and raids on the Italian posts along the Libyan frontier to force the enemy onto the defensive and to dominate the frontier and beyond. The RAF offensive on supply lines and troop concentrations aimed to delay the Italian invasion of Egypt. While eminently successful, this could not prevent the inevitable, and on 13 September the Italians made a tentative and ponderous advance into Egypt. General O'Connor's small force could not afford heavy losses and so executed with great skill a planned fighting withdrawal to prepared positions at Mersa Matruh. At the same time, RAF Blenheims and Wellingtons bombed the enemy columns as they moved eastwards. The Italian Army, with five divisions, advanced only 65 miles over four days, and then halted at Sidi Barrani. The town consisted of only a few buildings and a landing ground and it was here they dug in. The advance had not caused any anxiety to Wavell and a week later he ordered the planning for an offensive to recapture Sidi Barrani and an advance into Cyrenaica. At the same time, with the Support Group of 7th Armoured Division to hold the enemy advance, small ad-hoc formations of armoured cars, artillery and infantry known as 'Jock' Columns were formed to harass the enemy.[7]

The British armoured force was operating to the south of the Mersa Matruh defence line to prevent any outflanking move by the Italians. Western Desert Force only possessed one armoured car regiment and they had been carrying out their specialised role of far-ranging reconnaissance, the modern version of light cavalry, as part of the Support Group of 7th Armoured Division. The regiment was The 11th Hussars (Prince Albert's Own), the 'Cherry Pickers', and they were under the command of Lieutenant-Colonel John Combe. They were equipped with 1924-pattern Rolls Royce armoured cars and a few Morris armoured cars used as command and wireless vehicles. The strategic information they gathered was filtered back to General Wavell at Middle East Headquarters in Cairo.

The Regiment had been actively engaged ever since the outbreak of hostilities. Eighteen hours after the declaration of war by Italy, a venerable Rolls-Royce armoured car of the 11th Hussars had positioned its bonnet up against the 12-foot wide and five-foot high boundary fence of barbed-wire and steel pickets that marked the Egypt-Libya border, and after a few nudges the fence gave way and the cars moved through. A few hours later, they returned, having taken 61 Italian soldiers prisoner.

The constant operational demands on the 11th Hussars had, however, been taking a toll on vehicles and crews. Because of their success, they were now being specifically hunted by the *Regia Aeronautica*, with an entire Italian air squadron was given the sole duty of pursuing them. The threat of air attack was all the more fearsome as the Italians were using explosive bullets in their attacks on the relatively thin-skinned armoured cars. To sustain the Regiment, it required reinforcements that had the experience and expertise to operate successfully in desert conditions. The most obvious solution was to make use of the RAF Armoured Car Companies. Number 2 Armoured Car Company had worked with the 11th Hussars during the Palestine disturbances and was at Ramleh continuing with its routine 'peacetime' work. The 11th Hussars history continues:

> Before long the very serious shortage of armoured-car 'runners', which resulted from overstrain combined with this constant hunting by Italian aircraft, was remedied in a novel and inspired manner. The Eleventh's old friends from the RAF in Palestine came down to help them. Up to date the airmen's own Rolls-Royces had been sadly pottering up and down the Iraq pipeline and the Saudi Arabian frontier, until Air Chief Marshal Sir Arthur Longmore offered them to General Wavell for more active duties... and for many weeks afterwards the airmen and the cavalry fought side by side.[8]

On 17 September, three days after the Italians had crossed the Egyptian frontier, 'A' and 'B' Sections of No 2 Armoured Car Company were given notice that in two days' time they were to be ready to move to No 1 Sub-Depot Royal Armoured Corps at Abbassia in Cairo, prior to proceeding to the Western Desert of Egypt. 'A' Section had been at Ma'an, and drove all night to reach Ramleh after a 14-hour trip. On 20 September at 0500 hours, the two sections, consisting of five officers, 16 NCOs and 36 airmen, under the command of Flight Lieutenant Michael Casano, with ten Fordson armoured cars, four wireless tenders and six armed tenders, departed from Ramleh. A day later, after stopping for the night at Ismailia on the Suez Canal, they arrived at Abbassia. The next few weeks were spent fitting the armoured cars with Boys anti-tank rifles, wireless sets and extra armour in the rear to enlarge the armoured space, and repainting the cars in Western Desert camouflage.

The move to Egypt was some compensation for the disappointment the officers and airmen had felt at being left out of the 'real war'. For those remaining in Palestine there was some frustration. Haifa was bombed by the *Regia Aeronautica* during July and the air defences were strengthened with No 2 French Fighter Flight of the *Forces Aériennes Françaises Libre*, equipped with a few French aircraft.[9] Flying Officer Richard 'Dickie' Skellon had been serving with No 2 Company for a few months when he was ordered to proceed to Haifa to act as the British Liaison Officer to the Free French formation. He was selected for this job as he had a reasonable knowledge of French, his father having been a linguist. The French pilots expressed a certain degree of *joie de vivre*, and one of his tasks was procuring wine for breakfast in the mess. Haifa was also convenient location as the pilots spent a lot of their spare time in its local nightclubs.[10]

On 24 September, the detachment in Cairo were inspected by Air Chief Marshal Longmore, and six days later, the No 2 Company Commanding Officer, Squadron Leader John Page, and Flight Lieutenant Casano, attended an interview with General Wavell where they explained the characteristics of their armoured cars. Earlier in January 1940, with the chassis and engines of their Rolls-Royce armoured cars reaching the end of their useful lives, the decision had been taken to remove the armoured hulls and turrets, and then to fit them on the chassis of a modern Fordson truck. Though a relatively good fit, the armour was extended over the platform behind the turret and this extra space was used to house the wireless equipment. 'B' Section had been the first to receive the Fordsons and by September 1940, 20 cars had been converted at RAF Helwan and returned to the sections, along with four reserves.

On 5 October, the two sections departed from Abbassia and travelled west

The AOC-in-C Middle East, Air Chief Marshal Sir Arthur Longmore, inspects No 2 Armoured Car Company, now equipped with Fordsons, shortly before leaving for the desert to join the 11th Hussars (© IWM CM 150).

through the green of the Nile Delta and then out along the coast road into the desert; to their right, the white dunes and pink-hued salt marshes, and the occasional glimpse of the rich blue of the Mediterranean. To their left, the flat plain of the Western Desert, with its gravel and fine sand, in parts dotted with camel scrub, extending south for many hundreds of miles. Following the coast road, they reported to the 7th Armoured Division HQ at El Daba, and then travelled on to Maaten Bagush.

On 8 October, Pilot Officers Alan Douglas, Francis Richardson and Edward Spearing, with three Fordson armoured cars, reported to Advanced HQ of the 11th Hussars. Here they were assigned to work with 'B' Squadron while they settled in to their new area of operations. To be consistent with cavalry nomenclature, the No 2 Armoured Company detachment would be known as 'D' Squadron and the Sub-Sections as Troops. The task of the 11th Hussars was to maintain active touch with the enemy and to probe the Italian defences all along the line from Sidi Barrani on the coast, to Sofafi, 60 miles inland (Map 19, p. 249).

On 11 October, 'D' Squadron established an advanced patrol base at Sanyet Iznin, 20 miles east of Sidi Barrani, and 10 miles from the Italian forward positions at Maktila. The following day, Pilot Officers Douglas, Spearing and 2nd Lieutenant Dyer of the 11th Hussars with two armoured cars set off along the Matruh-Barrani road on their first operational mission, where they reported a small amount of enemy activity and came under enemy shellfire, but suffered no casualties or damage. Pilot Officer Francis Richardson, with Sergeant Hoyland of the 11th Hussars, proceeded towards Alam el Hatshi, where the 11th Hussars had established an advanced observation post. Two days later, three patrols were sent out and Pilot Officer Richardson, with his Section, observed 23 enemy transport vehicles moving from the Tummar camp out to Alam el Hatshi. A second patrol with Flight Sergeant Ault and Sergeant Hoyland, had returned to Alam el Hatshi, and were soon being shelled. However, they had the satisfaction of watching the Royal Artillery return fire, and the enemy vehicles soon retired back to the fortified camp. Not all the Fordsons were completely ready for use with the 11th Hussars; therefore, Flight Lieutenant Casano returned to Abbassia with six cars to have Army No 9 Wireless sets fitted.

For the next few weeks, the RAF armoured cars worked alongside 'B' Squadron, returning each day to the points overlooking the Italian fortified camps at Tummar and Nibeiwa. Their task was to report back on any signs of forward movement by the occupants of the camps and the size and direction of any columns that emerged from them. Intelligence reports had suggested that 14 October would be the day that the Italians would resume their advance, and the 11th Hussars and 'D' Squadron were warned to be vigilant. The veracity of this seemed reliable when a number of motorised columns were seen to be moving east, including one with a dozen vehicles that moved from Point 90 towards Sergeant Lewis' observation post at Alam el Hatshi, but then withdrew. At the same time, Pilot Officer Spearing was patrolling near Sidi Barrani, and was heavily shelled, with 14 shells falling within 150 yards of the cars. In response, the RAF then bombed one of the enemy transport concentrations and then Spearing screened an 11th Hussars detachment as they salvaged some of the abandoned Italian vehicles.

On 17 October, a column of 60 Italian vehicles was observed by Pilot Officers Douglas and Spearing operating north of the coast road. These large movements often turned out to be reconnaissances in force, not a determined advance, and after a few hours the columns usually turned about and headed back home.

'D' Squadron spent the remainder of the month on patrols to Hatshi and the

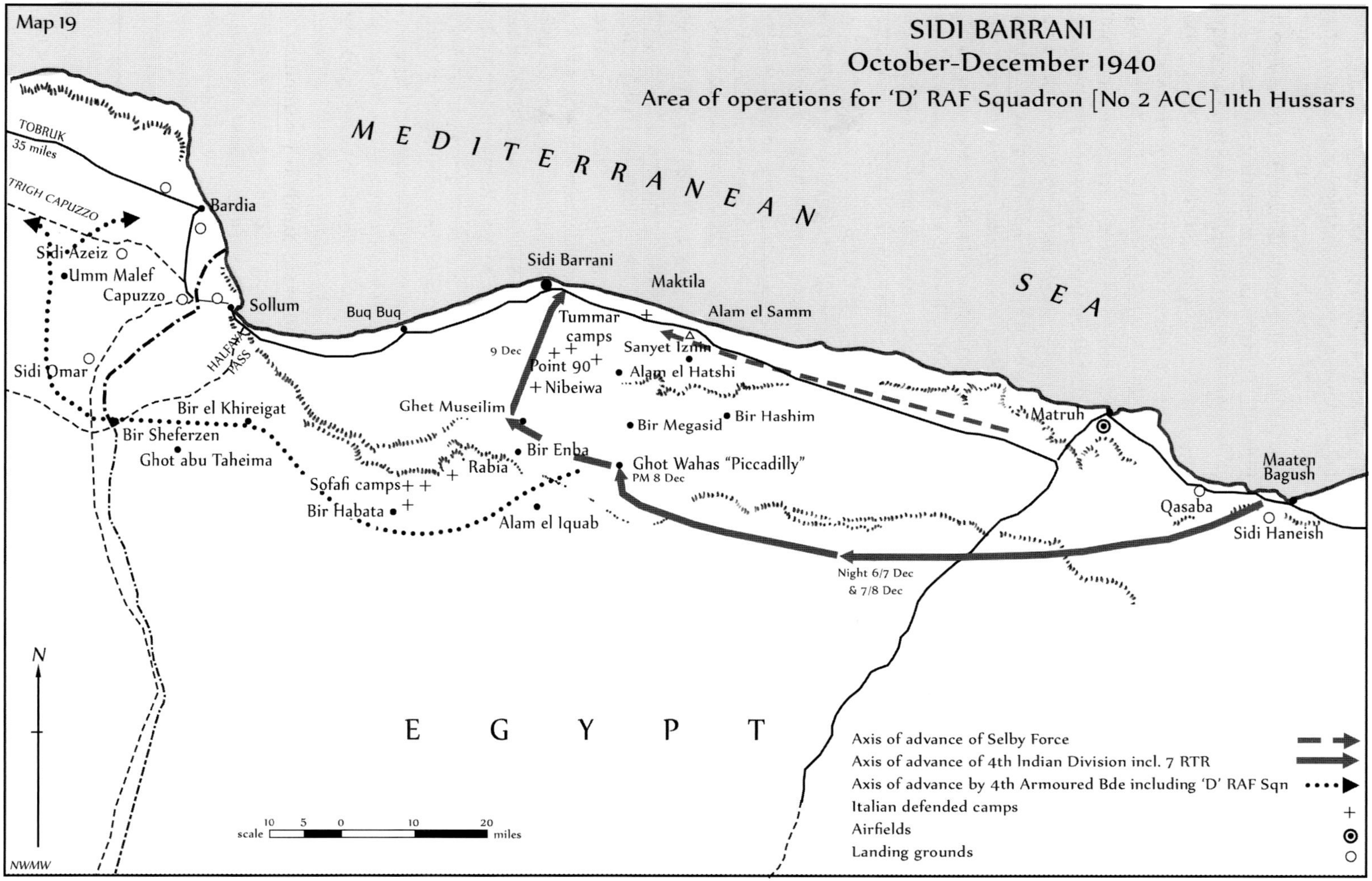
Map 19
SIDI BARRANI
October–December 1940
Area of operations for 'D' RAF Squadron [No 2 ACC] 11th Hussars
MEDITERRANEAN SEA
TOBRUK 35 miles
TRIGH CAPUZZO
Bardia
Sidi Azeiz
Umm Malef
Capuzzo
Sollum
HALFAYA PASS
Sidi Omar
Bir el Khireigat
Bir Sheferzen
Ghot abu Taheima
Buq Buq
Sidi Barrani
Maktila
Alam el Samm
Tummar camps
9 Dec
Point 90
Nibeiwa
Sanyet Izmin
Alam el Hatshi
Ghet Museilim
Bir Megasid
Bir Hashim
Bir Enba
Rabia
Ghot Wahas "Piccadilly"
PM 8 Dec
Sofafi camps
Bir Habata
Alam el Iquab
Matruh
Maaten Bagush
Qasaba
Sidi Haneish
Night 6/7 Dec & 7/8 Dec
EGYPT
N
scale 10 5 0 10 20 miles
NWMW
Axis of advance of Selby Force
Axis of advance of 4th Indian Division incl. 7 RTR
Axis of advance by 4th Armoured Bde including 'D' RAF Sqn
Italian defended camps
Airfields
Landing grounds

area around the coast road, west of the Italian forward positions at Maktila. There were further frequent small forays by the Italians but they seemed intent on staying put.

The arrival of the RAF armoured cars had been beneficial for the 11th Hussars, as they had been in continuous contact with the enemy since June. Four Troops of the Hussars were able to go into reserve and carry out much-needed maintenance, clean weapons and most importantly, allow their crews to have a good wash.[11] Squadron Leader Page, the Officer Commanding No 2 Company, came down from Ramleh, and Flight Lieutenant Casano arrived from Cairo on 3 November with the six Fordson armoured cars, now fitted with No 9 wireless sets. The following day, 'D' Squadron took over full responsibility for the northern patrols from 'B' Squadron of the 11th Hussars. The detachment was then organised into four troops each consisting of two Fordsons, with two more at Squadron HQ and two in reserve.[12]

General Wavell had planned to launch an offensive against the Italians, called Operation *Compass*, in mid-November. The diversion of troops and aircraft to Greece and Crete, and the slower than expected build-up of supplies, meant that he had to postpone the operation until the second week of December, when the moon would again favour a night attack. So the troopers and airmen, operating out between the lines, continued for another month with observation post duties, small-scale skirmishes and artillery exchanges.

On 5 November, the enemy made a determined attempt to clear the area east of Maktila. Pilot Officer Edward Spearing's' Troop was waiting in reserve when, just after dawn, an enemy aircraft passed overhead. They opened fire and the aircraft was hit and then lost height rapidly as it flew to the north-west, though no reports confirmed its demise. Nothing more occurred for two hours, until the enemy camp came to life, and two large mechanised columns were seen forming up. At 1100 hours they both began to advance; one from the west and the other from the south-west. At the same time, 18 *Regia Aeronautica* fighter aircraft flew over Pilot Officer Alan Douglas' Troop and their presence was reported back to No 202 Group. It appeared something significant was happening, so 'D' Squadron HQ and the two forward Troops withdrew back to the forward defensive positions of 7th Armoured Division. That afternoon, the westerly column was engaged by tanks of the 3rd Hussars, and the 1st Battalion, King's Royal Rifle Corps. This was clearly not to be the next big advance, as after half-an-hour, the two columns had been scattered, were in retreat, and being pursued by their assailants. By the end of the day, the area was clear and the RAF cars were able to return to their previous positions.

Active patrolling continued for the next few weeks, including a few unsuccessful attempts to draw the enemy into an ambush. Heavy artillery fire regularly fell on the forward posts and on one occasion forced the move of an observation post to a new location on the coast at Alam el Samm. As well as artillery, mines were also a problem. On 18 November, Flight Lieutenant Welham, with LAC Hoyles and Pinkham, set off down the coast road on a patrol but ran across a minefield. Four mines exploded under the car destroying the front end. Spearing, on patrol to the south, heard the explosions and picked up the crew and car and returned them to HQ, despite heavy shellfire. Fortunately there were no fatalities, with LAC Hoyles suffering only cuts and bruises, LAC Pinkham, shock, and Flight Lieutenant Welham a cut to his head, and shock.

During the first week of December, after having spent more than a month patrolling the coast road area, 'D' Squadron was ordered south into the desert, to

Alam el Iquab, to take over the watch on the camp at Rabia from another Squadron of the 11th Hussars. Here they took over the Hatshi and Bir Megasid patrols. A few days later, they moved closer to the track junction at Ghot Wahas, also known as 'Piccadilly'.

It was here that 'D' Squadron HQ was informed that the Western Desert Force was to attack the Italian camps on 9 December. Generals Wavell and O'Connor, while planning their counter-offensive, had relied heavily on the information flowing back from the reconnaissance work of the 11th Hussars and RAF armoured cars, in addition to that from the Hurricanes and Lysanders of No 208 Squadron RAF. Aerial reconnaissance had revealed that the Italian defensive positions were spread over a broad front, in fortified camps. However, they were not mutually supporting, being separated by large tracts of empty desert. Furthermore, the defence lacked depth and the main strength lay at the northern and southern ends of the line, with no second line of defence. General O'Connor had drawn up a plan which would exploit these weaknesses. The largest gap, some 20 miles wide, had been identified between Nibeiwa and the Sofafi-Rabia camps near Bir Enba.

Events outside the theatre also had a strong influence on the progress of operations. On 28 October, Mussolini had invaded Greece, and the British War Cabinet had immediately promised to provide military assistance. The British forces in Egypt would now be further stretched, and in particular the already limited air support had to be further thinned out and sent to Greece. Fortunately, Wavell was able to convince his political superiors to support his offensive. Operation *Compass* aimed to recapture those parts of Egypt held by the Italians up to the frontier. His case was so convincing that he also obtained some additional resources. Along with more aircraft, transport and extra artillery, the armour was reinforced with light, cruiser and heavy tanks from the United Kingdom, the most important being 45 of the 27-ton Matilda Infantry Mark II ('I') tanks of 7th Royal Tank Regiment. These tanks were General O'Connor's 'secret weapon' and had not been seen in North Africa before. Their thick armour made them virtually impervious to any of the Italian field or anti-tank guns.

For Operation *Compass*, there was not only 7th Armoured Division, but also the highly regarded 4th Indian Division. While one Indian brigade attacked Nibeiwa, the Support Group of 7th Armoured Division contained the camps in the south at Sofafi, whilst the remainder of the two divisions were to pass through the Enba gap. Fourth Indian Division, supported by the Matildas of 7th RTR, would fall on the camps at Tummar from the rear, and 7th Armoured Division would move north and cut the road between Sidi Barrani and Buq Buq. This would separate the Italians from their reserves at Sollum. The attackers would have to pass across 70 miles of open desert to reach the camps. As a consequence, dumps of water, petrol and ammunition were concealed in the forward areas beforehand. These had been built up throughout November under the close watch of the armoured car patrols, and had gone unnoticed by the Italians, to the great credit of the 11th Hussars and 'D' Squadron. The cars had ensured that the Enba gap remained open and reported any attempts by the Italians to establish intermediate defence posts.

Surprise was essential for the success of the offensive. Because of the distances involved, the attacking force took two days to reach their appointed positions, laying up for one day under camouflage nets. To keep the *Regia Aeronautica* away, the RAF flew patrols overhead and bombed the Italian forward airfields. The RAF had received reinforcements including new Hurricanes, and now had six fighter squadrons operating with No 202 Group, two army co-operation squadrons under Army control, and four bomber squadrons under RAF Middle East.[13] The offensive was timed to start at dawn. Late in the afternoon of the previous day, 'D' Squadron was placed under the command of 4th Armoured Brigade. Pilot Officer Spearing, in Fordson A105, with his driver, LAC Coupethite, and gunner, LAC Baillie, were however, given a specific task that was vital for the success of Operation *Compass*. They were to guide in the Matilda 'I' tanks, and lead them to a position from which they could launch the first attack on Nibeiwa the following morning (Map 19, p. 249).[14]

General O'Connor said of the role of 7th RTR: 'The whole plan depended on their success.'[15] They had only been in Egypt since September and very few officers and men had been in the desert before. Spearing and the crew of Fordson A105 rendezvoused with the tanks at their leaguer in the Enba gap, 12 miles from Nibeiwa, where they had lain up after the two-day approach march from Matruh. The noise of roaring engines and squeaking tracks was masked by RAF aircraft flying over the camps. On a moonlit, bitterly cold night, the crew of Fordson A105 completed the task without incident. The 'I' tanks were in position at Ghet Museilim, south-west of Nibeiwa by midnight and A105 was back at 'D' Squadron HQ by 0330 hours. At 0735 hours, following a short artillery barrage, the Matildas rolled into the Nibeiwa camp, just ahead of the 11th Indian Infantry Brigade and within an hour the camp had fallen, with 4000 Italian prisoners taken.

While the Support Group bottled up the forces at Sofafi, the Royal Navy bombarded Sidi Barrani and Maktila, and the RAF intensified the attacks on enemy airfields and supply lines from Malta and Egypt. Fourth Armoured Brigade dashed through the Enba gap and was heading northwards for the coast. By 11 December, all the camps had fallen or had been evacuated, and troops now had to deal with prisoners of war numbering in their thousands. So many, that they could be more easily estimated in acres, than in numbers. Some 38,300 Italian and Libyan prisoners were taken along with 237 guns and 73 tanks

Given the success of the three-day Battle of Sidi Barrani, General O'Connor now decided to pursue the enemy vigorously with the 7th Armoured Division and cut off their line of retreat. The aim was not only to drive the Italians out of Egypt, but also to move on to take Bardia and Tobruk, and capture the forward airfields of the *Regia Aeronautica*. Once these airfields had been captured, the *Regia Aeronautica* could take little part in the campaign. However, to add to General O'Connor's problems he was told that 4th Indian Division was being withdrawn immediately for an offensive in Italian East Africa, and so the pursuit for the time being would be made by the 7th Armoured Division alone, albeit the 6th Australian Division had nearly completed its preparations and would join Western Desert Force in late December. In contrast to the intricate planning and the carefully crafted troop and supply movements of the last few weeks, the advance into Libya would face an acute supply problem. Twenty-times the expected number of prisoners had been captured and they all had to be fed and watered and transported back to prisoner of war camps. General O'Connor had, therefore, to divert half his scarce transport to this task.

The rapid successes of what had been planned as a 'five day raid' had exceeded expectations. Seventh Armoured Brigade was ordered to move along the coast road to take Sollum, while to the south, 4th Armoured Brigade was sent off along the escarpment with orders to probe the frontier posts, attack any of the enemy caught in the open, and then strike north and east and cut the Bardia-Tobruk road.

OPERATION COMPASS
October 1940–February 1941

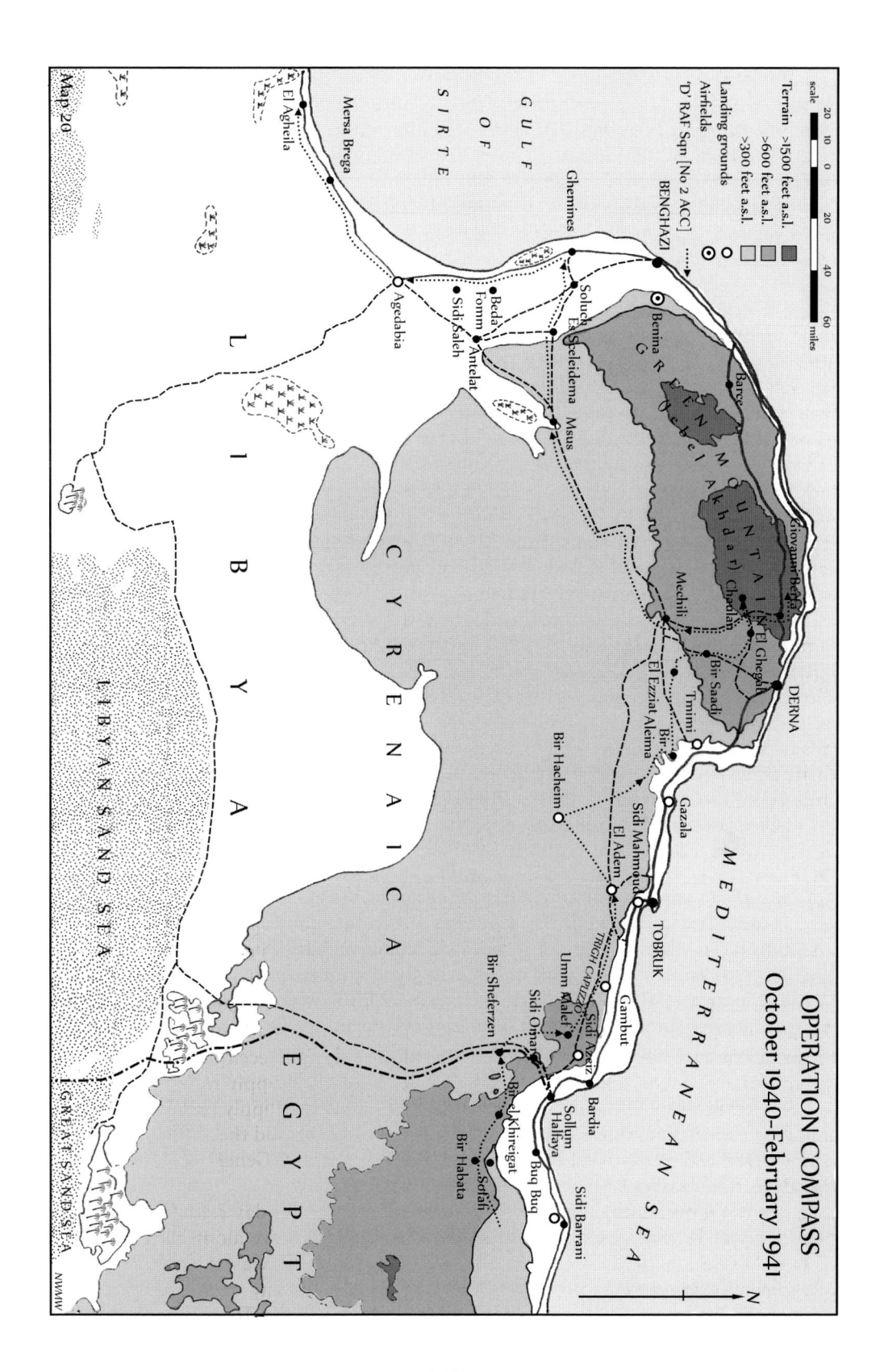

Map 20

'D' Squadron, as part of 4th Armoured Brigade, travelled up onto the escarpment and reached Bir Habata at 0400 hours on 10 December without meeting any opposition. Pilot Officers Richardson and Spearing patrolled forward and found the area east of the frontier free of the enemy, while 4th Armoured Brigade concentrated on the plateau at Bir el Khireigat, 15 miles from the frontier. The Brigade was formed up as two columns; 'Birksforce' consisted of 'A' Squadron, 11th Hussars, and 'D' RAF Squadron and 'Combeforce' with 11th Hussars (less two squadrons), the 2nd RTR and two batteries of 4th Royal Horse Artillery.[16] The task was to cut the enemy lines of supply and the path of their retreat. This was however, a light force for such a bold move (Map 20, p. 253).

A sandstorm had blown for the morning of 12 December, which despite its ferocity and discomfort, at least kept the *Regia Aeronautica* away. The next day was spent searching the area north to Halfaya for the enemy. While most of 'D' Squadron leaguered at Khireigat, Flight Lieutenant Welham and Pilot Officer Spearing went off on a night patrol to report on an enemy camp near Bir Sheferzen, which proved to be unoccupied. Eight miles away they spotted a number of vehicles, guns and a wooden observation tower. They were in turn seen by the enemy and the cars were heavily shelled. LAC Hoyles had been blown up on a mine less than a month ago, and was in the armoured car that was hit, but it managed to push on until out of the shellfire and temporary repairs could be made.

By the end of the day, it was clear that the Italian forces had departed from Egypt. Sidi Omar, on the frontier, was found to be held in strength, but the order was given to bypass the post and move with all speed into Cyrenaica. The advance was delayed for a few hours due to the late arrival of supplies for the tanks, and after three days of constant action, the troops could barely stay awake. Nevertheless, just after midnight on 14 December, with wireless silence enforced, the two columns set off for the frontier. The 11th Hussars 'A' Squadron took the advanced and right flank guard, while 'D' RAF Squadron moved on the left flank of the flying column. Once they had crossed the frontier, they made a wide sweep to approach Bardia from the west.

By dawn they were well inside Libya, but they were soon spotted by an enemy reconnaissance plane. The *Regia Aeronautica* reacted strongly to this swift and bold advance of 7th Armoured Division, and the enemy fighters and bombers arrived soon after. For the rest of the day, the RAF and 11th Hussars armoured cars came under a succession of violent air attacks. 'D' Squadron was bombed ceaselessly and at one time no fewer than 50 bombers and fighters were over them. A number of the RAF armoured cars were hit by shrapnel, but miraculously no-one was hurt. The force had no anti-aircraft guns, nor was the ground easy enough to dig slit trenches, and to quote Brigadier Caunter of 4th Armoured Brigade, "the situation of 'Birksforce' was somewhat exciting, to say the least."[17] 'Combeforce' was sent off ahead, crossed the Trigh Capuzzo, and moved down the escarpment to the Bardia-Tobruk road which, despite air attacks, it had cut by mid-morning. The flow of traffic on the road was stopped, but surprisingly the Italian ground forces made no attempt to clear the road block.

'D' Squadron arrived at Umm Malef, 20 miles west of Bardia by mid-afternoon and took over from 'B' Squadron, 11th Hussars. Pilot Officer Francis Richardson then took a patrol out to the airfield at Sidi Azeiz, with orders to watch to the south and west. At the same time, 'A' Squadron of 11th Hussars watched the Trigh Capuzzo for any attempt by Graziani to relieve Bardia or send reinforcements. 'Birksforce' and 'Combeforce' would have been hard-pressed to repel any determined effort by an Italian force to reach Bardia as their weaponry was extremely light. The air raids recommenced and a large number of bombs were dropped, while the cars were subjected to strafing attacks by the enemy fighters and were hit repeatedly. Again there were no casualties. The armoured crews had replied with their Lewis guns and had scored many hits but none were brought down. The 11th Hussars had not been as lucky and on the same day lost six vehicles, a Squadron Sergeant-Major killed, and six wounded. It was a hard day, and it was only when night fell that the air attacks ceased.

The following day, 'D' Squadron HQ moved about five miles south to get out of the bombing area, although Corporal Dunn and LAC Lloyd were attacked whilst proceeding to collect petrol. They took cover and escaped without injury, although their tender was hit in a large number of places by shrapnel. The RAF fighter squadrons had been absent for the last few days over the British ground forces, as the advance had outstripped their capacity to move forward, but on this day a Savoia SM79, a three-engine bomber, was shot down by a Hurricane. The pilot, the only survivor, was picked up by an RAF armoured car, brought back to 'D' Squadron HQ and given medical attention and a hot meal, before being sent back to base.

On 16 December, Flight Lieutenant Wilfred Stevenson arrived to take command of 'D' RAF Squadron, and despite moving Squadron Headquarters, the Italian bombing recommenced, with some dropping within 30 yards of the cars. This time, however, an enemy aircraft was hit by return fire. Meanwhile, patrols under Pilot Officer Richardson acted as guide and protector to Army units rounding up damaged transport and tanks. General O'Connor had a severe shortage of transport vehicles so any enemy 'runners' that were found were immediately put to use.

By the end of the day 'D' Squadron had been told that they would be relieved. Their armoured car patrols were recalled that evening and by midnight they had arrived at the frontier, and the detachment moved back into Egypt to join 11th Hussars HQ at Ghot Abu Taheima. After a couple of days' rest and recovery, 'D' Squadron went back into Cyrenaica in heavy rain and sticky 'going', and patrolled along the Trigh Capuzzo at night, and to Gambut airfield during daylight. On one occasion they reclaimed the staff car belonging to Group Captain Leslie Brown, the Senior Air Staff Officer with No 202 Group, which had been abandoned during a strafing attack by Italian fighters two days earlier.

On 22 December, No 2 Armoured Car Company suffered its first casualty in action against the Axis forces. Fordson A128 had developed mechanical troubles while on patrol, and was attacked by two fighters while returning to HQ. A bullet pierced the armour plate of the turret, missing all but LAC Baillie, who was badly wounded in the arm and back.

The last two weeks of 1940 had seen a pause in the campaign. The Italians had departed from Egypt or had surrendered. Western Desert Force was renamed XIII Corps and Bardia was invested by 7th Armoured Division. Sixth Australian Division had begun concentrating opposite Bardia by late December, and this was completed on New Year's Day 1941. They then readied themselves for their first engagement of the war.

The 11th Hussars, with 'D' Squadron, were sent out to the north and west, watching out for any attempt by Marshal Graziani to relieve Bardia from Tobruk or further west. Number 202 Group established its headquarters at Sollum and the bombers and fighters moved to airfields in the surrounding area, with No 208

Squadron RAF and No 3 Squadron RAAF further forward at Gambut. The small port at Sollum was reopened and the Royal Navy began moving supplies up by sea. Number 202 Group however, was still reliant on movement of aviation fuel and bombs from Mersa Matruh, and at times this limited the scope of operations.

On the last day of 1940, a Caproni 310 twin-engine reconnaissance aircraft was shot down over a patrol of 'D' Squadron by a nearby anti-aircraft post. The Italian aircrew, some of whom were badly injured, were picked up by the RAF armoured cars and medical assistance was sent from the headquarters of 11th Hussars.

At dawn on 3 January, the attack was launched on Bardia, and by dusk the town had been captured. The following day, the Italian garrison had surrendered, yielding another 45,000 prisoners, 462 guns and 129 tanks. Seventh Armoured Division had been responsible for fixing the Italian positions on the northern perimeter by launching a feint attack, but as soon as the defences were breached, General O'Connor launched his armour in a westward dash to isolate the next fortress, Tobruk. The tanks and armoured cars by-passed Tobruk with little hindrance and blocked the Derna road. A few days after its victory at Bardia, 6th Australian Division followed and invested Tobruk. It would, however, require two weeks to build up supplies for both the Army and RAF, before the next attack could be launched.

The threat from the patrols of 11th Hussars had driven the *Regia Aeronautica* to abandon the forward airfields at Gambut and El Adem. Evidence of the effectiveness of the raids by No 202 Group on enemy airfields soon became apparent. At El Adem, the occupiers discovered 87 damaged enemy aircraft, many having been shot up or bombed by the RAF, which the Italians had been unable to repair. This was to be a scene repeated on every captured airfield. By the end of the first week of January, the Italians had been forced to give up the airfields between Derna and Tmimi, and were now located well back at Benina near Benghazi, putting the *Regia Aeronautica* at great disadvantage.

Enemy air activity was fortunately sporadic, as many of the RAF squadrons were still some 150 miles behind the army. The RAF was operating where and when it could, and yet still managed a higher operational tempo than the *Regia Aeronautica*, which had now been reduced to 119 aircraft. On 11 January, the airmen of No 2 Company were cheered when a Hurricane flew over 'D' Squadron HQ, though this was followed on successive days by enemy reconnaissance aircraft. The armoured cars of 11th Hussars and 'D' Squadron were sent deep into the desert below Tobruk. The latter to investigate the landing ground at Bir Hacheim.

Flight Sergeant Lewis and his 'D' Squadron patrol were assigned to protect a landing ground party and a flight of Gladiators of No 3 Squadron RAAF, who were carrying out offensive patrols. The landing ground had been sown with hundreds of thermos bombs.[18] John Jackson, a pilot with No 3 Squadron RAAF wrote in his diary:

> Some of the RAF armoured cars were there and had some old Rolls Royce chassis now with Ford V8 engines, very solid looking jobs. The RAF armoured car chaps are all general duties, and they had all done flying courses [presumably the officers]. They are attached to the 11th Hussars who are always right out in front of all our other ground forces, and are continually carrying out tactical reconnaissance and lightning raids on the enemy and harassing their supply columns - they do a grand job. They live mighty hard and rough, and are dammed near as tough and waterless as

camels. One of the RAF blokes traded some tea (about a pound) for a lamb [with some bedouin]... We had the lamb in the form of half soup and half stew and it was good.[19]

Two days later, Lewis returned to escort No 3 Squadron and an anti-aircraft detachment further west to Bir Aleima.[20]

Tobruk held the first major port on the Mediterranean coast west of Alexandria and capture of this town would make it possible for General O'Connor, with help from the Royal Navy, to speed up the advance. By the time of the attack on Tobruk by 6th Australian Division, 'D' Squadron was 70 miles to the west at Bir Saadi, south of Derna, having travelled through El Ezziat.

There were two possible routes to Benghazi, the next objective after Tobruk. The northern route lay along the coast road from Tmimi to Derna, through Giovanni Berta and Barce, while the southern route lay across the desert to the south of the Jebel Akhdar (or Green Mountain), through Mechili and across the desert to Msus. The 11th Hussars and 'D' Squadron were moving along the tracks south of the Jebel Akhdar, with the aim not only to watch the left flank of XIII Corps, but also because Wavell wanted know if it was possible for a motorised column to travel the desert route across the 'bulge'. In one bold stroke, the aim was to trap those Italian troops left in Cyrenaica. A thrust by this route would quickly open the way to Benghazi, reach the shores of the Gulf of Sirte, and block the coast road. The track was however, some 200 miles long and there were no watering points for the entire length.

The fighter and bomber squadrons of No 202 Group moved forward to Sidi Mahmoud and Gazala, which had fallen on 14 January, and the army cooperation squadrons to Tmimi. The jumping off point for the dash across the 'bulge' was the small fort of Mechili, the meeting point of a number of camel tracks. To support this move, Flying Officers Douglas and Richardson and Flight Sergeant Lewis were constantly out on patrol around the area south of Derna reporting on the nature of the ground, and watching for enemy traffic on the Tobruk-Derna road. A series of long reconnaissances were carried out, but the strain of the stretched supply lines was becoming apparent, and the armoured car crews were now living an almost hand-to-mouth existence, as recounted by one airman:

> Food was brought to us by supply tenders. Sometimes it did not arrive. Then there was nothing to do but tighten-up our belts. In the big operation around Derna we had no rations for five days. We carried emergency rations for two days and we stretched them out for three-and-a-half days. Then we just waited. We rationed out half a gallon of water per day. We always thought that food was on its way, as we were in constant touch by wireless. I would have eaten anything. In the end it came - bully-beef and biscuits.
>
> For a full six weeks we were constantly on the go, hardly ever meeting or speaking to anyone except our companions in the car. You can imagine how the four of us got to know each other's family histories. At night we slept on the ground behind the car, each one taking a turn at guard duty.[21]

Marshal Graziani now had only one division and an armoured group of 160 tanks remaining of his once great *Tenth Army*, but this force occupied a strong position astride the coast road in front of the town of Derna. The desert route south of Derna had been wide open but Graziani had despatched an armoured group to hold the

Mechili Pass. Seventh Armoured Division only had a few tanks left but was asked to hold a position around Mechili and engage and hold the Italian armoured force, while the Australians advanced up the coast road to Derna. To General O'Connor's disappointment, the Italian force at Mechili was successfully withdrawn on 26 January, and despite harassment by the RAF in the narrow mountain passes and pursuit by 4th Armoured Brigade, lack of petrol, food and ammunition, breakdowns of tanks needing major overhaul, and inclement weather, meant that the Italians escaped north through the hills to the coast road. This did however, expose the flank of the Derna position, and opened the direct route across the 'bulge'. Graziani decided to abandon Cyrenaica and, as a consequence, withdrew his armour in the Jebel to the main Derna to Benghazi road.

On 26 January, Squadron Leader Casano, who had been leading 'D' RAF Squadron, was appointed as Officer Commanding No 2 Armoured Car Company, while his predecessor, Squadron Leader John Page, went off to RAF Habbaniya to become second-in-command and later Officer Commanding No 1 Armoured Car Company. Michael Casano, known affectionately by his fellow officers and men as 'Cass', was a colourful and dashing figure.[22] He was born on 7 June 1913 at Folkestone and was educated at Dover College. He had always wanted to join the RAF, but in his own words 'was a lazy bugger and failed the entrance examination for Cranwell.' An old friend convinced him to join The East Kent Regiment 'The Buffs' as a private soldier. However, he still yearned to join the RAF, and after three years he purchased his discharge from the Army and was given a short-service RAF commission as an acting Pilot Officer. In June 1935, he was posted to Egypt to be trained as a pilot, but crashed his Hawker Fury trainer, suffering concussion and a fractured skull. Assessed subsequently as 'unlikely to become an effective service pilot,' his flying career was over and he was posted to No 2 Armoured Car Company in April 1936. Squadron Leader 'Cass' Casano was to lead the Company with great élan through most of the next two years of the North African campaign.[23]

'D' Squadron maintained patrols on the Mechili to Derna road, and on one occasion drove off two Fiat CR 42 fighters that attacked the cars with anti-aircraft fire. On 29 January Flight Sergeant Lewis went to relieve 'C' Squadron, 11th Hussars, and while doing so A111 entered a minefield and was badly damaged. The driver, LAC Stewart, was slightly injured but the rest of the crew had only minor cuts and bruises. While Alan Douglas went to recover the car, the rest of 'D' Squadron moved on to Mechili to link up with 11th Hussars HQ.

Derna fell to the Australians on 30 January and the RAF and the armoured cars soon reported seeing large enemy columns moving west from Giovanni Berta. As the Australians advanced down the coast road, the RAF armoured cars made contact with their left flank. For the next three days, Flying Officer Richardson, an Australian, patrolled up into the foothills of the Jebel Akhdar to Chaulan and El Ghegab and reported the area clear of the enemy.

On the morning of 4 February, with the 11th Hussars as vanguard, the 7th Armoured Division, with 40 cruiser and 80 light tanks and only two days' rations, set off from Mechili, and headed south-west across the southern side of the stony foothills of the Jebel Akhdar. The first 50 miles of the track was strewn with slabs of rock and boulders, the occasional patch of soft sand, and steep wadis, which all combined to take a toll on the column's vehicles and thereby delay the advance. The Italians had also sown thermos bombs on the track and these also had to be avoided. It was no wonder therefore, that the wear and tear on the RAF Fordson armoured cars, after an unrelenting four month period of activity, began to be felt. A few days earlier, A108 had broken both front springs, A100 was unavailable after having been driven into a tank trap on returning from the LAD, and A105 burst a petrol tank. As the Squadron moved along the difficult track, A105 then broke both front springs, and A119, a steering arm. Then, a few days later, A116 broke a rear spring and had to be evacuated to the rear. Despite the difficult track conditions, 'D' Squadron reached the small fort of Msus after a journey of just under 12 hours.

As 7th Armoured Division replenished supplies and concentrated its armour around Msus that evening, reconnaissance reports from No 208 Squadron RAF revealed that large columns of the enemy were leaving Benghazi for the south, in full retreat. Although short of ammunition, petrol and food, the Division ordered the despatch of a flying column of armoured cars, infantry and artillery, again known as 'Combeforce' to move to Antelat and then to cut the Benghazi to Agedabia road in the region of Sidi Saleh.

'D' Squadron and 'A' Squadron 11th Hussars, were placed under the command of the Support Group and 4th Armoured Brigade. The Squadron had just been joined by Flying Officer 'Dickie' Skellon. He had discharged his duties as Liaison Officer to No 2 French Fighter Flight at Haifa as they had been sent to Cairo to train on Hurricanes. Skellon and Richardson were sent directly west to the Italian outpost, Es Sceleidima, which they found to be occupied. The RAF armoured cars were ordered to press on and cut the coast road at Ghemines. Es Sceleidima was found to have been evacuated that morning following a probing attack by the 1st King's Royal Rifle Corps. The King's Royal Rifle Corps, two batteries of artillery and Flying Officers Spearing and Skellon's sections proceeded to Ghemines and not only found it occupied, but also took the surrender of the town, along with 500 prisoners. With only a troop of two Fordson armoured cars to guard this host, the carrier platoon of the Rifle Brigade was quickly despatched to assist with their disposal. Skellon recalls the indignation of the Italian commanding officer of his newly-acquired battalion of prisoners:

> They were all wandering around lost... The Italians, when they left Benghazi, took everything out they possibly could; even their 'dancing girls', as we called them. General O'Connor issued an order that anyone caught taking anything from the Italians would be immediately arrested and court-martialled.
>
> We'd been out for nearly two days without any sleep, doing the job. The Italian Colonel came up to me and said I was a disgusting looking officer and that he wanted a better looking, and more senior one, to give himself up to. I said 'I'm afraid you're wrong there.' He was wounded in his bottom, and so I made him sit on the back of the armoured car while they took him back to the Regimental Aid Post, where he was looked over.
>
> The battalion was then taken over by an Italian Captain who was very good. The funny thing about him was that he came up to me and he said 'I've got a small dog here, and we can't keep it,' and so I said 'I'll ask somebody here if they want to take it over,' and one of our chaps looked after it. It stayed with us for a very long time doing patrols etc.[24]

Further spoils of war were found by Pilot Officer John Secter:

> The three Italian fencing swords - a foil, a sabre and an epée... may have

been liberated from an Italian officer during this episode... I do remember at one point writing my wife a letter on the stationery of the Mayor of Benghazi while seated at the desk in his office in the Town Hall. I had been searching the building. It was empty and everything was neatly in place. I opened the drawer and there was his stationery ready for use.[25]

Meanwhile, to the south, 'Combeforce' had reached Sidi Saleh at midday on 5 February, and was astride the Benghazi to Agedabia coast road; 4th Armoured Brigade was in the area of Beda Fomm, a few miles to the north and moving rapidly to attack the eastern flank of the Italians, 7th Armoured Brigade was on its way down to Antelat to the north-east and 7th Armoured Division Support Group with 'D' Squadron was closing in from the north from Ghemines and Soluch. In between these columns and the sea, was a pocket about 40 miles deep, and at the bottom about five miles wide. Contained in this pocket was all that remained of the *Italian Tenth Army* and with them a large portion of the Italian population of Benghazi.

'Combeforce' had reached the road just one-and-a-half hours before the first vehicles of the Italian column arrived from the north. The road had been sown quickly with mines, and the leading Italian vehicles were stopped in their tracks as the mines took their toll. The machine-guns of the 11th Hussars and King's Dragoon Guards, and the 25-pdrs of the Royal Horse Artillery joined in, and in a short time, many enemy vehicles were ablaze. The Italian infantry threw themselves a number of times at the Rifle Brigade and 11th Hussars positions, but were beaten back. Combe realised that these were only the lead elements and the bulk of the column had yet to arrive.

The battle continued the following day, with 4th Armoured Brigade arriving on the Italian flank just before dawn. The British tanks fired on the column from a series of ridges to the east of the road. An Italian armoured group arrived and threw themselves into a series of attacks and 4th Armoured Brigade was fought almost to standstill, but the bulk of the column was contained. Hemmed in from the flank and

Pilot Officer John Secter (Secter).

with Combe's force in the south, and the advance of the northern detachment of the Support Group, including the RAF armoured cars, the enemy's plight was desperate. The following morning, a final determined effort was made to break through the southern cordon, but after a short but intense struggle, it was clear the attack had failed. White flags appeared amongst the jumbled mass of tanks, guns and lorries, and the entire column surrendered. Some 25,000 prisoners were taken, leaving 112 tanks, innumerable light tanks, 216 guns and 1500 wheeled vehicles on the battlefield.

Benghazi fell to the Australians on 6 February. 'D' Squadron had reached Ghemines the same day. They reconnoitred south along the coastal track, while 'A' Squadron, 11th Hussars and the Support Group took the main road towards the battlefield of Beda Fomm. Ahead of them stretched 20 miles of the confused mass of the enemy column, many waving white flags.

The victory was almost complete, and the 11th Hussars and 'D' Squadron proceeded south to the air landing ground at Agedabia, and the following morning moved to El Agheila, which marked the boundary with the western Libyan province of Tripolitania. Egypt and Cyrenaica had been cleared of the enemy. The Italian forward outposts were located just east of Sirte, 120 miles up the coast road, while the remainder of the Italian Army was 300 miles away near Tripoli. Despite the heavy rain, the Hussars' and airmen's spirits were high as they had just taken part in the rout of an entire army.

In just two months, the Army of the Nile, with a force that never exceeded two divisions, had advanced over 500 miles. The Italian Army of four Corps, with nearly ten divisions had been destroyed. The tally in prisoners reached 130,000, while 400 tanks and 1290 guns along with the ephemera of battle had been captured. The British, Indian and Australian casualties were extremely light. Five-hundred had been killed, 1373 wounded and 55 were missing. Despite inferior numbers, the RAF had achieved complete air superiority and had enabled the free movement of the ground forces, which had suffered little interference or loss from the *Regia Aeronautica*. Air Chief Marshal Sir Arthur Longmore and Air Commodore Raymond Collishaw had provided the closest cooperation with the Army with 'energy and optimism'.[26]

Seventh Armoured Division, General O'Connor's spearhead, had endured a three month campaign and had shown great tactical effectiveness and powers of endurance. Despite the technical efforts of the mechanical and ordnance personnel it was now a skeleton force. The Division had been in the vanguard of the advance, and the lead element had always been the armoured cars of the 11th Hussars, ably assisted by their friends of 'D' Squadron from No 2 Armoured Car Company RAF. When General Wavell wrote his despatch on the campaign, note was made of their contribution:

> Special mention must be made of one unit, the 11th Hussars. As the only armoured car regiment in the force it was continually in the Western Desert for a period of about nine months, from the entry of Italy into the war till the fall of Benghazi. During this period it always supplied the most advanced elements in close contact with the enemy. Seldom can a unit have had a more prolonged spell of work in the front line or performed it with greater skill and boldness.[27]

First warning of the arrival of the German *Luftwaffe* had been given to the airmen of No 2 Company, just east of Mechili, when at mid-morning on 21 January,

The crew of A115 after many weeks of operations in the Western Desert (© Crown copyright. RAF Regiment Museum).

12 Junkers Ju 88s had flown low over the 'D' Squadron HQ. The officers and airmen of No 2 Company were visited by General Richard O'Connor on 11 February, and congratulated them on their work. Patrols were suspended for one day and the enemy air force seemed to have gone completely. 'Dickie' Skellon recalls O'Connor's visit:

> ... they sent us out to this place called El Agheila. We were put up there and told to stop and have a rest. This was an Italian airfield, with a road at the centre and a fort over the road with an Italian munitions dump. General O'Connor came to see the 11th Hussars and thanked us all for what we had done for his, then famous, victory. He said we could arrange a football match on the airfield. We had a church service, and just after that we were getting ready for the football match, when somebody looked up in response to a buzzing noise and said 'Look, there are aircraft'. And right over the top of us, to our horror were Stukas. They dived in and started to bomb. They dived on this fort and on us... and they screamed down and hit the Italian ammunition dump and blew the thing to smithereens.
>
> The order came to disperse. Normally, when we stopped anywhere we dug a slit trench, but we hadn't dug any as we were all quite happy, and the main thing had been to organise the football. When the Stukas came, we had nowhere to go, and so of course, after that we all started digging like hell.

The next few days were spent resting and recovering from the pursuit. A dawn reconnaissance led by Flying Officer Spearing, reconnoitred down the road towards Tripoli, to look for the enemy, and report on the suitability for tank movement, but it came back after a few hours having seen nothing. Flying Officer Skellon recalls another such reconnaissance:

> I carried out an extended reconnaissance beyond Agedabia and on the route the Germans were supposed to take if they were coming. If they were coming, my job was to clear out quickly and inform on what was happening. Nothing did happen though on that trip. [28]

The relationship of No 2 Company with the 11th Hussars had always been good, but there were the odd tensions at times. Skellon continues:

> Myself, Alan Douglas, and another chap were sent out on a long range reconnaissance by the CO of 11th Hussars. We must have been out for about a week, and when we came back we'd all grown beards. When we got back, there was a message from the Adjutant of the 11th Hussars saying that their CO wanted to see us. We were expecting a pat on the back. When we got there he said that his people shaved in the morning and we had to go away and shave now! We couldn't find any water, we only had a puddle in the middle of the road that used to run right through the area, and so we used that as a shaving bowl.[29]

The *Regia Aeronautica* had withdrawn to airfields in Tripolitania, and it seemed that an advance on Tripoli could not fail to succeed. However, the lack of success by the Italians in Egypt had become a matter of serious concern for the German High Command. They had been determined that they would not get entangled in an African venture, and had received assurances from Mussolini that the Italian Army would fight for every square foot of Libyan soil. To indicate his determination, Mussolini despatched two of his best divisions, the *132nd (Ariete) Armoured* and *102nd (Trento) Motorised Divisions* to Libya. Hitler directed that *Fliegerkorps X*, which had been operating from Sicily against British shipping, should be sent to Africa to help the Italians check the British armoured force and they were deployed to Libya in mid-January.[30] Hitler also ordered that an armoured force also be sent as reinforcement.

The airfield hangars, *Carabinieri* barracks, fort and other dwellings, which had provided such a comfortable residence after months living on the desert floor, were too obvious a target and the RAF armoured cars moved three miles to the south. Three days later, 16 Messerschmitt Bf 110s, with their engines switched off for a silent approach, swept in at 50 feet, without warning, and machine-gunned the fort and hangar at El Agheila. The armoured cars had never before experienced such a determined and ferocious attack. Retaliation was difficult as there was also a dust storm blowing at the time.

Flying Officer Spearing was patrolling between El Agheila and the border with his two Fordsons, and was strafed by the same aircraft. Spearing's driver, LAC Campbell, was wounded in the foot and the car was badly damaged. Flight Sergeant Lewis, in the second car, showed great presence of mind and opened fire as they attacked and brought down one of the Bf 110s. A captured German pilot, whose Bf 110 had been shot down by the 11th Hussars, inadvertently gave away the *Luftwaffe's* plan for another raid by his agitation when told he was to be held in the fort for 'about a week'. Twenty Stukas arrived in the late afternoon and spent the next 15 minutes attacking the fort, while the 11th Hussars suffered, there was no damage recorded for the RAF armoured cars.

The intense air attacks caused the RAF armoured cars, along with 11th Hussars, to move even further back to Mersa Brega, 25 miles to the east for the night, as the position was clearly too exposed. On the return journey to El Agheila the following morning, A103 overturned and Flying Officer Francis Richardson sustained a compound fracture to his right leg. The run of misfortune continued when two days later, Flight Lieutenant Welham and Flying Officer Edward Spearing were returning to Cairo with A119 and a Fordson tender. Only a few miles into the journey an Army lorry clipped the vehicle driven by Flying Officer Spearing. Unfortunately, he had his elbow outside the vehicle and suffered a severe arm injury which necessitated his admission to Derna hospital. The situation with regard to the Fordson armoured cars was now becoming dire. Many had been returned to Cairo for repairs. Of the 12 that had originally driven from Cairo in October only four now remained operational.

On 16 February, the 11th Hussars received their orders to return to Cairo. They had been on active operations since the outbreak of hostilities with Italy. The long period of cooperation with the RAF armoured cars did not go unmentioned in their regimental history:

> Very soon afterwards the Regiment paraded for the start of its thousand-mile drive to Egypt, and the time had come to part company with the old friends of the RAF Armoured Car Company ('D' Squadron) who were returning by a different route. The two had fought together for the past four months, all the way from Sidi Barrani to Tripolitania, and the parting left behind it many a memory of the thrilling days in the conquest of Cyrenaica.[31]

As the 11th Hussars departed, they were greeted by cheers from a column of the armoured cars of the 1st King's Dragoon Guards (KDGs) going in the opposite direction. Number 2 Armoured Car Company detachment now had a new responsibility. They were to handover to the KDGs, but first they needed an introduction to the desert and the RAF was given the job. The KDGs were the armoured car regiment for the untried and inexperienced 2nd Armoured Division which had arrived in a convoy from the United Kingdom in late December. Their regimental history describes the new arrangement:

> An armoured car squadron [sic] composed of RAF personnel (this was before the days of the RAF Regiment) had been operating under command of 11th Hussars, and this was now passed under command of the Regiment; it was a cheerful and efficient body of men, but as they had been in the desert a long time, and their few remaining armoured cars were overdue for refit, they shortly followed 11th Hussars back to the Delta. However, they were of great assistance for the first few days while the Regiment was finding its feet...[32]

In mid-February, Marshal Graziani, despondent from his crushing defeat, was replaced by General Gariboldi. There were four Italian divisions concentrated near Tripoli, and the German *5th Light Division* sailed from Italy. More importantly, the German unit was reinforced with a full armoured division. This strong armoured formation, to be known as the *Deutsches Afrika Korps*, was led by Generalleutnant Erwin Rommel, who had distinguished himself in command of the German *7th Panzer Division* in France in 1940. On his arrival in Tripoli he set about preparing a counter-offensive.

Unfortunately, higher level strategy dictated that the advance of XIII Corps could go no further. General O'Connor had been gathering his forces, and had been awaiting the order for a further advance. General Wavell, on the other hand, continued to juggle his resources to meet competing demands in Greece, Italian East Africa and Libya. His primary focus had shifted to Greece, and air and ground reinforcements that were arriving from the United Kingdom, Australia and New Zealand were directed to that theatre. Libya was stripped of the experienced formations that had routed the *Italian Tenth Army*, and these were returned to Cairo to rest and refit, or sent off to the Balkans. A foothold in southern Europe was judged more precious than the defeat of the Italians in the deserts of North Africa.

An easy and successful advance into Tripolitania was not a foregone conclusion, and the arrival of the *Afrika Korps* was then unknown. The British armour was worn out after a 500 mile advance and there was not enough mechanised transport to support a further advance of even a small force over a similar distance. In the air and on the sea, the enemy force still outnumbered the RAF and Royal Navy, even without counting the newly-arrived *Luftwaffe* units. Whether a further advance by O'Connor into Tripolitania in early 1941 would have succeeded and paid unknown dividends is one of the great imponderables of the Desert War.

XIII Corps was renamed Cyrenaica Command, and was reduced to a garrison force of two inexperienced and untried divisions. RAF Cyrenaica was formed in mid-February, under the command of Group Captain Leslie Brown. This was a shadow of the former No 202 Group. By March, there remained only No 3 Squadron RAAF and Nos 55 and 73 Squadrons RAF with one flight of No 6 Squadron. None of these were located near El Agheila to protect the forward troops but were dedicated to the air defence of the ports of Benghazi and Tobruk.

Number 2 Armoured Car Company could not sustain further operations in forward areas without a period to repair its vehicles and rest those officers and airmen who had been operating at a high pitch for such a long period. In the second half of February, as the KDGs had their first encounters with the *Afrika Korps*, the Fordson armoured cars that remained set off back down the road to Cairo. The officers and airmen went on to Amman, where the Company Headquarters and remaining two sections had been stationed since January. The Fordsons remained in Cairo and underwent extensive repairs, were fitted with extra armour, and in light of campaign experience, had improvements made to the chassis. The Fordsons that had remained in Palestine and Transjordan were sent off to the RAOC workshops in Haifa to be fitted with Boys anti-tank rifles and to have the armour extended to accommodate a wireless, in preparation for their eventual use in the Western Desert.

In Cyrenaica, matters had worsened. It was apparent that there had been a steady movement of enemy forces towards the British lines at El Agheila during March. There was certainty that an attack would come, but its timing and size were unknown. On 31 March, Rommel seized the initiative, and three enemy Divisions drove back the light screen maintained by 2nd Armoured Division and the El Agheila line collapsed. The RAF in Cyrenaica did their best to impede the advance. However Group Captain Brown had seen the inevitability of the withdrawal and had prepared his units for this eventuality. Benghazi fell on 28 March and the tanks of 2nd Armoured

Division were gradually worn down by mechanical breakdowns and enemy action; consequently a general withdrawal was ordered. Mechili fell on 6 April and with it the Headquarters of 2nd Armoured Division. In a crushing blow, General Richard O'Connor, the architect of victory at Beda Fomm was captured by a German patrol near Derna.

While the remnants of the 2nd Armoured Division fell back to the Egyptian frontier, the 9th Australian Division withdrew back into Tobruk and on 10 April was cut off and besieged. Western Desert Force was reconstituted, with 22nd Guards Brigade and four mobile columns from 7th Armoured Division, and was ordered to hold the frontier positions on the escarpment at Sollum, Sofafi and Halfaya and the defensive line at Mersa Matruh. By the end of April 1941, all the gains of the previous winter had been lost, Bardia had fallen, and the enemy held a line from Halfaya to Sidi Omar. Fortunately, Tobruk held in the face of determined attacks by armour, infantry and aircraft, and as the supply lines lengthened and the momentum slowed, Rommel decided to halt.

Number 204 Group RAF was formed at Maaten Bagush on 12 April, under command of Air Commodore Raymond Collishaw, and absorbed the remnants of RAF Cyrenaica. By 8 May, the last Hurricane had left Tobruk and the small RAF contingent, despite the best efforts to support the Army, was back in Egypt, around Mersa Matruh.

In the first week of April, the Company Headquarters and two sections at Amman, under the command of Flight Lieutenant Alan Douglas, with nine Fordson armoured cars and 20 tenders were ordered to proceed by road to Helwan. The remainder of the Company travelled by train and the reconditioned Fordsons were collected from Cairo. The Company then moved west, with the intention of moving into Cyrenaica. Events in Libya had, of course, overtaken that plan and they were sent to work with No 204 Group RAF. By mid-April, three of the sections of No 2 Armoured Car Company, each with three Fordson armoured cars and two tenders, were deployed in Egypt on aerodrome defence at Sidi Haneish and Fuka and the forward landing ground at Sidi Barrani. The remainder of the Company was at Maaten Bagush. With the *Afrika Korps* approaching the frontier, and enemy reconnaissance elements possibly moving further east, routine patrols were initiated to the south and west of the aerodromes.

The Company was back into its desert routines and could have been forgiven for thinking that their immediate future lay with the RAF in the Western Desert. Events of great significance to the maintenance of the position of Great Britain in the Middle East were however, occurring 1000 miles away to the east in Iraq and Syria. On 5 May 1941, No 2 Armoured Car Company received orders to return with all speed to Amman.

Notes
1   D. Clarke, *The Eleventh at War* (London: Michael Joseph, 1952), p. 126.
2   A. Longmore, *From Sea to Sky: Memoirs 1910-1945* (London: Geoffrey Bles, 1946), p. 218.
3   More correctly, *Regia Aeronautica Italiana*, or the Royal Italian Air Force.
4   B. Pitt, "O'Connor," in *Churchill's Generals*, ed. J. Keegan (New York: Grove Weidenfeld, 1991), p. 185.
5   The nine squadrons were Nos 30, 45, 55, 113 and 211 with Blenheims, Nos 70 and

216 with Valentias and Bombays, No 208 with Lysanders and No 33 equipped with Gladiators. Numbers 80 and 112 with Gladiators were located further back defending Cairo. When the Italian Army advanced into Egypt the RAF lost the airfields around Sidi Barrani. These had served as a staging post for reinforcement aircraft from Britain.

6 Air Commodore Raymond Collishaw later Air Vice-Marshal Raymond Collishaw CB DSO & bar OBE DSC DFC (1893-1976).
7 So named after Lieutenant-Colonel 'Jock' Campbell (later Major-General 'Jock' Campbell VC), the Commanding Officer of the 4th Regiment, Royal Horse Artillery.
8 D. Clarke, *The Eleventh at War*, p. 126.
9 The Free French Air Force.
10 Wing Commander R.C. Skellon RAF Retd, *Interview with the author*, 2010. Richard Skellon had been in No 2 Armoured Car Company since mid-1940. He had joined the Territorial Army in the late 1930s and had served as an officer in the 6th Battalion, The Hampshire Regiment, and later completed courses at Sandhurst and with the Royal Engineers at Chatham. Peacetime soldiering began to pale and he became frustrated that his requested transfer to the REs hadn't come off. He was interested in flying, as his brother had been in the RAF, therefore, after completing a flying training course at Gatwick, then a small airfield, he put in for a transfer to the RAF. He was confirmed as a Pilot Officer in January 1940. He was then posted to the No 4 Flying Training School at Abu Sueir in Egypt, where he was put on to twin engine aircraft, Airspeed Oxfords. Unfortunately, Richard Skellon, in his words: "was very bad at landing, and the RAF said it would be better if you find something else to do, because you are not going to make a very good bomber pilot. We'd like you to go to an Armoured Car unit in Palestine. Which I accepted as I thought this was quite good." He proceeded to Ramleh to join No 2 Armoured Car Company, and was stationed there when "the war bubbled up in North Africa."
11 WO 169/220 *11 Hussars (Prince Albert's Own) September 1939-December 1940*.
12 The detachment was organised as follows: Advanced HQ, Flight Lieutenant Casano; No 1 Troop, Pilot Officer Alan Douglas; No 2 Troop, Pilot Officer Edward Spearing; No 3 Troop, Flight Sergeant Ault and No 4 Troop, Pilot Officer Francis Richardson.
13 No 3 RAAF and Nos 6, 33, 45, 55, 113, 208(AC) and 274 Squadrons under No 202 Group with Gladiators, Hurricanes and Blenheims; Nos 37, 38, 70 and 216 Squadrons under RAF Middle East, with Wellingtons and Bombays. Number 73 Squadron was due to arrive in early December.
14 I.S.O. Playfair *et al.*, *The Mediterranean and Middle East, Vol. I*, History of the Second World War (London: HMSO, 1954), p. 267, states: The precision with which these difficult and important night marches were done reflected great credit on staff and troops, and was largely responsible for the subsequent success.
15 Quoted in B.H. Liddell Hart, *The Tanks: The History of the Royal Tank Regiment and its predecessors Heavy Branch Machine-Gun Corps, Tank Corps and Royal Tank Corps, 1914-1945, Vol. II* (London: Cassell, 1959), p. 42.
16 So named after the 2i/c of 4th Armoured Brigade and acting Brigade commander, Colonel Horace L. Birks, and Lieutenant-Colonel John Combe, Officer Commanding 11th Hussars, respectively. The Brigade Commander was Brigadier J.A.L. 'Blood' Caunter, but he was temporarily in command of 7th Armoured Division.
17 Liddell Hart, *The Tanks, Vol II*, p. 52.
18 Thermos bombs were dropped from the air in dozens. The impact made the firing mechanism sensitive and if picked up or bumped the four pounds of explosive would explode. They were designed to maim or blind rather than kill, but would blow the track off a tank or the wheel off a lorry. They were more a nuisance and caused few casualties.
19 P. M. Jackson and A.J. Jackson (eds.), *A Lot to Fight For: The War Diaries and Letters of Squadron Leader J.F. Jackson DFC* (Toowoomba: Church Archivist's Press, n.d. [c. 1996]), p. 68.
20 On 9 January the Company Headquarters of No 2 Armoured Car Company was moved from Ramleh to Amman.

21 *Life in an Armoured Car in the Desert*. Magazine article (no source information), RAF Regiment Museum Archives.
22 HO 144/1447/307522 *Nationality and Naturalisation: Poublon, Albert Victor Edouard Marie (known as Albert Casano), from Belgium. Resident in Folkestone. Certificate 4,097 issued 18 June 1919*. Considerable debate and misinformation has circulated as to the ethnic origin of Casano. Casano's father, Albert, was born in Belgium to Belgian parents, and moved with them to London when he was one year old and had received his Certificate of Naturalisation in 1919. Albert was a musician and had studied at the Brussels Conservatoire of Music. Casano's father's surname had originally been Poublon, but his grandfather, had changed it to Casano for professional reasons, as he was an opera singer. This was Casano's great grandmother's maiden name, who was Spanish by birth. His mother's maiden name was Harriet Katinakis and she was born in London and was of Greek origin.
23 Excerpt from eulogy delivered by Air Commodore Peter J. Drissell, Commandant-General RAF Regiment, at the Memorial Service commemorating the life of Squadron Leader Michael Peter Casano MC. Held at St Clement Danes, London, 26 November 2006.
24 Skellon, *Interview with the author*.
25 J.J. Secter and J.P. Secter, *Recollections: Narrative reflections on the life and times of John J. Secter* (Victoria [BC]: Privately published, 2001), p. 16.
26 General Sir Archibald P. Wavell GCB CMG MC, 'Operations in the Western Desert from December 7th, 1940, to February 7th 1941', Supplement to the *London Gazette*, 1946, p. 3269.
27 bid., p. 3268.
28 Skellon, *Interview with the author*.
29 Ibid.
30 An independent force consisting of 200 aircraft of all types; Junkers Ju 88s, Heinkel He 111s, Junkers Ju 87s and Messerschmitt Bf 110s.
31 D. Clarke, *The Eleventh at War*, p. 155.
32 D. McCorquodale, B.L.B. Hutchings and A.D. Woozley, *History of the King's Dragoon Guards 1938-1945* (Glasgow: Printed for the Regiment by McCorquodale & Co., 1950), pp. 44-45.

Chapter Thirteen

Habbaniya 1941
'Steadiness Under Fire'

"Finally my report would indeed be incomplete if I failed to record the outstanding services rendered by the Iraq Levies under the command of Lieutenant-Colonel Brawn, the 1st Battalion of the King's Own Royal Regiment and the RAF officers and airmen of No 1 Armoured Car Company…"

Air Vice-Marshal John D'Albiac AOC Iraq[1]

"The most remarkable thing about the rebellion was the fact that we should have lost the battle, but didn't, and I often wonder if it was due to the hand of Providence."

Aircraftman Charles Spybey, No 1 Armoured Car Company[2]

Habbaniya, from the Arabic, meaning 'of the Oleander tree', was situated on the south bank of the Euphrates and located approximately in the centre of Iraq. Work on its construction as an RAF station had begun in 1934 under a clause of the Anglo-Iraq Treaty that permitted a British military base west of the Euphrates. It lay some 50 miles west of Baghdad on the desert road through Falluja, and about 80 miles south of the oil pipeline from Kirkuk. The station extended for two and a half miles along the river bank and was surrounded by about eight miles of a high angle iron fence, curved at the top, to keep out intruders. Interspersed were blockhouses every 300 yards. There were six large hangars, an Aircraft Depot with two large repair shops, a Supply Depot, fuel and ammunition dumps, and a hospital and outside the perimeter fence, to the south, the airstrip. The airbase was self-contained, having its own water supply that rose on a 60-foot tower above the camp, a sewerage system and power station. Two miles south of the station was Lake Habbaniya, of about 100 square miles in extent. The lake was the location of a hotel and rest house, and staging station for the flying-boats of the British Overseas Airways Corporation (BOAC), operating on the Egypt-Basra-India route. RAF Habbaniya had been built as a peacetime air base.

The RAF had been established at Habbaniya since January 1938, when Hinaidi had been handed over to the Royal Iraqi Air Force. Conditions on the camp were wonderful and provided everything one could wish for to defeat the boredom of life on the edge of the Iraqi desert. There were air-conditioned buildings, a well-appointed officers' club, two indoor and three outdoor cinemas, a golf course, a polo ground,

The gate sign at RAF Habbaniya (RAF Habbaniya Assn).

a race course, swimming pools, one with three different heights of diving boards, a Garrison Church and also a Yacht Club at the lake up near the plateau. The camp had been created from a bare patch of desert, but after irrigation there were 28 miles of tree-lined avenues, with hedges of pink and white blossoming oleanders, bearing the names of streets and RAF airfields of the Home Counties. It was, however, a difficult station to defend from the ground, particularly from the south. The major weaknesses were the long perimeter and the large commanding plateau, 100 to 200 feet high, located a few hundred yards south of the airfield.[3]

RAF Habbaniya was the location of Air Headquarters Iraq and had a population of about 1000 airmen, plus 1200 Assyrians and Kurds of the Iraq Levies, while the cantonment contained some 9000 civilians, European, Iraqi and Assyrian, including the wives and children of the British servicemen and the Iraq Levies. The air units of the RAF in Iraq were under the command of Air Vice-Marshal H.G. Smart and consisted of No 4 Service Flying Training School (No 4 FTS), a Communications Flight at Habbaniya, and No 244 (Bomber) Squadron at Shaibah.[4] The School was under the command of Group Captain W.A.B. Savile, who had previously been Officer Commanding No 1 Armoured Car Company from late 1938 until December 1940. Number 4 FTS possessed the largest portion of the RAF aircraft in Iraq. Most, however, were training aircraft; 32 Hawker Audaxes, eight Fairey Gordons, five Hawker Hart trainers and three tired Gloster Gladiator biplanes, along with 29 Airspeed Oxfords and a Bristol Blenheim. Of these, only four could not be considered obsolete or suited only to training. Similarly, the Vickers Vincents of No 244 Squadron were mainly communications aircraft and could hardly be considered as frontline aircraft.

In the days following the declaration of war on 3 September 1939, No 1 Armoured Car Company had been busying itself providing the escort to ground

Airmen of No 1 Section with HMAC Diana at the oil pumping station at H3 in 1940 (© Crown copyright. RAF Regiment Museum).

parties of No 4 FTS, which it had been decided should be transferred from Abu Sueir in Egypt to RAF Habbaniya. Numbers 1, 2 and 3 Sections were stationed at RAF Habbaniya (Photograph p. 599), while No 4 Section was permanently located at RAF Shaibah. The Sections at Habbaniya were the escorts for the ration convoys to Oil Pumping Stations and Desert Staging Posts at H3 and LG 5, respectively, which were garrisoned by the Iraq Levies. Flight Lieutenant 'Ted' Frith recalls the work:

> The war broke out, and we had to guard the pipeline to Haifa, so we went out and patrolled, right up to Transjordan, because we feared the pipeline would be sabotaged. I went out with a company of Levies, under the command of Captain John Frost.[5] They were tremendous troops...
>
> We had a base in H2 or H3 and were the eyes. We patrolled from it and the Levies were our back up should trouble arise.[6]

The patrols were relatively routine and quiet, with one exception when a patrol was attacked by a party of armed Arab bandits. The Desert Staging Posts had been established by No 1 Armoured Car Company at LG 3, LG 5, Rutbah and H3, during September 1938. This had occurred at the height of the Munich Crisis following Hitler's annexation of parts of Czechoslovakia. Were a war with Germany to materialise, the Company would be required to provide escorts for troop movements westwards towards Palestine, Transjordan and Egypt.

Fordson trucks had replaced some of the Rolls Royce Wireless Tenders, but the Rolls Royce Armoured Cars were still the mainstay of the Company. The officers and airmen of No 1 Company must have expressed frustration as they spent August 1939

Airmen laying cement to mark out Landing Ground 3 (upper) and the finished result (lower) (Rolph, RAFACA).

escorting the flying units of Iraq Command, Nos 30, 55 and 70 Squadrons, with whom the Company had fought side-by-side for so many years, to join battle in the Western Desert and Greece.

In April 1940, a heavy melt of the snows in the mountains caused the Euphrates to burst its banks and the personnel of Habbaniya had to be evacuated to a temporary camp on the plateau. The Company, with 13 officers, 184 men and 45 MT vehicles moved rapidly in one and a half hours and then provided routine protective patrols around the temporary plateau camp for a number of days until the flood abated.

Some of the airmen who were serving in No 1 Company following the outbreak of war had arrived on the 'Boat' in March 1939. One of them was LAC Ken Basham. He had responded to a 'Standing Orders' request around RAF stations in the United Kingdom for motor transport drivers who wished to volunteer for the Armoured Car Crew course. He continues:

> The drivers chosen were eventually assembled at No 1 Air Armament School, Eastchurch, Isle of Sheppey. Under the instruction of Sergeant 'Tiny'

The officers of No 1 Armoured Car Company in 1940. Front row (left to right): Flt Lt R.C.J. Waters, Flt Lt D.C. Hellard, Sqn Ldr C.V. Lock (2i/c), Wg Cdr W.A.B. Savile (OC 1ACC later 4FTS), Flt Lt R.J. Payne, Flt Lt E.L. Frith (Adjt), Fg Off B.F. Pyne (© Crown copyright. RAF Regiment Museum).

Tregunna we were taught semaphore, Aldis lamp, Vickers and Lewis 0.303 machine-guns, rifles and revolvers. This was a six-week course beginning in November, with a Christmas break, finishing in January when everyone returned to their stations to wait for 'the Boat'. The trooping season was at this time confined to September to April.

February saw the arrival of 'the Boat', this being the well-known SS *Somersetshire*, which left Southampton bound for Karachi. Troops for Iraq transferred to the SS *Varela* for the journey up the Gulf to Basra, onward to Baghdad, and the road to Habbaniya. On arrival, in March 1939, we were allocated to one of our three sections (No 4 Section being at Shaibah). Yours truly, in No 2 becoming part of the crew of 'Tail End Charlie', HMAC *Jackal*, with Car Commander, Flight Sergeant 'Jumbo' Ellis (ex-boxing champ RAF).

Having settled into our routine, in early April, No 2 Section was allocated a 'recco' down to Shaibah. Leaving Habbaniya with an early start, we were on the outskirts of Baghdad before 9 am when a British Embassy car raced past the convoy and brought it to a halt. It appeared that King Ghazi had been killed early that morning when his car hit a tree and we were advised to return to Habbaniya, as stories were circulating that the British were implicated.[7]

Back at Habbaniya temperatures were beginning to rise and the summer routine meant on parade 6 am to 8 am, breakfast, and then 9 am to 12 o'clock finish, followed by 'tiffin'. Afternoons were spent quietly as sport was not recommended before 4 pm in the hot weather. Evenings were spent at the cinema, open-air in the summer, indoors in the winter, or at the NAAFI.

In the general run of events Sections, in turn, would spend five days at a training ground about 35 miles away for firing practice, or at an emergency landing ground (LG5) about 100 miles away on the way to Rutbah Wells.

One of the duties of No 1 Armoured Car Company was to visit the pumping stations on the oil pipeline from Kirkuk (K1) to Baiji (K3) where it branched off to the 'H' Line to Haifa or the 'T' Line to Tripoli. Sections made these visits in turn.

The 'Prize Recco' particularly in summer, was up north to Mosul on the River Tigris, with the biblical city of Nineveh on the opposite bank and on up to Arbil.[8] From here turning left up into the hills, 12 hairpin bends up and the same down the other side and on to Rowanduz Gorge, something like Cheddar, and into Kurdistan country near the Turkish border.[9]

The Treaty of Alliance and Mutual Support which had been signed in 1930 required Iraq, in the event of war, to come to the aid of Great Britain. Furthermore, the agreement granted the right of transit for British troops and supplies and the use of Basra for the Royal Navy. The country was required to provide all possible aid, including the use of railways, rivers, ports and airfields. There were no British troops stationed in Iraq and the internal security of the country was the responsibility of the Iraqi Government. The RAF retained a presence through the air bases at Shaibah and Habbaniya, which were important staging posts for the air route between Egypt and India. As well as her oilfields, and pipelines that moved oil to the refineries at Haifa, Iraq was also a strategically important alternative transport route to the Red Sea, which was subject at this time to interference from Italian forces in Abyssinia and Somaliland.

Airmen of No 1 Company cleaning and maintaining a Lewis gun (Rutter, RAFACA).

At the time of the declaration of war, Iraq was ruled by the four year old King Feisal II of Iraq, the son of the late King Ghazi. The political power however, laid with the Regent, Feisal's Uncle, the pro-British Amir Abd al Illah. While the Iraqi Government had broken off diplomatic relations with Germany, they had not taken similar steps against Italy in June 1940, and the Italian Legation in Baghdad had remained open. From this, and the Japanese Legation, as evidenced by decryptions of Italian diplomatic traffic, the Axis was fomenting Arab Nationalist and anti-British sentiments among the tribes and political movements of Iraq.[10]

This was helped considerably by the German successes of 1939 and 1940 in Poland, France, the Low Countries and Norway and the establishment of a Vichy French Government in Syria. British prestige was at the lowest ebb. In late 1940, British Intelligence warned the Chiefs of Staff that the position of the Regent was deteriorating and that there were several senior political and military figures that were notably pro-Axis in their sympathies. The Prime Minister, Rashid Ali El Gailani, was pro-Italian and together with The Grand Mufti of Jerusalem, Haj Amin el Husseini, who had been exiled from Palestine, was in contact with, and receiving funds from, the Germans. The German ambassador in Baghdad, Dr Fritz Grobba, had been cultivating a close relationship with the Iraqis since the 1930s. Rashid Ali had been a major participant in Iraqi politics for some years, and had begun conspiring with four Colonels of the Iraqi Army and Air Force, known as 'The Golden Square,' to seize power.

In the first week of April 1941, matters worsened. Rashid Ali resigned, but was replaced by one of his supporters. On 31 March, the Regent, learning of a plot to arrest him, and fearing for his own life, sought safety in the American Embassy in Baghdad. From there he was transported to RAF Habbaniya, hidden in the car of the American Ambassador. Once in the safe hands of the RAF, he was flown to Basra and given refuge with the Royal Navy on HMS *Cockchafer*.

General Wavell, with limited resources, had been doing his best to avoid military involvement in Iraq, and had sought resolution through diplomatic and economic measures. On 3 April however, Rashid Ali, with the support of 'The Golden Square', seized power in a *coup d'état*, formed a clearly pro-Axis government, and proclaimed himself 'Chief of the National Defence Committee'. He then proceeded to stir up anti-British feeling, which was already high. Consequently, the British Cabinet decided that a stronger line needed to be taken in Iraq. Despite Wavell having to deal with the German invasion of Greece, an expected attack on Crete, Rommel's rapid thrust into Cyrenaica, and the final battles of the campaign in Italian East Africa, the Chiefs of Staff ordered him to take military action in Iraq.

If the British Army in Libya had been left in difficult straits after being denuded of troops and aircraft to send to Greece, the situation in Iraq was dire. Wavell indicated that he could not spare even a battalion from Palestine and therefore, the Indian Government was asked to provide reinforcements. Tenth Indian Division had been earmarked for Malaya, but to Wavell's relief, the convoy conveying it was diverted at short notice to Basra. A further critical arrival was just under 400 infantrymen of the 1st Battalion, The King's Own Royal Regiment (The King's Own) of the 20th Indian Infantry Brigade. The first flight of the battalion was flown from Karachi to Shaibah on 17 April in the DC2s and Vickers Valentias of No 31 Squadron. The following morning, the first ships conveying the Headquarters of 10th Indian Division, under the command of Major-General W.A.K. Fraser, and the remainder of 20th Indian Brigade docked at Basra without incident. Fraser then assumed command of all Army

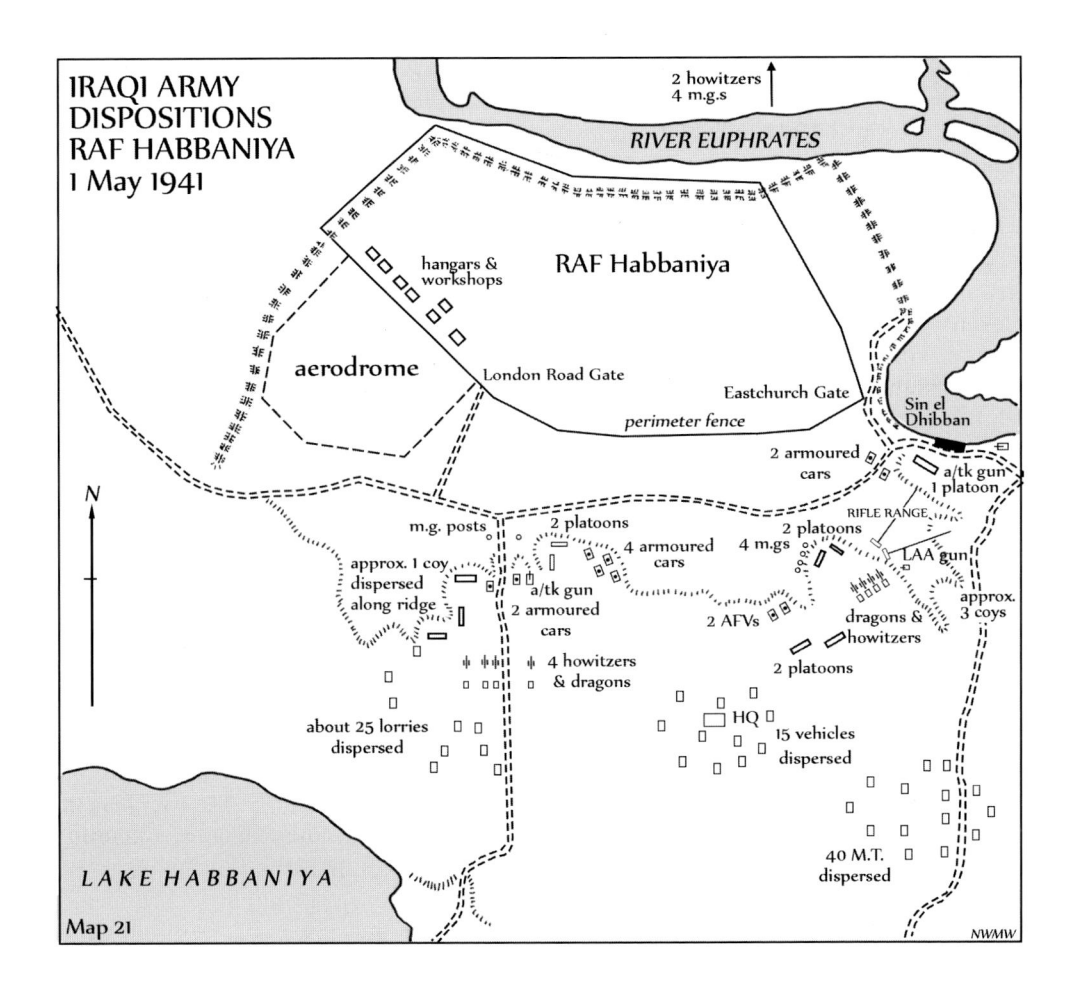

IRAQI ARMY DISPOSITIONS RAF HABBANIYA 1 May 1941

Map 21

forces in Iraq. Ten days later, after relief by an Indian battalion, the King's Own were flown on to RAF Habbaniya.[11]

Facing the RAF in Iraq were 50 or so aircraft of the Royal Iraqi Air Force predominantly based at Rashid airbase (previously RAF Hinaidi), near Baghdad. Iraqi ground forces consisted of four Divisions, two at Baghdad, one at Kirkuk and one in the Middle Euphrates area. The Army possessed 16 Fiat light tanks, 14 British-built Crossley armoured cars and two mechanised infantry battalions.

On 2 April, with the political situation deteriorating, Air Headquarters Iraq ordered No 1 Armoured Car Company to establish an observation post on the plateau, one mile to the west of the Canal Turn, on the Falluja-Baghdad road. A Rolls-Royce armoured car and a wireless tender, were sent out and placed on a 12-hour rotation. As a further safeguard on 7 April, a Dragon tank, manned by the Company, was placed at each of the London Road and Eastchurch Gates. Patrols were sent out along the Ramadi-Habbaniya road and another observation post was established three miles west of the cantonment. In late April, with the increasing threat that the Germans might attempt to land airborne troops on or near the airfield, an 'anti-aircraft duty' section comprising six Rolls-Royce armoured cars, the two old Dragon tanks and an Albion tender, was established outside the cantonment perimeter near the London Gate. Interestingly, the operational instruction indicated that despite the actual task being to watch for airborne troops, it had to be called 'anti-aircraft duty', presumably so as not to cause alarm and despondency in the cantonment.

On 21 April 1941, the Iraqi Army under Rashid Ali's instruction, occupied the Kirkuk oilfields, cut the flow of oil through the pipeline to Haifa and reopened the pipeline to Tripoli in Vichy-French Syria. A request by the British Government to land the remainder of the 10th Indian Division at Basra was also refused and this heightened the tension to breaking point. The first hostile move by the Iraqi forces was made in the early hours of 30 April, when the British Embassy sent a wireless message to Air Vice-Marshal Smart at Habbaniya, reporting that a large body of 6000 to 8000 Iraqi Army troops, and vehicles, were moving westwards from the city. With the Air Headquarters Iraq wanting to avoid an escalation of the conflict, at 0400 hours, the No 1 Armoured Car Company observation post at the Canal Turn and the cars on 'anti-aircraft duty' were withdrawn into the cantonment, but with the entire Company being placed on stand-by.

Flight Sergeant Mornington Wentworth describes the events of the next few hours:

> The Rolls-Royce armoured car and wireless tender were called back into camp from the observation posts. The alarm went off and we were ordered to man the cars. They were in the bays and we sat there until daylight.
>
> And when we looked up on the top of the plateau, there was the long line of the Iraqis, with huge guns, facing the camp... a nasty looking situation.[12]

Dawn reconnaissance flights revealed that an Iraqi infantry brigade with field, anti-tank and anti-aircraft artillery, machine-guns and armoured cars, had invested RAF Habbaniya, having occupied the plateau and towns of Falluja to the east, and Ramadi, 15 miles to the west. Further reinforcements were proceeding in a steady flow along the Baghdad to Falluja road and the key bridges over the Euphrates and Tigris were held by the Iraqi forces. Iraqi field guns and howitzers threatened the station and it was now completely cut off from land communications with the outside world (Map 21, p. 276).[13]

A view across the airfield at RAF Habbaniya looking towards the plateau where the Iraqi forces first appeared on 1 May 1941 (Gudgeon Coll., RAF Habbaniya Assn).

The arrival of the Iraqi Army had not been unexpected and steps had immediately been taken to disperse the aircraft. Since the beginning of April, preparations were being made by No 4 FTS for an outbreak of hostilities. The Audaxes, Gordons and Oxfords had all been modified to carry significant bomb loads so that they could undertake offensive action. Considerable resourcefulness and ingenuity was shown by all hands to adapt the aircraft for operational use, while intensive courses were begun on bomb-aiming and air-gunnery. The aircraft would be crewed by the instructors and pupils of No 4 FTS and would be known as the Habbaniya Air Striking Force.

At 0600 hours that morning, an Iraqi Army officer bearing the white flag, presented himself at the Station gates with a message from his Commander, demanding that all flying should cease and that no one should leave the cantonment, otherwise shelling would commence. Unsurprisingly, Air Vice-Marshal Smart rejected the ultimatum and indicated that any interference with normal training would be treated as an act of war. On a further visit at 1130 hours, Smart was accused of violating the Treaty. Unsuccessful diplomatic efforts were made that day by the British Ambassador in Baghdad and by Air Vice-Marshal Smart to the local Iraqi commander, but they failed to persuade the Iraqis to withdraw. Smart was also concerned that he had within the cantonment, a large group of women and children, both residents and evacuees from Baghdad. While he had been instructed that the situation could not be allowed to escalate, Smart was also aware that his main strength lay in the aircraft he possessed. These would be most effective during daylight and he was concerned that the Iraqi forces could attack at night and overrun the limited defences of the air base when the main strike force, the aircraft would be ineffective.

The ground defence force for RAF Habbaniya was small when compared to their Iraqi opponents, and consisted of Headquarters and six Companies of the Iraq Levies, with 1200 men, the newly-arrived regulars of 1st King's Own with 364 men, under the command of Major (later Lieutenant-Colonel) E.N. Everett, and the 21 Rolls-Royce armoured cars of the three sections of the No 1 Armoured Car Company, with 12 officers and 160 men, under the command of Wing Commander M. Lowe.[14] On 1 May, Colonel Ouvry Roberts, a staff officer of 10th Indian Division, was given overall command of the force.[15] It was considerably outnumbered by its opponents but quite experienced, exercises having been held with No 1 Armoured Car Company and the Iraq Levies during October 1940 for what was known as the Habbaniya Defence Scheme.

Smart was instructed that, as all peaceful efforts had failed he was to take the necessary steps to ensure the withdrawal of the Iraqi troops from the plateau. From the Prime Minister, Winston Churchill, he received the message; 'If you must strike, strike hard'. Therefore, at dawn on 2 May, eight Wellingtons of No 70 Squadron and others of No 37 Squadron from Shaibah began the air bombardment on the Iraqi positions on the plateau. Soon after the Wellingtons, the 33 aircraft of No 4 FTS took off to attack the enemy. The Iraqi artillery retaliated immediately and shelled the cantonment damaging a few parked aircraft. The positive consequence of this was that the artillery positions were revealed to the attacking aircraft. Over the course of the day, nearly 200 shells fell on the station. LAC Ken Basham recalls the first Iraqi barrage:

> After three days at about 6 am, two 'Wimpeys' appeared and dropped the first bombs on the Iraqis, this brought a salvo of shells, one of which, but for a eucalyptus tree, would have made the Officers' Mess just that - literally!

The end of that shell ricocheted towards HMAC *Jackal* in which we sat, but it stopped a few yards short.[16]

Flight Sergeant Wentworth continues:

So we were told to take all the cars out, park them on the rugby field and batten ourselves in the car and from then on for about six hours it was just continual shelling. They were bursting all around us but they did no damage. We were absolutely unprepared. There wasn't a rifle per man and the only automatic weapons were the machine guns on our armoured cars. There were some on the odd aircraft but most were for flying training.[17]

With the Habbaniya Air Striking Force operating over the Iraqi lines, the RAF armoured cars, Levies and the King's Own had begun their own ground operations. A platoon of No 8 (Kurdish) Company of the Iraq Levies crossed the Euphrates and knocked out three Iraqi artillery pieces that had been firing on the camp from the Burma Bund to the north. In the southern sector, at 1000 hours, Flight Lieutenant B.F. Pyne with the six Rolls Royce armoured cars of No 3 Section went out on a sortie to attack a group of Iraqi armoured cars that had been observed by the Levies to the south of the airfield, at the foot of the escarpment. The cars opened fire from 400 yards with armour piercing bullets and made five attacks, hitting all the cars but not knocking any out. Enemy fire hit the Rolls-Royces causing several tyre punctures but no casualties.

The main airfield now lay in 'No Man's Land' and taking off and landing was a difficult, if not deadly, proposition. Thus a proportion of the aircraft were now using the golf course and polo pitch to the north of the cantonment as a make-shift airstrip. This, at least allowed the aircraft to be hidden behind a line of trees and away from the direct line of sight of the Iraqi artillery observers.

The Wellingtons of Nos 37 and 70 Squadron had been a welcome reinforcement. They had been despatched from Egypt, had flown to Shaibah and had made the first attacks on the positions up on the plateau at dawn on 2 May. Seven of the bombers were able to return to Basra following their sorties over the Iraqi positions on the plateau; however, all were unserviceable due to intense anti-aircraft fire. The eighth Wellington, flown by Flying Officer Ian Anstey, was hit in the engines, while carrying out a low-level attack on enemy artillery and vehicles, but he made a good forced-landing on the main airstrip at Habbaniya.[18] The Wellington was now under the immediate gaze of the Iraqis. The crew piled out of the aircraft and sprinted for the safety of the hangars, with machine-gun bullets kicking up spurts of dust at their heels as they ran. Having reached safety of the hangars, the next problem was to recover the Wellington that now sat alone and in full view of the Iraqi positions on the plateau, and with a full bomb load still on board.

Possessing nothing as specialised as a Wellington bomber tow bar, the next best option was to send out a tractor with a strong rope. With machine-gun fire and now the Iraqi artillery ranging on the airstrip it would have been suicidal to drive out onto the airstrip on a lone airfield tractor. To protect the driver therefore, three Rolls-Royce armoured cars from No 3 Section, with Flight Lieutenant Bernard Pyne, Sergeant Bird and Corporal Whitbourne, commanding RRACs *Lion*, *Adder* and *Astra* respectively, were placed in a close vee formation around the tractor and the exposed driver. By the time the Wellington was reached the rifle and machine-gun fire was intense. Furthermore, five of the Iraqi armoured cars that the section had fired on an hour earlier, were now working their way along the tarmac on the southern edge of the aerodrome towards the stricken bomber. Despite the bullets zipping past him, the tractor driver succeeded in getting the tow rope attached to the tail of the aircraft. At that moment a machine-gun bullet pierced the petrol tank of the tractor and the Iraqi artillery also found their range. The tractor exploded in flames and the bomber was bracketed by shells, and within seconds the tractor and Wellington were flaming wrecks. Any further attempts at towing would be futile. The driver, though stunned by the explosions, was unharmed and he, along with the pilot, was quickly bundled onto RRAC *Lion* and the Section returned at high speed to the hangars. Luckily, the cars were halfway across the tarmac before the bomb load on the burning Wellington exploded.

While RRAC *Lion* headed back to the camp with the pilot and driver, RRACs *Adder* and *Astra*, linked up with the six Rolls-Royce armoured cars of No 1 Section, under the command of Flight Lieutenant David Hellard, and turned to face the Iraqi armoured cars that were moving across the trip from the foot of the escarpment. After half an hour, using machine-gun fire, and the Boys anti-tank rifle, they were able to drive the enemy off and force them back onto the plateau. Aircraftman Charles Spybey, a wireless operator with No 1 Armoured Car Company, recalls how close run the outcome was:

> Our equipment consisted of 50 training aircraft, 18 armoured cars, and a few machine guns. We had no field guns or anti-aircraft guns, except for two cannons that were used in the last war and which were unserviceable. The aircraft had to take off on open ground between ourselves and the surrounding plateau. We did manage a temporary makeshift for very light aircraft on the football pitch!
>
> It would have been the easiest thing in the world for the Iraqis to cross the open strip of ground, about half a mile in length between the plateau and the camp, during the first night and wipe us out completely…
>
> A dozen Iraqi armoured cars ventured across the open ground during the afternoon, but six of our cars went out and gave battle. We completely riddled eight of them with armour piercing bullets, and the other four fled.[19]

Despite the intense fire the cars had experienced, their armour had stood up well, with only two airmen suffering minor gunshot wounds. The successes of the Company that day were of some comfort to the armoured car crews, as the differences in performance of the two types of armoured cars had been the subject of some ridicule by the Iraqi troops in more friendly days. This is described by LAC Dennis 'Harry' Hawkins, then serving with No 1 Armoured Car Company:

> The Iraqi leader at that time was Rashid Ali, and he travelled around in a Crossley armoured car, supplied by Britain between wars. It had six wheels and was four-wheel drive, so consequently, did not get stuck in the sand as easily as ours did. Any time that we encountered Iraqi armoured cars, members of their crew would hold a hand up with thumb and forefinger about one inch apart, indicating that their armour plating was one inch thick, and they knew ours was only a third of an inch thick. But it was discovered by our colleagues when they were fighting at Habbaniya, that

a direct hit, using only ball ammunition would penetrate the Iraqi armour, whereas ours could only be penetrated by a direct hit with an armour-piercing bullet. I think our pals of Nos 1, 2 and 3 Sections had quite a hard time during the fighting at Habb. What with the Luftwaffe strafing and the Iraqi's shelling them, I think they did very well to get out on patrols and back again safely.[20]

The final task of the first day was performed by Flight Lieutenant Hellard, with RRACs *Jackal*, *Diana* and *Conqueror* when, late in afternoon, they were sent out to tow in a Gladiator, the most modern fighter the garrison possessed at that time, that had come to a halt on the runway. Whereas Nos 1 and 3 Section had been dealing with the defence of the airfield, No 2 Section, under the command of Flight Lieutenant Ronald Waters, had been out with three Rolls-Royce armoured cars on a reconnaissance along the Falluja Road noting the positions of enemy transport and machine-gun posts. Six more airmen had manned the two venerable Dragon tanks, *Walrus* and *Seal*, which were posted permanently at the Eastchurch Gate and had spent the day exchanging rifle and machine-gun fire with the nearby enemy posts.

The first day of the siege had passed for the Company without any serious casualties. The aircrews of the Habbaniya Air Striking Force had not fared as well. The Iraqi Air Force had joined in the battle during the day and some of their aircraft had performed well. Number 4 FTS had made 193 sorties, five aircraft had been destroyed and several others were put out of action, but losses had been heavy with 13 killed and 29 wounded, including nine civilians. Further to the south, Number 244 Squadron had lost two Vincents during an attack on the enemy positions around Shaibah.

It was apparent however, that the bombardment had not been as effective as

The tanks manned during the siege by personnel from No 1 Armoured Car Company. The two large tanks are HMT Walrus (first from the left) and Seal (second from left) and were Dragon Mark I artillery tractors. Both had been in Iraq since 1924. The smaller vehicle to the right is a Carden-Lloyd Mark VI tankette (Rutter, RAFACA).

feared and that the Iraqi Army was not showing any intention of advancing on the station. Air attacks the following day were therefore also directed against the Iraqi Air Force at Rashid airfield in Baghdad, and the Army's lines of communications on the road to Falluja. The air attacks on the Iraqi airfields soon began to pay dividends.

Number 3 Section was on the airfield at dawn the next day to cover the take-off of the Air Striking Force Later in the day, along with No 1 Section, they escorted working parties out to the airstrip to carry out repairs to the many shell holes in the tarmac. The cars also collected unexploded Iraqi bombs and shells. Meanwhile, HQ Section with two Rolls-Royce armoured cars, under intermittent shell fire, escorted two tractors that brought in the wreckage of the burnt-out Wellington and some Oxfords that had come to grief the previous day.

Iraqi Air Force Savoia SM79s bombed the cantonment around midday, while that night the Iraqi artillery resumed shelling, beginning at 2200 hours, and continuing intermittently for the next six hours. A few shells fell on the Armoured Car Lines and one airman suffered a minor leg wound. Aircraftman Charles Spybey recalls the Iraqi artillery and aerial barrage:

> Hundreds of shells were pumped into the camp… Later in the day, the Iraqis sent their own aircraft over and bombed us, one bomb hitting my billet. Nobody was in it at the time. Our water supply was stored in a huge tower, and we realised that if that was hit we might have a hard time of it. I was ordered to go to all the huts in our section and fill all the baths and sinks and buckets with water and in doing so had to duck the gunfire which rained down on us continually – really scary! The bombing and shelling went on for five days…
>
> One of the shells landed on the edge of the V shaped slit trench in which a number of us were taking cover, and it caved in, burying several of the lads. We dug them out with all haste, and only one lad was hurt in any way.[21]

Flight Lieutenant 'Ted' Frith, the Company Adjutant, recalls the shelling, his bewilderment at the Iraqi tactics and the effect that the air attacks was having on their supply lines:

> They came up onto the plateau; they were shelling us like mad, like there was no tomorrow. Oh, they meant business. They were probably firing our own shells. We had the idea that they would go for the water tower. They only had to pierce the water tower and we would have been out of business, but they didn't, because they wanted the camp.
>
> The next thing was that No 4 FTS took on a bombing role. Someone had the idea that the bridge at Falluja should be bombed to stop their supplies coming up. But we discovered that the Iraqis, when we took prisoners, had their leather pouches for their ammo stuffed with dates. They were being sustained on dates![22]

Other Iraqi prisoners had also commented that they had neither food nor water for more than two days. This, combined with the incessant air attacks and harassing patrols from the King's Own and Levies, had sapped their morale.

The escort tasks for the armoured cars were maintained for the next three days. The numbers at the station had been further swelled by the arrival of British women and children who had been evacuated from Baghdad. On one occasion, the cars escorted three Douglas DC2s of No 31 Squadron that were flying out parties of British and Assyrian civilians to Palestine. To protect aircraft from shell and machine-gun fire from the plateau, the armoured cars would drive out onto the airfield and stir up a screen of dust between the airstrip and plateau so that taxiing and take off could occur in relative obscurity.

The Air Striking Force maintained its attacks on the Iraqi positions and reinforcement aircraft had been arriving in limited numbers; ten more Wellingtons of No 37 Squadron were flown to Shaibah and Blenheims of No 203 Squadron, escorted by two long-range Hurricanes that had arrived from Egypt, carried out low-flying strafing attacks on Rashid and Baghdad airfields. It was becoming clear by 4 May that the enemy was not in an aggressive mood. The following day, No 1 Section waited from dawn until 0700 hours, on stand-by at the airfield, ready to provide escort to any aircraft that needed to scramble. All seemed quiet, and the Section was not called upon, and they returned to their lines.

The Iraq Levies were kept busy manning the blockhouses on the perimeter, locating enemy artillery positions, and having regular engagements against enemy machine-gun posts and snipers. Neither they, nor the King's Own, had confined themselves to defensive tasks, as they had also been carrying out regular aggressive nightly patrols. On the evening of 5 May, the King's Own carried out a grenade attack on the Iraqi positions, while No 3 Section transported and covered a patrol of the Iraq Levies as they moved up into the foothills of the plateau. From the reports sent back by this and other patrols, it was thought that the enemy were gathering their force for a final assault on Habbaniya.

As dawn broke on Tuesday 6 May however, the expected attack did not materialise. Number 1 Section was sent out on a reconnaissance to the south as far as the BOAC Rest House and the tarmac road on the plateau, but all they found were a

Vehicles recovered from the plateau following the withdrawal of the Iraqi Army (© Crown copyright. RAF Regiment Museum).

Conqueror after it became wedged on a concrete block near the road.

Numbers 1 and 3 Sections had moved with King's Own into the village, and were ordered to return to Habbaniya just after midday. In doing so, the cars had to pass back through Sin El Dhibban. As RRAC *Jackal* passed through the village it came under fire, and a bullet entered a gap in the armour of the turret and ricocheted around inside. The Car Commander, Pilot Officer Edward Petley, was hit in the chest and his driver LAC Vickers, suffered a scalp wound. Despite a punctured tyre, Vickers drove the vehicle on, and took Petley directly to the Station Hospital.[26]

The only other casualty in the Company was Flight Sergeant Paige of No 3 Section who suffered a minor gunshot wound to the leg. Levy casualties up to this time had been one killed and 17 wounded. The King's Own had fared worse, losing five men killed and five wounded. The attack had however, resulted in the capture of 26 Iraqi officers and 409 other ranks. It was decided that a defensive plan for the village could not be implemented that night and so the cars of No 2 Section covered the withdrawal of the King's Own and No 4 (Assyrian) Company of the Levies back to the cantonment.[27]

Surprisingly, the enemy made no attempt to reoccupy Sin El Dhibban, but now made a disorderly withdrawal to Falluja in the east and Ramadi in the west. Later in the day, a motorised infantry and artillery column was seen moving up from Falluja. Forty of the aircraft of the Striking Force were sent out to attack these reinforcements, and after a low-level bombing and machine-gunning attack, all that remained was a 250 yard long line of burning lorries and exploding ammunition, and many more prisoners. Mornington Wentworth had been sent out to report on the results of the bombing:

> I didn't realise what had happened until the next morning, when I was sent out in an armoured car, as escort to the King's Own, to clear up the mess. And what a mess! Not one of those convoys reached us. There were vehicles in the wadis, either side of the road, hardly any in one piece, they'd set fire to them; there were dead bodies. After that, we never had any fears that the Iraqis would get through.[28]

The following day, a salvage party of the Levies moved back into Sin El Dhibban, covered by five Rolls-Royce armoured cars of No 2 Section, and recovered six 3.7-inch howitzers, four Crossley armoured cars and a number of vehicles. RRAC *Conqueror*, now recovered, moved through the village towards Falluja and returned to report the presence of Iraqi infantry in the town.

For the next few days, salvage parties led by Warrant Officer Tomkins and Sergeant Bell with the Albion and Crossley tenders of the Company were kept busy salvaging the large amounts of materiel, of all kinds; field guns, trucks, and small arms ammunition, which had been left behind by the Iraqi Army.[29] Mornington Wentworth continues:

> We went out to mop up, it was shocking. There were dead horses and of course out there in the heat they'd swelled up and the smell was terrible.[30]

With the Iraqi Army having vacated the plateau, it was necessary to determine where their forces were now concentrated. A brigade each was located at Falluja and Ramadi, and a division was near Baghdad. The Iraqis had blown the bunds near

Falluja and those near Ramadi, causing considerable flooding, as well as destroying the Suttaih Bridge on the road to Ramadi. To secure the garrison's western flank and maintain road communications, Flight Lieutenant Pyne and three Rolls-Royce armoured cars from No 3 Section accompanied a detachment of the King's Own and the Habbaniya artillery to occupy the bridges in the vicinity.

The Iraqi demolitions were intended to hinder the movements of the British forces, but they also served to neutralise the threat to Habbaniya from Ramadi, as the Iraqi garrison was now surrounded by water. This had also cut the main road from Transjordan, and an alternative route had to be found for any columns proceeding from there. The most likely path of approach was the southerly route around Lake Habbaniya. On 10 May therefore, No 1 Section escorted Lieutenant-Colonel Everett and a party of the King's Own to Mujarra, at the southern tip of the lake. A strengthened trestle bridge was to be constructed over the Mujarra canal which drained from the Lake, and this was completed after six days. The plan was for a relief column from Palestine to turn south at the 25 kilometre post on the main Rutbah to Ramadi road, skirt around the western side of Lake Habbaniya, cross the canal at Mujarra, and then to head north to Habbaniya, thus by-passing the Iraqi brigade at Ramadi.

To improve the dispersal of the aircraft of the Striking Force, the Levies and King's Own assisted with the preparation of a new emergency landing ground to the south-west of the cantonment, constructing defences and anti-aircraft posts. It was also essential that the garrison maintain control of the internal lines of communications within the 10-mile wide and four-mile deep pocket that it now held. The Iraqis were sending in army and police dressed in civilian clothes to report on the locations of posts and troop movements. To counter this, by 15 May, the Iraq Levies

A Lewis machine-gun on an anti-aircraft mounting manned by airmen of No 1 Company at RAF Habbaniya during the siege (Jackson, RAF Habbaniya Assn).

had placed five platoons from Suttaih Bridge near Ramadi to Canal Turn, just west of Falluja, with No 1 Armoured Car Company assisting the Levies in sweeps of known pockets of these infiltrators. Flight Lieutenant Ted Frith recalls the threats facing the armoured car crews:

> The frustrating thing is that we were being bombed by our own types of aircraft. Although the Iraqis had some Italian Savoias, they also had Gladiators that were more modern than ours. We could provide only limited AA fire to try and shoot them down. We hadn't got the mountings on the cars. We rigged up a lot of stuff from our funk holes but the Lewis guns we had overheated. They were a 14-18 model.
>
> We patrolled the perimeter, the bund, which was vital, as all they had to do was trip that and we'd have been flooded.[31]

No 1 Armoured Car Company had carried out 23 sorties during the first four days of the siege including recce patrols, protection of working parties repairing the airfield, AA duties, and protection of aircraft taking off and landing. Along with the AA duty, the tasks were to keep watch on enemy movements, ensure that the roads were clear of enemy parties and infiltrators, report on the levels of water in the flooded areas, and provide escorts to senior officers. To the east, the patrols covered Sin El Dhibban, Canal Turn and Hammonds Bund; and to the west the road to the BOAC Rest House, Rocky Point, and on to the Suttaih Bridge.

The lack of success of the Iraqi Army had become a concern for Rashid Ali, and he now appealed to the Germans and Italians for assistance. The Germans were however, preoccupied with the preparations for the invasion of Crete and the attack on the Soviet Union, having been content to broadcast messages of support to the Arab movement. The Italians, although established in Syria with their Armistice Commission, were also slow to act. More interest was shown once the *coup d'état* had occurred, but the problem was how to deliver practical assistance in the form of money, arms and air support to Iraq.

Political support arrived in the form of the ex-German Ambassador, Dr Fritz Grobba, who arrived in Baghdad on 11 May to set up the German Military Mission, On 13 May, the first trainload of weapons arrived in Mosul, having travelled via Turkey. Following German pressure, the Vichy Government in Syria agreed to allow the refuelling of German aircraft, moving to Iraq from the island of Rhodes, on Syrian airfields. The Iraqis were told to hold out for a fortnight until the bulk of the commitment of the *Luftwaffe* would arrive. Two German bomber units were to be sent. Nothing of substance had been achieved by 6 May when the investment of Habbaniya had been abandoned, although the next day, three German reconnaissance aircraft landed at Damascus. A small detachment then flew on to Mosul on 11 May. However, their arrival met with misfortune when the Iraqi anti-aircraft guns opened fire on the Heinkel of the mission leader, Major Axel von Blomberg, the son of Generalfeldmarschall Werner von Blomberg, as it came into land at Baghdad. He was hit in the throat and was killed. The initial force of 14 Messerschmitt Bf 110 fighters and seven Heinkel He 111 bombers had also been spotted by RAF reconnaissance aircraft on Syrian airfields on 12 May and the following day, German fighters and bombers were reported at airfields at Arbil and Mosul. With the discovery that the Axis aircraft were staging through Syria, the RAF were given permission to attack the Syrian airfields, although, at this time no formal declaration of hostilities with the

Vichy French had been made.

The siege of Habbaniya had been lifted by the efforts of its own garrison; however, much fighting remained. The Iraqi Air Force posed a limited threat, and their Army held the road to Baghdad, and positions around Ramadi. On the evening of 7 May, Air Vice-Marshal Smart had received a message of encouragement from the Prime Minister: "Your vigorous and splendid action has largely restored the situation. We are all watching the grand fight you are making. All possible aid will be sent. Keep it up."[32]

By 10 May, the Iraqi Air Force had been virtually eliminated, but on 13 May, three German He 111s bombed Habbaniya, and were faced by a single Gladiator. Unfortunately, the fighter was shot down within minutes, when caught in the crossfire between the three Heinkels. This single raid caused more damage than all the previous sorties by the Iraqi Air Force. The Heinkels returned on 22 May and the next few days after that. For those on the ground the raids were an uncomfortable experience. Corporal 'Mel' Melluish was an armourer on No 1 Armoured Car Company and had been selected for guard duties at the Station powerhouse. He continues:

> ...this was a 24 hour guard. The usual shifts prevailed of two hours on and four off. The power house was one of the most important locations on the camp, being the source of electricity and fresh water for the whole of the camp and including the civil cantonment which contained the work force of cleaners, labourers etc., and their families. Any interruption to this supply would make a catastrophic difference to the efficient running of the camp. A 250,000 gallon tank elevated to some 60 feet, stored the fresh water. A smaller tank of 50,000 gallons contained the fuel oil required by the four massive generators housed in a very large building situated in the centre of the compound.
>
> The guard as usual were armed with 303 rifles with a clip of five rounds of ammo. Coming from No 1 Armoured Car Company where men on guard were equipped with a 455 Webley revolver when doing guard in our own lines, I was allowed to be armed the same way. None of the arms were loaded; permission to load had to be given by the duty officer. Makes you think doesn't it? A serious incident in progress, men being killed, and I as guard had to get permission to load my gun if by some chance parachutists were to attack the compound. If, as guard, you were not to leave your post without permission, how was I able to contact even the NCO i/c guard let alone the officer?
>
> This particular day I was on the 10 am to midday shift, bored to tears, no-one to speak to, no-one to see, and no shelter from the blazing sun. Suddenly the air-raid siren sounded. What was I to do? Stay where I was, on guard, or get in the slit trench that had been dug a few feet away from the fuel tank. Looking up I could see three Heinkels flying serenely over the camp, as though choosing the choicest targets. Also visible were tracers being fired by the only defence, Lewis guns![33] Flying around at 10,000 feet, the enemy had no fear of them as the tracers were curling well below the planes. I also saw a Gladiator labouring to make altitude and join in the defence against the intruders. A couple of sticks of bombs fell on the camp and made up my mind for me. Into the trench I jumped...
>
> I could hear the distant crackle of machine-gun fire as the Gladiator came

The fort at Rutbah, Iraq, under attack from Bristol Blenheims of No 84 Squadron RAF, based at H4 landing ground in Transjordan. Casano's cars fought a successful action with an Iraqi Army column in the area around the fort (© IWM CM 822).

Matters worsened that evening, when the Arab Legionnaires saw a Very light arc into the sky to the east, which was answered from inside the fort. To Glubb's annoyance this turned out to be the Iraqi relief column for Rutbah. It arrived to a fanfare of cheers, wild rifle and machine-gun fire and Very lights from the defenders. The Arab Legion, with only light weapons, could do little to prevent the column entering the fort. Now outnumbered by two to one, isolated by some 300 miles from the main echelon of 'Habforce', and with no hope of storming the fort without more support, Glubb returned to H3. He continues:

> It was already daylight on May 10, 1941, when our column came once more in sight of H3. We were pleasantly surprised to find No 2 RAF Armoured

Car Company there. They had been sent up to our support, pending the arrival of the main column.

The imperturbable Casano was in command of the armoured cars. I explained the situation to him, the ineffectiveness of the bombing and the arrival of the relief column from Baghdad. Casano decided to go on to Rutbah and see the position for himself. I promised to signal H4 to send him air support, but he did not seem particularly interested.

Casano set off with his armoured cars on a reconnaissance to Rutbah early that morning, and went into action against a group of Iraqi vehicles located south-east of the fort. The RAF armoured cars had inflicted casualties on the Iraqi column, but had been unable to cross a deep wadi and unable to pursue them further returned to H3. Glubb continues:

It turned out that the relief column consisted of trucks armed with machine-guns. Half of them were under Fawzi el Qawukji, a man who had acquired a considerable reputation as a guerrilla leader in the Palestine rebellion, while the other half of the column consisted of Iraqi Desert Police.[40] Casano's armoured cars fought an action with them outside Rutbah fort the same day. The engagement did not appear decisive, but nevertheless, the relief column disappeared again to the east the same night, abandoning the garrison of Rutbah to its fate.

If the spirits of the garrison at Rutbah had been elated by the arrival of Fawzi's relief column, they were equally depressed by his retreat 24 hours later after the engagement with Casano's armoured cars. The same night the RAF tried a night bombing and succeeded in dropping some bombs into the fort. Later in the night of May 10-11, the garrison slipped out in the darkness. When day dawned on May 11, Casano, still skirmishing on the plains outside, noticed that the great gate of the fort was standing ajar.[41]

Two of the RAF armoured cars had been sent off from H3 that following morning and took possession of Rutbah. The fort had been sacked, with everything smashed and overturned. The building had been fouled and the smell of filth permeated the buildings, while the Nairn Transport building had been looted. The cars remained there until relieved by a detachment of the Arab Legion. The first obstacle on the road to Habbaniya had been eliminated and the RAF armoured cars returned to H3 where they linked up with 'Kingcol'. The column crossed the Iraqi frontier on 13 May and reached Rutbah 36 hours after it had been occupied.

With the Iraqi Army holding Ramadi, the column proceeded south-east to the southern tip of Lake Habbaniya, to Mujarra, where it could then head northwards to Habbaniya. Five hours after leaving Rutbah the column was attacked by Blenheims that were 'believed British', but fortunately the Fordsons were unharmed.[42] By nightfall, they were only 35 miles from Ramadi. The following day, three Fordson armoured cars moved off as advanced guard to the column and camped five miles south of Ramadi. The next day, 16 May, the Fordsons turned south and despite crossing a belt of sand, easily reached the bridge at Mujarra by that evening. This had been strengthened by the engineers in anticipation of the arrival of 'Kingcol'. Camped on the knoll beyond the trestle bridge over the canal was a company of the pith-helmeted soldiers of the King's Own; their Lewis guns mounted on AA tripods and pointing skywards, and a pair of Rolls-Royce armoured cars of No 1 Armoured Car Company.

Unfortunately, the rest of the column was not able to move as fast, and the other three Fordsons were still back with the supply lorries near Ramadi. The three-tonners of the column had encountered a large patch of soft sand and once having broken through the crust had battled to make any progress whatsoever. 'Kingcol' was in a vulnerable position and was soon subjected to air attacks from the *Luftwaffe*. The lorries had bogged axle deep, and could only be moved in short dashes after strenuous digging. With temperatures of 50°C in the shade this was almost intolerable, the advance being made during the hottest recorded weather of the last 25 years. To add further discomfort, a hot and dusty *khamsin* blew for long periods during the journey.

The first attack by two Bf 110s on the column had again caused no loss to the three armoured cars, though there were fatalities in the other parts of the column. The pace of 'Kingcol' since leaving Transjordan had been reasonable but the troubles in the sand belt had considerably slowed the momentum. By afternoon, it was clear that the path chosen could not be followed, and the force had to withdraw exhausted and disappointed. A far easier route to the south was reconnoitred by the Arab Legion and despite being strafed again by two or three Bf 110s of the *Luftwaffe*, by the end of the next day, the remainder of 'Kingcol' had reached Mujarra.

All three sections of No 1 Armoured Car Company had been travelling regularly to Mujarra over the last week, escorting the King's Own and their supply lorries. On one occasion three Rolls-Royce armoured cars of No 3 Section, under the command of Flight Lieutenant Pyne, and accompanied by the Company Commander, Wing Commander M. Lowe, escorted two Army lorries to Mujarra. While there, they found an abandoned German Messerschmitt Bf 110, which they salvaged and which Wing Commander Lowe then flew back to Habbaniya. LAC Ken Basham recalls assisting with the recovery of a German aircraft:

> After three days the enemy began to retreat towards Baghdad and breached the Euphrates behind them. This flooded the main road for about 10 days, being monitored each day by RRAC *Jackal*, the Duty Car... In this period the alarm sounded when a pilot flying up from the south and avoiding Baghdad, spotted a plane down on the desert. Having noted its position we took a compass course across the desert and arrived to find a Bf 110 that had made a landing with its 'undercart' up, this was about 25 May, the plane having left the Augsburg Messerschmitt works on 24 April 1941. The following day, with a team from the workshops, we returned to the scene and after digging to tracks down, and in line with the wheels, they were lowered by hand and the aircraft pulled to a position where it could be towed back to camp, a rather tricky job as we had to negotiate a narrow defile from the plateau down the road and across the 'drome to workshops. Here it was stripped and serviced and the props straightened and eventually flown to a Flying Training School in Rhodesia.

Number 3 Section had also taken Colonel Roberts to the Mujarra crossing in anticipation of the arrival of the column on 15 May but had been disappointed to learn of the difficulties with the supply lorries and the withdrawal of the column. Three Rolls-Royce armoured cars and a Rolls-Royce wireless tender of No 3 Section, under the command of Flight Lieutenant Pyne, then proceeded north-west from Mujarra to a location two miles west of Ramadi two days later, and awaited the arrival of the remainder of the column. The enemy were not inactive and the cars were sniped at and later shelled as they waited.

As a consequence of the attack by the Heinkels on 16 May, one section was engaged on anti-aircraft duties back on the aerodrome. The mode of operation was somewhat stressful, as between two and six Rolls-Royce armoured cars from No 2 Section were ordered to take up positions amongst the dispersed aircraft, and then maintain a constant watch from dawn until 1930 hours. This was carried out every day for the next seven days, during which the cantonment was attacked six times. However, the attacks were concentrated on buildings in the cantonment rather than the airfield, and few targets presented themselves. When the *Luftwaffe* failed subsequently to appear, it was decided that the threat had receded and the Section was assigned to other tasks.

By Sunday 18 May, 'Kingcol' had arrived at Habbaniya in its entirety, and thus the lifting of the siege from the west had been achieved. A further welcome arrival was a detachment of the 2/4th Gurkha Rifles, of 20th Indian Brigade, which had been flown up from Shaibah. Their arrival had coincided with that of a new Air Commander, Air Vice-Marshal John D'Albiac.[43] He had replaced Air Vice-Marshal Smart when he had been injured in a road accident caused by a bomb blast and, along with his wife and daughter, was evacuated by air to Basra.[44] Major-General Clark, of 'Habforce' was also flown up from H4. The arrival of the force from Palestine had not only provided the garrison with much needed supplies, but the strength had now doubled, and it possessed field, anti-aircraft and anti-tank artillery. The remainder of 'Habforce' arrived over the next week and a half.

Major-General Clark and Air Vice-Marshal D'Albiac arrived to find that the Habbaniya garrison had not been idly awaiting the arrival of the column but, under

Looking south towards the bridge over the Euphrates River at Falluja (Rutter, RAFACA).

Colonel Roberts, had been actively planning for an attack on Falluja, as a preliminary move to the advance on Baghdad. The arrival of 'Kingcol' would help facilitate these plans. Falluja, 15 miles from Habbaniya, was the key to Baghdad, and was important because it possessed a long steel girder bridge over the 300 yards wide Euphrates. It was still intact, but if destroyed, the advance would be seriously hindered. The plan was therefore, to send out columns to make a three pronged attack to the north and south to encircle the town. Extensive flooding caused by the Iraqis blowing the bunds, had limited the options for manoeuvre; however, the garrison would make use of its engineering expertise and aircraft to overcome these difficulties. About a thousand Iraqi troops were thought to be in Falluja, along with a large civilian population.[45]

Four of the columns moved out on the night of 18/19 May to approach Falluja by road from the north, west and south (Map 22, p. 297). A fifth was landed by air two miles to the east of the town and prior to the opening of the ground attack the following day. The columns were composed as follows:

'G' Column, with No 1 (Assyrian) Company, Iraq Levies, under the command of Captain Alistair Graham, and supported by a troop of six 18/25-pdrs of 237 Battery RA, would approach Falluja from the south-west by crossing the gap in Hammonds Bund;

'A' Column, with No 2 (Assyrian) Company, Iraq Levies, under the command of Captain Anderson, would cross the Euphrates at Sin el Dhibban and advanced along the north bank of the river towards Falluja;

'S' Column, with a detachment of 2/4th Gurkha Rifles, under command of Major Strictland, and one troop of Habbaniya artillery with five captured Iraqi 3.7-inch howitzers, and mule transport, would follow up the advance of 'A' Column;

'V' Column, Lieutenant Rees with 'C' Company, 1st Battalion, The King's Own Royal Regiment were to be flown to a landing ground two miles to the north-west of Falluja and would then move on Falluja from the north-east;

'L' Column, under the command of Flight Lieutenant David Hellard, with No 1 Section, No 1 Armoured Car Company, and a platoon of the King's Own would cross the Euphrates behind 'S' Column, advance north along the Burma Bund and then east to the Notchfall Regulator to support 'V' Column.[46]

As a preliminary to the operation, the two telephone lines from Baghdad to Falluja were cut by two Audax aircraft from Habbaniya. One flew though the wires at several points, and the other, by use of pliers held by the pilot, who climbed onto the top wing of his landed plane, while the gunner took to the poles with an axe. Meanwhile, 57 aircraft of the Habbaniya Air Striking Force bombed the Iraqi positions around Falluja. Leaflets were also dropped on the town calling on the garrison to surrender, to which there was no response.

At dawn on 19 May, the infantrymen of 'V' Column were safely landed to the north of Falluja in two Valentias and four Bombay troop carriers. They quickly disembarked and cut the road to Baghdad to prevent any Iraqi reinforcements from reaching Falluja. 'G' Column moved along the south bank of the Euphrates, down to the Canal Turn and on to Hammonds Bund. They then crossed the three-quarter mile wide break that the Iraqis had blown in the bund. Some on an improvised ferry,

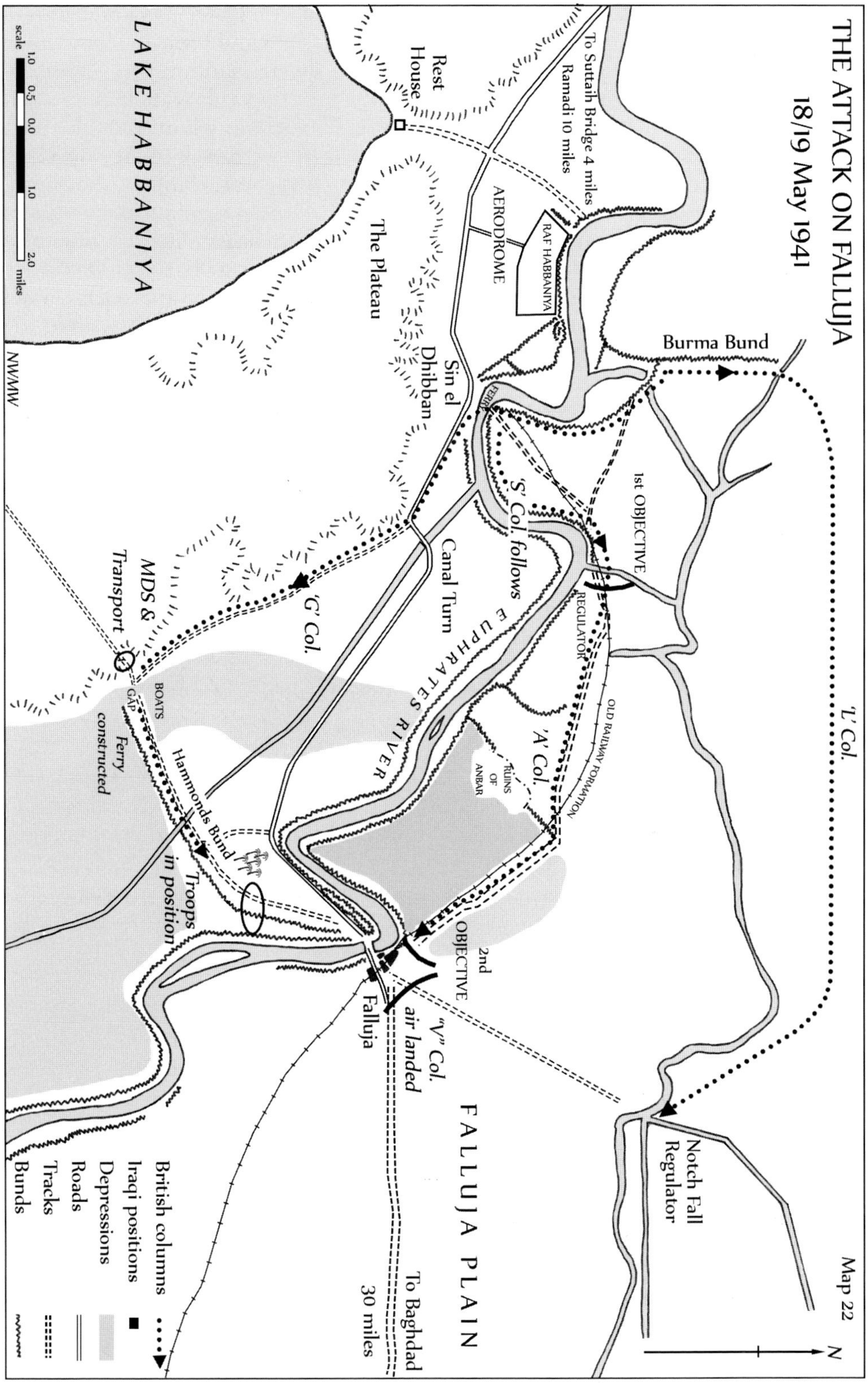
THE ATTACK ON FALLUJA
18/19 May 1941
Map 22
Burma Bund
'L' Col.
Notch Fall Regulator
To Suttaih Bridge 4 miles
Ramadi 10 miles
Rest House
AERODROME
RAF HABBANIYA
The Plateau
LAKE HABBANIYA
Sin el Dhibban
FERRY
1st OBJECTIVE
'S' Col. follows
Canal Turn
REGULATOR
'G' Col.
EUPHRATES RIVER
OLD RAILWAY FORMATION
'A' Col.
RUINS OF ANBAR
MDS & Transport
BOATS GAP
Ferry constructed
Hammonds Bund
Troops in position
2nd OBJECTIVE
Falluja
"V" Col. air landed
FALLUJA PLAIN
To Baghdad
30 miles
British columns
Iraqi positions
Depressions
Roads
Tracks
Bunds
scale 1.0 0.5 0.0 1.0 2.0 miles
N

others waded through the flood-water pushing equipment on rafts made from oil-drums, or some on an assortment of pleasure boats gathered from Lake Habbaniya.

Meanwhile, the two northern columns crossed the swiftly flowing river at Sin el Dhibban, on a flying bridge made up of pontoons working on wire hawsers that had been constructed by a detachment of Queen Victoria's Own Madras Sappers and Miners, which had been flown up from Basra. 'A' Column then set out along the north bank of the river. 'L' Column had the furthest to travel and had set off at 1900 hours the previous evening. Number 1 Section, with Flight Lieutenant Hellard, the six Rolls-Royce armoured cars and two Rolls-Royce wireless tenders, accompanied by six other vehicles, crossed the Euphrates at Sin el Dhibban. The dilapidated state of many of the roads and bridges and the soft going slowed the move and it wasn't until 0430 hours the next morning that the last car was ferried across the Euphrates. The column then completed a large hook across the high ground to the north, and east and pushed on to Notchfall, which was reached three and a half hours later. The RAF armoured cars were, however, unable to go any further, owing to the floods, so the accompanying troops went on ahead to reinforce the King's Own of 'V' Column. Albeit from a distance, the cars provided flank protection to the Column as it moved down to Falluja. Early on 20 May, however, while the section was returning to Burma Bund it came under attack from four Bf 110s that came in at low level, damaging some of the vehicles and wounding one airman.

'A' Column with mule transport had made heavy work of their advance through the floodwaters, but Falluja was now threatened by columns closing in from all sides. Support by the RAF had been significant with ten tons of bombs dropped in 134 sorties from before dawn. In mid-afternoon, 'G' Column reported back that they were within 50 yards of the iron bridge which spanned the Euphrates. Following a furious bombing attack by the RAF, and under the fire support from the six 18/25-pdrs of 237 Battery, Captain Graham and his Assyrian Levies rushed across the open boggy ground and captured the bridge, intact and without incurring a single casualty. The columns moved into the town and the Levies and King's Own then set about improving the defences of the town while others, assisted by the now numerous numbers of Iraqi prisoners, worked feverishly on the crossing at Hammonds Bund.

To everyone's surprise, the Iraqi Army launched a major counter-attack on Falluja two days later, intending to destroy the bridge. Two companies of the King's Own and the Levies were in Falluja but the position was poorly prepared for a defensive action and the outcome was finely balanced for a time. Fiat light tanks rumbled up the road before dawn and by daylight, the enemy had gained ground inside the town. The position was soon restored, in the words of the AOC Iraq, by 'a stout-hearted counter attack' by the Iraqi Levies, which inflicted heavy casualties on the enemy. A second attack looked like succeeding, but for the timely arrival of Brigadier Joe Kingstone with 'C' Squadron of the Household Cavalry Regiment and two companies of the 1st Essex Regiment, from 'Kingcol', who helped repel the attackers. Then the Iraqi reinforcements moving up the Baghdad road were attacked from the air. The enemy suffered heavy casualties and withdrew leaving six light tanks and 300 prisoners. Casualties to the Levies amounted to seven killed and 11 wounded, while the King's Own had lost one officer and 16 other ranks killed and four officers and 25 other ranks wounded. Falluja was secured and the advance on Baghdad could begin.

While 'Kingcol' focussed on the advance to Baghdad, a concentration of Iraqi troops still remained at Ramadi. Late on 24 May, Flight Lieutenant Alan Douglas took two Fordsons and a troop from 'B' Squadron of the Household Cavalry towards Ramadi. Their task was to watch the village and report on the effects of a bombing raid planned for the next morning and to stop any Iraqis that might attempt to escape. At dawn the following morning, the Household Cavalry came under sniper fire from the hills east of the town and were forced to withdraw under the covering fire of the RAF armoured cars. The Iraqis did not let up, and at mid-morning a force of around 100 Iraqi irregulars belonging to Fawzi el Qawukji, began to heavily snipe the Household Cavalry positions. Following this they put in an attack on the troopers' positions and they were forced back. Regrettably, in covering the withdrawal, the two armoured cars became stuck in soft sand. The crews came under heavy fire, suffering three minor casualties, and despite attempts to recover the cars, they were forced to abandon them, and fight a dismounted action back to the Household Cavalry positions. Another Troop, accompanied by an RAF tender, was sent out to join them. One of the cars was recovered early the following morning, but the other was taken by the Iraqi Army. Sadly, on the return journey to Habbaniya the column was machine-gunned by an RAF Gladiator and one of the troopers was killed.[47]

Platoons of the Iraq Levies were placed at various points to the east of Ramadi. Number 1 Armoured Car Company escorted Royal Artillery to positions closer to the town, where they were sniped at, and on one occasion No 2 Section, under Flight Lieutenant Waters, provided covering fire to an infantry attack at Suttaih Bridge and later joined in with the artillery to pour fire on the Iraqi positions. The Company also sent regular patrols to the Suttaih Bridge to watch the Ramadi garrison which still posed a threat to Habbaniya while the operations around Falluja and towards Baghdad were underway.

A first step in the advance had been made on 23 May, when Flight Lieutenant David Hellard of No 1 Section, with two Rolls-Royce armoured cars and a Rolls-Royce wireless tender, was ordered to escort eight trucks and two home-made armoured cars of the Arab Legion and a Royal Engineers Officer, to Samarra. The orders were to break up the Mosul-Baghdad railway line. The raiding party was ferried over the Euphrates, and then travelled throughout a burning hot day over bare desert. The journey was not without incident, as the Rolls-Royce Wireless Tender *Mercury* ran a 'big end' and RRAC *Diana* ran off the road on a bend and became stuck fast in mud. The engine and other important parts were salvaged, but the armour and chassis were left. RRAC *Jackal* and RRWT *Pathfinder* were sent out as replacements. The patrol concealed themselves in a hollow amongst eight-foot high bushes; Iraqi aircraft passed over at intervals, but were more intent on attacking Habbaniya. The patrol then moved at sunset towards a point on the railway line about six miles south of Samarra. David Hellard and the Sapper officer went forward to the railway line but were unable to find a bridge worth blowing up and, as explosives were scarce, they simply disconnected and removed a section of rails (Map 23, p. 300).

The effect of this raid may not have, at the time, seemed to have been of great consequence; however Glubb noted later that the Iraqis had been fully prepared for an advance from Falluja towards Baghdad. They had been surprised by the reports of a British force on the Tigris near the railway. Rashid Ali had also been awaiting the arrival in Baghdad of trainloads of French munitions, sent from Syria via Mosul. This limited cutting of the railway by a small raiding party had destroyed this hope.[48]

The following morning the party moved back towards Habbaniya, but weren't yet finished. Slightly frustrated that they hadn't caused more havoc, it was decided

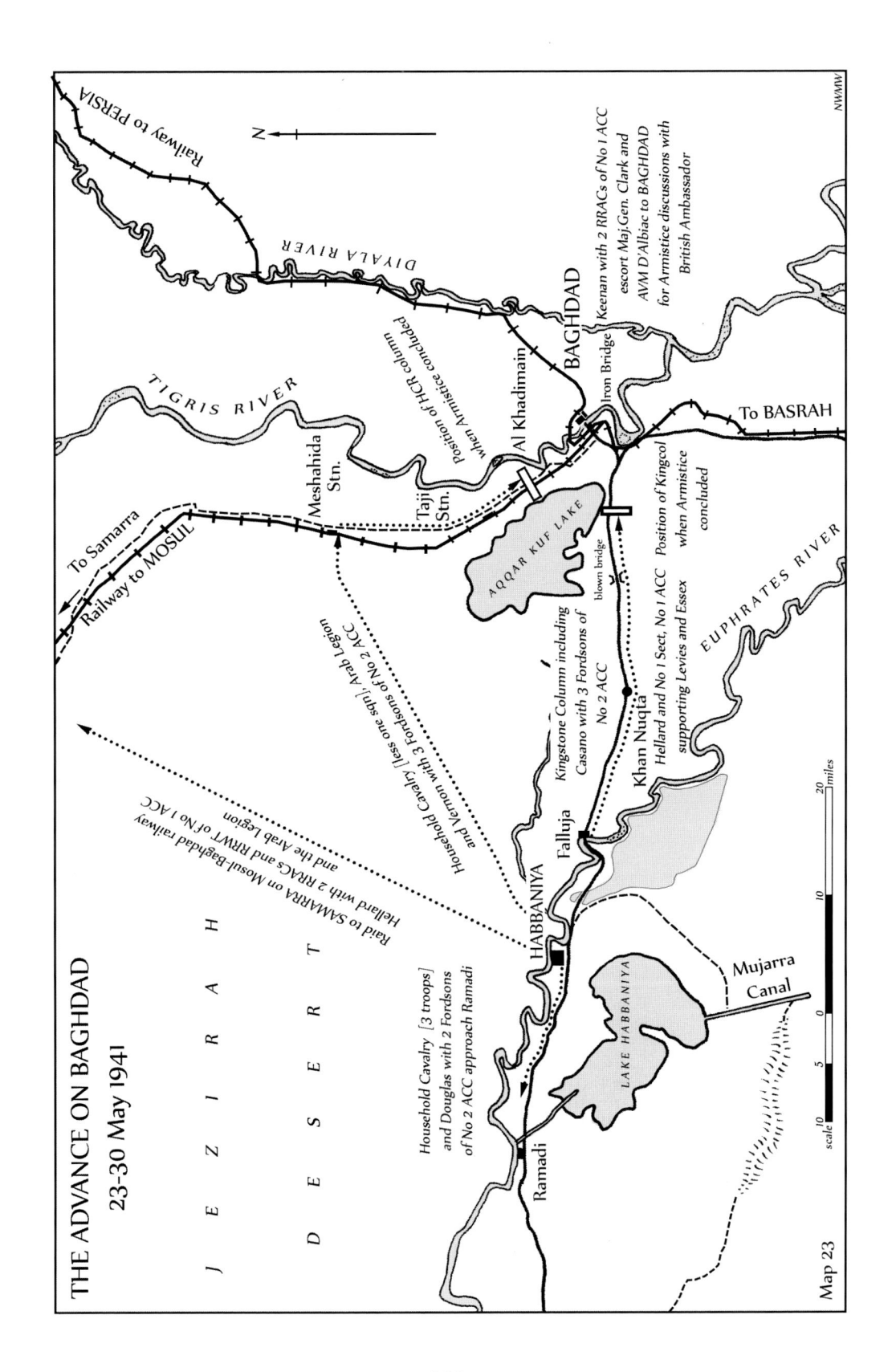

THE ADVANCE ON BAGHDAD
23–30 May 1941

Map 23

to set up an ambush position on the route followed by the supply columns to Ramadi. They were soon rewarded by the appearance of two Iraqi trucks and after a short pursuit they were halted. An officer and four Iraqi other ranks who were out attempting to salvage derelict lorries were taken prisoner.[49]

The fear of a German airborne attack still prevailed, and the advance on Baghdad had to be implemented as soon as possible, despite the force only possessing 1500 men as against the 20,000 of the Iraqi Army. For the move on Baghdad, General Clark decided on two lines of advance. He wished to avoid the Holy City of Karbala, and the resentment that the presence of his forces might cause, so a southern route was unacceptable. The ease with which the RAF armoured cars and Arab Legion had reached the railway line convinced him that a northern advance was a feasible option. A column led by Brigadier Joe Kingstone was ordered to push on up the main Baghdad road, while a second column, under Lieutenant-Colonel Andrew Ferguson, commanding the Household Cavalry Regiment, was sent on a path to the north to reach the Baghdad-Mosul railway and then to advance into Baghdad from the north-west.

The Northern Column consisted of the Household Cavalry Regiment, less 'C' Squadron, with one troop of 237 Battery under command, three Fordson armoured cars of No 2 Company, under the command of Flight Lieutenant Vernon, the Arab Legion, a detachment of a Field Troop RE, and an ambulance, and was ferried across the Euphrates on the evening of 27 May. Attempts had been made to repair the breach in Hammonds Bund, but had to be abandoned. The Southern Column therefore, under the command of Brigadier Joe Kingstone, comprising the rest of 'Kingcol'; two companies of the Essex, 'C' Squadron, the Household Cavalry Regiment, a troop of 237 Battery, and three RAF armoured cars under Casano, all had to be ferried across the gap on makeshift rafts and barges.

Ferguson's column set off early on 28 May and safely reached the railway line at Meshashida without incident. Here, the Arab Legion came under fire from the railway station and while they occupied the enemy, the main part of the column

Indian Sappers and Miners operate the ferry transporting a Fordson of No 2 Armoured Car Company across the Euphrates River (Smiley).

crossed the railway and headed south. At Taji railway station, the RAF armoured cars came under fire from Iraqi armoured cars and two tanks near the station but after exchanging fire the enemy, withdrew. The Household Cavalry came under fire three miles down the road from Iraqi armoured cars. The lead troop dismounted and advanced along the railway embankment under the covering fire of machine-guns of the RAF armoured cars. Two hundred yards short of the fort that protected Taji station, the enemy ceased firing and as the Troop reached the station made a quick getaway in several cars.

The Column proceeded southward, but the Iraqis had set up a number of water obstacles by filling irrigation ditches, flooding the nearby desert, and digging wide trenches across their path. These were covered by machine-guns and the RAF armoured cars were constantly being sniped at and shelled. The Northern Column, with Vernon's detachment, was finally stopped by a tank ditch 15 miles from Baghdad. An attempt was made by the Household Cavalry to take the next town, Al Khadimain, but the position was strongly held, possibly because it is one of the holiest sites of Shia Islam, and no further progress was possible. But for a few hours delay, the column might have been able to enter Baghdad, but the Iraqis had sent in a large force to oppose them and the column advance was halted.

Meanwhile, the Southern column, with only two steel barges to move the armoured cars, 18/25-pdrs and 3-tonners across the gap, had taken two nights to assemble on the eastern side of the break in the bund. At dawn on 28 May, the column passed through the wire that surrounded Falluja and fanned out into the desert plain. Squadron Leader Casano's three armoured cars took the lead, followed by the Household Cavalry and then the Essex. The armoured cars proceeded across the Falluja Plain, being continuously shot at from dawn until sunset. The cars encountered a company of the Iraqi Army, halfway between Falluja and Baghdad, but this was settled quickly when the accompanying 18/25-pdr of 237 Battery sent a few rounds into the position. The Brigade HQ entered the enemy camp, which had been rapidly vacated, to find a delicious smell which led to the discovery of breakfast still on the cooker. Progress slowed as the column moved from the desert to the cultivated area closer to Baghdad. The area had been flooded and the cars came up against many blown irrigation canals and other tank obstacles, and only 10 miles was made during that day.[50]

On 29 May, the column reached the Abu Ghuraib canal, only 14 miles from Baghdad. The bridge over the canal had been demolished and as two of the RAF armoured cars approached it, they came under heavy fire. Flight Lieutenant Alan Douglas and the crew of the second armoured car were all wounded and the car was forced to withdraw. Captain Somerset de Chair describes the action:

> There was good deal of machine gun fire going on along the canal where it cut the road about a mile ahead of us; and presently one of the armoured cars came back with a man [Douglas] standing up in the conning tower, with blood all over his white shirt. Joe [Brigadier Kingstone] spoke to him, and the armoured car went in search of the field ambulance section…[51]

The engineers were set to work and the armoured cars waited for the whole day while the bridge was repaired. At midday on 30 May, 'C' Squadron of the Household Cavalry and two of the RAF armoured cars took up the advance, and although the domes and minarets of Baghdad could now be seen, they were only able to move three miles before they were again held up by enemy fire. The Household Cavalry deployed from their trucks along each side of the road. Another tank obstacle was encountered and the cars were machine-gunned and heavily shelled. De Chair continues:

> Between us and Baghdad stretched three miles of flat open space, cultivated ground, intersected by many dykes, and crossed by the curving tarmac road, to the left of which the ground was flooded. I looked through my binoculars… [at] the telegraph wires which lined the road. I could see along this to where Casano's armoured car was driving as far as it could go. It appeared to have reached some obstacle and was turning round. As it did so the sharp chatter of machine-gun fire came across the open ground. 'C' Squadron of the Household Cavalry were now in front and were dismounting from their trucks just below us and moving down into the dykes to cross the open ground.[52]

Casano continued to demonstrate his calibre as a leader of the armoured cars. As the advance guard for the Column, No 2 Company had often been moving along a single confined and often flooded road. On a number of occasions, he and the other

Squadron Leader 'Cass' Casano (in the turret) waits outside Baghdad as the campaign reaches its successful conclusion (© IWM CM 923).

car commanders had brought their cars into close and hazardous contact with the enemy.

'Kingcol' had been halted yet again. Although the lines of communications of 'Kingcol' were tenuous, particularly with all supplies having to come across the break at Hammonds Bund, and the force was outnumbered, the two columns had created the impression that a large force had surrounded Baghdad. An interpreter found a telephone line to Baghdad that was in working order and this was used to spread alarm and despondency with exaggerated stories of the columns' size. Ferguson's Northern Column, despite the small size, had cut the road and railway to Mosul and this had caused great anxiety to Rashid Ali. Iraqi communications' buzzed with the news that the British were advancing on Baghdad with 50 tanks, when in fact it could only have been the three Fordsons of Casano's detachment or the Quads of the Royal Artillery.

In the meantime, No 1 Armoured Car Company had not been idle, and had also been running reconnaissances and supply escorts to Al Khadimain and Abu Ghuraib. Flight Lieutenant Hellard's Section was called out to a location a few miles southeast of Falluja on 28 May, to assist the Levies and the Essex to overcome an Iraqi battalion that had dug-in at the regulator on the Abu Ghuraib. Artillery fire, bombing by aircraft and dropping of leaflets calling on them to surrender had all failed. The two Rolls-Royce armoured cars made three attacks, suffering one minor casualty and seven punctures, and for RRAC *Jackal*, a punctured radiator, and despite their efforts the attack had to be called off and the armoured cars and Levies were forced to withdraw, without having overcome the position.

On 30 May, a signal was received from the British Embassy in Baghdad that Rashid Ali and his supporters had fled into Persia. A truce was called and two Rolls-Royce armoured cars of No 1 Armoured Car Company, under the command of Flying Officer Keenan, escorted Major-General Clark and Air Vice-Marshal D'Albiac, from Habbaniya to the Iron Bridge near Baghdad, where with Glubb Pasha, and Sir Kinahan Cornwallis, the British Ambassador, the Armistice terms were drafted and Cornwallis returned to Baghdad to present them to the Iraqi provisional administration.[53]

The agreement was lenient so that friendly government relations could be re-established rapidly. Hostilities ceased and the Iraqi Army returned to their peacetime stations. At 1900 hours, it was announced that an Armistice had been declared, although this was followed by rioting and looting in Baghdad by the local populace. 'C' Squadron of the Household Cavalry moved the last few miles into Baghdad, while Casano and the crews of his three cars formed a camp on the roadside 10 miles from the city. The Northern Column with Vernon's detachment were ordered to return by the way they had come back to Habbaniya,

While the garrison at Habbaniya had been fighting for its survival, No 4 Section of No 1 Armoured Car Company, stationed at Shaibah, had also been fully occupied with their own war, protecting RAF facilities and supporting Army operations. The first signs of trouble had become apparent during April, when the Section patrols reported increasing troop train movements by the Iraqi Army. On 4 April, as Rashid Ali took power, the Section activated the Shaibah Defence Scheme. An armoured car was placed at each of the two main gates of the cantonment as reinforcement to the Arab Company of the Iraqi Levies. At the same time, patrols were sent out to ensure the track to Zubair, the nearest town to Shaibah, was clear of any Iraqi troops or civilians.

On 1 May, British civilian evacuees had begun arriving at Shaibah from Baghdad by air and were then conveyed in the Section tenders to the port where they were embarked upon HMT *Nevasa*. Basra was also home to a large British civilian population and it was essential that they also be evacuated. Flying Officer Ernest 'Henry' Ford of No 4 Section had been serving in the Company since November 1938, and was assigned to the task:

> We had the responsibility of rounding up all the British civilians in the city and taking them into safe custody. I was told to go and ensure all the Europeans were okay. Having been in Shaibah all those years I knew where they all were as I used to go and visit them, so I went round to the bank managers, exporters… We brought them all into the safety of the camp. It was too dangerous for them to return, so they were shipped home.[54]

With Habbaniya besieged, the British and Indian forces in southern Iraq took their first offensive action against the Iraqi military and police units in Basra. They were to secure the communications and port facilities that were essential if the remainder of the 10th Indian Division was to disembark. No major operations had been possible in the first instance, as there were not enough troops and they were only able to hold the airfields and the power station at Margil. The 21st Indian Brigade was due to arrive on 8 May, and the 2/7th Gurkha Rifles of 20th Indian Brigade were given the task of securing Ashar, the port area of Basra. At 0200 hours, on 7 May, two companies moved against the town, along the river bank from the north, to secure the wharf. The other two companies moved from Margil, and entered the town from the west with orders to occupy the power station, police station, telegraph office and banks.

One half of No 4 Section had remained at Shaibah and patrolled the airfield perimeter, while the other sub-section of three cars, under the command of Flying Officer 'Henry' Ford, were attached to 20th Indian Brigade and were to support the Gurkhas. Although the Iraqi population and authorities would be hostile to this move, the force been told to expect little resistance. This optimism proved unfounded and it was met by heavy fire. By 0415 hours, one armoured car with the Gurkhas in support was in position at Al Hamra corner. Ford describes the task:

Number 4 Section, No 1 Company, at RAF Shaibah, March 1941, with HMACs Cleopatra, Jaguar and Curlew. Front row, left to right, (starting sixth from left): Sgt Rutter, FS Paige, Fg Off E.L. Ford, Flt Lt R.J. Payne (OC No 4 Sect), Plt Off O.R. Pilsworth (killed in air accident, 25 June 1941), Sgt Robson. LAC Hawkins is third row back, third from left (RAFACA).

I was detached by the No 4 Section commanding officer and told to report to the Brigade Commander and take my instructions from him. We went in having laid down the battle plan. The Brigadier told me where he wanted my armoured cars positioned and what role he wanted me to play. We had a backing role to the Gurkhas. We went in at dawn and came up against much stiffer opposition than we had thought… Actually the Arabs put up a very good fight, I was quite surprised really, by the ferocity of their resistance and I think the Brigadier as well. I thought it would be just a walkover.

Soon after occupying the post, an Iraqi police car tried to rush them and the armoured car and Gurkhas came under heavy and concentrated machine-gun and rifle fire from the police car, the surrounding buildings, and from all sides. LAC Dennis Hawkins describes what happened next:

I remember we were called out to go to assist two of our vehicles that were caught in cross-fire in the centre of Basra. One of these vehicles had a bullet enter the drivers small windshield slit, this went round and round inside the turret and not one person was injured. One car got caught in the crossfire from the rooftops and suffered punctured tyres.

We'd been there to bring in the Gurkhas. They were straight into it. We saw the Gurkhas whip the heads off the Arab gunners at the top of the building, with their kukris. We all gave our thanks to the wonderful Gurkhas who climbed the buildings. They silenced these guns to get those cars out…[55]

This provided some relief and the armoured car crew were then able to change two punctured tyres, albeit under sniper fire, and made temporary repairs to the shattered radiator with chewing gum.

By the end of the day, the Gurkhas were holding the western side of the town and business quarter, but the bazaar was still in Iraqi hands, and resistance was strong. Under threat of artillery bombardment by General Fraser the sniping ceased and the Gurkhas and RAF armoured cars were sent in to test the opposition.[56] Flying Officer Ford continues:

We fought from dawn till about midday, and I was then told by the Brigadier to go out and take the Iraqi Police Post. Of course, the Iraqi Police were just as powerful as the Iraqi Army. They played a very aggressive role during the campaign. They were very courageous too.

I decided to take just two armoured cars and leave the other in reserve. It was rather sticky and they had an enormous armoury in there. I just went in and demanded that they hand over the entire armoury. They tried to argue with me that they would have to phone Headquarters in Baghdad and I said 'No I'm not having that at all'. I ordered my men in and we kept them covered with guns, took all their armament away, put it on the back of the armoured cars and took one of the Iraqis as a prisoner for interrogation. I left the rest there.

I'd gone round and taken the Police Station with all the arms and ammunition and prisoners back to Divisional Headquarters and then after that the Gurkhas were stationed at strategic points, such as the bridges all over the city, and I'd placed my armoured cars at strategic points as well.[57]

Early on 8 May, the first battalions of the 21st Brigade were landed at the port area of Ashar, doubling the force available for offensive action. The Division and the two brigades then set about consolidating the positions around Basra. The 20th Brigade went to Shaibah and the 21st to Basra. They then dealt with those remaining pockets of resistance and Iraqi units that might have been moved north to attack Habbaniya. A few days later, the Section assisted the 3/11th Sikhs and 2/10th Gurkha Rifles to secure Safwan and Jebel Sanam on the southern border with Kuwait.

On 16 May, Major-General William Slim took command of 10th Indian Division after Major-General W.A.K. Fraser fell ill.[58] Slim was ordered to advance on Baghdad as soon as possible. Subsequently, on 27 May, the 20th Indian Brigade moved against Jalibah, Tel el Lahm and Ur Junction, about 80 miles north. Number 4 Section, under the command of Flight Lieutenant R.J. Payne, with seven Rolls-Royce armoured cars, two Fordson tenders, and two wireless tenders, set off as the advanced party to the brigade (Map 9, p. 97).

Jalibah station was found to be unoccupied, but the following morning as the Section approached Ur Junction they came under fire. In a rather confused skirmish, the RAF armoured cars returned fire and then sighted several white flags being flown from post. The airmen then approached the Iraqi positions under their own white flag but were fired upon and forced to retire. It seemed that the Iraqi civilians in the station wished to surrender but not the soldiers and police. The arrival of the Brigade artillery regiment with their field guns settled the issue and the Iraqis withdrew.

The following day, No 4 Section continued the move up the Basra to Baghdad railway and was involved in a number of skirmishes. Flying Officer Ford describes one such action:

> I was told by General Slim to recce, to see what the position was for the Gurkhas... because they wanted to secure the railway of course. So I took three armoured cars, and we came in at various angles to the railway and took them by surprise. But I was also taken by surprise, because I thought there would be quite a contingent of Iraqis there. Possibly with some German backing, but as it happened there were three men who'd probably seen or heard our approach and suddenly shot out of the Station and jumped into an open wagon with a machine-gun in the back. [They] started blazing away at us and we blazed away back. We hit them and they went up in smoke. All killed.
>
> I naturally 'recced' on a few miles further ... over the hill. To see if there were enemy forces that I hadn't noticed, but we returned to the Army Headquarters and reported to General Slim that [the station] was secured and all was okay.
>
> From there we proceeded north and the next skirmish we had was at Diwaniyah. And as I remember it, we were proceeding across the desert, and there was a road running north to the right of us ... It had a screening for the enemy and General Slim wanted us to see exactly what was there ... [and] to see what enemy forces the Gurkhas were going to be up against.
>
> I, first of all, advanced in a line abreast, a straightforward advance. Of course you get all this mirage in the desert, and it was difficult to see what you were up against. We approached the line of the enemy, who were hiding

in a palm tree plantation, whereas we were in the open. I suddenly came under very heavy gunfire. My car had its Vickers gun blown clean out. The bullets grazed down my shoulder at the back, but apart from that the crew were okay.

Some of the other armoured cars were coming into trouble so I immediately gave a vee-formation signal ... they would cut back, and so we could form a spearhead. But the others were also lying back so I could bring them up as a reserve and in-fold the arrowhead ... If the leading armoured cars got into trouble then I could invert the vee and come back. This we had to do, because we were up against superior forces. We came under withering fire from some tanks. Of course the Iraqis themselves were equipped with Bren guns, which we had none of, at the time. All we had was the Vickers water-cooled, and the Lewis gun on the back. Both very old guns and liable to stoppages, which we had to clear.

I realised the position was hopeless so I gave the order for my cars to retreat. All my cars were in trouble ... The Vickers were overheating and jamming. I was forced to give the order to retreat, but not before I had inverted the vee and I brought the cars up. We'd managed to establish that there was a pretty strong enemy force, with a few tanks, along this road. Of course we hadn't come against tanks before, and this caused a bit of dithering in the ranks, because there were thought to be no tanks out there.

I went back and reported to General Slim and told him what we were up against ... He actually left them alone and progressed north, and just ignored the forces that were lying there. I believe he left behind a company of Gurkhas to contain them in case they tried to come through and cut off his supply lines.

On 30 May, 25th Indian Brigade arrived from India and landed at Basra, thus completing the order of battle of 10th Indian Division. With the signing of the Armistice, 20th Indian Brigade moved north to Baghdad on 10 June and relieved 'Habforce' and 'Kingcol' from further tasks in Iraq. The Iraqi forces never made a significant stand but the advance from Basra had been very slow due to extensive flooding, the demolitions of essential railway installations and the removal of hundreds of sleepers by the retreating Iraqis.

Twentieth Indian Brigade then relieved the remainder of 'Habforce' from its responsibilities at Mosul, Kirkuk, Haditha and Rutbah. Number 4 Section remained at Ur Junction until mid-June when it returned to Shaibah. It had been decided, however, that the entire Company should be concentrated at RAF Habbaniya, and so on 5 July 1941, No 4 Section left Shaibah.

If the revolt in Iraq had been allowed to succeed it would have placed the British position in the Middle East in extreme jeopardy. The Axis would have gained a strong foothold and the situation for the British presence may have become irretrievable. Wavell's resources were already tightly stretched, and he was initially unable, and subsequently unwilling, to commit sizeable forces to the struggle. Three factors, however, led to the ultimate success of the campaign. The first was the determination and gallant defence by the garrison at RAF Habbaniya. They immediately took the offensive, both in the air and on the ground, and seized the initiative from the enemy. The second was the arrival of reinforcements in the form of 10th Indian Division to Basra and 'Kingcol' to Habbaniya. The latter allowed the momentum that had been generated by the attack on Falluja to carry the offensive on to Baghdad. The third factor was the lack of clear objectives, indecisiveness and poor intelligence information of Rashid Ali and his supporters.

How close run was the campaign, is best summed up in both the words of a humble Aircraftman of No 1 Armoured Car Company, Charles Spybey:

> The most remarkable thing about the rebellion was the fact that we should have lost the battle, but didn't, and I often wonder if it was due to the hand of Providence.

And those of General Wavell, writing in his Despatch:

> We may consider ourselves exceedingly fortunate to have liquidated what might have been a very serious commitment with such small forces and with little trouble. Rashid Ali and his adherents seem to have lost heart at the weakness of the support accorded to them by the Germans. The gallant defence of Habbaniya and the bold advance of 'Habforce' discouraged the Iraqi Army, while the Germans in their turn were prevented from sending further reinforcements by the desperate resistance of our troops in Crete, and their crippling losses in men and aircraft.[59]

The two RAF armoured car companies both played significant roles in the ultimate success of the campaign. The RAF armoured cars possessed the only light armour of any substance in the British arsenal. Both companies were highly-trained and effective reconnaissance and offensive units. Number 1 Armoured Car Company was familiar with the ground over which it had to fight. The effect of the defeat of the Iraqi armoured cars during the skirmish on the first day of the siege cannot be underestimated. If used more aggressively, and coordinated with infantry attacks and the artillery barrage, the Crossley armoured cars of the Iraqi Army could have caused havoc among the aerodrome facilities, the parked aircraft, and the cantonment, as the garrison had nothing heavier than a handful of Boys anti-tank rifles to defeat them.

The manner in which No 4 FTS had rapidly transformed their collection of training aircraft to an effective strike force was a major reason for the initiative being ceded to the garrison. RAF Habbaniya could not however, have been held without the presence of an effective ground defence force. The last word is left therefore, to the AOC Iraq, Air Vice-Marshal D'Albiac, who concluded his report on the campaign with the following paragraph:

> Finally my report would indeed be incomplete if I failed to record the outstanding services rendered by the Iraq Levies under the command of Lieutenant-Colonel Brawn, the 1st Battalion of the King's Own Royal Regiment and the RAF officers and airmen of No 1 Armoured Car Company ... I would like however to pay tribute to their work before 'Habforce' arrived. It was on these units that the close defence of Habbaniya cantonment depended and right well did they carry out their task. Their steadiness under fire, their dash and complete disregard for danger in attack provided a valuable complement to the action of their comrades in the air and helped materially towards demoralising of a vastly superior enemy force.[60]

(Aldershot: Gale & Polden, 1952), p. 20. Wyndham describes him as a fine guerrilla leader and a formidable and ruthless opponent. Fawzi was a Syrian Arab, who was serving as Rashid Ali's War Minister at the time. He had been educated at St Cyr (the foremost French Military Academy) and had fought in the Turkish Army during the First World War and later became involved in the Palestine disturbances of 1936. With German funds, he happily resumed his favourite pastime of fighting the British.

41 J.B. Glubb, *The Story of the Arab Legion* (London: Hodder & Stoughton, 1948), p. 266.
42 AIR 29/55 *Operations Record Book: No 2 Armoured Car Company January 1940-October 1946*.
43 Later Air Vice-Marshal Sir John D'Albiac KCVO KBE DSO (1894-1963). D'Albiac had been involved in the action against the Wahhabis at Ziza in Transjordan during 1924, when a pilot of No 14 Squadron RAF.
44 Smart has come in for severe criticism for his handling of the defence of Habbaniya, particularly in Dudgeon's book, *Hidden Victory* (A.G. Dudgeon, *Hidden Victory: The Battle of Habbaniya, May 1941* (Tempus Publishing: Stroud, Gloucestershire, 2000). This was disputed by Smart's daughter and others who were serving at the time. His daughter, Naida, was so incensed at the manner in which her father's role had been portrayed that in July 1999 she wrote the following letter to 'Air Mail': Error - please get your facts straight before blackening an honourable man's name. My father was neither distraught, nor was he hospitalised, nor was he evacuated after the bombing against the Iraqis commenced on 2-5-41. He was in fact injured in a car crash caused by bomb blast several days after the hostilities began. She then quotes Churchill's message of 7 May.
45 Colonel Nichols of the 1st Essex Regiment described Colonel Ouvry Roberts' plan as 'one of the most brilliant operations in the history of the 1939-1945 war.' T. Martin, *The Essex Regiment, 1929-1950* (Brentwood, Essex: The Essex Regiment Association, 1952), p. 49.
46 AIR 23/5921 *Coup D'Etat, April 1941: defence of RAF Station, Basrah 1941*.
47 AIR 23/5982 *Habbaniya: operations by No. 1 Armoured Car Company 1941*. A notice was sent out to the Sections of No 1 Armoured Car Company at Habbaniya warning that the Iraqis now possessed a captured Fordson armoured car and might try to use it to infiltrate the British positions.
48 de Chair, *The Golden Carpet*, p. 214.
49 Glubb, *The Story of the Arab Legion,* pp. 282-283. John Glubb describes this incident and noted that following the capture, a celebratory cup of tea was made, and shared with their prisoners. On their return to Habbaniya the prisoners were presented to the Regent, who had just arrived.
50 J. Bartlett and J. Benson, *All the King's Enemies* (Boston, Lincolnshire: Richard Kay, 2000), p. 93.
51 de Chair, *The Golden Carpet*, p. 75.
52 *Ibid.*, pp. 87-88.
53 Cornwallis had remained inside the British embassy in Baghdad for the last month. The Embassy wireless had been confiscated by the Iraqis soon after the outbreak of hostilities.
54 E.L. Ford, *Interview 4614* (London: IWM Sound Archive, 1980)
55 D. Hawkins, *Interview with J. Rolph, RAF Armoured Cars Association*, 2008.
56 J.N. Mackay, *History of the 7th Duke of Edinburgh's Own Gurkhas Rifles* (Edinburgh: William Blackwood & Sons, 1962), p. 140. The 2/7th Gurkha Rifles had lost five killed and 13 wounded by midday.
57 Ford, *Interview 4614*. Ford's party confiscated 18 Mauser rifles, two British Army pattern rifles, eight Webley revolvers, three shotguns, three bayonets and 600 rounds of SAA.
58 Later Field Marshal, The Viscount Slim of Yarralumla KG GCB GCMG GCVO GBE DSO MC (1891-1970). Slim would go on to earn great fame leading the Fourteenth Army to victory in the Burma campaign.
59 General Sir Archibald P. Wavell GCB CMG MC, 'Despatch on Operations in the Middle East, from 7th February, 1941 to 15th July 1941', Supplement to *The London Gazette*, 3 July 1946, p. 3439.
60 D'Albiac, *Report on Operations in Iraq*.

Chapter Fourteen

Syria 1941
'... A Long and Difficult Business'

"If they had gone into Syria when I wanted to... this time last year - after the fall of France, with Tricolour flying from the armoured cars and the rest of it, we should have been all right. Now I am afraid it is going to be a long and difficult business."
Brigadier 'Joe' Kingstone, 4th Cavalry Brigade[1]

"If anyone had predicted two months ago, when Iraq was in revolt and our people were hanging on by their eyelids at Habbaniya, and our Ambassador was imprisoned in his Embassy at Baghdad, and when all Syria and Iraq began to be overrun by German tourists, and were in the hands of forces controlled indirectly but none the less powerfully by German authority - if anyone had predicted that we should already, by the middle of July, have cleaned up the whole of the Levant and have re-established our authority there for the time being, such a prophet would have been considered most imprudent."
Winston Churchill, Prime Minister[2]

While the campaign in Italian East Africa was coming to a successful conclusion, the British position in the Middle East had not improved. Two days after the surrender of the Italian forces in Abyssinia, the Germans had launched the airborne invasion of Crete. Despite desperate fighting by the British, Australian, New Zealand and Greek forces, the island was lost once the key airfield at Maleme had fallen to the German airborne forces. Wavell had no other option than to order the evacuation of the island by the Royal Navy on 27 May and this was completed on 1 June, two days after 'Kingcol' had entered Baghdad. The Luftwaffe now held airfields in Cyrenaica, Crete and the Dodecanese Islands of the Aegean, and could launch air attacks on the Suez Canal, depots in the Nile Delta area and Alexandria, the home of the Mediterranean Fleet. Cyprus was threatened with the same fate that had befallen Crete. Given the difficulties facing the British forces, it was hard to comprehend why the Axis did not make a greater effort to deliver a fatal blow to the Allied position in the Eastern Mediterranean and Iraq.

In Iraq, it was essential once the Armistice had been signed, that British control be re-established over the Kirkuk oilfields and the flow of oil to Haifa be restored. When the *Luftwaffe* had been operating out of Mosul airfield, this threat had to be neutralised, but the Germans had, however, departed from Mosul in haste. Their attempt at providing air support for the Iraqi *coup-d'état* had been poorly planned and implemented. The incessant RAF air attacks, combined with a lack of coordination, inadequate fuel and supplies, poor facilities and the absence of an effective anti-aircraft defence for Mosul, meant that by 29 May the *Fliegerführer Irak* possessed only two Heinkels capable of flying, four bombs, and not a single serviceable fighter. Italian support had only been welcomed by the *Luftwaffe* late in the month and furthermore, the *Regia Aeronautica* had only been given permission by the Vichy French to fly in 12 CR42 fighters, across Syrian territory on 27 May. By the time the Iraq campaign had concluded, the Germans had lost 14 Bf 110s and five He 111s, and the Italians three CR42s.

The officers and airmen of the two RAF armoured car companies were allowed little time to rest and recover before they were despatched to further duties (Map 24, p. 317). Number 1 Armoured Car Company remained in Iraq to aid in restoring the British position in the country and the four sections were soon fanning out from Habbaniya. On 2 June, 'Gocol', under the command of Major R.E.S. Gooch, with 'B' Squadron of the Household Cavalry Regiment, two 3.7-inch howitzers, and RASC transport, escorted by six Rolls-Rolls armoured cars of Flight Lieutenant David Hellard's No 1 Section of No 1 Armoured Car Company, set off for Mosul. As 'Gocol' moved north, they passed through units of the Iraqi Army coming from Ramadi, who all seemed perfectly friendly. Hellard's section reached Mosul early on 3 June, where they were met by an RAF detachment and two companies of 2/4th Gurkha Rifles that had been flown into Mosul to assume the defence of the aerodrome. Later in the day they were joined by the 1st Battalion, The King's Own Royal Regiment, who had motored up from Habbaniya. The Section spent the next few days patrolling to the west to Tel Awainat and Tel Afar, and villages surrounding Mosul, as well as reconnaissances to check on the state of nearby landing grounds at Ain Zala and Quiyara. Despite some initial uncooperativeness from the local Iraqi Army commander, the handover proceeded relatively smoothly. Flight Lieutenant 'Ted' Frith recalls the return to Mosul:

The men of 'Gocol', 'B' Squadron, 1st Household Cavalry Regiment and No 1 Section of No 1 Armoured Car Company, prepare for departure for Mosul (Smiley).

'Gocol' arrives at Mosul air station as the transport carrying the 2/4th Gurkha Rifles circles for landing (Smiley).

We had to take over Mosul. The Germans had evacuated it, and the Iraqis remained. I went up with Wing Commander John Hawtrey who had served in the Iraqi Air Force, and was to become Officer Commanding RAF Mosul. When we returned to Mosul we met the officers of the Iraqi Air Force. Now, all their officers, from the Station Commander, Mufti Aziz, down, were trained at Cranwell. There were no guns firing at all, no shots fired in anger. The Iraqis were happy to hand it over.[3]

The next objectives were the apprehension of Rashid Ali, Dr Grobba, the Head of the German Military Mission and Fawzi el Qawukji. Soon after their arrival at Mosul, Major-General Clark, the 'Habforce' commander, ordered Major Gooch to apprehend Dr Grobba, the Head of the German Military Mission who, having fled Baghdad following the collapse of the Rashid Ali government, was now trying to stir up trouble with the tribes on the Iraq-Syria border.

The first attempt to apprehend Grobba was when a Rolls-Royce armoured car from No 1 Section was sent east from Mosul, along with a troop of the Household Cavalry Regiment under the command of Lieutenant David Smiley. They were moving along the Mosul to Arbil road when they were overtaken at speed by a car containing four senior Iraqi Army officers. Smiley took off in pursuit and was able to force the car off the road down a six-foot drop. Their followed a considerable row and the indignant Iraqi officers were arrested and returned under escort to Mosul.[4] Proceeding on to Rowanduz, they set up a further road block on the junction of roads that led to Turkey or Persia. The Household Cavalry Regiment history describes 'three very pleasant few days there, bathing and drinking with the local Kurds. Nobody passed, and after three days they returned to Mosul.'[5]

While the entry of British troops into Syria was forbidden, it was agreed that Gooch would be sent the code word "Grafton" as soon as it was clear for him to do so. This operation perhaps epitomised the unusual nature of the conflict between the British and Vichy French. 'Gocol' were to move directly, with all speed, to Qamichliye, 35 miles inside Syria, where Grobba had last been reported. On 7 June, Gooch

The hunt for Dr Grobba. A car carrying senior Iraqi Army officers that was forced off the road (Smiley).

received the code word "Grafton" and 'Gocol' set off for Qamichliye hoping to surprise Grobba, who would think himself safe inside 'neutral' Syria. Accompanied by a Rolls-Royce armoured car of No 1 Section, they unintentionally disturbed a French military frontier post and to prevent any warning of their approach, cut the telegraph wires after they had passed. On reaching Qamichliye they were challenged by the local French commander, Buisson, who possessed a substantial mixed force including aircraft, and forbade them to enter the town. Courtesies were exchanged, though Buisson demanded to know why they were in French territory. Disappointingly, he informed Gooch that Grobba had left some days previously, but he did offer 'Gocol' safe conduct back to the frontier which was accepted given the size of the force facing them. On crossing the frontier they were sent a message by despatch rider from the

Major Gooch of the Household Cavalry confers with the local French commander, Buisson, on the outskirts of Qamichliye on 8 June 1941. Rolls-Royces of No 1 Section are parked to the rear (Smiley).

Map 24

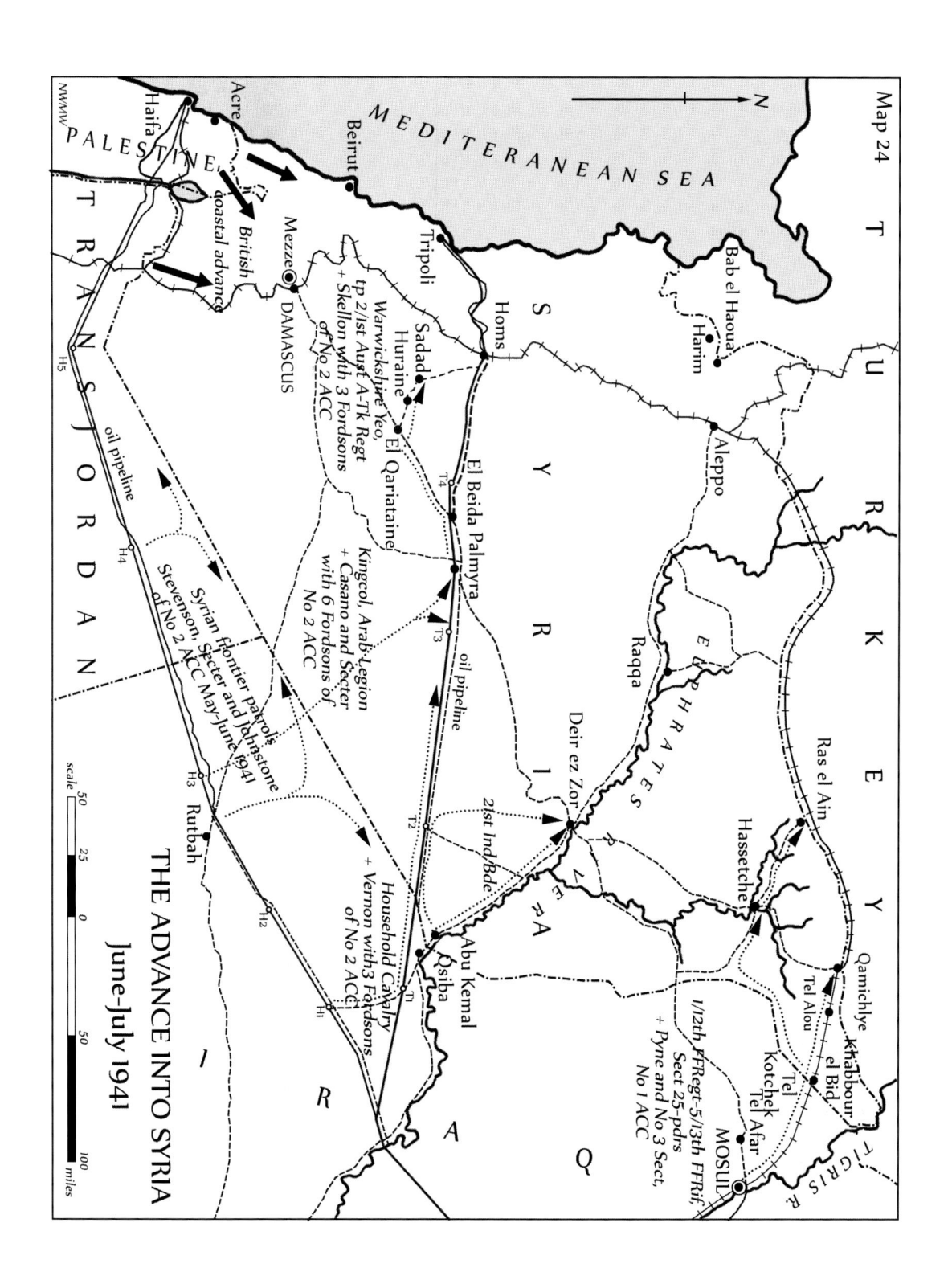

THE ADVANCE INTO SYRIA
June–July 1941

French Frontier Post Commander asking that they not cut his telegraph wires next time they passed.[6]

Meanwhile on 6 June, two Rolls-Royce armoured cars of No 2 Section of No 1 Company departed Habbaniya as part of 'Mercol', under the command of Major E.J.H. Merry. Consisting of 'A' Squadron of the Household Cavalry Regiment, two 4.5-inch howitzers from the Habbaniya artillery, some sappers and RASC transport, the task was to capture the guerrilla leader, Fawzi el Qawukji. On 24 May, a troop of the Royal Wiltshire Yeomanry escorting a supply column to Habbaniya had been ambushed by a force of Fawzi's irregulars. Despite offering stiff resistance the column was outnumbered. Seven lorries were captured and driven off, but not the drivers. Their mutilated bodies were recovered a few days later.[7]

'Mercol' proceeded to Hit and then Haditha, an important traffic, oil pipeline and telegraph junction, and where Fawzi and his armed gangs had been reported to have dispersed following their departure from Ramadi. 'Mercol' was also to determine the best 'going' to attack any armoured thrust from Syria that might come through Palmyra. This signalled that a threat now existed from the Vichy forces in Syria, and provided a clear indication to the next campaign for the Household Cavalry Regiment and the RAF armoured cars.

They encountered Fawzi el Qawukji with 500 followers in 70 heavily-armed trucks, near Abu Kemal and after an artillery engagement he was pursued to the Syrian border. At this stage, the Column had not been given permission to enter Syria and the chase was halted. Using the radio from a captured armoured car, Fawzi called up 'Habforce' and sent the message 'see you in Syria'.[8] After a few days of observation, awaiting a chance to apprehend him should he re-enter Iraq, they were recalled as the Iraqi Government attempted a rapprochement with Fawzi. This approach inevitably proved fruitless and Fawzi would re-appear within a matter of weeks to fight the British yet again.

It was now clear to Wavell that the Vichy French in Syria could not be regarded as a neutral presence. The Levant was remote from the main battle areas in Libya and the Aegean, however, the delivery of arms by the Vichy regime for the Iraqi uprising and provision of refuelling facilities for German and Italian aircraft on Syrian airfields en route to Mosul, could not go unchallenged. Despite the failure of the venture by *Fliegerführer Irak*, there was still a distinct possibility the Germans would establish themselves permanently in Syria, seriously threatening the Suez Canal and the oilfields of Iraq and Persia.

General Wavell had initially been ordered by the British Chiefs of Staff to undertake negotiations with the pro-Vichy High Commissioner in Syria, General Henri Dentz, with a view to jointly repelling any German incursion. Dentz was however, entirely subservient to the Vichy Government and was unlikely to oppose any German penetration, nor would he acquiesce to British demands. At the same time therefore, Wavell set about assembling as large a force as practicable that could operate against Syria if necessary. The Vichy forces in Syria consisted of 35,000 well-trained and experienced troops; 8000 being French, and the remainder Foreign Legion and colonial troops, predominantly African Sénégalais, Tunisians, Algerians and Moroccans. The majority had Vichy sympathies, and most of the officers were professional soldiers who would do their utmost to resist any invasion, both as a matter of pride and to perhaps help to restore the reputation of the French Army that had been lost in June 1940.

Independent action against Syria had been initiated by the RAF from 14 May, when No 84 Squadron attacked German aircraft near Damascus, followed a few days later by attacks on Rayak and Palmyra. At the same time in the House of Commons, Anthony Eden warned Vichy of the consequences of allowing German air units to use facilities in Syria. By this time, Wavell could barely scrape together a force capable of mounting a Syrian expedition as he had been forced to allocate most of his reserve and all of his transport to the relief column for RAF Habbaniya. This left most of the remaining troops in Palestine immobile and any further troops would have to come from Egypt, which would seriously weaken the defence against Rommel in Cyrenaica. Wavell was also receiving confusing intelligence from contacts in Syria as to the willingness of the Vichy forces to fight, and false claims that conditions were ripe for a *coup d'état* by Free French supporters. Furthermore, he had received imperious signals from General De Gaulle, the Leader of the Free French, asking him why he had delayed launching the Free French Division into Syria during May.

Nonetheless, by mid-June the Iraq crisis had been settled, and Wavell resolved to advance into Syria primarily to secure the main airfields. The force for Operation *Exporter* was composed of the Free French 'Division' (in reality only half a division in strength with only six battalions of infantry, one artillery battery and a squadron of tanks), two brigades of the 7th Australian Division, the 5th Indian Brigade, two cavalry regiments (one still on horses) a squadron of armoured cars of the Royals, three artillery regiments and a commando battalion. The air contribution consisted of one light bomber squadron, one army co-operation squadron and two and a half fighter squadrons from the RAF and one fighter squadron from the Fleet Air Arm.[9] Opposing them was a numerically superior and well-equipped French army, of 18 battalions, with 120 guns and 90 tanks, and an air force with 30 bomber and 60 fighter aircraft of modern design, later doubled by reinforcements from French North Africa.[10]

Paradoxically, one of the main reasons for concern over Syria, the presence of Axis forces, was resolved the day before the offensive was launched, when they withdrew their aircraft from Syria. German interest in the Middle East had soon faded, as their main focus switched to Operation *Barbarossa*, the invasion of Russia.

While Squadron Leader Casano had taken half of No 2 Armoured Car Company

A Fordson armoured car of No 2 Armoured Car Company on patrol on the Syrian border (© Crown copyright. Chester, RAF Regiment Museum).

319

to Baghdad with 'Kingcol', the other half of the Company, under the command of Flight Lieutenant Wilfred Stevenson, had remained at H4 and Rutbah, maintaining routine patrols along the Syrian border. With Syrian airfields being used as staging points for Axis aircraft, it was important that a watch be kept on any threats that might have arisen to the left flank and rear of the supply columns of 'Habforce'.

Two-car patrols were sent out regularly from 15 to 30 May, led by either Flight Lieutenant Wilfred Stevenson or Pilot Officers John Secter and John Johnston. As hostilities had not yet been initiated against Syria, amicable contact was made regularly with frontier patrols of the Vichy French. On 23 May, Flight Lieutenant Stevenson, along with two intelligence officers, rendezvoused with a French party of seven officers and three NCOs, accompanied by their wives, travelling in 11 Chevrolet trucks and escorted them over the frontier. They had expressed a wish to fight with General De Gaulle's Free French. The negotiations with this group had begun three days earlier when a patrol, led by Pilot Officer Secter, had encountered the Frenchmen, driving a staff car, and armed with only two light machine guns, three miles inside the Syrian border. The Captain leading the party had met them again the next day, and arranged for the escort to Transjordan.

On 26 May, diplomatic relations between Vichy Syria and the British were severed and the Vichy French troops were ordered to occupy planned defensive positions. Meanwhile, the invasion force was placed under the command of Lieutenant-General Sir Henry Maitland Wilson, GOC Palestine and Transjordan, and advanced across the Syrian border on 8 June. Three columns were sent into the mountainous south-west corner of Syria and the Lebanon through terrain that strongly favoured the defenders. The first, 21st Australian Infantry Brigade moved up the coast from Haifa to Beirut. The other two columns followed an inland route, with 25th Australian Infantry Brigade moving towards Merdjayoun and the other, 5th Indian Brigade, towards Deraa. The Free French contingent was to pass through the Indian Brigade the next day and advance on Damascus.

It had been hoped that a show of force would lead the Vichy French to make a token effort to repel the invasion and then speedily capitulate. This was not the case and the fighting became bitter and casualties were heavy, particularly between the Free French and Vichy forces. A great tragedy was realised when French Foreign Legion and Sénégalais troops of the Free French Division came into open combat against their Vichy counterparts. The Vichy forces were prepared for the attack and knew the terrain well. Resistance stiffened once the initial surprise had been overcome and when the weakness of the Allied columns became apparent. The Vichy troops then launched a series of successful counterattacks which drove some of the columns back. Rather than inducing them to surrender, the presence of the Free French Division had stiffened the resolve of Dentz's troops. Many deeply mistrusted the British because of their actions at Oran and Dakar in 1940. They considered De Gaulle was at best a misguided patriot, and at worst a leader of a traitorous faction defying the legal government of France, fighting with the British in a lost cause.

After a week of slow progress, it was clear that three small columns could not achieve their objectives, the Vichy superiority in tanks and familiarity with the terrain having halted the advance. The Free French were held up ten miles from Damascus, the 5th Indian Brigade had suffered heavily and the Australians were facing tough resistance through the mountains. Consequently, the 16th Infantry Brigade from 6th British Division and another light bomber and fighter squadron were sent from Palestine as reinforcements to support the advance in the west.[11]

At the same time, Wavell had instructed Major-General Clark to send 'Habforce' into Syria, with the goal of capturing the ancient desert oasis of Palmyra, and then to cut the Damascus to Homs road and harass the French lines of communications between Damascus and Beirut.

After handing over responsibility for Baghdad, Mosul and Kirkuk to 10th Indian Division, 'Habforce' was ordered to concentrate for the operations against Palmyra, more than 150 miles to the north-west. The Brigade Intelligence Officer, Captain Somerset de Chair, described the departure from RAF Habbaniya, down the now open road to Ramadi and the Syrian border:

> The vehicles were beginning to draw out on to the road.... At the signal ... I started off up the winding hill onto the plateau, turned left for a few hundred yards, and then descended abruptly to the road which skirts the aerodrome. Here I turned left and drew into the right-hand side. All across the aerodrome, head-on to the famous London-Baghdad signpost, were arrayed the grey Air Force armoured cars of Casano's squadron [sic]. They were old friends, dusty, bullet-scarred, square-ended bonnets and the men, in greasy white overalls, lolling out of the conning towers. The Lewis guns were pointed to the sky, but the machine-guns and anti-tank rifles pointed sharply in the direction we were going.[12]

To deceive the enemy as to his intentions, the 'Habforce' commander, Major-General Clark, sent the Household Cavalry Regiment on a feint up the west bank of the River Euphrates, then westward from Abu Kemal on the Syrian border, towards Palmyra. They were to make a show of force and distract French attention from the main thrust through Palmyra.

Accompanying the Household Cavalry Regiment was Flight Lieutenant Vernon with his three Fordson armoured cars. They had moved off to join 'A' Squadron at T1 on 10 July, travelling via K3 and H1. From there, they moved up to Qsiba and assisted in the attack on Abu Kemal. At dawn on 16 July, the Household Cavalry Regiment was attacked by four enemy armoured cars which were driven off by two of Vernon's cars. Vernon then established an observation post five miles north of the town in preparation for the next stage of the advance to watch for any enemy counterattack. Deception as to the size and role of the Column was assisted by BBC broadcast of reports, intentional or otherwise, that a large British armoured column was being sent up the Euphrates. As a decoy however, the Column was relatively ineffective as the French possessed excellent air reconnaissance and they were easily dissuaded of the possibility that an armoured column was advancing from the east.

On 20 July, two of Vernon's Fordsons along with 'A' Squadron, Household Cavalry Regiment, reached T2 and went forward to demand the surrender of the outpost. This was refused so the position was bypassed, although the troop of 237 Battery accompanying them sent 20 shells into the pumping station before departing. This had the desired effect and the defenders capitulated.

The main body of 'Habforce', 'Kingcol', had been renamed the 4th Cavalry Brigade Group. It had concentrated around Rutbah, H3 and H4 pumping stations, still under the command of Brigadier 'Joe' Kingstone. The Royal Wiltshire Yeomanry and Warwickshire Yeomanry had been protecting the long supply lines of 'Kingcol' as it moved towards Habbaniya and Baghdad. However, with the return of the column, these two regiments were given a central role in this operation. Accompanying the yeomanry regiments, each with only two 'sabre' squadrons, was 237 Battery, Royal Artillery, a newly-arrived Australian anti-tank battery equipped with 2-pdr anti-tank guns, three sections of No 2 Field Squadron Royal Engineers, four troops of the Arab Legion and Casano's nine Fordson armoured cars.[13] The Brigade Group departed before dawn on 21 June. Brigadier Kingstone's orders were to capture Palmyra that day, as it was assumed, falsely as it turned out, that the desert outpost was only lightly-held and would be easily captured.

The Arab Legion provided wide sweeping patrols of the route to Palmyra, while Squadron Leader Casano with half of No 2 Armoured Car Company, organised his nine cars in three sections, each being allocated a different task. One section moved with the advanced guard of the Column, the second with the main body and headquarters, while the third was away to the east working with the Household Cavalry Regiment.

Casano had by then become a valued member of the Brigade command group, and Captain Somerset de Chair wrote a fond and vivid description of him:

> Casano, who commanded the RAF armoured cars, was first met at H3... Casano's face was thin and sallow. He resembled Mephistopheles in every respect, with a thin pointed nose, arched black eyebrows and mocking dark eyes. I see him now, when we were back at H3 after sharing every variety of adventure, preparing for another campaign. An oil lamp illuminated the intent faces of five of us at Poker... and there was Casano leaning forward in the lamplight, as if he were the devil himself, and saying in a long-drawn out whisper 'Go-the whole-hog'.[14]

At a planning conference for the advance on Palmyra the previous day, Brigadier 'Joe' Kingstone had turned to his now trusted ally:

> 'You, Casano, will guard the flank and, if there is trouble, you go at once to the sound of the guns'.[15]

Prior to departure Casano had, however, expressed his concerns about the operation to Captain de Chair:

> Casano remained in our mess. His sharp Lucifer features revealed a satanic doubt.
> 'I don't like this "no air support",' he said. 'I know something about those French aircraft. The Potez 630 is a bloody good bomber. They have 400 aircraft in Syria.'[16]

However, this did not distract him for long as he had another important mission in mind; to improve the firepower of his Company. De Chair continues:

> ... Casano was a permanent and honorary member of our mess now; and was intrigued by reports of a case loaded with 2-inch mortars which was addressed to the Household Cavalry. As the 'lumpers'[17] were still far away, Joe, who suspected that the heavy case probably contained champagne, told Casano he could open it up and help himself. Casano was pathetically grateful. He had been all round the units of the Brigade trying to swap

anti-tank rifles (soon to be officially known as The Boy's anti-tank 'pistol' due to its ineffectiveness against all but the lightest of armour) for 2-inch mortars.[18]

Casano's section, along with the Royal Wiltshire Yeomanry, departed late on 20 June, as the advanced guard, to reconnoitre to the frontier ahead of the main column, while Pilot Officer Secter and his three cars accompanied the main body with the Warwickshire Yeomanry and the remainder of the Brigade. The element of surprise was soon lost. The Arab Legion had captured the small outpost at Juffa, but a French aircraft was seen to fly off from the nearby airfield which had no doubt raised the alarm.

Casano's cars spent the night on the Syrian border and then set off again at 0200 hours. At 0700 hours they were spotted by a French reconnaissance aircraft, well before they had completed their 150-mile approach march to Palmyra. In the early afternoon, the RAF armoured cars came in sight of Palmyra, but came under heavy machine-gun fire and accurate shelling as they motored up the main road to the town. Casano tried unsuccessfully to locate the guns and it was clear that the outpost was strongly held, so he withdrew to the main column. He made two more attempts later that day to find the guns, and again the next morning, but received a similar reply from the defenders. The yeomanry then moved up and attempted to take the town, while the RAF armoured cars watched for any intervention by the French along the tracks to the west.

Palmyra was an Arab town that possessed a large French fort and barracks, 'the Poste Weygand', and an aerodrome on its outskirts. The town had a number of features that made it a natural defensive position. The famous Roman ruins lay to the south-west, and high rocky ridges dominated to the south-west, north and north-west. On a hill to the north, and visible for miles around, was a Roman fortress known as the Chateau Oumêre. A large salt pan, impassable to vehicles, lay to the south. Any plan to encircle the town would rely on the capture of adequate water supplies and these were to be found at the oil pumping stations on the pipeline running to the east of the town at T1, T2 and T3 (Map 25, p. 323).

The French were in great strength and consisted of the *1st Light Desert Company*, some armoured cars, and two companies of the *6th Regiment* of the Foreign Legion. They were accommodated in concrete pill boxes, machine-gun and sniper posts; all set up to fire across the bare and open desert at an attacking force. Further obstructions to the advance were the tank traps to the north and in the south, closely-planted palm

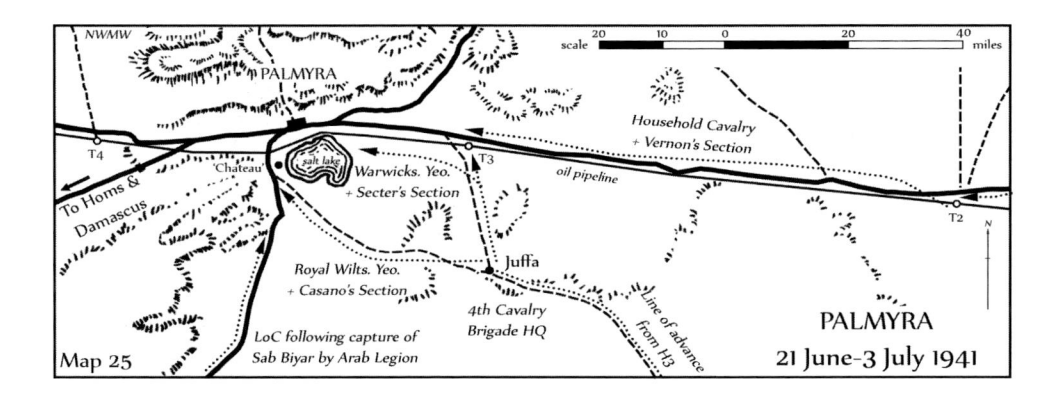

Map 25 — PALMYRA, 21 June–3 July 1941

groves with walls up to 18 feet high, and a jumble of Roman sandstone ruins that were ready-made as defensive positions. The French defenders could also call on 20 Potez 63 bombers and a number of Dewoitine 520 fighters.

The Vichy garrison put up a staunch resistance and defied capture for the next 12 days. The salt lake to the south of the town had forced the Royal Wiltshire Yeomanry to move around to the west where they came up against a ridge that ran south and west of the town and there they met heavy opposition. With the advance halted, the 4th Cavalry Brigade Headquarters found itself in an exposed and uncomfortable position. It established itself in a defile between high sandstone hills near Juffa to the south, while the remainder of Brigade moved to the east to link up with the Household Cavalry Regiment as it approached T3 from the east.

It was now apparent to the Vichy French where the threat to Palmyra lay, and on the second day of the operation, a major part of the French Air Force in Syria set out to smash the Brigade. The main body of the Column, still 23 miles to the south, came under attack from a force of French bombers and fighters, and the advance came to a complete standstill. Possessing only a few Bofors anti-aircraft guns, retaliation was inadequate, and despite increasingly strident calls for air protection to Army Headquarters by Brigadier Kingstone, none could be spared, as the RAF was occupied with the main coastal advance. The Column lay exposed in the open and came under repeated air attack, losing men, vehicles and supplies. The attacks continued unabated for the next two weeks. The Brigade Headquarters, the Royal Wiltshire Yeomanry, the Warwickshire Yeomanry and the Household Cavalry Regiment were subjected to repeated and devastating attacks. One troop of the Royal Wiltshire Yeomanry, after one air attack, had only four vehicles remaining out of the 17 they had set off with.

Attempts were made, with some difficulty, to place a stranglehold on the ancient city. This was made all the more complicated as the supply lines were open to attack from enemy parties on the ground and from the air, and hence the RASC vehicles could only move at night. In a vigorous action however, the Arab Legion routed a detachment of French 2nd *Light Desert Company* and captured the post at Sab Biyar. Located halfway between the Transjordan frontier and Palmyra, this at least allowed the 4th Cavalry Brigade to operate a shorter and safer supply line.

Meanwhile, Pilot Officer John Secter and his section had been ordered to accompany the Warwickshire Yeomanry to T3. He describes how Casano approached him about an operation and his inspirational style of leadership:

> Near the end of this encounter in the Syrian desert, Casano took me aside and said, 'It's time that you got some experience!', as though the preceding weeks were just water under the bridge, so to speak! To this I replied, 'sure, what do you want?' We had a special target that was required to extract us from a position of extreme hazard at Palmyra. He said 'I want you to take this patrol', and gave me one quarter of our cars. I went out with this small force...
>
> He would take you by the arm, pat you on the back or hold his arm around your shoulder. He was so inspiring that I could barely believe that he could talk like that in such a romantic and improbable manner and get away with it! He was an incredible leader![19]

The T3 pumping station lay 35 miles to the east of Palmyra and possessed a typical French desert fort, defended by the Foreign Legion and Sénégalais troops. On

The ancient city of Palmyra. To the left is the Chateau Oumêre, the castle built by the Mamluks in the 13th Century, and to the right the ruins of the 1st Century Temple of Baal. The modern village and French military barracks were further to the right (Library of Congress, Prints & Photographs Division [LC-DIG-matpc-01423]).

21 June, Secter, with his Section of armoured cars, moved up to draw fire from the fort and ascertain the strength of the garrison. Unfortunately, Casano's fears about the French Air Force had been realised. The armoured cars were spotted and strafed by six Vichy French fighters. Caught in a hail of cannon shells and machine-gun bullets, two Fordson armoured cars were rendered completely unserviceable, and the Company suffered its first fatalities of the campaign. Corporal Lishman was killed immediately and LACs McWalters, Wigley and Wood suffered head and arm injuries. LAC Walter Holl, the driver of a Fordson armoured car, was hit in the back by a Dewoitine cannon shell which went between the car commander's legs and straight into his back. He was asked about his condition, and he said "Yes, I'm all right. I'd like to get out though". However, once he was lifted out of the Fordson, it was clear that he was badly wounded, but he still said to an officer, "Oh no, it's all right Sir". Casano came up in his vehicle and took him away for treatment.[20] Holl had suffered serious multiple gunshot wounds and was evacuated in a poor state. Sadly, his condition worsened and he succumbed to his wounds a fortnight later following evacuation back to Ramleh.[21]

The accompanying troop of 25-pdrs of 237 Battery was brought up, and shells poured into the fort at T3. But this had little effect, and the Warwickshire Yeomanry attack had to be called back. The Column leaguered for the night and buried their dead in the bomb craters, lit by the glow of the burning vehicles that had been struck by the French air attacks. The following morning the decision was made to leave a small covering force, bypass the fort, and move on to Palmyra.

A single troop of the Warwickshire Yeomanry remained, but they soon came to grief due to an act of treachery by Fawzi el Qawukji and his band. Having escaped capture by 'Mercol' earlier, he had fled to Syria, but had renewed his campaign against the British, with Vichy and German encouragement. The following day, after the main column had moved on to Palmyra, the Troop was approached by some Chevrolet trucks, which according to the Warwicks were under the white flag. As a Yeomanry officer went forward to parley, the vehicles to the rear opened fire and then moved forward to sweep the Warwicks trenches with machine-gun fire. The Boys anti-tank rifle was knocked out and as further resistance seemed hopeless, the Troop surrendered. Those troopers who were unharmed were marched off to become prisoners of war, but in a further example of poor behaviour by their captors, two wounded troopers were left in the desert. They were rescued later by a party brought back by a trooper who had escaped capture.[22]

The Yeomanry were only equipped with light trucks, and the Troop had possessed only one anti-tank rifle and two outdated Hotchkiss light machine guns. Had two or three RAF Fordsons been allocated to assist the Troop, this misfortune may not have befallen the Warwicks. In previous incidents, the Fordsons had shown that they could hold themselves well against the French armoured cars and machine-gun mounted trucks. Fawzi el Qawukji continued his personal campaign after this incident but was caught in an air attack by a Hurricane on 19 July. Despite being wounded in 14 places, none were mortal, and he was flown out to a hospital in Berlin for treatment.

Flight Lieutenant Vernon's three Fordsons had finished their work with the Household Cavalry Regiment, and were sent to link up with the reinforcements of the 1st Battalion, Essex Regiment and escort their transport as they moved north towards T3. With little progress being made in the capture of Palmyra, the battalion had joined the Brigade from 'Habforce' reserve.[23] The column was bombed and machine-gunned four times during the day, fortunately without loss. The troubles at T3 were revealed and Vernon was sent to watch the fort and search for the Troop of the Warwickshire Yeomanry that had inexplicably gone missing. They brought to safety a trooper of the Warwickshire Yeomanry who had been wounded in an earlier air attack. The following day, his Section escorted 27 RASC vehicles bringing supplies to the main column, while Secter with his cars escorted a column of wounded back to the Brigade Headquarters at Juffa, and then on to the relative safety of H4. Surprisingly, no plans had been made for the evacuation of the wounded, as it had been assumed that Palmyra would fall on the first day.

The conditions were severe. It was the height of summer and for the troops in their slit trenches or vehicles, the threat and reality of air attack, the extreme daytime temperatures and dust storms made movement and the completion of their daily tasks almost unbearable. The wounded in particular suffered badly. Among them were some gunners who had suffered severe burns during an air attack when their artillery quad, under which they were sheltering, exploded in flames.

Casano and his section had been fully occupied at Palmyra. At the beginning of each day of the siege, his armoured cars motored out to test the reaction of the garrison and to probe for weaknesses in the defence. Little progress was being made in the capture of the fort as the force was not strong enough to overcome the resolute defenders. However, early on the morning of 29 June, Casano's section intercepted and blew up a French ammunition convoy on the Palmyra to Homs road. The convoy was bringing much needed supplies to Palmyra and this may have been a turning point in the battle as this event, and the defeat of the *No 2 Light Desert Company* a few days earlier by the Arab Legion, had a significant impact on the morale of the defenders.

On a patrol a few days later, Casano's section came under very accurate and heavy shell fire for nearly an hour and the cars suffered four punctured tyres, before they could retire to safer ground. Other patrols were just as eventful. In one instance, the airmen came across a roadblock of stones. As they set about clearing them away they were fortunate to discover that the roadblock had been booby-trapped with a number of bombs. With the road opened up they proceeded further on until one of the Fordsons became stuck in soft sand in sight of the enemy. Fortunately, the car was towed out by a friendly Bren carrier from the 1st Essex.

The strain on Brigadier Kingstone due to the repeated air attacks, to which his Brigade had little reply, had been intense, and on 24 June, he became ill and collapsed. He was replaced temporarily as Brigade Commander by Major Gooch of the Life Guards, until the arrival of Brigadier Tiarks. Repeated requests for air support, and protests about the complete absence for 'Habforce', had finally borne fruit on 25 June.[24] Eight Tomahawks of No 3 Squadron RAAF were despatched to H4, where they refuelled and then flew on to patrol over Palmyra. The Brigade was further heartened a few days later to see the RAAF Tomahawks escorting Blenheims to attack Palmyra. In full view of the Brigade, and to great cheers, the Tomahawks proceeded to shoot down six Vichy French Martin Maryland bombers. The same day, the infantrymen of the 1st Essex captured the Chateau Oumêre and thereby established a foothold on the high ground to the north-west of Palmyra. The RAF Fordsons were then used to ferry senior officers to and from the position so that the next move could be planned. The Royal Wiltshire Yeomanry struggled for three days to capture the ridge overlooking the town and to penetrate into the maze of walls, trees and houses from the west, but met with limited success. The battle had reached a stalemate.

Over to the west however, Damascus had fallen to the Australians on 21 June; the same day the 4th Cavalry Brigade had set off from H3. Early on 3 July, with no hope of relief, and having decided that honour had been satisfied, the 165-strong garrison of Palmyra surrendered. The following day, the 22 defenders of T3 also capitulated. To their credit, just under 200 Vichy soldiers, mostly mercenaries, had held off attacks for 12 days by a force of three cavalry regiments and an infantry battalion.[25]

With the fall of Palmyra, the 4th Cavalry Brigade was ordered to move on toward Homs. Pilot Officer John Secter and four airmen returned to Transjordan and were relieved by Flying Officer Skellon with nine airmen, having travelled from Amman. As part of the move of 4th Brigade towards Homs, Skellon's four Fordsons joined two troops of the Warwickshire Yeomanry and a troop of 2/1st Australian Anti-Tank Regiment and were to drive through El Beida and El Qariataine, and on to Huraine and Sadad.[26]

At dawn on 9 July, Skellon, with his two Fordsons, moved off at the head of a column comprising one Australian 2-pdr anti-tank gun, the anti-tank Troop HQ and one troop of the Warwickshire Yeomanry. Flight Sergeant Lace, with the other two Fordsons, was sent to watch for movement to the west. Skellon's group drove towards Sadad where they encountered a detachment of French armoured cars mounting 2-pdr guns and came under high-explosive and machine-gun fire from only 500 yards. Armed with only Vickers and Lewis machine-guns and the Boys anti-tank rifle, Skellon withdrew his cars to a wadi. From here the Australian anti-tankers engaged the enemy while he directed the two Fordsons to attack from the flank. This was sufficient to force the enemy to retire.

Flight Sergeant Lace's half section was recalled, but an hour and a half later they and came under heavy fire as they encountered the same group on a ridge east of Sadad. Skellon sent Lace around to the left flank while he and his two cars moved to the right. To add discomfort to the manoeuvre, a French 75-mm field gun, the famous 'soixante-quinze', known to be a very effective weapon against armour, opened fire at them from north of Sadad. After an hour however, the enemy cars withdrew. Skellon and his section retired to a ridge, 4 miles to the east. At midday, they set out on a forward reconnaissance to the north of Sadad. In mid-afternoon, the enemy cars attacked again and this time succeeded in knocking out one of the Australian anti-tank guns. Skellon seeing this, took the Boys anti-tank rifle and returned fire. To his and his crew's surprise, he knocked out one of the French armoured cars. Flying Officer Skellon continues:

> There were rumours of a French armoured car which was making a nuisance of itself and they sent me off to put it down. Which I did, and I got a nice little pipe out of that; because I was a pipe smoker in those days. The French officer dropped his pipe and I picked it up and used it myself. It was an actual armoured car, it was an extraordinary looking thing, but it did work. It saw us coming and then we knocked it out. The crew had gone, they'd left it.[27]

It was clear that the Vichy French were determined to hold Sadad to delay any further westward movement. The following morning, plans were made for the capture of the village by the troop of the Warwickshire Yeomanry. Skellon and his cars occupied the high ground behind the enemy and cut their line of retreat, and at 0740 hours the Fordsons moved off to attack the village. They soon came under fire on the outskirts from four enemy armoured cars. Skellon again split his Section, and sent one half off to the left flank. The move was successful and another enemy armoured car was captured and the village was taken. Mid-morning, the enemy were reported approaching Sadad from the west. The Fordsons were sent out to reconnoitre and sighted a French column of three armoured cars and 20 lorries. However, they soon retired and no further action occurred. A quarter of an hour after seeing off the French column, the Fordsons were ordered to return to base. For No 2 Company the Syrian campaign was at an end.

With successes for the British, Australian, Indian and Free French to the west, it was now becoming clear that the campaign was drawing to an inevitable conclusion. Success had not been as easy and quick for 'Habforce' as had been first thought. A handful of French and colonial troops had held them at bay for a fortnight. The reasons for this were three-fold. The troops for the most part were inexperienced and untrained in mechanised and desert warfare. Only the 1st Essex, the Household Cavalry Regiment and the RAF armoured car crews had seen action previously.[28] The battle for Palmyra had been fought at the height of summer and the heat of the desert during the day, the freezing cold at night and a paucity of water had taken a heavy physical toll. Last, but most important, was the lack of air support which meant that the modern French bombers could attack the columns at will.

On 1 July, a third phase of operations had been launched against the Vichy French position in the east of Syria. General Slim's 10th Indian Division, which had taken over positions at Haditha, Baghdad and Mosul from 'Habforce', was ordered to send the 21st Indian Infantry Brigade up the Euphrates to take Deir ez Zor, and

Flight Lieutenant Bernard Pyne (right) of No 3 Section on a pre-War exercise (Rutter, RAFACA).

to threaten Aleppo. Transport was as ever, at a premium, and the advance had only begun when vehicles could be scrounged and borrowed from the limited pool in Iraq. Air support was pitiful, consisting of only four Hurricanes, four worn-out Gladiators from No 127 Squadron RAF and four Blenheim bombers. This was only slightly more substantial than that given to 'Habforce', and these were soon lost in the first days of the advance. Severe dust storms for the first few days and later air attacks from the well-equipped Vichy air force slowed the progress of the Division.

On 1 July, a sub-section of No 1 Section of No 1 Armoured Car Company moved west from Mosul with two companies of the 2/8th Gurkha Rifles and some sappers from 20th Indian Infantry Brigade, as part of a feint towards Deir ez Zor, to distract the enemy from the main advance of 21st Indian Brigade along the Euphrates. A 'demonstration' by the RAF armoured cars towards Balad Sinjar discovered a small party of half a dozen Vichy French and Syrian soldiers. The other half of the Section followed the next day with the rear column. Disappointingly, they found that the bridge over the Khasin River had been destroyed after the advanced column had passed through and there was no option but to return to Mosul.

Another column of the 20th Indian Brigade was also sent from northern Iraq to evict Vichy forces from a series of 'Beau Geste' style forts in the *Bec du Canard* ('duck's bill'), as the far north-eastern province of Syria was known. This region bordered Turkey, and along its length ran the Mosul-Aleppo railway. On the night of 2/3 July, No 3 Section of No 1 Company, under the command of Flight Lieutenant Pyne, with a column of the 1/12th Frontier Force Regiment and a section of 25-pdrs from 3rd Field Regiment RA, set off from Mosul. An official history of the campaign describes the RAF armoured car contribution to the column as follows:

> They had with them... an armoured wing of exactly three RAF armoured cars a little past their fifteenth birthday. The cars proved the most valuable element in the attack. Despite their antiquity, the Rolls-Royce engines would effortlessly send them cavorting over the desert at 70 miles an hour as long

as petrol was forthcoming; at such a speed the sand they churned into the air became a cloud which covered acres, and the watchers from the forts could be forgiven for thinking that at least a squadron of tanks was rushing towards them.[29]

They occupied Tel Kotchek, seized the railway and set about preventing any sabotage of the line by the Vichy French. The French garrison was taken by complete surprise and fled. The railway and a large quantity of rolling stock were captured intact but it was found that several bridges had been wired for demolition. A similar fate befell Tel Alou, although this time the garrison of 150 were captured after a long period of parleying with the French officers, and then only after the artillery sent a few shells over the fort to encourage the surrender. Further on, at Tel Hadi, the three Rolls-Royce armoured cars arrived to see the French cavalry detachment disappearing over the horizon.

The advance was then resumed towards Qamichliye, along with a company of the 5/13th Frontier Force Rifles and troop of artillery. Arriving at dawn, the French Tricolour still flew over the fort of Khabbour el Bid. The three armoured cars formed up in line-abreast in preparation for an advance, at which point the garrison took to their horses and fled, pursued by the Rolls-Royces.

On 7 July, RRACs *Lion* and *Virginia* entered Qamichliye, where they halted on the main bridge. An ultimatum was issued by the French commander to retire; the RAF offered a counter-ultimatum, and then withdrew to await their decision. The artillery could not be used as an inducement for two reasons; the potential loss of civilian life in the town and because some shells would undoubtedly be 'overs' into Turkish territory, and this could lead to an international incident. Turkey had been watching the German invasion of Russia with some unease and while not assisting the Axis, it had completed a pact of friendship with Germany ten days after the British advance into Syria. The cars awaited the French decision, and at midday the Tricolour was seen being lowered and the garrison surrendered. Number 3 Section quickly entered the town, removed the road blocks and occupied the barracks.

Returning to the base at Tel Kotchek, No 3 Section then departed for Hassetche on 8 July as part of a fast moving column of the 1/12th Frontier Force Regiment. The French garrison had already left and the column moved on to Ras el Ain which was easily occupied. The breakdown of French civil order was evident in the fort of the latter town as it was found to have been looted by the locals. Flight Lieutenant Pyne played a major role in the surrender; receiving the local notables and participating in the speeches of welcome which were exchanged. The armoured cars of No 3 Section returned to Mosul two days later.

Back on the Euphrates, the main body of 10th Indian Division had made hard work of their advance. Frustrated, General Slim threw caution to the wind, and launched two columns of 21st Indian Brigade on Deir ez Zor on 2 July. Despite suffering from air attacks, the main column which had followed the Euphrates, opened a frontal attack on the town and the second, including an Indian cavalry regiment, 13th Duke of Connaught's Own Lancers, equipped with old Indian-pattern Crossley-Chevrolet armoured cars, and the 4/13th Frontier Force Rifles, made a 100 mile-wide outflanking move to the left and cut the road to Aleppo. By the following morning 100 prisoners and nine guns had been taken, while the remainder of the garrison had departed during the night. This complete and bold use by Slim of his motorised units shortened the campaign by three weeks. The 21st Indian Brigade then moved further up the Euphrates to threaten Aleppo and the Syrian villages along the Turkish frontier.

The advance of 20th and 21st Indian Brigades now had to be halted as supplies of ammunition, food and petrol were running low. The desert across which the Indians had travelled was strewn with the hundreds of lorries that had come to grief from Vichy air attacks, breakdowns or broken front springs. North-eastern Syria had, however, been successfully and peacefully occupied by use of rapid movement, courage, tact and more than a little bluff.

The Syrian campaign was nearing the end. To the west, the Australians, assisted by a bombardment from a naval squadron, had fought hard to capture Damour, thus threatening Beirut, and the 6th British Division was progressing along the road to Rayak. It had become clear to General Dentz that Beirut was lost, his air force had been severely mauled, and the RAF had railways, ports and airfields under constant attack. Homs and Aleppo were now threatened from many directions; by the Free French from the south, 4th Cavalry Brigade, from the east and the columns of the 10th Indian Division from the north-east. Dentz was told by the Vichy Government to expect no more reinforcements, and so the same day, he sent emissaries to discuss terms.

On 12 July, the Armistice was signed at Acre by General Maitland Wilson and General Andre de Verdilhac. Syria came under Allied occupation, with administration divided between the British and Free French authorities. British casualties, including prisoners, had been about 3300 and the RAF had lost 27 aircraft. The Free French had fought in difficult and unpleasant circumstances and had suffered similar losses to their Vichy counterparts. Sadly, given the choice of joining De Gaulle and the Free French or repatriation to France, only 5668 of the 37,736 Vichy French military chose the former. Considerable civil unrest ensued as the Syrians saw one unpopular French regime replaced with another.[30]

The successful conclusion of the Syrian campaign brought to an end more than two months of intense action for Nos 1 and 2 Armoured Car Companies. The officers and airmen of No 2 Company made their way back down through the flat lava belt of black rock to Transjordan and RAF Amman to rest and refit. The Fordson armoured cars required repairs and much needed maintenance and were despatched to Haifa and Cairo for repairs. New drafts of airmen arrived from the United Kingdom and a new armoured car crew course was commenced to bring them up to a suitable level of competence.

Numbers 1, 2 and 3 Sections of No 1 Armoured Car Company continued with the task of re-establishing British control in Iraq, visiting the oil pumping stations, accompanying aircraft recovery units scouring the deserts of Iraq and Syria for the remains of the aircraft lost in the two campaigns, and escorting large petrol and supply convoys to the many units of the Indian Army now located all over the country.

Horrendous sandstorms had assailed Iraq during the last week of June, particularly in the south, and it was during one of these storms that a Vickers Vincent of No 244 Squadron was reported missing on a flight to Kuwait. On board was Flying Officer Owen Pilsworth from No 4 Section. Flight Lieutenant Pyne went out with the Section from Shaibah to search for the aircraft, but poor visibility made the task difficult. It was two days before the crashed aircraft was located. Footprints were found later in the sand, but petered out on the shores of the Khor es Zubair waterway. The armoured cars went out and found the pilot, Flight Lieutenant Stephenson, still alive, but sadly, however, the body of the rigger, LAC Goodsal, was found lying on a beach by a searching aircraft. The body of the third member of the crew, Flying Officer Owen Pilsworth, was never found.

This was the last task carried out by No 4 Section from RAF Shaibah as it was moved permanently to RAF Habbaniya in early July. Number 4 Section, which had been stationed at Shaibah since 1934, joined No 2 Section. Numbers 1 and 3 Sections were sent north to RAF Mosul. Further changes occurred in August, with the appointment of a new Company Commander, Squadron Leader W.O. 'Jonah' Jones.

The activities of No 2 Armoured Car Company in Iraq and Syria had not gone unrecognised, with Squadron Leader Casano and Flight Lieutenant Wilfred Stevenson both awarded the Military Cross. Stevenson had first led the Company detachment that had worked alongside the 11th Hussars during the victorious advance against the Italians in Libya during early 1941. He was recognised for his inspirational leadership and personal disregard for danger during eight months of near-continuous operations in Egypt, Cyrenaica, Iraq and Syria.[31]

As the advance guard for 'Habforce', Casano had personally led his armoured cars into battle and had shown great foresight and organisational skill to keep his small unit operational. He had often placed himself in close proximity to the enemy and had displayed 'greatest gallantry'. The successes of the Company in Iraq and Syria were credited largely to his 'zeal and devotion to duty.'[32]

Despite the loss of Greece and Crete and the threat posed from Libya by the *Afrika Korps*, the victory in the campaigns in Iraq and Syria, lasting in total just over two months, had considerably strengthened the British strategic position in the Middle East. On 15 July, the Prime Minister, Winston Churchill, addressed the Houses of Parliament on the war situation:

> The conclusion of this brief Syrian campaign reflects credit upon all responsible - upon General Wavell, who was able to spare the Forces first to put down the revolt in Iraq, and afterwards to act in Syria... I hope it will soon be possible to give fuller accounts to the public than they have yet received of the Syrian fighting, marked as it was by so many picturesque episodes, such as the arrival of His Majesty's Lifeguards and Royal Horse Guards, and the Essex Yeomanry [sic], in armoured cars, across many hundreds of miles of desert, to surround and capture the oasis of Palmyra.[33]

In his Despatch on the Syrian campaign, Wavell wrote the following:

> We must be again considered fortunate in achieving our objective with forces which were really insufficient for their task. It was only skilful handling and determined fighting that brought about success.[34]

Iraq and Syria were now safe, but preparations were now underway in Egypt to strike a severe blow against the German-Italian Army in Libya, and so the focus of operations for the both RAF Armoured Car Companies now swung firmly to the Western Desert.

Notes

1. S. de Chair, *The Golden Carpet* (London: Faber & Faber, 1944), p. 182.
2. Winston Churchill, 'Speech to the House of Commons, 15 July 1941', *Hansard, Vol. 373*, cc. 463-7.
3. Air Vice-Marshal E.L. Frith RAF Retd, *Interview with the author*, 2007.
4. H. Wyndham, *The Household Cavalry Regiment: The First Household Cavalry Regiment* (Aldershot: Gale & Polden, 1952), p. 33.
5. *Ibid*.
6. *Ibid.*, p. 34.
7. J.R.I. Platt, *The Royal Wiltshire Yeomanry 1907-1967* (London: Garnstone Press, 1972), p. 98.
8. *Ibid*. This may have been one of the Fordsons of No 2 Armoured Car Company that was lost in the action near Ramadi on 24 May, referred to in Chapter 13.
9. No 11 Squadron, with Blenheims; No 80 Squadron and one flight of No 208 Squadron, equipped with Hurricanes; No 3 Squadron RAAF, newly-equipped with Tomahawks; 'X' Flight with Gladiators and No 803 Squadron, Fleet Air Arm with Fulmars and flight of Beaufighters of No 252/272 Squadron.
10. These included the Potez 63, which was considered a very effective bomber.
11. Further air reinforcements for the final phase arrived from Egypt following the end of the *Battleaxe* offensive. These consisted of No 45 Squadron with Blenheims and two newly-formed composite Hurricane Squadrons, Nos 450/260 and No 806/33. Wellingtons of Nos 37, 38, 70 and 148 Squadrons began operations against Beirut and Aleppo.
12. de Chair, *The Golden Carpet*. p. 168.
13. Platt, *Royal Wiltshire Yeomanry*. p. 100.
14. de Chair, *The Golden Carpet*,. p. 16.
15. *Ibid.*, p. 176.
16. *Ibid*.
17. So called because the Household Cavalry Regiment was a combined regiment of the Life Guards and Royal Horse Guards (The Blues)
18. de Chair, *The Golden Carpet*, p. 177.
19. J.J. Secter and J.P. Secter, *Recollections: Narrative reflections on the life and times of John J. Secter* (Victoria [BC]: Privately published, 2001), p. 27. John Secter was born in Winnipeg, Canada, to Ukranian-Jewish parents and had enlisted in the RAF while working in Palestine in December 1939.
20. Wing Commander R.C. Skellon RAF Retd, *Interview with J. Rolph*, RAF Armoured Cars Association, 2011.
21. Corporal Jemieson Lishman was buried at the Aleppo War Cemetery and LAC Walter Holl at the Ramleh War Cemetery.
22. Anon, *Yeoman Yeoman: The Warwickshire Yeomanry, 1920-1956* (Birmingham: The Queen's Own Warwickshire and Worcestershire Yeomanry Regimental Association, 1971), pp. 28-29.
23. T. Martin, *The Essex Regiment, 1929-1950.* (Brentwood, Essex: The Essex Regiment Association, 1952), pp. 62-63.
24. According to the *Army Narrative of the Campaign* [quoted in Air Ministry document, *Ground Defence*, Chapter 3, p. 40, RAF Regiment Museum Archives], the Gloster Gladiators of No 127 Squadron had flown to H3 on 22 June to operate against Palmyra, following the arrival of RAF ground personnel and equipment. However, there was no capability for ground defence of the forward landing ground, and as a consequence the AOC Palestine ordered them to be withdrawn to Lydda.
25. J.R.I. Platt, *The Royal Wiltshire Yeomanry,* p. 106. The French prisoners taken at Palmyra consisted of six officers, 87 legionnaires and 48 airmen and 24 camel troopers.
26. Flying Officer Skellon had been in Alexandria when the call had come for No 2 Armoured Car Company to proceed to Iraq. He had then returned to Amman but had contracted

dysentery en route. He was treated in the Australian General Hospital in Palestine.
27 Wing Commander R.C. Skellon RAF Retd, *Interview with the author,* 2010.
28 J.R.I. Platt, *The Royal Wiltshire Yeomanry,* pp. 93, 98. The troopers of the 4th Cavalry Brigade had only given up their horses four months earlier. Rifles were in such short supply that some drivers were issued with pick handles as weapons. The two Squadrons of the Royal Wiltshire Yeomanry could only muster 78 men for the attack on Palmyra on 29 June.
29 Anon, *Paiforce: The Official Story of the Persia and Iraq Command 1941-1946* (London: HMSO, 1948), p. 48.
30 I.S.O. Playfair *et al., The Mediterranean and Middle East, Vol. II,* History of the Second World War (London: HMSO, 1956) p. 221.
31 WO 373/47 *War Office and Ministry of Defence: Military Secretary's Department: Recommendations for Honours and Awards for Gallant and Distinguished Service (Army), Military Cross.* Flight Lieutenant W.J.L. Stevenson.
32 *Ibid.,* Acting Squadron Leader Michael Peter Casano.
33 Churchill, 'Speech to the House of Commons, 15 July 1941'. The reference to the Essex Yeomanry is not correct. It was of course 1st Battalion of the Essex Regiment and the armoured cars referred to were those of No 2 Armoured Car Company, RAF.
34 General Sir Archibald P. Wavell GCB CMG MC, 'Despatch on Operations in the Middle East, from 7th February, 1941 to 15th July 1941', Supplement to *The London Gazette,* 3 July 1946, p. 3441.

Chapter Fifteen

Operation Crusader

"For the first time, British and Empire troops will meet the Germans with ample equipment in modern weapons of all kinds. The battle itself will affect the whole course of the war"

Winston Churchill, Prime Minister[1]

"...these aeroplanes... they shot the unit up completely, absolutely everything; every car had a ruddy bullet hole in it. There were several injured and there was one killed"

LAC Vic Morte, No 2 Armoured Car Company[2]

Notwithstanding the successful outcomes from the Iraq Revolt and the Syrian Campaign, Egypt still faced the major threat from German and Italian forces in Libya. The fortress of Tobruk had been besieged since April, and its garrison of Australian, British, Indian and Polish troops, had repelled major assaults. Despite heavy losses in shipping, the Royal Navy had kept up the steady delivery of supplies through the small and battered seaport. With Tobruk in Allied hands, Rommel could not consider a move into Egypt; however, General Wavell also could not contemplate a major advance until reinforcements of personnel and aircraft had arrived from the United Kingdom.

Despite the distractions of the campaigns in Iraq, Syria, Crete and East Africa, the Western Desert Force had launched two limited offensives into Libya. Operation *Brevity* was launched in mid-May with a small force of two brigades equipped with patched-up tanks and borrowed transport. The objectives were to drive the Germans from Sollum and Capuzzo, and, if possible (as was the Prime Minister's fervent hope), to relieve Tobruk. Rommel had just received crucial reinforcements in the form of a second armoured division, the *15th Panzer Division*, and the British High Command were apprehensive that he would soon use his newly-arrived armour to strike deep into Egypt. After three days of fighting, Rommel sent in the German panzers. Despite having reached all their objectives, the few British tanks could not hold off the determined German armoured counterattack, and the British infantry, after having captured Halfaya Pass, were exposed on the open ground above the escarpment. There was no option but to return to the previous positions and Operation *Brevity* was called off.

Before the remainder of the *15th Panzer Division* could reach the Front, Wavell was determined to launch another offensive, Operation *Battleaxe*. Churchill pinned great hope on the success of this operation and had rushed a convoy of tanks through the Mediterranean. *Battleaxe* was launched on 15 June, with two armoured and two infantry brigades. By the second day however, the British armour suffered a severe reverse and again failed to halt the German counter-thrust. Wavell lost nearly half of the 190 tanks that were sent into battle. The Matilda 'I' tanks, which had proven formidable against the Italians, lost the reputation as the invulnerable queen of the battlefield, having been easily accounted for by a handful of German 88-mm anti-aircraft guns quickly adapted for use in the anti-tank role. Within two days, the British troop and transport columns were withdrawn to Sidi Barrani. The RAF had provided intensive air cover over Western Desert Force, but had lost 33 fighters and three bombers. The timing of this operation had consequences for other theatres, and in particular for Operation *Exporter* and for 'Habforce', as it was only after *Battleaxe* had concluded that RAF squadrons could be sent to support the forces in Syria.

Whilst these limited offensives had inflicted more damage on the enemy than at first thought, Churchill was unhappy with the conclusion. General Wavell had been dealing with the huge Middle East Command for some two years, and Churchill decided that he was tired and in need of a rest. The inconclusive outcome for Operation *Battleaxe* had settled matters, and in July 1941 he exchanged places with General Sir Claude Auchinleck, Commander-in-Chief India.[3] The Western Desert Force became the Eighth Army in early-September 1941, and Lieutenant-General Alan Cunningham, fresh from victories against the Italians in Abyssinia was appointed as its commander. Auchinleck, as the new Commander-in-Chief Middle East, was immediately urged by the Prime Minister to 'renew the offensive in the Western Desert,' if possible before the fighting in Syria ended.[4] 'The Auk' however, was determined not to be rushed. Control over Iraq had to be re-established, Syria stabilised, and the defence of Cyprus against airborne attack assured, before he would contemplate an offensive in the Western Desert. The British Chiefs of Staff offered 150 new American tanks, 40,000 men, and the diversion of scarce shipping as an inducement to hasten his plans. Auchinleck accepted these but set about planning the new offensive, to be known as Operation *Crusader*, for early November. Auchinleck was also fully conscious of the swift progress of Hitler's Operation *Barbarossa* in Russia. He recognised that should it be maintained then Syria, Iraq and Palestine would be threatened by a German advance south through the Caucasus. Priority was therefore given to defeating the *Afrika Korps* in Libya so that the British forces could then turn and deal with the potential threat from the north through Syria.

The Air Commanders in the Middle East were also replaced, and the newcomers proved to be exceedingly good appointments. In May 1941, Air Marshal Longmore was replaced as AOC-in-C RAF Middle East by his deputy, Air Marshal Arthur Tedder.[5] Longmore, to his credit, had directed a small professional air force on active service over three continents that had operated on improvisation and to some extent bluff, with a pioneering spirit and a piratical flare. Tedder would however, take the best aspects of this force and forge a modern instrument of air power. He believed firmly that the Air Force should closely cooperate with the Army, but he was also determined that it should provide air support on a sound tactical basis, and not be subservient to the numerous and nefarious demands of the Army. The RAF was to provide full support to the Army's plans for an offensive, but the methods were to be left to the air commanders.

Air Headquarters Egypt, with responsibility for local air defence of Cairo and surrounds, was formed from No 202 Group, while No 204 Group was reorganised as Air Headquarters Western Desert, and from October became known as Western Desert Air Force, shortened to Desert Air Force in 1943. Air Commodore Raymond Collishaw had also left the desert in July when his overseas tour had expired, and his place as AOC, Western Desert Air Force was taken by Air Vice-Marshal Arthur 'Mary' Coningham.[6] Coningham and Tedder formed a strong, successful and lasting partnership. Both were ardent believers in the importance of army/air cooperation and, to emphasise this, Coningham immediately moved his Air Headquarters to Maaten Bagush, to stand beside the Eighth Army Headquarters. For the coming offensive, the Western Desert Air Force would have 29 squadrons and also be able to call on the Wellington bombers of No 205 Group. To further improve air support for the Army, mobile Air Support Control units were created with both RAF and Army staff which would operate closely at Corps and Divisional level.

From July onwards, the RAF in the Middle East was reinforced, with new squadrons and personnel hailing from all the corners of the Empire and the Globe; Australians, Canadians, New Zealanders, Rhodesians and South Africans, along with Poles and Free Frenchmen. Seven South African Air Force squadrons moved to Egypt from April onwards following their successes in the campaign in Italian East Africa. Obsolescent aircraft were also replaced as new aircraft types and marks arrived; Hurricane IIs and Wellington IIs from the United Kingdom, and Tomahawks, Kittyhawks, Marylands and Bostons from the factories of the United States.[7] Tedder set about improving the training, supply and technical organisation, and demanded the despatch of radar, wireless observer, repair, maintenance and salvage units from the United Kingdom. In June 1941, the Middle East Air Force had comprised 34½ squadrons but by October this had risen to 52 squadrons with 846 aircraft of which 780 were up-to-date types.

In his Despatch on the First Western Desert Campaign, Air Marshal Longmore had identified the prime importance that had to be placed on the mobility of the RAF fighter squadrons.[8] The fighters of the Desert Air Force had only a short range, and it was essential, given the speed with which the Army motorised and armoured units could move that the squadrons be able to keep pace with them to provide effective and near continuous support. Numbers 258 and 262 (Fighter) Wings, therefore became self-contained and mobile, with administrative and support units under command. Each wing had control over two to six squadrons and was able to operate quickly from forward landing grounds which could be rapidly occupied and readied for flying operations.

By September, the Army still had only a precarious hold on the frontier but fully cooperated with the establishment of the fighter squadrons on the landing grounds in the Sidi Barrani area. Radar stations (known at the time as AMES) were established well forward and the Eighth Army anti-aircraft defences at Mersa Matruh were considerably reduced and brought forward to protect the airfields.[9] The land offensive of Operation *Crusader* was timed to commence on 18 November. The RAF had launched limited sorties for the previous month against Axis shipping, supply lines, and the enemy fighter and dive-bomber airfields in Cyrenaica, and provided patrols and interception over the army units that were moving into position for the offensive.[10]

Air Marshal Tedder was still concerned about the ground defence capability of the Air Force as he pushed his squadrons forward during a rapidly moving offensive...'I felt that our anti-aircraft defences in general, and our aerodrome defences in particular, were our weakest spot, and a vital one.'[11] He wrote later:

> 'I was satisfied that the Army had genuinely done their best to provide for defence of forward aerodromes, and I myself had denuded our aerodromes in the Delta most drastically of machine-guns. The [RAF] armoured cars had been brought all the way from Habbaniya and would go forward to support the anti-aircraft defences...'[12]

The Wings and Squadrons had been provided with more 3-tonners for transport and these columns were long and vulnerable. The role of Nos 1 and 2 Armoured Car Companies would now change. Now that the Army had an adequate number of their own armoured car units, the RAF armoured car companies could concentrate on providing observer screens and protection to the landing grounds of the Desert Air Force. The RAF armoured cars were to have an active role in supporting the RAF fighter force and would be an essential protective and shepherding force for RAF headquarters units, ground parties and transport columns as they moved forward.[13]

No 2 Armoured Company spent August and September 1941 at RAF Amman in Jordan. A final reconnaissance and tactical training exercise with both the experienced and newly-arrived airmen was made to Qasr al Kharanah. Time was then spent preparing for the move back to the Western Desert and, after only a two-

The Fordson armoured cars and tenders of No 2 Armoured Car Company move off across the Libyan frontier at the beginning of Operation Crusader, November 1941 (© IWM CM 1409).

338

month break from operations, the Company arrived at Air Headquarters Western Desert at Maaten Bagush on 12 October and reported for duty with the Western Desert Air Force. Despite more than a year of war in Libya, it must have been with a mixture of mirth and frustration, that the 'old hands' in the RAF armoured car crews returned to the same localities from which they had set off in pursuit of the Italian Army in December 1940 (Map 26, p. 341).

With only 12 days to go before the launch of Operation *Crusader*, half of No 2 Armoured Car Company, under the command of Flight Lieutenant Wilfred Stevenson, moved up to Sidi Barrani to work with No 258 (Fighter) Wing, from whence they escorted the fighter force to LG 110, a few miles south.[14] Armoured car patrols were immediately sent out far to the west along the Libyan frontier. Rommel had launched a surprise armoured thrust towards the frontier during September and the threat from probing enemy reconnaissance units was ever-present, particularly as the build-up for *Crusader* was underway. For the next two weeks this RAF armoured car observer screen kept watch for the *Afrika Korps* and *Luftwaffe*. Surveillance was not made easy by relentlessly raging sandstorms. Other tasks included establishing aircraft homing points for new forward landing grounds, assisting the Royal Engineers to clear away wrecked aircraft, and marking out a decoy airfield. LAC Vic Morte of No 2 Company describes the routine of the armoured car sections once the cars were 'in the blue':

> ... In the Desert, the usual daily duties were that you did a guard every night. There was one section picked to do the guard and we each did an hour's stag. There was a laager of about 30 vehicles all facing outward as much as possible. The idea was that you patrolled the laager armed with a 303 rifle. You walked round at a great distance, but you couldn't go too far or you could get lost. The light in the desert was funny. On a number of occasions I'd got lost and panicked because I couldn't find the way to get back to the laager.
>
> There were long periods where we saw nothing. That means we were in a certain area and all we were doing was standing patrols every day. There was always a section picked to do post for one week. Consequently, from there we went out every day practically for as much as 30 miles, scouting a certain area. And then when we got to a certain time of the day, we'd return. These were really good luck exercises.[15]

Meanwhile, on 24 October, at RAF Habbaniya, No 1 Armoured Car Company was given four days to prepare a detachment of two sections to send to Egypt. The Company had been placed at the disposal of the Air Marshal Tedder by the AOC Iraq, Air Vice-Marshal John D'Albiac, who informed him that 14 armoured cars would be available at 48 hours' notice from 26 October 1941. The offer was gratefully accepted by Tedder. The No 1 Armoured Car Company Detachment, as it was known, was under the command of Squadron Leader 'Jonah' Jones and comprised Nos 1 and 3 Sections, under Flight Lieutenants S.W. Griffiths and J. St.C. Olliff-Lee, respectively.[16] It consisted of six officers, six NCOs and 77 airmen, with a Ford utility, 14 Rolls-Royce armoured cars, four Rolls-Royce wireless-tenders, a Fordson wireless tender and six Fordson tenders. The long journey from Habbaniya, which began on 28 October, through Transjordan, Palestine and on to RAF Helwan in Egypt, was not without incident as the aged and weary state of many of the vehicles was revealed.

Painted in the diagonal Caunter-style camouflage, the venerable Rolls-Royce armoured cars of the Western Desert detachment of No 1 Company prepare to leave Habbaniya for Egypt in October 1941 (RAF Habbaniya Assn).

Owing to a shortage of Rolls-Royce spares in Egypt, the Company took two-month's supply with them from Iraq. As the Detachment moved along the road to Cairo, mechanical failures to Rolls-Royces and Fordson tenders necessitated repairs to axles, a steering column, a gearbox, a burnt out generator, a half shaft, and in two cases required the complete replacement of the engines.[17] Four more Rolls-Royce armoured cars were allocated on arrival in Egypt which took the total to 18. In only four days at Helwan, they carried out repairs, fitted the three leading section Rolls-Royces with the newer Vickers K gas-operated machine-guns *in lieu* of the antiquated Lewis guns, and exchanged the 1933-vintage No 1 radio sets for the more modern and longer range No 18M Collins sets. The Detachment then set off for Maaten Bagush, and arrived one week before the date set for the start of the offensive.

The first offensive by the Eighth Army, Operation *Crusader*, was launched on the stormy night of 17/18 November. The poor weather, of unprecedented violence, served to immobilise a large proportion of the German armour and waterlogged the enemy airfields, thus giving the Eighth Army complete surprise. To the north, XIII Corps, with the 4th Indian and New Zealand Divisions and 1st Army Tank Brigade crossed 'the wire' south of Sidi Omar and moved north to isolate the German and Italian positions at Sollum, Halfaya and Sidi Omar. Further to the south, XXX Corps, with 7th Armoured Division, 4th Armoured Brigade Group, 1st South African Division and 22nd Guards Brigade crossed at Fort Maddalena, under the protection of a swarm of fighters, and set off towards Tobruk with the task of bringing to battle and defeating the German and Italian armour and then linking with up with the besieged garrison as it broke out.[18]

Rommel's focus had been firmly fixed on the capture of Tobruk since April, and he initially treated the new offensive as a small raid. It took three days before he realised the seriousness and intent of the offensive and sent the *Afrika Korps* off to meet the thrust from Egypt. The battle now developed into a series of furious

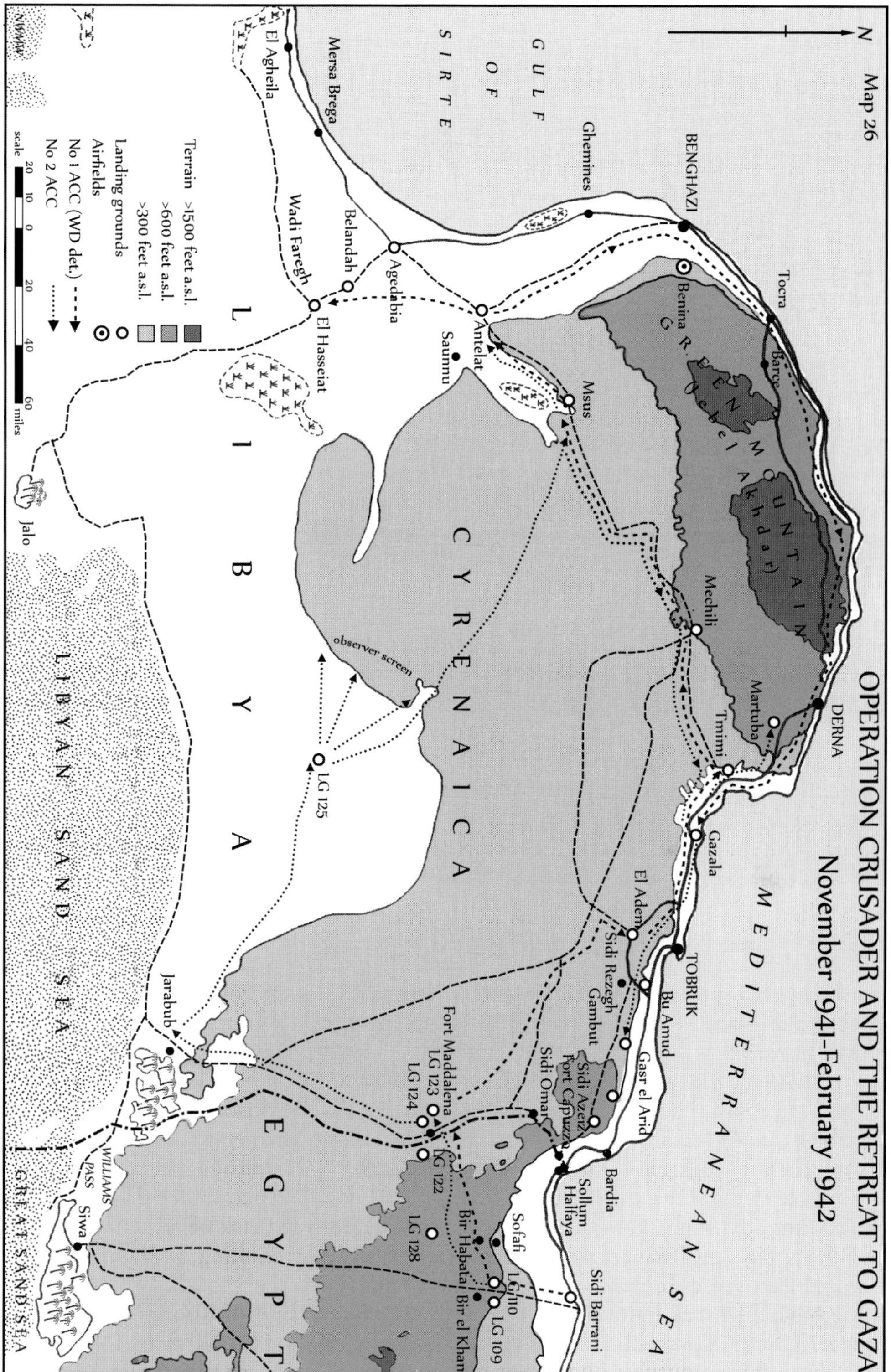
Map 26
OPERATION CRUSADER AND THE RETREAT TO GAZALA
November 1941–February 1942
N
MEDITERRANEAN SEA
GULF OF SIRTE
BENGHAZI
Tocra
Barce
Benina
GREEN MOUNTAIN (Jebel Akhdar)
DERNA
Martuba
Tmimi
Gazala
Mechili
Msus
Antelat
Saunnu
Agedabia
Belandah
El Hasseiat
Ghemines
Mersa Brega
El Agheila
Wadi Faregh
L I B Y A
C Y R E N A I C A
observer screen
LG 125
Jalo
LIBYAN SAND SEA
El Adem
TOBRUK
Sidi Rezegh
Bu Amud
Gambut
Gasr el Arid
Sidi Azeiz
Fort Capuzzo
Bardia
Sidi Omar
Sollum
Halfaya
Fort Maddalena
LG 123
LG 124
LG 122
LG 128
Sofafi
Sidi Barrani
Bir Habata
Bir el Khamsa
LG 110
LG 109
Jarabub
E G Y P T
WILLIAMS PASS
Siwa
GREAT SAND SEA
Terrain >1500 feet a.s.l.
>600 feet a.s.l.
>300 feet a.s.l.
Landing grounds
Airfields
No 1 ACC (WD det.)
No 2 ACC
scale 20 10 0 20 40 60 miles

and confusing struggles to wrest control of various features on the escarpment overlooking the road to Tobruk, in particular the airfield at Sidi Rezegh. General Cunningham, despite having been successful in the East African campaign, had no experience of tank warfare, and unfortunately allowed his armoured brigades to be dispersed and defeated in detail. Furthermore, the inadequacy of the British tank guns in range and penetration, and the effectiveness of the German anti-tank tactics had taken a heavy toll.

After seven days of struggle, the Eighth Army was in dire straits. The Western Desert Air Force did what it could to support the Army with its hard-earned air superiority. The Air Support Control system, despite having been so carefully planned, was found to have some flaws. For example, as air and land units intermingled, clarifying a safe bomb-line beyond which the RAF light bombers could attack enemy troop concentrations without harming their own was often impossible. Overall, however, the RAF cooperation with the land forces was used to great effect.[19]

The RAF armoured cars had been fully committed from the first day of Operation *Crusader*. Number 1 Armoured Car Company had been sent to relieve No 2 Company, with a section each going to LG 109 and LG 110 just south of Sidi Barrani. Each day, a Rolls-Royce armoured car was also sent 15 miles out to the south-west of Bir el Khamsa to protect an AMES. Number 2 Company departed for a special mission deep in the desert.

On 19 November, No 258 Wing, as planned, moved up to LGs 122 and 123, located on the mud flats and salt pans near Fort Maddalena on the Libyan frontier. Until mid-1941, the most forward airfield for the fighters was at Sidi Barrani, but with the increasing number of squadrons planned for *Crusader,* this single airfield was inadequate. Over the preceding few weeks, four new airfields had, therefore, been carved from virgin desert, 60 miles to the south and 'under the enemy's nose.'[20] This placed them well away from the torrential rain on the coast and in line with the planned advance of the British armour.[21] Rain had fortuitously waterlogged the enemy airfields on the first day of the offensive, but these landing grounds were unaffected. The Wing was escorted by No 1 Armoured Car Company over a poor track that was soft with recent rain and made heavy work for the Rolls-Royces and Fordson tenders, which suffered again from a few cracked chassis and a punctured petrol tank. Notwithstanding the difficult 'going', the Company went out immediately on arrival to set up an observer screen.

Despite early successes, the British armour had been frittered away in small packets against the German anti-tank screen and Rommel had seized the initiative. Sidi Rezegh was recaptured by the *Afrika Korps*, the British armour fought itself to near exhaustion, and a South African infantry brigade was practically annihilated by a German panzer attack. By 23 November, General Cunningham's confidence had been severely eroded, and he was thought to be near breaking point. General Auchinleck had become concerned that Cunningham would be no longer able to press the offensive.[22]

However on 24 November, Rommel, rather than dealing with the remnants of the British armoured brigades, made a bold but inexplicable decision, and turned his armour and motorised units away from the battlefields south of Tobruk and towards the Egyptian frontier. The *21st Panzer Division* was sent eastwards towards Sidi Omar, while the Italian *Ariete* and *Trieste Divisions* were directed on Fort Capuzzo. His aim was to destroy the Eighth Army supply dumps and maintenance centres south of Sidi Barrani, in particular the railhead at Bir Habata, thus cutting off the

British armour and infantry from their supply bases and moreover, cause alarm and anxiety in the Eighth Army High Command.

General Cunningham narrowly escaped capture by one of these columns as it overran XIII Corps Headquarters. The rear echelons of Eighth Army were thrown into complete chaos and panic. As the Germans were now using many captured vehicles, the Western Desert Air Force, in attempting to check the advance, found great difficulty in distinguishing between hostile and friendly forces, as they raced in an easterly direction. Furthermore, the RAF fighter squadrons concentrated at the Maddalena landing grounds lay in Rommel's path, and yet had lost the W/T links to various Army Headquarters as they were overrun or scattered. Consequently, there was a serious delay in notifying Air Headquarters Western Desert and subordinate RAF formations of these developments.

Group Captain 'Bing' Cross, the officer commanding 258 Wing, first learned of the threat to his squadrons when his fighter commanders reported a German column moving eastward at a fast pace. Eighth Army Headquarters scoffed at the idea that the enemy could be in this location; however, one of his squadron leaders, an Australian, Peter Jeffrey, assured him 'well tell them that the tanks have big black crosses on them...' [23] This was confirmed when an SAAF squadron commander reported following a reconnaissance that there was a mass of vehicles where none were supposed to be, and they appeared to be heading directly for the Maddalena landing grounds.[24]

Air Vice-Marshal 'Mary' Coningham took the view that he had been left high and dry by the failure of the Army High Command. He had no guarantee that they would protect his frontier airfields. Cross had flown to see Coningham, who informed him that he 'had asked the Army to alert the brigade assigned to airfield defence, only to be told that it had been sent elsewhere.'[25] The situation was obscure and rich in rumour and misinformation. He ordered his fighters to withdraw. At this very moment it had also been recognised that the Western Desert Air Force had achieved and was maintaining air superiority over the battlefield, but as Coningham told Tedder, 'I was loath to do any moves at all, but the force is so valuable that it could not be risked'. To the Army he had stated firmly, 'in the prevailing confusion and lack of information', little else could be done.[26]

An hour before sunset on 24 November, the eight fighter squadrons at landing grounds 122, 123 and 124 were warned that Rommel's armour had broken through and lay only 10 miles to the north. Swarms of fighters took to the air and flew 20 miles east to LG 128 and beyond. Many had never been to their new location and incorrectly came down only ten miles further on at LG 122. That night, fearing an attack by German parachute troops, the pilots slept under the wings of their aircraft, which were parked wing-tip to wing-tip.

While the aircraft had been pulled back, the ground crews had stayed at LGs 122 and 123. The only weapons they possessed were rifles and pistols, and most were not trained or equipped to defend the airfields. Number 1 Armoured Car Company remained to stiffen the defence and the few anti-aircraft gunners sited their guns to engage tanks.

Any airfield with aeroplanes on the ground is in a vulnerable position, and 175 aircraft now sat weakly protected and exposed on a single landing ground. Should the German columns have discovered them, the large majority of the fighter force could have been destroyed on the ground in a very short time. After having spent the night anticipating an attack, No 1 Company sent out a patrol screen, five miles to the north and west, but the armoured car crews were no doubt relieved to see no sign of the enemy.

The following evening, the threat had become even more serious, and the RAF ground echelons were sent away from the landing grounds and out into the desert. Here they remained under the watchful eye of the RAF armoured cars until it was determined that it was safe to return to the landing grounds at first light. The crew of RRAC *Dhibban* had some difficulty while out on a night reconnaissance. The armoured car suffered a fractured sump plate. This was successfully replaced but as all the oil had drained away the engine seized after the car had travelled only a short distance. There was no other option but to abandon the car and walk back to LG 122. The following morning the Rolls-Royce was recovered and sent back to the rear echelon for repairs, but not before the working back axle was exchanged with that from another car that had been damaged, thus illustrating the degree of cannibalisation now required to keep an adequate number of the RAF Rolls-Royces up to establishment. The loss of an armoured car was soon rectified by the now homeless crew of *Dhibban* who transferred all their equipment to another Rolls-Royce that had been discovered at a nearby Army salvage dump.

At this point, with Rommel threatening the line of communications and supply dumps of the Eighth Army and the forward landing grounds, all could have been lost. However, General Auchinleck realised that General Cunningham had lost control and removed him from command, appointing his Deputy Chief of Staff, Major-General Neil Ritchie, in his place.[27] Auchinleck wanted no let-up in the offensive or withdrawal, and ordered an all-out attack. The New Zealand Division struck west to recover the airfield at Sidi Rezegh, to relieve Tobruk, and at the same time to deprive the *Luftwaffe* of airfields around Gambut. The Western Desert Air Force was no longer required to refer to Eighth Army Headquarters for orders, and was told to act on its own initiative. Tomahawks and Hurricanes were sent off from the Maddalena airfields to strafe Rommel's columns, and this was followed up with a pounding by the Blenheims and Marylands.

As a consequence, Rommel's 'dash to the wire' ran out of steam. He had outpaced support from his air force, his columns were running short of fuel, and his armour was being frittered away in charges against the 25-pdrs of the British field artillery. Axis Forces besieging Tobruk were threatened by the renewed offensive by Eighth Army, so Rommel raced back there to prevent the New Zealand Division linking up with the fortress garrison as it broke out. Despite inflicting heavy losses on the New Zealanders, the effort proved fruitless as reinforcements arrived and the German and Italian troops neared exhaustion.

The threat to the Western Desert Air Force forward landing grounds had abated. Number 1 Company spent the next few weeks on patrols and protecting landing ground decoy parties on the Libyan border. On 1 December, one of the patrols discovered an armoured car that had been abandoned by the Army. Refitted and repaired it was christened *Norfan* and yet another armoured car that had belonged to the Army entered service with the RAF.

A week before the opening of the *Crusader* offensive, a further element of the operation had been put in motion from the oasis at Jarabub, 80 miles south-west of Mersa Matruh and some 20 miles into Libya. 'Oasis Group', composed predominantly of the 29th Indian Infantry Brigade and under the command of Brigadier Denys W. Reid, had been formed to protect the British-held oases at Siwa and Jarabub. During the offensive, its tasks were two-fold; first, to stage a feint towards the Axis-held oasis at Jalo to distract Rommel's attention and suggest that a large column threatened his southern desert flank (to this end the Group was supplied with a number of mocked-up dummy tanks), and second, to support the operations of a special RAF detachment. It was to move west and capture Jalo oasis. The departure of the column was carefully broadcast in a report by the BBC as part of the bluff and described as a substantial armoured force.[28]

This detachment was led by Wing Commander Eric Whitley, and was known as 'Whitforce'.[29] It consisted of long-range Hurricanes of No 33 Squadron and Blenheims of No 113 Squadron, and was to operate from an advanced landing ground, LG 125, located deep in the Cyrenaican desert behind enemy lines, 110 miles west of Jarabub along the track to Jalo. The Hurricanes and Blenheims were to launch attacks on transport and troops moving along the coast road of the Gulf of Sirte and thereby disrupt the Axis supply lines to eastern Cyrenaica. Should the offensive by Eighth Army towards Tobruk go as planned, they would attack vehicle and troop concentrations on the enemy line of retreat. To support this move, Oasis Group formed a mixed column, 'Force E', and was composed of lorried infantry, South African armoured cars and artillery. Indian Army supply convoys, protected by the South African armoured cars, had begun transporting petrol, water and supplies to the landing ground in mid-October.

In the last week of October, Squadron Leader Casano, with two sections of No 2 Armoured Car Company, moved south to Jarabub to support the operations of 'Whitforce'. On 1 November, while the two sections of the Company were

Casano (centre) briefs his officers before a patrol including Flight Lieutenant Stevenson MC (second from right) (© IWM CM 1413).

occupied with aerodrome defence duties at Jarabub, Squadron Leader Casano and Flight Lieutenant Alan Douglas set off on a four-day reconnaissance to LG 125. A week later, Flying Officer Mosley went out to clear and mark the landing ground to facilitate the arrival of the aircraft of 'Whitforce'.

Meanwhile, the 7th South African Reconnaissance Battalion had been ordered to take over the protection of the aerodrome, with the assistance of No 2 Armoured Car Company. The Battalion's Commanding Officer, Lieutenant-Colonel Grobbelaar, had been told a few weeks earlier to prepare for a special mission and that '… in view of the arduous nature of the operation it would be advisable to get in some special desert training'.[30]

On 17 November, the eve of the opening of Operation *Crusader*, Grobbelaar was ordered by Eighth Army Headquarters to strike north and raid Mechili. Located well behind the Axis front lines and timed with an RAF bombing raid, it was hoped this would cause disruption and panic in the enemy rear areas. The South African Official History notes that Brigadier Reid assigned the RAF armoured cars (No 2 Company) to his command, but Grobbelaar later stated, "The RAF armoured cars which were to form part of the raiding force were 'very old military types and not very mobile from a desert-going point of view'".[31] Number 2 Armoured Car Company was therefore left behind at Jarabub and the raid was entrusted entirely to the South African armoured cars, crewed by what Grobbelaar described as 'amateurs but possessing boundless enthusiasm.'[32] Given the obstacles to movement of a large armoured column, the raid through difficult terrain was considered barely achievable. After two days' struggle and with few of the South African armoured cars in a fit state to proceed, the column was forced to retrace its steps and returned without having engaged the enemy.

The South African Marmon Herrington cars, despite possessing four-wheel drive, weighed some 6 tons (2 tons more than the Fordsons of No 2 Armoured Car Company), and therefore experienced great difficulty in moving through soft sand. Progress was slow and it was fortuitous that the raid was called off as the result might have been disastrous had they been committed to battle. However, the considerable desert experience of the officers and airmen of No 2 Armoured Car Company could have been of great use to the column in pursuing the mission had they been allowed to accompany them.[33]

The preponderance of South African armoured cars with 'Force E' was more a result of an enthusiasm for action rather than an attempt to create a balanced force. The 7th South African Reconnaissance Battalion, under the command of Lieutenant-Colonel Grobbelaar, possessed 49 Marmon Herrington armoured cars. The major problem faced by 'Force E', as the vehicles wallowed through the soft sand on the northern boundary of the Great Sand Sea, was the rapid consumption of petrol and this predicament was exacerbated by the presence of the large number of the heavy South African armoured cars and field guns.

The remaining two sections under Flight Lieutenant Welham of No 2 Company, having been relieved of their responsibilities on observer screen duties with No 258 Wing on 12 November, moved south to join up with Squadron Leader Casano and the rest of the Company. LAC Vic Morte describes the journey south to Jarabub:

> We went into the desert, and of course there was always this business of looking after your rear. There was always about half a dozen blokes or more who were kept back. I was one. It was a good posting because we

The view through the visor of a Fordson as it arrives at Siwa Oasis (© Crown copyright. Chester, RAF Regiment Museum).

were at Sidi Haneish with the Air Stores Park. We were there about a week or so and it was decided that we'd got to go up and join the unit. So we went from Sidi Haneish, to Maaten Bagush, to Mersa Matruh then we cut a path across the desert right down as far as Siwa, and from Siwa we cut across the dry land and then climbed up to Williams Pass, down the other side and into Jarabub.[34]

Located just over the Libyan frontier on the northern fringe of the Great Sand Sea, Jarabub was a mud-walled village with the tomb of a saint of the Senussi sect, and an Italian fort, surrounded by numerous date palms. The least attractive features were the millions of flies and the high Epsom salts content of the water, 'occasioning a universal looseness of the bowels'.[35] LAC Vic Morte continues:

It was rather fantastic really. It was an exciting trip. It was one of those trips you would not have missed. From Jarabub, what was so interesting about it really? We stayed there for two or three days. It was the Kingdom of the Senussi tribe, and it was quite a sacred place. There was a shrine there and actually all the water was drawn from a well in the middle of the town and after we'd been out for some distance, sometimes about 30-40 miles, the lads went back one day for some water and the Royal Engineers who had been pumping it up said 'Oh, we've found three dead Italians in the well.'[36]

With No 2 Company now concentrated at Jarabub, it set off for LG 125 on the morning of 19 November following the departure of 'Force E' which had left

Airmen of No 2 Armoured Car Company bivouacked with their Fordson armoured car while on a patrol (© IWM CM 1547).

the previous day. They were charged with escorting the ground parties of Nos 33 and 113 Squadrons, No 3 Refuelling Party, a W/T unit, and two sections of No 9 Light Field Ambulance.[37] The landing ground was reached the following day. Number 2 Company remained at LG 125 while 'Force E', including the 7th South African Reconnaissance Battalion, continued on with great difficulty over sandy and rough 'going' to attack Jalo, which was captured on 24 November along with 670 prisoners. The movement difficulties encountered by 'Force E' had made a mockery of the original intention of the military planners in Cairo to send a major armoured thrust through Jalo and to the coast road of the Gulf of Sirte.

Meanwhile, 'Whitforce' set about preparing for air operations against the coast road. The Hurricanes of No 33 Squadron flew in to LG 125 from Jarabub late on 20 November and No 2 Company was charged with defending the airfield from interference from both Axis air and ground forces. Consequently, the following day the Company moved 40 miles to the north-west and established observer screens and sent out defensive patrols.

The movement of 'Force E' was advertised to the enemy so that it would provide a distraction to the main thrust of XXX Corps. The *Luftwaffe* was, therefore, determined to prevent the force from carrying out its role and this was to have fatal consequences for some in 'Whitforce', as over the next three days, a series of air attacks were made on LG 125.

Half-an-hour before noon on 21 November, No 2 Company was attacked by 10 Messerschmitt Bf 110s. A wireless tender, carrying the supply of water, was burnt out, and another wireless tender and two Fordson armoured cars damaged. Flight Lieutenant Alan Douglas showed considerable bravery and coolness under fire when he left his armoured car and ran to one of the unarmoured wireless tenders and endeavoured to send a message calling for assistance from the Hurricanes at LG 125. The tender then came under attack and so he ran to two armoured cars that had become the primary target of the German fighters and directed the fire from the two Fordsons at the attacking aircraft. One of the Bf 110s was hit and crashed five miles away but the enemy aircrew made good their escape when another of the Bf 110s landed and picked them up. Surprisingly, the only casualties were AC1 Matthews and AC2 Lowe who were both wounded. They were returned to LG 125 for evacuation by Blenheim to Jarabub, and two wireless tenders sent out to replace the damaged vehicles.[38]

The following day, the Company was not to be as fortunate. Eleven Messerschmitt Bf 110s, a Junkers Ju 88 and a Cant 1007 arrived at eight in the morning and for the next hour-and-a-half attacked the Company in its observation position 40 miles to the north-west of the landing ground. Three more tenders, one with the unit petrol and water supply, and the staff pick-up were destroyed, including the two tenders sent out the previous evening, and one armoured car was burnt out. Alan Douglas won further admiration from his fellow airmen for his coolness as he assisted the wounded from a burning tender while still under attack.[39] All the remaining Fordson armoured cars were damaged with half the tyres written off. One Bf 110 was damaged in reply. Flight Lieutenant Mosley, Pilot Officer Johnston, LACs Powell and Webb and AC2 Norris were all wounded. Sadly, LAC George Webb's wounds were mortal. Vic Morte recounted the events of the day:

> In Jarabub, a few of the blokes stayed back, but the rest pushed out to Landing Ground 125, and it was at 125 that I think 'Cass' [Casano] met his Waterloo. He started to push out patrols, but he didn't realise that at 12 o'clock every day they had a shufti and came over taking photographs. The following day the complete unit was brought together, idiotic, and these aeroplanes... came from Crete. And they shot the unit up completely, absolutely everything; every car had a ruddy bullet hole in it. There were several injured and there was one killed... I know Johnston got shot... he got five rounds in his backside...
>
> This chap Webb, it was rather unfortunate, he got sprayed in the back. It shows you just how silly people can be, the edict was that he should have been treated professionally, and he had received these terrible wounds and some silly bugger tried to sterilise it with iodine. He was in agony, he died shortly afterwards.
>
> I always remembered we buried him right out in the desert. He'd been hit with shrapnel in the back... Anyway they dug a shallow hole, put him into a blanket, put him down there, and when I drove away, it must have been half a mile away, and you couldn't even see... it blended into the desert. God knows how he was ever found. It was completely flat desert, no features.
>
> It's funny really, he belongs to someone, and when you actually bury them there's just a little mound of sand, and it's there, and when you drive away you look at it about a mile of driving and you think 'Good, God' there's nothing there, it's never ever going to be found. I can remember this so well.[40, 41]

The armoured cars were vulnerable to attack from the air, and Casano had developed tactics to deal as best they could with aircraft and weapons that could not have been contemplated when the cars were constructed 20 or more years earlier.

> The cars were dispersed. 'Cass' didn't have a car, so he was running around giving orders. He was telling them to get a sight lined up and then when he's [the enemy aircraft] coming towards you, just keep going straight and then when he starts to come down at the bottom of his dive and is about to release his bomb, port 90 or starboard 90 and you'll be the best part of a hundred yards before he hits. Driving towards the aircraft, the car commander would look up and as the bomb was released the commander would yell port 90 or starboard, and the bomb always fell behind.

At a time of great misery and difficulty Morte and his fellow airmen also found time to see some humour in events of the day:

> There's always a funny story, there was a wireless tender... and the driver of the truck, he could see that it was on fire at the back, dived out and this other chap, the electrician called Robin. He was sat there, and the doors were open, and the truck was moving, moving, moving and couldn't understand it, there was no one driving it.

The Company set off back to LG 125 and were attacked again by two Ju 88s, one of which was shot down and the crew captured. Morte continues:

> These aeroplanes had come down from Greece, and we shot one down. It came down, and belly landed. The front gunner was crushed in the fuselage and there was no way of getting him out, and he was in agony, and so the

A photograph of a German air crewman recovered from the Ju 88 shot down at LG 125 (© Crown copyright. Chester, RAF Regiment Museum).

pilot asked one of the officers, and he said, 'Well, this is over' ...so he got his gun and he blew his temple out.

With the thankful cover of night, the Company made it back without further incident, although the Ju 88s returned the next morning, slightly wounding LAC McKeown and damaging another car with its tyres shot up.

The two RAF squadrons were flying sortie after sortie from LG 125 against the supply columns of the Germans and Italians on the coast road, but the Hurricanes of No 33 Squadron also had to put in a lot of effort merely to defend the landing ground from incessant enemy bombing and strafing attacks. The Hurricanes took heavy toll on their attackers, but the flying squadrons did not go unscathed, when two Hurricanes and two Blenheims were lost on the ground. Late on 24 November, seven Hurricanes of No 73 Squadron arrived and were given the sole responsibility for defending the landing ground so that Nos 33 and 113 Squadron could concentrate on the attacks on the coast road and flying patrols over 'Force E', as it struggled across difficult country to Jalo. Despite the effectiveness of the attack on the Axis supply lines it was decided that the losses in Blenheims at LG 125 were too high and No 113 Squadron was withdrawn after a few days.

After the trials of the previous few days, No 2 Company dedicated a day to refitting, and by the following day it was able to send out four cars to resume the observer screen. Flying Officer Lucas went 20 miles out and brought in Flying Officer Anderson, who had crash-landed his Hurricane. The destruction of the previous few days was fortunately not repeated and the Company spent the remainder of December on observer screen duties with no further excitement. The threat of attack from Axis ground columns was now a possibility and the car patrols, led on various occasions by Flight Lieutenant Welham and Flying Officer Skellon, Sergeants Hoyles, Lawn and Smith and Corporals McWalters, Coultate, Ross and Green went out daily to the north-west, north and north-east in a 40 mile radius from the landing ground.

The operations of 'Force E' had however, caused only minor distraction to the Axis command and it made little difference to the outcome of the battles being fought around Tobruk. Brigadier Reid, following his successful capture of Jalo, was ordered to push on to Agedabia on 27 November to threaten the rear of the German-Italian Army. The Eighth Army command however, was still unaware of the great difficulties in moving the light motorised column across the difficult terrain to the coast road, let alone the problems with petrol and supplies that faced 29th Indian Brigade. Brigadier Reid therefore, had to content himself with sending out light reconnaissances towards Agedabia, and the force remained at Jalo until 20 December on half rations while conserving its meagre fuel reserves.

By the second week of December, the Axis forces around Tobruk were in a difficult situation. Petrol and ammunition were in short supply. The British armour and infantry were concentrating south of Tobruk and were now numerically superior on the ground as well as in the air. On 9 December, Rommel called off further attacks and ordered a withdrawal to positions at Gazala, thus bringing to an end the eight-month siege of Tobruk. Rommel left the Italian divisions to hold a line near Gazala. This was easily breached by the New Zealanders and Poles, and the Eighth Army moved westwards across the bulge. Benghazi changed hands for the third time in less than a year. Despite the rapid withdrawal, the *Afrika Korps* was in good order and not dispirited and the Axis formations consolidated in defensive positions at Agedabia.

The Western Desert Air Force was able to move into Cyrenaica and could now demonstrate its mobility. As a consequence, No 1 Armoured Car Company prepared to move as escorts to ground parties of the fighter force. On the day that Rommel had called off the siege of Tobruk, No 1 Section of No 1 Armoured Car Company with the advanced parties of the fighter squadrons, moved forward to the abandoned Italian aerodrome at El Adem.[42] They were joined a week later by HQ Section. After crossing 'the wire' into Libya the armoured cars passed over the battlefields of the previous three weeks including Sidi Rezegh, where the main struggle had occurred. The desert was strewn with disabled and burnt out tanks, strafed and bombed trucks, some still with their incinerated crews on board. The blowflies were breeding in profusion in the bodies of the dead and the smell of death, which hung heavily in the air, was ever-present. The *Luftwaffe* and *Regia Aeronautica* were still active and the columns were continually on the alert for air raids.

By 20 December, the HQ Section reached Mechili where the day was spent preparing the aerodrome for the arrival of the fighters the following day. Number 3 Section moved up from the landing grounds on the frontier and had in turn taken over El Adem from No 1 Section which had moved forward to join the HQ Section.

The transport columns of the RAF had been organised so as to move forward rapidly and occupy captured airfields, and at Mechili, had arrived on the airfield as the enemy fled westward in a cloud of dust. There were however, few supply vehicles to spare as the Army had first priority to transport the columns pursuing the retreating Axis ground forces. It was only by stripping Western Desert Air Force headquarters and other units of their cars and lorries that fuel for the aircraft could be moved forward. By this means, a convoy with 15,000 gallons of fuel arrived the day after Mechili was occupied, by which time the airfield had been cleared of obstructions. The next day, a rudimentary wireless network and anti-aircraft defence was functioning and four fighter squadrons of No 258 Wing were operating from the airstrip. Another four squadrons waited further back ready to move forward to the next bound of the advance.[43]

The commander of the Western Desert Air Force, Air Vice-Marshal 'Mary' Coningham, did not want his force to remain at Mechili for long. His reconnaissance aircraft had reported that there were potential landing grounds near Msus, 70 miles further west, but the first 'mud flat' selected was found on closer inspection to be a shallow lake. A better site was found further west, and fighters of No 258 Wing were operating from there the next day. The movement forward of the ground parties was not as easy and the Rolls-Royce armoured cars and tenders experienced problems in negotiating the difficult 'going' that was in parts, rocky and hilly and in others, flooded mud flats. The wear and tear of the advance meant that the crews were dealing with cracked chassis, damaged clutches, broken axles and burst petrol tanks, and at any time between one and four of the Company vehicles were under repair or out of action.

The HQ and No 1 Section of No 1 Armoured Car Company reached Msus on 24 and 26 December respectively, and were followed a few days later by No 3 Section. The last days of 1941 were spent searching for a crashed enemy aircraft shot down by the RAF Kittyhawks. This was found but all the crew had perished and only one could be buried as the remainder had been consumed in the explosion following the crash.

As a consequence of the capture by Eighth Army of the airfields in the bulge of Cyrenaica, 'Whitforce' at LG 125 had fulfilled its purpose. The sorties of the

Blenheims and Hurricanes had been fruitful despite the incessant attacks by the *Luftwaffe*. The small force had accounted for several hundred vehicles, including some petrol tankers on the roads and tracks along the Gulf of Sirte and had destroyed more than 30 enemy aircraft in the air and on the ground during sweeps over the Axis airfields around El Agheila.[44] Casano's armoured cars had also been out on road-watching task, monitoring enemy vehicle movements. Flying Officer Skellon, who had recently rejoined No 2 Company, describes one such patrol and the hazards of navigation in the desert:

> We settled at LG 125 for quite a long time, actually, and we carried out patrols to see what German vehicles we could see. I went out on one of these patrols one day and sat on the coast road and watched and counted them going up and down the road. This was about 150 miles behind the German lines. It was on Christmas Eve, and when we had finished and we set off to return to base, and I got lost coming back. We used a sun compass, and of course, the chaps were getting very antsy and rather bolshie. I had to get on the R/T, which we were never supposed to use, as there had to be complete radio silence. I said "I'm lost" and so they said "We'll send up a flare" and to my relief we were only about half a mile away.[45]

Skellon and his section escorted the advanced party of No 33 Squadron across to Msus on 27 December to join No 258 Wing and No 1 Company. Casano arrived with the remainder of the Company and No 33 Squadron on the first day of 1942. In a rare occurrence in the 20-year history of the RAF Armoured Car Companies, both were to spend New Year's Day 1942 at the same airfield, although neither of the two Companies Operations Record Books makes mention of there being any meeting.[46]

The German-Italian Army reached Agedabia in mid-December had held it until 12 January. Before the Eighth Army could launch an assault on these positions, Rommel commenced a further withdrawal, and covered by sandstorms, minefields and aggressive rear guard actions, the Axis forces retired to strong positions at El Agheila. Operation *Crusader* had succeeded in its aim of clearing the enemy from Cyrenaica. Rather than a decisive and crushing British victory, the struggle had been long and costly for both sides. By the time the Eighth Army approached the enemy positions, the supply difficulties had grown enormously and the thrust was spent. The Eighth Army could barely gather one weak armoured division to launch an attack. The German-Italian Army in Africa had not been destroyed and was now readying itself for a quick and decisive riposte.

Notes
1. Quoted in R. Owen, *The Desert Air Force* (London: Hutchinson, 1948), p. 74.
2. Vic Morte, *Interview with the author*, 2008.
3. Field Marshal Sir Claude Auchinleck GCB GCIE CSI DSO OBE LLD (1884-1981). The letter of dismissal for Wavell was written on 21 June, the day that 4th Cavalry Brigade set off for Palmyra.
4. Quoted in W.E. Murphy, *The Relief of Tobruk* New Zealand in the Second World War 1939-1945 (Wellington, NZ: War History Branch, 1961), p. 11.
5. Marshal of the RAF Lord Tedder GCB (1890-1967). Tedder had been appointed Deputy AOC-in-C Middle East in December 1940.
6. Air Marshal Sir Arthur 'Mary' Coningham KCB KBE DSO MC DFC AFC (1895-1948).

Coningham had been a fighter pilot in the RFC during the First World War. Born in Brisbane, Australia, he grew up and was educated in New Zealand. He served in the New Zealand Expeditionary Force in Somaliland and Egypt, but was invalided out of the army in 1916. Determined to fly he paid his way to England and joined the Royal Flying Corps. He was credited with 19 kills over the Western Front. His nickname, 'Mary', was thought to be a corruption of 'Maori', by which he was known in the RFC, and which referred to his New Zealand origins.

7   Despite this reinforcement the British fighters were still outclassed in speed and climb by the German Messerschmitt Bf 109F.
8   Air Chief Marshal Sir Arthur Longmore, Air Operations in the Middle East from January 1st 1941 to May 3rd 1941, Supplement to *The London Gazette*, 1946, p. 4689.
9   RAF radar stations were given the name, Air Ministry Experiment Stations, so as not to disclose their function.
10 No 205 Group with Wellington bombers was carrying out the nightly 'milk run' to Benghazi and other ports, while the light bombers of No 3 (South African) and 270 Wings bombed rear supply dumps and airfields at Gazala and Tmimi during daylight hours.
11 A.W. Tedder, *With Prejudice: The War Memoirs of Marshal of the Royal Air Force, Lord Tedder* (London: Cassell, 1966), p. 172.
12 *Ibid.*, p. 189.
13 For Operation *Compass* the previous year, the Western Desert Force had only the equivalent of two-and-a-third reconnaissance regiments; the 11th Hussars, No 2 RAF Armoured Car Company equipped with Rolls-Royce, Morris and Fordson armoured cars and the 6th Australian Divisional Cavalry with Bren gun carriers. The latter only coming into use in January and was used for divisional reconnaissance. The RAF armoured cars had therefore made up one-quarter of the Army's reconnaissance assets. By November 1941, the Eighth Army had nine regiments and battalions in the order of battle for reconnaissance and patrolling; the 1st King's Dragoon Guards, 11th Hussars, 3rd and 7th South African Reconnaissance Battalion, 4th and 6th South African Armoured Car Regiments all equipped with South African Marmon-Herrington armoured cars, the Central India Horse with Bren gun carriers and light trucks and New Zealand Divisional Cavalry Regiment with Bren gun carriers and a few Mark VI light tanks.
14 Squadrons were no longer attached to a particular Wing but were handed over to the established Wing as the other Wing moved forward.
15 Morte, *Interview with the author.*
16 Nos 2 and 4 Sections were to remain behind to continue with the Company's responsibilities at Habbaniya and Mosul.
17 The replacement engine fitted to RRAC *Avenger* seized a few days later.
18 The Axis forces were composed of the German *15th* and *21st Panzer* and *90th Light Divisions*, and the Italian *Ariete Armoured Division* and *Pavia, Bologna, Brescia, Savona, Sabratha, Trieste* and *Trento Infantry Divisions*.
19 A view expressed in *Luftwaffe* Intelligence summaries at the time. Cited in R. Owen, *The Desert Air Force*, p.76.
20 AIR 23/1345 *Western Desert Operations 1941-1942*. Quote from correspondence: Air Vice-Marshal Coningham to Air Marshal Tedder, 5 January 1942.
21 K. Cross and V. Orange, *Straight and Level* (London: Grub Street, 1993), p. 149
22 J.A.L. Agar-Hamilton and L C.F. Turner, *The Sidi Rezeg Battles 1941* (Cape Town: Oxford University Press, 1957), p. 313.
23 Quoted in K. Cross and V. Orange, *Straight and Level*, p. 159.
24 *Ibid.*, pp. 159-160.
25 *Ibid.*, p. 160.
26 Quoted in V. Orange, *Coningham: A Biography of Air Marshal Sir Arthur Coningham* (Washington DC: Center for Air Force History, 1992), p. 86.
27 J.A.L. Agar-Hamilton and L C.F. Turner, *The Sidi Rezeg Battles 1941*.
28 'E Force' was under the command of Brigadier Denys Reid and comprised the 3/2nd Punjab

Regiment; one squadron, 6th South African Armoured Car Regiment and two companies, 7th South African Reconnaissance Battalion, both equipped with Marmon-Harrington armoured cars; 4 Battery, 2nd South African Field Regiment; a battery of anti-tank guns of 73rd Anti-Tank Regiment; 6 Light Anti-Aircraft Battery with Bofors guns, and two sections of Indian sappers and an Indian field ambulance.

29 H.L. Thompson, *New Zealanders with the Royal Air Force, Vol. III* (Wellington, NZ: War History Branch, Dept of Internal Affairs, 1959), p. 47. Wing Commander (later Group Captain) Eric W. Whitley DFC DSO (1908-1973) was a New Zealander serving the RAF.
30 Harry Klein, *Springboks in Armour* (Cape Town: Purnell & Sons, 1965), pp. 197, 199.
31 *Ibid.*, p. 199.
32 *Ibid.*, p. 200.
33 *Ibid.*, p. 199.
34 Morte, *Interview with the author.*
35 AIR 49/48 *Middle East Command, AHQ Western Desert, Miscellaneous Reports July 1941-January 1944.* Report of Medical Officer, Oasis Group ('Whitforce') to Senior Medical Officer Air Headquarters Western Desert, 9 January, 1942.
36 Morte, *Interview with the author.*
37 'F' Troop, 6 South African Field Battery, equipped with 25-pdrs, and 'X' Troop, 6 (Coleraine) Light Anti-Aircraft Battery with Bofors LAA guns, accompanied the RAF armoured cars.
38 AIR 29/50 *No 1 Armoured Car Company, Habbaniya; before 1 Apr 1930 Armoured Car Wing, Hinaidi; from 3 Oct 1946 No 1 ACC incorporated in RAF Regiment, redesignated No 2701 Squadron.* Two Fordson wireless tenders were sent by No 1 Armoured Car Company to Jarabub to replace those that had been lost by No 2 Company.
39 WO 373/47 *War Office and Ministry of Defence: Military Secretary's Department: Recommendations for Honours and Awards for Gallant and Distinguished Service (Army), Military Cross.* For the 'great gallantry shown in the face of the enemy' during this campaign and for his 'great leadership and unfailing cheerfulness' Flight Lieutenant Alan Douglas was awarded the Military Cross.
40 V. Morte, *Interview with J. Rolph*, RAF Armoured Cars Association, 2008. LAC Webb's body was not recovered as his name is recorded on the memorial at the Commonwealth War Cemetery at Alamein.
41 Morte, *Interview with author* and *Interview with J. Rolph.*
42 No 1 Squadron RAF Regiment would be presented with its first standard at RAF El Adem in 1959.
43 AIR 23/1345 *Western Desert Operations.*
44 H.L. Thompson, *New Zealanders with the Royal Air Force, Vol. III*, p. 59.
45 Wing Commander R.C. Skellon RAF Retd, *Interview with the author,* 2010.
46 There is no mention of a meeting between the Companies at Msus in either of the Armoured Car Company Form 540s.

the command of Group Captain 'Bing' Cross, to take responsibility for the air force units in Cyrenaica. As of 20 January, nine single-engine fighter squadrons were located at Antelat, and four more were further back at Benina, Derna, El Adem and Tobruk protecting ports and shipping. Moves were also being made to establish the fighters and a radar station further south at Belandah. The day bomber force had been reduced to two squadrons at Gambut and Bu Amud due to withdrawals for re-equipping and transfer to other theatres. In total, the fighter force could call on 445 aircraft of which 280 aircraft were serviceable against the German and Italian total of 515 of which 300 were available.[5]

As well as supply limitations, the weather now conspired to help turn the tables against the British. On 19 and 20 January, Antelat was bombed by the *Luftwaffe* but with the loss of only one petrol tanker. However, more seriously, this was followed by heavy rains, hailstorms and flooding, which curtailed any further flying. LAC Vic Morte describes the conditions at Antelat:

> We had come across desert. It was quite a long journey and arrived at a place called Msus. We were only there for a few days, and then all of a sudden we went to a place called Antelat, which was just behind the Eighth Army. We were doing landing ground protection. Number 1 Company under Jones had gone ahead a day or so before us. Unfortunately, when we got to Antelat, conditions were really bad, it was raining terribly and we were subject to a lot of dive bombing. It was really terrifying for a time.[6]

The rain fell in lengthy downpours of half-an-hour to two hours in duration. The runways, which were simple, graded strips, were soon transformed from hard

Antelat landing ground, five days before Rommel launched his counter-attack. Australian airmen of a Kittyhawk squadron dig drains around their tent following a heavy downpour (AWM 023320).

red earth into quagmires of crimson mud, which made aircraft take-off or landing impossible. The tracks from the headquarters and dispersal areas became impassable for vehicles. Even walking was frustrating and time-consuming, as at each step the airmen sank up to their thighs in mud, which was described as having the consistency of 'a chocolate blancmange'.[7]

In contrast, the enemy air force was operating from strips located closer to the coast on light sandy soil that drained quickly. Consequently, the British fighter force was helplessly stuck on the ground and utterly vulnerable to air and ground attack. The airstrips possessed a thin defence of light anti-aircraft Bofors but these were inadequate against a determined and large-scale attack by the *Luftwaffe*. This also left XIII Corps completely without fighter cover and the air commanders recollected the disasters of Greece, Crete and Syria of the previous year where the Army had been left exposed to unrestricted enemy air attack. Fortunately, the rain eased on the afternoon of 20 January and with everyone pitching-in, the worst patches on the Antelat airfield were filled with stones and bushes collected from the surrounding sparse vegetation. By midday, after a huge effort by some 2000 airmen, a strip 500 yards long and 30 feet wide had been made serviceable.[8]

The British fighters were however, still at rest in their dispersal areas. To allow them to take off, each aircraft had to be manhandled by 12 airmen, lifting under the wings, to the prepared strip. The Army also assisted with the use of their Bofors gun tractors to tow the aircraft through the mire. In this manner, a substantial portion of the fighters got off the ground. All but one squadron flew to Msus, the other going to Gazala. In a magnificent effort, only four Kittyhawks and two Hurricanes had to be left behind due to lack of aircrew and minor mechanical problems. All six were destroyed to prevent them falling into enemy hands before the airfield was vacated.[9]

In an astounding piece of good fortune, the *Luftwaffe* did not appear over Antelat during this period. It was becoming clear however, that the enemy ground forces were gathering for an attack. RAF aerial reconnaissance aircraft reported seeing a large mass of vehicles near Mersa Brega and further inland. On 21 January, Rommel ordered the *Panzerarmee Afrika* to launch what was considered a reconnaissance in strength.[10] The Axis forces were divided into three columns. The *Marcks Group* advanced up the coast road towards Agedabia, *Ariete Armoured Division* moved in the centre, and *21st Panzer Division*, and the furthest south, progressed along the axis of the Wadi Faregh. The British columns fell back as planned but were soon in trouble due to the bad 'going', attacks from dive-bombers and desert inexperience. By 22 January, the *Marcks Group* had reached Agedabia and Rommel, seizing the opportunity, decided to drive on towards Antelat and Saunnu. The planned move of the fighters to Belandah was no longer possible. Corporal 'Mel' Melluish of No 1 Armoured Car Company was now a gunner on a Rolls-Royce wireless tender and he and his crew were ordered to proceed to the forward airstrip and to destroy the aviation fuel stocks that had been secretly placed there.[11]

While the ground parties were preparing the rudimentary Antelat strip on 20 January, Flight Lieutenant John Olliff-Lee and No 3 Section of No 1 Company departed from Antelat and headed south towards the airfield at El Hasseiat, presumably to make contact with the army and ascertain the proximity of the threatening enemy columns. The heavy rain slowed their journey and only 30 miles was made before all the vehicles became bogged. The following morning, at the same time that the Axis ground forces were launching their attack, the Section moved south, with some difficulty, towards El Hasseiat, taking 5½ hours to cover the remaining 60 miles.

After only an hour in occupation, Olliff-Lee was instructed to leave as the enemy were in close proximity and the Section therefore departed along the track heading to the north-west and the coast road. Progress was reasonable and the Section spent the night 55 miles south of Benghazi. The state of the vehicles again became of concern and RRWT *Pathfinder* had to be cannibalised to provide spare parts for RRAC *Cossack* and then abandoned. Notwithstanding their rapid move towards Benghazi, enemy columns were reported to be only five miles away and No 3 Section moved further back towards Msus.[12]

On 21 January, the same day that the ground crews at Antelat were struggling to get the fighters onto the makeshift strip, No 2 Company was engaged on ground sweeps, also in an attempt to contact the enemy. The *Luftwaffe* made one attack but that was only on the nearby fort, early that morning. With the enemy threat intensifying it was decided to withdraw all the RAF units at Antelat. Consequently, at 1630 hours, No 2 Company, escorting the Headquarters of No 258 Wing, set off for Msus, arriving the following day.

Notwithstanding the poor weather, the Desert Air Force stayed on the offensive. Light bombers, escorted by the fighters that had reached Msus, struck at the Axis camps, strongpoints and lines of communications while the Wellingtons of No 205 Group attempted to destroy the main enemy petrol dumps. Their efforts were of little avail and the German columns rolled on.

The enemy thrusts, in spite of their relative weakness, had caught the Eighth Army off balance, and wireless links started to break down due to poor atmospheric conditions. The Axis columns were too strong for XIII Corps and there was no choice but to fall back. The 1st Support Group was overrun and the 200th Guards Brigade on their right flank was forced to withdraw. The 2nd Armoured Brigade fought to clear the position around Antelat and Saunnu, but was badly mauled and suffered heavy casualties, losing a large part of its tank strength.

News of the rapid withdrawal of the Army was however, not conveyed to the RAF. The first and only warning that the enemy was approaching Antelat was received at 1300 hours on 22 January, when XIII Corps sent the simple message 'Move back at once, enemy coming'.[13] A party of airmen had stayed behind at Antelat to ensure that any remaining aircraft could get away and spent the night listening to the German tanks moving only a few miles from the airfield. Everything had been packed up ready to leave and, as a deterrent to the enemy, bombs had been scattered over the runways. The enemy were already closing in and, as the last aircraft departed, shells began to fall to the west of the airfield.

The only defensive unit remaining at Antelat was No 1 Armoured Car Company, under the command of Wing Commander Jones, with HQ and No 1 Section and their six Rolls-Royce armoured cars and a wireless tender. Small ground parties from the fighter squadrons still remained and were ordered to destroy the stocks of fuel that had been so carefully stockpiled over the last few weeks. Unfortunately, it was not possible to destroy everything and much of the 100,000 gallon stockpile had to be left behind. At 1530 hours, the armoured cars moved back to a slight rise 2 miles to the north-east as the enemy was reported to be only 5 miles away. The Germans were however, closer than thought and it was only when a shell from a nearby hill exploded on the strip was it clear they were now in close proximity. The Company held their ground for half a day, presumably only succeeding in delaying the enemy as they thought it was some kind of trap. Later that afternoon, a skirmish developed and, as one of the Rolls-Royce armoured cars was sent forward, it received a direct hit from a German shell and was put out of action. The Rolls-Royce armoured car, *Hawk*, went out to recover the crew who were all miraculously uninjured. In the course of this, Corporal Ryan, the vehicle commander of RRAC *Hawk*, was hit in the face by shell splinters. He was safely evacuated back to Ghemines Hospital, nearer to Benghazi, for treatment.

Despite the high rate of fire from the Vickers 0.303-inch machine-gun in the turret and the 0.303-inch Vickers K for anti-aircraft defence, the heaviest weapon was the 0.55-inch Boys anti-tank rifle. The thin armour of the armoured cars had only been designed for 'bullet-and-brick-proof' patrolling in the mandated territories, at a time when the armour-piercing projectile had barely been conceived.[14] The Rolls-Royce armoured cars could do little to halt or even delay the advancing enemy panzer and motorised units. It was wisely decided that 'it was time to beat a diplomatic retreat' and make their way towards Benghazi.[15] AC Charles Spybey was with the No 1 Section and describes what happened next:

> When we reached the main road, we were shelled again, so we turned back and made our way across the hilly desert. We were going along quite nicely in convoy the next day when some enemy tanks came over a hill and split the convoy. The rear section (mine) managed to escape, while the front section was trapped and there was nothing we could do to help them.[16]

Wing Commander 'Jonah' Jones and five airmen along with the RRACs *Bloodhound*, *Mosul*, *Norfan* and *Lalliyah* could not be accounted for following this action. The Operations Record Book on No 1 Company gives little detail and so the circumstances surrounding these events are unclear. The history of No 112 Squadron, the famous 'Shark Squadron', that flew Kittyhawks however, recounts in more detail the events that followed the ambush as reported by a ground party that had the closest of escapes:

> That day some stragglers returned to the squadron, eight airmen who had been left behind in the retreat. They had been packing gear and servicing the remaining aircraft and MT vehicles when an officer of an RAF armoured car unit drove up and told them that an enemy column was nearby. This column, which was holding an escarpment on the Msus side of the Antelat road, had already lobbed some shells at the landing ground. Ammunition and aircraft were now being destroyed and that evening the armoured cars moved off towards the Benghazi road in a north-easterly direction. Around midnight they caught up with a mixed bunch of Artillery and Ordnance Corps.
>
>   When they reached the main road they were strafed by a Bf 109. They hid in a wadi and after about 10 minutes the road was shelled. Uncertain what to do they decided to return to Antelat arriving back during the afternoon. Two armoured cars went forward to investigate but they bogged down in the soft sand. Just as they had been dug out nine German tanks appeared, firing as they came. The armoured cars, 10 [more likely two, RRACs *Bloodhound* and *Mosul*, commanded by Jones and Clay] of them in all, old Rolls-Royces dating back to 1921 armed with one .303 machine gun each, bravely turned to face them and the trucks departed as fast as they could. They [the trucks] were chased for about 45 minutes and only four vehicles got away. Having

A pre-war photograph showing the Rolls-Royces Bloodhound and Hawk in the garage at RAF Habbaniya. Both were involved in the engagement at Antelat on 22 January 1942 (Rutter, RAFACA).

refuelled they waited to see if anyone else would turn up, but no one did.[17]

The degree of surprise was such that the Army anti-aircraft detachments were also caught unawares and two sections of a Heavy AA Battery were captured. As always in battle situations, the perspective of different participants can vary widely. Corporal 'Mel' Melluish wrote:

> Wing Commander Jones had decided to ambush the oncoming enemy patrol, a mistake because the tanks came over the top of the escarpment and saw the two armoured cars waiting and the first shell hit the CO's car in the engine.[18]

Support for the story that the Rolls-Royces engaged the German tanks came from Squadron Leader 'Cass' Casano who wrote some years later:

> Unfortunately they were put in the bag. Bad luck I hear. They were caught in the unusual floods… No 1 Armoured Car Company, before being captured, engaged the enemy tanks.[19]

No 2 Company were soon aware that trouble had befallen No 1 Company. LAC Vic Morte recalls:

> News came back that actually, in the first place he'd [Jones] been captured and in the second he'd been killed. It transpired later that he had been

captured with five more men. We were there, but we were within 10 miles or so. Hard to imagine, but the area was immense...[20]

That the Desert Air Force fighter force had nearly been caught undefended on the ground was of great concern. Air Vice-Marshal Coningham signalled Group Captain 'Bing' Cross of No 258 Wing the day after the evacuation from Antelat as follows:

> Personal from AOC to Group Captain Cross - As you are aware I am most concerned at circumstances whereby bulk of your force might have been destroyed by enemy ground forces. I have discussed with Army Commander and Corps Commander the vulnerability of your bases and the position is appreciated.
> It is your personal duty however to ensure, by consultation with Corps Headquarters that enough direct protection can be made available for your base to ensure (1) comparative immunity from sporadic raiding by small ground forces and (2) a holding action against larger forces that will give you reasonable warning to move.
> If after representing your views you have any doubts about your security from ground attack you are to refer to me or to the senior officer acting for me. The protection of your base is a primary army commitment.[21]

Flight Lieutenant Olliff-Lee and No 3 Section of No 1 Company reached Msus safely and then proceeded on towards Mechili on 24 January. Two more Rolls-Royce armoured cars, *Lion* and *Avenger*, failed en-route and were disabled and abandoned as the enemy were still close behind. The following day, RRAC *Ajax* and *Explorer II* and a Fordson tender were sent off back to Gambut for repairs while the remainder of the party made for Gazala, which was reached on 26 January. Here they were rejoined by No 1 Section which made its way back through Benghazi and past Giovanni Berta without further incident. AC Charles Spybey was in this party:

> We fortunate ones eventually managed to reach Benghazi, only to find that the British were evacuating the city. We joined the escapees, and only just in time, for Benghazi was captured by the Germans the very next day. We travelled for 400 miles through Cyrene and Derna to Gazala, just south of Tobruk. When we arrived, we found some more of our lads and learned that two of the three [sic] trapped cars had managed to escape and make their way to safety.[22]

There was still no news however, of the fate of the CO and the missing airmen. The following morning, in awful weather that began as rain but turned into the gritty, unending misery of a sandstorm, Flight Lieutenant S. Griffiths, commanding No 3 Section, returned to Mechili in the hope of locating the party, but he was unsuccessful. With Wing Commander Jones missing, Flight Lieutenant Griffiths assumed acting command of the Company. A week later, with hope fading, the detachment signalled RAF Habbaniya that Wing Commander Jones and the crews of RRACs *Bloodhound* and *Mosul*, Corporal C.T. Clay, LACs D.F. Lister, A. Kessack and S. Cook and AC1 F. Burn were missing, having been last seen in action at Antelat.

It was later learned that they had all been captured and were now prisoners-of-war of the Italians. Following their capture they had been transported to the port of

General Rommel inspects one of the Rolls-Royces of No 1 Armoured Car Company lost in the action at Antelat on 22 January 1942 (RAFACA).

Tripoli, and along with 288 other British prisoners-of-war that had been captured in the fighting in Cyrenaica, they were embarked on the 4200 ton Italian freighter *Ariosto*. During daylight on 13 February 1942, the *Ariosto*, a German freighter *Atlas* and an escorting destroyer and motor torpedo boat, en route from North Africa to Italy, were sighted by a Maryland reconnaissance aircraft. Three Albacores of the Royal Navy were sent out that evening to intercept the small convoy. Only one aircraft made a successful attack, and a torpedo struck the forward hold of the *Ariosto*, into which the Allied prisoners had been crammed. The ship was left smouldering and disabled and three hours later the Royal Navy submarine, *P-38*, delivered the *coup-de-grace*. British intelligence was unaware that there were prisoners-of-war on board and of the 410 prisoners and crew, 158 did not survive.[23] Among those who perished were LACs 'Sandy' Kessack and Stanley Cook of No 1 Company. The remaining four airmen, along with most of the survivors, were rescued by an Italian naval ship and were sent to POW camps in Italy.[24]

Lister subsequently escaped from captivity and made his way safely back to the Allied lines, where during his post-escape interrogation, he recounted the details of the events surrounding the deaths of the two airmen. Wing Commander 'Jonah' Jones, following imprisonment in Italy, was able to make his way to Switzerland and later returned to the United Kingdom. A letter he wrote in February 1943 while in captivity expresses some remorse at having allowed the detachment to be captured.[25] Corporal Clay and AC1 Burn were not able to escape when the Italian Armistice was signed in September 1943, and were transported to Germany to spend the remainder of the War as prisoners of the Germans.[26]

XIII Corps had intended to launch an armoured attack to retake Antelat and

Saunnu but the speed of the enemy advance towards Msus forced an abandonment of those plans. On 27 January, Rommel sent a feint towards Mechili, but diverted the larger part of his force northwards to capture Benghazi. The 4th Indian Division had no choice but to break out to the south of the encircled city, and with the fall of Benghazi, so too went the chances of holding western Cyrenaica. Rommel did not allow his troops any rest, and launched armoured car and motorised units towards Tocra and Barce and into the Jebel Akhdar.

The RAF continued to be hindered by the weather which had made the withdrawal difficult. It had when possible however, been providing air cover to the Army units as they fell back. Nevertheless, the enemy air forces had also found it difficult to support the rapid and unexpected advance by Rommel's columns. As a consequence, the RAF fighters and bombers were met with very little opposition and during February the Axis air forces were almost inactive. It was only on 5 February that the *Luftwaffe* established itself on the Benina airfield near Benghazi.

Meanwhile, at Msus, Flight Lieutenant Skellon and Flying Officer Lucas of No 2 Company spent 22 and 23 January carrying out sweeps to the west and south-west of Msus. The airfield was extremely vulnerable, and by 24 January, reports were coming in that the German motorised columns were approaching the airstrip. With no units of the Eighth Army between the enemy and the fighters at Msus, the officer commanding No 211 Group, Group Captain 'Bing' Cross saw no alternative but to move 80 miles further back to Mechili. The ground crews were nearing exhaustion as many had spent the last 48 hours in the horrendous journey through the mud from Antelat. The other alternative however, was to stay and become prisoners-of-war. Skellon therefore took half the Company and escorted No 258 Wing Headquarters while Squadron Leader Casano and the remainder of the Company remained at Msus to protect a refuelling party of No 208 Squadron. The Hurricanes of this squadron were acting as aerial rear-guard and providing tactical reconnaissance. They stayed there until the following day and the ground parties were then escorted by the Company to Mechili.

Following their arrival, No 2 Company established routine patrols on the Msus to Mechili track to watch for the enemy. Flight Lieutenant 'Dickie' Skellon was sent out with his Section to await the imminent arrival of the *Afrika Korps*. He continues:

> The Germans began to attack and all the vehicles were coming down a little wadi. They were from all the regiments… I was told to go there and set up at night and keep my eyes open for the Germans. And to be prepared to clear off if it happens. And one night, I think it was the second night, and we were sitting out there and it was very dark and we'd had all these vehicles had come through. We'd just sat there and watched, and suddenly there was an awful commotion in front and a hell of a din, and somebody shouted out "Tanks!" And so we all stood there, and my Sergeant said to me "Well, what are we going to do, now sir?" and I said "What we are going to do is, we are going to load a Very light, and if these chaps come any nearer we'll fire the Very light at them and that'll blind them. And then we'll clear off." And that's precisely what we did. Unfortunately, it wasn't a German tank, it was the Coldstream Guards in an old broken-down lorry and, having fired the Very light at them, they were furious.[27]

While moving back along the track to Mechili, an incident occurred that has gone down in the folklore of No 2 Armoured Car Company and its successors. Squadron Leader Casano was approached by an officer from an armoured regiment who informed him that a number of tanks had been left some distance back and they could not be brought away through lack of drivers. He immediately turned the Company about and they returned down the track to the tank park. Casano and five of his armoured car crews then collected the tanks, LAC Vic Morte recalls:

> It was one of the big retreats. There was no such thing as convoys, everyone was making their best. The heavy vehicles were dropping behind and the lighter vehicles going on ahead. We kept overrunning vehicles, tanks and armoured cars that had run short of petrol. The tanks had been abandoned; they'd just been left, the drivers never even set them on fire.
> Our chaps volunteered to drive straight away. We examined them very carefully for booby traps and we discovered that every one of them had run short of petrol. We were carrying a fair amount of fuel, so we put all our spare petrol into the tanks, started them up. 'Cass' drove one. I can always remember two friends of mine who seemed to laugh like devils driving these tanks.[28]

The airmen, escorted by the Fordsons, then drove the tanks for some 60 miles until they handed over to an armoured regiment headquarters that had the requisite fuel and drivers. Casano's exploit with the tanks did not go unnoticed at Air Headquarters Western Desert, as Air Vice-Marshal Coningham wrote in a letter to Air Marshal Tedder on 5 February. Tensions had clearly intensified between the Army and Air Force due to the problems experienced by the RAF in determining the threat from the advancing enemy columns. He wrote:

> There are signs that my bad temper spreads to Army and my jocular appointment of Casano of Armoured Cars as Air Commodore in charge RAF armoured brigade has spread.[29]

The fighter force could not remain for long at Mechili, as late in the day on 28 January, an enemy column was reported to be closing-in and the decision was made to move to Gazala. Fearing a repeat of the fiasco at Antelat, XIII Corps Headquarters, which had packed up and was on the move, had told the fighter wing at Mechili to do so as well. The diarist of No 112 Squadron noted that the 'mysterious withdrawal in the face of Rommel's alleged inferior forces begins to assume something uncomfortably resembling a disordered and inexplicable retreat'.[30] Unfortunately, this led to a delay and a large gap in the provision of air cover over the withdrawing troops as the squadrons moved back.[31] Flight Lieutenant Skellon recalls the events surrounding the urgent departure from Mechili:

> It was on the way near Fort Mechili. We then all going back, the whole Army was going back and we were at this Fort and we sat there and then we were told over the R/T to clear out because otherwise we would all be in the bag by tomorrow. So we weren't going to be taken prisoner, under any circumstances. The CO said to me "You take your people and get off back, out now". And we went off at dusk and it took us all night to get back. We were on the side of this wadi… but we got through but we saw the

main road, which was of course covered with vehicles, because they were all going back…[32]

The rest of No 2 Company had escorted the ground parties of No 258 Wing eastwards to Gazala where three new strips were constructed astride the coast road. While Skellon halted at Gazala with half the Company, Casano returned with the remainder of the Company to Martuba, where he was to escort the Headquarters of No 258 Wing back to Gazala. Skellon was then sent out to watch for the arrival of the *Afrika Korps*:

The 4th Indian Division, having evaded encirclement in Benghazi, was making its way back along the coast road through Derna and on to Martuba. With the fall of Benghazi, the enemy sent columns across the desert through Mechili towards Gazala, while another was sent along the coast towards Derna in pursuit of the 4th Indian Division. It was feared that the enemy column coming through Mechili might move north and cut the coast road along which the Indians were moving. It was therefore vital that the Army delay the desert columns as long as possible and the fighter force maintained its fierce rear-guard action. The roads were choked with the numerous lorries, tanks and armoured cars of 4th Indian and 1st Armoured Divisions. LAC Vic Morte recalls the arrival at Martuba:

> We were sent there to guard an airfield. We'd been pushed up there to reinforce this situation that was absolutely hopeless. It was just scrub and goodness knows. The Germans were pushing and so we had to retreat. It was difficult country, covered in huge boulders that almost wrecked the cars. And we developed a puncture so we needed to change the wheel. We were going along, and we picked up this enormous convoy. There were literally thousands of vehicles crowded down this road. The mass of vehicles was half a mile wide, nose to tail. The awkward thing was that, like the present day, a traffic jam always forms when you got into an awkward place all the vehicles had to fit into a small area. And this Jock Ross, he was a panicker, and he didn't like to be caught with a soft tyre. So he decided that he'd change the wheel, so we took the tyre off, and put the good one on.
>
> But in the meantime, on top of hill about 3 miles away there was an escarpment, and the Germans had got up there and one of these '88-mm' guns was firing over the top of us, and it kept hitting one of the vehicles. If it hit a petrol tank it went whoosh! There was so much happening. There was three of us; the car commander, Ross, a bloke called Bennett, and myself, all changing this wheel with the tyre levers. These anti-aircraft shells, they were flashing over the top.
>
> I could get a feeling. All of a sudden I just realised that one was going to fall short. Bennett and myself immediately sensed this and jumped up and ran like bloody hell. Ross was a bit older and he was a bit late and he couldn't move as fast, and all of a sudden this thing burst, and a piece of shrapnel hit him behind the calf. I shouted to him and he said "I've been hit". So we went back to have a look at him and he was on his side. I looked at his leg and his foot was twisted round and you could see the bone in his calf. So we strapped it up as much as we could and our officer, a decent chap, immediately gave him some morphine. He was in very intense pain, but there was nothing we could do with him.

With pennants flying, Fordsons of No 2 Armoured Car Company set out on a patrol from a forward landing ground (AWM MED0047).

Of course all the vehicles on the road were full up. Our officer dashed out and saw an Indian officer and we stopped an ambulance. We opened the doors at the back and there was about 15 wounded Indian troops lying there, all on top of each other. So we got Jock Ross and lifted him up into the ambulance and sent him off.[33]

On 3 February, Casano set off westward yet again, this time towards Tmimi to watch out for the enemy columns. Meanwhile, it had been decided that the airstrips at Gazala were too far forward for safe operation of aircraft and so the fighter force had to be placed further back. As a consequence, Flight Lieutenant Skellon and a half section escorted No 258 Wing from Gazala to Gambut with Flying Officer Mosley's half section remaining at Gazala until well after sunset and then following.

The successful attack from El Agheila could not be sustained by the German and Italian troops as the usual problems of supply and fuel began to take effect. Rommel grounded his panzers and air support and sent his motorised units on ahead, but the advance soon lost momentum as the attacks from Desert Air Force took heavy toll on the columns.[34] The German vanguard reached Tmimi on 10 February, but XIII Corps reached prepared positions between Gazala and Bir Tengeder and the front soon stabilised. The enemy motorised units could only dig in and await the arrival of reinforcements.

Air Vice-Marshal 'Mary' Coningham expressed his frustration however, that the airfield at Gazala had come under enemy shelling and had been evacuated as a result. He also pushed for British columns to be sent out towards Mechili, Martuba and in front of Gazala to delay the enemy advance to the Gazala Line.[35] Allied air operations had been very successful, despite the lengthy periods of alternating rain and dust storms, and the recurring requirement to move to landing grounds further back. This had been primarily because the flying squadrons were repeatedly threatened by ground attack and XIII Corps had had difficulties providing reliable information on the location and level of threat posed by Rommel's armoured and motorised columns.

The fighter force was established at Gambut and El Adem, with Gazala to be used as a forward refuelling field. El Adem was later found to have a dust problem and subsequently the airfields at Gasr el Arid were used in its place. An improved early warning system was implemented and this allowed adequate time for interceptions over the forward areas. Radar coverage was greatly improved, and as a consequence a mobile radar unit was sited as far forward as was possible, on the seashore at Ain el Gazala.

With matters settled for the time being, No 2 Company spent the remainder of February with two sections forward at Gazala while the remaining two sections patrolled the Gambut landing grounds. Number 510 AMES, up to this time, had been dedicated to providing cover for shipping convoys going along the coast to Benghazi; however, on 10 February it was moved to Gazala and an acceptable controlled air-interception system was put in place. With a range of 60 miles, it was able to detect and plot aircraft taking off from Martuba, the forward airfield for the *Luftwaffe*.[36] Being located so close to the enemy front line however, the radar station was considered vulnerable to attack from ground troops, a sea landing or parachutists. Therefore one section of four Fordson armoured cars of No 2 Company and a detachment of Bofors guns were specifically tasked with its protection.[37]

The presence of RAF facilities so close to the front line was quickly realised by the enemy and they reacted swiftly. The day after the arrival of No 510 AMES at 1130 hours, 10 Ju 87 Stukas, escorted by 12 Messerschmitt Bf 109Fs dive-bombed the Gazala No 2 airstrip, including the Air Operations Room. The Section of No 2 Company assigned to aerodrome defence duties came under attack and Fordson A116 received a direct hit, burst into flames and was completely destroyed. LAC

Getting under the deck. The crew of A117 dig an ARP hole (from left to right): Ross, Ivor Chester and AC2 James Maltman. Maltman was killed in action a few weeks later (© Crown copyright. Chester, RAF Regiment Museum).

The crew of A125 scan the sky for enemy aircraft. To improve the AA defence, the Fordsons had been equipped with twin rather than a single Lewis machine gun (AWM MED0029).

John Scholes was killed immediately and Flight Lieutenant Alan Douglas and AC2 James Maltman were both badly wounded. Considerable bravery was shown by Flight Sergeant B.W. Smith and Corporal R.C. Griffith who rescued the airmen from the burning vehicle while still under persistent attack from the enemy dive bombers. Maltman's wounds were severe and he died the following day in hospital, while it would be several weeks before Douglas could return to the unit. LAC Vic Morte remembers the burial party for the fallen airman:

> The idea was to bury the dead near telegraph poles, so the tanks wouldn't run over the graves. So if you put their heads towards the poles there was a good chance the tanks wouldn't disturb them. If they were buried shallow the tanks used to remove the sand. The Italians used to bury shallow and there used be a number of places we used to pass where you could see the Italians feet stuck out of the ground.
>
> So this bloke we were burying. Six of us carried him in a blanket, and we got him almost to the telegraph wires and all of a sudden a German plane came over strafing us. We all dropped the bloody blanket and ran like hell.
>
> When we got near the grave some said who's got the bible? Nobody had got a bible. So somebody dashed off and came back with a prayer book. 'Cass' didn't know where to find the service. He kept flicking through the pages. Then he put it down and said "I can't understand this lot!" He then

The burning wreck of the Fordson armoured car soon after the air attack that killed LAC Scholes and mortally wounded AC2 Maltman (© Crown copyright. Chester, RAF Regiment Museum).

conducted a very simple service saying how much we missed our long departed brother.[38]

On the same day, Squadron Leader 'Cass' Casano's armoured car had come under attack and sadly his constant companion, his dog 'Butch', was killed in a strafing attack. The two had been inseparable and he accompanied his master everywhere he went.[39] He was so well known within RAF circles in Cairo that his sad demise was announced in a Cairo newspaper as follows:

> 'Butch' dearly loved mascot of an RAF armoured car squadron [sic]. He died on the battlefield in Libya on February 11th. A Middle East veteran 'Butch' was the friend of hundreds of Royal Air Force personnel. He was unofficially awarded the Military Cross when his master received that honour. 'Butch' died gallantly barking defiance at the enemy during a dive bomber attack on a forward landing ground. Loyal and devoted to the last his loss will be mourned by all who knew him.[40]

The strafing and bombing attacks continued on an irregular basis against Gazala and Gambut throughout the month, but the Company suffered no more fatalities. Later in the month, Flying Officer Lucas reported an enemy tank concentration while on a forward patrol out from Gazala. Preparations were made for a section of Fordsons to stand by the AMES site and to make ready for a rapid departure if the column appeared. Fortunately, the tanks failed to materialise. The latter half of the month at Gambut was spent in preparing for a possible attack by parachute troops. The routine at Gazala and Gambut continued during March but enemy air activity declined. Finally, on 24 March, the RAF armoured cars of No 2 Company left Gazala having handed over responsibility for the protection of the AMES to the South Africans. At Gambut, the remainder of the Company formed up and set off for RAF Helwan in Egypt. Only a few days were spent in Cairo and by the end of the month the Company was safely ensconced back at the station it had called home for

As winter waned in the desert and the rains became less frequent, the mud dried and so came the extreme heat and dust of summer. Poised halfway between each other's main supply ports, the Allied and Axis armies began a race to gather supplies, vehicles, tanks, aircraft, men and equipment to determine which side could launch the next offensive.

Notes

1. Quoted in R. Owen, *The Desert Air Force* (London: Hutchinson, 1948), p. 56.
2. The 1st Armoured Division consisted of 2nd Armoured Brigade, 200th Guards Brigade and 1st Support Group. Fuel was in such short supply that the armoured brigade had been forbidden to do any training or exercises.
3. The *Deutsches Afrika Korps* as of 30 January consisted of *15th* and *21st Panzer Divisions* and the *90th Light Division*. A complicated command meant that General Rommel did not directly command the Italian armoured and infantry formations.
4. AIR 23/1345 *Western Desert Operations January 1941- December 1942*. As of 3 January 1942, Nos 258 and 262 Wings were composed of Nos 2 and 4 Squadrons SAAF and 250 Squadron RAF with Tomahawks, Nos 3 Squadron RAAF and 112 Squadron RAF with Kittyhawks and Nos 80, 94, 229, 238 and 260 Squadrons RAF with Hurricane IIs. Number 33 Squadron RAF with Hurricane IIs and No 272 Squadron RAF with Beaufighters were under command of Air Headquarters Western Desert.
5. I.S.O. Playfair *et al.*, *The Mediterranean and Middle East, Vol. III*, History of the Second World War (London: HMSO, 1956), p. 140.
6. V. Morte, *Interview with J. Rolph*, RAF Armoured Cars Association, 2008.
7. *Ibid.*
8. K. Cross and V. Orange, *Straight and Level* (London: Grub Street, 1993), pp. 168-170.
9. AIR 23/6200 *RAF operations in the Western Desert and Eastern Mediterranean, 18 November 1941 to 19 May 1942*, p. 42.
10. Rommel's command had been renamed *Panzerarmee Afrika* on 22 January. It consisted of *Deutsches Afrika Korps: 15th Panzer, 21st Panzer, 90th Light; 10th Corps: Bologna, Brescia; 20th Corps: Ariete Armoured, Trieste Motorised; 21st Corps: Pavia, Trento and Sabratha Divisions*.
11. E. Melluish. Correspondence: Letter to Squadron Leader S. Miller, OC No 1 Squadron, RAF Regiment, RAF St Mawgan, 16 November 2002, RAF Regiment Museum Archives.
12. V. Morte, *Interview with the author*, 2008. Morte recalled seeing HMWT *Pathfinder* lying derelict on the roadside as No 2 Company withdrew towards Msus.
13. AIR 23/6200 *RAF operations in the Western Desert and Eastern Mediterranean*.
14. B.H. Liddell Hart, *The Tanks. The History of the Royal Tank Regiment and its predecessors Heavy Branch Machine-Gun Corps, Tank Corps and Royal Tank Corps, 1914-1945 Vol. I* (London: Cassell, 1959), p. 213.
15. E.C. Spybey, Correspondence: Corporal E.C. Spybey, No 1 Armoured Car Company to his brother Harry, 4 January 1944.
16. *Ibid.*
17. R.A. Brown, *Shark Squadron: The History of No 112 Squadron RFC RAF 1917-1975* (London: Crécy Books, 1994), pp. 53-54. Further corroboration for these events is provided by mention in the official history of the campaign, which states: "The airfield came under shell-fire as the last aircraft took off, and the remaining maintenance parties were rescued by Nos 1 and 2 Armoured Car Companies RAF" and Playfair *et al.*, *The Mediterranean and Middle East, Vol. III*, p. 142.
18. Melluish, Correspondence. It is unclear whether Melluish was in this party.
19. Correspondence: from Squadron Leader M.P. Casano, 27 February 1997; recipient's name not indicated, Archives of the RAF Armoured Cars Association.
20. Morte, *Interview with J. Rolph*.

21. AIR 23/1782 *Location plan for RAF units withdrawing from Cyrenaica 1942, January-December 1942*. Correspondence: from Air Vice-Marshal Coningham, AOC Air HQ Western Desert, at Advanced Air HQ to OC No 258 Wing, Group Captain Cross, and copied to XIII Corps HQ through Eighth Army.
22. Spybey, Correspondence.
23. C. Shores, B. Cull and N. Malizia, *Malta: The Spitfire Year 1942* (London: Grub Street, 1991), p. 82.
24. The names of LACs Kessack and Cook are recorded on the memorial wall at the El Alamein Commonwealth War Cemetery. LAC Kessack had served in the RAF since 1936, and for some years in No 1 Armoured Car Company. He came from the town of Buckie in Moray in Scotland and LAC Cook from Farlington in Yorkshire.
25. W.O. Jones, *Document 12373, Letter 02/43/1, Private Papers of Wing Commander W.O. Jones*, 2 February 1943 (IWM Document Archive). Correspondence: Letter to Squadron Leader H.F. O'Neill DFC. 'What a BF I was to get myself in this mess…' Jones eventually made his way Switzerland where he was interned, after either escaping or being released following the Italian Armistice of September 1943. He returned safely to England and had a post-war career in the RAF Regiment.
26. According to AIR 20/2336/3 *British, Dominion and Allied prisoners-of-war in Germany and German occupied territories: alphabetical list. Section 1: RAF Airmen*, Clay was sent to *Stalag VIIIB* at Lamsdorf, while LAC Burn went to *Stalag Luft III* at Sagan.
27. Wing Commander R.C. Skellon RAF Retd, *Interview with the author*, 2010.
28. Morte, *Interview with J. Rolph*.
29. AIR 23/1345 *Western Desert Operations*. Correspondence: Air Vice-Marshal Coningham to Air Marshal Tedder, 5 February 1942.
30. Brown, *Shark Squadron*, p. 55.
31. AIR 23/1345 *Western Desert Operations*. Correspondence: General Auchinleck to Air Marshal Tedder. 30 January 1942. 'I was infuriated to hear of this avoidable mistake. Blame rests entirely with XIII Corps which ordered the move themselves but did not ascertain the conditions under which the fighters were working. They were much influenced by what happened at Antelat and feared a recurrence but I can see no excuse for what was a blunder'.
32. Skellon, *Interview with the author*.
33. Morte, *Interview with J. Rolph*.
34. AIR 23/6200 *RAF operations in the Western Desert and Eastern Mediterranean*, p. 369. During air attacks on 27 January it was estimated that the Tomahawks, Hurricanes and Kittyhawks of the Desert Air Force had destroyed or damaged more than 120 MT vehicles and had killed or wounded more than 200 of the enemy.
35. AIR 23/1345 *Western Desert Operations*, Correspondence Air Vice-Marshal Coningham to Air Marshal Tedder, 5 February 1942.
36. Cross and Orange, *Straight and Level*, p. 178
37. AIR 29/180 *Air Ministry & Ministry of Defence Operations Record Books: Miscellaneous Units - Air Ministry Experiment Stations*.
38. Morte, *Interview with J. Rolph*.
39. According to his obituary, on one occasion Casano entered Shepheard's Hotel in Cairo with 'Butch' to be told that dogs were not allowed. Casano responded: "Well, you had better put him out then", and the two marched off to the bar. *The Telegraph*, Obituary, 26 September 2006.
40. Extract from *The Egyptian Gazette*.
41. Spybey, Correspondence.
42. Lt.Col. T.E.H. Helby RA, *Notes on the Defence of Landing Grounds*, RAF Regiment Museum Archives.
43. AIR 23/6200 *RAF operations in the Western Desert and Eastern Mediterranean*, p. 376.

across the Mediterranean to Tripoli. By early May, the Gazala Line was being held by XIII Corps with 1st South African Division, 50th (Northumbrian) Division, along with 9th Indian Brigade Group and two Army Tank Brigades equipped with Matilda and Valentine infantry tanks. The 2nd South African Division was at Tobruk, and XXX Corps now consisted of two armoured divisions, the 1st and 7th, with three armoured brigade groups, the 2nd, 4th and 22nd, along with 201st Guards (Motor) Brigade[3], 1st Free French and 29th Indian Brigade Groups and 3rd Indian and 7th Motor Brigade Groups.

From February until May 1942, the Desert Air Force was constantly in demand for operations. At the same time, it had been undergoing a process of rest, re-fitting, training and reorganisation. The instrument of war that Tedder and Coningham had fashioned from mid-1941 had worked well during Operation *Crusader*, but they set about further refining its effectiveness. In late March, Air Vice-Marshal 'Mary' Coningham reorganised the fighter force by reforming No 211 Group, which had been dissolved when Cyrenaica was overrun. This was to take operational control of three new mobile fighter wings: Nos 233 and 239 Wings, equipped with Kittyhawks and No 243 Wing with Hurricanes.[4] While the day-bombers of No 3 Wing SAAF perfected their bombing technique with the new Bostons, the fighters had been modified to become fighter-bombers, with each aircraft being equipped to carry a single 250-lb bomb.[5] No 6 Squadron RAF had arrived in theatre and was equipped with the new Hurricane IID which mounted two 40-mm cannon and was specifically designed as a 'tank-busting' aircraft.

New methods of land marking were developed to aid pilots in fixing their position. Distinguishing friend from foe from the air was still a problem and the use of a bomb-line was only successful as long as the opposing ground forces did not become intermingled; a common feature of desert fighting. The RAF roundel was

The Duke of Gloucester inspecting No 4 Section, No 1 Company, while on his tour of Iraq in May 1942. Following the withdrawal to Gazala, Company HQ and Nos 1 and 3 Sections returned to Egypt to await a replacement for the Rolls-Royces. Meanwhile, Nos 2 and 4 Sections operated from Habbaniya and Mosul carrying out training, routine patrols and making route reports across the Southern Desert and Northern Iraq (© Crown copyright. RAF Regiment Museum).

to be painted on the roof of each British vehicle to aid identification but many had not been so marked before the battle started and as both sides used large numbers of captured vehicles, the markings were often of little use.

Despite airstrips at Gazala and El Adem being closer to the front line, it was decided to concentrate the fighter force on the Gambut airfields, about 12 miles from the day-bombers at Baheira. The location of the Gambut airfields well back from the Gazala Line would facilitate earlier warning of raids by the *Luftwaffe* and *Regia Aeronautica*. A considerable amount of engineering work was completed by the RAF and Army Engineers to improve the airfields and satellite landing grounds, with miles of perimeter tracks, numerous dispersal lanes and pens in the shape of a horseshoe, constructed from 50-gallon drums filled with earth and stacked two high. An entire dummy landing ground, dotted with disabled enemy aircraft, was constructed three miles from Gambut, and equipped with elaborate deception devices, fake anti-aircraft positions and unoccupied tentage. An operations room for No 211 Group was chiselled from solid rock in 12 days. By April, the Desert Air Force had a well-prepared and organised base for operations.[6] The typical RAF desert airfield was described as follows:

> The usual desert airfield was nothing but a large space of desert scraped smooth and hard, around the edges of which were scattered a few tents and trucks, the aircraft and the protecting RAF armoured cars. Large square marquees housed the various messes, the operations control and the orderly room. Around them were dispersed ridge tents and little bivouacs as sleeping quarters, each with its V-shaped slit trench handy as an air-raid shelter. The rest of the 'outfit' stood on wheels; the office of the Commanding Officer was a caravan trailer; signals, that life-blood of the whole force, operated from a few specially fitted vehicles beneath portable aerial masts; workshops of the engineers were fitted into lorries; the cookhouse itself was often a trailer with a field kitchen dumped outside. The whole camp, tents and all, could be bundled into trucks and be on its way within an hour.[7]

The problems that faced Air Marshal Tedder and Air Vice-Marshal Coningham were not dissimilar to those they had dealt with the previous summer before Operation *Battleaxe*. The Army needed a period of reorganisation and rebuilding, and as a consequence, the Air Force had to carry the fight to the enemy through attacks on airfields, supply lines, transport and troop concentrations. The Wellington bombers of No 205 Group continued to pound the port of Benghazi during night raids, at least to slow the unloading of cargo, but were also ordered to attack the major airfields at Martuba. They were assisted in this by the light bombers and Kittyhawk fighter-bombers that attacked the enemy airfields during daylight. As well as offensive tasks, the fighters were carrying out light bomber escorts, defending the port of Tobruk, as well as patrolling over the narrow coast road and railway from Egypt, and Allied shipping moving up the coast from Alexandria. Tactical reconnaissance of troop and supply dispositions was still being carried out by No 208 Squadron, in association with the newly-arrived No 40 Squadron SAAF.[8]

Although having to maintain a high level of activity, the lull did allow the Desert Air Force to send ground and air units and personnel back to the Delta to rest and recover. Number 2 Armoured Car Company, having been on operations since early October, arrived back at Ramleh in Palestine at the end of March. It was given only five weeks to rest, re-train, absorb new officers and airmen, and to repair and re-fit the worn and damaged armoured cars and tenders which had covered many thousands of miles of rough desert over the last five months. The No 1 Armoured Car Company Detachment remained in Egypt at RAF Helwan and received replacement personnel from RAF Habbaniya, and while some airmen returned to Iraq, a large group of time-expired personnel departed on postings to the United Kingdom.

One of the new arrivals on No 2 Company at Ramleh was a relative veteran of the RAF, Corporal (later Warrant Officer) Harry Fenwick. Harry had served in the RAF in France during May 1940 as a driver, and had managed to make it safely back to England before the fall of France. He was then sent to Scotland and was embarked on a ship destined for the ill-fated operations in Norway. Fortuitously, before the convoy could depart, the Germans overran the country. Subsequently he was put on a ship to the Middle East. Harry continues:

> I landed in Suez and was sent into transit at RAF Abu Sueir. After a few days rest I was detailed to take a tanker of either petrol or water to Tobruk. In those days someone in authority just pointed the direction and God help the one who did not arrive.
>
> I think the journey took two days, due to lots of movement back to Cairo, and when I arrived no-one took any interest in me and advised me to get out. This I did and 'in the blue' I met No 2 Armoured Car Company for the first time and followed them to Sidi Haneish. Once again there was nothing but confusion, and for a short time I lived with the Company and was then sent to the No 73 Squadron Officers' Mess as Mess Manager and Clerk of Works. Not only did I build them a Mess, I also managed it for a short time.

Having met the officers and airmen of the Company, he had set about obtaining a posting to join them and in a very short time he was on his way to Palestine to join No 2 Armoured Car Company.

> I have never forgotten the reception I received on my arrival at Ramleh… Of course my days in the desert, with them had been a great help and soon I was settled in as a 'new boy'.
>
> First, I was introduced to all the officers; Squadron Leader Casano, Flight Lieutenants Newland, Skellon, Douglas, Johnston, Mosley, Blake, Parker and Richardson. Then the NCOs Lawn, Drabble, Smith, McNair, Williams, Garbut, and in a short time I knew everyone.
>
> As I arrived alone my training was severe and good, with no rest. Driving up and down the Seven Sisters and down to Jericho, I gave my instructor a good fright one day coming down the Sisters – I missed a gear, panicked a little, and had to travel down in neutral all alone, as my instructor had bailed out. I was really amazed, when I got back to camp, expecting to be crucified. I was complimented for my presence of mind and for bringing the car back in one piece.
>
> Armament instruction was the same as driving, hard; stripping, cleaning and firing every day. I remember having 12 Vickers breech blocks stripped down trying to find out how to assemble them. I did succeed in my training and passed with flying colours, to end up as spare gunner to Sergeant 'Zeke' Williams.[9]

By the middle of May, it had become apparent to Middle East Command that despite the intensive preparations the Eighth Army had been making for a new offensive, Rommel's *Panzerarmee Afrika* would be ready to attack first. Intelligence reports and aerial reconnaissance suggested that the *15th* and *21st Panzer Divisions* were now well forward. The *Luftwaffe* increased attacks against RAF airfields to an almost daily basis and enemy fighter sweeps endeavoured to prevent British reconnaissance aircraft from flying over the Axis positions. The German and Italians possessed some 497 serviceable aircraft, but could draw on just under 800 aircraft from around the Mediterranean, whereas the Desert Air Force had only 190 serviceable had another 739 aircraft with the rest of the RAF in the Middle East. The British were therefore outnumbered both on the Libyan front and in the Mediterranean; moreover, the latest Messerschmitt Bf 109F was superior in performance to both the Kittyhawk and Hurricane.

On 12 May, with the offensive looming, Flight Lieutenant Alan Douglas, who had recovered from his wounds, and had rejoined the Company in mid-March, led No 2 Armoured Car Company once again down the road towards Egypt, across the Sinai, then the Suez Canal and up the coast road. Leaving the Repair detachment at Qasaba, they crossed the Libyan frontier and rejoined the Desert Air Force just behind the Gazala Line. Harry Fenwick continues:

> A few days after I completed my training we moved back up to the Desert via Ismailia and Amiriya. The journey was very quiet and peaceful, everyone had had a good rest and most were broke, and nights were spent drinking the rum ration and tea in groups round the cars.[10]

Following their arrival on 17 May at Gasr el Arid airfield, 35 miles south-east of Tobruk, the Company was joined by Squadron Leader Casano, who had been in Cairo. Deploying without delay on ground defence duties, two armoured car sections remained with No 233 (Fighter) Wing at the airfield, while another section, under

Flight Lieutenant 'Dickie' Skellon (left) and his driver at Bir el Gubi (Skellon).

the command of Flight Lieutenant Skellon, travelled just over 30 miles south-west to Bir el Gubi. Here there was a low ridge, about 15 feet high and two miles in length, but in an otherwise flat and featureless desert it gave some elevation and allowed observation to the west. Here also, was the junction of a number of tracks; the Trig el Abd from the north-west which passed through the central minefields of the Gazala Line, the Trig Bir Hacheim from the Free French Brigade 'Box' to the west, and track leading northwards to the El Adem 'Box'. Bir el Gubi was also on the likely path that the German armour and motorised forces would follow if they were to attempt to strike directly towards the airfields at Gambut and Gasr el Arid. As a consequence, a detachment of either one or two sections of the Company was stationed at Bir el Gubi for the next 12 days (Map 27, p. 384).

On 21 May, Casano led half the Company a few miles north to the Gambut airfields where they came under operational control of No 211 Group. For the armoured car crews at Gambut, being based around Headquarters units could have its perils, as Harry Fenwick was to find out:

> I was always embarrassed to have to dig a hole in the desert and sit over it. One day on a visit to Group HQ I spotted a toilet marked "OFFICERS" and thought I would have time to relieve nature quickly. I just got sat down when to my horror, in came Air Vice-Marshal Coningham. I leapt off the seat, gave him a salute with my shorts down and froze solid. I remember him saying "Well it's not the place to talk shop, sit down, where are you from, etc." I left him sitting, with a salute – very embarrassed I was. He smiled.[11]

General Auchinleck had carefully marshalled his resources, despite transfers of men and materiel to the Indian Ocean for the war against Japan. The launch of the British offensive had been planned for 5 June, but he was fully aware that with the more favourable supply lines, Rommel had won the race and would be able to attack first. Auchinleck's plan was to meet this offensive and then launch a counter-offensive as soon as the enemy had been halted.

And so it was that on the afternoon of 26 May, *General Crüewell's Group*, consisting of the *Italian 10th and 20th Corps* and the *15th German Rifle Brigade*, supported by dive-bombers and artillery, closed up to the northern sector of the Line between Gazala and Sidi Muftah. The impression was to be given that this was the main attack; however, that night, under a bright moon, Rommel launched the *15th and 21st Panzer Divisions* of the *Deutsches Afrika Korps*, *90th Light Division* and the *Ariete Armoured* and *Trieste Motorised Divisions* on a sweep southwards through Bir Hacheim. There was little surprise for the British commanders in this move as it was being shadowed by South African armoured cars and a column of the 7th Motor Brigade, though this information seems not to have always been passed effectively on to those it might directly concern. At the same time, the enemy air forces launched widespread attacks on British airfields.

The following morning, the enemy turned northwards overwhelming the unfortunate 3rd Indian Motor Brigade and forcing 7th Motor Brigade to vacate the Retma 'Box' and move back to Bir el Gubi. The 4th Armoured Brigade was launched against the German armour and a fierce tank battle ensued. The Headquarters of 7th Armoured Division was overrun, causing some confusion, and the XIII Corps Headquarters was forced to seek shelter in the El Adem 'Box'. The 2nd and 22nd

Armoured Brigades were ordered south to meet the threat but suffered heavily.

Notwithstanding the losses in armour and infantry, the British higher command was satisfied with events after the first 24 hours of the Battle of Gazala. The Axis forces were, on the other hand, in a parlous state. Despite one column of *21st Panzer Division* having reached Sidi Rezegh, and the *90th Light Division* being reported only 30 miles from Gambut, Rommel had lost a third of his tanks, and his two Panzer divisions were now trapped behind the extensive minefields to the west, and menaced to the north and east by the British armoured brigades. The *90th Light Division* was lost somewhere south of El Adem, the *Trieste Division* was in trouble in the minefields, and the Free French 'Box' at Bir Hacheim was valiantly resisting the efforts of the *Ariete Division* to subdue it. Axis fuel supplies were low and the supply echelons were not getting through from the south due to the effectiveness of low-level air attacks from the Kittyhawks of the fighter wings and the Boston day-bombers of No 3 Wing.

By the second day of the offensive, the threat from Rommel's thrust was such that orders were issued that evening for the evacuation of the fighters from Gambut.[12] According to a pre-arranged plan, the anti-aircraft guns were placed around the landing ground in an anti-tank role. Flying Officer Patullo of No 2 Company was sent out with two Fordsons to patrol the escarpment south of Gambut and to keep watch for enemy incursions. An Axis column was reported to be in the vicinity; however, it veered away and by morning only friendly troops were seen in the area. The reason for the evacuation was unclear and there was some confusion in the fighter squadrons. One explanation proffered was that it was merely a precautionary move; however, there was also a rumour of a planned German paratroop landing and another of a threatened moonlight bombing raid. Harry Fenwick continues:

> Very soon I had my own car with Mick Durell, as driver, Nick Carter on the radio, and Flight Lieutenant Parker, the car commander; me, gunner....[13] Most of the first two or three weeks were just spent on patrols. Then things really did begin to brighten up. The Company was deployed around Group Headquarters, and one night, to avoid the bombing, Group Captain Carter decided to move out for the night only and did not advise Squadron Leader Casano of his intentions. The Company immediately thought they had retreated and plundered the Group HQ. The next morning when they came back, it was ever so sad. Fortunately, everything but food and drink was returned with much embarrassment on both sides. A friend of mine really liked the Group Captain's pyjamas.[14]

By 29 May, the Eighth Army was well placed to destroy the Axis armoured force that was now trapped in the pocket between the minefields and the boxes to the north, west and east. Rommel was in a difficult situation with the *Afrika Korps* now at the end of a long and tenuous supply line. He concluded that his best option was to break through the minefields to the west to shorten the route for his supply convoys to his fuel-starved panzers. Not only would he have his back to the British minefields, but the 'box' held by 150th Infantry Brigade at Sidi Muftah was directly in his path. And so on the night of 29/30 May, he ordered the German panzer divisions to temporarily halt the advance towards Tobruk and El Adem. They were concentrated west and south-west of Knightsbridge and formed a thick anti-tank screen facing east. Rommel then set about reducing the 150th Brigade 'Box'. Despite

Morale was high in the RAF, particularly in No 239 Wing at Gambut, which considered itself the spearhead of the fighter force. Ground crews on the airfields worked feverishly to maintain the maximum number of sorties in support of Bir Hacheim. But under ceaseless shelling and air attack, Bir Hacheim became untenable and so on 10 June, the RAF provided air cover as the defenders were evacuated from the 'box'. Despite the valiant struggle of the Free French, the loss of Bir Hacheim had opened up the front to the south and Eighth Army now faced attack from the south, as well as the west. A key feature of the Gazala Line had fallen and the outcome was reaching an inevitable conclusion. Rommel had planned to reduce the fortress in one hour on the 27 May. It had however, held out for 15 days and as it turned out, this delay was critical in disrupting Rommel's timetable for the capture of Tobruk and the advance into Egypt.

While the RAF concentrated its efforts on Bir Hacheim, the British armour positioned itself for the clash against the *Afrika Korps* for what would be the final decisive act of the battle of Gazala. When the sandstorms finally abated on 3 June, the armour of the two armies faced each other around the 'Cauldron'. The British unsuccessfully counter-attacked on 5 June and suffered further heavy losses in both armour and infantry in poorly-planned, uncoordinated attacks. On 11 June, the Bostons of No 3 Wing SAAF along with the Kittyhawks of No 239 Wing focussed all their attention on the *21st Panzer Division* south-west of Knightsbridge and the following day attacked *90th Light Division*. The newly-arrived Hurricane IID 'tank-busters' of No 6 Squadron joined the desperate air onslaught but failed to stop the German armour.

Rommel, seeing an opportunity, sent his armour north-west towards the 201st Guards Brigade 'Box' at Knightsbridge and a heavy armoured engagement developed the following day. As in previous engagements, the 2nd, 4th and 22nd Armoured Brigades suffered severe losses as the fighting drifted north to Acroma. The ground crews at Gambut could hear the tanks slogging it out only a few miles away, and the

Skellon (in white overalls) and some of his section in front of a knocked-out German tank (Skellon).

LAC Vic Morte (left) (RAFACA).

artillery duels going on day and night. Corporal Harry Fenwick was in a Fordson armoured car watching the armoured battle spread out below him:

> Knightsbridge was a sight I shall never forget and the terrible slaughter of the British tanks. My car sat on an escarpment and watched the whole battle. In fact we became so interested we forgot the serious side of the situation and were the last in the area. The Germans must have had mercy on us and let us get away.
>
> The strangest part about life in the desert with No 2 Armoured Car Company was we never seemed to be on the right side of the line and yet never came to any serious harm.[17]

The RAF armoured cars patrolled continuously on the edge of the battle. They had been out constantly on watch, signalling back details of the best targets and standing out in the open to report on the results achieved by the fighters and bombers. They had to be continually on their guard for enemy columns, particularly German reconnaissance units, which in the majority of cases possessed superior vehicles and weaponry. LAC Vic Morte describes the routine when out on patrol with the cars:

> You were reporting absolutely anything that was hostile. You didn't meet a lot, but on many occasions, you couldn't believe that you were no more than three miles away from a German armoured column, and they were moving fast... You did a turning circle to move around the back to get behind them, and as long as you actually kept the enemy in sight, that was

GAZALA
Evening 15 June 1942

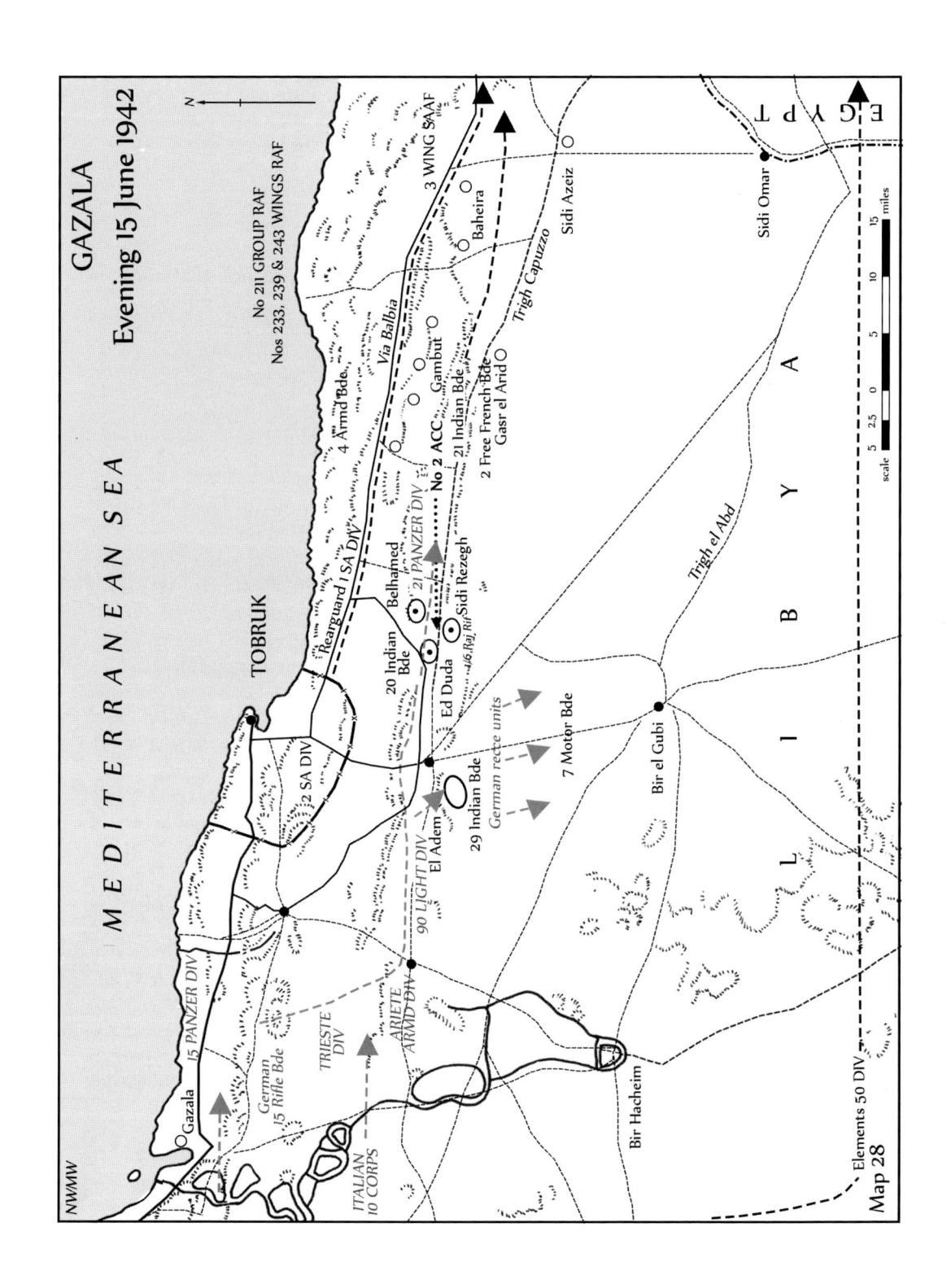

No 211 GROUP RAF
Nos 233, 239 & 243 WINGS RAF

Map 28

the most important thing. These turning circles were usually quite big... The idea was to keep them in view.

The wireless operator was completely tuned-in to the net all the time... and at a chosen minute every hour he called up the Headquarters and gave a little report. But if anything was an emergency he'd break silence and call up the CO. Casano was there in the control car and he knew exactly to the minute which car was which, and of course every car was reporting to him every hour on its position and what the situation was like at the time. Consequently, when anything really serious happened you broke your radio silence...

Each section was a unit. It was generally one car in each section that had contact with HQ. The main thing was to keep the air as free as possible. I don't know of any occasion where anyone was actually out of place. Occasionally a car was lost, that had vanished, but eventually it found its way back. We were all kept under close scrutiny. It was simple system and nobody could do anything wrong. You were in a section of four cars, and the officer in charge had to answer for anything that was not quite right. [18]

By 14 June, with Rommel having defeated the British offensive against the 'Cauldron' and Knightsbridge, and with the rear echelons of the northern sector of the Gazala Line threatened, Major-General Ritchie had no option but to order the 1st South African and 50th (Northumbrian) Divisions to retire at dusk. The latter broke out to the west and then headed south into the desert and then cut east, while for the next two days and nights, a mass of troops, lorries, guns and armoured cars of the 1st South African Division streamed back along the Via Balbia. The fighters from Gambut flew just under 300 sorties over the South Africans and prevented serious interference from the *Luftwaffe*. Meanwhile, the garrisons at El Adem and Acroma continued to hold out against repeated attacks by the enemy motorised infantry and tanks, which were in turn being harassed by British 'Jock' columns operating from the south.

Until 15 June, the airfields of the Desert Air Force had not been directly threatened by the Axis land advance. On this day however, Rommel swiftly turned eastwards, away from Acroma, bypassed the strongpoint at El Adem and sent his panzers towards Sidi Rezegh. His aim was to isolate Tobruk, but it also placed his armour only a short bound away from the entire fighter force. By early morning, there were reports of up to 30 German tanks with infantry only 20 miles from Gambut (Map 28, p. 388).

Flying Officer Blake's patrol from No 2 Armoured Car Company had seen this enemy transport moving eastward. Flight Lieutenant Skellon and his section were also out to the west near Sidi Rezegh, and through the heat haze of summer could see the enemy tank columns. These were the advanced elements of the *21st Panzer Division* with tanks, armoured cars and hundreds of lorries following behind. Skellon continues:

We were doing the work for the Desert Air Force, keeping them in touch with what was going on, because in that period no one really knew what was happening.

I had to spend the night out and I was just fiddling around trying to find something to report and then I saw these vehicles coming along the escarpment. I recognised them as German armour, which was an appalling thing to see. There was a great line of them along the escarpment. They all stopped and began to refuel, and I thought, aha! That's it!

So I got in touch with 'Cass' and he said to get in touch with No 6 Squadron, which had recently been issued with the new anti-tank gun mounted Hurricanes. He said "Get onto them quickly and give them a full report as to position and everything else". Well they'd already had this apparently, but I confirmed it.[19] And I then had to brief them over the radio on what was happening, and I saw them all take-off in line to attack this force of German armoured vehicles. They flew right over me. Going the right way, as far as I was concerned!

I never saw them attack as I had to shove off, but I was told afterwards by the Squadron CO that the attack had been successful. I remember, I went in to see Six Squadron that evening and they gave me a couple of beers to thank me for what I had done.[20]

Skellon's patrol had maintained continuous touch with the enemy columns for several days calling in air strikes from the Hurricanes, Kitty-bombers and Bostons and were forced to retire only when, on a number of occasions, they came under heavy shellfire. Flight Lieutenant Newland's patrol was however, also in contact with the same column. Perhaps of all the officers during this period; Flight Lieutenant J.H.F. Newland was most vividly remembered by his fellow officers and men and with some humour. LAC Vic Morte served in 'Bill' Newland's Section, and recalls some of his idiosyncrasies and eccentricities:

Flight Lieutenant Skellon shortly after his exploits around Sidi Rezegh on 14-17 June 1942. The official photographer wrote 'The RAF Armoured Cars have done magnificent work in every Middle East theatre of war... Typical of this work was the recent exploit of a young Flight Lieutenant from Bournemouth, who from a far advanced position spotted enemy tanks and hundreds of MT. He passed on the information to base and within a short time Kitty-bombers and Bostons attacked the Axis column, knocking out tanks and nearly 40 vehicles' (© IWM CM 2955).

I was with 'Bill' Newland, on 'B' Section; called the 'Suicide Section'. He was an ex-Indian Army officer, 50 year-old, blind in one eye, and he could be a bit rash at times, but he was a character. I'd become really a good map reader and navigator. I had an interest in maps... I used to read them in the quiet, so I knew exactly where we were. He had difficulty reading maps. His favourite saying was "The man that made this map did not know how to do his job!"

He used to issue all his orders the 'decks' way. When on patrol and he wanted to issue orders he used to shout to me, in good Naval style, "Morte! Hail alongside". Of course the cars would then pull up in line abreast about 12 inches apart and the roofs of the four radio compartments made a platform that he could walk over.

One time we managed to get our hands on some very good captured German binoculars. Unfortunately, they were damaged and had only one good lens which matched his bad eye, so they weren't any use to him.[21]

Flight Lieutenant Skellon also recalled Newland:

Yes, I remember, he was an elderly gentleman, he was ex-Indian Army, and he was a bit mad. Used to scare his own airmen. He was quite a character... I remember one occasion I was being chased by a German armoured car, going like blazes, and I threw them off. Soon after, I was coming down the track that led to HQ and looked across and there was Newland and his Section having a picnic. The Germans could have jumped on them at any moment.

Harry Fenwick also knew him:

Flight Lieutenant Newland was known as 'Old Bill' and had a big reputation from the Indian Army and in the cars.[22] Everyone considered he was blind as a bat. He always managed to get into the wrong area on patrol. His dress was unknown in any service book. On one occasion the Field Security picked him up and Squadron Leader Casano was asked to identify him and stated that he had never seen him before. Newland was locked up. On another occasion he got lost he signalled back to base "I have made contact with the enemy". Casano's reply was "Blast your luck". But in words not printable.[23]

On 16 June, while Eighth Army Headquarters was moving back to Sollum on the Egyptian frontier, Air Vice-Marshal Coningham declared his intention to keep Advanced Air Headquarters Western Desert and the fighters at Gambut to control operations until the very last moment. The South African Campaign History describes this moment:

The new tank-destroying Hurricanes were also out, and fighter bombers were operating in full force from the Gambut group of airfields which were getting uncomfortably near the ground fighting... General Ritchie's failing grip on the reins was reflected in a screen of patrols of No 2 Armoured Car Company of the RAF in front of four infantry battalions and three and half anti-aircraft batteries allotted to close defence of the landing grounds, and Air Vice-Marshal Coningham himself remained at Gambut. Cooperation between the Army and Air Force was thus, quite literally, very close and *21st Panzer Division* suffered considerable losses in men and material in repeated attacks by Hurricane IIDs with their 40-mm cannon, which gave the Panzer crews a taste of a new medicine. With the Eighth Army's disorganisation increasing hourly, the Desert Air Force was playing an increasingly important role in the battle.[24]

Gambut was the birthplace and testing-ground of the Desert Air Force. Over the preceding few months it had perfected the tactics for escorting the day-bombers, refined air control and enhanced the mobility of the squadrons. It was here that the 'Kitty-bomber' was developed and its use in close air-support refined. The fighters continued providing full air support to the El Adem 'Box' and cover for the withdrawing ground forces but this could not have been continued had the force moved back from Gambut. The decisions made over the next few days by Coningham concerning the Desert Air Force would be crucial, not only to its effectiveness in slowing Rommel's advance, but would determine its actual survival. Morale was high among the ground and air crews, who worked feverishly night and day to sustain the sortie rate, but it was to be an anxious period. In the words of the Senior Air Staff Officer, Group Captain George Beamish, "The price of the gamble taken was the entire fighter force; the decision was courageous."[25]

There was no adequate ground force in front of Gambut that could deal with either an armoured advance or even a raid by enemy reconnaissance forces. The value of the infantry 'boxes' had been brought into question in the previous weeks as one 'box' after another had been overrun by the German and Italian armour. Most of those remaining had been issued with a few of the puny 2-pdr anti-tank guns only a few days earlier. The reconstituted 4th Armoured Brigade had about 90 tanks, and moved up to a position 10 miles south-east of Sidi Rezegh on 17 June. It had been cobbled together from disparate units and to its credit, fought another pitched battle against the two Panzer divisions, but was heavily outnumbered and it was driven back towards Gambut.

Skellon's patrol returned the next morning and resumed the watch on the German column as it moved eastwards along the escarpment. The day was hot with temperatures of around 60 °C out in the sun, so the temperatures inside the steel-plated cars must have been almost unbearable. The enemy were approaching the Sidi Rezegh 'box' held by an Indian Army battalion of the 20th Indian Brigade and the enemy artillery had begun to register. He continues:

> 'Cass' used to send me out on every damned patrol there was. I suppose he thought I was good at them. The crews of mine were only too pleased to get out. Because as you know we slept out on the ground alongside the cars and we did our own rations.
>
> Everybody was in these 'boxes' and 'Cass' called me on the R/T and told me to go and get in touch with the Colonel of 1st Rajputana Rifles.[26] So I went up to see him, and asked "Was their anything that we could do for them?" and he said "No, you can clear off, we'll manage" and he said "Well we're not going to stay here too long, believe me it's all too hot". The German's kept on coming over and bombing.

We were quite happy where we were, but he said "Well I shall be leaving tonight so get the hell out and leave whenever you like." So we stayed put, I don't know why, but we stayed for the night; we had a chap out on guard. In the morning, when we got up, we thought, it's damn quiet. So we sent somebody to have a look and they came back and said they've gone. All the people in the box had disappeared. We were left on our own there, which was a bit exasperating. So I got in touch with 'Cass' and he said "Right stay around and see what you can see, and then clear off as quickly as you can".

Well we were sitting in a wadi and I was staring around and suddenly from where the Germans were, near this 'box', a little vehicle came out, snooping around, and it stopped. It had a crew of three and a chap got out and went off to have a leak. I thought that's it. We had a 0.55 in Boys anti-tank rifle and I thought as much for fun I'd shoot at them. A bit unfair, but anyway, so I fired off a shot with the Boys and that made them clear off quickly.

The funny thing was that as we went off, to my amazement there appeared a great long line of vehicles, 3-tonners, with an RASC Captain in charge, who said "I've come to pick up the Rajputana Rifles?" I said "They've gone", He said "Well Christ, I better get back" and they all turned around and went off.[27]

At Belhamed and Ed Duda were the two remaining battalions of 20th Indian Brigade, which along with the 1/6th Rajputana Rifles had arrived only ten days earlier after a 1500 mile drive from Iraq. As the front collapsed, the Brigade was ordered to retire to the east. While the Rajputana Rifles successfully evaded capture that night, the two other battalions were ambushed by German tanks and armoured cars as they left their 'boxes'. Both suffered heavy casualties and the majority were made prisoners-of-war.

By remaining at Gambut, Coningham was also able to deal a decisive blow to the *Luftwaffe*. A morning reconnaissance flight reported large numbers of German aircraft had established themselves on the Gazala No 2 airfield shortly after its capture. Number 239 Wing launched a surprise attack with 31 Kittyhawks and Kitty-bombers and in a swift low-level sweep claimed to have severely damaged more than a third of the 30 or so Messerschmitt Bf 109s and 110s drawn up on the strip. This significantly reduced the enemy fighter efforts for the next few days, but it could not halt the land advance.

During the night of 16/17 June, the El Adem 'Box' was evacuated allowing the enemy force around Sidi Rezegh to be reinforced. Air Headquarters Western Desert was only notified of the loss of El Adem at 1500 hours the following day, with the airfields having been exposed for 14 hours to any columns that might bypass the last remaining defence positions at Sidi Rezegh and Belhamed. The sound of gunfire could now be heard clearly on the dispersals at Gambut, and the ground crews could hear the explosions of the bombs being dropped by the Bostons. The fighter force however, could no longer be risked. Acting on information being radioed back by Flight Lieutenant Skellon, and with the enemy only 12 miles away, the fighter squadrons departed in the late afternoon and headed to a new landing ground at Sidi Azeiz. Number 3 (Bomber) Wing with a fighter wing in support remained at Baheira (few miles further east) until first light on 18 June, when the bombers departed for LG 07, back near Mersa Matruh, and the fighter wing for LG 76.

Grabbing what they could to keep the planes flying, the RAF ground crews joined a mad rush of Army and RAF vehicles. Trucks, wireless vans, bowsers, fuel tankers, heavy and light anti-aircraft guns and ambulances raced eastwards across the desert towards the next airfield. The salvage and demolition parties remained at Gambut until just before midnight to deny any material and equipment to the enemy. When the tanks of *21st Panzer Division* rumbled across the airfield in darkness they found nothing of consequence but the wrecks of a few burnt-out Kittyhawks. The fighter force had gone, swiftly and silently. Casano remained to watch the entry of the enemy onto Gambut, and then spent the night astride the Trigh Capuzzo at Gasr el Arid watching for any further advance by Axis reconnaissance units. Air Headquarters Western Desert reached Sollum safely, and following discussions at Eighth Army Tactical Headquarters it was concluded that the fighters at Sidi Azeiz could not be protected from fast-moving enemy columns and they were to withdraw back into Egypt. The next morning, the fighters flew off and No 211 Group Headquarters, escorted by No 2 Company, departed by road for LGs 75 and 76, located 30 miles south of Sidi Barrani and from where Nos 233, 239 and 244 Wings were to continue operations.[28] The maintenance of the Desert Air Force well forward had not been in vain as it had been able to strike serious blows against the Axis ground and air forces. Between 11 and 20 June, the fighters launched 2171 sorties and the bombers 280 and 231 sorties during the day and night, respectively.[29]

On 20 June, the bulk of the German and Italian Divisions turned on Tobruk. After much debate and vacillation, Generals Auchinleck and Ritchie had determined that the only option was to hold Tobruk for military, political and prestige reasons. Rommel surrounded the fortress with his Italian infantry and then prepared for an armoured breakthrough with the two Panzer divisions. The Eighth Army could do little to aid the garrison of South African, British and Indian troops. The move of the RAF fighter force to landing grounds in Egypt now meant that they could not reach Tobruk. The Desert Air Force could only send over a few of the Bostons of No 3 Wing to bomb the *Deutsches Afrika Korps* as it gathered for the attack on the fortress. The role of the fighters, at the limit of their effective range, was to protect the frontier positions that were now held by a thin Eighth Army rear-guard. Supported by artillery and Stuka dive-bombers, the enemy attacked the south-eastern corner of Tobruk on a narrow front early on 20 June. Despite a gallant defence and counterattack the enemy prevailed. With his troops facing annihilation at the hands of the German panzers, and with few of his troops having the vehicles to organise a breakout, the commander of the Tobruk garrison, General Klopper, saw no option but to authorise the surrender of the 33,000 men under his command. Some battalions fought on until the next day but the outcome was inevitable.

After much debate amongst the German High Command, they decided that rather than launch the planned assault on Malta by airborne troops, Rommel should be given full reign to pursue the Eighth Army and to continue until they were totally destroyed. Mussolini was also attracted to the prospect of reaching the Suez Canal. By the time the decision to advance had been confirmed, Rommel's forces were already well into Egypt. The *Luftwaffe* was caught by surprise by the plan to keep the advance going into Egypt and made only a few attempts to deal fatal blows to the retreating Eighth Army columns.

The British planned to delay the advance with as strong a force as they could muster in order to gain time for reinforcements to arrive from Syria and Iraq. Rommel crossed the Egyptian frontier on 23 June, by which time the planned 'delaying action'

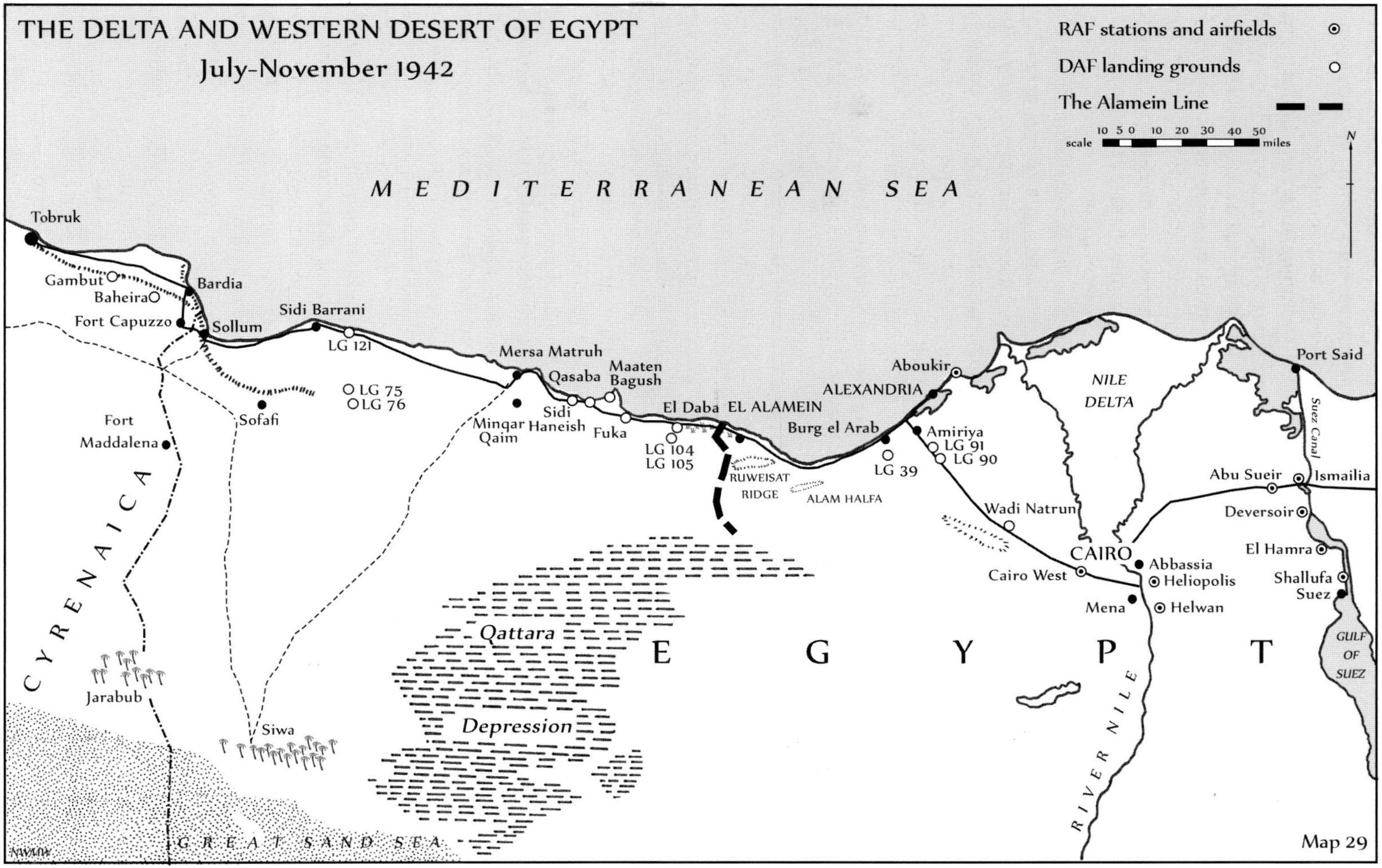
THE DELTA AND WESTERN DESERT OF EGYPT
July–November 1942
RAF stations and airfields
DAF landing grounds
The Alamein Line
scale
10 5 0 10 20 30 40 50
miles
N
MEDITERRANEAN SEA
Tobruk
Gambut
Baheira
Bardia
Fort Capuzzo
Sollum
Sidi Barrani
LG 121
LG 75
LG 76
Sofafi
Fort Maddalena
CYRENAICA
Jarabub
Siwa
GREAT SAND SEA
Mersa Matruh
Minqar Qaim
Qasaba
Sidi Haneish
Maaten Bagush
Fuka
El Daba
LG 104
LG 105
EL ALAMEIN
RUWEISAT RIDGE
ALAM HALFA
Qattara
Depression
Burg el Arab
LG 39
ALEXANDRIA
Aboukir
Amiriya
LG 91
LG 90
Wadi Natrun
Cairo West
CAIRO
Abbassia
Heliopolis
Helwan
Mena
RIVER NILE
NILE DELTA
EGYPT
Port Said
Suez Canal
Ismailia
Abu Sueir
Deversoir
El Hamra
Shallufa
Suez
GULF OF SUEZ
NWMW
Map 29

had quickly degenerated into a withdrawal.

The Eighth Army transport columns were moving down the coast road *en masse* and were reaching the bottlenecks through the passes at Sollum and Halfaya. Here they were coming under attack from Stuka dive-bombers as the roads became congested. To avoid this, it was considered wiser for the RAF armoured cars to move inland, down into the desert, and then to head east to the frontier landing grounds. Stores, in particular petrol and ammunition, had been stockpiled at Misheifa railhead in Egypt, near Sofafi, in readiness for the now aborted Eighth Army June offensive, and these now had to be cleared or destroyed. Much was moved back towards the east, but 500,000 gallons of petrol was deliberately leaked into the sand. Water points were wrecked and the remaining ammunition blown-up. Vic Morte and 'B' Section of No 2 Company were withdrawing back into Egypt and he recalled the chaos of retreat and the destruction of these large stores dumps:

> This business of petrol was fantastic. We went to a place called Sofafi, on the way back; supplies were spread out all over the place. There was the most gigantic petrol and bomb dump. The petrol was stacked in huge squares, all tins, about six high, and apart from that, there was ammunition for 25-pdrs. As we got there, the Royal Engineers were there detonating them. I stood on the side of car to help guide the driver through the smoke. I could feel the heat scorching my back as we went through. It took a mile or so to get through here, and then we stopped to survey damage, and then went on another 10 miles or so.
>
> All of a sudden we looked back. The Germans had large 8-wheeled armoured cars, marvellous, on four independently-mounted axles. We could see a half a dozen of these very fast armoured cars coming up behind. Every one shouted "Scarper! Get out of it!" We drove like bloody hell. They only thing is that they were much better than what we had in soft sand. So we were having to pick our way through, looking in front, finding where on the sand it was possible to go. And we realised that in the distance was a shallow hill, but quite steep towards the top. The first car decided to climb it, with no instructions, nothing at all.
>
> They [the RAF armoured cars] all had the common sense to go back in file. The first car went, and almost got to the top. But at the top was soft sand. The wheels were going chomp, chomp, but he just managed to pull himself over. The other four cars did the same thing, they followed up. We stood at the top and looked down on these Germans vehicles, with the sole satisfaction, well if we just about got up, they couldn't get up!

Air Vice-Marshal Coningham planned to fall back on a chain of landing-grounds, stocked with fuel and ammunition, and with small parties of ground crews. This would allow the Desert Air Force to provide continuous air cover to the retreating army. There would be no repeat of the pauses in provision of air support that had been experienced in the retreat from Antelat to Gazala in January. Landing grounds were prepared at Mersa Matruh, Maaten Bagush, Sidi Haneish, Fuka, El Daba, Amiriya and Wadi Natrun. Meanwhile, aircraft and squadrons were despatched from the Nile Delta to increase the strength of the Desert Air Force. To sustain the offensive, the Wellingtons of No 205 Group, led by flare-dropping Albacores of the Fleet Air Arm as pathfinders, attacked the Axis troop concentrations by night (Map 29, p. 395).

The RAF was to continue its attack from landing-grounds as far west as possible, while the Eighth Army would prepare to fight a battle at Mersa Matruh. However, the German advance was rapid and at this stage unstoppable, and so for the next three days, No 2 Company covered the withdrawal of No 211 Group from LG 75 as it moved back to Maaten Bagush, just beyond Matruh. Landing Ground 75 was used for as long as possible, with the RAF again leaving only minutes before the German panzers rumbled onto the aerodrome.

The Eighth Army hastily established a stable defence line at Mersa Matruh under X Corps with elements of the 50th Division, 10th Indian Division and the New Zealand Division, which had only just arrived from Syria. The gravity of the situation had become such that General Auchinleck decided to take personal command of the Eighth Army and on 25 June he took over from Major-General Ritchie. Auchinleck then ordered a further withdrawal as it was clear he had neither the tanks nor the artillery to hold the Matruh position.

Harry Fenwick and his section were cheerfully making their way back towards Matruh, but they were very much dependent on their own resourcefulness and a fair amount of luck to reach the safety of the British lines:

> When the retreat did take place it was really good fun. We were never so well off in our lives. Like vultures we watched NAAFI stores, ration dumps, from a short distance then moved in and plundered like Danes. One day we jumped a little too soon and got a bill for what we had taken!
>
> The strange thing about life in the Desert was no-one appeared to think about the war in a serious manner. No-one feared the Germans [or] spoke with pride of Rommel. Obviously, the bombs and shells made life a little unpleasant but day to day life went on without grumbles. Health was extremely good and everyone survived coughs, colds, etc. without any real hardship. They had to, no MOs.
>
> Coming back to Mersa Matruh… we were diverted way down south for some unknown reason and got lost. God really was on our side, we ran out of petrol and on our last gallon found an abandoned truck with one can full of petrol, the other half full, no signs of the driver. Lost, broken down, and foolishly he'd left his truck, maybe he died. Next refuelling point was an abandoned Bren gun carrier, and then it looked a clear run to home. This was not so, for we hit a minefield. We could not go west because of the Germans, so we had to enter the minefield. We took turns driving, in case we triggered a mine, while all other crew members sat on the turret. We made it in sweat and silence.

The rapid advance of the *Afrika Korps* soon outflanked the infantry divisions holding Mersa Matruh and they were forced to break out through the Axis columns lying out in the desert or blocking the coast road behind Matruh. On the evening of 26 June, Air Headquarters Western Desert received the shocking news that a German armoured column had passed through a gap in the line south of the Mersa Matruh defences and was now within 20 miles of the airfield at Maaten Bagush. With darkness falling there was no time to get the squadrons off the ground and set them down again at the next landing ground. The scenario that had been played out at Gambut and LG 75 was again repeated. 'Mary' Coningham sent the RAF armoured cars out to the west of the landing grounds to form a screen where they waited, watched and

Fordson A123 of No 2 Armoured Car Company pulls up next to General Auchinleck as he watches the Eighth Army coming back down the coast road after the withdrawal from Mersa Matruh, 2 July 1942 (© IWM E13877).

reported back. They could provide a warning of a possible enemy advance and at least some of the fighters might get away. The Advance Headquarters was moved back as a precaution, but the Mobile Operations Room was held back to maintain control should the fighters have to be flown off in the darkness.

Despite a noisy and anxious night, Rommel did not push on, and at dawn the fighter force flew further back to safety at El Daba. The ground crews and pilots of No 239 Wing continued to work tirelessly to maintain offensive sorties. However, by 29 June, columns of the *90th Light Division* were reported to be within 15 miles of El Daba and a screen of Fordsons from Flight Newland's Section were again out reporting back on the speed and position of a menacing column of tanks, MT and light wheeled armoured cars. The fighters at El Daba stayed to cover the elements of X Corps retreating from Mersa Matruh until the last moment and then set off back to the new defensive line where the Eighth Army would make its final stand, El Alamein. Harry Fenwick continues:

> The retreat to El Alamein was amusing, hazardous, and at times a very independent move of the armoured cars. No one knew what was happening, and often it was a case of moving in the wrong direction. On one occasion my car was heading west towards a NAAFI dump, saw some tanks approaching in the opposite direction, and it was not until a very late decision that we

realised they were German and we beat a very hasty retreat.

One very sad incident occurred. We were laagered on an escarpment. High in the sky was a German fighter patrol and returning from a sortie was an RAF fighter squadron. Like vultures the Germans came down and shot all the RAF planes down. We buried the dead in their chutes and kit. To bury the dead was not an unusual task for the armoured car crews.

The Alamein Line, a misnomer at this stage, as it was more a series of defended features, was named after an insignificant halt on the railway line from Alexandria. The location was chosen as it was one of the few places that could not be outflanked. The sea prevented this to the north and 38 miles to the south lay the Qattara Depression, a morass of mud and salt flats and sand dunes that was impassable to a large mechanised army. Auchinleck was preparing to hold the enemy, and as soon as possible strike back at the now tiring and badly-depleted enemy divisions. As the

The sun sets over the desert battlefield (King).

divisions of the Eighth Army arrived they were fed into the line. Number 2 Company reached LG 39 near Amiriya on 29 June. Harry Fenwick continues:

> The cars just got back before they closed the Alamein line … the last car through, was stopped by General Auchinleck and he asked Flight Lieutenant Newland what the 'gen' was. We finished up near Amiriya and stayed here during the lull in activities.

Despite Rommel's determination to reach Cairo, the *Panzerarmee Afrika* was exhausted and understrength. The German supply lines had become stretched and were attacked by over 700 sorties a day by the Desert Air Force, as well as harassment by the 'Jock' Columns of Eighth Army; as a result, Rommel's advance ran out of momentum. The Alamein Line was now held by the 1st South African Division, 5th Indian Division, the New Zealand Division, which had fought its way back from Matruh after encirclement, and the newly-arrived 9th Australian Division. The remnants of 1st and 7th Armoured Divisions waited behind the line as a mobile reserve.

On 1 July, Rommel commenced his attack and after two days of desperate fighting on the land and in the air, it was clear that the Axis forces could not break through, and they were fought to standstill. The threat to Egypt was countered for the time being and the only option for the German and Italian divisions was to dig in, await reinforcements, and prepare for another push.

In his despatch on the campaign, General Auchinleck paid generous tribute to role played by the Desert Air Force during the retreat to the Alamein Line. He wrote:

> Our air forces could not have done more than they did to help and sustain the Eighth Army in its struggle. Their effort was continuous by day and night and the effect on the enemy was tremendous. I am certain that, had it not been for their devoted and exceptional efforts, we should not have been able to stop the enemy on the El Alamein position, and I wish to record my gratitude and that of the whole of the Eighth-Army to Air Chief Marshal Tedder, Air Marshal Coningham and the air forces under their command.[30]

The RAF armoured cars had played a small, but essential part in the protection of the Desert Air Force fighter force for nearly a year now. A report written by Army Staff during April 1942, just prior to Gazala, comments rather grudgingly on the contributions made by the RAF Armoured Car Companies:

> There were also available in the recent operations, some RAF armoured cars, usually about 12. Some of these had seen service in the last war and most them were unreliable. They were heavy and in soft ground or sand they were apt to stick and their W/T did not often work satisfactorily. Where little is available everything helps but it would be an error to assess these vehicles as being anywhere on a par with the modern armoured car unit. It is understood that the armoured car unit is in the process of refitting at base and is due to return to the desert shortly.[31]

If only half of these criticisms had been accurate, then this would have made the vital contribution of the RAF armoured cars and their crews even more remarkable.

Only 10 days after the Axis advance had been halted at El Alamein, Air Chief Marshal Tedder, AOC-in-C Middle East, felt it important enough to mention the significance of their role to the achievements of the Desert Air Force in correspondence with Chief of the Air Staff, Air Chief Marshal Sir Charles Portal[32]:

> Though he did not know it, Rommel's push had met its real breaking point on 2nd July. I was at this time again in the Desert and returned on 6th having had a most stimulating stay with 'Mary' Coningham's force. I described my visit in a letter to Portal on the 12th:
>
> ...Of course the crux of the whole matter as regards maintaining the fighter effort both in retreat and in advance is security of advanced landing grounds. Recently the Army have paid lip service to the paramount importance of this point, but in fact have done nothing except in regards anti-aircraft. As I think I told you, on two occasions at least it was only our Armoured Car screen that saved the fighter force from being wiped out on the ground by enemy land forces. Our armoured cars have done yeoman service, and under the present conditions it would be quite impossible to accept the risks of operating fighters from really advanced landing grounds if we had not got our own armoured car screen. There is no doubt that under conditions of mobile warfare armoured cars are an essential part of the RAF in the field...[33]

Notes

1. AIR 23/1179 *RAF Operations during withdrawal from Gazala to El-Alamein: Report, January-December 1942*.
2. A.W. Tedder, *With Prejudice, The War Memoirs of Marshal of the Royal Air Force Lord Tedder* (London: Cassell, 1966), pp. 309-310.
3. 201st Guards Brigade had been renumbered from 200th Guards Brigade. It had previously been renumbered from 22nd Guards Brigade as this had led to confusion with the 22nd Armoured Brigade.
4. Number 233 Wing consisted of Nos 2, 4 and 5 Squadrons SAAF and 260 Squadron RAF, No 239 Wing, Nos 3 and 450 Squadrons RAAF and Nos 112 and 250 Squadrons RAF, and No 243 Wing, Nos 33, 73, 238, 274, 213 Squadrons RAF. Number 211 Group was reformed on 12 March 1942 under the command of Group Captain 'Bing' Cross and then from 5 April 1942, Group Captain G.L. Carter AFC.
5. No 3 Wing SAAF consisted of Nos 12 and 24 Squadrons SAAF with Boston IIIs and No 223 Squadron RAF with Baltimores.
6. AIR 23/1179 *RAF Operations during withdrawal from Gazala to El-Alamein*. In all nine landing grounds were provided with perimeter tracks and dispersals lanes. New landing grounds were constructed at Baheira Satellite 1, Sidi Azeiz Satellite at Bir Uazan and two at Bir Hacheim. A dummy was constructed at Gambut. The landing grounds at Gasr el Arid, Baheira Main, Gambut Satellite 1, 2 and 3 and Gambut dummy were all extended. Heavy rains delayed work and repair parties were kept busy for many weeks filling in ruts made by movement of vehicles across the strips when waterlogged.
7. H.L. Thompson, *New Zealanders with the Royal Air Force, Vol. III Mediterranean and Middle East, South-East Asia*, New Zealand in the Second World War 1939-1945 (Wellington, NZ: War History Branch, Dept of Internal Affairs, 1959), p. 48.
8. No 208 Squadron had the nickname 'The Flying Shuftis'.
9. H. Fenwick, *Reminiscences* (Archives of the RAF Armoured Cars Association, 1972).
10. *Ibid*.

11 *Ibid.*
12 J.A. Brown, *Eagles Strike: The Campaigns of the South African Air Force in Egypt, Cyrenaica, Libya, Tunisia, Tripolitania and Madagascar 1941-1943, Vol IV* South African Forces World War II (Purnell & Sons: Cape Town, 1974), p. 153.
13 Flying Officer Parker joined the Company on 24 January 1942, along with Flight Lieutenant J.H.F. Newland.
14 Fenwick, *Reminiscences.*
15 R. Owen, *The Desert Air Force* (London: Hutchinson,1948), p. 94. Major-General Ritchie asked the RAF to take responsibility for Bir Hacheim while the British armour was directed on the 'Cauldron'. Ritchie feared that diversion of the armour to the south would split his force and weaken the planned attack against Rommel's panzers.
16 *Ibid.*, p. 95.
17 Fenwick, *Reminiscences.*
18 V. Morte, *Interview with the author*, 2008.
19 AIR 23/1782 *Location plan RAF units withdrawing from Cyrenaica 1942, January-December 1942.* The RAF Wireless Observer Units had also reported the presence of the column.
20 Wing Commander R.C. Skellon RAF Retd, *Interview with the author*, 2010. According to AIR 23/6480 *Withdrawal from Cyrenaica: report*, No 239 Wing (including No 6 Squadron) claimed 12 tanks and fired 27,500 rounds of 0.5-inch ammunition.
21 V. Morte, *Interview with J. Rolph*, RAF Armoured Cars Association, 2008.
22 WO 372/14/204928 *Medal Card* J.H.F. Newland. Flight Lieutenant John Henry Frankland Newland had served as a subaltern with the 48th and 32nd Sikh Pioneers in Iraq, and in particular Kurdistan. He left the Indian Army in the late 1920s with the rank of Captain. He was granted a commission as a Flight Lieutenant in the RAF Volunteer Reserve as of 1 September 1939.
23 Fenwick, *Reminiscences.*
24 N. Orpen, *War in the Desert, Vol. III* South African Forces World War II (Cape Town: Purnell, 1971), p. 292.
25 AIR 23/1179 *RAF Operations during withdrawal from Gazala to El-Alamein report, 1942.*
26 Lieutenant-Colonel J. West.
27 Skellon, *Interview with the author*. The 1st Battalion, 6th Rajputana Rifles had been attacked that night by 1000 infantry supported by tanks. One company had been overrun but the remaining companies in the 'box' had held out for over two hours. Their resistance had forced the enemy to call off the attack until daylight, however, the orders for the battalion to retire were received during the night and they slipped away in the darkness. W. Hingeston and G.R. Stevens, *The Tiger Kills*, (Bombay: Government of India Press, 1944), pp. 204-205.
28 AIR 23/6480 *Withdrawal from Cyrenaica: report.* Notes on operations of No 2 Armoured Car Company
29 *Ibid.*
30 General Sir Claude Auchinleck GCIE, GB, CSI, DSO, OBE, ADC, Commander-in-Chief, The Middle East Forces, Operations in the Middle East from 1st November 1941 to 15th August 1942, Supplement to *The London Gazette*, 1948, p. 59.
31 WO 201/2099 *Protection of operational landing grounds in forward areas April 1942-January 1943.* Landing ground defence, p. 4.
32 Later Marshal of the RAF, Viscount Portal of Hungerford KG GCB OM DSO & bar MC (1893-1971).
33 Tedder, *With Prejudice*. Tedder was promoted to Air Chief Marshal on 1 July 1942.

Chapter Eighteen

El Alamein

"The Allied Air Forces have today started the battle. The whole of our air and ground personnel is involved. The victory you are going to win will be decisive in the land battle."
Air Vice-Marshal 'Mary' Coningham, AOC Western Desert[1]

"I really enjoyed those days. Somehow it was my life; it was something that gave you a bit of zest. Almost every day was exciting…"
LAC Vic Morte, No 2 Armoured Car Company[2]

For the last months of the summer of 1942, the fate of the British position in the Middle East hung in the balance. Either the Axis would prevail, and Cairo and the Suez Canal would fall into German hands, with all the consequences for the British position in the Middle East, or the Eighth Army would drive the enemy back from Alamein. The German panzer divisions however, were down to only a couple of dozen tanks, and the infantry divisions down to fewer than 1500 men each. During the first week of July, Field Marshal Rommel's exhausted and depleted force attempted to break through to capture the important feature of Ruweisat Ridge.[3] The attacks were held by the mobile columns of the 5th and 10th Indian Divisions, the infantry brigades of the South Africans and New Zealanders and the depleted regiments of the British armour. With the advance of *Panzerarmee Afrika* halted, there could be no further movement until supplies and reinforcements could be rushed forward. The Germans and Italians, therefore, set about erecting fortified strongpoints and laying mines.

General Auchinleck was determined to drive the enemy back, and so from 10 to 26 July 1942, the Eighth Army launched a series of attacks against the severely-depleted Axis divisions. However, due to poor armour-infantry coordination by Eighth Army, many of these battles ended indecisively and after a fortnight of attack and counter-attack, both sides were exhausted. Consequently, the British and Commonwealth troops dug themselves in to regain their strength and to await reinforcements.

Rommel had failed to reach the port of Alexandria, and his lines of supply now stretched back along the Egyptian coast and through Cyrenaica to the Libyan ports of Tobruk (370 miles), Benghazi (660 miles) and Tripoli (1420 miles). In contrast, the Eighth Army and Desert Air Force were only 70 miles from their major supply depots. Thus by October, advantaged by this favourable supply situation, the Desert Air Force had gained an overwhelming superiority over the *Luftwaffe*.

The Prime Minister, Winston Churchill, was still deeply concerned by the Middle

East situation and visited Cairo from 4 to 10 August to see matters at first hand. The disasters of the summer that had occurred under General Auchinleck's purview could not be allowed to continue. 'The Auk' had twice in the last year saved the situation by his own intervention. Whilst he had halted Rommel and seized the initiative, it was clear that he had difficulty choosing and managing the right people to command the Eighth Army. Churchill was also impatient for a renewed offensive, and saw that there needed to be a change, and so Auchinleck was removed as Commander-in-Chief Middle East. Churchill's choice for command of the Eighth Army was an old desert hand, Lieutenant-General 'Strafer' Gott, but he was killed when his aircraft was shot down, while flying back from the desert to Cairo take up his new appointment. On 13 August therefore, Lieutenant-General Bernard Montgomery[4] arrived from the United Kingdom and took command of the Eighth Army. Two days later, General Harold Alexander was appointed Commander-in-Chief Middle East.[5] Persia and Iraq were removed from Middle East Command and formed into a separate command so that Alexander could concentrate fully of the war in North Africa. The Air Force commanders, Tedder and Coningham, who continued to work so well together, and through whose efforts the Army retreat had been covered, both retained their positions.

At the July meeting of Army Commanders, before Auchinleck's removal, Tedder had been forthright in his views on the poor performance of the Eighth Army with regard to cooperation with the Desert Air Force during the previous six months:

> Auchinleck remained in command in the Desert, while I attended the monthly meeting of the Army Commanders on 16 July. After Major-General Thomas Corbett, recently appointed Chief of General Staff in place of Arthur Smith, had pointed to some lessons of the recent debacle, I indulged some plain speaking on the air aspect. I told them that on three occasions our fighter force, without which their retreat would have become a shambles, had only been saved by the RAF armoured cars from being overrun… Two or three of them came up to me after and said it was about time there was some plain speaking on the subject, but I noticed that to try and make an impression on the Army was rather like hitting a wall of cotton wool.[6]

The frustration with the lack of support for ground defence of landing grounds had already been noted in a major report prepared the previous March by the Officer-in-Charge of the AA defences of the fighter landing grounds, before the rout at Gazala. It had been widely circulated:

> Whenever infantry was available for the duty of mobile reserve on the LGs, the armoured cars were used for such recce and patrolling as the situation might demand. When no infantry was available however, the bulk of the Armoured Cars had to be retained as a mobile reserve, being the only troops available for this duty. It usually happened that the occasion on which no infantry were available were the very times when extensive patrolling was most necessary.[7]

While No 2 Armoured Car Company had been actively involved in the Battle of Gazala, the No 1 Armoured Car Company Detachment, under the command of Flight Lieutenant Olliff-Lee, had been stationed at RAF Helwan with responsibility

'Gladiator' of No 1 Armoured Car Company. The Humber Mark I armoured car was the replacement for the Rolls-Royce armoured cars of Nos 1 and 3 Sections (Waddington, RAF Habbaniya Assn).

for protection of airfields around Cairo. However, as events turned to disaster around Gazala, No 3 Section of the Company was called forward to protect the landing grounds along the Egyptian coast road that were supporting the effort in Libya. On 1 June, as the tank battles raged in 'The Cauldron', the Section travelled to LG 121, west of Sidi Barrani where it remained until 23 June. Meanwhile, the other section remained on airfield protection at Wadi Natrun and Cairo West. Other tasks included aircraft salvage operations and protection of landing ground construction parties as the Desert Air Force prepared for the return of the fighter and bomber wings to airfields near Cairo and Alexandria (Map 29, p. 395).

Number 1 Company had continued to operate the Rolls-Royces following the return from Libya in early-1942, but it was becoming increasingly difficult to maintain them on operations, particularly due to a scarcity of spares. These ageing armoured cars were now neither suitable nor reliable enough for modern mechanised desert warfare. Consequently, in the first week of July, the Company began re-equipping and training on Humber Mk I armoured cars. Over the next two months, they also received Chevrolet 3-tonners in place of the Fordson tenders that had first been issued in 1939. This was further complemented by other means when Flight Lieutenant Olliff-Lee recovered a Humber Mk III armoured car which had been found abandoned by the Army in the desert near LG 91.

With the Eighth Army now ensconced at Alamein, the RAF established operational bases near Amiriya in a large cluster, some 20 miles south of Alexandria. The RAF light bombers and fighters now returned in great strength over the battlefield in their key tactical role, interdicting the Axis columns moving inexorably eastwards towards the Nile (Map 29, p. 395).

Rommel launched his first attacks on the Alamein Line on the first day of July; at this time a line in name only, as it was more a series of defended localities that could be bypassed. The two sections of No 1 Company were therefore called forward to Advanced Air Headquarters Western Desert at LG 91. Two half-sections, each with two Humbers and a tender, were sent out on observer screen duties 25 miles to the south-west and west, while an armoured car and tender went off to guard an AMES codenamed 'Jumbo'. The Company continued these tasks for the next two months until mid-September when it was ordered to join No 212 Group HQ.[8]

Rommel made his final attempt to take Egypt on 30 August, in what became known as the Battle of Alam el Halfa. Leaving two Italian and a German infantry divisions to hold the line in the north, the *Deutsches Afrika Korps* with *15th* and *21st Panzer Divisions* and *33rd Reconnaissance Unit*, the *90th Light Division* and the *Ariete* and *Littorio Armoured Divisions* skirted the Allied positions in the south and then wheeled northwards towards the sea, with the aim of cutting off the Allied infantry divisions in the Alamein Line. The Eighth Army, as planned, offered little resistance and fell back as the enemy columns advanced. Rather than sending his armour out to attack the Panzers, Montgomery held it back, and the armoured and infantry brigades of the Eighth Army were thus able to fight the battle on ground of their own choosing.

The Desert Air Force, using Wellingtons by night, and the light bombers during the day, pounded the German and Italian columns. The incessant air attacks were more than human nerves could stand. Two senior German field commanders became casualties, with one wounded and the other killed amongst the chaos caused by the bombing and a subsequent dust storm. The Eighth Army defensive positions held and the Panzers were halted. By 1 September, the plain south of Alam el Halfa was marked by the black smoke from countless burning vehicles. Rommel had run short of fuel as his supply vessels were being sunk in the Mediterranean by the RAF coastal group and air and naval attacks from Malta. With little fuel in reserve for an outflanking move, he was forced onto the defensive. After three days fighting, and with no prospect of making further progress, the enemy withdrew to the west of the British minefields.

The enemy operated fighters, bombers and dive-bombers from airfields at El Daba and Fuka, while heavier enemy bombers flew from Crete. On the eve of Alam el Halfa, the *Luftwaffe* launched a series of heavy attacks on the main RAF landing grounds at Amiriya, Wadi Natrun and Burg el Arab. The aim was to subdue the efforts of the Desert Air Force. On the third day of the battle, 95 bomber and 220 fighter and dive-bomber sorties were recorded, but these soon dwindled as the offensive was halted and the enemy withdrew. The *Luftwaffe* attempted to mimic the efforts of the Fleet Air Arm Albacores by dropping streams of flares during night raids to mark targets but this had been too hastily organised and had limited success.

The intense night raids on the airfields began in the last week of August and continued intermittently through September, with nine air raids reported by Nos 1 and 2 Companies over this period. While no great harm was done to No 1 Company other than a raid when a W/T tender was damaged by shrapnel and a tent set on fire, No 2 Company suffered more serious harm. At 0430 hours on the night of 29 August, Fordson A102 suffered a near miss, was set on fire and totally destroyed. LAC G. Dixon was seriously injured and Sergeant Jock Ross slightly injured by bomb shrapnel. Some revenge was extracted as a Junkers Ju 88 was seen to crash nearby soon afterwards. LAC Vic Morte had gone to the aid of Sergeant Jock Ross when he had been badly wounded during the 88-mm shelling incident in February at Martuba. Ross had recovered from his wounds by August and had just returned to the Company. Vic Morte continues:

> The Germans were doing a new type of bombing. They were sending aeroplanes over dropping flares and the complete area was as bright as sunlight. It was marvellous with all these things cascading down on parachutes. They could bomb us fairly accurately and there were two to three vehicles knocked out. We were laid out at the side of car, with no protection, nothing at all. The shrapnel was coming down like confetti. Jock Ross was beginning to panic and he kept saying "It's getting more intense", but myself and 'Johnnie' Johnston, he was from Dumfries and a very nice lad, were tired and we just wanted to sleep. So, after a while, Jock Ross said "I am ordering you to get in the car!" And we realised that something was going to happen, and we heard this scream of this Stuka coming down. 'Johnnie' said "How do we get in?" I said "I think I tip you in head first; that's the way we just have to, and deal with it afterwards"…
>
> So we dived in… I had closed the main front visor, but I hadn't closed the vision port. We could see the bomb burst right in front of the car. All these flames and everything went up. We'd been sensible and jumped inside, but we didn't know who'd gone through the rear or the escape hatch. We had no idea. But Jock Ross had dived underneath, and when this bomb dropped, it blew the radiator out, and the front tyres went. After a minute I shouted out "Are you all right Jock?" and he replied "Nay, I'm hit!" We both jumped out. The car had dropped down a bit and it was almost on his shoulders. These cars, they've got a huge flat plate underneath, from the engine right down to the rear axle, and it was 1 inch thick. It was strapped to the bottom of the car, just in case, if a mine went off it didn't blow up the transmission.
>
> His feet were just visible, so 'Johnnie' and myself pulled him out. When we got him out I said "What's wrong Jock?" and he said "It's me arm". These bits of shrapnel, they're only the size of a half a crown, but they do so much damage. It's razor sharp and by the time it's finished… it makes a hell of a mess. He was in a bad way, bleeding terribly. We were on our own and we had no medical assistance at all.
>
> There was a small mound and 'Cass' and all the officers stood there watching all the bombing. So I said to 'Johnnie', "I'll put him over my shoulder and you get his arm and hold it up as high as you can so the blood will run back." So I carried him the best part of a mile towards the hill. And when I got there, 'Cass' shouted down, "Who is it?" and I said "Sergeant Ross." He replied "What, Sergeant Ross again!"[9]

LAC Vic Morte had another close call, when seeking cover during another of the German air raids:

> There were quite some hectic carry-ons with these cars. It makes you realise the hazards of the job, and how easy it is to get injured or killed. There was a big square petrol tank at the bottom rear of the car that was far too low to the ground. We were having lunch and a lot of dive bombers came up and

1923. He then participated in the preparation and redesign of the new armoured car, the GMC Otter and later rejoined Casano for the advance to Tunis.[15]

LAC Vic Morte had been with the Company since late 1941. He remembered the moment when his time in the RAF armoured cars ended:

> I will say I really enjoyed those days. Somehow it was my life; it was something that gave you a bit of zest. Almost every day was exciting. There were three of us; a chap called Tinsley from Southport, a nice lad, a good driver, and another Scotsman called Sinclair, a very good armoured car bloke, quite an aggressive lad. But anyway, 'Cass' realised that we'd had enough in the Desert. We didn't want to go, but he called us up to the Orderly Room tender and thanked us very much for what we'd done. He said "I've gone out of my way in the Middle East to personally get you a good posting while you are waiting for the boat."
>
> He sent us to RAF Heliopolis, just outside Cairo. It was really nice. My mate, Sinclair, didn't want to be on a base station but they were forming some transport companies with very heavy American vehicles called Whites. So he went to be a driver on those. I never saw him again.[16]

To improve AA defence the Fordsons were fitted with twin Browning 0.303-inch aircraft machine guns on the turret. Some had also been fitted with an American 0.5-inch Browning aircraft machine-gun in the mounting previously occupied by the Boys anti-tank rifle. A sun compass, used for navigation in the desert, can be seen to the right hand side of the turret (King).

Meanwhile, Casano had been giving thought to improving the limited firepower of the Fordsons, particularly when dealing with strafing attacks. Harry Fenwick continues:

> The Fordson armament was the pride of my gunner, 'Lofty' Garbut, and it pleased him when the Lewis was replaced with twin Browning 0.303s, the Boys anti-tank rifle with a Browning 0.5-inch, and we obtained a few personal weapons that would have been the envy of Al Capone.
>
> There was something about the Rolls/Fordsons that gave a crew pride… I know the Germans were really amused by them. One day we picked up the crew from a German '88' [88-mm anti-tank gun]. Very young and pleasant men. I feel sure when we arrived we had them baffled. The appearance of a real antique car, stuffed with everything. My Wireless-Op had his feather mattress wrapped round it in one place, kettles, pans and other items

LAC Len King (left) and long-serving member of the No 2 Company, Sergeant 'Pop' Carlton (second from left) (King).

Flying Officer Bill Prentice (second from left) and the airmen of 'B' Section (King).

dangling from the car and the crew dressed in half British and half German clothing. Amazing as it may seem, the first thing we did was brew up – all had a cup of tea, something to eat, and we then took the Germans to an Army camp.

LAC Len King, who had been on the Company since early 1942, recalls the arrival of the new Brownings:

With desert conditions, when you were a gunner, your job first thing every day was to overhaul and clean all the guns. Once you'd had your breakfast then you went through the lot. If you got sand in them, then you couldn't get them to work.

We had twin-Brownings on the top by then. Their rate of fire was 1000-plus, each gun [this had doubled the AA firepower as the Lewis gun could only fire 500-600 rounds per minute].[17]

The experiences of the previous summer had made it clear that greater coordination was needed between the various elements of the Desert Air Force ground defence forces. During September, No 2 Armoured Car Company moved to LG 90 to prepare to support No 211 Group. Meanwhile, each of Flight Lieutenants Lucas, Skellon and Newland's sections spent four to five days at Wadi Natrun on Army airfield defence schemes with the 12th Anti-Aircraft Brigade. Here they completed navigation exercises, rifle and machine-gun training and their annual musketry practice. In a further indication of changing tactical air control methods, newly-arrived Flying Officers Herbert Blake and Bill Prentice took four armoured cars to Wadi Natrun where, under the instruction from No 211 Group, they did a 'vectoring' exercise with the Hurricane IID 'Tank Busters' of No 6 Squadron, guiding them on to ground targets.

The Desert Air Force had further improved the capability of the fighter wings to move forward rapidly and keep pace with the Eighth Army as it advanced. Administrative problems meant that only a small, compact and tough striking force with strong anti-aircraft defences could be sent forward to defend the forward landing grounds. To further enhance operational flexibility each unit was split into forward and rear sections. To support the move forward there was an Air Ammunition Park, two Supply and Transport Columns, two Air Stores Parks, an Aircraft Salvage unit, an Advanced MT Light Repair unit and a Refuelling Party in three sections. All units were to be capable of operating for a maximum of three weeks without reinforcements.

The responsibilities of the RAF armoured cars during the advance were four-fold: the protection of advance parties of No 211 Group as they moved forward and occupied or established landing grounds, the screening of the captured landing grounds, covering the movement of the heavy and light AA regiments of the 12th AA Brigade, and the protection of the forward-most fighter squadrons' ground parties and the supply and transport columns of the Desert Air Force.[18] These tasks had to be covered by only two sections of Humbers of No 1 Company and the three sections of Fordsons of No 2 Company. They were, however, to be ably assisted by the newly-formed flights of the RAF Regiment that were to accompany the ground parties.

For the advance from Alamein, No 211 Group was divided into three operational sections: Sector A and the A and B Parties. The Sector A Party would move in advance of the two parties and consisted of three specialist signals vehicles, for the R/T control of the fighter aircraft and maintenance of radio links to the rear, a Wireless Observer Unit and one or two AMES radar units.[19] Protection of this party would be the specific role of the No 1 Armoured Car Company Detachment. The Sector A Party prepared to move forward as soon as the breakthrough occurred.

At 2140 hours on Friday 23 October, the decisive battle of the North African campaign began when nearly 900 guns of the field and medium artillery of the Eighth Army opened a massive barrage. The infantry stood up from their slit trenches and

Casano addresses the gathered officers and airmen of No 2 Company (© IWM CM 2954).

After a refit and re-armament, No 2 Armoured Car Company parades before going forward at El Alamein (© Crown copyright. RAF Regiment Museum).

went forward. Montgomery launched the infantry of XXX Corps; the 9th Australian, 51st Highland, 2nd New Zealand and 1st South African Divisions, across the minefields. At the same time, XIII Corps, comprising the 7th Armoured and 44th and 50th Infantry Divisions, launched a feint in the south. Despite forcing two gaps in the minefields, the British armour could not break through the enemy anti-tank line and matters reached a stalemate. After a stubborn land battle lasting four days, Montgomery ordered Eighth Army to regroup for a renewed attempt at a breakout, to be known as Operation *Supercharge*.

Meanwhile, the RAF was launching sortie after sortie over the battlefield and repeatedly broke up German tank formations as they attempted to concentrate for counterattacks. In the north near the coast, the Australians launched a drive to the sea and cut off large numbers of Axis troops. On 2 November, Montgomery launched Operation *Supercharge* and after two days of heavy and bitter fighting, Rommel began to contemplate a withdrawal. Early on 2 November, the New Zealanders, with the tanks of the 9th Armoured Brigade moved against the Axis anti-tank screen and by nightfall, with the help of 1st Armoured Division, they had broken through. The RAF fighter squadrons were reporting that the coast road from Daba to Fuka was lined with burning vehicles and a multitude were streaming westwards. Early the following day, aerial reconnaissance suggested that the enemy was withdrawing and by 4 November, they were in full retreat.

Notes
1   Quoted in, J. Hetherington, *Air War against Germany and Italy 1939-1943* (Canberra: Australian War Memorial, 1954), p. 369.
2   V. Morte, *Interview with J. Rolph*, RAF Armoured Cars Association, 2008.
3   Rommel had been promoted to Field Marshal on 26 June, 1942.
4   Field Marshal Viscount Montgomery KG GCB DSO (1887-1976)
5   Field Marshal Harold Alexander Field Marshal Harold Alexander, 1st Earl Alexander of

Tunis KG PC GCB OM GCMG CSI DSO MC CD PC(Can.) (1891-1969)

6 A.W. Tedder, *With Prejudice: The War Memoirs of Marshal of the Royal Air Force Lord Tedder* (London: Cassell, 1966), p. 312.
7 Lt.Col. T.E.H. Helby RA, *Notes on the Defence of Landing Grounds*, RAF Regiment Museum Archives.
8 On 14 September 1942, the officers and senior NCOs of No 1 Company carried out tests on the diminutive Beaverette armoured car. No report is made but one can surmise that it must have caused some consternation from seasoned armoured car campaigners who had been driving the Rolls-Royce and now Humber Mk Is.
9 V. Morte, *Interview with John Rolph*.
10 V. Morte, *Interview with the author*, 2008.
11 Brigadier Percy G. Calvert-Jones DSO MC.
12 H. Fenwick, *Reminiscences* (Archives of the RAF Armoured Cars Association, 1972).
13 The composition of the Desert Air Force on 27 October 1942 was as follows:

Fighter
No 211 Group ('Force A')
No 233 Wing (Three squadrons of Kittyhawks and one of Tomahawks).
No 239 Wing (Five squadrons of Kittyhawks including one from US 57th Fighter Group).
No 244 Wing (Three squadrons of Spitfires and one of night-flying Hurricanes).
US 57th Fighter Group (Two squadrons of Kittyhawks).
Two tank-destroying Hurricane squadrons.
No 212 Group ('Force B')
No 7 (SAAF) Wing (Four squadrons of Kittyhawks).
No 243 Wing (Four squadrons of Hurricanes).

Day-bomber
No 3 (SAAF) Wing (Two squadrons of Bostons and one squadron of Baltimores).
No 232 Wing (Two squadrons of Baltimores).
US 12th Medium Bombardment Group (Three squadrons of Mitchells).

Reconnaissance
No 285 Wing
Two tactical reconnaissance (Hurricane) squadrons.
One strategical reconnaissance (Baltimore) flight.
One survey reconnaissance (Baltimore) squadron.
One photographic reconnaissance (Spitfire) flight.

14 AIR 5/1212 *Armoured Cars Policy: Palestine, Transjordan and Iraq, 1933-1942*.
15 Flying Officer A.J. Gregory had signed up in 1921 and qualified as a Fitter, Driver Petrol. He served in No 1 Armoured Car Company in Palestine in 1923, and when No 1 Company was disbanded transferred to No 2 Armoured Car Company. He served in Palestine and Transjordan until the mid-1920s. In 1940, as a Corporal in the Balloon Branch, he was commissioned and sent to the Middle East where he joined No 2 Armoured Car Company.
16 V. Morte, *Interview with J. Rolph*.
17 L. King, *Interview with author*, 2008. Len King had joined the RAFVR in 1938. He had been sent to France in late 1939. He returned to the United Kingdom on the last boat from Brest, following the fall of France. After completing the six-week intensive training course for RAF Armoured Cars at No 2 (Ground) Armament School at RAF Manby in August 1941, he sailed to Egypt via Durban. The first leg to Durban was on the troopship, HMT *Mauretania* where he helped man the AA machine-guns on eight-hour shifts. On arrival at Suez in early 1942, he was sent straight up to the Company which was operating near Gambut at that time.
18 There were four Supply and Transport Columns used during the advance; Nos 5, 6, 10 and 11.
19 Nos 510, 608, 609 and 610 Air Ministry Experiment Stations, at various times.

Chapter Nineteen

The Road to Tunis

"Ground parties went ahead in small convoys escorted by RAF armoured cars, tracking over the desert to select the new site… Yet, hot though the pace was, the Desert fighter squadrons never fell behind and never failed to carry out their assignments."

New Zealand Official History[1]

"I tell you, we never have any fun anymore, of course it's grand having the new General Motors armoured cars, but playing around Tunisia isn't what it used to be in the desert"

Squadron Leader 'Cass' Casano, OC, No 2 Armoured Car Company[2]

On 23 October, the first day of the second battle of El Alamein, No 2 Armoured Car Company had been ordered to be on stand-by at 15 minutes' notice to move. This, as events as turned out, proved to be optimistic; however, on 2 November, the Company moved off as escort and guide to 12th Anti-Aircraft Brigade. By evening, they reached LG 105 at El Daba which was raided several times that night by the *Luftwaffe*. Harry Fenwick recalls the move forward across the battlefield:

> The big push from Alamein saw the cars out in front, too far once again and the grimmest night ever spent with the unburied bodies of Germans and British and the flies in the area, due to the fact the Germans were next door.[3]

The scale of the victory was evidenced by the fuselages of scores of discarded and damaged Bf 109s and Ju 88s, as well as the aircraft that had simply run out of fuel, on the Fuka airfields. This scene was to be repeated at each captured landing ground. In a stroke of misfortune, heavy rain began to fall continuously for the next 24 hours. The desert became a quagmire, and LG 105 was inundated, forcing the RAF armoured cars to move from their flank and anti-aircraft defence positions. The following three days of incessant rain also unfortunately stopped two of the outflanking thrusts by X Corps, the British *corps de chasse*, and severely hampered air operations (Map 29, p. 395).

The following morning, 3 November, the three sections moved off on separate tasks. Flight Lieutenant Newland's section went off up the coast road to reconnoitre the airstrip at LG 104, as flooding had made LG 105 completely unusable. Here there

South of Fuka, November 1942. A100 'The Yellow Peril' of No 2 Company pulls out another Fordson after bogging in ground sodden with the heavy rains that fell on the first few days of the pursuit (Prentice).

were another 100 Axis aircraft littering the airfield, a sad testament to the hurried nature of the enemy retreat and the disorganisation in the *Luftwaffe* aircraft recovery and salvage system. Flight Lieutenant Lucas' section moved further westward to Sidi Haneish, and Flight Lieutenant Parker's section set off for a rendezvous with 16th Light AA Regiment. By 10 November, the Company, proceeding with the advance parties of the fighter squadrons, and as escort to supply and transport columns, reached LG 75, though Parker was yet to find the Light AA Regiment. His task was made very difficult by tracks made impassable by the heavy rain, and movement on the coast road that was hampered by heavy traffic. Moreover, there were now large parties of German and Italian soldiers, many disillusioned, parched, hungry and bedraggled making their way on foot or in their own vehicles towards the wire-fenced compounds to become prisoners of war.

The use of mines had gradually increased over the past two years of the war in North Africa and during this period they became a frequent problem. The first armoured car was lost to a mine seven miles east of Mersa Matruh, when Corporal Ivor Chester's car, A115, was blown up, albeit no casualties were reported. More mines were to be encountered, and the car crews would also see the increasing use of booby traps left on or amongst discarded enemy vehicles, equipment and rations. Despite the threat, there were some good finds to be made, as Len King recalls:

> When we first moved to Alamein, the Germans just moved out. Some people got cameras and things like that. I didn't, I got food. The first thing I found was two 7-lb tins of Danish butter which went in our rations. But you had to nip off and get it and get back on, because we were moving up quite quickly by then. We'd stood still for a long time.[4]

On 6 November, with the *Panzerarmee Afrika* in full retreat, No 1 Armoured Car Company and the Sector A Party passed through the now quiet battlefield of Alamein. Two days later they reached Sidi Haneish near Mersa Matruh.[5] Although the Company had three officers with experience in Libya and Iraq, Squadron Leader John Olliff Lee and Flight Lieutenants Keenan and Weeks, the remainder were relatively new Pilot Officers: A.V. Attfield, R.H.B. Pellew, W.R.M. Smith and H.H. Tickler. They had been on the Company for only a few months and were serving in their first campaign with the RAF Armoured Cars.

Halfaya Pass was captured on 11 November, and General Montgomery launched four armoured columns from 7th Armoured Division across Cyrenaica. The first column was to secure the Martuba airfields, so that air cover could be provided to the *Stoneage* convoy which was bound for Malta with desperately needed supplies. Another was tasked to capture the roads through the Jebel Akhdar to Benghazi, and the remaining two to capture the Msus landing ground.

Having stayed at LG 76 near Sidi Barrani for two days, No 1 Company crossed the Libyan frontier on 10 November, passed through Sidi Azeiz, and by 13 November was established at Gambut. The fighter squadrons were not far behind, and on the same day, units of the 12th Anti-Aircraft Brigade were escorted further forward by Flight Lieutenant Weeks to Martuba where they were soon joined by No 211 Group. Despite the landing grounds being waterlogged at Martuba, the RAF was able to provide cover for the *Stoneage* convoy to Malta, using the aircraft at Gazala; the first to safely reach the besieged island in three months. Number 1 Company then moved on to Msus, allowing No 244 (Spitfire) Wing to fly in. A week later, with Rommel still withdrawing, and to keep pace with the Eighth Army, the armoured cars moved on to Antelat, the place where they had lost their CO and five of their fellow airmen the previous winter.

Meanwhile, on 11 November, Casano received orders to proceed with No 2 Company to a 'secret' forward landing ground deep in the desert and well behind the enemy lines, for a very special operation. This was LG 125, from which the Company had operated during *Crusader* with 'Whitforce'. The plan, purely an Air Force show, went under the name of Operation *Chocolate*. It was led by Wing Commander 'Jackie' Darwen DFC, the Officer Commanding No 243 Wing, and would comprise 36 Hurricane IICs of Nos 213 and 238 Squadrons RAF. Both squadrons were experienced in ground strafing, and were to attack the enemy ground forces as they fled down the coast road from Benghazi to El Agheila on the Gulf of Sirte. Hudsons and Bombays of No 216 Group RAF were to fly in most of what was needed, more than 100 ground crew, their equipment, stores and ammunition.[6] Others would make the journey across the desert in three-tonners loaded with the four-gallon 'flimsies' of petrol.[7] Some of the pilots of No 213 Squadron thought it sounded a 'suicide do' and went away to write cheerful final letters home, while others were envious of those picked to go.[8] The Hurricanes, Hudsons and Bombays departed for LG 125 on 13 November, led in by Group Captain Eric Whitley, who had been in command of 'Whitforce' on the previous operation and knew the location well (Map 26, p. 341).

Accompanying No 2 Company was the No 243 Wing Defence Flight of the RAF Regiment under the command of Flight Lieutenant Richard Cox. He continues:

> I took what was to become 'B' Squadron, RAF Regiment on a long sweep south and west covering a ground column around and behind the bulk of the Axis forces retreating along the coast road.[9] This column, of which Casano

was in overall command, was to support a skeleton No 243 Wing operation (under Wing Commander Darwen) which operated from a remote landing ground to harry enemy vehicles retreating westward.

The vehicles were heavily laden with water, aviation fuel, petrol, ammunition and some rations. Supplies were replenished at the landing ground by a daily Dakota flight and there was some interchange of Wing pilots and aircraft from our base landing ground near Alamein.

For this trip, the Command Medical Officer had entrusted a nursing orderly and a supply of sulphanilamide and morphine to my care. He hoped that I wouldn't need to use the latter items, but I was under strict instructions to bring the former back safely as they were in short supply![10]

Travelling south-westward from Sidi Barrani into the desert, No 2 Company crossed 'The Wire' at Fort Maddalena and proceeded to Fort el Grein, a few miles north of Jarabub. Casano then set a course due west. The journey was however, quite eventful. Two hours after crossing the frontier, they encountered a German Warrant Officer from a motorcycle unit, who they made their prisoner. His motorcycle had broken down at El Daba during the retreat and he had claimed to have walked back to rejoin the *Afrika Korps*. Harry Fenwick recalls:

Paddy Knox picked up a German Warrant Officer and actually had him in his car for a number of days. He lived like one of the crew and Paddy was sorry to see him go.[11]

Then, late in the afternoon of 13 November, the armoured cars were circled by four Hurricanes. After providing suitable recognition signals the aircraft landed. Casano was able to inform them of their own location. The RAF armoured car crews were no strangers to these parts and the pilots were sent on their way with a great sense of relief.

Prior to the arrival of the fighters, the Long Range Desert Group had made a reconnaissance of the area to ensure there was no enemy presence. Darwen's aircraft had arrived well before the land component which had to make the near 300-mile

A Hurricane of No 213 Squadron and a Lockheed Hudson of No 117 Squadron of No 216 Group prepare for take-off before heading to a forward landing ground (© IWM CM 4099).

journey from Egypt. The fighters had been in occupation of LG 125 for only a day, but possessed no ground radar, early warning or anti-aircraft defence, so there was some concern when a dust cloud appeared on the horizon. Flying Officer 'Bert' Houle, the Canadian flying ace, was a pilot with No 213 Squadron and remembered that day:

> A ground column was approaching and we took off to inspect them. If they were enemy, we were to put them out of commission as quickly as possible. They proved to be friendly, and shortly after, Squadron Leader Casano, an English Desert Rat, and his group of RAF armoured cars and mobile radio stations, joined us. We sure were glad to have them with us.[12]

Number 2 Armoured Car Company provided a welcome addition to the defence of the landing ground. Three days after receiving the order to move, and with navigation that was spot-on, the cars reached their destination. The landing ground was demarcated in an otherwise flat plain, by only by a few rusty oil drums. From 14 to 17 November, the three armoured car sections formed an observer screen, 50 miles out from LG 125, to provide warning of the approach of enemy raiding parties and hostile aircraft. Meanwhile Casano, with the Company HQ, remained at the landing ground to provide the only anti-aircraft defence. Len King recalls:

> There was nothing out there, way down 'in the blue'. We formed a sort of perimeter, just in case anything happened… We'd gone so far away from any fighting. We were spaced out quite a bit to give them warning so they could get the aircraft out the way.[13]

The Hurricanes meanwhile, took heavy toll on the Axis transport columns, attacking not only the coast road, but raiding the airfield at Agedabia.[14] On 15 November, the Hurricanes of No 238 Squadron completed another strafing attack on the coast road when they flew over an Italian column of 50 vehicles located only 60 miles from LG 125. It was thought this could be an enemy column moving on the landing ground and Darwen immediately ordered the Hurricanes to attack, causing considerable slaughter. On his return to base, he considered sending the RAF armoured cars to 'mop up' the remnants of the column and to pick up prisoners, but owing to the distance involved, some 60 miles, and the rough terrain it was decided not to proceed. Further sorties failed to find the column, and so the air and ground crews spent a wakeful night anticipating a possible ground attack. Nothing transpired as it seemed the air attacks had been so devastating that the column no longer posed a threat. It was later found to have been the Italian *Young Fascist Division*, which had garrisoned Siwa Oasis and which had been retreating back towards the coast.

On the third day, the Hurricanes flew south-west into the desert to Jalo Oasis, where they attacked numerous lorries and armoured cars. A further threat developed the following evening when the RAF armoured cars reported that nine bombers were approaching from the west at 9000 feet. The vehicles and ground crews at LG 125 were ordered to scatter and a flight of Hurricanes was sent out to look for them, but no raiders appeared. It was however, apparent that the element of surprise had been lost and the decision was made to withdraw the following day. With the force Darwen had, the landing ground could not be defended against an attack in strength from the ground or in the air. The decision to leave was made all the more frustrating for a large party of ground crew which had just arrived by lorry after a long journey

Operation Chocolate LG 125. Keeping watch for the approach of enemy columns or aircraft from the turret of a Fordson (Prentice).

from Mersa Matruh.[15] The following morning after one more strike on Jalo the force withdrew from LG 125.

The operation had however, been a great success. In the course of 119 sorties the Hurricanes had destroyed 138 lorries and armoured cars, damaged 173 and destroyed or damaged 15 aircraft on the ground and two in the air. Three Hurricanes and their pilots had been lost in action and four more aircraft had to be destroyed by ground parties before they departed.[16] The Hudsons flew out some of the ground crew, and the Hurricanes flew northwards to their new base at El Adem. A half section under Flying Officer Edwards escorted the ground parties of the Wing and Squadrons overland to El Adem which was reached after three days and nights along a severely flooded road. The remainder of the Company set off for Gazala and arrived late on the afternoon of 18 November. Richard Cox recalls the return trip:

> ... Navigation was the responsibility of Casano and his armoured car company crews. He was bearded like a pirate by the time of our return. He used a sun compass and knew the area... On the morning of the second day of our withdrawal, 'Cass' remarked that in the afternoon we should come

Airmen inspect a mine-damaged tyre after running across an unmarked minefield near Mechili. The steel plates that were fitted to the cars were essential as they partially dissipated the blast, otherwise the driver's feet and lower legs would be smashed as a consequence (Prentice).

across a row of ten 40 gallon drums, each a hundred yards apart. I was full of admiration for the Armoured Car Company navigation when in due course we found ourselves heading for the row of drums. Cass' dog 'Butch' was buried there and they picked up petrol and some ammo and rations which had been cached there.[17]

The stay was only short, as the Company moved on to Martuba where they remained for ten days before moving on to Mechili. On 21 November, Lucas and Newland and their sections moved off with No 6 Supply and Transport Column and No 211 Group Advanced Party to Msus. At around midday, the column came under attack and Corporal A. Allen shot down a Junkers Ju 88. Eleven days later, the remainder of the Company reached Msus. Flight Lieutenant Parker had some misfortune during the journey when his section ran across an unmarked minefield south of Mechili and A122 was irreparably damaged by a mine explosion and had to be abandoned.[18]

The Eighth Army and Desert Air Force were making steady progress into Cyrenaica and the cars quickly moved forward with Casano and No 2 Company escorting the forward parties of No 211 Group, Nos 239 and 244 Wings, and Nos 5 and 10 RAF Supply and Transport Columns to the landing grounds at Antelat and El Hasseiat. As these airfields and those at Agedabia and Belandah came into operation during the first week of December, the fighters and fighter-bombers attacked the enemy airfields to the west from Marble Arch to Nofilia.

Benghazi was entered for the third and last time on 19 November, representing an advance by the Eighth Army of 1000 miles in 18 days. Despite being harried by 7th Armoured Division, the *Panzerarmee Afrika* had intentionally drawn back to the Mersa el Brega to El Agheila position, which it reached on 23 November and where it planned to make a stand (Map 30, p. 425). The Desert Air Force spearhead, No 211 Group, closely matched the advance of Eighth Army. The captured airfields were rapidly cleared and repaired, notwithstanding the terrible weather which had made some airstrips unserviceable. As each newly-won airfield was occupied, an RAF reconnaissance party and Royal Engineers mine clearing and construction parties moved in, accompanied by a detachment of the RAF Regiment for local ground protection. In Cyrenaica, the Germans were determined to do their utmost to make airfields unserviceable by ploughing up runways, demolitions, the sowing of countless mines and by placement of ingenious booby traps. The newly-occupied airfields had to be carefully cleared of these devices before they could be opened, a long and

Number 1 Company passes along the Via Vittoria in Benghazi. The Cathedral dominates the skyline (© Crown copyright. Hannam, RAF Regiment Museum).

British airmen and soldiers of the New Zealand Division clear an airfield of mines and obstacles (AWM MED 1076).

tedious process. Where damage or threats from mines on established airfields was too great however, the Desert Air Force merely constructed an airstrip at a new location. The pattern for the establishment of a functioning airfield was described as follows:

> Ground parties went ahead in small convoys escorted by RAF armoured cars, tracking over the desert to select the new sites. The sand was levelled, soft patches were filled in with hard core, scrub torn out and burnt, rocks and boulders shifted and a landing ground carved out of the rough surface, often within 48 hours; then a radio message brought the aircraft forward. Moreover, the technique quickly improved. One landing-ground site, 1200 yards square, selected in the Bir Dufan area, was serviceable in three hours, enabling fighter formations to move forward in one hop of 140 miles; and at Tripoli itself, where the airfield was most thoroughly ruined by the enemy, three new grounds were carved out of the desert in 24 hours. All along the way the Army gave invaluable help; at one point the New Zealand Division detailed 2000 troops to pick up stones and make a landing ground; and there were cases where a whole brigade performed this service for the RAF; striking evidence that inter-service collaboration was now complete.
>
> With the advance, units had been continually on the move, operating from as many as a dozen different landing grounds within a month; and it is worth remembering that a squadron of aircraft with all the cumbersome necessities of petrol, bombs, servicing equipment, signals and operations control, does not move as easily as a squadron of tanks or armoured cars. Yet, hot though the pace was, the Desert fighter squadrons never fell behind and never failed to carry out their assignments.[19]

Inter-service collaboration had been complete and the intensity, urgency and danger of these operations can be seen in the casualties caused to the Army personnel. The 5th New Zealand Brigade Group lost 14 killed and 49 wounded under attacks by enemy fighter-bombers while picking up stones on one of these fields.[20]

Number 1 Company had spent the week at Antelat on patrolling, but also training on MT, W/T, guns and map reading. By 5 December however, they had moved on with the Sector A Party, towards Mersa Brega. The Army was still fighting for the town and the RAF column, with its charges, awaited the outcome. While passing through Agedabia, a tender struck a mine, but fortunately the driver, LAC Chambers, only suffered minor injuries and shock. Three armoured cars and a tender were detailed to protect No 510 AMES, which was established on Mount Tabilba, only a mile or so from the waters of the Gulf of Sirte. The position was, however, exposed to enemy artillery spotters, and when German 170-mm shells, fired from some 20 miles distant landed only 500 yards from the AMES, it was decided that the position should be vacated. An alternative site was established two miles to the north-east, but the radar coverage was not nearly as good. So after two days, the AMES returned to Mount Tabilba and continued its work directing fighters onto raids coming from the west, fortunately now without interference from the German heavy artillery. The sounds of frequent artillery exchanges could be heard by the armoured car crews as the Eighth Army prepared to launch its assault on the Axis positions and enemy aircraft strafed and bombed around their camp.

While every effort was made to repair and re-establish the port at Benghazi, the Eighth Army gathered its strength for the next attack. The fighter force operating from Antelat, Belandah, Msus and El Hasseiat, destroyed numerous enemy vehicles retreating along the coast road towards Tripoli. Reaching ever westward, the Kittyhawks and Spitfires succeeded in driving the enemy air forces from the airfields around Marble Arch to Nofilia.

The 7th Armoured, 2nd New Zealand and 51st Highland Divisions were given the task of taking the naturally strong El Agheila position, difficult to outflank due to belts of salt marshes and dunes. On 13 December, the New Zealanders were launched on a wide left hook around Rommel's southern flank, while 7th Armoured and 51st Highland Divisions attacked closer to the coast. Threatened by the outflanking

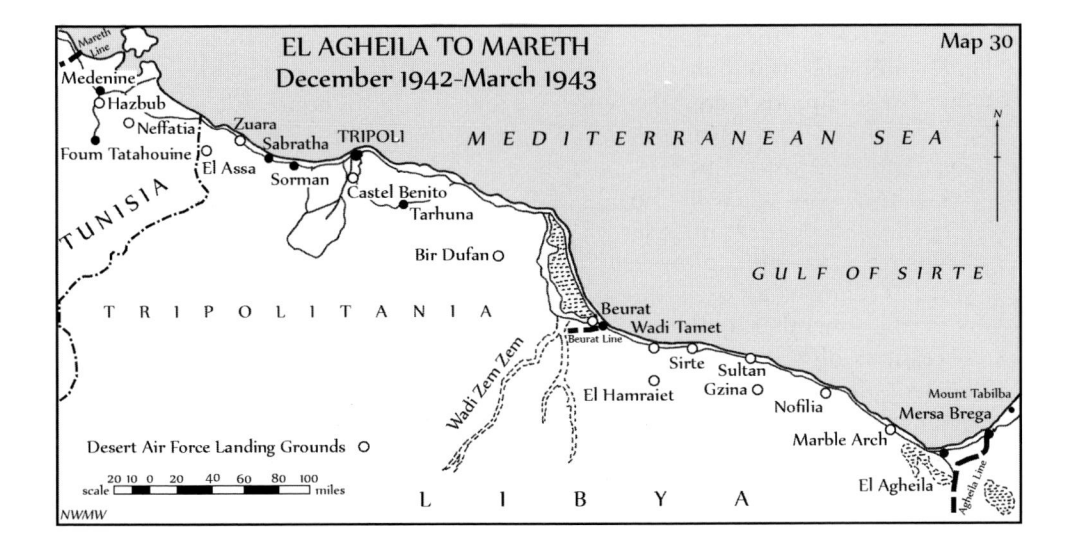

Map 30. EL AGHEILA TO MARETH, December 1942–March 1943

move, Rommel broke contact and withdrew to Nofilia and then to Buerat. The New Zealand Division experienced difficult 'going' on their desert flank and only reached the coast road in time to maul the seasoned enemy flank and rearguards as they withdrew along the coast road.

What had been achieved during Operation *Chocolate* at LG 125 was now to be attempted on a larger scale. The withdrawal of the Axis was followed up by the 2nd New Zealand Division, with 4th Light Armoured Brigade in the vanguard, and they moved on quickly towards Nofilia. To keep the most advanced troops of the New Zealand Division in range, the fighter wings were to be maintained as far forward as possible. Consequently, No 2 Armoured Car Company escorted the ground parties of No 211 Group and Nos 239 and 244 Wings, along with Nos 5 and 10 Supply and Transport Columns, towards Marble Arch.

At the same time, the No 239 Wing Advanced Party, R/T, W/T and radar equipment and ground crews were loaded onto the Hudsons of No 216 Group RAF at Belandah, while at El Adem enough petrol to keep a wing going for a day of intensive operations was loaded onto the Dakotas of USAAF 316th Carrier Wing, who were to be escorted by the Kittyhawks of No 239 Wing. As soon as the airfield was declared safe, the Kittyhawks of Nos 3 and 450 Squadrons RAAF and 112 and 250 Squadrons RAF began landing. Within two hours of their arrival the fighter-bombers were launching sorties against the enemy rearguards, which were now in range. The establishment of these airfields so close to the front line also facilitated the prompt air evacuation of casualties, thus saving many lives and the suffering for the

The RAF armoured cars were forced to make frequent detours off the roads and tracks as the frequency of mines increased (© Crown copyright. Chester, RAF Regiment Museum).

wounded from long jolting journeys over rough desert tracks.

Marble Arch airfield was so named after the ostentatious marble creation of Mussolini's that marked the boundary between the provinces of Cyrenaica and Tripolitania. More ominously, the Sappers found some 500 anti-tank and 360 anti-personnel mines that were quickly lifted to clear a large enough area to allow the fighters to land. So thick were the mines, it was difficult to find an area on the airfield where the ground parties could be safely accommodated. In one instance, an advanced party of ground staff arriving at the Marble Arch airfield jumped off the back of a truck to move some empty 44 gallon drums. As one of them alighted he landed right on top of a dreaded 'S' anti-personnel mine, detonating it, and killing three airmen outright, two more died later and three were badly wounded.[21]

Further progress westwards was difficult as the roads were sown with thousands of mines. When No 2 Company moved on to Nofilia, so heavily did the mines infest their chosen path, the column was forced to detour off the main road to avoid them. The pace of No 2 Company's move was however, so rapid that Casano arrived at Nofilia shortly after the enemy had departed. Here they were employed not only in the defence of the aerodrome but also assisted the New Zealand sappers in filling in the numerous mine holes in preparation for the arrival of the fighters.

A Humber Mark I armoured car of No 1 Armoured Car Company escorts the Sector A Party convoy beneath Mussolini's Marble Arch (© IWM CM 4232).

Number 2 Company, Christmas Dinner 1942, 40 miles south-east of Sirte. The menu was listed in Ivor Chester's photo album as: Soup - nil; Dinner – chips, Yorkshire pudding, baked beans, and pork (?); Sweet – rice pudding. In left hand photograph pork is on the plate and Yorkshire pudding is in the pan (© Crown copyright. Chester, RAF Regiment Museum).

Number 1 Armoured Car Company, with the Sector A Party, moved forward on 21 December and followed the coastal road, passing through Marble Arch and then Nofilia, making slow progress, because of the many bridges that had been blown and the thickly-sown mines. At one point, a long wait occurred while the New Zealand Engineers cleared a path so that the AMES vehicles could at least move off the road. The mines thickened and yet more delays occurred while they were cleared.

During the lull following the enemy's retreat, 7th Armoured Division took over the lead from the New Zealanders, and on Christmas Eve was in contact with the Axis rearguards south of Sirte. Again, there was the necessary pause to build up supplies, and to clear and construct forward landing grounds. Air Marshal Coningham was determined to move his squadrons forward as fast as the enemy moved back and if captured landing grounds were found to be ploughed and mined, then it would be quicker to build new ones.[22] The Eighth Army now had the support of three fighter wings, two day-bomber wings and a reconnaissance wing.[23] The enemy air force on the other hand, was having great difficulty maintaining its effort against the Allies, partly due to a serious shortage of aircraft and at times through a lack of fuel.

On Christmas Day 1942, Casano left by air from Marble Arch for Cairo, where he was to inspect some new armoured cars that had recently arrived in Middle

East Command for No 2 Company. For some there was the opportunity to have a Christmas Dinner. Len King constructed an oven and cooked a pork joint. However, others were less fortunate. On the same day, Flight Lieutenant Suckling and AC1 John Pedrick were travelling along the Nofilia to Sirte road when their jeep detonated a mine. The jeep was completely destroyed and 19 year-old Pedrick suffered severe injuries, from which he died a few minutes later. Suckling was extremely fortunate and received only minor injuries.

The advance was still proceeding at pace, and with 7th Armoured Division capturing Sirte, the way was clear for Flight Lieutenant Newland's section to escort the heavily loaded lorries of the RAF's No 10 Supply and Transport Column to Gzina, and onwards to El Hamraiet. The enemy air force had recovered from their earlier setbacks and again the RAF armoured cars did their best to protect the airfield working parties from persistent air attack. Len King recalls their convoy protection role:

> You had to be constantly watching all the time. Generally speaking if you were in a supply and transport convoy, your cars located on either side and you would shoot to one side. We escorted anybody that hadn't got any ack-ack support of any sort, because we were well equipped. I didn't know any other units that were as well equipped as the RAF armoured cars were.

After spending Christmas Day at Nofilia, two armoured cars from No 1 Company and a party from the AMES made a recce towards Sultan in the hope of finding an ideal site for radar. A location was selected, although after making contact with the New Zealand Divisional Cavalry, they were informed that enemy patrols had been reported in the area. Furthermore, the heavily-mined roads prevented any further move to Sultan and movement off the tracks was not possible with the heavy vehicles used to transport the radar equipment of the AMES.

It was on 30 December, that a section of cars finally moved on towards Sirte, again heavily mined. The landing ground was also found to have been ploughed up and was far too small for use by a full fighter wing. The decision was made that No 510 AMES had to be placed as near to the front as feasible and a suitable site found with the assistance and professional advice from the 131st (Queen's) Lorried Infantry Brigade of 7th Armoured Division. Meanwhile, the remainder of the Company settled at Wadi Tamet alongside the Advanced Air HQ, Western Desert.

On New Year's Day 1943, the airfield was raided twice by a few enemy aircraft, but five days later, the *Luftwaffe* returned in force. A large formation of aircraft appeared over the strip at lunchtime. Some of the enemy aircraft made a low pass over the AMES, at only 50 feet, and were immediately engaged by the Vickers K anti-aircraft machine-guns of the Humbers. One plane was hit by their bullets and was believed to have crashed; however, Pilot Officer Robert Pellew was hit during the attack and suffered serious wounds which necessitated his evacuation to the RAF Medical Receiving Station. The air raids continued on a daily basis for the next ten days, although they were intercepted by the Spitfires and Kittyhawks with varying degrees of success with the critical assistance of No 510 AMES.

From 9 January, operations for the Desert Air Force intensified which would only end with the fall of Tripoli. Rommel withdrew from the Buerat position and Allies (fighter-bombers by day, medium and heavy bombers by night), struck at his supply lines in the rear. They switched for a time to attacks on the main enemy positions around Wadi Zem Zem as the Eighth Army pushed forward, and then on to the German airfields. The latter proved costly in men and aircraft but they reduced the intervention of enemy aircraft over the battlefield.

On 16 January, No 1 Company, the Sector A Party and No 510 AMES, were given the order to move as near to Tarhuna as the military situation allowed. Tarhuna had fallen to 7th Armoured Division that evening and it was now fighting on the outskirts of Tripoli. The party camped the night, and then the following day, after a long wait, was allowed to join the long, slow-moving lines of Army vehicles making their way towards the Libyan capital. On 23 January, the Company arrived at Castel Benito airfield on the southern outskirts of the city, the same day that Tripoli fell to the Eighth Army. The jubilation of the airmen at reaching the Libyan capital was tempered by the unhappy news that Pilot Officer Pellew had died of his wounds.

At dawn on 23 January, three months to the day that the final Battle of El Alamein had begun, the first British troops of the Eighth Army entered Tripoli. The Allies had advanced 1400 miles, about the same as the distance from Moscow to Berlin. The dust of the desert was now left behind as the airmen entered a land of grassy plains, green mountains and cultivated olive plantations. The advance was halted for a period as the port of Tripoli, which had suffered under repeated bombing by the RAF and enemy demolition, was put back in order.

Number 2 Armoured Car Company resumed their advance towards Hamraiet on 14 January, and moved closely to the rear of the New Zealand Division escorting No 10 Supply and Transport Column and the advanced parties of No 239 Wing. The New Zealanders were held up for a time due to strong enemy rearguard action at Wadi Zem Zem, but eventually they reached Bir Dufan on 19 January and established new landing grounds. The country was becoming more difficult to navigate, with many wadis and rocky outcrops slowing progress, but Castel Benito was reached three days after the fall of Tripoli. The new Orderly Room Corporal, Ray Ferguson, only 20 years old, arrived on the Company at this time and recalls his first impressions:

> It took me about two weeks to get there from Alex [Alexandria]. I suddenly realised what it was all about. There was no going out on parade at 9 o'clock in the morning. There was no official lunchtime, and you didn't have to be in by an official time, because there was nowhere to go!
>
> We had a medic, he was only an LAC, and he'd worked for the Post Office in London, where they sorted the letters out. He was called 'Doc' Carter. The other guy was Flight Sergeant Davies; he was in charge of all the service vehicles.
>
> When I saw the guys and the way they worked I was fascinated, because you never went to bed in a barracks. You were on the move, there was no barracks. I had a stretcher on top of four oil cans, and a blanket, and I slept out in the open all the time.
>
> When I got to the unit eventually, I'd got about six months of mail waiting there. My Mum had put in cigarettes, some soap and a fruit cake. Sadly, the soap had infiltrated the cigarettes and the fruit cake was mouldy in the middle.
>
> There was already a guy in the Orderly Room from Manchester. There was hardly any paperwork for me to do, so I used to do most of the cooking. I used to make cakes. When our unit was stationary it used more petrol than when it was moving, because to cook you had to have a petrol can with the

sides sliced off. You'd put sand in it and some petrol, stir it in, and you got a fire.

I used to make the porridge in the morning. Flight Sergeant Davies used to like it with salt but I always put in sugar. That's how we lived. The 'bobajee',[24] in charge of rations, used to go and get all the food; but tins of this, and tins of that, you know, but no fresh vegetables. So you were in your shorts with your legs bare, and the slightest tap, and you got a desert sore.

They were a very happy crowd of guys. They used to play bridge all day. At night time we had this radio in the car and we would all crowd into the vehicle to listen to Doreen Villiers. Corporal Higgins, he was sitting next to me, and all of sudden it said "We've got a request here for Corporal Higgins" He jumped out of the vehicle and tore around telling everyone else, "My song's on the radio!"

I don't remember saluting anybody. Because the officers had to be on the vehicles with airmen, they had to make the effort to be friendly. With our arrangement, the Orderly Room, we only had four of us. We didn't have an officer so we were on our own.

Our commander, Squadron Leader Casano; everybody called him 'Cass'. He was very popular. You never had any facilities for washing your gear. The Orderly Room was in the back of a 3-tonner. I spent a lot of time in it, because there was nothing to do. 'Cass' would come up and say "I'm going over to 211 Group to play poker. I want a clean shirt." You wouldn't believe how popular that man was. Everybody showed him respect.[25]

The Eighth Army again drew breath; supplies and reinforcements were brought

Keeping up with the news. Listening to the BBC from 'Blighty'. Corporal Ivor Chester (right) (© Crown copyright. Chester, RAF Regiment Museum).

The Fordsons of No 2 Company are lined up for the final time at Castel Benito. A few days later the Company was re-equipped with GMC Otters (Elliot).

up in preparation for the next battle. For the two armoured car companies, a fortnight was spent on inspection, servicing and overhaul of their vehicles after their long and demanding journey from Alamein. Rather ominously, lectures on chemical warfare were begun at this time, suggesting that this may have been considered a threat, as the enemy became more desperate. For No 2 Company however, a significant change was afoot. On 9 February, 13 new GMC Otter light reconnaissance cars arrived from Cairo. Casano however, refused to accept them until they were properly prepared, as Len King recalls:

> If you went over a mine and it went off, it smashed your feet up. We had a bomb plate on the armoured cars, but if a mine detonated near front without one, then it would hurt the driver. 'Cass' wouldn't accept the new GMCs until they'd put on the bomb plates.

Accordingly, the Fordson armoured cars were to be handed in, but not without regrets. Harry Fenwick recalls:

> The Fordson cars, after the Rolls, really did the job well. Mainly because of the high standard of driving and servicing; drivers really took a pride in their cars. The Fitters were the best and no job was too big for them. I remember the back end of a Fordson being blown off and was then repaired by beg, borrow and steal.[26]

In a fortnight of busy activity, the equipment and ammunition was transferred from the old to the new vehicles which were taken out on training runs and W/T tests with new American radios.[27] The Operations Record Book notes the passing of the

A rare meeting between the members of Nos 1 and 2 Armoured Car Companies during the advance to Tunis (© Crown copyright. Chester, RAF Regiment Museum).

Fordsons with some sadness:

> The old armoured cars were sent away to the Motor Transport Repair Section at Tripoli. It was with regret that they went. These armoured cars were a modified version of the old Rolls Royce armoured cars, the armour and turrets being fitted to Ford commercial chassis' in June 1940. Since that time, although outclassed and outmoded by present day standards, they have travelled thousands of miles and have stood up remarkably well to the arduous conditions imposed on them.[28]

The Axis forces were now fighting on two fronts. The Allies had made successful landings in French North Africa in early November 1942, but their eastward advance to Tunis had been held by the Axis forces in the mountains. Rommel's Italian and German Divisions had linked up in February with General Von Armin's forces fighting the British, American and French Divisions of the First Army in Tunisia, but they were separated by a great distance. Rommel had taken command of a newly-created *Army Group Afrika* on 23 February, with responsibility for both fronts. With the shortened internal lines of communications the Axis troops, supplies and aircraft could now be easily transferred from one front to the other. The outcome of the campaign now seemed inevitable, but Rommel was determined to strike one final blow. He had already caused chaos and a near rout when he attacked the Americans at Kasserine Pass. Fortunately, this had been held and he now turned his attention to the Eighth Army.

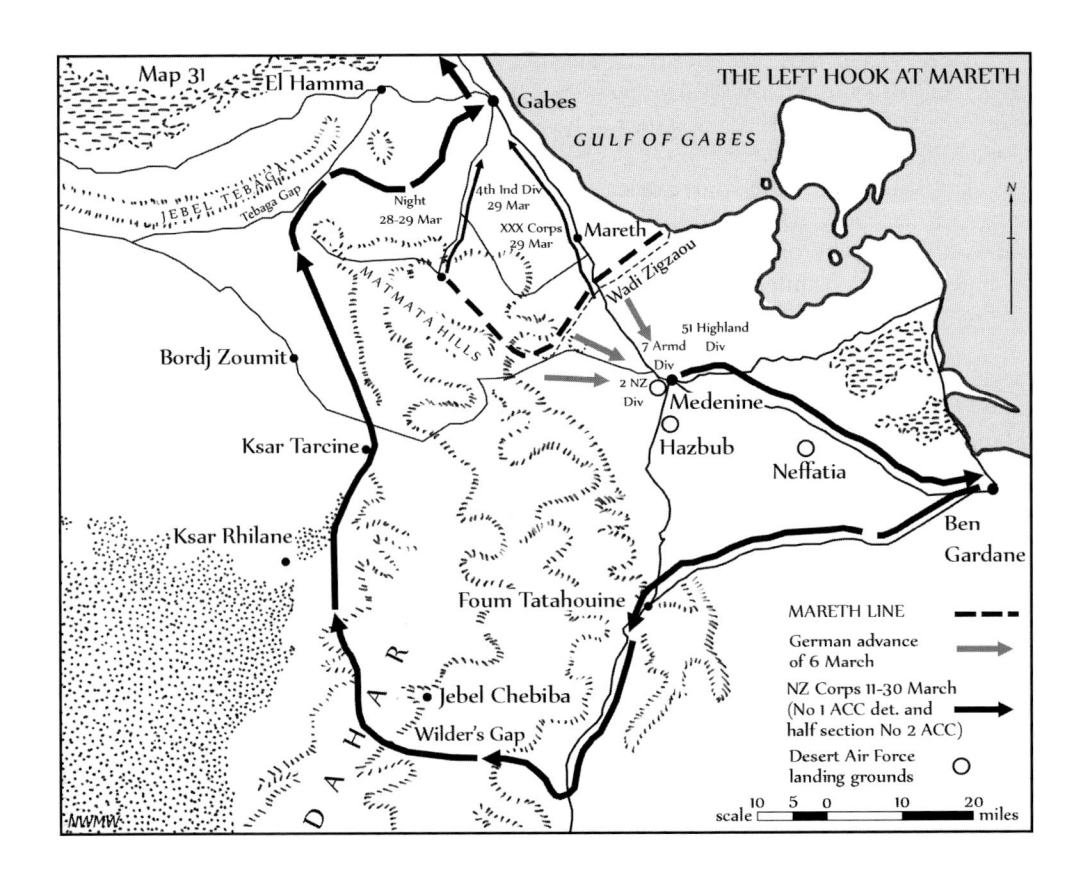

After the fall of Tripoli, with the Eighth Army unable to move forward as swiftly as hoped, the Axis forces had continued their ordered retreat to the west and established themselves on the Mareth Line. The Eighth Army crossed the Libyan-Tunisian border on 4 February thus bringing to an end Mussolini's great Italian Empire. Attacks by Rommel and General Von Armin to the north against the Americans in Tunisia had met with some success and the Eighth Army and the Desert Air Force were requested to apply pressure to draw off the enemy forces in southern Tunisia and prepare to repel an expected Axis offensive. The Allied position at Mareth centred on the town of Medenine, with its crossroads, tracks and airfields. The 7th Armoured, 51st Highland and 2nd New Zealand Divisions and 4th Light Armoured, 8th Armoured and 201st Guards Brigades were moved up by Montgomery and the Desert Air Force arrived at the same time to support the Army. Two fighter and fighter-bomber wings arrived at the rapidly cleared airfields at Neffatia and Hazbub, located south and east of Medenine. Unfortunately these airfields were located well forward and were in perfect view of observation posts of the enemy-held Matmata Hills, only a few miles distant (Map 31, p. 434).

Due to their close proximity to the front line, the enemy motorised units could easily move through the wadis and passes of the Matmata Hills and strike at the Desert Air Force forward landing grounds. The Army had the armoured cars of the Royal Dragoons and the carrier platoons of the infantry watching for enemy incursions, but it was vital that the RAF armoured cars be brought forward to concentrate on safeguarding the RAF assets. On 26 February, No 2 Company was ordered up with the Advance Party of No 211 Group and two sections were sent off to the airfield at Hazbub, just 3 miles behind the forward defended localities of the New Zealand Division. The GMC Otters were sent out to patrol the surrounding roads to protect convoys against strafing enemy aircraft. The Spitfires of No 244 Wing flew in and began patrolling the forward areas for aerial intruders.

Number 1 Company and the Sector A Party and radar station had arrived at Medenine only a few days before No 2 Company.[29] The arrival of both Companies coincided with a series of concerted attacks by the Axis air forces on the Allied forward airfields. The *Luftwaffe* had carried out a sneak raid a few days before the arrival of the Companies after they had slipped past Allied air patrols. The arrival of the cars with the accompanying AMES would therefore have been welcomed.

The enemy were not happy with their presence however, and the No 510 AMES position was strafed a few days later. All the anti-aircraft weapons on the station, including those of their protecting armoured car section, fired at the two groups of Bf 109s as they swept across the sky, destroying one of them. Leading Aircraftman Wilford, a fitter from No 1 Company, was hit in the abdomen but survived and was safely evacuated for treatment.

The site was again strafed later that afternoon. As often happened, the threat from these attacks hastened the digging of slit trenches and during the lull, all the Company's guns were overhauled. The enemy returned the following morning, and by this time the armoured cars had taken up position on top of a ridge and got in bursts of fire at the enemy fighters as they swept over them.

The enemy observation positions were so close that Hazbub airfield soon came under direct shellfire from 170-mm German guns located in the Matmata Hills. Aerial reconnaissance failed to locate the guns and little could be done about them as they were out of range of the British artillery. In the space of 90 minutes, some 25 shells fell on the landing ground dispersals causing casualties amongst the ground personnel of the flying squadrons and rendering the airfield unusable. A night-time evacuation of the Spitfire Wing was ordered and the ground parties and pilots rapidly moved eastwards as great muzzle flashes from the German guns were visible in the hills. Many aircraft still remained on the ground as it was impossible to fly them out under the concentrated shellfire. Number 2 Company remained on the landing ground, however, the following morning the shellfire intensified and as a consequence the entire armoured car detachment was ordered to withdraw.

Aerial reconnaissance had reported increased movements of panzers and infantry towards the Mareth line for some days, and Montgomery was warned by General Alexander, now in overall command of First and Eighth Armies as 18th Army Group, to expect a ground attack. On 5 March, the *Luftwaffe* returned in strength with orders to support the offensive by neutralising the Allied airfields. Rommel launched Operation *Capri* the following morning. While the newly-named *First Italian Army*, composed of *20th* and *21st Italian Corps* with *90th Light Division* held the 51st Highland Division in the north, he sent *10th*, *15th* and *21st Panzer Divisions* which debouched from the Matmata Hills, to attack the centre of the British line.

Further south, elements of the *164th Division* and the *3rd* and *33rd Reconnaissance Units* moved up the Wadi Goraguer to cut the Foum Tatahouine to Medenine road.

For the RAF Armoured Car Companies, the heavy shellfire on the misty morning of 6 March heralded the beginning of Rommel's offensive. The bombardment had become so intense and accurate over the previous days that No 1 Company and the AMES had been forced to temporarily withdraw, but only until the fire slackened, and a few hours later they returned to the site. The Company was also able to watch with some satisfaction the RAF successes in numerous dogfights overhead, no doubt vectored in by the Sector A Party they were watching over.

The southern part of the line was only thinly-held by a battalion of the King's Royal Rifle Corps and a few tanks and armoured cars of the Fighting French Flying Column, the 'Colonne Volante'. This unit fought a pitched battle along this road against the *10th Panzer Division* and German Reconnaissance elements on the night of 5 March and into the next day.[30] There was apprehension that there might be an outflanking move from the south-east and consequently a section of cars from No 1 Company was despatched on road block patrols on the Medenine to Tatahouine road.

The day before the launch of Operation *Capri*, No 2 Company pulled its HQ back to Neffatia. The intense shellfire on Hazbub forced its evacuation, and Neffatia, with No 7 Wing SAAF, became the most forward landing ground. The bothersome 170-mm guns continued to rumble in the hills and were only neutralised by the 4th Indian Division a few days later when it launched its attack into the Matmata Hills.

There developed a real fear, however, that the enemy would make a ground strike at Neffatia. A few weeks earlier at Kasserine, the Germans broke through and struck at Thelepte airfield, forcing the Americans to destroy 34 aircraft on the ground to prevent their capture.[31] The defences of the landing grounds were considerably bolstered when 24 3.7-inch heavy anti-aircraft guns and 42 40-mm Bofors and the exotically-named Free French 1er Bataillon d'Infanterie de Marine du Pacifique[32] were brought up to Neffatia. Ground and aircrews were also issued with rifles and sub-machine guns.[33]

Flight Lieutenant Newland, with the cars of No 2 Company, patrolled constantly to the north, north-west and north-east in search of enemy columns. Neffatia however, came under direct and repeated air attack on the first day of the offensive. The heaviest raid occurred at 1430 hours that afternoon when, with screaming aero engines, the crack of cannon shells and sprays of tracer, 18 Ju 88 bombers and 24 Bf 109 fighters struck with considerable fury. Harry Fenwick remembers that day:

> … It must have been one of the worse baptisms of fire the Company ever was in… The planes came in waves, bombs and bullets came down like rain.

There was the whistle and crump of exploding bombs, the thundering belch of the 3.7-inch guns and the Bofors guns barking in reply all adding to the eardrum splitting cacophony. Casano's luck had finally run out and he was badly wounded in the right side. AC1 Radcliffe was also wounded, in the left forearm. One armoured car was hit by shrapnel but fortunately there were no further casualties.[34] Len King recalls the air attacks:

> I can remember several times being strafed. We were spaced out and fired back, but we never hit anything. Before you could really get to your guns

A jeep, Fordson armoured car, tender and the Chevrolet CMP 3-tonner 'Orderly Room' of No 2 Armoured Car Company (King).

they'd gone because of the speed they travelled. Some airmen were quicker than others; it depended where you were located. Some got quite a few shots off as they were good at getting on target quickly.

Corporal Ray Ferguson on the Orderly Room lorry had nothing to fire back with and remembers the air raid:

We weren't expecting anything, but one of the guys on our lorry, Corporal Wiggins, whenever we stopped, he dug what he called a 'ARP hole'; which was a trench. So I dug one as well. We were suddenly attacked. We just got down in the hole. The noise; I don't know if there was an anti-aircraft unit there but the noise was terrific![35]

The raids continued and as night fell the Company took up defensive positions in anticipation of a ground attack. The ground defence officer for the airfield had a plan that if threatened all soft vehicles were to withdraw while the anti-aircraft guns formed a 'semi-circle of steel' to repel German armour should it break through.[36]

The Kittyhawks and Spitfires launched sortie after sortie to attack the oncoming panzer columns. One RAF armoured car patrol however, had reported that enemy fighting vehicles had been seen only 12 miles off. A flap ensued, with soft vehicles of the RAF and SAAF squadrons streaming eastwards and anti-aircraft guns moving forward and preparing for anti-tank actions. As the enemy ground offensive petered out, the order was sent out for the vehicles to return. Surprisingly, some had nearly reached the Libyan border before they were halted. With Casano's medical evacuation, John Newland returned to Neffatia, was promoted to Squadron Leader, and assumed command of the Company.

As the shellfire intensified on the morning of 6 March, the cars of No 1 Company were required to escort the Sector A Party away from Medenine. Despite this, the AMES was non-operational for only a few hours before it established itself ten miles further east. Twenty-four hours later, with the threat having subsided, they were back at Medenine. Two Humber armoured cars still maintained constant 'road block' patrols to the south-west of Medenine.

In one of Montgomery's most successful battles, the enemy were delayed by dummy minefields and then halted by the concentrated fire of 350 field and medium guns and 460 well-emplaced anti-tank guns of the Eighth Army. Three fighter wings were flown in support of Eighth Army, attacking the enemy motorised columns and intercepting large swarms of the Messerschmitt and Maachi fighters escorting Junkers bombers and dive-bombers of the *Luftwaffe* and *Regia Aeronautica*. The Axis ground attacks were, uncharacteristically, poorly coordinated, easily repelled and eventually petered out, leaving 50 tanks lying on the battlefield. The Allied armour had not been needed and the Eighth Army suffered few casualties. Despite a bold attempt at driving the Eighth Army back, Rommel had made his final attack and it had failed. He could not retrieve the position of the Axis in North Africa. He handed over command to Colonel General Hans-Jürgen von Armin and flew back to Germany in poor health and low morale, never to return. The panzers were called back lest there not be enough troops and vehicles to defend the Mareth Line.

Montgomery now set about planning his own Mareth offensive, Operation *Pugilist*. This was not to be as easy as the defensive battle. The Axis defence line, a 'desert Maginot', had been constructed by the French military before the war to face a possible invasion from the Italian Tripolitania and the Germans had hastily repaired and improved the many prepared positions, engineered and natural tank obstacles and concrete pill boxes. To the north was the Wadi Zigzaou, which with banks 20 feet high, was a major obstacle to an armoured advance; while in the south overlooking the British positions were the Matmata Hills. Along its 19-mile length were tens of thousands of mines.

Unlike at Alamein, the Mareth Line could be outflanked to the south. The route, located on the northern edge of the Sahara, had been identified by patrols of the Long Range Desert Group. General Bernard Freyberg's 2nd New Zealand Division reinforced with medium and anti-tank artillery, the King's Dragoon Guards, the 8th Armoured Brigade, the 'Colonne Volante' and General Leclerc's Free French 'L' Force, a mixed force of infantry, artillery and armoured cars which had arrived after a gruelling march across the Sahara from Chad, was grouped as New Zealand Corps. The New Zealanders were to move south by night from Medenine to Foum Tatahouine, then turn westwards and outflank the Matmata Hills, and then move across the waterless desert via Wilders Gap, Ksar Rhilane, Ksar Tarcine and Tebaga Gap to then threaten the El Hamma coastal plain. The country was difficult for a mechanised army to cross, with ragged rocky outcrops and long stretches of deep white sand. The latter raised a dust cloud that clogged eyes and nostrils with its caustic powder. Vehicles were repeatedly bogged and had to be towed or dug out.[37] However, the outflanking move by New Zealand Corps was planned only as a diversionary operation. The main attack by 50th Division was launched along the coast and was intended to smash through the wadi defences and then advance on Gabes (Map 31, p. 434).

Air Marshal Coningham was now commander of the North-West Tactical Air Force and charged with coordinating the activities of all the British and American air forces in the Tunisian theatre.[38] He ordered the Desert Air Force to concentrate on providing the "maximum assistance to the Eighth Army."[39] The Desert Air Force contributed 41 of the 75 squadrons involved. The Allied air forces now had an overwhelming superiority in aircraft and it became possible to refine and develop the new ground support role. At Hazbub, Medenine and Neffatia were the Kittyhawks and Hurricane tank-busters that could strike at the enemy armour and infantry and the Spitfires that had the job of maintaining air superiority against the Messerschmitt Bf 109s and the newly-arrived Focke-Wulf Fw 190s. With the air cleared of enemy fighters, Wellington bombers could then attack the Mareth Line by night and the Bostons, Baltimores and Mitchells by day.

The main coastal thrust was launched on 16 March but after five days it was clear that the British infantry could not break through as none of their supporting tanks and guns had been able to cross the Wadi Zigzaou. Furthermore, with German reserves arriving in larger numbers, an Axis counterattack was imminent. The New Zealand Corps, comprising 27,000 men and 6000 vehicles, began moving from Medenine from 11 March and gathered to the west of Wilders Gap ready for the advance by 19 March.

The Sector A Party and No 510 and 606 AMES were ordered to accompany this move to provide radar coverage and fighter control for the New Zealanders as they made their secret move around the desert flank. On 13 March, Squadron Leader Olliff-Lee and Nos 1 and 3 Sections of No 1 Company set off with this convoy for Foum Tatahouine leaving the HQ Section at Medenine. Flight Lieutenant Herbert Tickler was sent forward with an armoured car to New Zealand Divisional HQ to provide forward communications with the Sector A Party. The remainder of the Detachment followed in the tracks of the New Zealand Division. Early the next day, after making contact with Tickler, Squadron Leader Olliff-Lee moved ahead coming across tracks that had been mined by the enemy which led to constant detours and the need to make fresh tracks. Their presence was now known to the Axis air forces and over the course of the day, they observed dogfights above them between the RAF and *Luftwaffe*.

The Desert Air Force was now in the ascendant and was planning a series of concentrated low-level attacks against the enemy positions just prior to the ground advance by the New Zealanders. In one of several RAF raids that day in support of New Zealand Corps, 40 aircraft were sent to bomb a group of enemy tanks. Following this action, the RAF armoured cars recovered two wounded pilots who had been shot down and transported them back to the nearest RAF Medical Receiving Station in the Detachment's soft vehicles. One of the pilots had been helped by local Arabs and some Humber armoured cars were sent off to thank them for their help on behalf of the RAF.

With the failure of 50th Division to break through on the coast, Montgomery switched his main effort to the outflanking move by the New Zealanders. Some of the senior commanders feared that after the triumphant progress from El Alamein, the Eighth Army would stall and be left floundering on the Mareth Line.[40] The 50th Division was ordered to withdraw from the Wadi Zigzaou and the Eighth Army Reserve of X Corps HQ, under Lieutenant-General Brian Horrocks, and 1st Armoured Division were ordered to join the New Zealanders. In the centre, the 4th Indian Division struck through the Matmata Hills.

The enemy now sought to impede the outflanking manoeuvre and consequently No 1 Company Detachment was raided at night by the *Luftwaffe*. The AMES was established at Jebel Chebiba for four days and then moved on through Bir Soltane and on to Bordj Zoumit. The New Zealand Corps completed the outflanking move and

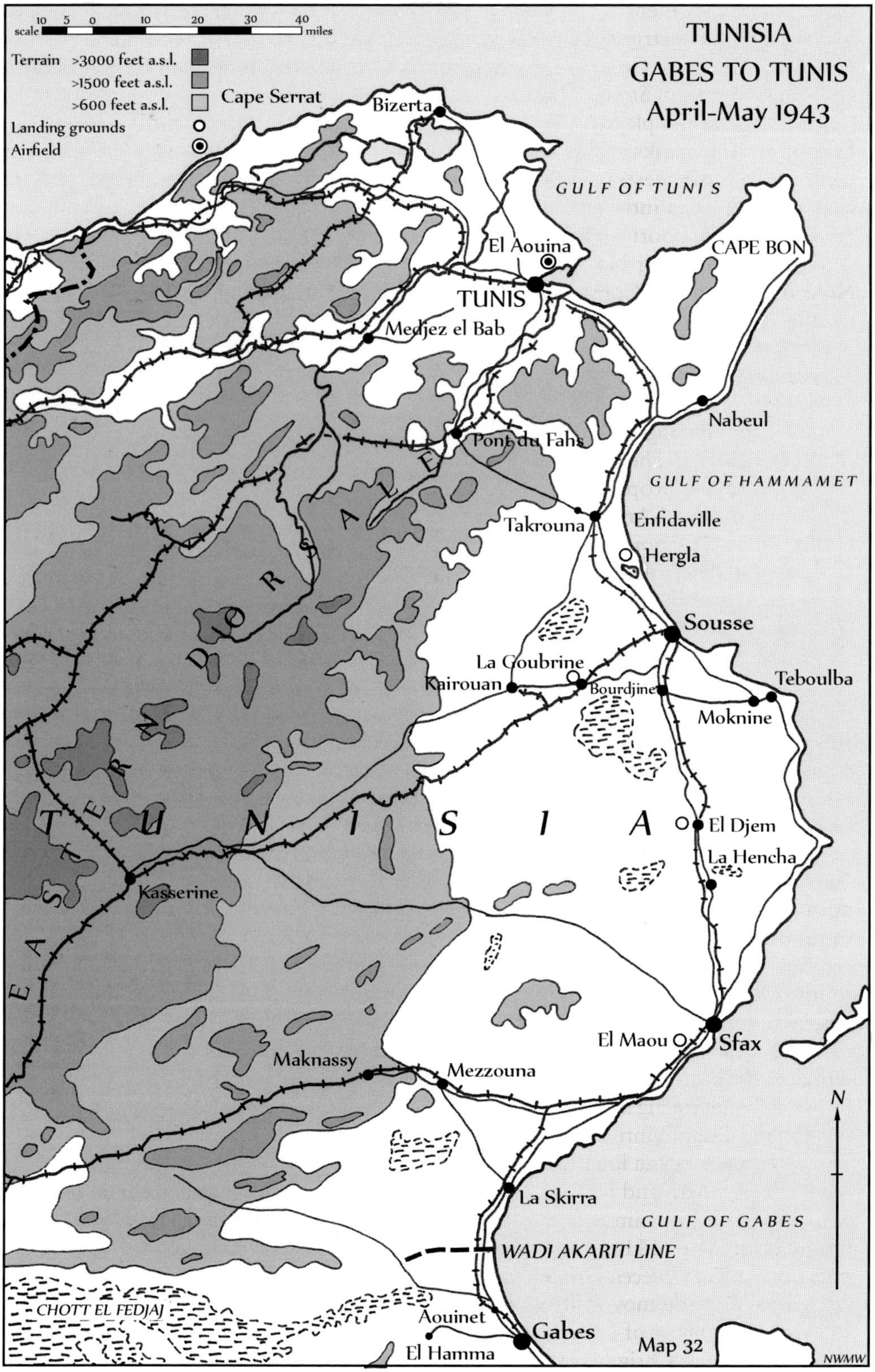
TUNISIA
GABES TO TUNIS
April-May 1943
scale 10 5 0 10 20 30 40 miles
Terrain >3000 feet a.s.l.
>1500 feet a.s.l.
>600 feet a.s.l.
Landing grounds
Airfield
Cape Serrat
Bizerta
GULF OF TUNIS
El Aouina
CAPE BON
TUNIS
Medjez el Bab
Nabeul
Pont du Fahs
GULF OF HAMMAMET
Takrouna
Enfidaville
Hergla
EASTERN DORSALE
Sousse
La Goubrine
Kairouan
Bourdjine
Teboulba
Moknine
TUNISIA
El Djem
La Hencha
Kasserine
El Maou
Sfax
Maknassy
Mezzouna
N
La Skirra
GULF OF GABES
WADI AKARIT LINE
CHOTT EL FEDJAJ
Aouinet
Gabes
El Hamma
Map 32
NWMW

made contact with enemy at the five-mile wide Tebaga Gap. This fortified position had been first constructed by Roman legionaries and had been modernised by the French and Italians. General Freyberg now set about organising the breakthrough to be called Operation *Supercharge*.[41]

Montgomery's plan for *Supercharge* was to launch a 'blitz' attack delivered by massed artillery, tanks and aircraft. Air Vice-Marshal Harry Broadhurst had assumed command of the Desert Air Force in mid-February and was prepared to provide overwhelming and intimate air support for the Army.[42] To assist in coordination of the direct air support control, Wing Commander 'Jackie' Darwen DFC, now the Officer Commanding No 239 Wing, and a VHF/HF-equipped armoured car from No 2 Armoured Car Company were sent to join New Zealand Corps HQ. This was mentioned in a letter to Freyberg and Horrocks from Montgomery's Chief of Staff, Major-General Francis De Guingand, sent on 25 March, though it seems the car was given insufficient time to arrive before the battle was due to start:

> We are sending over Darwen… to help you tie up the air support for *Supercharge*. The RAF have ordered an armoured car to report to NZ HQ and it is proposed that Darwen should be located 'cheek by jowl' with commander 8th Armoured Brigade or whoever else is in a position to get the latest information as to how the air support is working. It is important that he should be able to see the battle area from a good OP, and he will then be able to give the pilots the lowdown as to how they are doing.[43]

Flight Lieutenant Tickler from No 1 Company moved forward with New Zealand Division HQ, while Squadron Leader Olliff-Lee set off on 26 March to make contact with the air support control expert, Wing Commander 'Jackie' Darwen. He was supposed to be located with 8th Armoured Brigade HQ, but unfortunately, Darwen proved elusive as he had flown to see the 6th New Zealand Brigade before Olliff-Lee arrived. The crew of these three forward armoured cars did however, have a front seat view of the ensuing battle from 8th Armoured Brigade HQ.

On the same day that the New Zealand Corps launched their assault at Tebaga Gap and 13 days after the No 1 Company Detachment departed to join in the outflanking move, Flying Officer Thomas Stockdale of No 2 Company was ordered to proceed to No 211 Group where his armoured car was fitted with a VHF/HF R/T receiver and transmitter. After testing, he was ordered to move with his three cars to join New Zealand Corps HQ. In an exceptional piece of driving, they set off just before midnight and after an all-night drive had covered 216 miles over a difficult route of undulating scrub-covered country, wadis and dunes of soft sand. The path had already been traversed by an entire Corps but they reached General Freyberg's HQ late the following afternoon. They made contact with Wing Commander Darwen, but to their disappointment they were not used.[44]

The attack began late in the afternoon of 26 March, as the first squadrons of the RAF, RAAF, SAAF and USAAF roared overhead. The Boston and Baltimore bombers were first and then came wave after wave of more than a dozen squadrons of Kitty-bombers and one of Hurricane tank-busters. As the aircraft flew away, 200 field and medium artillery pieces opened fire with a half-hour barrage and the tanks of 8th Armoured Brigade moved forward with two brigades of the New Zealand infantry following a quarter-of-an-hour later.[45] After a bitter struggle, the New Zealanders and 8th Armoured Brigade overwhelmed the German and Italian positions and the

Squadrons but it had only just been adopted by the Eighth Army.

After bloody struggles by 4th Indian and 2nd New Zealand Divisions, it became apparent that the Enfidaville line could only be broken at great cost. This came as a disappointment for the Eighth Army and the Desert Air Force, for after the 1800 mile journey from Egypt the soldiers and airmen had dreamt of a victorious entry into Tunis from the south. The mountainous crags and valleys, however, provided new obstacles to the motorised divisions of the Eighth Army which had proved more suited to the wide outflanking moves of the desert. The mule had now become more important than vehicles. As a consequence, on 29 April, General Alexander transferred the main attack to the front in the north.

During the last week of April, Alexander launched a major offensive by First Army, Operation *Vulcan,* with the aim of breaking the German defensive line in the north. Initial progress was slow despite hard fighting and the expected breakthrough did not transpire. Montgomery was ordered to send his freshest and most experienced formations, 7th Armoured and 4th Indian Divisions and 201st Guards Brigade to reinforce the First Army. Alexander regrouped his forces and the final attack against the Axis forces in North Africa was launched on 6 May. In one final effort, the entire North African Tactical Air Force[49] and the medium bombers of the North African Strategic Air Force provided direct air support to the 18th Army Group. With the addition of the newly-arrived Eighth Army divisions they broke through and struck towards Tunis, while the Americans moved on Bizerta. By 7 May, the final enemy defences around Tunis were pierced and the city fell to the British 6th and 7th Armoured Divisions, led by No 2 Company's old comrades the 11th Hussars 'The Cherry Pickers'. There were still pockets of resistance to the south and east of Tunis and so General Alexander, in a clever move, sent the 6th Armoured Division around the coast road of Cape Bon. The defenders were encircled, and with it the hopes for the enemy of a last ditch stand with their backs to the sea.

The southern front at Enfidaville remained too strongly-held by the Axis forces and the advance by the Eighth Army was not ordered until the 6th Armoured Division had completed the rout of the enemy. The Desert Air Force fighters and light-bombers were flying numerous sorties but with no hope of a breakthrough from the south, they could only await the surrender of the Axis units to their front. In the afternoon of 12 May, General Von Armin informed the Italian General Messe that he intended to surrender his headquarters and that of the *Afrika Korps*. About one hour before midnight, the sounds of the guns gradually died away as the gunners completed their fire programmes. Although some enemy units, the German *90th Light* and Italian *Young Fascist Divisions* chose to fight on until overrun, the end was in sight. Late in the evening, signals were sent from Alexander's 18th Army Group HQ stating that the war in North Africa was over, and all resistance had ceased. The following day, the Italian General Messe, the commander of *First Italian Army,* was granted an honourable surrender. The *Luftwaffe* and *Regia Aeronautica* had withdrawn to airfields in Sicily, and with the Axis unable to organise a Dunkirk-style evacuation to extricate its ground forces, some 250,000 men became prisoners of war of the Allies.

The fall of Tunis came as something of an anti-climax for the soldiers and airmen of Eighth Army and the Desert Air Force. After the victorious advance from Alamein, they had been unable to break through the Enfidaville line. The city fell to the thrust from the west by First Army. On 12 May however, three armoured cars and two tenders from No 1 Company escorted a party of No 211 Group on the six hour journey to Tunis. They returned after only two days and soon after the No 1

Equipped with the new GMC Otters, No 2 Company watch the convoys of Eighth Army move forward to Tunis (© Crown copyright. Chester, RAF Regiment Museum).

Armoured Car Company Detachment received orders to return to the Nile Delta.

For the officers and airmen of No 2 Company at Hergla, their experience of the battle was the constant drumming of the Allied artillery as they awaited the end. They had prepared to face a ground attack on the airfield should the enemy attempt to break out to the south but by 10 May with Tunis having fallen, the Company was ordered to make haste through Enfidaville and Pont du Fahs to Tunis. They were to escort the Middle East Aircraft Intelligence Unit.[50] Sadly, their gallant leader of three campaigns, Squadron Leader Casano was not with them as he had been evacuated to hospital following his wounding in the air attack at Neffatia, and so was prevented

A GMC Otter of No 2 Armoured Car Company parked near a wrecked German Henschel ground-attack aircraft on El Aouina airfield near Tunis (© Crown copyright. Chester, RAF Regiment Museum).

from seeing his Company into Tunis.

Arriving later that afternoon, they received a great welcome from the citizens of Tunis and then proceeded on to the El Aouina airfield five miles north of the city. This was the largest and best of the Tunisian airports but was now littered with more than a hundred wrecked and smouldering aircraft, particularly Ju 52s and Me 323 transports; the product of the strafing and bombing attacks by the Allied Air Forces.

Over the next few days, the cars moved out to surrounding landing grounds in search of enemy aircraft, some intact and others already destroyed. On 12 May, the entire Company travelled towards Cape Bon on a reconnaissance for enemy aircraft and reached Nabeul on the southern shore. This gave further opportunities for 'plunder', with two German Auto Union armoured cars and six captured lorries and light cars being taking on strength. These types of enemy armoured car had often been their greatest threat and had been widely used by their adversaries over the past two years. Comments in the Operations Record Book described the exceptional design and utility of the captured cars which can be contrasted with the less refined nature of the Fordsons and GMC Otters:

> The Auto Union armoured cars which are low built, have four-wheel drive and four wheel steering, independent springing and are much superior to our own in respect of quality, speed and armament. The armament consists of a 20-mm cannon and 0.30-inch machine-gun mounted on a revolving central pillar. Their height is much lower than the GMC Armoured Cars thus enabling a better approach to enemy positions and facility for camouflage.

The campaign in North Africa was finally over after an epic two and a half year struggle. The RAF armoured cars had been there from the early days of the campaign and had played a part in all the subsequent operations. Number 2 Armoured Car Company moved forward with General Wavell's 36,000 in December 1940 alongside the 11th Hussars, as the 'eyes and ears' of the Western Desert Force. There followed an intense three month sojourn in Iraq and Syria where they joined No 1 Armoured Car Company to help defeat the Axis intervention in Iraqi politics and neutralise the Vichy French in Syria. Both Companies rested for only a short time before they were ordered to the Western Desert. This time the two companies had a defined role in support of the Desert Air Force in reconnaissance and ground and anti aircraft defence. They provided the Air Commanders with direct and immediate information as to the threats to the advanced landing grounds. Indeed, on a number of occasions, their presence was vital in averting disaster for the Allied fighter force. Having learnt many lessons, the RAF Armoured cars awaited the breakthrough at Alamein and moved forward with the lead mobile elements of the RAF. Support was provided to radar and fighter control units, and for successful operations behind enemy lines that harassed the enemy as they retreated for the third and final time down the coast road of the Gulf of Sirte. The enemy's extensive use of mines and the relentless air attacks had caused casualties to mount in the Companies, as the depleted units of the *Luftwaffe* and *Regia Aeronautica* struck back. Vic Morte gave his impression of what had happened:

> You were fortunate. There were lots of casualties but spread out. Some of these people were prone to accidents. My only problem was a fantastic toothache! You'd got to have your wits about you, as it was so easy to end

up in trouble.

I saw the Orderly Room Clerk and he was saying what a record the unit's got. Number 2 Company was about 96 strong, and he said that between 1940 and the later part of 1942, there were 143 casualties, includes grazes and bangs, several killed and some in rather unfortunate circumstances. All the, what I would describe as, the independent lads were all right but sometimes if anyone was going to get injured or killed, it was the married bloke with a family, and it was terrible really.[51]

Air power had come to play an increasingly important part in the North African campaign and it was the control of advanced landing grounds that was a key factor in the sustaining the land advance and for the protection of vital Malta convoys. Possession of landing grounds was of as much of significance as the capture of wadis and mountains. By May 1943, Air Chief Marshal Tedder at Mediterranean Air Command had 3241 operational aircraft at his disposal; this contrasts with the 371 aircraft that had been under the control of Air Marshal Longmore in 1940. The two RAF armoured car companies were however, still there.

RAF Middle East Command had really only begun to set the RAF Regiment on a sound footing in the latter months of 1942. So other than the *ad-hoc* attachment of Army units, the RAF armoured cars were the only mobile and armoured ground defence force available to Tedder and Coningham on a reliable basis for protection of the Desert Air Force forward tactical fighter wings and the air control and radar assets. New techniques in air support control that were unthinkable during the early years of the campaign had been refined and developed, and the RAF armoured cars played an important role. The RAF armoured car companies consisted of a handful of men in antiquated or often worn-out vehicles, but their constancy and ubiquity during the crucial days of the campaigns in the Middle East cannot be overestimated.

Notes
1. H.L. Thompson, *New Zealanders with the Royal Air Force, Vol. III* New Zealand in the Second World War 1939-1945 (Wellington, NZ: War History Branch, Dept of Internal Affairs, 1959), p. 95.
2. Quoted by R. Busvine, War Correspondent, 'They fought with the armour of Lawrence of Arabia', *Chicago Times?* c. 1943.
3. H. Fenwick, *Reminiscences* (Archives of the RAF Armoured Cars Association, 1972).
4. L. King, *Interview with author*, 2008.
5. At the same time, the flights of the RAF Regiment were going forward from El Alamein for the first time. The defence flight from No 40 Air Stores Park was the first unit to reach El Daba airfield. On 8 November, as the RAF Armoured Car Companies and the RAF Regiment flights moved off, squadrons and flights of the RAF Regiment were landing at the other end of the Mediterranean as part of Operation *Torch*, the British and American landings in French North Africa.
6. The aircraft of No 117 Squadron RAF that were flying into LG 125 were under the command of Wing Commander R.G. Yaxley who had been awarded the was awarded the MC while serving with No 2 Armoured Car Company during the Palestine disturbances of 1936. He had commanded Nos 252 and 272 Squadrons flying Beaufighters in Egypt until early 1942 and was awarded the DFC and DSO. He returned to the United Kingdom in February 1943, having received promotion to Group Captain, but was shot down and killed over the Bay of Biscay on 3 June 1943 whilst returning to the Middle East in a

The airmen of No 1 Company watch a football match at Habbaniya. A German battle flag captured as a trophy is placed on the side line (Moyes).

and if you hear things, stop breathing, because if you stop breathing you can hear someone else breathing." He was right; you could hear people breathing quite a long way away.

Of course we started with dogs as well. They weren't official ones but they were good. We picked em up in Egypt. We were good at picking things up. They trained with us, and were used for going round with the guard at night. They'd picked up an Arab long before you did. You wouldn't even know he was about. As we treated them well they were all right.[15]

With the conclusion of the final sessions of the Cairo conference in the second week of December, the VIPs departed. On 10 December, with the VIP protection task over, No 2 Company departed for Amman, and No 1 Company Detachment returned to Habbaniya.

Number 2 Company spent the remainder of 1943 and early 1944 at RAF Amman, with the main emphasis on training and maintenance, search and recovery of crashed aircraft and surveys of landing grounds, where they operated under the direct command of Air Headquarters Levant (renamed from Air HQ Palestine and Transjordan on 1 December 1941). In December 1943, a noteworthy event occurred when Flight Sergeant A.H. Davies was promoted to Warrant Officer; the first such appointment of an armoured car crewmen to this rank. In February 1944, the Company was moved with HQ and two sections going to RAF Ramleh and the remaining two sections moving to the village of Al Bassa 12 miles north of Acre.

Early in April 1944 however, there was a mutiny of Greek Army and Naval units stationed in Egypt. The mutiny stemmed from Republican sympathies among some members of the Greek forces, but was exploited by the Greek Communist group, EAM.[16] An appeal for unity by King George II of Greece, Head of the Greek government-in-exile, and his agreement to submit to a national plebiscite on Greece's future political system was to no avail.[17]

On 10 April, two sections of No 2 Armoured Car Company were ordered to proceed to Amiriya in Egypt without delay while Squadron Leader Murch flew

GMC Otters of 'B' Section of No 2 Company at Al Bassa, March 1944 (King).

by air to Alexandria and reported to the AOC Defences, Eastern Mediterranean to receive further instructions. The RAF armoured cars were ordered to standby to take action if mutiny should spread to the Royal Hellenic Air Force. There was particular concern that No 13 (Hellenic) Squadron, stationed at LG 91, which was equipped with modern Baltimore light bombers, might join the mutiny. Two sections of the Company arrived at 1700 hours and were kept strictly concealed in order not to provoke the Greek airmen. The Greek Squadron was kept under surreptitious observation for the next five days, but fortunately there were no signs of the mutiny spreading (Map 29, p. 395).

The Greek Army units were however, still in a belligerent mood and on 17 April the RAF armoured cars were attached to 7th Armoured Brigade. They were allotted the task of blockading the 1st Greek Brigade camp, which was being held by rebels in strongly-defended positions, including a dominating ridge. Loyalist elements, including their senior officers, were also being held prisoner in the Camp. The Greek rebels were running short of food, and with a long perimeter it was not possible to prevent parties of the rebels leaving or entering the Camp. The two RAF armoured car sections were sent to patrol the open south-western corner and the crews entered into the task with great enthusiasm. Despite the extensive area to cover there was a large degree of success, mainly due to excellent wireless communications. The situation was very delicate and no firing was allowed. The airmen did not allow this to dissuade them from taking action and the GMCs were used to ram or intimidate, sometimes at speeds of 40 to 55 mph, to bring at least a portion the rebel vehicles to a halt. The GMCs stood up well to the chases at high-speed and collisions with vehicles ranging from jeeps to tracked Bren Carriers. The constant watch prevented rations reaching the Camp and in one instance they captured several rebel leaders, a

Number 2 Armoured Car Company escort a column of Greek soldiers rounded up during the mutiny of April 1944 (King).

large sum of money and a store of civilian clothing.

General Sir Bernard Paget, C-in-C Middle East, had postponed using force against the mutinous Greek Army units, but resolved to act on 23 April.[18] An ultimatum was issued that a full-scale attack would be made if surrender was not made unconditionally. Sherman and Stuart tanks, artillery and infantry moved up. The RAF armoured cars' role was to cut off any escape attempts and distract the rebels' attention from the main attack. As night fell, flares were fired into the air and the tanks moved in. By morning the rebel emissaries had offered an unconditional surrender and bloodshed was avoided. Forty Greek soldiers were intercepted by the cars and the remainder of the day was spent disarming the entire Greek Brigade and escorting columns of vehicles into POW cages.

For the next few weeks, the armoured cars were retained at No 102 Maintenance Unit where they were to assist in dealing with armed bands of thieves that had begun operating in the vicinity of the desert airfields. However, by the end of May the entire unit was back at Al Bassa and RAF Ramleh.

Only a few days after the last Section had returned from Egypt, No 2 Company, along with four RAF Regiment squadrons, were sent to Syria as part of Operation *Turpitude*. By early June the Company was laagered at Bab el Haoua, the Turkish border crossing 50 miles west of Aleppo, and operating under the command of 87th Armoured Brigade of Ninth Army. This Brigade was composed of dummy tanks and was a further part of the deception plan (Map 24, p. 317).[19]

The RAF armoured car crews had anticipated that this was the beginning of an advance into Turkey, and hence the Balkans, but on arrival at Aleppo it was apparent by the quality of the British troops and their equipment that this was not an invasion force. The aim of *Turpitude* was to convince the Turks to throw in their lot with the Allies, and for the Germans, that the British were planning an invasion of northern Greece with a substantial military force. Meanwhile, the British Operational Orders and Conferences were to conceal the deception from the British soldiers and airmen, both for security reasons and to maintain enthusiasm. The ORB of No 2 Company records however:

> This policy was difficult to support in this Unit since the officers and airmen were too observant and experienced to remain convinced for more than a short time that the whole operation was nothing more than a somewhat thin attempt at deception.[20]

From 6 June, for a period of four weeks, the four sections were located along a 90-mile length of the Turkish frontier between the Mediterranean coast and Harim, one third of it mountainous and dissected by river valleys or rocky terrain, making mobility for vehicles difficult. The cars were to operate patrols near the Turkish border to 'tickle' the Turkish frontier observers' curiosity, including the extensive use of signalling lamps and lights at night. They were also to observe and report any abnormal activity, troop or vehicle concentrations or aircraft operations on the Turkish side of the frontier, and map the location of all Turkish posts. Any unauthorised personnel crossing from Syria to Turkey and vice versa were to be detained. Len King recalls the period on the frontier:

> We spread ourselves along the Syrian border and stayed there on watching operations, that's all. And there was no move through Turkey. It didn't happen. It's like a lot of things in wartime you spend a lot of time just waiting for something to happen. You're there in case. At times you must have been getting quite useful information but it wasn't obvious to the

A Corporal of No 2 Company has an amicable meeting with Turkish soldiers on the Syrian-Turkish border during Operation Turpitude (King).

ordinary erk. You'd see something and the officer in charge would radio where he thought the information needed to go.[21]

The frontier was not clearly marked in places, as Harry Fenwick recalls:

This trip was nearly my last one for the duration of the war. I was sent on a foot recce to get as close to the border as possible and I did. I finished up in Turkey and escaped by the skin of my teeth. We stayed here quite some time, keeping the Turks interested in us, and did a really good job of it.[22]

The Company's 'tickling' activities were reasonably successful and resulted in increases in the number of Turkish frontier guards. In one instance, 'B' Section, under Bill Prentice, quite innocently carried out firing practice with their Solothurn 20-mm cannon, and as a consequence caused the local Turkish guards to desert their posts and the inhabitants of a nearby Turkish village to be evacuated. This provided encouraging evidence that *Turpitude* had not been conducted in vain and that the activities of the cars had caused considerable nervousness. The task was however, tedious and trying on men and vehicles. Thankfully, despite the highly malarial nature of the area, no airmen contracted the disease nor did any vehicles suffer from any serviceability problems.

By early July, Operation *Turpitude* had partly served its function and with the

Flight Lieutenant Bill Prentice (Prentice).

Officers and NCOs of No 2 Armoured Car Company. Middle row second from left: Capt J.W.G. Grey, Flt Lt A.V. Attfield, Flt Lt S.F. Richardson, Sqn Ldr P.F. Murch, WO A.H. Davies; Flt Lt W.W. Prentice. Davies was the first WO to be promoted to that rank from within the RAF Armoured Cars (King).

success of Allied operations in Normandy, Italy and Southern France, the Operation had become superfluous and was quietly wound down. The Company returned to Ramleh, with one section going to Al Bassa as the entire unit could not now be accommodated at the former location.

Since the end of the North African campaign it had become apparent to Murch that the Company had no clear role in the RAF in the Middle East. With the creation of the RAF Regiment in 1942, many of the roles that the Armoured Car Companies had fulfilled prior to 1942 been assumed by the new Corps. Indeed, the field squadrons of the Regiment possessed their own AFV Flights, some equipped with the same GMC Otter, while in North-West Europe the RAF Regiment Armoured Car Squadrons were operating successfully with Humber light reconnaissance cars. The main focus of the War had moved on to Italy and France, and the RAF armoured car companies in the Middle East had reverted to their peacetime tasks.

By 1944, No 2 Company was experiencing great difficulty obtaining personnel, particularly trade-trained airmen, and by middle of the year was 40 men short of establishment. This was further exacerbated by the impeding loss of 30 time-expired airmen due to return to the United Kingdom. The shortage of armoured car crews was crippling the unit and Murch considered placing half the GMCs in storage as there were insufficient airmen to crew them, exacerbated by courses, guard duty, leave and sickness. This deficiency had been foreseen months earlier but there had been no response from higher authority to correspondence on the subject. In one instance, 35 of the 39 airmen sent as replacements were found to be unsuitable. Murch also believed that the flow of volunteers was being frustrated. In January 1945, Murch wrote:

> It is considered that in a number of cases Commanding Officers of Units are preventing airmen's applications from proceeding... There have been many instances of this reported through airmen of his Unit whose friends and

acquaintances in their own trade have made applications.

Volunteers are urgently required, and it is considered that there are a large number of suitable airmen who wish to transfer... the higher trade group and the more interesting work appeal to the better type of airman which is possibly why Unit Commanders are unwilling to recommend their applications.[23]

The GMC vehicles were also under considerable strain, with transmissions, axles and chassis having covered a total of 18,000 miles in Egypt, dealing with the Greek mutiny and then in Syria on *Turpitude* over rough and difficult terrain. Murch suggested that a search begin for a suitable replacement armoured car. This was of such concern that Squadron Leaders Alan Douglas and Philip Murch toured Army units in the Delta looking at a possible replacement vehicle which had been designed for desert reconnaissance and artillery observation.[24] A range of AFVs were trialled and evaluated over the next two years – the Staghound, Marmon-Herrington Mark IV, Humber Mark III, Daimler Mk II and the GMC Fox Mark I armoured cars, but none were ever found to be suitable or available in adequate numbers to replace the GMC Otters.

By August 1944, Squadron Leader Murch was becoming frustrated that the Company appeared not to be considered part of the Command Defence organisation of Air Headquarters Levant. The ORB noted:

There has been a singular lack of information or intelligence upon the Unit's role, or the intentions of Higher Authority with regard to the operational employment of the Company.[25]

Furthermore, Murch had noted in correspondence that his Section officers, some with seven years' experience, were not being selected for promotion to Staff positions. These positions were going to RAF Regiment officers who were ex-Army or RAF with no Armoured Car experience and most had only been commissioned during the early years of the War. Murch corresponded routinely and held regular meetings with Senior RAF Officers and Command Defence Officers to define a role for the RAF armoured car companies. 'Ted' Frith believed also that the roles of the two Companies had diverged over the course of the war:

No 2 Company tried to get us interested in aircraft cooperation but I was so keen that we should be 'spot defence' and 2 Company became [observers] for the aircraft people, but I was keen to look after our ships [aircraft on the ground].[26]

By late 1944, Murch had set about training No 2 Company for a number of roles within Air Headquarters Levant. The Company began experimenting with VHF and HF radio and carried out Exercise *John* with the brigades of the 5th Infantry Division and on Exercise *Scylla* working with the trainee army cooperation pilots of No 74 OTU to develop its air support capability, or "Rover-Tentacle patrols" as it had become known. The Company had possessed this capability during the final stages of the North African campaign but it seemed to have lapsed. Tactical reconnaissance exercises with pilots and Army liaison officers were organised, and the experience of those airmen who had performed the same task during the operations in Tunisia

As had happened since 1922, 'C' Section of No 2 Armoured Car Company make a halt at Qasr al Kharanah while on a training run, January 1944 (Prentice).

proved invaluable.

Murch had anticipated that internal security operations would become more common at the War's end and organised full-scale night exercises near Acre to provide training in convoy escort procedures. Road blocks, mines, booby traps and live mortar smoke bombs and gun cotton made for a realistic performance. It further reinforced the concept that GMCs operating singly were extremely vulnerable. Further to this end, the Company began familiarising itself with the Police wireless methods and frequencies in Palestine. During November 1944, the Sections were required to make nightly patrols at Nos 120 and 142 Maintenance Units. Two cars operating at the former were sent out singly; furthermore, two of the crew were ordered to do foot patrols by an officer at the MU, leaving only one crewman with the GMC. He would have been easy to overpower, and weapons and ammunition stolen. This was brought to the attention of the Command Defence Officer and there was comment that the advice of RAF Armoured Car officers with seven years' experience was being ignored and overridden by relatively junior officers of the RAF Regiment.

As RAF armoured cars were often called out to assist in the search for missing aircraft, Murch also arranged for an AFV at Al Bassa to be permanently tuned to the frequency of Air-Sea Rescue aircraft and High-Speed Launches so that they could remain in touch and act in concert with them should a search become necessary.

Number 1 Armoured Car Company, unlike No 2 Company which had moved all its personnel to Egypt and Libya during the fighting of 1941 to 1943, had been required to continue with its work in Iraq, while at the same time maintaining the HQ and Nos 1 and 3 Sections with the Western Desert Detachment. Thus, Nos 2 and 4 Sections in Iraq had alternated during 1941 and 1942 between RAF Habbaniya and Mosul.

The occupation of Iraq and Syria in 1941 had removed the direct threats to the British position in the Middle East. Furthermore, the August 1941 invasion of Persia by British and Russian forces had secured oilfields and the Abadan refineries, as well as providing a path to send weapons and supplies to Russia. However, the German successes in Russia meant that the British Command remained apprehensive about an enemy attack developing through Turkey and/or Iran via Anatolia or the Caucasus, thus threatening the oilfields around Mosul and Kirkuk.

The Tenth Army, formed in early 1942 was given the task of developing the defences of northern Iraq to meet this threat, albeit with limited numbers of troops, predominantly from the Indian Army. The British Commanders did not possess an adequate force to create a complete defence line, and so an armoured division and an infantry division were positioned around Mosul, and an infantry brigade at Zakho on the frontier, as well as in further defences to cover the passes and defiles across the Kurdish and Persian mountains. Concrete and barbed-wire defensive positions, anti-tank ditches and communications lines were constructed over the next few months.[27]

Advanced aerodromes and landing grounds were constructed in northern Iraq by the Indian Engineers for the RAF. The directive was that Iraq should be prepared to support a force of ten divisions and 30 RAF squadrons. However, in mid-1942, only two Indian infantry divisions and one Indian armoured division were available. With the burgeoning demands from other theatres, the RAF in Iraq was never composed of more than one or two squadrons with Hurricanes and Blenheims and a few flying boats.[28] The major part of the Tenth Army had been from the Indian Army; however, by late 1942 the Command had gained the 5th and 56th British Divisions, the 7th Armoured Brigade and later the Polish Army of the East, composed of Poles who had been evacuated from Soviet Russia after harsh treatment by Stalin (Map 2, p. 24; Map 6, p. 51).

Two landing grounds had been constructed to the north and south of Mosul and a sub-section each was given responsibility from August 1941, for Ain Zala and Quiyara, respectively. The former was located only a few miles south of the Turkish frontier, while the latter was 35 miles south of Mosul, on a long, flat, desolate plain overlooking the Tigris River. Apart from an airstrip, there was little more than a few dispersal huts and a couple of mud huts and a few tents.[29] Quiyara was never home to more than an army cooperation or light bomber squadron. The troops and airmen toiled in a climate of extremes with winter temperatures dropping to -9 °C and through the long heat of summer with day temperatures reaching 50 °C.

The RAF armoured cars provided constant protection to the landing grounds, patrolled the petrol and bomb dumps in the area and made local reconnaissances, road, bridge, and ferry inspections. Tactical exercises were held with the often changing Army units camped nearby, with such famous names as the 17th Poona Horse, as well as with their constant companions the Iraq Levies. In the case of the former, Nos 2 and 4 Sections unsuccessfully defended Mosul airfield against a mock attack by 30 armoured cars of the Poona Horse. A more mundane task was assigned to a single Rolls-Royce armoured car for a week, to clear the local natives from the firing range at Quiyara each morning to allow the Rhodesian Hurricane squadron to carry out firing practice.

There were still suspicions about Iraqi loyalty after the failure of the revolt led by Rashid Ali. In late June 1942, No 4 Section travelled out to Tel Kotchek on the Syrian border to investigate the movements of two Iraq Air Force Gladiators. They had landed and then immediately taken off again, and had then circled the landing ground at Ain Zala, suggesting that they were reconnoitring the local landing grounds. Their activities and intentions were concealed as much as possible and for what purpose was never revealed.

Sections travelled to the north and west of Mosul, out into the desert or up into northern Kurdistan to Rowanduz, to Qamichliye in Syria. While the major focus for operations now lay to the north, the new RAF armoured car crews gained experience on patrols into southern Iraq over the stamping grounds of old, to Basra and westward to Rutbah. On two occasions, during January and December 1942, the armoured cars escorted various RAF units farther afield into Iran to Kermanshah and Teheran.

The reorganisation of the Middle East Command in August 1942 led to the creation of Persia and Iraq Command, commonly known as 'Paiforce'. By late 1942, the threat of German invasion from the north had lessened as resistance on the Russian front stiffened and with the ensuing victory over the Germans and Italians at El Alamein. Following these successes, the size of 'Paiforce' gradually declined through 1943 as it was stripped of formations needed in other theatres. Ain Zala and Quiyara airfields became less important and the Company ceased patrol work at these locations, with the Sections spending much of the remainder of the year at Habbaniya. The No 1 Armoured Car Company Detachment that had been stationed at RAF Cairo West finally returned to Habbaniya during December.

The Rolls-Royces had continued their loyal and unflagging service, along with a few new Fordsons. However, in September 1943 the inevitable occurred and they were replaced entirely by the GMC armoured cars. During 1943, newly-arrived personnel were sent to the Armoured Car Course at the No 3 (Middle East) Training School at Amman.[30]

While the greater strategic problems had passed in Iraq, there still remained the ethnic and religious differences that had occupied so much of the time of the RAF from 1921 to 1932. In November 1943, the Company was visited at Mosul by the AOC Iraq and Persia, Air Vice-Marshal R.P. Willock CB. This would have been a memorable occasion for Willock as he had been the first commander of No 4 Armoured Car Company from 1922 to 1924 during the operations against Sheikh Mahmud in Southern Kurdistan when he had been mentioned in despatches.

During the dark days of 1941 and into 1942, the Kurds had caused little anxiety to the Iraqi Government or British forces. However, coincidentally only a few weeks after Willock's visit there was an uprising in Northern Kurdistan by the Kurds who had become increasingly concerned as to their place in the Iraqi state. Led by Mullah Mustafa, the brother of Sheikh Ahmed Barzani, his grievances were mostly related to local problems – amnesties for gaoled family members and alleviation of the devastating famine that was afflicting the villages under his protection. At a more strategic, political level he was also demanding the creation of a Kurdish governorate separate from that currently being administered from Mosul. With the Baghdad Government's promises of help with food aid failing to materialise, he rallied his tribes and having obtained weapons after overrunning police and frontier posts, he launched an insurgency. The Iraqi Army reacted violently, shelling and bombing Mustafa's villages and exacerbating the starvation of his people. The Iraqi Army for celebrations for VJ Day, 15 August, were postponed due to the Company being placed on an operational footing due to disturbances with the local Kurds. The event was finally marked on 3, 4 and 5 September with a dinner and a two-day holiday.

Squadron Leader David Hellard, now an RAF Regiment officer, having transferred from the General Duties Branch, and who had led the armoured car sorties from RAF Habbaniya in May 1941, had assumed command on 22 September 1945 from Squadron Leader R.J. Payne. On the same day, a Farewell Party was held in the Officers' Mess as the RAF was to withdraw permanently from Mosul airfield. Mosul had been the Company's home for two years with at least one section of No 1 Armoured Car Company resident from the cessation of the revolt in May 1941, and the HQ and two or more sections from November 1943. At 0730 hours on 1 October 1945, the RAF armoured cars departed Mosul for the last time and returned to RAF Habbaniya, being bade farewell by the Officer-Commanding No 1 Squadron of the Royal Iraqi Air Force and the AOC's representative.

The Allied forces that had been stationed in Iraq and Persia from 1942 onwards, had played an unglamorous but an important part in the overall victory. They had kept open the overland route for supplies to the Russian armies on their southern front. The all-important Middle East oil supplies had been assured, thus delivering the essential fuel needed for the forces fighting on the sea, land and in the air.

Meanwhile in Palestine, many of the officers who had been with the No 2 Armoured Car Company for the duration of the war were departing. Flight Lieutenant Bill Prentice, an Australian from Queensland, had been with the Company since El Alamein and had been 'B' Section commander since July 1943. His wife, 'Paddy' who served in the Women's Auxiliary Air Force, remembered how well he took to the job:

> He had spent years roaming the deserts with No 2 Armoured Car Company – a choice he'd made after being told he was too old for flying duties in the RAAF, but could be seconded to the RAF Armoured Cars. This suited his outdoor nature – having previously been employed on cattle stations; the last as Manager of 'Cork', a big holding in outback Queensland. A bush experience from which his crew were to benefit and appreciate as he

The King's Birthday Parade 1945 in Jerusalem, led by Flight Lieutenant Bill Prentice (King)

had more expertise in improvising whatever sources were available when provisions ran short and he was a 'dab hand' at making dampers![35]

Len King recalled Bill Prentice:

He always wore an Australian bush hat. He was in charge of the Section for a long time. But when you went gazelle hunting he was the man who used to butcher them for us. He was a quite a character and very well liked.[36]

Bill Prentice's last major task, only six days before being posted from the Company for repatriation to Australia, was to lead 12 GMC armoured cars from No 2 Company as the 'RAF Mechanised Detachment' in the King's Birthday Parade on 14 June 1945 in Jerusalem. All the cars had been specially spray-painted, tow chains burnished and tyres cleaned with graphite, all of which gave them a very smart appearance. The High Commissioner to Palestine, Field Marshal Lord Gort, took the salute, and in a congratulatory signal sent to the Company he said:

Nobody who witnessed the parade could fail to be impressed by the military bearing of the veterans of many campaigns and by the peacetime turnout of their war scarred vehicles.[37]

The two RAF Armoured Car Companies ended the war at their pre-war stations of Habbaniya and Ramleh. At the cessation of hostilities, Great Britain had fought a costly war that had left it drained of funds, resources and manpower. Within a few months, the vast majority of the Allied air forces in and around the Mediterranean had to be sent home and a peacetime RAF re-established. The Levant had been relatively free of domestic troubles, or at least they had been suppressed during the war years, but as it reached its conclusion two conflicts came back into prominence; the political future of Syria and the intractable problem of reconciling the Arab and Jewish struggle over Palestine.

Notes

1. AIR 29/52 *1 Armoured Car Company, Mosul, Iraq; Form 765A daily operations and statistical summary. Appendices only, February-August 1944.* Correspondence: Disposal of Applications made by DMT's [Drivers, Mechanical Transport] for posting for Training as Armoured Car Crew, P.F. Murch to Air HQ Levant, 21 January 1945.
2. L. King, *Interview with the author*, 2008.
3. The Italians were from the ADRA or *Arditi Distruttori Regia Aeronautica*. The tip-off as to their location came from local Senussi tribesman
4. Nos 2912, 2916, 2917, 2918, 2919, 2926, 2927, 2933 Squadrons RAF Regiment.
5. AIR 29/51 *1 Armoured Car Company, Habbaniya, Iraq; appendices only, mostly Movement Orders, includes three photographs of armoured cars May 1946; includes appendices for 4 Section, 1 ACC and 1 ACC Detachment Western Desert, May 1936-June 1943.*
6. The Auto Union cars were kept on the establishment until 1947, by which time the remaining car was being used as the staff car of the CO, Squadron Leader Kennedy.
7. R. Ferguson, *Interview with J. Rolph*, RAF Armoured Cars Association, 2008
8. *Ibid.*
9. *Ground Defence Narrative, Chapter III*, RAF Regiment Museum Archives.

10. The Company was reorganised at this time into three sections: Flight Lieutenant Prentice 'B' Section; Flight Lieutenant Attfield 'C' Section and Flight Lieutenant Edwards HQ and 'A' Section.
11. Later Colonel Joyclyn William Gladstone Gray, was born in Durban, Natal in 1909. He had been a regular officer in the South African Artillery and had evaded capture when his Regiment was overrun during the Battle of Gazala in the dark days of June 1942.
12. C.J.C. Molony *et al.*, *The Mediterranean and Middle East, Vol. V,* History of the Second World War (London: HMSO, 1973), pp. 570-571.
13. The remaining 15 Rolls-Royce armoured cars, five Rolls-Royce wireless tenders and six Fordsons were handed over in Egypt during September 1943.
14. Air Vice-Marshal E.L. Frith RAF Retd, Interview with the author, 2007. Air Commodore T.C.R. Higgins CB CMG (1880-1953) was the Chief Staff Officer for Iraq Command during the operations against the Ikhwan in the Southern Desert during 1930.
15. L. King, *Interview with the author*.
16. AM or the National Liberation Front was the principal resistance organisation in occupied Greece and was largely controlled by Communists.
17. W.G.F. Jackson *et al.*, *The Mediterranean and Middle East, Vol VI, Part 2,* History of the Second World War (London: HMSO, 1987), p. 206.
18. *Ibid.*, p. 207.
19. Nos 2902, 2908 & 2924 Field Squadrons and 2932 LAA Squadron RAF Regiment. The Army component of the deception was known as Operation *Reviver*.
20. AIR 29/55 *Operations Record Book: No 2 Armoured Car Company, January 1940-October 1946*.
21. L. King, *Interview with the author*.
22. H. Fenwick, *Reminiscences* (Archives of the RAF Armoured Cars Association, 1972).
23. AIR 29/52 *1 Armoured Car Company, Mosul, Iraq*. Correspondence: Disposal of Applications made by DMT's for posting for Training as Armoured Car Crew, P.F. Murch to Air HQ Levant 21 January 1945.
24. AIR 29/56 *2 Armoured Car Company, appendices only; September 1923-July 1946*.
25. AIR 29/55 *Operations Record Book: No 2 Armoured Car Company*.
26. Frith, Interview with the author.
27. Anon, *Paiforce: The Official Story of the Persia and Iraq Command 1941-1946* (London: HMSO, 1948), pp. 424-426.
28. I.S.O. Playfair *et al.*, *The Mediterranean and Middle East, Vol. III,* History of the Second World War (London: HMSO, 1960), pp. 416 and 424. Air HQ Iraq in November 1941 had three squadrons: No 52 at Habbaniya (Audaxes); No 244 Squadron at Shaibah (Vincents) and No 261 Squadron at Mosul (Hurricane Is). By September 1942, little had changed with Air Vice-Marshal H.V. Champion de Crespigny having only one tactical reconnaissance squadron stationed at Mosul. At the end of the year, there were two light bomber squadrons in Iraq, while Persia had received two fighter squadrons and tactical reconnaissance squadron.
29. M. Lax, *Alamein to the Alps. 454 Squadron RAAF 1941-1945* (Wanniassa [ACT]: Published by the author, 2006), p. 14.
30. Armoured Car personnel were on longer being trained in the United Kingdom, other than with the RAF Regiment and the responsibility now lay with RAF Middle East.
31. D. Gore, *On Kentish Chalk: A Farming Family of the North Downs* (Newbury [Berks]: Published by the author, 2006), pp. 93-94, and C. Tripp, *A History of Iraq* (Cambridge: Cambridge University Press, 2000), p. 111.
32. R. Ahmed, *History of the Baloch Regiment, 1939-1956* (Uckfield, UK: Naval & Military Press, 2004), p. 36.
33. WO 169/14974 *1/10 Baluch Regiment, December 1943* and 169/18977 *1/10 Baluch Regiment, January 1944*.
34. Relations between the Iraqi Government and Mullah Mustafa, Sheikh Ahmed and 3000 followers soon soured and they were forced into exile in Kurdish Iran. When the war

ended, the Iranian Government turned on the Kurds, and Mustafa then moved to the USSR. He returned to Iraq in 1958 following the successful coup against the Hashemite monarchy where he led the Kurdish Democratic Party. His continued pursuit of autonomy for Iraq's Kurds again led him into conflict with the central Government, and by 1974 he and his followers had again crossed back into Iran. He spent the remainder of his life in Iran and died from lung cancer in 1979 while being treated in Washington DC. He was then buried in Iranian Kurdistan; however, in October 1993, his remains were returned to Iraq. They were presented to his grandson Nerchevan Idris Barzani, now the major power-broker in the Kurdistan Regional Government, and they were interred in his hometown of Barzan, north of Rowanduz. An RAF Regiment officer in the party invited to witness the return of the remains was Squadron Leader Russell La Forte who was then serving for six months with the Military Coordination Centre in Northern Iraq. Under the umbrella of the Coalition's (US, UK, France and Turkey) Operation *Provide Comfort 2* (known by the UK as Operation *Warden*), this was a small team of Allied personnel monitoring the security situation in the Kurdish Autonomous Zone following the First Gulf War. La Forte was subsequently appointed an MBE for distinguished operational service whilst in Northern Iraq, from where immediately following his return in June 1994 and until December 1996, he went on to command 1 Squadron RAF Regiment, the successor to No 1 Armoured Car Company.

35 Phyllis 'Paddy' Prentice, *A Story to Tell - Paddy Prentice (O'Brien) (Gold Coast, Qld: Unpublished Memoirs, 1986)*. 'Paddy' Prentice (née O'Brien) was an Australian and served in the Women's Auxiliary Air Force in Egypt during the Second World War. She worked in Codes & Cyphers in Unit Signals at Headquarters RAF Middle East Cairo and achieved the rank of Squadron Officer. Damper is a simple bread made from flour and water and was commonly prepared by Australian stockmen and drovers working in remote areas.

36 W.W. 'Bill' Prentice served in No 2 Company from August 1942 to June 1945.

37 AIR 29/55 *Operations Record Book: No 2 Armoured Car Company.*

Chapter Twenty-One

Palestine 1945-1948
An Insurgency Re-ignited and Transition to the RAF Regiment

"Armoured Cars were invaluable... their mobility and fire power were important factors in the defence of Stations and of the scattered buildings we occupied in Jerusalem."

Air Vice-Marshal W.L. Dawson, AOC Levant[1]

"You'd never done anything or been in that sort of country before. It was exciting, I wouldn't have missed it."

AC1 Bert Bayliss, No 2 Armoured Car Squadron, RAF Regiment[2]

Five and a half years of total war had led to the decisive defeat of the Axis powers, but there still remained unresolved pre-war conflicts in the Middle East. The conflict in Palestine was renewed with increasing vigour, new political movements had arisen in the Middle East, and Arab nationalism was resurgent. Moreover, there were new fears over the expansionist aims of the Soviet Union, in particular its intentions towards the oil resources of Iran, Iraq and Saudi Arabia. British post-war military policy in the Middle East was two-fold; firstly, the protection of the sea, land and air communications between the United Kingdom, India and the Far East and secondly, maintenance of the security of oil installations and transport routes.

The Middle East therefore remained a strong focus of the post-war RAF activity. Palestine was an important base for the British Army and the RAF and as a consequence there had been an extensive airfield construction programme. At a strategic level, the defence of Palestine was considered necessary to secure Egypt, the main British base in the Mediterranean, as well as oil pipelines and land communications to Transjordan and Iraq. The number of RAF assets had significantly increased during the War years and the task of protecting these required a larger force. A newspaper article written at this time wrote in glowing terms of the RAF armoured cars:

'ONE OF THE BEST JOBS IN THE RAF'
That is the opinion of all ranks in No 2 RAF Armoured Car Company in Palestine… With the end of the war the company has not finished its job. It goes on in an unobtrusive manner, doing a multitude of jobs in a quiet efficient way. Day and night, sections rumble out from base to patrol many hundreds of miles of barren hill country and tortuous mountain roads … Each individual crew member is a specialist, not in one, but in many jobs.[3]

Number 2 Armoured Car Company resumed its role in Palestine and Transjordan but with an increased internal security task. Rifle squadrons of the RAF Regiment were soon required to join them. By mid-1945, Number 2 Company had its Headquarters and two sections at RAF Ramleh, another section at RAF Ramat David in northern Palestine near Nazareth, and the fourth at RAF Amman. The detachment at Ramat David continued with Air-Support Control training with the pilots of the resident fighter squadron and the section at Amman concentrated on desert training, navigation and field firing. Each section rotated through these locations at three-monthly intervals.

With the departure of the airmen from No 2 Company who had served for the duration of the War, new RAF armoured car crews had to be found. Squadron Leader Murch remained frustrated at the shortage of personnel, partly the result of changes in the ground defence organisation of the RAF consequent upon the formation of the RAF Regiment. The recruitment and training structure for the armoured car companies no longer existed and the number of volunteers had either dried up or a proportion of those that arrived had proven unsatisfactory. Murch was eventually given permission to obtain armoured car crews using his own officers and, during

HQ staff and 'A' Flight of No 2 Armoured Car Squadron parade outside the Armoured Cars garage at Ramleh in early 1947 (Lock, RAFACA).

unrest, strikes and street-fighting between Syrian and French troops in the large towns. This led ultimately to the bombardment of the mosques and the parliament in Damascus by French artillery and aircraft, causing many civilian casualties and much destruction.

The British had been observing this situation and by late May 1945 had determined to act to prevent any further bloodshed. This was despite French suspicions that this was merely an attempt to extend British influence into Syria. General Sir Bernard Paget, C-in-C Middle East Forces, was therefore placed in overall command of all Allied forces in Syria, including French colonial troops, and ordered by Churchill to intervene. On 1 June, British troops of the 1st Division, in full fighting equipment and with vehicles emblazoned with the Union Jack, crossed the Syrian border and joined those already there, including the 31st Indian Armoured Division. Ostensibly they were there to carry out manoeuvres and exercises; however, a curfew was imposed, French offices were picqueted by British soldiers, while French colonial troops were ordered to cease fire and were confined to barracks.[4]

Detachments of No 2 Armoured Car Company had been in Syria since mid-May for exercises with a brigade of the 1st British Division near Damascus. 'Lofty' Hodge recalls:

> From Amman I was posted to RAF Ramat David in Northern Palestine where 'D' Section was serving. I did about four weeks as a gunner and then a chap went home and I was immediately put on as a driver.
>
> In that month, 'D' Section went to Syria. The French were having a terrible time with the Arabs – they were bombing Damascus. The French were on Mezze airfield, two miles outside Damascus. And they were taking off in their medium bombers and bombing suburbs in Damascus, only two miles away... so we were sent to that airfield, but we didn't go anywhere near the French, we camped just inside the wire.

The complexity of the Syrian situation was brought home to the airmen when they were required to collect their rations which were located at the Army depot in the middle of Damascus. Hodge continues:

> We had to send a 3-ton Dodge into Damascus every day to pick up our rations. And believe you me that was really scary. One of us had to go with a driver. We took turns in that. And you couldn't take any weapons with you. You drove into Damascus and a huge mob used to roar down this street at you, and they jumped on your running boards – and all you could do – if you were French you were [cut across throat] - if you were English you shouted out "Englezi! Englezi!" and they'd let you go on and you could collect the rations.

During May and June 1945, one of the principal activities for No 2 Company was operating as Forward Control Posts in Air-Support exercises in Syria with 1st British Infantry Division and 31st Indian Armoured Division of Ninth Army.[5] 'Lofty' Hodge continues:

> While we were there, the British Army put on a huge war game involving a division that was near to us at Mezze. They also involved a squadron of

Spitfires from Ramat David, our camp. And we actually had one of their officers with us, one of the pilots. And we had to go up into the hills and observe this battle going on. It was all put on to impress the Arabs in Syria.

The Spitfires came from Ramat David. It was only 20 minutes flying from there. They used to bring our mail up which was always in a big cigarette tin with a streamer on it; and before they did this they'd come whizzing down; they used to shoot us up first and nearly take the whip aerials off the cars. Of course we had VHF sets and we were talking to em, and this RAF officer who was with us would say, "You stupid bastards, you want to see what it looks like from down here."

When we went back to the airfield at Ramat David, we didn't go straight back down the main road, we went to Beirut. It's not far, about two hours, and believe it or not, at Beirut there were all sorts of explosions. We had a South African who was our Section CO, Pat Gray, and he went down in his jeep and had a look and when he came back said "We're going round the outside." He took us round the back route, but we could hear it all going on.[6]

For the first time since operations in Tunisia and Tripolitania in 1943, the Company was called on to provide direct air-support control. Although not used to the extent hoped for, the GMCs were often used purely as signals vehicles for airfield control and to maintain HF radio contact between columns and formations and the Advanced Air Headquarters Levant, situated in Beirut.

A two-car detachment of 'A' Section established itself at RAF Aleppo in the first week of June where they guarded aircraft and cooperated with the Indian Armoured Division, They were relieved by two more Forward Control Post Cars from 'C' Section while the detachment of 'A' Section, under the command of Flight Lieutenant Richardson, moved further into Syria to join 'Scottforce'. They headed eastwards through Palmyra, the battleground where in 1941 No 2 Company had fought the Vichy ground and air forces with such a limited force and in such trying circumstances. At Palmyra and other towns they passed through, the RAF armoured car crews received an enthusiastic reception from the Syrian locals. At Raqqa, an insubstantial town of a few single-story Arab dwellings and some irrigated fields on the banks of the Euphrates, they joined the main body of 'Scottforce', comprising the tanks of the 3rd Hussars, and 144th Field Regiment RA. Their task was to restore civil order and ensure the safe evacuation of the French military, civilians and families from the scattered desert outposts in eastern Syria. While limited in numbers, the aim of 'Scottforce' was to give the impression of greater strength than in fact they possessed, and in more than one place at the same time. A case for the armoured cars of *plus ça change, plus c'est la même chose*.[7]

Richardson's detachment of two GMCs then moved further down the Euphrates to operate with 'Bedouforce' at Deir ez Zor, which was primarily concerned with preventing French or Syrian patriotism or injured national pride flaring into wholesale slaughter. The detachment operated in conditions of considerable discomfort with temperatures of 50°C, dust storms and high winds. As they were the local RAF representatives, the detachment of only eight or so airmen was placed under some duress when they were required to provide accommodation and catering for any RAF visitors or personnel, including, on one occasion some 30 officers and airmen of No 32 Squadron and No 226 Mobile Signals Unit. The detachment had been living in the garden of the house occupied by 'Bedouforce' Headquarters, and to cope with the influx were given permission by Advanced Air Headquarters Levant to occupy the buildings on the nearby French airfield. They also signalled the Company Headquarters to send cooking utensils and furniture; the nearby Army units being unable to provide for them. Their presence was however welcome as in one instance they had maintained the only link with Ninth Army Headquarters, due to a delay of 24 hours in setting up the Army Signals network, and later due to extreme heat causing failure in the Army wireless equipment. The radio systems of the Company, on which considerable effort had been expended, were shown to be very effective with American Collins 18Q HF radio equipment proving capable of reaching the 500 miles from Deir ez Zor to Ramleh.[8]

As the Syrian situation headed towards a satisfactory conclusion due to the British intervention, the detachments at Aleppo and Deir ez Zor were recalled in mid to late 1945. The League of Nations Mandate for Syria was allowed to lapse and French power gradually ebbed away. After a period of intense diplomacy, agreement was reached for the withdrawal of both French and British forces (allaying any suspicions that the British were taking over) and the process was completed by August 1946.[9]

As the war had drawn to a close, the pre-war enmity between Arabs and Jews in Palestine was re-ignited. The British Government had been completely unsuccessful in meeting the aspirations of either the Arabs for independence or the burgeoning Jewish population's desire to create a Jewish state. Five years of war and Nazi persecution had created a vast group of homeless and stateless Jews in Europe who wished to settle in Palestine. The President of the United States of America, Harry S. Truman, was therefore pressuring the British Government to immediately admit more Jewish immigrants into Palestine.[10] The British Government considered this unacceptable due to the hostility it would engender with the Arabs. An effective organisation to infiltrate Jews into Palestine was set in train and there was an increase in acts of terrorism against the British administration and forces. The British forces were to receive little support or goodwill from the population and would suffer opprobrium and resentment for decisions made by their Government in the United Kingdom.

The concept of Air Control had been proven not to be practicable in Palestine, and by 1945 the means by which an insurgency operated had significantly changed. Most Jews in Palestine lived in settlements where they had formed their own defence organisations, and many had received military training from the British forces during the war, with some serving with distinction. But with the advent of peace they turned their efforts to the creation of a Jewish state. A number of Jewish paramilitary organisations, the Haganah[11], Palmach, and more ruthless groups such as the Irgun Zvai Leumi, Lochmei Heruth Israel and the Stern Gang launched an insurgency with the aim of the expelling the British. Many of the personnel were experienced and skilled saboteurs, who had learnt their trade operating in resistance movements while fighting the Germans in occupied Europe. The first strike had been by the Stern Gang with the assassination of Lord Moyne, the British Minister of State, in Cairo on 6 November 1944, who was targeted for his unsympathetic views on the plight of the Jews in Europe.

The first insurgent attacks were made in Palestine during October 1945, although as 'Lofty' Hodge recalls, in the early months of that year, relations with the Jews already in Palestine had been reasonably friendly:

Actually we used to work on kibbutzes before the war finished. Nothing happened till then. There was one outside Ramat David and, if you had a day off, you used to go up there and work. The terrorists, they had a truce with the British until the Germans were defeated.[12]

The situation would however, deteriorate quickly and develop into a terrorist campaign against the railway system, government, military and police, with robberies, kidnappings, shootings and bombings. The British Garrison was reinforced with the 6th Airborne Division and by January 1946 there would be more than 80,000 troops in Palestine. The main tasks of the RAF were air-cooperation with the Army during cordon and search operations in villages and towns, locating and identifying the ships bringing Jewish would-be immigrants to the shores of Palestine, and patrolling the oil pipeline from Iraq to Haifa and the single, very vulnerable water pipeline to Jerusalem.[13]

With the role of the RAF in these operations having been identified by the Jewish insurgents, RAF installations were soon being targeted. During August 1945, No 2 Armoured Car Company and some RAF Regiment gunners were detailed to provide escorts to contractors' vehicles conveying high explosive between RAF airfields, where there was considerable building activity, and local quarries. These and the arms and ammunition convoys were proving tempting targets for the Jewish insurgents. As the year drew to a close, and the situation deteriorated, the demands placed on the Company for convoy escort increased, as did the need for more Forward Control Post work as the number of fighter squadrons in the Levant increased. Night patrols of RAF Stations were instituted and with the increasing threat from mines, bomb-plates were re-fitted to the armoured cars for the first time since 1943. Despite all these demands, the section in Transjordan found time to complete a survey of several hundred miles of rough and difficult desert tracks.

In January 1946, all RAF units in the Levant were brought to a state of maximum defence readiness. This placed immense responsibility on the RAF Regiment squadrons and No 2 Armoured Car Company, having to spread themselves thinly across hospitals and medical and maintenance units, signals installations and radar sites as well as airfields. Number 2 Company began dusk to dawn patrols at the Air Headquarters Levant Telecommunications Centre at Ramleh and RAF stations at Ramat David, Petah Tiqva and Aqir. Usually of two cars, one would patrol the hangars and aircraft, while the other went around the airfield perimeter. Whereas the RAF Regiment rifle squadrons would concentrate on static and close protection of RAF installations, the most appropriate role for aerodrome defence for the RAF armoured cars was as a mobile reserve on RAF stations and very profitably as convoy escorts.[14]

Only three days after issuing the alert, there was an abortive attack on the radar station known as No 5 Air Ministry Experiment Station on Mount Carmel. On 28 January, the Irgun attempted to steal 600 Sten guns and ammunition from No 160 Maintenance Unit; however, their escape was thwarted when their truck became bogged. Undeterred, the Haganah struck at the radar station on Mount Carmel again on 20 February and succeeded in making it unserviceable. Further weapons were also taken from No 10 Medical Rehabilitation Unit in Tel Aviv.

Far worse was to come when on the night of 25/26 February there were simultaneous attacks mounted against RAF stations at Qastina, Petah Tiqva and Lydda. The RAF suffered its heaviest losses on the ground since the Luftwaffe offensive in the Ardennes on 1 January 1945, with 11 Halifaxes, seven Spitfires, two

Ansons and three Army Austers destroyed or damaged beyond repair.

The Spitfires belonged to Nos 32 and 208 Squadrons at RAF Petah Tiqva. The first sign of the attack was at 2040 hours when the air was rent with explosions among the dispersed Spitfires. Three GMCs of No 2 Company were on patrol that night under the command of Flying Officer H.E.G. Price. Price immediately took his cars towards the exploding aircraft and came under carefully prepared direct fire from outside the perimeter wire. He had however, noticed that the damage had been caused by delayed-action bombs made from sticks of gelignite placed in the radiator intakes of the Spitfires. Showing a cool temperament and great courage he was able to dismantle one such device before it could detonate. He then took his cars on an extensive search of the airfield perimeter. Despite not finding any saboteurs he did discover two cuts in the perimeter wire, one of which was found to be booby-trapped.[15]

The attacks had been carefully planned and executed and this brought home the serious inadequacies of the defence of RAF Qastina, Petah Tiqva and Lydda airfields. With the rapid demobilisation and the release of all 'hostilities only' airmen, RAF Levant was suffering from serious undermanning. This included the RAF in Palestine in general, and the RAF Regiment rifle squadrons in particular. They were often composed of men who had survived six years of war and had had enough, or were 'raw and untrained boys' in the words of the AOC Levant, Air Commodore William Dawson CB CBE.[16] This had its recurring problems as technical staff faced increasing demands for night guard duties while still performing their daytime tasks. Security and alarm procedures were tightened and a further RAF Regiment Wing, No 1320, with Nos 2771 and 2908 (Rifle) Squadrons, was brought in during March 1946 from their role in the occupation force in Austria. A further addition was No 2742 Armoured Car Squadron which arrived from the United Kingdom. Rather surprisingly however, it was disbanded after only a few months.

Number 2 Company had its recurring problems of obtaining replacement officers and airmen as others departed, including the loss of experienced senior NCOs. The shortage of trained personnel made it necessary to temporarily disband 'A' Section for a period during early 1946. Some idea of the degree to which Number 2 Company was fully stretched can be seen in the ORB during February. As well as having detachments at Ramleh, Ramat David and Petah Tiqva on aerodrome defence, a detachment proceeded to the landing ground at Wilhelma to meet a Lockheed Ventura carrying Jewish prisoners, who were then handed over to the Palestine Police and escorted to Jerusalem. Armoured cars had travelled to Ramallah and Nablus, patrolled at Kolundia, made a road recce in Northern Palestine, provided convoy escort to Lydda railway station while others were on Forward Control Post work with 6th Airborne Division.

As early as September 1942, there had been a proposal that the RAF Armoured Car Companies be amalgamated into the RAF Regiment. The absence of a higher formation to control training, planning for replacement of crews and vehicles, and of a main base for refitting and retraining had been noted at that time. Many of these problems however, had recurred through 1943 until 1946, with a fair number of *ad hoc* responses to changing theatres of operations, personnel and equipment. A policy for supply of suitable officers together with consideration of their position relative to RAF Regiment officers was discussed but not clearly resolved. The armoured car company officers were to be over 33 years of age, or if under, unfit for aircrew. To preserve the history and identity of the armoured car companies it had also been suggested that they be allotted a distinctive badge; however, nothing came of the proposals.[17] Despite the problems, the men of the RAF armoured cars were still highly regarded at this time, as Dick Lock recalls:

> We were well received at the various RAF camps we were detached to and were also made very welcome by the Palestine Police with whom we patrolled Tel Aviv and Jerusalem. At a more exalted level we were less enthusiastically welcomed. Number 2 Armoured Car Company was directly controlled by AOC Levant (we carried a signed 'chitty' to that effect in each car) and the deployment of our cars was in the hands of each Flight Commander. This led to difficulties with the RAF airfield commanding officers who tried to order our crews to alter their positions or guard routines without consulting our officers. This did lead to some Station Commanders being required to account for their actions to the AOC himself. On the other hand many officers and NCOs at bases were detached to work with us so they could appreciate our particular problems of being 'lodgers', often at short notice, and went out of their way to help us.[18]

By the final year of the war, the RAF Regiment had formed a total of six armoured car squadrons equipped with the Humber Mark IIIA light reconnaissance car for service in North-West Europe following D-Day. Meanwhile, the Armoured Car Flights of the RAF Regiment Field Squadrons deployed to Italy and Greece had been used productively in a number of roles similar to those performed by the Armoured Car Companies. It therefore seemed inevitable that the Companies would either be disbanded and disappear altogether from the RAF Order of Battle, or that they would be amalgamated into the RAF Regiment.

The first sign of change in the wind was that RAF Regiment officers and airmen began arriving on the Companies as replacements. The most significant manifestation of this being during March 1946 when both No 1 and No 2 Armoured Car Companies received new Commanding Officers, both of whom were RAF Regiment. The command of the former was assumed by Squadron Leader J.S. Deag, who arrived at RAF Habbaniya to replace Squadron Leader Hellard, and the latter by Squadron Leader C.G.E. Kennedy, who assumed command of No 2 Armoured Car Company from Philip Murch. Murch had been Officer Commanding since 30 August 1943 and some credit must be given to him for his tenacity in regularly keeping his superiors at Air Headquarters Levant aware of his Company's existence and its diverse capabilities or deficiencies in equipment or personnel, as evidenced by the copious correspondence found in the ORB.

With the departure of personnel who had chosen not to remain with the armoured cars, 'Lofty' Hodge had soon reached the rank of Flight Sergeant. He continues:

> I was at RAF Ramat David when the change to the Regiment happened. We had a Group Captain, from the RAF Regiment, who came around and told us all about it. And shortly after that we had the options; you could either stop serving on the cars, or you could go in the Regiment.
>
> But I'd lost three guys and I had to have those replaced of course. So we went to Jerusalem and settled in there. I was three bods short, so I ended up with three gunners from the RAF Regiment, and I can always remember it when they came. They brought 'em in a 15-cwt from Ramleh and they

The view over the Old City of Jerusalem from the airmen's billets at Air Headquarters (Hodge).

dropped them off and they started walking up and they'd got big boots on and gaiters. And I said to them "Are you coming to join the Company?" I said "The first thing you can do is take those gaiters off, I'm not having you trampling all over my cars with those bloody great boots on." So I said "Put your shoes on and don't wear gaiters." They said "Do you mean it?" I said "Of course I mean it." And they fitted in lovely, they were good guys.[19]

A few weeks later, Squadron Leader Kennedy made a complete inspection of 'A' and 'B' Sections and lectured the men on the local situation, dress and discipline, although his attempts to change to Regiment ways met with disapproval from some.[20] Courses were begun for RAF Regiment gunners arriving from the United Kingdom and RAF personnel were posted as they become surplus to establishment.[21] The exodus of armoured car crewmen from the companies at the end of war had made the on-going operation of the armoured car companies difficult. Furthermore, there was a pool of trained gunners coming through from the RAF Regiment Depot who could readily perform the job.[22] Dick Lock was a Wireless Operator/Mechanic on 'A' Flight of No 2 Armoured Car Company. He had trained at Cranwell as an Aircraft Apprentice from 1943 to 1945 and joined the Company in March 1946 where he underwent 'on the job' training. As he recalls:

> Morale was affected by the sudden transfer of the Company to the RAF Regiment with far too little thought given to the wisdom of sending untrained personnel to a unit heavily engaged in high profile patrols with the Police, and other exacting duties. It is to the credit of our Flight Commanders and of the incoming NCOs and men that after a month or two the Company was able to perform to its normal high standards and to continue its particular regard for teamwork and adaptability without resorting to harsh discipline.
>
> We were fortunate in that all our Flight Commanders were very experienced and forceful leaders. Among them was Flight Lieutenant 'Jimmy' James, an extrovert Welshman who was my Flight CO for much of the time.... LAC

O'Keefe, a lorry driver and nutter, managed to overturn a 3-tonner. Flight Lieutenant James supervised matters. Two cars with hawsers attached to the lorry, and a third car restraining the lorry as it was hauled upright. There was only damage to the paintwork, so the incident was treated as a lesson in vehicle recovery and the bother of paperwork avoided.[23]

Some of the officers and airmen of the armoured car companies who had signed up as RAF personnel had no intention of converting to RAF Regiment, many for sensible reasons due to concerns over maintenance of their trade qualifications. Fred Morris was one of many who had been aircrew under training, while others were ex-aircrew, and who had become surplus to requirements. There were plenty in the pipeline by the time they joined up and the dreadful losses, particularly in Bomber Command, had now abated significantly. Remustering to Driver, he waited six months for a course and on completion was posted to Egypt. He joined No 2 Company from Al Maza Transit Camp in Egypt following a request for volunteers and arrived in Palestine in January 1946. For many like him, when the announcement was made about the conversion to RAF Regiment, it was yet another change after many and most had had enough of this and were just happy to do their time as RAF and go.[24]

It also needs to be understood however, that in the early years of the RAF Regiment there was considerable resentment among some RAF tradesmen at being posted to

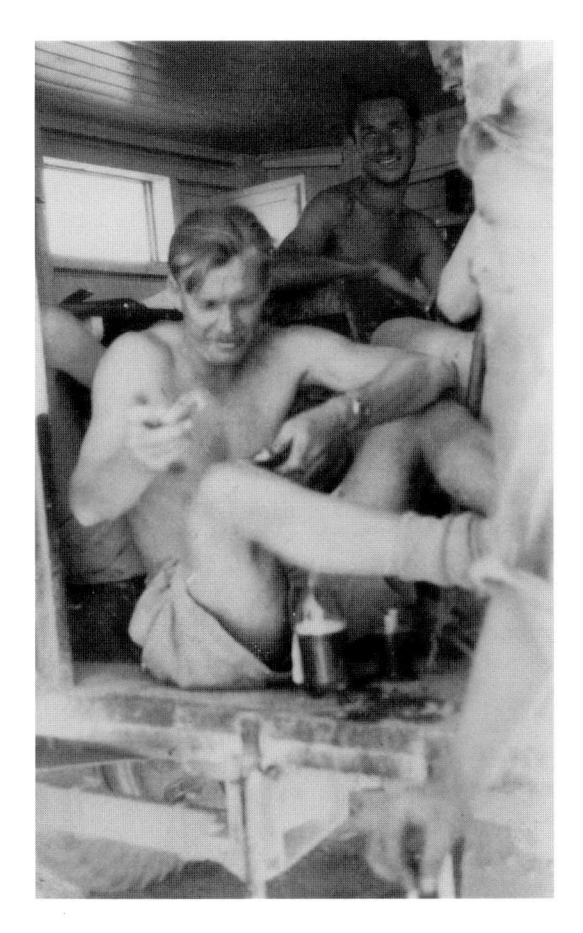

Flight Lieutenant 'Jimmy' James enjoys a gazelle steak washed down with 'Gold Star' (Bayliss).

a Regiment squadron. The Corps did not enjoy the respect of other branches and trades which it holds today. Nevertheless, the decision was eventually made and on 3 October 1946 the two Companies were renumbered as 2701 and 2702 Armoured Squadrons, RAF Regiment.[25]

The change of name from 'Armoured Car Companies' to 'Armoured Squadrons' and the renumbering to the rather cumbrous four-figures, caused considerable discontent among many of those who had served or were serving on 'the cars'. It was felt that the new Squadron number plates, Nos 2701 and 2702, did not allow the continuance of the proud and distinguished histories of the RAF armoured car companies. As 'Lofty' Hodge recalls:

> Well it became '2702 Armoured Squadron', and we kicked up hell about that because we'd lost the name.[26]

Fortunately good sense prevailed and only four months later, in February 1947, it was decided that the two units would be again renumbered as Nos 1 and 2 (Armoured Car) Squadrons, allowing the two Regiment squadrons to take their foundations back to the earliest days of the independent air force, 21 years before the formation of the RAF Regiment.[27]

Bert Bayliss was one of the first airmen to join No 2 Company as an RAF Regiment Gunner reaching the Company eight months before the amalgamation:

> I got called up in October 1945, when I was 21 years old. I'd taken up an apprenticeship at 14 and I had been in the Air Training Corps. I went to Sudbury in Suffolk for four weeks RAF training.
>
> The Sergeant came out one day with his clipboard and said "What do you want to do?" There were cooks, batmen, drivers, all sorts of things, and amongst them was 'Gunner'.
>
> A couple of blokes that I'd got together with as mates said "I wonder what Gunner is?" So we put our names down for that.
>
> Well there were about 200 blokes there and on the last day the Sergeant put us on parade and he called out "All those for cooks over there, all those for drivers, over there, all those for batmen, all over there…" and there was just three of us left.
>
> Then he said "And who's the three idiots who want to be Gunners!"
>
> We said "Here that's us."
>
> And he said "Well I'll pity you. Tomorrow, you're off to Belton Park in Lincolnshire".
>
> Well, we'd never heard of the RAF Regiment. That's where we went, and it was like a prisoner of war camp. It was really rough, and apart from RAF Regiment instructors, they also had half-a-dozen from 6th Airborne and a few Coldstream Guards. And it was really hard, it was. They had big fire bells outside each hut and they'd ring those at all hours of the early morning, like 2 o'clock, and you had five minutes to get out fully dressed and out on some sort of manoeuvre, and at that time of year it was really rubbishy weather. One chap from East London hung himself on a lavatory chain. He'd got so fed up with it all, couldn't face it.
>
> Anyway, we had two months of that and then they said "We've got an armoured car company and a parachute unit at Wombleton [in North

Bert Bayliss (left) and his good mate, Jack Harris (right) (Bayliss).

Yorkshire]." So the three of us who'd become good friends, decided we'll go and drop out of aeroplanes.

When we got to Wombleton we went into the office and they told us the parachute unit had been disbanded, but there was Armoured Cars. Well, they had small, very sleek Daimler armoured cars. So we learnt to use the cars all round Skegness. Then we went to Folkingham, not far from Belton Park, for a time to finish our training.

Eventually we went off to Toulon, in the south of France, and caught the boat, the *Empire Mace*, to Egypt, and were all sick as hell getting to Port Said. We then spent one night in a transit camp, just outside Cairo, and then went up the line by train to Ein Shemer. We stayed there the night and then we went by 3-tonner to Ramleh and arrived sometime in March 1946. It was rather a shock when we saw these big 13-ton armoured cars, the GMCs, rather than the sleek Daimlers we'd been driving.[28]

The British sailors, soldiers and airmen serving in Palestine from 1945 were soon involved in a spiteful campaign involving cordon and search operations and the processing and detention of Jewish illegal immigrants as they arrived on shores of Palestine in their rusting hulks. Over the next three years, it would develop into a large-scale insurrection involving both the Arabs and Jews which eventually became impossible to control. The number of terrorist acts by the Jewish insurgents increased rapidly, from half a dozen during October 1945 to more than 30 in November the following year.[29] While the troops on the ground were dealing with a large scale and complex insurgency, intensive diplomatic efforts were being made to find an acceptable solution to the Palestine problem.

The most significant attack of the campaign by the Jewish insurgents was aimed at the very heart of the British Mandate in Palestine. In June 1946, the British Army had launched a vast search and arrest operation codenamed *Agatha*, which involved

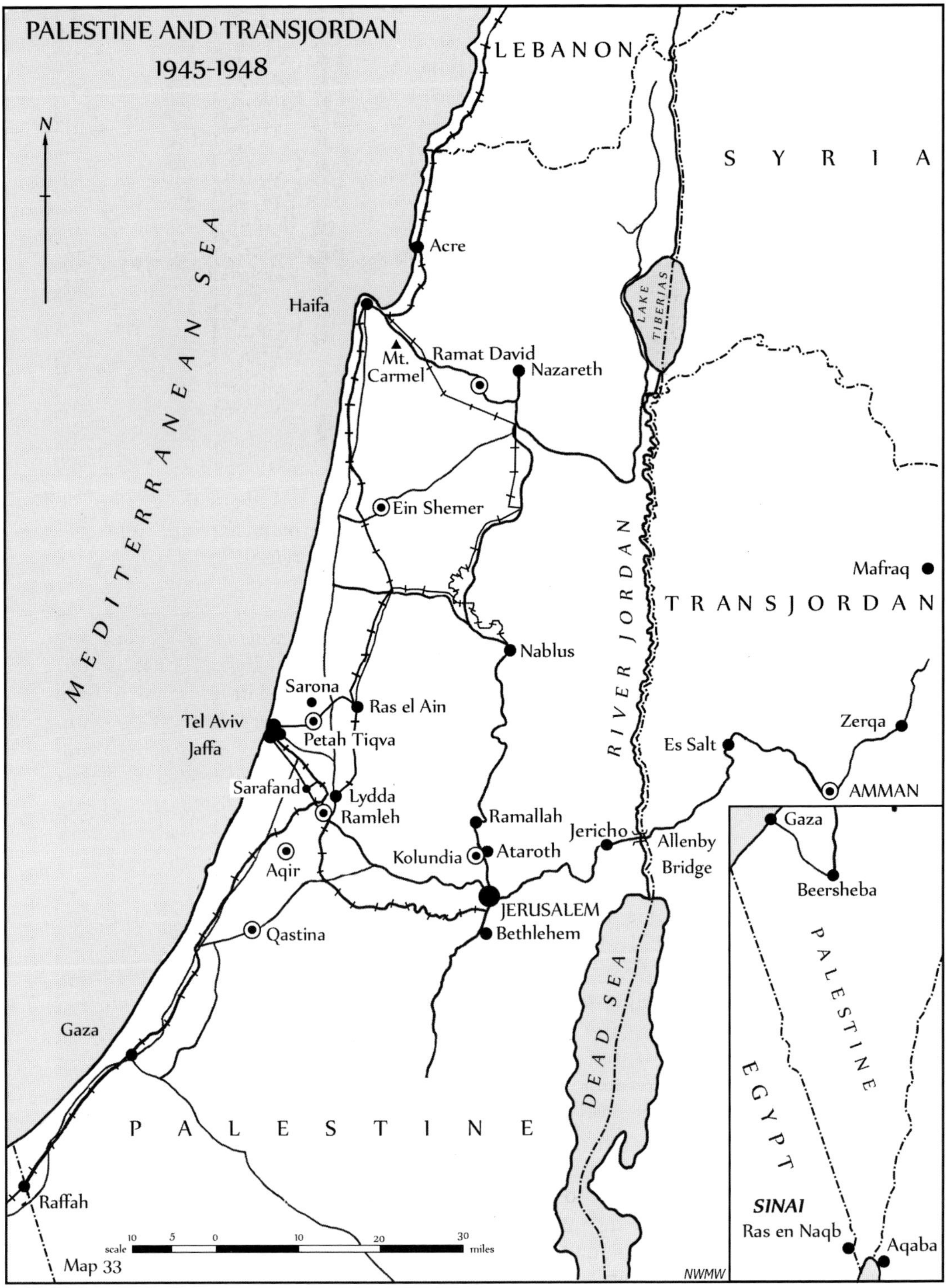

PALESTINE AND TRANSJORDAN
1945-1948
N
MEDITERRANEAN SEA
LEBANON
SYRIA
Acre
Haifa
Mt. Carmel
Ramat David
Nazareth
LAKE TIBERIAS
Ein Shemer
RIVER JORDAN
Mafraq
TRANSJORDAN
Nablus
Sarona
Ras el Ain
Tel Aviv
Jaffa
Petah Tiqva
Zerqa
Es Salt
AMMAN
Sarafand
Lydda
Ramleh
Ramallah
Jericho
Allenby Bridge
Aqir
Kolundia
Ataroth
JERUSALEM
Bethlehem
Qastina
DEAD SEA
Gaza
PALESTINE
Raffah
scale 10 5 0 10 20 30 miles
Map 33
NWMW
Gaza
Beersheba
PALESTINE
EGYPT
SINAI
Ras en Naqb
Aqaba

'British invaders – out of our country.' Two airmen from 'A' Flight display one of the banners put up by the Irgun. After many were taken down, the Irgun then put concealed charges behind, killing several British Sappers (Bayliss).

more than 100,000 troops. Poor security meant that the operation was not a complete surprise, although 600 weapons were found. In retaliation, the Irgun struck back at the very core of the British administration. The King David Hotel in Jerusalem housed the Secretariat of the Government of Palestine and Headquarters, British Troops in Palestine and Transjordan. Just after noon on 22 July 1946, 15-20 of the Irgun, dressed as Arabs, and pretending to be a work party, transported five milk churns containing explosive into the basement of the hotel. These were detonated directly under the Secretariat. The force of the explosion was devastating. Bert Bayliss was nearby with his Section when the bomb went off and recalls the subsequent events:

> They got up to some frightening things. You were looking over your shoulder all the time. I was there when the King David went up. That was a big bang. All cars, Army, Palestine Police, were up there as soon as it had gone off and we were put on guard. We parked the cars and we always left the car commander because he had the gun on top, but the rest of us were all out in the street. It was just a mass of rubble. They blew a whole wing off the building... We were up there for three or four days doing our six hour stint and mulling over bits and pieces. They killed 91 people, Arabs, Jews and British.[30]

Throughout the first half of 1946, No 2 Company maintained aerodrome protection of RAF Ramleh, Lydda, Aqir, and Ein Shemer, depending on the deployment of RAF flying squadrons (Map, 33, p. 488). By mid-1946, RAF Ein Shemer was home to the Spitfires of No 208 Squadron and the Lancasters of No 38 Squadron.[31] As part of Operation *Sunburn*, the latter were flying long-range maritime

A GMC of No 2 Armoured Car Company watches over Spitfires lined up at RAF Ein Shemer. 'Twenty-four hour guards, no perimeter, just sand dunes - very difficult to defend' (Hodge).

reconnaissance over the eastern and central Mediterranean searching for the Jewish immigrant boats coming from ports in Southern Europe. With the Jewish resistance groups doing their utmost to interrupt these flights, the RAF armoured cars were moved to RAF Ein Shemer to protect the aircraft both on the ground and at their most vulnerable when taking off. 'Lofty' Hodge of 'D' Section continues:

> At Ein Shemer there was a huge area of sand dunes to the south of the runway. It was a hell of a runway, it was very wide, and it ran for ages. The Lancasters could take off from it to do the boat spotting. But the Jews used to come up through those sand dunes and fire on the flights taking off.
>
> They got to the stage where we used to have an armoured car at one end of the runway and before they took off they'd give us a Very light. Then we use to belt down the runway on the other side and just rake the sand dunes with the turret 0.5 Browning or Bren to keep their heads down while the aircraft was taking off.[32]

'A' Section, which included Bert Bayliss, was ordered to move to Tel Aviv in November 1946, where they were to cooperate with the Palestine Police on road patrols, enforce the curfew and assist with car searches for contraband and weapons. He continues:

> I thought Ramleh was a reasonable camp; the main reason being they had a swimming pool and they had quite a good NAAFI. But you didn't spend much time there. There was nowhere to go outside. You weren't allowed out. Tel Aviv was about 6-8 miles past Lydda airport, but it was a trouble spot. There were three main troubles spots – Haifa, Jerusalem and Tel Aviv.

I was in 'A' Section and we used to do a stint of three months in Tel Aviv, and back to Ramleh for a fortnight. It was all something really new. You'd never done anything or been in that sort of country before. It was exciting, I wouldn't have missed it.

We spent three months at Tel Aviv, billeted with the Palestine Police in a place called Citrus House [the local British Military HQ]. I found that quite good, I mean I didn't like the situation but the place was okay. You got good food, you ate with the Palestine Police, and they had tablecloths and all. They were earning £60 a month. They were mostly British and they were a great bunch of blokes. There were some nice fellas and I lost seven good friends killed from the Police.

We had to learn a bit of Hebrew, "What's your name?" "Where are you going?" That sort of thing. If you were on the 12 midnight shift, they were six hour patrols. You might get a call to make a road block up. It might be 3 o'clock in the morning. It was unusual to see a car about at that time of night so it was suspicious. It was always two cars on duty out of the six. But you did have problems. I mean it's that time in the morning, all quiet, it was a dodgy thing to do, make a roadblock and then see a car coming towards you which could have terrorists in it.[33]

There were some successes for No 2 Company at Tel Aviv, with 'C' Section assisting the Police to capture four Jewish insurgents who were then delivered to the Criminal Investigation Department. 'Lofty' Hodge recalls one unusual patrol that could have had fatal consequences:

A car patrol went into one of the Tel Aviv suburbs. There was only one way into it. As they did the patrol around the area, a Jew came out and asked the car commander, Tony Courtney, if he could help him because his wife was having a baby and she needed to get to a doctor. So he made his gunner get on the roof and they got the pregnant woman into the gunner's position and then completed the circuit of the suburb. When they came to get out again they found the Jews had built a road block. They had completely blocked their exit. They were more or less in trouble. So Tony called over one of the Jews manning this road block and told the Jewish women to explain to them what they were doing. They immediately ripped the road block down and let them through.[34]

As Bert recounts, the Palestine Police had a difficult and dangerous job to do, and having made friends with many them, he also attended their many funerals:

We were on the same wavelength as the Palestine Police, so you could hear what was going on all the time. Over the radio came a call that a taxi had been stolen so look out for the such-and-such-a-number taxi.

Ten minutes later we were just patrolling the streets and got to the entrance to the Beit Hakerem road, to the west of Jerusalem, and about 100 yards away was a Police armoured car. Two of the crew were setting out to walk towards a car, which we thought might be the taxi. We were looking on as one of the Palestine Policemen opened the door of the car when there was an almighty explosion. It was booby-trapped, killing both policemen.

I couldn't believe what I had seen; when I think it could have been our car that had found the taxi.[35]

As the insurgents became more sophisticated, the threat from mines became more prevalent as Fred Morris recalls:

The GMC Otters had a sheet of steel underneath and you used to put sandbags around your feet. The worse thing to do was to be the first vehicle out of the camp in the morning to drive down the road.[36]

Number 2 Squadron was to suffer its first fatality in the conflict on 17 November 1946. At 2245 hours, a Palestine Police 15-cwt detonated a mine as it returned from a trip to the cinema at the 6th Airborne Division Camp at Sarona, on the eastern outskirts of Tel Aviv. The survivors were then fired upon as they attempted to escape the vehicle. Sergeant Herbert Olliffe of No 2 Squadron, 20 years old, was killed along with four Palestine Policemen. ACs Warrenger and Chisholm, also from the armoured cars, were wounded. A section of No 2 Squadron was called out but despite recces and patrols of the area no sign of the attackers was found. Olliffe was buried at Ramleh on 19 November with full military honours with the majority of the Squadron attending.[37]

By September 1946, the situation required further reinforcement and No 1 Armoured Car Company moved in its entirety from RAF Habbaniya to southern Palestine and RAF Qastina. The Company departed from Iraq with little fanfare, with it and its antecedents having operated successfully there for nearly a quarter of a century. The Company returned to Palestine where it had first operated in 1922. A few weeks later it assumed the RAF Regiment title of No 2701 Armoured Squadron.

While deployed at RAF Qastina the Squadron found time for exercises with the 2nd Infantry Brigade in Jordan at Zerqa and there was also sport with the Squadron soccer team defeating the Glider Pilot Regiment 2-1 and 3-1. During December, the Squadron ground parties of No 13 (Mosquito) Squadron were escorted from RAF Ein Shemer to RAF Kabrit, Egypt. The rapid transfer from Habbaniya had not been without its problems as the Squadron did not receive any spares for three months, the vehicles deteriorating and serviceability suffering. Despite the difficult times, 80 personnel from the Squadron were able to attend the Christmas midnight services in Jerusalem.

Throughout 1946, the British Government made intense efforts to find a politically acceptable solution to the Palestine problem. A joint Anglo-American Committee had been formed, but its recommendations of a single state and increase in Jewish immigration to 100,000 was rejected by Westminster. The post-war world was now very different to that when Britain had taken on the Mandate in 1921. The British decision ran counter to opinion of Zionists in many countries, and hardened their attitude in support of the military activities of the Jewish insurgents. The United States of America now carried considerable international power and President Truman, moving towards an election and dependent upon a sizeable Jewish vote, was supportive of the committee proposals. The Palestine problem was having serious ramifications for Anglo-American relations and was arousing considerable anti-British feeling in many quarters. With Great Britain having endured six years of war, and from which it now faced severe economic restraint and a long period of recovery, Palestine had become an extremely unattractive commitment. The British Foreign

Minister, Ernest Bevin, told the House of Commons in February 1947, "the Mandate had proved to be unworkable in practice and that the obligations undertaken to the two communities in Palestine had been shown to be irreconcilable".[38]

In the last three weeks of 1946, there was had been a short unofficial 'truce' with a pause in terrorist attacks. In Tel Aviv, 'C' Section of No 2 Squadron spent the daylight hours of New Year's Day 1947 at rest, but patrols were resumed as usual as night fell. However, the following day was eventful, with 20 incidents through the length of the country. In the early evening in Tel Aviv, a returning patrol came under intense automatic fire as they entered their compound at the Importers Building, next to Citrus House. Under cover of this fire, grenades were thrown at three Army vehicles parked outside the Headquarters of 1st Parachute Brigade, and a hail of bullets was sent into the officers' quarters on the third floor. The outgoing RAF armoured car patrol was just being inspected by their CO, Flying Officer Hawkins, when the firing began. Corporal Hyde and his crew mounted up immediately and returned fire, while Hawkins sent Corporal Manser off in his car to find the source of the trouble, which he found to be coming from the roof of some newly-constructed flats. Fifteen minutes later a jet of oil was sprayed from a home-made flame-thrower

A flight of No 2 Armoured Car Squadron at the Importers Building next to Citrus House in Tel Aviv. This was site of the attack by the Irgun on 2 January 1947 on 'C' Flight. Note the 6-pdr anti-tank gun on the roof. According to Dick Lock, this was manhandled there by the Coldstream Guards who occupied the building. It was determined, however, that even with the barrel fully depressed, any shell fired from it would land somewhere out in the Mediterranean Sea (Lock).

onto the RAF vehicles, including Corporal Hyde's GMC, but fortunately due to a faulty ignition mechanism the oil failed to ignite. Hyde and his crew ignored this and continued pouring in accurate return fire. The operators of the flame-thrower quickly jettisoned their equipment and departed in haste.

The battle raged on for a further three-quarters-of-an-hour with the standby armoured car crews maintaining accurate and heavy Bren gun fire from defensive positions on the roof of the compound. From his rooftop OP, Hawkins directed their fire onto the enemy positions as they were identified. After half an hour, the insurgents fired a red Very signal which was seen by Hawkins and there was a lull in the firing. This allowed him sufficient time, in concert with Flight Sergeant Allen, to ascertain the number of Section casualties, and surprisingly given the intensity of enemy fire, there were none.

The lull was only brief before a green Very signal was seen and the attack was renewed from a different direction. From his OP, Hawkins could see Corporal Manser engaging the enemy from his GMC in a nearby street. An hour after it began, the firing ceased. Two cars were sent out to search and patrol the area, while Hawkins led a six-man foot patrol of his section to thoroughly search the abandoned positions. The attackers were later learned to be from the Irgun Zvai Leumi, but none were found as they had melted away into the surrounding town.[39]

The prompt action of the airmen had prevented serious loss but the cars had also performed a further crucial role. The Police radio equipment had completely failed during the engagement and all communications with patrols had then been maintained by an armoured car of the section, which acted as a central control under Police supervision. Flying Officer K. Hawkins later wrote in his report on the action:

> This patrol was not without risk and I highly commend the men who accompanied me. Their behaviour was outstanding. The same may be said for the crews of the vehicles engaged.
> During the whole of the attack, the morale of my Section was of the highest order, and here, I would like to specially commend Corporal Hyde, AC Goodwin, AC Shenton, Corporal Manser, AC Hitchin, Flight Sergeant Allen and LAC Drye.[40]

The terrorist acts and sabotage and the threat to British personnel had reached such a state in early 1947 that the decision was made to evacuate the remaining Service families and civilians from Palestine. Just prior to Christmas 1946, some families from Haifa had been escorted by detachments of No 2 Squadron into a safe enclave in the RAF quarters in Jerusalem. In the following February however, the High Commissioner ordered that all British non-essential personnel be evacuated from Palestine. Parties were brought to RAF Aqir in a convoy under escort by No 2 Squadron and were airlifted out in Halifaxes and Dakotas of 113 and 78 Squadrons. Some went to Cyprus and Egypt, while others returned to the United Kingdom to await developments. A few families were accommodated at RAF Amman after being escorted by No 2 Squadron to Allenby Bridge on the River Jordan, and from whence they safely proceeded without escort to the Jordanian capital, while another group were escorted to the Syrian border town of Hakoura.[41]

By January 1947, the threat to Air Headquarters Levant, located at Air House in Jerusalem was such that a flight of No 2 Squadron was sent on a permanent detachment (Map 34, p. 495). The cars began familiarising themselves with the

Map 34

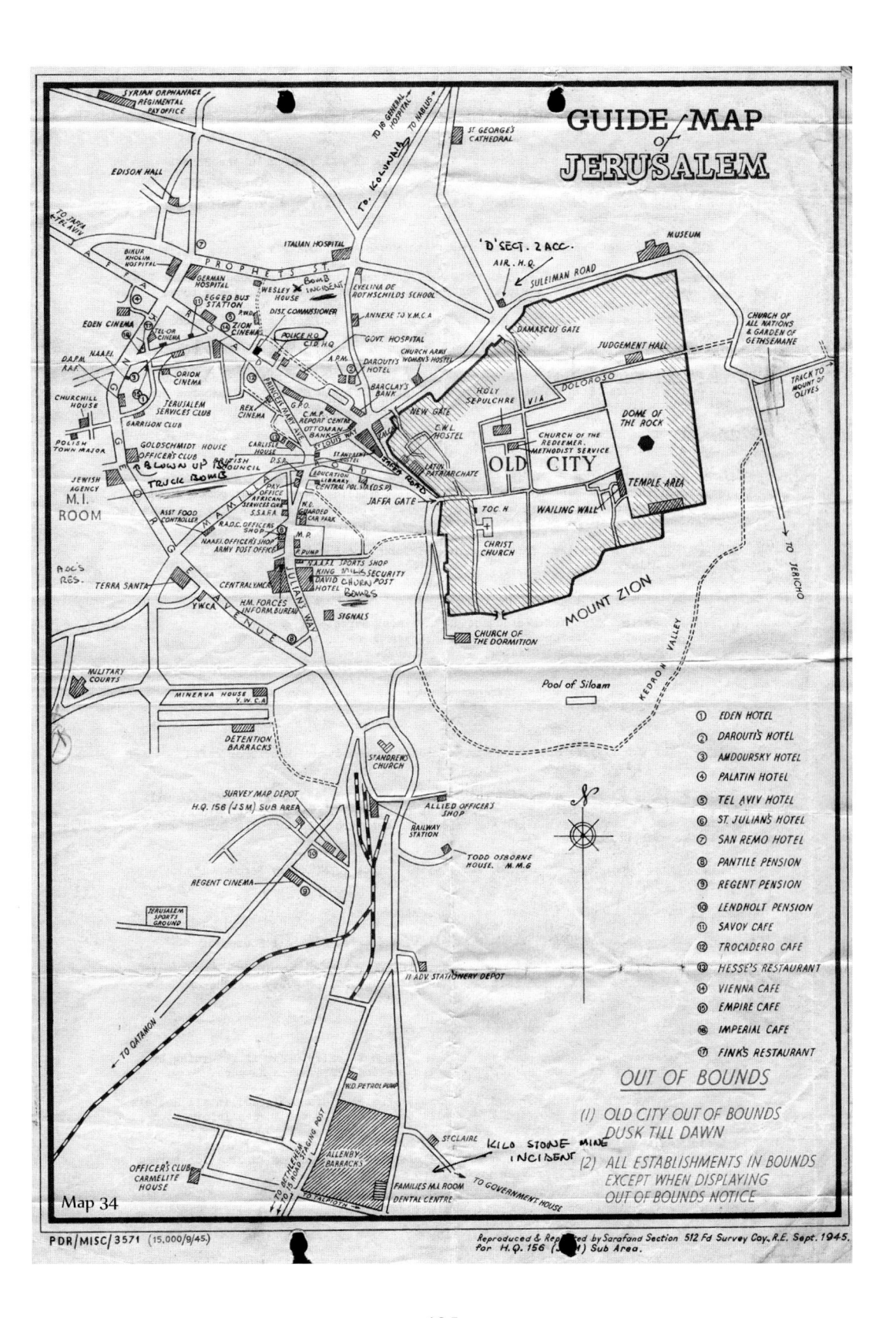

Holy City. Two of the six cars in a flight were always allocated to the Jerusalem Operational Patrols (or the JOP) as they were known. Flight Sergeant 'Lofty' Hodge and 'B' Flight was assigned to this task.[42] He continues:

> For myself I did seven months on JOPs, with the Palestine Police. Of course that was in addition to the normal escorts and patrols we did to anywhere in the Levant. Kolundia airport was only two miles away on the Jerusalem side of Ramallah and the brass hats were always coming in on Avro Ansons. You were at it all the time.
>
> My section covered two shifts on a daily basis. One car did 0600 hours to 1400 hours; another did 1400 hours to 2200 hours. That was non-stop except for a quick coffee and kebab at an Arab café. We just stood by the car for that. We had a Palestine policeman in the car with us for those patrols. Nearly every patrol you were being fired at from somewhere, it was not boring!
>
> Every time the city sirens went, which was frequently, we had to turn out and standby with the available cars backed up to the Old City Wall next to Damascus Gate. You got out of that courtyard, as you were trapped in there. You could then watch all the approach roads. You then used whatever intelligence you'd got, which was mainly listening. Ah, big bang or machine gun fire etc... Then you'd send a couple of the cars over there to see what

'What? The bloody sirens again?' 'D' Flight of No 2 Armoured Car Squadron deploy outside Air Headquarters Levant in Jerusalem opposite the Damascus Gate on the Old City Wall. Note the 0.5-inch Browning and searchlight. The airman, middle front, is an RAF Regiment gunner from a rifle squadron who wandered over from the gate and got in the photo (Hodge).

was going on.

The Army had got a 3-inch mortar, and if the sirens went at night they used to fire parachute flares up and it used to light the whole of Jerusalem. They lasted about five minutes or so. They were a Godsend they were. We had 2-inch mortars on some of the cars and we could also fire parachute flares with them if needed.[43]

On 1 March 1947, there were more than a dozen incidents against the British forces involving mines, mortar and gunfire attacks and bombings. 'Lofty' Hodge was out on patrol in mid-afternoon when the Irgun struck, killing 13 soldiers and civilians. He continues:

I was with the CO, Flying Officer 'Dusty' Miller, doing a little recce near the Jewish Agency. We had dismounted from the car and were standing on the pavement having a discussion about the next day's ops when a huge explosion blew us both of our feet. We soon got up because everything that had been blown into the air was starting to come back down again! The Goldschmidt Officers' Club just around the corner had been blown apart by a huge truck bomb.[44]

Not all of the insurgent attacks were successful however, and on 20 April, the

The results of the truck bomb at the Goldschmidt Officers' Club (Hodge).

armoured cars did help thwart an attempt on the life of the High Commissioner, General Sir Alan Cunningham. 'Lofty' Hodge continues:

> One day on JOP my car was directed to investigate an incident at Allenby Barracks playing fields. So we went there with all possible speed. When we arrived there, I took a look at the situation. There was a sloping grass bank up to the playing fields with a big hut at the top and an Arab dancing about, hands in the air. So I instructed the driver to take the car up there. On the floor in the hut was a dead Arab. They were both caretakers, Right in the distance, going down through some rocks, about three or four hundred yards away was obviously some Irgun Zvai Leumi. I couldn't do anything about them because we couldn't go down the rocks anyway, and I was more concerned about the Arabs.
>
> So we stopped and tried to talk to the remaining caretaker and we got the idea that the Jews had come in and shot one of them as they were trying to take over their shed. Then he pointed to this thing on the ground. I thought "Christ!" So I said to him "You want to be safe so you go back to the Barracks." I called up to Police Headquarters in Jerusalem telling them that we'd discovered an unexploded mine. It was quite a big thing.
>
> Thirty minutes later an Army Bomb Disposal Major arrived in a jeep. He dismantled the bomb on the spot whilst I had to stand there with him and watch what he did and radio his every move over the R/T. It seemed like forever.
>
> It was amazing what came out of that thing. The bomb was full of nuts, bolts, nails etc. and enough sticks of gelignite to blow up AHQ Levant. The top part of the bomb was disguised as a kilo-stone, even down to the correct distance recorded on it. The Irgun were going to replace the existing stone on the nearby road with this bomb. There was only one building down there and that was the High Commissioner's Residence. They'd already got the wires on it and they were going to set it off from the caretakers hut and blow the High Commissioner to kingdom come when he went by. Oh they were clever.[45]

By April 1947, it was apparent that there was little hope of a peaceful resolution in Palestine between the two parties. While the diplomats and politicians sought a resolution, the violence continued with no abatement to the sabotage, killings and arrests. British troops were being killed at the rate of two per day. Fewer troop reinforcements could be expected as the reduced defence spending had meant further reductions in the size of the armed forces and these were required in other places. It would soon become near impossible to impose martial law in the Mandate and thereby maintain law and order.

On the ground in Palestine, lives were being lost in increasing numbers while attempts were made with little success to resolve the conflict. The Jewish insurgents began a campaign of kidnappings and assassinations of British soldiers and airmen. In the early days, it was possible to go out in 'civvies' but with a .38 revolver tucked into your belt, but this became more difficult as the insurgency worsened, as 'Lofty' Hodge recalls:

> You didn't go out. At one time in Jerusalem you had to go out in fours and

you had to always have your sidearm of course. And then an order came out, you weren't allowed to go out at all. Of course if you're British your life was in danger every hour of the day and night. The hot points were in the cities supplementing the Palestine Police patrols.[46]

The British Government of the time was unable or unwilling to impose a solution by force and as a consequence the opinion formed that the matter should be referred back to the United Nations. In November 1947, the United Nations voted 25-15 for the partition of Palestine. The British Government announced that it was not prepared to enforce any plan in the absence of an agreement between the Arabs and Jews and that it would leave Palestine and the Mandate would end on 15 May 1948.[47]

As a consequence, the RAF presence in the country was to be gradually thinned out. Many larger aircraft could easily fulfil their tasks flying from Malta, Cyprus and Egypt. By mid-1947, only five flying squadrons remained, Nos 32 and 208 Squadrons, flying Spitfires, and Nos 37 and 38 Squadrons, with Lancasters, at RAF Ein Shemer, and Austers from No 651 Air Observation Post Squadron at Qastina and Haifa. Notwithstanding the reduction in flying units, the RAF Regiment retained a significant presence in the theatre with No 20 Wing, one flight of No 1 Armoured Car Squadron and Nos 58 and 66 (Rifle) Squadrons protecting Ein Shemer. Other Regiment units were deployed at Air Headquarters Levant and airfields at Kolundia, Qastina and Ramleh and Nos 120 and 160 Maintenance Units at Ras el Ain and Aqir, respectively. Protection of these and the smaller supporting units, such as No 3 RAF Hospital, proved to be a time-consuming commitment for the Regiment as they were particularly vulnerable to terrorist attack and sabotage. By 1 July 1947, there were 1183 RAF Regiment personnel controlled by Air Headquarters Levant with Nos 19 and 20 Wings, Nos 52, 53, 54, 58 62, 65 and 66 (Rifle) Squadrons and Nos 1 and 2 Armoured Car Squadrons, the latter two with their Headquarters at Qastina and Ramleh, respectively.[48]

Number 2 Squadron had spent the second half of 1947 at Ramleh and Jerusalem, while No 1 Squadron moved its HQ and one flight from Qastina to Ramleh and also took over responsibility for Police work in Tel Aviv from No 2 Squadron. By the end of the year however, and despite the burgeoning security task, there was insufficient manpower to retain the eight RAF Regiment squadrons. Numbers 52, 58, 62 and 66 (Rifle) Squadrons remained, but Nos 53 and 65 existed in name only. A similar plight had befallen the Armoured Car Squadrons and so the decision was made that on 1 December 1947, No 1 Squadron would be disbanded and those airmen who had not completed their posting would be sent to No 2 Company.[49]

With the British Government stating their determination to leave Palestine and the announcement of the Partition Plan by the United Nations, there was a considerable increase in unrest. The British Government's aim was now to withdraw from Palestine in good order. The soldiers and airmen now faced a deadline for their departure from Palestine and the Arabs and Jews feverishly prepared for the inevitable conflict. Number 2 Squadron continued with the JOP. Dick Lock recalls his time at Jerusalem during July 1947 and particularly his 21st birthday:

In the event of trouble in the city, an alarm was raised. We dropped everything and rushed to the cars. First there got to drive! We then deployed to pre-planned locations and set up road blocks. On the morning of July 18 valuable materiel was at No 120 Maintenance Unit at Ras el Ain. Before the Mandate ended, the RAF had to move as much as possible of the accumulated stocks of arms, ammunition and high explosives from Palestine to Egypt and Iraq. As a consequence, No 2 Armoured Car Squadron found itself busy for the remaining months of the Mandate on numerous convoy escorts. With the deterioration in law and order the convoys were increasingly exposed to ambush or interference, and it was essential that this materiel did not fall into the hands of the Arab or Jewish protagonists. As 'Lofty' Hodge recalls:

> My two cars got orders to go to No 120 Maintenance Unit from Amman and pick up this convoy. It was huge. Another two cars from our Section came and joined us from Ramleh. I finished up with four armoured cars and at least 30 of these thundering great Macks, Whites and Studebakers. I was told it was the AOC's furniture… but we all knew damn well what it was. At that time they were taking every available piece of high explosive and ammunition out of Palestine.[54]

On one of these convoy trips, the savagery of the conflict was brought home to the airmen. Just after dawn on 9 April, a convoy under the command of Flying Officer D.J. Cronin of 'A' Flight was returning back to No 120 Maintenance Unit on the Gaza bypass when they were hailed down by a Lieutenant and 14 sappers from the Field Park Squadron of the 6th Airborne Division. The Lieutenant's convoy had been ambushed by a party of Arabs the previous night and he requested a lift for him and his men to Sarafand. Collecting them up, Cronin's detachment continued northwards and soon came upon the site of the ambush where they found the remains of the column's vehicles and disturbingly, the mutilated body of a Sapper Corporal. Having been shot in the throat, he had been stripped of all his clothing and his eyes had been gouged out. The corpse was recovered and the sappers driven to Sarafand and the unfortunate Corporal's body delivered to the mortuary.[55]

Readying themselves for the coming struggle, the Arabs and Jews coveted the vehicles, stores, arms and ammunition at No 120 Maintenance Unit, and as a consequence every attempt was made to obtain them.[56] However, patrols at this site more commonly dealt with wanton vandalism, looting and theft, rather than terrorist acts. Prior to the arrival of the RAF armoured cars, the situation at Ras el Ain was chaotic with non-Regiment airmen doing their best to repel attacks by large groups, mainly of Arabs, that were attempting to break in. This proved to be the most difficult station in Palestine to defend and to evacuate cleanly. 'Lofty' Hodge and his Flight were sent there for guard duty:

> It was a large area, with hangars dotted about all over the place. A great big perimeter fence and part of it was mined, but there was a path inside the wire you could drive around. We used to do that all night. They used to cut the wire and then put sheaves of straw each side of the gap, and then take camels in and rob these warehouses, or try to, and then out again with the loaded camels. After dark you had orders to shoot on sight.[57]

The cars were forced at times to open fire on trespassers inside the perimeter wire to disperse them. On one occasion, a fire broke out in one of the storage areas and the cars, while covering the firemen as they fought the blaze, came under fire from the intruders who had decided to take pot shots at them. With good planning and organisation, most of the equipment was recovered from the site by No 51 MT Company RAF, and the station was finally abandoned on 16 April as no purchaser could be found. It was immediately taken over by an Arab military force, the Arab Liberation Army.[58]

If materiel could not be found in large quantities from stores or armouries there were those who were able to find other sources. Their adversaries became quite brazen in their attempts to procure arms, uniforms and documents, as Dick Lock recalls:

> We were required to carry rifles sometime in 1947 as both Arab and Jewish factions became more militant. We slept with the guns under our mattresses but at one location a couple of lads after a night out leaned their rifles against the barrack wall near a window and they were stolen. Twenty-eight days detention followed.
>
> At another camp [RAF Aqir], intruders entered the billet at night and made off with most of the battledress, wallets and identity cards. The Flight's dog mascot had raised the alarm but had a boot thrown at it for its trouble.[59]

The aspirations of the insurgents in Jerusalem had few limitations. On 25 April, only a few weeks before the withdrawal, a party of Jews managed to steal one of the Squadron's GMC Otters, albeit while in the care of the Royal Warwickshire Regiment. Dick Lock continues:

> One night, a lorry bearing Army Engineer markings drew up at the gate. Two men in battledress and cockney accents showed the guards a document allowing them tow away the RAF armoured car, and take it to the Army Workshops for an urgent repair. The Army guard let them in and they towed the car away.
>
> Next morning the RAF armoured car crew arrived and said "Where's our car?" and the alarm was raised. A Police patrol spotted it a few days later in the narrow backstreets of an orthodox Jewish quarter, but it was deemed too risky to attempt to recover – it was probably booby trapped. The feeling on the Flight was relief that it was not our fault that it had been taken. Huge chains and padlocks were issued to secure the cars' steering wheels, forthwith.[60]

Once the decision had been made to leave Palestine, all the RAF installations had to be either handed back to the original owners or sold. Most equipment was to be cleared from the site but before this could happen they were seen as fair game by local Arabs looking for loot. Although no longer resident at Ramleh, a Section of No 2 Company on a passing patrol caught some Arabs breaking into the building storing petrol, oil and lubricants. Many fled in disorder once the cars arrived, but the airmen were able to catch and arrest some of the thieves, along with their six carts and seven horses. A few weeks later, they were called to extinguish a fire in the old Officers' Mess after receiving a distress call from the Egyptian Red Cross, who occupied the building.

Much the same situation arose at RAF Aqir, south of Tel Aviv, although the large amount of valuable equipment particularly that used for aircraft maintenance and parachute training had been removed. On 12 March, four days before it was due to handed over to the new buyer, there was a wave of Arab looting and rioting. Squadron Leader Childs was in charge of the handover:

> I had a bearer who had been with the Squadron for 19 years. And he was an absolute first class source of intelligence. And he came to me one morning and said "There's going to be big troubles today. It's in the local paper that Aqir is lost forever, because the Jews had bought it." And this was in the Arab territory supposedly.[61]

The Arabs had indeed read of this in their newspaper, under the headline "LOST FOREVER" and were incensed that the airfield had been sold to Jewish contractors. By that afternoon they had set fire to ten derelict aircraft fuselages in the aircraft dump, while others set about smashing windows and removing corrugated iron from the roof of a hangar. Childs continues:

> The bullets were flying about all over the show and what-have-you, and the AOC, Air Commodore Dawson, rang me and asked me if I wanted to pull out. I said "No, we're going to stick it out". And this went on all day and all night.[62]

A nearby cornfield, some two feet high, was suspected of hiding the people responsible for the trouble. The following morning there was some amusement when the first bomb of a 2-inch mortar shoot designed as a show of force fell into the field, and 20 or so looters were seen to leap to their feet and flee back across the fields. For the next two days, the cars kept a close watch on the encroaching looters and on many occasions had to fire bursts from their Brens to drive them off. Childs decided to act:

The handover of RAF Aqir to the new owners, March 1948. GMCs of No 2 Armoured Car Squadron escort the last RAF vehicles from RAF Aqir (Lock).

In the end I got Awed, my bearer, to come round to the local villages with me where I asked to see the local Mukhtars. I told them that this nonsense had to stop or else I was going to take serious action against them, but I would make sure that they knew when we were going to pull out. That satisfied them.

Things quietened down afterwards. Peace reigned until we went. And the day we went, we went out to the Sarafand crossroads where I had a rendezvous point and by then Jews were in.[63]

The departure from Ramleh was similarly chaotic. The station was due to be taken over by the Palestine Survey Department, but they had no more than unarmed supernumeraries as guards. A rumour had spread among the local Arab population that it had been sold to the Jews and as a consequence there was a large influx of local Arabs intent on dismantling the station and removing the remaining equipment. Squadron Leader Childs recalled being sent by Air Commodore Dawson to Ramleh with a detachment of RAF armoured cars from RAF Aqir and a platoon of the local Army garrison to sort out the mess:

When the treaty was coming to an end and we'd decided to pull out I had the job of taking these cars round to the airfields that had been sold to either the Arabs or the Jews. One exceptional place was Ramleh itself. About four or five days after we had evacuated Ramleh the AOC Levant rang me and said "Joe... what can you do about getting Ramleh back?" But, he said "No gunfire, no fighting or anything of that. It's got to be done craftily and cunningly".

So anyway I thought about this and I arranged for six armoured cars to arrive at Ramleh, with myself, at dusk. As you know armoured vehicles are no good after dark. So I knocked on the gate of Ramleh. It was answered by the chap I'd handed the camp over to and I asked if I could have a night's lodging, as I daren't go any further. Relying on the Arab custom to offer hospitality to travellers, he agreed to accommodate us for the night. After we'd got in we took over the Officers' Mess, which had become literally a s..thouse. The urinals were full of crap and what not. You couldn't imagine the difference in the place in a few days. But after we'd got it cleaned out we moved in. As dawn broke, the armoured cars were located at key points and we now had complete control of the base.[64]

The situation was soon resolved, although not before a local employee of the Works Department had been killed and the last lorry load of steel stolen while on the way to Lydda Station. According to Dawson's report on the incident:

Several Arabs were killed before they were driven off, and when the local Mukhtars were interviewed they replied bluntly that their villagers were out of control, and, from their point of view, it was a pity that the numbers killed were five and not 50. This incident, however, was a useful lesson on the risks of leaving any Station, even for a short period without an RAF guard strong enough to deal with the local situation.[65]

The final handover for RAF Ein Shemer was on 25 April, when the RAF armoured cars, with Nos 58 and 66 (Rifle) Squadrons, departed quietly and without loss from the Station. As the column left, skirmishes could be heard breaking out between the Arab and Jewish forces, both sides having been awaiting the opportunity to loot, destroy or occupy the site and buildings.

By early 1948, the civil government, legal and financial system was near collapse. During March and April, 'B' Flight was assigned the job of escorting some £7 million in bullion and £1 million in banknotes to and from Kolundia airport from Barclays Bank in Jerusalem.

Once the decision to end the Mandate had been made, the British troops were no longer the prime targets for attack, although constantly coming across Arab and Jewish road blocks made journeys between camps rather tense at times. The policy for the last few months was to remain neutral between the Arabs and Jews, which involved a considerable degree of tolerance and patience on the part of the servicemen. Intervention was only permitted to allow communications to remain open to maintain some semblance of a normal society. The opening rounds of a deadly conflict were being played out before them, but the sailors, airmen and soldiers were frequently torn between being ordered to remain distant while villages or kibbutzes were sacked or intervening to save lives of the innocents caught up in the struggle.

The plan for the departure from Palestine was for a gradual withdrawal from the bases in the south, with the units remaining gradually concentrating in an enclave around Haifa. All that remained for the RAF by April was Ramat David, with Nos 32 and 208 Squadrons, and Air Headquarters Levant in Jerusalem with the small airstrip at Kolundia. With No 2 Squadron Headquarters and 'C' Flight permanently located at Amman, 'A' Flight would take responsibility for defence of Ramat David, and 'B' Flight, Air Headquarters Levant in Jerusalem. The No 2 Squadron Operations Record Books describes the work of April 1948 as follows:

> The main feature of the month's activities was the safeguarding of RAF lives and property. The extensive camp patrols were carried out by the AFVs at RAF Stations that were closing down. The patrols, by virtue of their extreme mobility, were instrumental in minimising looting by Arab and Jew alike.
>
> Numerous escorts to various parts of Palestine and the Egyptian border have been accomplished without casualty or incident.
>
> Since the evacuation of Palestine, No 2 Armoured Car Squadron has taken on defence and escort duties and has seen the successful withdrawal of all personnel from the following stations: RAF Ramleh, RAF Aqir, No 120 MU, RAF Ein Shemer… On each occasion No 2 Armoured Car Squadron was the last to leave the Units and the handing over the new authorities were accomplished by the Squadron.[66]

For the last fortnight at Ramat David, 'A' Flight had maintained constant patrols around the airfield and as the deadline approached, escorted a number of petrol convoys into Nazareth and Haifa. On 8 May it took the last remaining RAF personnel into Haifa and then handed over to the Army. The following day, the Flight set off for Kolundia with No 52 (Rifle) Squadron RAF Regiment, and with a Spitfire escort. They remained there only a day before they moved off down the road from Jerusalem, crossed the River Jordan at the Allenby Bridge, and reached RAF Amman on 11 May, reuniting with Squadron Headquarters and 'C' Flight.

'B' Flight was the last detachment of No 2 Squadron remaining in Palestine. The Jerusalem Operational Patrols had ceased and the main activities of the Flight for the remaining weeks were the defence of Air Headquarters Levant and provision of VIP escorts to and from Kolundia airstrip and around the Holy City, particularly for the AOC, Air Commodore Dawson. A feature of life at Kolundia was listening to the whistle of mortar bombs as they passed from the nearby Arab village to the Jewish settlement on the far boundary of the airfield. The Flight was kept busy right up until the last days before the end of the Mandate. The last few RAF convoys were being escorted to Amman and to the Egyptian border at Raffah, the latter usually with a detachment of three GMCs leaving around 0600 hours from a Jerusalem - a 13-hour round trip. A constant vigil was kept at Kolundia until everyone had been safely evacuated, as Childs recalls:

> The final days we picked up the remaining staff from Jerusalem – Arabs, Jews, and what have you, and we ferried them by road from Jerusalem to Kolundia [from where they] were flying them out in an Anson.[67]

Surprisingly, there were few incidents during the days that remained, other than the theft and recovery of a unit 3-tonner at Nazareth and the odd random shots at the cars on convoy duty. Both sides were simply waiting for the British to go. On 13 May, preparation began for the final evacuation of Kolundia and the departure from Jerusalem. A large convoy of the final elements of the British Royal Navy, Army and RAF was to be assembled.

Lieutenant-Colonel E.J.B. Nelson DSO MC was in command of 'North Group', an all-arms column of armoured cars, Comet tanks, a Bailey bridge, bulldozer, lorries, ambulances and a tank transporter, composed of the 1st (Guards) Parachute Battalion, 42 Commando Royal Marines, 2 Air Support Signals Unit, elements of 6th

The last morning in Palestine, 14 May 1948 (© Crown copyright. II Squadron RAF Regiment History Room).

Field Regiment RA, 4th/7th Royal Dragoon Guards, 17th/21st Lancers, 4th Royal Tank Regiment, 1st Airborne Squadron RE, the RASC and various government officials, the Palestine Police, 'B' Flight, No 2 Armoured Car Squadron and No 62 (Rifle) Squadron RAF Regiment.

At reveille, at 0500 hours on 14 May, at Kolundia airstrip, all-round defence was taken up by most of 'B' Flight's GMCs, while the remainder were detailed to act as barriers where the runway crossed the main Jerusalem-Ramallah Road. The car crews cooked and ate their breakfasts on their own vehicles. Smoke was laid for the aircraft by the GMCs at the barriers, to reduce visibility to any watchers in the surrounding hills. The cars remained in their positions until North Group had brought the last VIPs from Jerusalem to the airstrip and the last aircraft had taken off. The British High Commissioner, General Sir Alan Cunningham, departed that morning in his Avro Anson for Haifa, escorted by a flight of Spitfires and Lancasters. Later that day, he embarked on the cruiser HMS *Euryalus* and sailed from Haifa harbour.

Their task accomplished, the seven GMCs, a petrol and water bowser and an LAD vehicle, took up their positions in the North Group column. Along with No 62 (Rifle) Squadron, they were placed at the rear. Flight Lieutenant H.M. Gibson was car commander of the leading RAF armoured car, with Flight Lieutenant 'Jimmy' James and Pilot Officer H.G. Robson in the two rear cars. The latter were designated to destroy any vehicles that fell out. The engines roared into life and the convoy slowly but steadily progressed westwards along the long, precipitous and bitterly-disputed road corridor from Jerusalem towards the coastal plain. Apart from being sniped at as the destroying party set a disabled ambulance ablaze, no serious trouble was encountered. The column reached Ramleh, where the RAF armoured cars and rifle squadron peeled off and went to the south, reaching Sarafand by mid-afternoon, while most of North Group made speed towards Haifa.

At Sarafand they joined a column, known as 'Findforce', made up predominantly of the 2nd Battalion, The Royal Irish Fusiliers. The following morning, with vehicles serviced and refuelled, they were piped out of Sarafand by the battalion's pipers. More than 120 assorted vehicles set off down the coastal road for the Canal Zone of Egypt. Progress was again steady, and the GMCs maintained regular contract with their escorting Spitfires via their VHF radios until Raffah, on the Egyptian frontier, was reached at dusk. As the RAF armoured cars crossed the Palestine-Egypt frontier for the final time, a simple but poignant signal was sent off by Pilot Officer Hamish Robson on Morse key to No 2 Armoured Car Squadron Headquarters at RAF Amman:

-.-. .-.. . .- .-. / --- ..-. / .--. .- .-.. . ... - .. -. .

"CLEAR OF PALESTINE"

At midnight on 14 May 1948, the British Mandate in Palestine had expired. The next day, 15 May, the Jews proclaimed the establishment of the State of Israel, which was recognised immediately by the USA and USSR. The Arab League declared that a state of war existed with Israel, and the Arab armies of Egypt, Syria, Iraq and Jordan marched into Palestine on three fronts. The final evacuation of British personnel occurred on 30 June when Air Commodore Dawson and GOC Palestine moved their

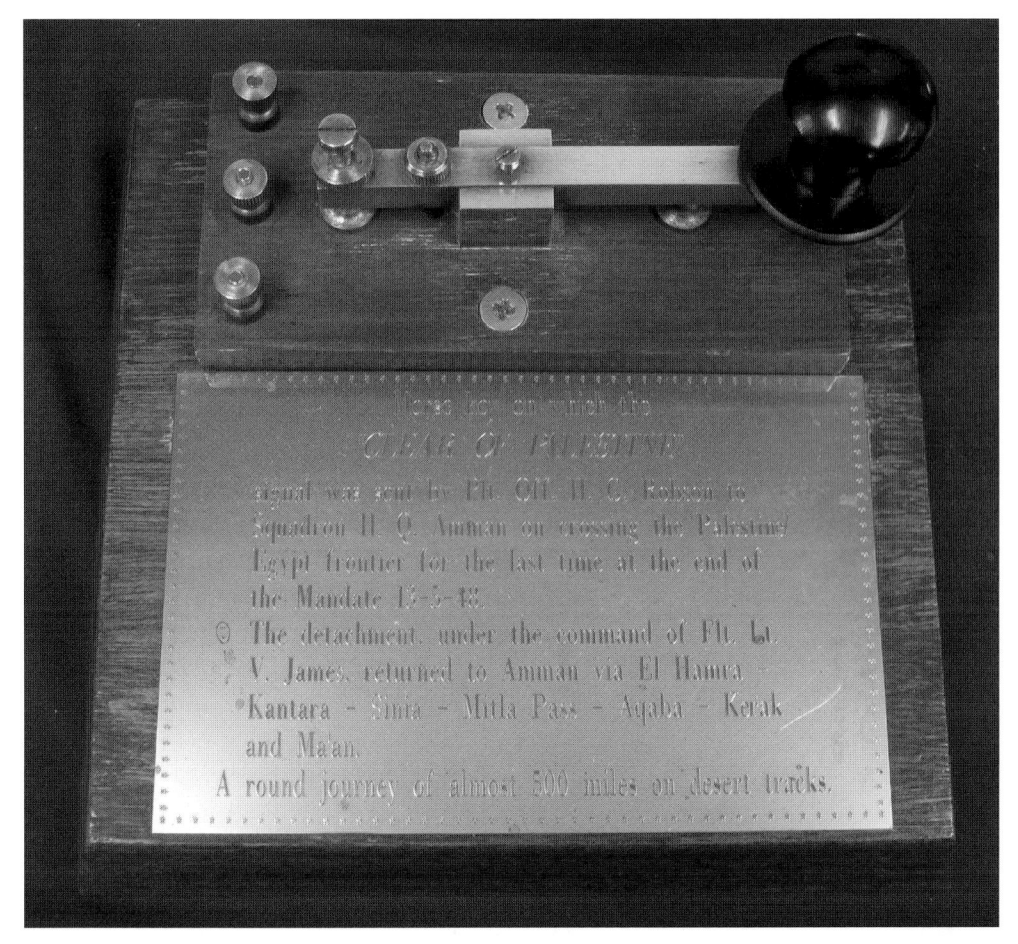

The Morse key, held in the II Squadron History Room, on which the 'CLEAR OF PALESTINE' signal was sent by Pilot Officer Hamish Robson to Squadron HQ Amman on crossing the Palestine/Egypt frontier for the last time at the end of the Mandate 14 May 1948. The detachment under Flight Lieutenant James completed a round trip of 500 miles, primarily on desert tracks (Author).

headquarters onto HMS *Phoebe* and sailed from Haifa harbour, thus bringing to an end almost 30 years fulfilling the League of Nations Mandate.[68]

Once in Egypt, the RAF Regiment contingent proceeded on independently to RAF El Hamra, passing the Egyptian Army on the way as it moved northwards into Palestine. After a few days to repair and service vehicles, the convoy, codenamed 'Dry Trek', comprising 32 vehicles and 150 officers and airmen of 'B' Flight and No 62 (Rifle) Squadron, set off across the Sinai. On the first day, they successfully cleared a number of sand drifts that had covered the road and which particularly hindered the progress of the 4 x 2 lorries in the convoy. The 20 miles of descending road near the Mitla Pass was completed safely, as was the last steep descent from Ras en Naqb, although it tested the brakes of the heavy GMCs. After three days, they reached Aqaba and settled in to the bungalow used as a rest house by the RAF armoured cars crews on the shores of the Gulf.[69] They moved north on the track to Ma'an the following morning. Despite road washouts from winter rains, a sandstorm, a few overheating engines, and after a near round-trip of 500 miles, they drove into RAF Amman at 1730 hours on 25 May, to be met by their OC, Squadron Leader Childs.

As Jordan was now at war with Israel, there was some apprehension that the Israelis might make a retaliatory attack. A strike force of GMCs was kept on the alert and as further insurance four Bofors guns were brought over from Mafraq to stiffen up the anti-aircraft defences. These were to be manned in turn by airmen from No 2 Squadron and No 62 (Rifle) Squadron. The attack however, came in the early hours of 1 June, before the guns could be deployed, as Dick Lock recalls.

> Life was enlivened when we awoke one night to the sound of a string of bombs straddling the camp, dropped by a lone Israeli aircraft. There were no injuries, and the only damage to our Unit was the shattering of a window in the Signals Workshop, and a piece of shrapnel found lodged in the casing of the transmitter in the Radio-Van, having passed through the woodwork of the vehicle. A souvenir at last!

Despite manning the Bofors and preparing to reply to any low-level strafing, there was no further trouble and a few days later, the Squadron celebrated the end of the campaign. Dick Lock continues:

The reunion parade held at RAF Amman on 9 June 1948, following the return of the remainder of the No 2 Armoured Car Squadron from Palestine. In the foreground are the ME21 Signals vehicles (Lock).

The Squadron was now together again... and a parade was ordered. That night we held a massive barbecue, met friends from the other flights and introduced our new boys, and together celebrated the end of another chapter of the "life with the cars". Thankful we had led a charmed life during the past few years.

The contribution of the RAF armoured cars had as usual not gone unnoticed, and as the AOC Levant, Air Commodore Dawson, noted in his final report on the campaign:

> Armoured Cars were invaluable. They escorted inter-station and evacuations convoys. In some cases they had to escort labourers to and from villages; they helped the Army to keep open the Kolundia road, and their mobility and fire power were important factors in the defence of Stations... and of the scattered buildings we occupied in Jerusalem.[70]

The RAF armoured cars had served in a difficult, nasty and unrewarding campaign which had seen much hatred and violence, the unhappy consequences of which we still see today. The last word on these events should however be left to a 21-year-old airman, who perhaps best summarised the absurd nature of the struggle that had enveloped Palestine between 1945 and 1948:

> During our last days in Jerusalem I was in the turret of a car tactfully shepherding a peaceful band of Arab protesters along a narrow street. Looking up at a balcony I spied a young Jew holding a Mills bomb over my head. He gave me a wave with a huge grin. I bade him a quick 'shalom' as we moved away.[71]

Notes

1. AIR 23/8350 *Report on the evacuation of RAF from Palestine, Air Vice-Marshal W.L. Dawson, AOC Levant, October 1948*. Later Air Chief Marshal Sir Walter Dawson KCB CBE DSO (1902-1994).
2. B. Bayliss, *Interview with author*, 2008.
3. 'One of the best jobs in the RAF,' Newspaper article published Palestine c. 1945. A. Hodge Collection.
4. D. Fieldhouse, *Western Imperialism in the Middle East 1914-1958* (Oxford: Oxford University Press, 2006), pp. 275-276, and D. Hopwood, *Syria 1945-1986: Politics and Society* (London: Unwin Hyman, 1988), pp. 29-30.
5. The detachments were usually composed of two or three GMCs and later an ME21 Signals vehicle was added.
6. A. Hodge, *Interview with the author*, 2008, and J. Lunt, *Imperial Sunset* (London: MacDonald, 1981), pp. 81-82, 164-165. Gray remained with the Company until 1947. He then joined the Arab Legion as a contract officer and became commanding officer of the 3rd Mechanised Regiment. He was subsequently decorated for gallantry by King Abdullah after the fighting in Palestine against the Israelis in the 1948-1949 war. Dismissed by King Hussein in 1956, along with all other British officers in the Legion, he then took up a position with the Sultan of Oman's Armed Forces. He was killed and his wife wounded in 1966 by two disgruntled soldiers while serving as the Commanding Officer of the Hadhrami Bedouin Legion in the Aden Protectorate, a month before the end of his seven year contract. Dick Lock recalled: I believe he had no commitments back home, and...

(this was a planned civil settlement that was built on the landward side of the isthmus),
3. For up-country trips doing escort and reconnaissance.

The Section was initially accommodated at RAF Khormaksar, while the new facilities were constructed at Steamer Point, to which they moved in June 1929. They also received a new, though at that stage experimental, Crossley 6-wheeler armoured car fitted with W/T and R/T.

The majority of the RAF 'air control' operations were conducted in the north against recalcitrant tribes in the mountainous hinterland towards the frontier with Yemen. The first major trip by the Section, 'up country' as it was called, was made on 13 February 1928, when a Crossley and a Rolls-Royce armoured car escorted the AOC Aden, Group Captain W.G.S. Mitchell and the Principal Works and Buildings officer, to open up a trade route to Dhala, the largest town near the Yemeni frontier.[8] However, at the foot of the Khureiba Pass, where the track rises from the coastal plain, the road was found to be unsafe to ascend until it had been reinforced and widened. A few months later, presumably with the road suitably repaired, a Crossley armoured car took Group Captain Mitchell and the British Resident, Colonel George Symes, to investigate the report of raid on a border village by the Zaidi tribe from Qataba in Yemen.

The problems of movement by mechanised transport and the heavy armoured cars, particularly on the rudimentary and winding mountain roads around the Western Aden Protectorate, were soon apparent. In one incident, quite close to home, an armoured car fell 75 feet into a ravine after the edge of the road gave way under the weight of the car, when returning from the firing range located only a short distance from Steamer Point on the Aden Peninsula. Surprisingly, the injuries to the crew were slight, with the most serious damage being a fractured shoulder.

While the Rolls-Royces ran as usual with no trouble, the lack of power and unreliability of the Crossley 6-wheeler armoured cars was soon apparent, with

The Crossley six-wheeled armoured cars, AC1 and AC2. The main equipment of the Armoured Car Section, Aden from 1928 until 1939 (© Crown copyright. RAF Regiment Museum).

A Crossley six-wheeled armoured car negotiates the winding and difficult roads of the mountainous hinterland (© Crown copyright. RAF Regiment Museum)

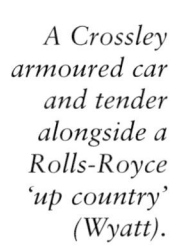

A Crossley armoured car and tender alongside a Rolls-Royce 'up country' (Wyatt).

frequent mechanical problems on each trip into the hinterland. The Crossleys were never satisfactory for the task; as well as the reliability problems, they were far too large and unwieldy for the terrain and tracks they had to traverse.

By 1930, a need for more landing grounds 'up country' had been identified and the Section was sent to assist with their preparation. During March, a Crossley escorted the Royal Engineers of the Aden Fortress Company to Musemir in the Wadi Tiban to upgrade the landing ground to a higher standard and later to prepare a landing strip at Al Masana. Several of the Sappers, the Section Commander, Flight Lieutenant Dickson, and AC1 Swaddle, came down with malaria. This disease would be a recurring problem over the years for the car crews working in the Protectorate.

Closer to the Aden Colony, the annual April activity during the early-1930s was standing by at RAF Khormaksar to deal with any disturbances that might arise during the fair held each year at Sheikh Othman. Further civil order work with the Police was required in May 1932, when tensions arose between the Arab and Jewish communities in Crater. The two Crossley armoured cars carried out long patrols over the next few days and nights in the disturbed areas to suppress street-fighting and looting; their arrival had an immediate calming effect and the cars were not interfered with.

The local populace inspect the cars of the Aden Section after entering a town in British Somaliland (Wyatt).

unit, was making the return trip for company. He heard their tale and was just as excited as us, though the officer seemed to be rather doubtful as to the prospect of making a chase without permission from his senior officer… We camped for the night just inside the border and listened to the many stories and jokes of that happy go lucky Rhodesian Sergeant, who I don't think I will ever forget.

On return to Berbera, maintenance was carried out, though not without mishap, as LAC Wyatt recalls:

Everyone has been very busy putting the cars into tip-top condition. Gunners have also been very busy, for we never know when we may be called upon to go out again. We had some bread today, vile stuff it was too. After digesting it I am firmly convinced that my stomach has a cast iron lining, or will I get punished in years to come? This evening one of the cars caught fire whilst being refuelled with petrol and Corporal Thomason was slightly burnt. Extinguishing it was pretty easy, though we had to work flat out into the night putting the car serviceable again.

On 29 March, the complete Section set off again from Berbera to Hargeisa. They were accompanied by three platoons of a clandestine unit of the Special Operations Executive, known as 'G(R)', which consisted of Somali irregulars led by British officers.[15] The objective of the column was to round up a large group of Italian Somali 'Banda' which locals had told the airmen were heading towards the British Somaliland-Abyssinian frontier at Sigudan. The pursuit was successful, and the following day the 'Banda' were caught 45 miles south of the frontier, as LAC Wyatt recalls:

At midday the enemy were sighted and engaged. Every crew of each car had many stories to tell of what happened in their sector of the fighting. We

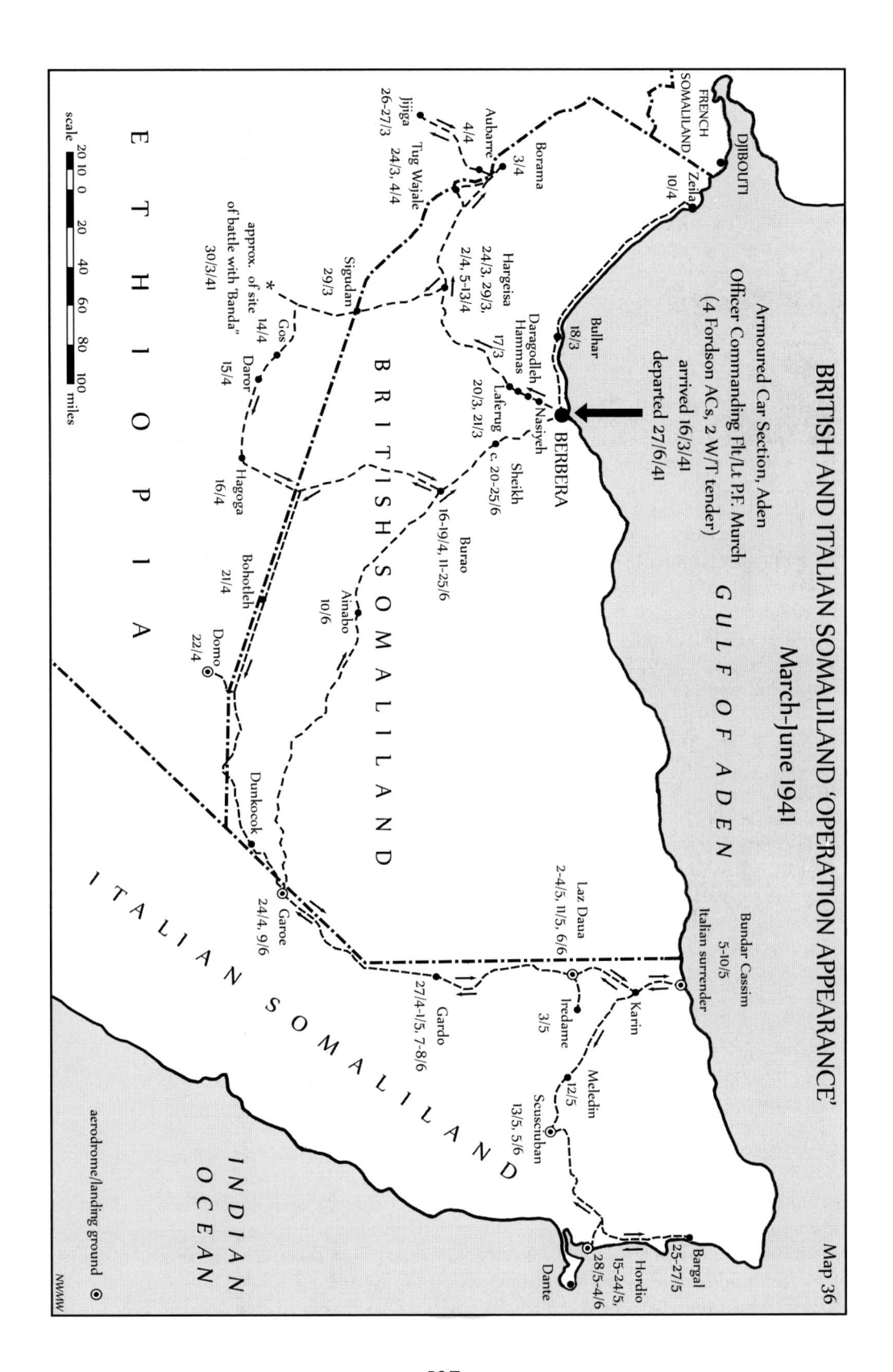

BRITISH AND ITALIAN SOMALILAND 'OPERATION APPEARANCE'
March–June 1941

Map 36

The G(R) unit of Major Musgrave guarding 'Banda' prisoners captured after the battle over the frontier in Abyssinia on 30 March 1941 (Wyatt).

> on AC10 had a puncture in the height of the battle and though amusing to relate it was not funny at the time, crawling around in an attempt to change a wheel when the inconsiderate 'Banda' tried to put us out of our agony. Fortunately everything came out right and we were soon able to resume fighting.[16]

The operation took half an hour and resulted in 12 enemy dead, four wounded and 96 prisoners, with no casualties to the British force. Seven hundred camels, three machine-guns and large quantities of ammunition, including hand grenades, were also captured.[17] Wyatt continues:

> John Harrison's car yesterday was missing after the fighting, and leaving the G(R)s in charge of the prisoners, several of us spread out in lines abreast to search for them. After we had progressed about half a mile, bullets started flying at us from apparently all directions and although we lay flat on our guts we had some narrow escapes. Shortly afterwards we discovered the missing car and on returning learned that a prisoner had made an attempt to get away. The Somalis fired tommy-guns at him and he was practically shot to pieces… We returned to our camping ground of the previous night where the village chief killed and cooked a sheep in our honour.
>
> Early next morning we began the return journey, arriving at Hargeisa, where we had a royal welcome from all the natives. Many things needed replacement and repair. Two Scarff rings were broken and all spare tyres had been used. Two other cars also had tyre bursts from hard stumps of trees that point up out of the ground in this semi-jungle country and are almost invisible to the drivers. Another general trouble was engines overheating, and AC10's brake cable was broken.[18]

The Section spent the first ten days of April with G(R) force on further patrols from their new Headquarters at Hargeisa to Tug Wajale, and later arrested four

Italians at a post at Aubarre on the Abyssinian frontier. Conditions were however, unpleasant as LAC Wyatt recalls:

> With the coming night came the rain, the thunder and lightning was most severe. I had had some good fortune to receive letters from home and to some of them already replied though goodness knows if they will ever arrive at their destination. We have also had to start guards. The natives are pilfering everywhere and making themselves a general nuisance…

The cars set then off on a four day trip with Lieutenant-Colonel Smith, the Chief Political Officer for Somaliland, to visit the Italian posts at Gos and Daror and then back through Burao. The journey was not completed without mishap on the poor roads, as LAC Wyatt recalls:

> We left early this morning heading south, the track was pretty bad owing to recent rain. At one place which was worse than most, the CO decided to wait till all cars got through and ride on the last. Corporal McKenzie, an interpreter and myself were on the leading car, which unfortunately skidded into a big hole and overturned. What seemed so funny was that this was the first and only time that the CO has left his car to go without him. Fortunately no-one was hurt though all were pretty wet.

On 13 April, the Section Commander, Flight Lieutenant Murch, returned from Berbera with orders that they were to accompany the G(R)s on a ten-day operation. After the Section had carried out three days of maintenance and repairs on its vehicles, they were ordered to travel the 145 miles to Bohotleh to rendezvous with Major Musgrave and his G(R) force. With three Fordsons, two W/T tenders and two Morris trucks they were to form 'Muscol'. The task of the column was to move eastward, accept the surrender of any Italian forces, and report on the state of the

A mishap to Fordson AC10 on a road in British Somaliland, 13 April 1941 (Wyatt).

captured aerodromes in north-eastern Italian Somaliland.

On 21 April, 'Muscol' set off along the Abyssinian frontier for the 62 miles to Domo, and then headed north-east to Dunkocok and Garoe following the border with Italian Somaliland. At Garoe, they took the first surrender of an Italian outpost. The armoured cars deployed for action but the remaining occupants of the fort wisely surrendered without opposition, as LAC Wyatt recalls:

> We left camp after making tea and were told that we had to take a fort today. On sighting it, the cars dashed in at full speed, but they had to cross a wadi before getting to the fort. The leading AC10 got stuck and only the united effort of the G(R)s released it. Naturally everyone was panicking and the CO cursed McKenzie better than anyone could from the Billingsgate Market. Anyhow, no resistance was made by the three Italians in occupation. The CO took the flag down to keep as a souvenir.
>
> The excessive heat here is pulling us all down, as yet it is definitely the hottest place I have ever been to… The name of this place is Garoe and apart from the fort contains a few mud houses, but everyone is in dire poverty and I should imagine hungry.

The column then moved off for Gardo the next morning, which although only 135 miles away, took some two days to reach due to the rough track. They arrived to find the Union flag flying, with a South African Air Force aircraft having arrived before them. Gardo did have some redeeming features. LAC Wyatt continues:

> No Italians were in residence and we surmised that they had probably gone to Dante. We found a large spring that the enemy had mined so that after a certain amount of water had been withdrawn the explosion would occur. We soon [made it harmless] and then had a jolly nice swim.

The following morning, 30 April, they set off in pursuit of some local 'Banda' who had been looting, successfully recovered 300 camels and several hundred sheep. The arrival of the armoured cars had been announced by their dust plumes as they crossed a wide plain and the 'Banda' had fled by camel into the hills. The airmen did, however, find some badly wounded Somalis who were taken back to Gardo.

The task was still at hand and the cars then proceeded north to Laz Daua and Iredame. At the former, they cleared the landing ground to allow two Vickers Vincents from No 8 Squadron to land after having flown over from Aden. The aircraft were attached to 'Muscol' to provide air support for the ground operations, and the following day, the Vincents set off for Bundar Cassim on the coast, to drop a message advising the garrison to surrender. While one of the aircraft landed, the second returned to Laz Daua, as Wyatt recalls:

> At 0700 hours one plane returned with the message that the other plane had landed and we were to proceed, as no opposition was to be entertained. It was a distance of 80 miles through the hills and the Italians showed great skill in the beautiful road they had cut and planned all the way. At one point they had built a trap which, had they the guts to have held out against us, would most probably held up the advance indefinitely.
>
> At 1600 hours, we drove into the town and I watched the Italians lower

the flag for the last time, a very impressive ceremony. Many warnings were issued about bathing in the sea because of the sharks, though very few of us took any notice and had a very cool swim. In the evening with the others we paid the Italians a visit. They welcomed us as friends and made us some very nice chai although like us they had no milk. Judging from the amount of coffee roasters about I could see that they, like myself, were great consumers of this very satisfying drink.

Although encountering little opposition, large stocks of rifles, machine-guns and ammunition were found. Here they guarded the Italian prisoners until 10 May, when a Royal Navy ship arrived to collect them and landed rations. The inadequate ration situation and the incessant heat, poor water supply and malarial conditions were taking a toll as Wyatt recalls:

Frank Bushel had a touch of sunstroke today, and McAngus is ill with malaria. In the evening, I passed a great deal of blood when going to the lavatory and was sent to the doctors, for what good he did, I might just as well not have gone. I felt pretty groggy and went to bed. I did not think McAngus ill though, as he would not stop laughing. He was delighted to think that others were beginning to break down under the rough conditions.

Those that were unwell remained at Bundar Cassim, including Wyatt, and were treated by the Italian doctor, but ten days later he was flown out to receive medical treatment in Aden.

Meanwhile, the remainder of the Section made their way back towards Hordio

'John' Wyatt of the Aden Section at Sheikh Pass in British Somaliland (Wyatt).

and Bargal on the eastern coast of Somaliland. An amicable agreement was made with the Italian commander at the former location in that he would hand the town over intact as long as 'Muscol' did not use the radio station, oil and installations for military purposes. The promise was given and the column occupied the area without opposition. The acceptance of the Italian commander's terms had been a wise decision, as it became apparent that every important point had been heavily mined and readied for demolition. The Section moved to Bargal on its own to find the Italians had gone, but returned after three days to Hordio with nine captured vehicles.

After 20 days at Hordio, the column, having repaired the captured vehicles, set off on the return trip to British Somaliland, travelling through heavy sand and badly rutted tracks. Looting was now rife among the native population, but the Section was unable to help with the limited size of the force available. At Garoe, they made contact with the Somaliland Camel Corps garrison and then reached Burao on 11 June after a near 500-mile journey over six days. Here they received orders to return to Aden but were able to enjoy the delights of the hill station at Sheikh for a few days before their departure. The Section sailed from Berbera on 27 June on the SS *Tuna*, *Cola* and MV *Sofala* and arrived at Aden the following day.

The return from Somaliland ended one of the most intensive and trying periods of operations for the Armoured Car Section. The G(R) unit, assisted by the RAF armoured cars and later a pair of Vickers Vincents, had operated across large swathes of British and Italian Somaliland, and killed, captured, or otherwise neutralised, approximately 20-times their own number.

Other than the operation in Somaliland, the early years of the Second World War had been relatively uneventful for the Aden Section. Once the Italian East African Empire had fallen, the direct threat of attack had gone, and the Mediterranean front became the main focus of the war in the Middle East. Aden was to provide a refuelling port and air cover for the convoys moving between the United Kingdom, South Africa, Egypt, India and Australia as they passed across the Red Sea. During most of 1942 and 1943, the main focus for the armoured cars was on training with some road trips up-country, particularly with the establishment of the RAF leave camp at Dhala. The role of the Section during this time was however, focussed mainly on local defence of the aerodromes and other RAF facilities at Khormaksar and the surrounding area.

Flight Lieutenant Murch, who had led the Section during and after Operation *Appearance*, was soon promoted to Squadron Leader and went off to Egypt to take command of the No 1 Armoured Car Company Detachment in Egypt for a short time, before moving on to command No 2 Armoured Car Company. His place was eventually taken by Flight Lieutenant C.A. Mortimore until early 1943, when Pilot Officer G. Curran, who had been serving on the Section since August 1942, took command. Within two months, Curran had been promoted to Flight Lieutenant, and was active in leading the Section on operations beyond the bounds of the Aden Colony and the nearby airfields. The Section moved from Steamer Point to Seedaseer Lines at RAF Khormaksar in August 1942 and then on to RAF Hiswa (known previously as Little Aden) from January 1943. This was only a short stay, and by June it had returned to Khormaksar which provided superior accommodation and better technical, recreational and sporting facilities.

In the last two years of the war, the Section began to be used more regularly in assisting the local British Political Agents in civil control, showing the flag, the

The Section sets up camp near a village in the Western Aden Protectorate (Wyatt).

settlement of disputes, and establishment of truces between warring tribes in the Protectorate. An interesting note, however, was that for a period during early 1943, there was a clear caution by the civil authorities over the Section's movements in the hinterland, and whether its presence might inflame any tribal aggression. The Section was instructed on one occasion that on no account was it to accompany or approach RAF leave convoys proceeding to and from Dhala. Furthermore, any movement by the Armoured Car Section had to be proceeded by a note, to be sent to Headquarters British Forces Aden, requesting permission to travel and which would then be passed on to the Chief Secretary for approval.[19]

Even by 1943, there were still few navigable roads in the Western Aden Protectorate and there was a clear need for a better understanding of the condition and suitability (unsuitably was more often the case) of the routes in the north, west and east of the Protectorate. Consequently, from mid-1943 the Section, usually in a detachment of two armoured cars and two tenders, began exploring these routes. The first trips were across the Western Aden Protectorate to Bir Maknuk, Khor Umeira and beyond as far as Sheikh Said and the island of Perim. This route had never before been traversed by wheeled vehicles. On their return from one of these expeditions, the AOC British Forces Aden commented on the evidence of 'zeal, enthusiasm and persistent effort in overcoming considerable physical and climatic conditions' as shown by Flight Lieutenant Curran and his Section, and added his 'commendation and appreciation of their good work'.[20] Other tasks included routine reports on the road to Dhala, and on one occasion conveying a Medical Officer up to the Rest Camp there to arrange for the evacuation by road of a sick RAF officer, as air evacuation was not possible.

The Fordsons continued to give reliable service until April 1944 when they were handed over to the APL and replaced with GMC Otters. Further trips were made in early 1944 to the east of Aden, along the coast to Shuqra, and beyond to Ahwar. This route was partly along the beach and required careful use of tide tables to avoid trapping the cars in the wet sand. An important task was confirming the accuracy of the maps then in use, as they were often imperfect and misleading. Many of the places they stopped at had not been visited by the RAF in more than a decade, while some had never seen the RAF before.

The RAF Armoured Car Section had been under-utilised as the ground component of air control in the hinterland for the first 15 years of its existence. However, from early 1944 it was to become an essential component of the work of the Political Agents. Correspondence written at the time by Major B.W. Seager OBE, the British Agent for the Western Aden Protectorate, indicates that they had begun to appreciate that they had an instrument with which to demonstrate the power of the Crown to the local inhabitants.[21] This was easily manifested following their arrival at a village with a Bren gun fire display and mock armoured car assault by the Section. However, sick parades for the locals, particularly their children, were also routinely organised by the airmen or an RAF Medical Officer, as these were an effective means of spreading goodwill. The Section was later sent to assist with anti-locust spraying campaigns in areas where agriculture was being encouraged to provide secure food sources. The aim was to demonstrate that the armed forces 'could just as easily turn their hands to peaceful and constructive pursuits' (Map 35, p. 517).[22]

These 'showing the flag' visits were clearly successful, as on their return to the villages the armoured cars were often met by spontaneous native drumming and dancing. Old friendships would be renewed with the heads of tribes and villages, often in areas where officials had previously been met with doubt and suspicion. On one run up-country, the Sultan of Lahej supplied the crews with eggs, chickens and goats for each day of their stay.

Later trips took the Section further along the coast as far as Irka and Dar Dahukha, and then to Ras Quseir in the Western Hadhramaut. Once the coastal routes had been followed, the Section began to open up roads to the villages of the hinterland, improving civil administration and allowing more effective famine relief. In May 1944, the Section, now commanded by Flight Lieutenant Brian Pemberton-Pigott, completed a highly successful tour of the Western Aden Protectorate to

The Aden Section moves 'up-country'. The role of the Aden Section in civil control in the Western Aden Protectorate increased significantly during the later years of the Second World War (© IWM CM 5249).

Dathina and adjacent areas. This region was considered to be the most backward and insecure in whole Protectorate, but the Section was able to assist Major Seager, the British Political Agent, to conclude two truces, detain two hostages from among trouble-makers, and arrest a notorious murderer. The armoured car crews found a common feature of conflicts in these isolated areas were the blood feuds between the various tribes, and they became involved in trying to calm these matters. While visiting Irka, several murders were committed, and two Arabs came in with bullet and dagger wounds.

This success of the British Agents was attributed in large degree to the show of force provided by the armoured cars, and the Governor, writing to the AOC British Forces Aden, expressed his gratitude for the armoured car section's valuable support and cooperation. Furthermore, he observed that the Armoured Cars 'are fitting in admirably as a support to the political staff in the field and that their employment not only increases security but can save bombing in accessible areas...'[23]

During April 1944, there was a disturbance up-country at a village called Khalla, which was located near Dhala. A disagreement had broken out between three tribal parties which led to open conflict, and at the end of eight days of turmoil, there were 17 wounded and seven men dead. A coordinated operation was launched to restore order. A Vickers Vincent was sent up to conduct a photo-reconnaissance to ensure that the ground forces (the Armoured Car Section, an APL company, 40 Government Guards and a detachment of 20th Fortress Company RE) would not be ambushed as they travelled the road to Khalla. Some subterfuge was used to increase the impact of their arrival, with the RAF armoured cars firing their Brens in the air, and tossing grenades to give the impression that the Vincent and Beechcraft aircraft flying overhead were dropping bombs. The Royal Engineers prepared a dhar (a large stone fortified tower) belonging to one of the senior village figures for demolition, and from whence the first shot had been fired that sparked the unrest. The British Agent then addressed the gathered crowd, flanked by two GMC Otters, and gave a stirring speech. Then, at his signal, the sappers detonated their charges, blowing the dhar to pieces with an impressive explosion and a shower of debris.[24]

A month later, Flight Lieutenant Pigott with two GMCs and three tenders set off on a seven-day operation to the Jiblat al Faraj district near Lodar. The area was unmapped and had not previously been visited by motor vehicles, let alone armoured cars. The trip had initially gone well with Pemberton-Pigott and Major Seager, the Political Agent, taking a friendly breakfast with the Sultan of Shuqra before they headed into the hinterland. At one village a young cow was slaughtered by villagers for the delectation of the armoured car crews, and as a genuine sign of appreciation of their medical work. Seager was also able to organise the election of a new sheikh and to renew truces across the Meisari tribes.[25]

At the village of Husan Muhammad Husan however, a struggle broke out while negotiations were underway, and there was concern that shooting would start. The Brens of the GMCs were quickly trained on the dhars and a few grenades were detonated to quieten matters down. The column moved on, but the following day, Seager received a report that there had been an outbreak of robbery, looting and murder against passing camel trains by inhabitants of the village of Hasan Daran Sane. As a consequence, it was decided that punitive measures were to be taken against the bandits. The locals were moved from their houses to a safe distance and a dhar was filled with brushwood and then soaked in petrol and hand grenades hurled in. The building burst into flames and soon collapsed.

The Humbers are giving me problems with big end failures, burst radiators, transmission troubles and differential crown wheels stripping. I get exhausted, keep stripping bits out and doing the best I can with what few spares I can get. I have had to scrounge from the sergeants in the Patiala (Indian) Lancers as the RAF were so poorly stocked so there was quite an exchange thing going on with a few bottles of scotch etc. The worse thing is trying to jack up the vehicles in the soft sand to strip and remove the differential or crown wheel as you have to remove the front wheels and hubs to start to get the drive shafts out. The layrub shaft couplings are hard to get out and refit. Big ends always need to be scraped in to fit the crankshaft. It is no fun. Sweat pours off you and the sand finds every crevice in your body and you become sore in toes, bum, ears, etc. With this experience I should become a good fitter one day!

The engines on these armoured cars are the same as the Humber staff cars. They and the transmissions are not up to the job as they are not suitable for this heat or the country. We even had to remove the armour plates underneath as these made it hopeless to dig the damn things out when stuck in deep soft sand... Imagine how hot it is in these vehicles as the sun heats them up like an oven. The poor driver is the worst off as he sits below without any airflow – at least in the turret the gunner and I do get a bit of air.[28]

The hinterland of the Protectorate had been relatively quiet during the war years and no serious incursions had been reported from Yemen. Indeed, by October 1945, a three year truce had been negotiated successfully between the Meisari, Hassani and Dathina tribes and the Fahdli from Yemen. As the RAF official history noted:

This was probably the first time that these war-like tribes had ever been at

A parade with the Humber Mark IV armoured cars. As with the Crossley six-wheelers of the 1930s, the Humbers were too unwieldy for the roads and tracks of the mountainous hinterland (Author's Coll).

peace and much goodwill was evident: the RAF was warmly thanked for the not inconsiderable part played by its personnel and units, notably the Armoured Car [Section] and a number of staff officers who escorted the negotiators.[29]

The APL had been considerably expanded during the Second World War and by 1945 comprised the equivalent of ten infantry squadrons (equivalent to an infantry company) and a light anti-aircraft wing. The Levies had also been placed under the direct command of the RAF. British Army personnel were replaced by RAF Regiment officers and NCOs, and by 1946, the APL had formed two Mobile Wings. The Levies gradually established garrisons on the frontier with Yemen and at the airstrips at Dhala, Mukeiras and Beihan, while smaller posts were occupied in troubled tribal areas - such as Ataq, Lodar, Mafidh, Nisab, Rabat and the Jebel Jihaf – as the situation required. With the support of the aircraft of No 114 Squadron and the Aden Communications Flight, and the armoured cars of Aden Section, the RAF had at its disposal a considerable force for operations against local tribes and Yemeni incursions.

The situation in post-war Aden, though peaceful, was fragile, and there was always some simmering discontent among one or more of the tribes. In January 1946, tribal animosities again erupted. The source of the trouble was the Western Subeihi tribe, with whom a truce had been agreed in May 1945, and with whom relations were always delicate. Even the local Sheikhs had found this tribe's activities impossible to control. As a consequence, a force of two Humber armoured cars of the Section, two GMCs from the APL, and 180 Government Guards, as well as locally-trained men from Lahej, was despatched with orders to round up the miscreants and install a settled administration under the Sultan of Lahej. Air support was provided by Mosquitos of No 114 Squadron and Albacores of the Aden Communications Flight. The arrival of the column in overwhelming strength subdued the Subeihi and the matter was resolved without conflict after a period of consultation with the tribesmen. Forty-three suspected looters, murderers or raiders surrendered, 13 hostages were released and a number of village towers were destroyed as an example and fines levied.[30]

In June 1946, the Shairis, a small tribe living north-east of Dhala, rebelled against their Amiri overlords, refused to recognise the sovereignty of the Amir Nasr and his son Haidara, and refused to pay taxes. The Amiris then attacked the Shairis with their own guards and Amiri and Radfan mercenaries. They were successful, but after a time the mercenaries turned their hands to robbery and looting on the trade routes over which they now had control. In a sign of the complexities of politics in this region, the mercenaries by various intrigues allowed the Shairis to return to the villages from which they had been driven only a few weeks earlier.

The security of the region was now in a perilous state and consequently, the Political Agent, Major Seager, and the RAF Political Intelligence Officer at HQ British Forces, Squadron Leader Peter Bellerby, were despatched with an escort from the Armoured Car Section to negotiate a truce. Continuous air cover was provided by the Mosquitos of No 114 Squadron. Flight Lieutenant V. 'Jimmy' James was now in command of the Section and he was charged with escorting the negotiators to the area.[31] The column, comprising the OCs jeep, three Humbers and four lorries, set off on the morning of 26 June. After two days of negotiations it was decided to conduct a 'demonstration bombing' of the old RAF Rest Camp by six Mosquitos, to convince the Shairis of the Government's determination in the matter.[32] Sergeant 'Pete' Petrie continues:

> We are to make a run up to the area of Dhala in the mountains as the Sultan is showing off a bit. On the first day, after the usual loading of supplies and servicing we started away at 0700. The first part of the run was fairly easy and we passed the Palace (or fortress) of the Sultan of Lahej about midday. He was one-hundred per cent for the British and had been schooled in England and was a friend to our Royal Family. We used the track to get near to the crossing into Mount Jeman and then on to the lesser tracks toward Dhala stopping to make camp about 1630.
>
> We moved off slowly about 0830 the next morning and finally came to the Dhala Pass. It is marked on the map as passable for vehicles but it does not say so for the clumsy armoured Humbers. I have since thought that if the locals were given a good 20-mm cannon we could have been slaughtered as we crawled up the pass as it twisted and turned with rocks scraping the armour as we climbed up...
>
> We finally made the valley in the mountains. It was fertile and cool. It rained and we just happily stood there in it. It was nice to be cool and wet! The Government House at Dhala was on a small hill opposite the gates to the city and we made camp there with the guns pointing towards the gates. The building that the Sultan was after was below us and to the left. Squadron Leader Bellerby started to make the usual parley talks to the lower Arab officials sited at the bottom of the hill.
>
> Early in the morning of the seventh day, we laid out the aircraft markers for the arranged Mosquito attack who were to use rockets and 250-lb bombs on the Government buildings. We spoke to the pilots on the VHF

Sergeant 'Pete' Petrie (far left) and Squadron Leader Bellerby, the Political Intelligence Officer (in cap) (Petrie).

radio to guide them through the mountains. We felt good that the building would soon be rubbished. But surprise, surprise, they rocketed us by mistake. Luckily none of us was hurt but I am sure that the pilots and crew learnt some new language to go with their burning ears. On the next run in, the bombs and rockets went into the right places, but not that they did much good as, these buildings are made of thick stone and also, some of the bombs did not go off. Pity – it was a good try.

We fired at the building with our own big gun (37-mm) but the shells did no better than the rockets... Flying Officer Brace, myself, and LAC Jones then went down and set explosives in the building and made a better job of it. We also blew up a couple of 250-lb bombs that had not exploded.[33]

To further reinforce their determination, the following morning the Armoured Car Section organised an impressive firing demonstration of their own. Petrie continues:

What we did during the night was to hide a 45 gallon drum with about 5 gallons of petrol in, behind a camel-thorn bush, but taking very great care not to get scratched by the bush. If you did you were due for a quick festering sore. In the morning we gave a very noisy demonstration with our machine-guns, and as a grand finale, fired the big gun with a tracer shell at the hidden drum. By now the sun had baked the fuel and as the shell hit the bush it exploded in flames with a mighty bang. This was all show and we did not tell them that our shells were not capable of blowing up their walls; we just let them think that if we fired at them, this would be their fate. We then left with a warning to behave or else – it usually worked.[34]

The demonstrations proved almost too effective, and the Shairis immediately departed from the area and moved their families, cattle and household goods over the frontier to Yemen. Their hope was that the Government would take over their lands completely and expel the Amiris. The Amiris were however, invited to occupy the vacant land. To encourage the Shairis to return, the Government offered them fair treatment and government aid, and subsequently they began to drift back.[35]

During September, the Section and the Political Officers were again back at Dhala coordinating a further demonstration by the Mosquitos and making a 'flag march' into the frontier areas. In this case, a fly-over was timed to coincide with the visit by the Governor and the Amir of Qataba to the Political Officer's Bungalow to impress on the latter the Government's resolve. These operations were to become more frequent over the next few years and served to highlight the complex tribal and political factors that were continually played out in the civil administration in Aden.[36]

Although the RAF Armoured Car crews were rarely if ever called on to fire their weapons in anger, the local tribes-people did not hesitate to take pot-shots at the airmen while on operations 'up-country' as Sergeant Petrie recalled:

If a local tribe stepped out of line we would camp outside the village. It is against our rules to engage with these people in any form, enter their villages or camps, even any sort of confrontation so as to avoid making ourselves a target for them. If you got into a situation where a gun was fired, and you should miss, then you would be laughed at…

The Arabs have a lot of old fashioned French rifles and were always keen to try us on with them. They were excellent at trying to steal our ammunition and by necessity they were very good at making their own. It is not wise to take chances with them in any way.

During the day, these people were mostly a quiet and peaceful lot but were not averse to firing a few shots into camp. Most of their bullets were lead dum-dums and when they hit the armour on the vehicles they left a lot of hot lead but no serious damage. But if they hit you, they would cut you in half. The night was the worst time for this.[37]

While there was a high tempo of operations there were periods for vehicle maintenance and some relaxation, as Petrie recalls:

Apart for a couple of minor jobs, we had a breather so we were able to carry out really necessary servicing and repairs to our equipment – such as oil changes and gun cleaning. Some much needed rest and even swimming at the NAAFI in Steamer Point. There was a shark net around the swimming area for our safety so everyone quite happily ran and swam in the water without worry. One day the tide went out and we saw a gaping hole in the wire mesh. I hope that the sharks never found out about it. We met our submariner friends from the Royal Navy a couple of times and invited them up to our camp and we had a few good evenings of quite merry hospitality.

There was also the need for inspections and VIP visits. One of these was, however, to cause considerable irritation as 'Pete' Petrie continues:

One stupid thing was that a VIP was visiting Aden and we told to paint our armoured cars green. Unfortunately the paint that they supplied to us would not dry, so we drove in the parade in clean shirts and shorts but were soon covered in paint - but no one could see that as we stood in the turret. As we went past the stand we were required to turn the turrets and lower the gun in salute. I think that almost all of us felt like shooting that VIP.[38]

On 3 October 1946, the Aden tour of Sergeant 'Pete' Petrie and three other airmen had expired and they boarded the SS *Windsor Castle* to return to the United Kingdom. Petrie recalled with great fondness the officers he had served under in the Section:

One of the things that I have not said anywhere is that our officers, Flight Lieutenant Brace, and latterly Flight Lieutenant James, have been a great source of leadership and help. I could not have wished to serve under better men. They always did their best at all times.[39]

The Section had moved yet again during March 1946 to RAF Wali Road, however, a more significant change was now to occur. On the same day that Petrie and the others had departed, the Armoured Car Section, Aden, as with Nos 1 and 2 Armoured Car Companies, was absorbed into the RAF Regiment and became No 4001 Armoured Car Flight.[40] Despite, the change in affiliation, the tasks of the Flight remained the same. The Flight moved again in January 1947 to Singapore Lines at RAF Khormaksar.

By late 1946, it had become clear that the Humber Mark IV armoured cars were worn out and unsuited to the tasks required. Consequently, the Flight had to temporarily loan two GMC Otters from the APL until seven more GMC Otters arrived as replacements in March 1947.

Aden still remained relatively quiet but there were intermittent outbreaks of troubles which were easily dealt with by No 8 Squadron, the APL and No 4001 Armoured Car Flight. Regular trips were made up the Dhala road which remained the major area of trouble. The main action for 1947 concerned Haidara, the rebellious son of the Amir of Dhala. Due to the relative weakness of his father, his son was able to prosecute a campaign against the Government. He ignored all attempts at negotiation and withdrew to a mountain stronghold at Jebel Jihaf near Dhala. During February, a column comprising an entire Mobile Wing of four squadrons of the APL, a 3-in mortar flight and two armoured cars of No 4001 Flight was sent in. In a quick and decisive operation, Haidara was driven from his stronghold but was able to flee across the border into Yemen.

The Flight continued with route reports, patrols and provision of escorts to the Political Agent, and while the usual runs were made to Musemir and Dhala, it had been decided that more of the country had to be opened up. The Flight was therefore despatched on numerous operations to the far-flung corners of the Western Aden Protectorate. The cars explored the feasibility of opening up and improving the overland route to Beihan in the Western Aden Protectorate, and then reconnoitred and assisted in the construction of the road beyond Dhala, from Dathina to Habban, up to the Hadhina Plateau, which had been unusable by wheeled vehicles. The track was successfully constructed over difficult mountainous country by the armoured car crews during the three-week operation, but there was some tribal opposition and the road would not be useable until control could be exerted over the local tribes. Low-level defensive air cover was provided during this operation by the Mosquitos of No 8 Squadron, while the Albacores of the Aden Communications Flight dropped

Vehicles and airmen of No 4001 Flight RAF Regiment at Khormaksar in 1948 (Price).

rations and spares parts to the armoured cars by parachute.

The operations into the hinterland continued into 1947. Lodar was visited and the old landing grounds on the Mukeiras Plateau were inspected to determine their usefulness for future operations. In mid-1947, newly-arrived personnel were taken on runs to Shuqra, Zingibar and the Amyan area for driving and signals training.

In late 1947, responsibility for the Air-Land Rescue task was given to No 4001 Flight and two of the GMCs were fitted with VHF radio to allow them to communicate with aircraft and HQ British Forces in Aden while on operations. During November, the Flight was ordered to Al Milah to support a seven-day operation in the Quteibi area being carried out by Tempests and Avro Lincoln bombers.

In April 1948, the Governor had ordered No 8 Squadron to carry out operational sorties against the Al Yehya, a sub-section of the Haushabi tribe, who were disturbing the peace in the Haushabi and Abyan areas. A detachment of the Flight was required to stand by to respond in instances where aircraft had crashed, and the following rescue operation illustrates the particular difficulties that the RAF armoured cars encountered in the barren, mountainous terrain of the Western Aden Protectorate. On 12 April, a signal was received that a Hawker Tempest on a ground attack mission had crashed near Dar ad Daula, only ten miles from its target.[41] Three GMCs, *Zebra*, *Able*, and *Baker*, a jeep and a 15-cwt, under the command of Flight Lieutenant B.J. Betham, set off with an RAF medical officer and a nursing orderly. Another GMC, *Easy*, would follow with an Engineering Officer.

It was originally planned to reach the Tempest by road via Lahej, which was reached in only two hours. However, this route proved impassable, and even the flight commander's jeep nearly overturned. Circling aircraft indicated the cars were eight miles from the crashed aircraft. Then, a promising track was found, but after a mile or so they were brought to a halt by a 30-foot sheer drop. By this time, it was getting dark and petrol was running low. With the dangerous route conditions, there was no option but to retrace their path to the road and move to Shaka. They made camp for the night and awaited the arrival of much-needed petrol. There was an attempt by an APL Major to reach the Tempest with a camel party but this failed at the first hurdle as he was unable to hire any from the Sultan of Lahej.

At 0200 hours, four 15-cwt lorries of the APL arrived at Shaka with petrol and a flight of the APL. Half an hour later, Pilot Officer Frank Thomsit BEM arrived in *Fox* escorting a 3-ton lorry with petrol, oil, rations and water. The force immediately set about refuelling and by 0430 hours, the 11 vehicles had set off towards Al Milah. From here, the force followed a dry wadi bed covered with large boulders and with speed limited to 2 to 3 miles per hour, progress was slow. To their frustration, a circling Anson informed the column that they were still eight miles from the crashed aircraft, so little seemed to have been gained.

By 0915 hours, they had reached the village of Dar ad Daula, only to find it deserted. Betham ordered the APL to deploy into all-round defensive positions. After a short halt, the cars set off again and proceeded another three miles where they came to open country. From there, the Anson was able to direct them towards the site of the crash. The pilot, Flight Lieutenant Wilson, had only superficial head injuries and he had been well supplied with food and water. The armoured car crews set about assisting the Corporal Wireless Fitter to dismantle and remove the VHF radio from the aircraft. The breech blocks of the 20-mm cannon were also removed and then after the vehicles had moved away a distance the aircraft was set alight.[42]

The column set off for Aden, with the pilot travelling in an APL GMC, and the

Medical Officer in a jeep, reaching base at 0100 hours the next morning. As Flight Lieutenant Betham wrote:

> ... I should like to compliment the car crews, especially the drivers, including those of the APL Force on their fine performance during this trip. It is not generally appreciated that they were driving continuously for 25 hours with few halts and little food over the worst country imaginable; it was entirely to these drivers that the force arrived at the aircraft in the remarkably short time it did.[43]

While the majority of the work carried out by the Flight was in support of operations up-country, there was work to do around Aden itself. A troop of GMCs from the Flight was required to patrol Khormaksar Beach to search for survivors of a Boeing B-29 Superfortress of the United States Air Force; one of three on a round-the-world trip that had crashed into the sea on take-off from RAF Khormaksar on the night of 27 July 1948. After four days of searching, one survivor and several bodies had been recovered.

With the lessons learnt from the operations at Dar ad Daula, it was clear that the Air-Land Rescue organisation had to be modified so that the armoured cars were located up-country near to where the flying operations were being carried out so the response to air crashes could be made more quickly and more efficiently. The Flight continued to provide this role in support of military operations that were increasing in intensity in the Western Aden Protectorate. From 16 to 29 August, the Flight was heavily committed to an operation in support of the APL against a Saqladi Sheikh who was refusing to negotiate with the Government. While a Rear

A typical 'dhar' (Price).

Rescue Team consisting of *Charlie*, *Fox* and *George*, and two jeeps, along with a small Levy force with four camels, was stationed at Nobat Dakim, an Advanced Rescue Team consisting of *Zebra*, *Able*, *Baker* and *Dog* and two jeeps led by Flight Lieutenant Betham, set off for Dhala, where it linked up with a convoy of the APL. The following morning, they set off on the short journey to Khalla where a base was established. An advance on Al Ukla was planned with *Zebra*, *Able* and *Baker*, along with No 3 and 4 Squadrons APL and a small force of Government Guards.

On the morning of 17 August, following information from friendly tribesmen that a hostile group had occupied some of the dhars in the village, the Levies debussed three miles from the objective, while the GMCs escorted the vehicle carrying depth charges that were to be used for building demolitions. A thousand yards from the village, firing broke out and the cars deployed to the right flank to support the move by the Government Guards who had come under heavy fire. They then covered the advance of No 4 Squadron APL with fire directed at a dhar until the village was occupied. The vehicle carrying the depth charge was having trouble so the 250-lb charge and equipment was loaded onto *Zebra* which moved it into the village, coming under considerable sniper fire from nearby mountain sides during its progress. After a short time, the dhar was destroyed and the cars covered the withdrawal of the APL to their vehicles. A further dhar was then destroyed at Haza and they returned to base in Khalla. The remainder of the trip was routine, although sadly a Tempest crashed

The GMCs of No 4001 Flight in support of No 66 (Rifle) Squadron RAF Regiment c. 1948 (Price).

in the target area while making an attack and the pilot was killed. After a few days of maintenance and exercises, the cars of both teams retuned to Aden.[44]

During the last fortnight of October 1948, the Flight along with a detachment of Levies was sent via Shuqra to Ahwar airstrip where it was required to standby at 30 minutes' notice to move during the four days that operations were being carried out by No 2 Wing APL and No 8 Squadron against the Mansuri tribe. As was usual, warning was given by leaflets dropped from an Anson 48 hours before the attack. By this time, every person and head of cattle had been evacuated and the tribesmen then watched the operation from the safety of the nearest hillside. The Tempests carried out constant bombing and rockets attacks from dawn till dusk for three days. While no aircraft were lost, one Tempest did force-land at Ahwar suffering coolant troubles, but was able to proceed after a short time.[45]

During 1948, the GMC Otters had been fitted with VHF radio, and the cars were becoming proficient at air support control for No 8 Squadron. On a number of occasions during 1949, the Flight supplied a GMC as a control car for the Tempests when they were on rocket-firing exercises and training on the air bombing range. The perilous nature of this work was highlighted when one aircraft crashed into sea just off the range, killing the pilot. Time was also spent on escorts for the APL and RAF Regiment convoys travelling to up-country outposts. During April 1949, Flight Lieutenant G.G. Whittle DFM assumed command from Betham, and the Flight came under the direct command of the APL.

Civil unrest in the colony of Aden itself reached a peak during December 1947 when, as the troubles in Palestine worsened, tensions increased between the Jewish and Arab communities in Crater. While a section of the Flight was operating on Air-Land Rescue work in the mountains during the first week of December, the remaining section was on standby at RAF Khormaksar employed on airfield security. Firing was heard and huge fires raged in Crater and Ma'alla, and the three armoured cars were kept busy protecting supply convoys and dealing with looters. While most of the time was spent on standby or making a show of force, there were few instances of direct conflict with the rioters. Sixteen of the airmen were sent into Crater to help recover damaged goods from looted Jewish shops and transport them to a Central Depot for safe-keeping, but by the third week of December the situation had quietened. The Flight was stood down and was able to enjoy three days of Christmas festivities.

In January 1948, there was a large turnover in personnel, with 17 new airmen arriving on the Flight. With such a large influx, the first few months of the year were dedicated to training. May 1948 saw the arrival in Aden of No 20 Wing with Nos 58 and 66 (Rifle) Squadrons RAF Regiment, following the end of the Mandate in Palestine. These two squadrons were made responsible for security at RAF Khormaksar and Singapore Lines, and were assisted in this for a short time in the latter half of 1949 by No 62 (Rifle) Squadron. With two rifle squadrons of RAF Regiment and the eight squadrons of the APL, including their own armoured car flight, there were considered to be adequate resources to deal with protection of RAF assets, as well as any troubles that might arise in the colony or hinterland.

On 5 August 1950 therefore, Flight Lieutenant Zeylmans, his 2i/c, and 26 airmen loaded the seven GMCs of No 4001 Armoured Car Flight, RAF Regiment, onto the LST *Reginald Kerr* for the short sea journey to the port of Aqaba in Jordan, where it was to become the resident armoured car flight at Amman.[46] This ended 22 years of continuous service by this Flight, and its predecessor the Armoured Car Section, in the Aden Colony and beyond. Of all the theatres of operations in which the RAF armoured cars had operated, it was the terrain of Aden that had presented the greatest obstacles to their employment. There were no large sweeping areas of desert hard 'going' where the armoured cars could easily rout parties of raiding Bedouin, but instead a land inhabited by numerous hill tribes and penetrated by a few primitive roads, many impassable to wheeled vehicles. The RAF armoured cars had never been designed for this type of country, and had at first been limited in the roles they could perform by the ineffectiveness of the Crossley six-wheelers. Nevertheless, by the time they departed in 1950 they had come to play a significant part in the policing of Aden, despite these difficulties.

By 1953 however, there was a growing insurgency within the Western Aden Protectorate, supported by arms and finance from Yemen, Saudi Arabia and Egypt. The policy of 'air control' had never been designed to deal with a contingency of this extent and intensity, and the APL, lacking artillery, signals and engineers, found it increasingly difficult to carry out widespread and sustained military operations. When No 4001 Flight had departed, the garrison had retained the APL and No 20 Wing, RAF Regiment, with Nos 58 and 66 (Field) Squadrons.

Permission was eventually given for the expansion of the APL to three wings and in 1955, the formation of a specialist armoured car unit, No 10 Squadron.[47] The Squadron was equipped with the Ferret Mark II armoured scout car and, although part of the APL, was wholly-manned by RAF Regiment personnel from the United Kingdom. This unique unit in an indigenous Force wherein normally only the more senior officers were British, remained so manned until the 1960s, well after the Levies were transferred to the Army. Now, for the first time in more than 30 years, an RAF armoured car unit was equipped with a purpose-built vehicle that had been properly designed for the conditions experienced in the operational theatre. The Ferret was an ideal weapons platform for the 0.30-inch turret-mounted Browning machine-gun, had heavy-duty tyres, and was a reliable communications platform. Number 10 Squadron APL would go on to perform sterling deeds in Aden and personnel from the Squadron would be decorated for gallantry.

The British Army arrived in Aden in late-1955 and took a share of the internal security role and in up-country operations with the RAF Regiment and APL. During this time, there were few disturbances in the Colony, although there were the usual but occasional up-country tribal disputes or border skirmishes with the Yemenis, but these did not threaten the political stability of Aden and the Protectorates.

In 1957, the responsibility for APL passed from the Air Ministry to the War Office and the RAF Regiment's No 20 Wing (Nos 58 and 66 Squadrons) was disbanded. On 1 February 1957, the Officer Commanding the APL, Group Captain Alan G. Douglas CBE MC, who had earned his laurels while serving with No 2 Armoured Car Company during the North African and Iraq campaigns, and who had later commanded No 1 Armoured Car Company, handed over responsibility for the APL to Colonel D.W. Lister DSO MC of the British Army.

The APL became the Federal Regular Army of South Arabia in 1961, in preparation for the United Kingdom Government's aim to eventually shed all colonial possessions. It was only in the last years of the British presence in Aden when there were increasing outbreaks of rioting, street-fighting and terrorism that the RAF Regiment returned and were to remain there until the final withdrawal in November 1967, bringing to an end 128 years of British rule.

Notes

1. AIR 23/710 *Armoured Car Reconnaissance, April 1943-August 1944*. Correspondence from J. Hathorn Hall, Governor, Aden, to AOC British Forces, Aden, 25 May 1944. Later Sir John Hathorn Hill GCMG DSO OBE MC (1894-1979).
2. H.B. Jones, Extract from 'Aden – to be carried in the hand of every Airmen on arrival in England', n.d. RAF Regiment Museum Archives.
3. In Arabic, the 'khor makswr' or 'broken neck'.
4. J. Lunt, *Imperial Sunset* (London: MacDonald, 1981), p. 142 and R.A. Cochrane, 'The Work of the Royal Air Force at Aden', *Journal of the Royal United Service Institute*, LXXVI (1931), 88-99.
5. Cochrane, 'The Work of the Royal Air Force at Aden'. An estimated saving of £100,000 per year.
6. Lunt, *Imperial Sunset*, pp. 133-134. A locally-enlisted force, the Yemen Light Infantry, had been raised during the First World War when the colony was threatened by Turkish forces, but this had been disbanded in 1925. When the RAF took responsibility for Aden in 1928, the predominantly Indian Army garrison was replaced by the Aden Protectorate Levies (usually abbreviated to the APL) which was a British-officered infantry unit composed of locally-enlisted Arab tribesmen.
7. The Armoured Car Section, Aden, was established with two officers, a Sergeant, three Corporals and 27 airmen.
8. Later Air Chief Marshal Sir William G.S. Mitchell KCB CBE DSO MC AFC (1888-1944).
9. AIR 29/57 *Armoured Car Section, Aden, January 1928 to September 1946*.
10. Rather unusually, the Section was also responsible for the High-Speed Launch commanded by Flying Officer W.V. Hatey.
11. AIR 2/7221 *Aerodromes: use of armoured cars for aerodrome defence, 1940-1942*. The 11 Alvis armoured cars that had been sent to the Middle East in the late-1930s were all reconditioned and modified at the Alvis factory on their return to the United Kingdom. They were then dispersed across the country to various aerodromes of Fighter, Bomber and Coastal Command for local airfield defence. As spare parts were lacking, the cars had a limited service life.
12. The Striking Force consisted of: HQ Striking Force, 18 Mountain Battery, 1/2nd Punjab Regiment (less one company), 3/15th Punjab Regiment, Armoured Car Section - Aden, G(R) Aden, detachment REs and supply issue section.
13. D.J.E. Collins, *The Royal Indian Navy 1939-1945* (India & Pakistan: Combined Services Historical Branch, 1964), pp. 38 *ff*.
14. Patrick K. 'John' Wyatt, *Diary, Armoured Car Section, Aden 1941*.
15. HS 9/1080/2 *Report by Major G.R. Musgrave*. This unit had been formed in London in September 1940 as Military Mission 106 of the Special Operations Executive (SOE) and was sent to the Middle East, where it was re-reorganised and renamed as G(R). By March 1941, it was located in Aden. It had been destined for operations to foment an uprising in Abyssinia prior to the invasion by British forces but then was allocated to the Aden Striking Force. It was disbanded in August 1941. The unit was commanded by Major G.R. Musgrave. As cited in S. Anglim, 'MI(R), G(R) and British Covert Operations, 1939–42', *Intelligence and National Security*, 20(2005), pp. 631-653. The function of G(R) was described as follows: it is that section of the General Staff at GHQ Middle East … which is responsible for organising all irregular and guerrilla activities where these can be carried out by uniformed personnel, i.e. in enemy and allied countries where operations are in progress … When activities which in the first place had to be conducted covertly can, owing to changing circumstances, be conducted overtly, i.e. by uniformed personnel, they become the responsibility of G(R).
16. Wyatt, *Diary*.
17. AIR 29/57 *Armoured Car Section, Aden*.
18. Wyatt, *Diary*.
19. AIR 23/710 710 *Armoured Car Reconnaissance,* Correspondence: HQ British Forces,

Aden to Armoured Car Section, 3 May 1943.
20 *Ibid*. Correspondence: Air Vice-Marshal F.H. McNamara VC CB CBE (1894-1961) to Officer-Commanding RAF Station Khormaksar, 3 July 1943.
21 *Ibid*. Correspondence: British Agent, Western Aden Protectorate to HQ British Forces, Aden, 14 January 1944.
22 *Ibid*. Correspondence: British Agent, Western Aden Protectorate to HQ British Forces, Aden, 31 July 1944.
23 *Ibid*. Correspondence: J. Hathorn Hall, Governor, Aden, to AOC British Forces, Aden, 25 May 1944.
24 AIR 29/57 *Armoured Car Section, Aden,* Report on operation at Khalla, April 1944.
25 *Ibid*. Report on operational movement carried out by Armoured Car Section, Jiblat al Faraj and District, 12-19 May 1944. Some idea of the strain on vehicles and men when driving in Aden can be found in this report. It was estimated that 57 gear changes were required in one 5-mile stretch. This meant that for a 120 mile trip, some 6000 gear changes were required.
26 D.A. Petrie, *Reminiscences of Sergeant D.A. Petrie, RAFVR, No 2 Armoured Car Company (January to May 1945) and Aden Section (May 1945 to September 1946)*. Provided to the author by his son, David Petrie.
27 The Section eventually had five Humber Mark IV and a Daimler Mk II armoured cars.
28 Petrie, *Reminiscences*.
29 D. Lee, *Flight from the Middle East* (HMSO: London, 1980), p. 44.
30 AIR 29/57 *Armoured Car Section, Aden*.
31 'Jimmy' James would later serve in No 2 Armoured Car Squadron in Palestine.
32 AIR 29/57 *Armoured Car Section, Aden*. Escort force to Dhala area, 26 June to 16 July 1946.
33 Petrie, *Reminiscences*.
34 *Ibid*. Petrie was posted back to the United Kingdom in October 1946.
35 AIR 24/1678 *Headquarters British Forces Aden January to December 1946*.
36 AIR 29/57 *Armoured Car Section, Aden*. Reconnaissance and training to the Dhala area, 4-15 September 1946.
37 Petrie, *Reminiscences*.
38 *Ibid*.
39 *Ibid*. Flight Lieutenant Edward A. Brace MBE.
40 AIR 29/1414 *Independent Armoured Car Flight (No 2701 Squadron RAF Aden)* and AIR 29/1719 *No 4001 Armoured Car Flight, Aden*. From October 1946 until February 1947, the unit was known as the Independent Armoured Car Flight, No 2701 Squadron, when it was renumbered as No 4001 Armoured Car Flight.
41 No 8 Squadron's Mosquitos had been replaced by rocket-firing Hawker Tempest VIs
42 AIR 29/1414 *Independent Armoured Car Flight*, Report on Air-Land Rescue carried out by 4001 Flight between 12 and 14 April 1948.
43 *Ibid*.
44 *Ibid*. Report on Operation carried out by 4001 Armoured Car Flight Royal Air Force, August 1948.
45 *Ibid*. Report on Air-Land Rescue Operations at Ahwar carried out by 4001 Armoured Car Flight Royal Air Force, 17-27 October 1948, and D. Lee, *Flight from the Middle East* (London: HMSO, 1980), pp. 39-40.
46 LST, landing ship, tank. Flight Lieutenant Geoffrey Zeylmans had assumed command in December 1949.
47 K. Oliver, *Through Adversity: The History of the RAF Regiment* (Rushden, Northants.: Forces & Corporate Publishing, 1997), pp. 194-195.

Chapter Twenty-three

Farewell to Armour

"In a bloodless combined operation, the Trucial Oman Levies, vehicles of the RAF Regiment's No 2 Armoured Car Squadron, and jet Vampire fighter aircraft of No 6 Squadron, dispersed tribesmen from east of the Trucial boundary..."

Middle East Air Force Report, 1953[1]

Following the post-war reduction in size of the RAF in the Middle East and the withdrawal from Palestine, most of its operational units were concentrated in Egypt. The RAF stations at Amman and Mafraq in Jordan were to be maintained as staging posts between Cyprus and the Persian Gulf. Neither station hosted any flying squadrons but there were three Middle East Command training schools based at Amman; Officer Advanced Training, General Service and Physical Training. Defence of the RAF assets in Jordan was provided by No 19 Wing RAF Regiment with No 2 Armoured Car Squadron and No 62 (Rifle) Squadron (Map 3, p. 29).

The arrival of the entire No 2 Armoured Car Squadron at Amman in 1948 was indeed a homecoming. Flight Lieutenant T.P. Yorke Moore had established his section of Rolls-Royce armoured cars at Amman some 26 years earlier and either elements of, or the complete No 2 Company had been in residence for the majority of that time. On 22 May 1946, the Anglo-Transjordan Treaty was signed and the Mandate ended, with the country now known as Jordan becoming an independent state with His Highness Amir Abdullah assuming the title of King. The relationship between the RAF and the Hashemite Kingdom of Jordan had also been long and close, with the RAF armoured car crews having worked on many operations in both peace and war with the Arab Legion. The standing of the RAF in Jordan had remained high even throughout the troubles in Palestine. At their height, the AOC Levant, Air Commodore Dawson, could drive from his Headquarters in Jerusalem with a heavily-armed escort and then at the Allenby Bridge, dismiss them. Indeed, he would leave his personal weapons in the Jordanian guard post on the eastern side of the bridge, and proceed unprotected to Amman.

An armoured car flight from No 2 Squadron had been stationed at Amman for short periods during 1947, no doubt providing a welcome break from the intense civil disorder and counter-insurgency operations in Palestine. 'C' Flight participated in exercises with the Arab Legion at Aqaba during July, while in October, 'A' Flight took part in Operation *Duststorm*, at Dawson's Field, located on the mudflats a few miles north-east of Zerqa.[2] The aim of this operation was to test the ability of a fighter squadron to establish a base quickly at a new airfield in an isolated location

– a capability that had become *de rigueur* in the heady days of the advance of the Desert Air Force after El Alamein. 'A' Flight was ordered to proceed to the airfield to provide all-round defence and await the arrival of a squadron of Spitfires from Palestine. Various war games were then held with the Spitfires and the Arab Legion (Map 3, p. 29).

The Arab-Israeli conflict had raged in neighbouring Palestine until July 1948 and so at RAF Amman, No 2 Armoured Car Squadron had manned the four Bofors guns in turn with No 62 (Rifle) Squadron, following the Israeli air raid of the previous June. The struggle in Palestine had led to discontent amongst the population of Amman, much of it driven by the thousands of Palestinian refugees. There were isolated instances of rocks being thrown at RAF armoured cars as they passed through, and for a time British nationals were ordered to stay away from the centre of Amman. During July, a temporary truce was agreed between the Arabs and Israelis and the threat of air attack diminished, the Bofors were placed in storage, and the local unrest subsided. Matters quietened down and, as the truce held, there were few operational commitments for the remaining months of 1948.

Training became the main focus for Squadron Leader Childs of No 2 Armoured Car Squadron, and the Squadron was reorganised for this purpose. All the regulars were placed in 'B' and 'C' Flights, where they would undergo an extensive training programme, whereas the remaining airmen in HQ and 'A' Flight would be given maintenance and defence duties. Map reading and signals exercises were carried out to Mafraq, Ma'an and Aqaba. The good relations the RAF enjoyed with the Jordanians were further evidenced at the town of Es Salt. Whilst on an exercise practising patrolling techniques to intercept saboteurs, the cars of No 2 Squadron were surprised to find almost the entire Arab population had turned out to give them an excited and friendly welcome. In November of that year, there was recognition of the work of Squadron Leader Childs and Sergeant C.H. Webb during the operations in Palestine, with both being mentioned in despatches.[3]

The post-war presence of the RAF in Iraq had been governed by the treaty of 1930, whereby Britain gave administrative, economic and technical aid in return for the use of air bases at Habbaniya and Shaibah with its satellite at Basra (Map 2, p. 24). Habbaniya was being further developed into a magnificent desert air station with every amenity and facility to mitigate the oppressive heat and arid surroundings. Following the war, Air Headquarters Iraq at Habbaniya had also assumed responsibility for RAF Bahrain and for RAF Sharjah, Sharjah being one of the seven Trucial States on the coast of the Persian Gulf. All of the aforementioned stations were not only important staging posts for the increasing British military commitments in the Far East, but also locations from which to deploy British forces to trouble spots within the region.

With the end of the British Mandate in Iraq in 1948, a new Anglo-Iraqi agreement was signed in Portsmouth, with similar terms to that of the 1930 treaty – although this was repudiated within two weeks following serious civil unrest and the resignation of the Iraqi Government. Many Iraqis remained unhappy with the British presence in Iraq, and in the following years there were increasing numbers of demonstrations and outbreaks of rioting. By 1950, there had been a further resurgence of nationalism and an intensifying desire to review existing treaties. The increasing influence of the USSR on regional politics also exacerbated industrial and political unrest. In accordance with the Anglo-Iraqi agreement, the RAF could play no part in controlling civil disturbances and therefore concentrated on security and

Operation Duststorm at Dawson's Field, October 1947. 'A' Flight vehicles (upper), Spitfires arrive from Palestine (middle) and a Lancaster makes a fly-over (lower) (Lock).

defence of its stations.

Since the departure of No 1 Armoured Car Company for Qastina in Palestine in 1946, airfield defence on the RAF airbases in Iraq had been in the capable hands of the 1700 men of the Iraq Levies, who were organised in two wings of four squadrons, with their officers mainly drawn from the RAF Regiment. With the post-war rundown of British forces there remained not a single operational RAF squadron in Iraq. Various flying squadrons came and went, but the view was held that reinforcements, if needed, could be sent at a few hours' notice from the Canal Zone. In October 1948 however, No 2 Armoured Car Squadron was ordered to relocate to RAF Habbaniya, as Squadron Leader Childs recalls:

> ... I had to leave one flight behind in Amman and took HQ and the others down to Habbaniya. Periodically we'd go down to the Persian Gulf. Just a 'show of force' and we'd run the polished armoured cars round in a convoy just to show them that we were still there.[4]

During January 1949, the Squadron busied itself for the inspection by the Command RAF Regiment Officer and Force Commander RAF Levies Iraq, Group Captain H.M. Vaux MC. The GMCs were repainted for the occasion, and after touring the facilities and interviewing each officer, Vaux took the salute as the Squadron drove past. Sadly on a return flight from Amman a few days later, his plane came down in a dust storm and crashed in the Euphrates as it attempted to land. He and the pilot were killed and while the latter's remains were recovered with the aircraft, the Squadron spent the next few days scanning the Euphrates by day and night in the vain hope of finding Vaux's body. Memorial services were held for Group Captain Vaux, on 16 February at both St George's Church and then the Levies' Chaldean Church at Habbaniya. Vaux's body was eventually recovered from the Euphrates on 9 April and brought back for burial at RAF Habbaniya.[5]

An important role the Squadron performed at Amman and Habbaniya was as a ground component of the Desert Rescue Organisation. This comprised air traffic control personnel, search aircraft, and the Station Desert Rescue Unit. The latter operated recovery vehicles, and along with the duty armoured car flight, were ready to respond to any reports of downed or missing aircraft. Squadron Leader Childs recalls one such incident:

> The outstanding instance at Habbaniya was when we'd lost a Devon aircraft that was being delivered to the AOC Far East. They were ordered to come via Mafraq and refuel there, but instead of that they decided to make a short cut and come straight across to Habbaniya, and of course halfway across they ran out of fuel and put down in the desert.[6]

On 15 June, the Squadron was ordered out to search for the de Havilland Devon. A search aircraft located it deep in the southern desert, west of Nukhaib. While the uninjured crew were flown back to Habbaniya, Childs and No 3 Flight, with seven GMCs, five lorries, a group of heavy aircraft recovery vehicles including a crane, a Diamond T with trailer and two Mack 10-tonners, were sent off on a 400-mile return journey to recover the aircraft. Travelling through soft sand and across insecure local bridges, the site was reached after a long and difficult journey, particularly for the heavy vehicles.[7] He continues:

It took us about three days to find them and it took us five days to get out to the aeroplane and take it to pieces and bring it home. We had everything supplied by air. It was just parachuted to us. We weren't allowed to shave, or anything of that. Water was for drinking purposes only.[8]

The gunners set about dismantling the Devon under instruction from the RAF salvage technicians and with a shortage of packing to load the Devon safely for the return trip, the airmen were relieved of their bedding for that purpose. Childs considered this a mission of some success which deserved a celebration:

And when we got back to Habbaniya we were met by the Station Commander, who agreed to my request that the chaps wanted to keep their beards on till the following morning. This was granted and we had a hell of a night.[9]

Training remained a constant activity and field exercises were held on a regular basis. During this period, No 2 Squadron practised air-ground cooperation with No 84 Squadron while further exercises were held in Jordan with No 21 Light Anti-Aircraft Squadron RAF Regiment.[10] There were also annual exercises with the RAF Levies Iraq, as well as desert rescue and supply-dropping practice.

The maintenance of the Anglo-Jordanian relationship remained important for both sides. Britain had guaranteed to provide military assistance to Jordan should it be subject to aggression by its neighbours, and with a worsening of the relationship between Great Britain and Egypt, Amman and Mafraq were of increasing importance as alternative airfields should it be necessary to withdraw from the Canal Zone.

The resident armoured car flight that had remained at Amman was kept busy during 1949. There was some unease with the Israeli forces still active on Jordan's western frontiers, and later in the year there were strained relations with Syria, until a *coup d'état* in the latter calmed matters. In the north of the country, a detachment of GMCs was routinely sent to the satellite airfield at Mafraq. Interestingly, the airfield was shared with 18 aircraft of the Royal Iraqi Air Force as a consequence of the establishment of a joint command between Jordan and Iraq. The cars remained there for the first two months of the year until replaced by a Bofors detachment from No 52 (Rifle) Squadron.

In the south, the Israelis had reached the eastern edges of the Negev and their jeep patrols were constantly probing towards the port of Aqaba. All supplies, arms and large shipments of ammunition for the RAF in Jordan arrived through this port and were transported along the road from Aqaba to Amman. With the threat of further Israeli intrusions, there was a heightened concern over the safety of this supply line. There was considerable reason for caution as on 7 January 1949, four Spitfires of No 208 Squadron were downed by Israeli anti-aircraft fire and air attack. A Tempest searching the area for the missing aircraft was then also shot down. As a consequence, the cars from the Amman flight of No 2 Squadron routinely escorted the supply convoys. Two GMC armoured cars usually accompanied each convoy which usually comprised two dozen 3-tonners and 10-ton lorries, an MT breakdown vehicle, as well as a petrol and water bowser. They were assisted in their escort task at times by a troop of 42 Commando Royal Marines.

By April 1949, however, the threat of hostilities between the Arabs and Israelis had diminished considerably with an armistice having been signed by Israel with Egypt, Lebanon and Jordan. No further incidents occurred and the British

Government's formal recognition of the State of Israel in late January 1950 further reduced tensions.

In December 1949, Squadron Leader Childs had departed for the United Kingdom, and Squadron Leader L.G. Inglefield assumed command. By this time however, it was becoming difficult to maintain adequate numbers of airmen across the units in the Command and in the case of No 2 Squadron manning levels had dropped to 60%. The AOC Iraq therefore decided to withdraw the armoured car flight from Jordan and the entire Squadron was concentrated at Habbaniya.

The majority of 1950 was relatively uneventful in Iraq, with new airmen arriving and requiring training. After less than a year's absence from Jordan however, the armoured car flight returned. A disagreement had arisen between Israel and Jordan over the stretch of road between Aqaba and Amman. During October, the Israelis had driven a convoy down the road, which was in Jordanian territory, and a skirmish had developed with the Arab Legion. Although the RAF was not directly involved in the action, this road was still of major importance for the passage of supplies and ammunition coming from Aqaba to the RAF Stations at Amman and Mafraq, both of which had to be continually stocked and defended.

With the concentration of all three flights of No 2 Armoured Car Squadron at Habbaniya, the requirement for an RAF armoured car flight to be permanently stationed at Amman had to be met from elsewhere. During August 1950 therefore, the Squadron received notice that No 4001 Armoured Car Flight would be arriving at Aqaba from Aden on the LST *Reginald Kerr*. With two officers and 26 airmen and seven GMCs, this Flight was the to become the resident armoured car flight at Amman.[11] After a few weeks at Amman, No 4001 Flight travelled to Habbaniya where, under the supervision of No 2 Squadron, it underwent intensive training, and its GMCs, which were badly in need of an overhaul, were reconditioned in the Squadron workshops.[12]

Despite the political upheavals of the post-war years in the Middle East and the occasional resurgence of conflict with Israel, Jordan had remained relatively quiet. However on 20 July 1951, King Abdullah, who had ruled Jordan from 1921 with a

The GMCs of No 2 Armoured Car Squadron at RAF Habbaniya during the inspection of the station by the AOC Iraq on 1 February 1951 (© Crown copyright. RAF Regiment Museum).

Inspection of No 4001 Armoured Car Flight at RAF Amman by King Talal I of the Hashemite Kingdom of Jordan (fourth from left) in November 1951 with RAF officers (second from left to right): Flight Lieutenant G.N. Zeylmans Flight Commander, Air Marshal Sir John Baker KCB MC DFC Middle East Air Force, Group Captain E.J. Palmer OBE OC RAF Amman and Air Vice-Marshal G.R. Beamish CB CBE AOC Iraq (© Crown copyright. RAF Regiment Museum).

great degree of political acumen, was assassinated while visiting the Al Aqsa Mosque in Jerusalem. Fortunately, the situation did not develop into further bloodshed and he was succeeded by his first son, Talal. King Talal's reign was short-lived due to ill health, and following his abdication after only a year, Abdullah's grandson, the Crown Prince Hussein ibn Talal, at 16 years old, was proclaimed as the ruler of the Hashemite Kingdom of Jordan.[13]

During May 1952, perhaps in response to the threat of instability in Jordan, No 3 Flight under Flight Lieutenant John Simpson participated in a further large-scale joint exercise in Jordan with No 19 Wing RAF Regiment, the Arab Legion and two battalions of The Parachute Regiment. The Flight was given the task of linking up with airborne forces, securing the dropping zone, and then reconnaissance to establish contact with the enemy.

Since 1945, the major focus of operations for the RAF armoured car, field and light anti-aircraft squadrons had been in Palestine and Jordan countering the threats to RAF airfields and assets posed by the Arab-Israeli conflict. From 1950 however, there was a gradual shift in attention to Iraq, and instability in Persia, Kuwait, and the Trucial States of the Persian Gulf. Furthermore, with increasing commitments in the Far East, the RAF was considerably stretched and it was decided that rather than maintaining flying squadrons at each of the RAF stations across the Middle East, forces were to be deployed to trouble spots as required from either Egypt or Aden.

This operational posture was predicated in large part on the important role of RAF Regiment squadrons protecting the airfields wherever the flying squadrons were to be deployed in the theatre of operations. The first potential crisis in the Persian Gulf had arisen in early 1950 when the Amir of Kuwait became unwell and there was a fear of friction between his potential successors.[14] The British Government was apprehensive that this might lead to internal instability, which would have consequences for the security of the installations of the Kuwait Oil Company. Number 2 Squadron was therefore put on 24-hour notice to move, and on 28 January, loaded its vehicles onto railway wagons and was transported to Margil station in southern Iraq, from where they proceeded by road to RAF Shaibah.

No immediate move was made into Kuwait and so the airmen spent the next three weeks at Shaibah awaiting further instructions. In the meantime, they occupied themselves with training in and around the airfield and on vehicle maintenance. The succession of the ruler of Kuwait was eventually resolved without trouble. Indeed, on 23 February, the Squadron was given the order to proceed into Kuwait, not to carry out an internal security operation, but to participate in a 'courtesy visit' and ceremonial parade to celebrate the accession of Sheikh Abdullah III Al Salim Al Sabah.[15] The CO, Squadron Leader L.G. Inglefield, was also required to represent the RAF at the dinner given by the new Sheikh. The airmen were treated well by the local British families and were also given tours of the oilfields.

Following the partitioning of India in 1947, the RAF Regiment had received an influx of officers who had previously served as regulars in the Indian Army, prior to the granting of independence. Squadron Leader E.J.B. 'John' Brown, was one such an officer, and he arrived to take command of No 2 Armoured Car Squadron during December 1950. Another Indian Army officer joining in April 1951 was Flight Lieutenant P.D. 'Pat' Lee. He continues:

> I came from Egypt as a replacement officer, as the previous 2 i/c had broken both ankles. Being an infantry officer and new to armoured cars, it was agreed that I should learn something about armoured car tasks and tactics. So I went to the Senior Ground Defence Staff Officer in the Middle East and he arranged for me to go to the Royal Dragoons in the Canal Zone. They had the big Staghound armoured cars and their Warrant Officer took me on all the details. He was very good and I learnt about 2-pdrs and tactics and lines of observation.
>
> As 2i/c, I then had to teach my officers in the Squadron as well. John Brown knew what I was doing and he agreed with me. He was a trained infantry soldier as well and so he relied on me for a lot of these things.[16]

The immediate problem facing John Brown was that the Squadron had a serious shortage of NCOs, particularly gunner Corporals, qualified wireless operators and technicians. So dire had the situation become, that No 3 Flight had to be temporarily disbanded.[17] Furthermore, for a unit which had prided itself during the war years on its signalling expertise, it was having great difficulty obtaining either spares for the now ailing Collins type sets and the components needed to install the No 19 Army wireless sets.

The wartime service personnel had all gone and the Squadron was now composed of a few regulars and a larger group of airmen doing their stint of National Service. Airmen such as Jon Jordinson, Barry Walker, Ron Fairweather, and Ray Hill had been called up for National Service during 1951. As Pat Lee recalls there were two types of National Servicemen:

The GMCs of No 2 Armoured Car Squadron in the parade celebrating the accession of Sheikh Abdullah III Al Salim Al Sabah as Ruler of Kuwait in February 1950. (© Crown copyright, RAF Regiment Museum).

There were those who were going to accept it and did their best and enjoyed it and there were those who were going to moan and groan and say I'm wasting my time.[18]

Many saw it as an opportunity to improve their education level or learn new skills that they could then use in civilian life, as Ray Hill recalls:

I went to Cardington to get kitted out and then West Kirby to do our RAF Basic Training. And then after that they called us in for our separate interviews. So I said "Well if I've got to be in the forces I want to get something out of it. So I wouldn't mind learning how to drive." The interviewing NCO said "Well we can offer you driving, but the only way you'll get it is if you sign on for three years and you join the RAF Regiment." So I said fair enough, if that's what I've got to do, that's what I'll do. That's how I came to be in the RAF Regiment.

I hadn't got a clue what the Regiment was. So I went up to Dumfries for the RAF Regiment Basic Training and then when we'd finished that off I went down to Weeton to learn to drive through Blackpool at the height of the season which was a bit hairy anyway. Then after that we came back off leave and went off to RAF Innsworth (the RAF Personnel Despatch Centre) for kitting and then off to Iraq. We dropped into El Hamra in Egypt for about a fortnight and then they gathered us up and said you there, you there ... and we finished up in Iraq.[19]

The gunners of No 2 Armoured Car Squadron RAF Regiment at Basra (Walker).

Jon Jordinson had been a civilian driver before joining up but was required to complete the RAF driving course as well:

> I started my basic training at RAF West Kirby and I was already a civilian driver before I went in and they asked me what I wanted to do. They said you can get in the RAF for nine years. I said no way to that. I'd already signed up for three years then. Well they said "You can go in the RAF Regiment," so I said "That'll do me." I was nine weeks at the RAF Regiment Depot at Catterick and while I was there they took me on a driving test. There were only three of us that had civilian licences.
>
> I left RAF Lytham St Anne's, where you got all your inoculations, then went by train to Harwich, a troopship from there to the Hook of Holland, and then a troop train right through to Trieste. We then sailed on the SS *Empire Test* to Egypt. I was there doing various jobs before I got a posting to 2 Armoured Car Squadron.[20]

Ron Fairweather recalls the intricacies of National Service and what was necessary to be able serve in Iraq with No 2 Armoured Car Squadron:

> I joined up for three years… A tour overseas was two years, so if you only went in for the two years of National Service, then you didn't have to go overseas. That was why I went in for three years, so I could go overseas. Plus the fact that if you signed up for three rather than two years you became a regular, so your money was better. You were also classed as a 'regular' by the longer serving regular servicemen, so you were treated differently. You were considered one of them.

Reveille in the desert in 1952 (© Crown copyright. RAF Regiment Museum).

> I went to my basic training at Warton near Blackpool and from there they offered me a Signals Course at Compton Basset, which I enjoyed. So I came out from there as a Signaller.[21]

While many of the airmen reached Egypt and Iraq by train and boat, others were flown via Egypt or via Malta and Mafraq to Habbaniya. On arrival at Habbaniya, the men were posted to their new flights. 'Nick' Nixon had joined as a regular at 17½ years old in 1952 and arrived at Habbaniya in December of that year:

> I flew out from RAF Lyneham on a Handley Page Hastings. We landed on the airstrip on the plateau which had just been opened. After a week or so in the transit camp a truck came out and Flying Officer Haymes told us, "Go and get your kit out of the Reception Tent, you're going down to 2 Armoured Car Squadron." And I sort of objected to that a bit, I said "My kitbag's in the bay for Bahrain." He said "Well get it out because it's here where you are going."[22]

The influx of airmen allowed the Squadron to reform No 3 Flight entirely from the new arrivals. With so many new airmen arriving, the major focus was again on training to bring it up to a suitable state of readiness. 'Nick' Nixon recalls the daily routine and the responsibility placed on the young airmen:

> At Habbaniya there was always this ritual of daily inspections of vehicles. I had three vehicles on my charge. An 18-year-old! I had an armoured car, a Bedford QL and a petrol bowser. And I had to look after the necessary maintenance needs of all of these. They used to come down the yard, the MT Sergeant, with the officer, and he would say to somebody "Get underneath there and check that differential. See what the oil level is in that vehicle. Check those batteries." And woe betide you if they weren't up to the mark. You had to have the right level of fluid in the batteries and the gearbox had to have the right amount of oil.
>
> When your time wasn't spent doing that, you were up on the plateau doing training with the armoured cars – line abreast, line astern. Flight Lieutenant Simpson used to be there and he would offer a packet of ten Woodbines for the quickest crew.[23] You were all on a level start, and he was somewhere four to 500 yards ahead and we had to race up, stop in front of him. The quickest crew to get out that car and get set up with a Bren gun on the ground, won the cigarettes. There was one time when he offered a Mars Bar for the quickest crew. The weather was so hot you had to eat it with a spoon, it was just goo![24]

By the early 1950s, what the RAF official history called the 'quiet years' in Iraq were coming to an end.[25] Despite the larger issues of Arab nationalism and periods of political instability in Iraq, the RAF was untouched by these events. Gradually however, Iraq experienced increasing anti-British sentiment, although the relations of the airmen with the local Iraqis were generally good, as Jon Jordinson of No 3 Flight recalls:

> We finished all our training at RAF West Kirby and Catterick, but you

Armed and ready to go into action during the riot at Habbaniya in June 1952 (© Crown copyright. RAF Regiment Museum).

did the same thing all over again in Iraq, only more extensively. You were training all the time.

And then when we finished that, they were going to let us go to Cyprus for a week's leave. But with the troubles going on over there, they sent us instead up to Ser Amadia, the rest and leave camp. That's how we met the Kurdish people. They were brilliant; no bother with them at all. You joined in the festivities. They'd do anything for you and they were pleased to see you. No problems.

Anywhere we went in Iraq, out in the desert, the Bedouins, they always made you welcome. They didn't turn their backs on you. They made us welcome.[26]

However, one town where the airmen experienced hostility was Falluja. Surprisingly, a recce by Pilot Officer Robson and a section to Falluja a few days after the arrival of No 2 Squadron at Habbaniya in 1949 had been met by spontaneous and great excitement from the local population. With the RAF armoured cars having been absent from the country for three years, the response was gratifying. Three years later, however, Falluja had a different reputation, as Ray Hill recalls:

Going through Falluja wasn't very good. That was always a hot spot. We used to batten the hatches down when we went over Falluja Bridge. You were alright once you'd got through Falluja and into the plantations. It wasn't so bad in Baghdad and in the villages down towards Basra. But whenever we went through Falluja we used to have our wits about us, because you'd never know whether you were going to get a stone or a bullet.[27]

Meanwhile, serious and insoluble political problems had been developing

Looking towards the main gate from the turret of a GMC during the riot (Fairweather).

Squadron Leader E.J.B. Brown, while on an exercise with the Iraq Levies at Mujarra (© Crown copyright. RAF Regiment Museum).

in Persia, and in 1951, there was a push from the newly-installed government to nationalise the installations and oilfields of the Anglo-Iranian Oil Company. This had led to rioting, protest and loss of life, and as a consequence the Squadron was placed on alert to provide petrol-bowser drivers and refuelling teams for aircraft, should the British armed forces be required to intervene to safeguard lives and property. The de Havilland Vampires of No 6 Squadron and Bristol Brigands of No 8 Squadron were flown into Shaibah from Egypt and Aden respectively, to await developments. The Persian Government was determined to nationalise the oil company, yet Britain wished to avoid a military confrontation. After several months' negotiation therefore, it was agreed that the Anglo-Iranian Oil Company would be taken over by the Persian Government and that the many thousands of British oil workers would be evacuated.

The Anglo-Iraqi Treaty of 1930 had allowed for the maintenance of a British presence in Iraq, at the RAF stations at Habbaniya and Shaibah. By 1952 however, following the rise and fall of various Iraqi governments of varying friendliness, there was considerable unease about the future of the Treaty and the security and tenure of the RAF airbases.

Outside the gates of RAF Habbaniya was a civil cantonment of several thousand, which had developed rapidly following the establishment of the RAF station in the 1930s. This was home to a broad mix of the peoples of Iraq, including the families of the Iraq Levies. It also provided local employment for the Iraqis who provided services useful to the RAF, as Pat Lee recalls:

There were little shops and lots of them. There were laundries - I used to send my shirts down there to be pressed for Guest Nights and the like - hairdressers, silversmiths, goldsmiths and cheapjacks with knick-knacks which the airmen loved to buy.[28]

It was also where the airmen could get a taxi to Baghdad, though they would often spend some time haggling over the fare. On 8 June 1952, there was a disturbance in the civil cantonment and a strike was declared by the local Iraqis. The gates of the airbase were picqueted to prevent others going to work, and towards the end of the day, with no sign of the crowd dispersing, the police decided to move in to arrest the ringleaders. Number 2 Flight were called out in support with their weapons mounted and with all ammunition ready and were placed on standby should more serious trouble arise.

By early the following morning, large crowds had gathered at the gates of the camp and they soon moved forward and overpowered the police post, setting fire to a jeep and some motorcycles, and seriously damaging the Station fire tender, which had been brought up to assist with crowd control. With the police now cut off amongst a hostile crowd and in serious danger, two of the armoured cars were ordered to drive the crowd back. This was successful for a short time but the crowd surged back when they realised the GMCs had not opened fire.

Assuming that no mortal threat would come from the armoured cars, the airmen soon came under a hail of missiles thrown by the crowd. Flying Officer Haymes and LAC Byrne were hit on the head with pieces of brick and concrete and four other Station airmen were injured. With the lives of the armoured car personnel and police in imminent danger the Squadron CO, John Brown, along with Haymes, took up a rifle each and fired eight shots into the mob, wounding five of the demonstrators. This action caused the crowd to retreat and allowed the injured airmen to be sent to

The Humber Mark IIIA light reconnaissance car, 4 x 4, ready for service at RAF Habbaniya (© Crown copyright. II Squadron RAF Regiment History Room).

hospital for treatment.

A period of relative calm followed which allowed No 2 Flight to relieve No 1, with the former remaining on readiness for the rest of the night. In one incident that evening, Flight Lieutenant Lee and eight airmen successfully calmed a group of 200 rioters who were attempting to break out of the cantonment and into the Levy lines. Squadron personnel continued to man the gates and maintain order, handing over to the police when matters had quietened down.

For the next two days, the two Flights were held at instant readiness, and kept busy moving in and out of reserve as crowds gathered and dispersed. The cars were shuffled between the various gates of the airbase and assisted the police as they made arrests in the civil cantonment. By the morning of the third day, the crowd began to dissipate and the Iraqi workers began drifting back to their jobs in increasing numbers, until by the fifth day, the trouble had completely calmed and the armoured cars were stood down.[29]

During December 1952, Squadron Leader John Brown departed for the United Kingdom and he was replaced by P.D. Lee, who had been on the Squadron since April 1951 as 2i/c. He was told that the Squadron had two main areas of responsibility:

> The 'peacetime' tasks and duties were keeping the peace (the worst area being Basra), showing the flag, escorting convoys from Basra to Habbaniya and desert rescue of aircraft.
>
> The 'wartime' task, should this eventuate, was holding the line in Northern Iraq between Kirkuk and Mosul (with 21 armoured cars and Brens!) against

the Russian Army, until a brigade could arrive by air from Egypt. We were also to escort the Royal Engineers who were to mine the bridges. The thing that made us smile was that some of the bridges had no water flowing under them as the river was dry and people didn't go across the bridge they just went down onto the river bed and up the other side.[30]

The latter task was further manifested in June 1952, when the Squadron was called out on Exercise *Delay* to practise tactics to impede a fast-moving column approaching Habbaniya. The 'peacetime' tasks were routine and achievable, the latter task somewhat problematic, and fortunately for the Squadron it was not a task called on to perform in earnest. As to the state of the vehicles in his command, Lee continues:

At first we had the wartime GMCs, which I disliked as the only offensive weapon was a Bren gun, the wireless was adapted from an aircraft set and unreliable, but as our immediate enemy were usually tribesmen, we did have an advantage.

The GMCs were replaced with Humbers, another wartime product, but

LAC Barry Walker with one of the Bedford QLs (Walker).

Squadron Leader Pat Lee (far right) with his officers, Flying Officer P.R.T. Haymes (OC No 2 Flight), Flying Officer W.F. Turner (Adjutant) and Pilot Officer M.B.B. Hellings (OC No 3 Flight) on board the LST Evan Gibb (Hill).

collection of scallywags into a disciplined military force'.[45]

Squadron Leader Pat Lee had been in command of No 2 Armoured Car Squadron for less than a month when he received the order to move to RAF Sharjah. The operational order released on 3 January stated rather cryptically, presumably due to the politically sensitive nature of the move, that 'conditions of unrest exist and in the event of trouble it may be necessary to move forces to the affected areas' and that 'should a force be required in the event of a minor disorder it was the intention of the AOC to move No 2 Armoured Car Squadron to the affected area by rail from Baghdad'. Lee was therefore instructed 'to move... to the affected area.' but was unaware exactly what it was he was heading into, while the gunners of the Squadron believed they were going off on manoeuvres.[46]

A day later, the Squadron was issued with its first Land Rovers and these were quickly fitted with mounts from which to fire the Bren guns, and brackets for the TR1143 radio sets.[47] Squadron Leader Pat Lee continues:

> I was called to Air HQ and told to move as quickly as possible and take my Squadron down to Sharjah for operational purposes. I wasn't to be told what the job was until I got down there. So I said "Okay, I'll go straight down and across the desert." They said "Oh God, don't do that you'll cause a bloody war". You see I'd have to go through Kuwait, Saudi Arabia and Abu Dhabi. So I said "Well, how am I to get down there?"[48]

On 6 January, with movement overland impossible, the Squadron Headquarters, Nos 2 and 3 Flights, with their Land Rovers and Humbers, the Squadron 'B' Echelon and a group of maintenance vehicles of No 6 Squadron, set off by road towards

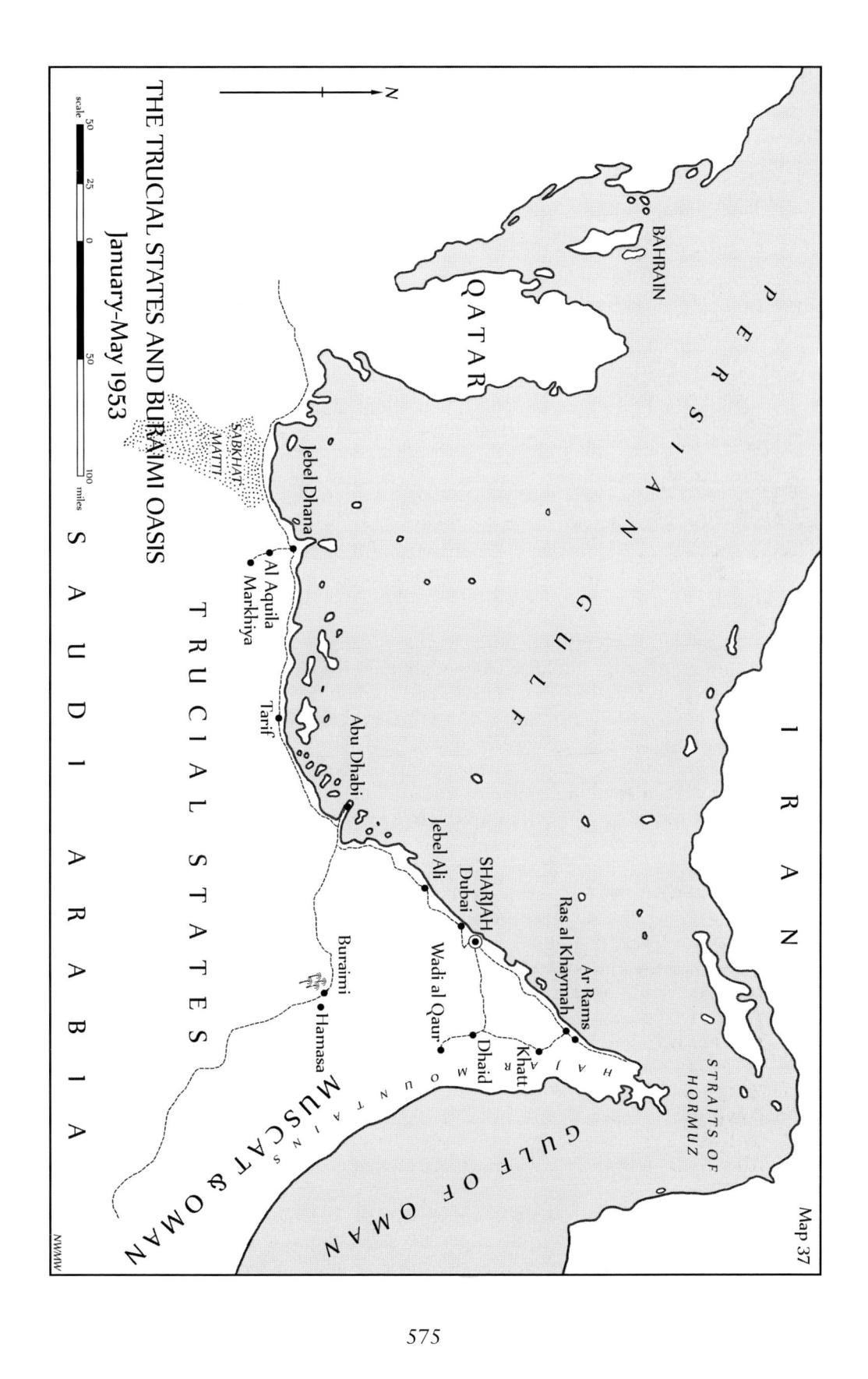

THE TRUCIAL STATES AND BURAIMI OASIS
January–May 1953

HMS Wild Goose lies off the beach at Jebel Ali, while the No 2 Armoured Car Squadron vehicles are unloaded from the LST Evan Gibb. Squadron Leader Lee stands in the water to the left of the ramp directing the unloading (Hill).

Baghdad where the vehicles were loaded onto railway flats. They moved by rail to RAF Shaibah and were unloaded. After a six-day wait they drove to the Basra docks, where the vehicles and stores were loaded through the massive bow doors of the tank landing ship, the LST *Evan Gibb*. Pat Lee had considerable experience in amphibious operations which came in very useful:

> I pushed them onto the landing ship. I took part in the invasion of Sicily and Italy as well, and when I went to the Indian Army I was a Staff Captain for the invasion of Malaya – Operation *Zipper*. I'd had to go and load up the ships for Malaya and all the various bits and pieces, then we went on, and so I was a natural-born chap for that job.[49]

The ship departed on 14 January for Bahrain and arrived the following day. After a further two-day wait, the LST *Evan Gibb* set off for Sharjah. It was an uncomfortable journey with inclement weather, making it necessary to repeatedly check and re-adjust the vehicle chains and to keep watch on the cargo of thousands of gallons of petrol and aviation fuel in flimsy four-gallon tins that had been stowed on the LST's upper deck.[50] Arriving off the beach at Jebel Ali on 18 January, the rough seas prevented the *Evan Gibb* from beaching for another two days. Barry Walker remembers the first few moments as the LST ran onto the beach:

> They opened the front up and one of the Flight Sergeants said "I'll show you lads how to get these vehicles off here." He went out, but unfortunately the Gulf is fairly shallow and they hadn't run the boat close enough on shore. His vehicle disappeared. Everybody was laughing as his head come out of the observation turret and he said "I'll get you lot!" So they took the boat

RAF Sharjah (Hill).

back out and ran it back on shore and further down.[51]

It took most of the day to unload the vehicles and manhandle the stores and fuel to land, with the RAF Regiment gunners ably assisted by the ratings from their naval escort, the sloop HMS *Wild Goose*. Pat Lee continues:

> I directed the loading on and off of the vehicles. The weather was very hot and the water was quite deep. We had no waterproofing on the vehicles and I wanted to make certain that I could get them through to shore quickly before they stalled. So once I'd got them to the end of the ramp we would hook on a winch cable from the Diamond T recovery vehicle of the LAD. They'd keep the engines running and we'd pull them up the beach one-by-one. The LST was gradually drifting and every now and again we pulled it off and it came up again onto the beach.[52]

After staying the night at Jebel Ali, the Squadron set off the following morning for RAF Sharjah, where they found the 12 Vampires of No 6 Squadron that had flown in that morning.[53] The ground crews and essential equipment of this squadron had arrived the previous day in ten Valettas. With the force in place, Lee's next task was to ascertain exactly what they would be required to do. He continues:

> When I got to Sharjah I got my instructions from a Brigadier on the Embassy staff in Bahrain. I never saw him; he just gave me my instructions on the telephone. My briefing was poor. All I was told was that oil had been discovered in Buraimi Oasis some miles south of Sharjah and the Saudis were claiming it to be theirs. I asked the obvious questions; how strong were they, and could I fire if necessary. I was told not to start a war, but stop them, and send them back from whence they came... which was not very helpful.[54]

Relations between Great Britain and Egypt had worsened by 1954 and this would lead ultimately to the departure of the British from the Canal Zone. As a consequence, Cyprus became the major British base in the Near East and the location of the Headquarters of the Middle East Air Force from October 1955. Meanwhile, the Iraqi Government's need to show solidarity with the Arab League and to meet the increasing demands of anti-British elements, led to the termination of the Anglo-Iraqi Treaty of 1930. A new international agreement, known as the 'Baghdad Pact' was signed in 1955 whereby the airbases at Habbaniya, Shaibah and Basra would be returned to Iraqi control.[89] Although the agreement provided for close defence cooperation and training, no British Forces would remain permanently in Iraq. The new alliance guaranteed mutual protection of Iran, Iraq, Pakistan, Turkey and the United Kingdom. The RAF retained a modest staging post at the (by now) Iraqi Air Force Base, Habbaniya until the Iraq Revolution of July 1958.

Thus, in April 1955, No 2 (Field) Squadron was ordered to prepare to move to RAF Nicosia on the island of Cyprus. The advanced and main parties departed by air to come under the control of Air Headquarters Cyprus, soon to be renamed Air Headquarters Levant. On 2 May 1955, the RAF air stations were formally returned to the Iraqi Government. Handover ceremonies were held at Habbaniya and Shaibah. Number 2 (Field) Squadron provided the Guard of Honour at Shaibah and ten days later, a further Guard of Honour on the arrival of the senior officers of the Iraqi Army and Air Force. The Rear Party of the Squadron departed by sea from Basra with the unit's Land Rovers on 10 May and the Squadron completed its concentration in Cyprus on 3 June.

RAF Habbaniya was finally vacated on 6 April 1956, with No 6 Squadron being the last complete RAF unit to leave.[90] The Baghdad Pact remained in place for another three years until further political strife made Britain's presence in Iraq unwelcome, and by 1959 there had been a complete withdrawal.

The armoured car operations in the Trucial States during early 1953 were the last in the Middle East for a unit directly descended from the RAF armoured car companies. Operation *Boxer* had been conducted by No 2 Armoured Car Squadron working in close cooperation with locally-raised levies, and supported from the air by Vampire ground attack-fighter bombers of No 6 Squadron, with air reconnaissance provided by Lancasters, Ansons and Valettas. The disagreement over Buraimi Oasis had been settled for the time being through the clever use of armed force and without bloodshed. This further emboldened the rulers and peoples of the Trucial States and allowed time for diplomatic negotiation. It was a final demonstration of the flexibility and capability of air power when used in coordination with the economical use of air-minded ground forces. An operation that Marshal of the Royal Air Force, Viscount Trenchard, would no doubt have recognised as the epitome of 'Air Control.'

Notes
1. FO 371/104279 Report by Frank Tinsley, Information Officer, MEAF, on the recent 'affair' in the Trucial Oman.
2. This airstrip gained notoriety in September 1970 as the site chosen by members of the Popular Front for the Liberation of Palestine to bring three hijacked passenger aircraft which were later blown up.
3. AIR 29/1714 *No 2 Armoured Car Squadron, Middle East, Transjordan and Iraq, February 1947-December 1950*.
4. L.A. Childs, *Taped interview*, RAF Regiment Museum Archives, n.d.

5   K. Oliver, *Through Adversity: The History of the RAF Regiment* (Rushden, Northants.: Forces & Corporate Publishing, 1997), p. 266. Group Captain Vaux was, as a Major, 2i/c of the 1st Battalion, The Durham Light Infantry, on the Island of Cos in the Dodecanese campaign of September 1943, the RAF Regiment's first full-scale battle after its formation in 1942. After the War, he transferred to the RAF Regiment. The Vaux Trophy, donated by his family business, Vaux Breweries, to the RAF Regiment in 1970 in his memory, is presented to the most improved student on the Junior Regiment Officers initial professional Training Course.
6   L.A. Childs, *Taped interview*.
7   AIR 28/1040 *Habbaniya Appendices April-December 1946, January 1948-August 1950*. In April 1949, an administrative change occurred with 'A', 'B' and 'C' Flights becoming Nos 1, 2 and 3, respectively.
8   L.A. Childs, *Taped interview*.
9   *Ibid*.
10 Number 21 Light Anti-Aircraft Squadron RAF Regiment, had been formed by the re-roling and renumbering of No 52 (Rifle) Squadron, presumably when the vulnerability of the airfields at Amman and Mafraq to air attack had been demonstrated by the Israeli Air Force.
11 The Royal Army Service Corps operated five of these LSTs in the Middle East as a consequence of the shortage of merchant ships following the end of the Second World War.
12 RAF armoured car operations in Aden from 1928 to 1950 are covered in Chapter 22.
13 King Talal I ibn Abdullah (1909-1972) and King Hussein ibn Talal (1935–1999).
14 Sheikh Ahmad Al Jaber Al Sabah KCIE KCSI (1885–1950).
15 Sheikh, later Amir Abdullah III Al Salim Al Sabah GCMG CIE KStJ (1895-1965).
16 Wing Commander P.D. Lee RAF Retd (1920-2013), *Interview with the author*, 2010. Pat Lee had begun his military career as a boy soldier in the 2nd Battalion of the Devonshire Regiment in 1934. He had spent the period from 1938 until November 1942 on Malta, where the Devons, part of the Island's military garrison, stood against the continuous aerial onslaught by the *Luftwaffe* and *Regia Aeronautica*. He had then gone on to see action with his battalion in the amphibious landings in Sicily and Italy. In 1944, the 2nd Devons retuned to the United Kingdom to prepare for the D-Day landings. While in the United Kingdom, Lee was sent to Sandhurst and received his commission. He was then posted to India where he joined the Royal Garhwal Rifles. He served for a time on the staff of South-East Asia Command for the planning of the invasion of Malaya, Operation *Zipper*, and later with his battalion, the 2/18th Royal Garhwal Rifles, during the difficult days of the partition of India.
17 Squadron Leader E.J.B. Brown had served in the Baluch Regiment of the Indian Army.
18 Lee, *Interview with the author*.
19 R. Hill, *Interview with the author*, 2008.
20 J. Jordinson, *Interview with the author*, 2008.
21 R. Fairweather, *Interview with the author*, 2008.
22 R.M. Nixon, *Interview with the author*, 2011.
23 Later Squadron Leader John C. Simpson MBE MSc.
24 Nixon, *Interview with the author*.
25 D. Lee, *Flight from the Middle East* (London: HMSO, 1980), p. 35.
26 Jordinson, *Interview with the author*.
27 Hill, *Interview with the author*.
28 Lee, *Interview with the author*.
29 AIR 29/2226 *Field Squadrons: No 2, with appendices, 1952*.
30 Lee, *Interview with the author*.
31 *Ibid*.
32 W.B. Walker, *Interview with author*, 2008.
33 The Humbers had been used by No 1 Armoured Car Squadron which had been reformed

at Sundern in Germany on 1 March 1948 with the renaming of No 4 Armoured Car Squadron RAF Regiment. The six Armoured Car Squadrons that served in North-West Europe with Humbers were Nos 2742, 2757, 2777, 2781, 2804, 2806.

34　AIR 29/2226 *Field Squadrons: No 2, with appendices, 1951*. The lack of storage was resolved by the addition of extra loading bins and racks for jerricans.

35　Ibid.

36　Ibid.

37　This Squadron had a long association with the RAF armoured cars having served in Iraq during the 1920s alongside Nos 3, 4, 5 and 6 Armoured Car Companies. It had then moved to Palestine where it worked with Nos 1 and 2 Armoured Car Companies during the Palestine disturbances of 1936-1939. It became part of the Desert Air Force during the North African Campaign and was the first to use the Hurricane IID 'tank busters' against the Afrika Korps in June 1942.

38　AIR 27/2592 *No 6 Squadron: Summary of Events 1951-1955*.

39　Ron Fairweather was on the guard of honour after requesting the duty.

40　R. Fairweather, *Interview with the author*, 2013.

41　Ibid.

42　Number 4001 Flight, resurrected in 1972, remains in existence as the Training Support Flight at the RAF Regiment Force Protection Headquarters at RAF Honington.

43　Fairweather, *Interview with the author*, 2013. Fairweather recalled that "Crown Prince Hussein would visit the RAF in Amman regularly – enjoying his time on the rifle range with the rest of us. When he became King Hussein our pay was increased by 3 shillings per week out of the King's own coffers. In later years, he commissioned a Jordanian commemorative medal to be struck with the King's head on one side and the reverse side the words 'For services to The Hashemite Kingdom of Jordan', for all those who could prove entitlement. I am proud to say I have mine. The King was very pro-British and a delightful man." This is known as the Jordan Service Medal or *Midalat al Kidmat al Urduni* was established with the approval of King Hussein for British military and police personnel who served in Jordan and in the Jordanian military forces between 1946 and 1957 and assisted in the protection of Jordan during the emergency and crisis in 1958.

44　Muscat and Oman became the Sultanate of Oman in August 1970.

45　J. Lunt, *Imperial Sunset* (London: MacDonald, 1981), pp. 91-93. Hankin-Turvin had served in the Palestine Police and then became a contract officer with the Arab Legion before being asked to form the Trucial Oman Levies.

46　AIR 29/2226 *Field Squadrons: No 2, with appendices, January 1953*. Numbers 2 and 3 Flights were under the command of Flying Officer P.R.T. Haymes and Pilot Officer M.B.B. Hellings, respectively. 'B' Echelon was composed of the unit's supply vehicles, LAD and heavy vehicles of No 6 Squadron.

47　The Land Rovers were allocated to No 3 Flight.

48　Lee, *Interview with the author*.

49　Ibid.

50　To add further drama, AC1 Batt was taken ill with acute appendicitis and had to be taken on board the escorting naval vessel, HMS *Wild Goose*, where the ship's surgeon performed a successful appendectomy.

51　Walker, *Interview with the author*.

52　Lee, *Interview with the author*.

53　No 6 Squadron was under the command of Squadron Leader Ernest J. Roberts.

54　Lee, *Interview with the author*.

55　FO 371/104276. The British forces were not to take any action against the Saudi Arabian people or provoke any action. They were however, to repel any attack on the undisputed territory of the Trucial States by Saudis or their sympathisers. Squadron Leader Lee's contact was Brigadier John E.A. Baird CBE, the Military Adviser to the Political Resident Persian Gulf in Bahrain.

56　Lee, *Interview with the author*.

57 FO 371/104278, Correspondence: 28 January 1953, Political Agency, Trucial States, Sharjah, to Sir Rupert Hay, Political Resident, Bahrain.
58 Lee, *Interview with the author*.
59 FO 371/104278, *Account of the incident at Wadi al Qaur*.
60 Later Sir Michael Weir KCMG (1925-2006) noted Diplomat and Arabist. FO 371/104278, Correspondence: 28 January 1953, Political Agency, Trucial States, Sharjah, to Sir Rupert Hay, Political Resident, Bahrain.
61 Walker, *Interview with the author*.
62 AIR 28/1270 *RAF Station Sharjah January 1951-December 1955*.
63 Lee, *Interview with the author*. Air Chief Marshal Sir Arthur Saunders GCB KBE (1898-1974).
64 Jordinson, *Interview with the author*.
65 Fairweather, *Interview with the author*.
66 Jordinson, *Interview with the author*.
67 Walker, *Interview with the author*.
68 Later Admiral Sir William Slayter KCB DSO DSC (1896-1971)
69 Lee, *Interview with the author*. Squadron Leader Pat Lee recalls paying an amusing visit to the Captain of HMS *Wild Goose* soon after his arrival at Sharjah. He continues: I was told to liaise with the Navy. I got the message that they may be able to support you with gunfire, should you need it. So I said "Oh, yes". This thing came in and I got into a pinnace and I went out to it, and it had just had a new wooden deck put in. I had hobnail boots on so they rolled a carpet down for me to walk on so I wouldn't make a mess of their deck. The Captain was a big chap with a beard and we had a nice chat. You know what the Navy are like. They're very pleasant and very peculiar in some ways. We started off on a bad footing because he said to me "Have a drink, its after 11". So I said "It could be after three Sir, but I don't drink. I'm a teetotaller, but carry on."

I then explained "I'm in charge of No 2 Armoured Car Squadron and we're doing etc." He said "Yes, I've got the message about what's going on. How can I help?" So I said "What can you do for me? What gun power have you got?" He replied "Oh, a four-inch" So I said "Oh that's good, how far will that fire?" He said "About six miles at the very most, but there is a problem". "What's that?" I asked. He then explained that "because of the shallowness of sea at this part of the Gulf I can't get within four miles of the beach. So I've got to stand-off. So my only target will be two miles." I said "Thank you for that Captain" and then I explained that the only thing he could do was use his men as soldiers. I said "If I wanted 50 soldiers in a hurry, could you send me them?" and he let out a gasp and said "Have you ever seen a sailor with a rifle? It's the most dangerous thing in the world!"
70 Air Commodore M.S. Witherow RAF (Retd), later Director RAF Regiment, Comments to author, May 2013. Even in 1957-8, when we had a bigger air fleet there for the Jebel Akhdar War, Sharjah did not have a hard surface runway. It was simply rolled sand sprayed with oil, repeatedly, and dried in the sun. To demarcate the 'runway' it was lined on its whole length and about 50 yards to each side with parallel lines of sand-filled oil drums.
71 FO 371/ 104278, Telegram: Bahrain to Foreign Office, 24 February 1953.
72 Wing Commander R.A.A. 'Dickie' Dawes MC had also served in the Indian Army before joining the Aden Protectorate Levies.
73 Walker, *Interview with the author*.
74 The Vampires of No 6 Squadron were used initially in this role but they were replaced by Meteors of No 208 Squadron assisted by a few Ansons and a Valetta and later Lancasters of Nos 37 and 38 Squadrons.
75 Two RAF Regiment rifle squadrons were also held in reserve in Egypt should they be required.
76 FO 371/104284 Telegram: Foreign Office to Bahrain, 26 March 1953.
77 Nixon, *Interview with the author*.

Regiment that provide Force Protection for the RAF.[3] Most recently in Afghanistan, they have performed a vital role in the protection of critical operating bases, particularly in ensuring the security of the air-bridge - where loss of a single troop transport to insurgent attack from a surface-to-air missile would have serious strategic and political consequences - and supporting the work of the Medical Emergency Response Teams on the Chinook helicopters.

The Royal Air Force Regiment, which came into existence in the United Kingdom on 1 February 1942 following the signing of the Royal Warrant by King George VI, was the title conferred upon the Corps within the Royal Air Force. Its personnel were drawn initially from the old Ground Defence Branch of the RAF, and its formation inevitably led to amalgamation with the RAF Armoured Car Companies that had been fulfilling this role, albeit on a smaller but effective scale, in the outposts of the Middle East for the past 20 years. The principal lesson learned from the fall of France, the debacle of Crete and the siege of Habbaniya was that secure airfields were vital to ensuring control of the air and thus campaign success, yet were especially vulnerable to attack by enemy ground forces; a dedicated defence force was essential during periods of high intensity operations.

The end of the Second World War and the withdrawal from Empire has not lessened this requirement. Indeed, the threat to RAF operating bases and facilities has evolved considerably, with adversaries now using far more sophisticated weaponry, tactics and techniques.

The RAF Regiment has been on continuous active service for more than 70 years and yet it has shown an impressive capacity to continually adapt itself to changing circumstances. It has been at the forefront of RAF operational deployments and has moved seamlessly between roles as light infantry, with armoured cars, on light anti-aircraft guns, Rapier missiles, light armour, on tactical air control, counter-insurgency and special forces operations. The agility and adaptability of the Regiment has been exemplified most recently by the rapid assumption of full responsibility for UK Defence CBRN.[4]

Royal Air Force Regiment squadrons have on many occasions in recent decades been called to operate in the same theatres as their predecessors in the RAF Armoured Car Companies, and in some senses history has come full circle. The RAF Regiment has clearly demonstrated in many theatres of war that a dedicated 'air-minded' force protection and ground defence force is critical to ensuring control of the air. Concomitant with this has been the necessity for armoured protection, mobility and firepower. Whether this is provided by a Rolls-Royce armoured car, a Scorpion or a Jackal armoured vehicle, the essential concept has changed little, and the élan and esprit de corps that existed with 'The Cars' from 1921 to 1953 provides clear inspiration to current and future generations of the RAF Regiment.

PER ARDUA

Notes
1 CVR(T), Combat Vehicle Reconnaissance (Tracked).
2 Nos 3, 4, 6 and 33 Wings; Nos 20, 26 and 66 (Rapier) Squadrons; Nos 1, 34, 51 and 58 (Light Armoured) Squadrons and II (Field) Squadron.
3 Nos 1, II, 3, 15, 26, 27, 34, 51, 58 and 63 (Queen's Colour) Squadrons RAF Regiment.
4 CBRN, Chemical, Biological, Radiological and Nuclear.

RAF Habbaniya, 1940: Nos 1, 2 and 3 Sections, No 1 Armoured Car Company (Rolph, RAFACA)

'Born 1915 - still going strong'. HMAC Jaguar, 1914-pattern Rolls-Royce, Iraq, 1935, with water chargals, signal flags, Type '0.2' compass, searchlight and Vickers. The Rolls-Royces would serve with No 1 Company until 1943 (© Crown copyright. Constantine, RAF Regiment Museum).

Around the campfire out 'in the blue' (© Crown copyright. Godsave, RAF Regiment Museum).

Air-land integration, airfield and landing ground defence, tactical air control, policing the tribes, 'showing the flag', counter-insurgency, aid to the civil power, route reports, track marking, reconnaissances and escorts. Thirty years of operations, in every place (King).

Appendices

Appendix 1

Commanding Officers

Armoured Car Wing HQ

3 November 1922	*Wing HQ formed*
	Wing Commander W.H. Primrose DFC
10 November 1924	*Disbanded*
1 April 1927	*Reconstituted*
	Squadron Leader A.H. Peck DSO MC
April 1928	Squadron Leader J.J. Breen
October 1928	Wing Commander J. McCrae MBE
March 1929	Squadron Leader D.E. Stodart DSO DFC
February 1930	Wing Commander C.H. Elliott-Smith AFC
1 April 1930	*Disbanded*

No 1 Armoured Car Company & No 1 Armoured Car Squadron RAF Regiment

19 December 1921	*Company formed. Attached to No 216 Squadron.*
1 February 1922	*Company becomes self-accounting*
	Flight Lieutenant F. Fernihough MC
April 1922	Squadron Leader A.J. Currie
1 December 1923	*Disbanded in Palestine*
1 April 1930	*Reformed in Iraq*
	Wing Commander C.H. Elliot-Smith AFC
November 1931	Wing Commander V. Gaskell-Blackburn DSC AFC
June 1932	Squadron Leader A.W. Fletcher OBE DFC AFC
December 1932	Wing Commander W.V. Strugnell MC
February 1935	Squadron Leader R.S. Sugden AFC
March 1937	Wing Commander T.S. Ivens
November 1938	Wing Commander W.A.B. Savile
December 1940	Wing Commander M. Lowe
May 1941	Squadron Leader J.J.J. Page
August 1941	Squadron Leader W.O. Jones
February 1942	Squadron Leader B.F. Pyne
November 1942	Squadron Leader A.G. Douglas
February 1945	Squadron Leader R.J. Payne
September 1945	Squadron Leader D.C. Hellard
March 1946	Squadron Leader J.S. Deag
3 October 1946	*Incorporated in the RAF Regiment and redesignated as No 2701 Armoured Squadron*
25 February 1947	*Renamed as No 1 Armoured Car Squadron RAF Regiment*
15 December 1947	*Disbanded and reformed during March 1948 at Sundern Germany*

No 2 Armoured Car Company &
No 2 Armoured Car Squadron RAF Regiment

7 April 1922	*Company formed*
	Squadron Leader M.G.D. Copeman
December 1922	Squadron Leader G. Blatherwick
March 1926	Squadron Leader A.N. Gallehawk AFC
December 1926	Squadron Leader J. Everidge MC
December 1927	Squadron Leader L.F. Forbes MC
April 1930	Squadron Leader H.G.R. Malet
December 1930	Squadron Leader E.B. Rice
April 1934	Squadron Leader J.P. Coleman AFC
August 1934	Squadron Leader J.R.I. Scambler AFC
July 1935	Squadron Leader D.G. Mulholland AFC
October 1937	Squadron Leader R.F. Shenton
July 1938	Squadron Leader C.H. Stillwell
August 1939	Squadron Leader W.T. Smail
March 1940	Squadron Leader J.J.J. Page
January 1941	Squadron Leader M.P. Casano MC
March 1943	Squadron Leader J.H.F. Newland
August 1943	Squadron Leader P.F. Murch
March 1946	Squadron Leader C.G.E. Kennedy
3 October 1946	*Incorporated in the RAF Regiment and redesignated as No 2702 Armoured Squadron*
25 February 1947	*Renamed as No 2 Armoured Car Squadron RAF Regiment*
September 1947	Squadron Leader L.A. Childs
December 1947	Squadron Leader L.C. Inglefield
December 1950	Squadron Leader E.J.B. Brown
December 1952	Squadron Leader P.D. Lee
May 1953	Squadron Leader B. Brooke
9 November 1953	*Renamed as No 2 Field Squadron RAF Regiment*
April 1955	Squadron Leader V.J.G. Cole
May 1955	*Departed from Iraq for Cyprus*

No 3 Armoured Car Company

3 November 1922	*Company formed*
	Squadron Leader F.H.W. Guard CMG CBE DSO
1 April 1925	*Disbanded*

No 4 Armoured Car Company

3 November 1922	*Company formed*
	Squadron Leader R.P. Willock
November 1924	Squadron Leader G.G.H. Cooke DSC AFC
November 1925	Squadron Leader G.E. Godsave
1 April 1927	*Disbanded*

No 5 Armoured Car Company

3 November 1922	*Company formed*
	Squadron Leader D. Harries AFC
April 1924	Squadron Leader D.O. Mulholland AFC
January 1925	Squadron Leader G.S. Trewin AFC
March 1926	Squadron Leader A.F.A. Hooper OBE
January 1927	Squadron Leader A.S. Morris OBE
1 April 1927	*Disbanded*

No 6 Armoured Car Company

3 November 1922	*Company formed*
	Squadron Leader J.W. Cruikshank OBE
	(died of typhoid 20 February 1925)
March 1925	Squadron Leader – Wing Commander E.W. Norton DSC
February 1926	Squadron Leader E.M. Pollard
	(died in air crash 26 July 1926)
August 1926	Squadron Leader F.R. Alford MC
March 1927	Squadron Leader A.H. Peck DSO MC
1 April 1927	*Disbanded*

Armoured Car Section, Aden & No 4001 (Armoured Car) Flight RAF Regiment

12 January 1928	*Formed as HQ 'D' Flight No 8 (B) Squadron RAF*
	Flying Officer V. Harris
29 January 1929	*Formed as Armoured Car Section, Aden*
	Flight Lieutenant C.N.C. Dickson AFC
March 1932	Flight Lieutenant E.H.M. David
November 1933	Flying Officer G.M. Gillan (temporary)
January 1934	Flight Lieutenant C.H. Appleton
November 1935	Flight Lieutenant R.B. Jordan
November 1936	Flight Lieutenant H.V. Satterly
May 1938	Flying Officer R.N.J. White
July 1939	Flying Officer-Flight Lieutenant W. Townson
March 1940	Pilot Officer-Flight Lieutenant P.F. Murch
September 1941	Flying Officer G.L.D. Cox
October 1941	Flight Lieutenant C.A. Mortimore
January 1943	Pilot Officer-Flight Lieutenant G.P. Curran
April 1944	Flight Lieutenant B.E.K. Pemberton-Pigott
January 1945	Flying Officer R. Wells
September 1945	Flying Officer-Flight Lieutenant E.A. Brace
June 1946	Flight Lieutenant V. James
3 October 1946	*Absorbed into the RAF Regiment and renamed Independent AC Flight No 2701 Squadron*

January 1947	*Renamed as No 4001 (AC) Flight RAF Regiment*
July 1947	Flying Officer H.B. Miller
August 1947	Flight Lieutenant R.A. Burgess
February 1948	Flight Lieutenant B.J. Betham
April 1949	Flight Lieutenant G.G. Whittle DFM
August 1949-July 1950	*No 4001 (AC) Flight under the command of Aden Protectorate Levies*
December 1949	Flight Lieutenant G.N. Zeylmans
August 1950	*No 4001 (AC) Flight departs for Jordan*
July 1952	Pilot Officer R.H. Barraclough
October 1952	Flight Lieutenant G.P. Dodd MC
March 1953	Flying Officer R.H. Barraclough
July 1953	Flight Lieutenant G.P. Dodd MC *(resumed command)*
20 July 1953	*Disbanded*

Appendix 2

Armoured Fighting Vehicles[1]

Car, Armoured, Rolls-Royce Standard Type A
(also 1914 pattern and 1920 pattern)

Weight	3.8 to 4.2 tons
Armour	9.5 mm
Crew	4. Commander, gunner, driver, spare driver-wireless operator
Engine	Rolls-Royce 65 bhp. 6 cylinder in-line, L-head, water cooled, petrol engine
Performance	4 x 2. 60 mph max, 35 mph cruise. Range 200 miles. The armoured car version of the Silver Ghost chassis had four extra leaves in the rear springs
Armament	Vickers 0.303-inch mg, elevation +40° to -13°, in rotating turret.
	Lewis 0.303-inch mg fitted to turret top on single pedestal – later mounted on Scarff ring.
	The Boys 0.55-inch anti-tank rifle mounted in the turret to right of the Vickers.
Units	Nos 1-6 Armoured Car Companies, Armoured Car Wing and Armoured Car Section, Aden
Notes	As well as the RNAS and Tank Corps supplied Rolls-Royces, the Air Ministry, independently of the War Office, built Rolls-Royce armoured cars to equip the RAF armoured car companies. They were armoured at No 1 Stores Depot, and bore the Air Ministry designation 'Car, Armoured, Rolls-Royce Type A'. The armoured shape was like that of the 1914 RNAS 40/50 Silver Ghost car but they had the 1920 turret. Mechanically, the three types were similar, but the heavier 9.5 mm armour instead of the 8 mm steel of the 1914-pattern, contributed to an overall increase in weight of 6 cwt and the reduction in speed of 5 mph. The 1914-pattern vehicles were fitted with turrets with lower sides than the 1920-pattern 'Standard Type A'. The 1920-pattern cars had slotted panels on the radiator doors and some were fitted with a ball-mounted Vickers in the turret.[2]
	The wheels of the 'Standard Type A' were disked rather than spoked, although all models were later changed to a heavier commercial pattern. Tyres gradually increased in width with large sand tyres being used from the mid-1930s. Twin wheels were fitted at the rear, but as the wider tyres were fitted they were replaced by single wheels.

Lancia Armoured Personnel Carrier

Weight	3.3 tons
Armour	9.5 mm
Crew	2-3. Commander or Commander/gunner, gunner, driver (+10 riflemen)
Engine	Lancia 4 cylinder 35 bhp
Performance	4 x 2. Speed 35-40 mph

Armament	Single Lewis 0.303-inch mg mounted to fire through aperture in cab front. Additional mountings for up to four Lewis guns at corners of personnel compartment
Units	Nos 1-6 Armoured Car Companies
Notes	Lancias were among the first armoured cars to be ordered by the Air Ministry. Some of the cars were similar to those used by the Police in Ireland, although they had been fitted with modern lighting equipment and a small searchlight added at the front. These cars were armoured personnel carriers or armoured trucks rather than true armoured cars. One version used in Palestine was a fully-enclosed armoured vehicle with a small multi-sided turret mounting one Lewis machine-gun.

The Lancias were used in Palestine and Iraq from 1922, but lasted only a few years, and had been phased out by the late 1920s. In contrast to the success of the Rolls-Royces, the Lancias were soon found to be too cumbersome and top-heavy, the springs and frames were inadequate for the weight of armour, the clutch gave problems, the tyres were faulty and had poor clearance with the armour, and the open top meant that the crew had inadequate overhead cover.[3] At Mosul, between July and September 1924, consideration was given to modifying a Lancia so that it could carry a 3.7-inch mountain gun portée style in the rear compartment. The aim was to provide a swifter mean of transport for the guns of the Frontier Striking Force. A Lancia was fitted out at Mosul by No 5 Armoured Car Company with ramps and fittings and a gun from the normally mule-transported 113 (Dardoni) Pack Battery, Indian Mountain Artillery. Despite clear enthusiasm from the RAF and Major Hill, the Battery Commander, there is no evidence they were used on operations.[4]

All Lancias surplus to requirements in Palestine and Egypt were sent to Iraq in August 1924.

Crossley Six-Wheeled Armoured Car
Crossley 30/70 hp (dome-shaped turret) - Crossley 38/110 hp

Weight	7.1 tons (30/70), 5.4 tons (38/110)
Armour	8 mm
Crew	3-4
Engine	4 cylinder, 70 bhp and 6 cylinder, 110 bhp
Performance	Speed 35-40 mph
Armament	Vickers 0.303-inch mg in turret
Units	Nos 1 and 2 Armoured Car Companies (limited use) and Armoured Car Section, Aden
Notes	The dome-shaped turret of the 30/70 hp possessed four mountings for the Vickers, though only two guns were carried. The six-wheeled chassis had dual rear wheels and these could be fitted with tracks to improve performance in bad going. No record has been seen of the tracks being used on operations. The spare wheels were mounted on either side of the chassis and projected below the level of the chassis frame. They were free to revolve and designed to prevent the vehicle "bellying" – a common problem with 6 x 4 vehicles. Number 2

Armoured Car Company had one Crossley on strength from 1928 to 1934. A further six-wheeled armoured car, the 38/110 hp Crossley IGA4 Mark I, was supplied to the RAF in 1930 and used a more powerful engine. The hull and turret were similar to the Lanchester Mark I used by the British Army but the Crossley had only one Vickers machine-gun. A Crossley Mark I had been supplied to No 1 Company for evaluation during the 1930s. The Mark I was also supplied to the Iraqi Army prior to the Second World War and during the siege of Habbaniya it was these vehicles that confronted the Rolls-Royces of No 1 Armoured Car Company on the morning of 2 May 1941.

Car, Armoured, Fordson

Weight	3.8 to 4.2 tons
Armour	9.5 mm
Crew	4. Commander, gunner, driver, spare driver-radio operator
Engine	Ford V8, 85-90 bhp
Armament	Vickers 0.303-inch mg in turret. Lewis 0.303-inch mg on turret top on single pedestal – later mounted on Scarff ring. Boys 0.55-inch anti-tank rifle. Twin Browning 0.303-inch AA mgs. Browning 0.5-inch mg in turret
Units	Nos 1 and 2 Armoured Car Companies and Armoured Car Section, Aden
Notes	By the beginning of the Second World War the Rolls-Royces of the armoured car companies were nearly worn out. Arrangements were made for the armoured hulls and turrets to be removed and fitted to a modern Fordson 4 x 2 commercial truck chassis. Twenty of the Rolls-Royces of No 2 Armoured Car Company were sent in batches between January and August 1940 to Cairo to be refitted. Two versions of the Fordson were constructed. One short wheelbase model was created, but the remainder were the more common long wheelbase model. As the Fordson chassis was longer than that of the Rolls-Royce, the hull was extended over the platform behind the turret, and the extra space was used to house the wireless equipment which was carried in most cars by this time. The Fordson armament was considerably upgraded in light of experience in Egypt and Libya.

Car, Armoured, Humber, Marks I & IV

Weight	7 tons
Armour	15 mm
Crew	3 [Mark I], 4 [Mark IV]
Engine	Rootes 6 cylinder, 90 bhp
Performance	Four-wheel drive. Maximum speed 45 mph. Range 250 miles.
Armament	Mark I - 7.92-mm + 15-mm Besa mgs. Vickers K 0.303-inch mg mounted for AA defence on turret roof. Mark IV – 37-mm gun + 7.92-mm Besa mg co-axial.
Units	Nos 1 Armoured Car Company (Western Desert detachment) [Mark I], Armoured Car Section, Aden and No 4001 Armoured Car Flight RAF Regiment [Mark IV].

Notes	The most important of the British-built armoured cars of the Second World War. The 15-mm Besa mg was however, not a success, and was prone to jamming. The Mark IV had a roomier turret.

Car, Light Reconnaissance, Canadian GM Mark I, Otter I

Weight	4.8 tons
Armour	12 mm
Crew	3
Engine	General Motors 6 cylinder, 104 bhp
Performance	Four-wheel drive. Maximum speed 45 mph
Armament	At various times two Bren 0.303-inch LMGs, twin 0.5-inch Brownings on an AA mounting on the turret and a 20-mm cannon mounted in the hull front or on the turret.
Units	Nos 1 and 2 Armoured Car Companies, Nos 1 and 2 Armoured Car Squadrons RAF Regiment, Armoured Car Section, Aden and No 4001 Armoured Car Flight RAF Regiment
Notes	A total of 1761 GMC Otters were built in Canada between 1942 and the end of the war. The Otters also equipped the AFV Flights of the RAF Regiment Field Squadron in Italy and Greece during the later stages of the Second World War.

Car, 4 x 4, Light Reconnaissance, Humber Mark IIIA

Weight	3.3 tons
Armour	10 mm
Crew	3
Engine	Humber 6 cylinder 87 bhp
Performance	Four-wheel drive. Maximum speed 50 mph
Armament	Bren 0.303-inch mg
Unit	No 2 Armoured Car Squadron RAF Regiment
Notes	First produced at the end of 1941, they had a specially-designed four-wheel drive chassis. Some 3600 Humber LRCs of all marks were built by the Rootes Group. The Marks III and IIIA were used by the RAF Regiment Armoured Car Squadrons in the campaign in North West Europe from June 1944 to May 1945. The Mark IIIA had extra vision ports. The Humber Mark IIIA was in service with No 2 Armoured Car Squadron in Iraq and Sharjah from November 1952 until May 1953. Two Humbers recovered from a bombing range were used for a time by the Squadron on Cyprus.

Car, Armoured, Alvis-Straussler, Type A

Weight	6.5 tons
Armour	-
Crew	3
Engine	6 cylinder Alvis 120 bhp with cooling by radiators located on each side

Performance	4 x 4 or 4 x 2 selective. Maximum speed 69 mph.
Armament	Vickers 0.303-inch mg in ball-mount in turret
Units	No 2 Armoured Car Company and Armoured Car Section Aden
Notes	Twelve of the AC3D cars were supplied to the RAF out of a batch of only 27 constructed. They were sent to Palestine and Aden in 1939. On the outbreak of war they were withdrawn and replaced with the Fordsons and returned to the United Kingdom where they saw out their days on aerodrome defence, until the limited supply of spare parts had been used up. These vehicles were the latest of a series designed by Nicholas Straussler, an engineer of Hungarian origin. The first type was built by the firm of Manfred Weiss, of Budapest, in 1933. A second prototype, AC2, much the same as the first, was made in 1935 and tested by the RAF in Iraq. This car had a specification much in advance of contemporary British armoured cars, including four-wheel drive, four or two-wheel steering, rear-mounted engine, transverse leaf spring suspension at front and rear, swing axle design and an armoured body which could easily be removed for the vehicle to be serviced. In 1937, Straussler linked up with Alvis Ltd of Coventry. The Alvis-Straussler AC3D was supplied to the RAF in 1939. Built by Alvis Ltd, it was generally similar in layout to the 1935 model but the armour was angled instead of curved and there was four-wheel steering.

SdKfz 222 Auto Union

Weight	4.7 tons
Armour	8 mm (14.5 mm on later models)
Crew	3
Engine	Horch 3.5-3.8 1itre, 8 cylinder, 80 bhp
Performance	4 x 4. Four wheel steering. Six forward gears, high and low ratio, and rear-mounted engine.
Armament	20-mm Solothurn + 7.62-mm MG34
Units	No 2 Armoured Car Company
Notes	Four Auto Unions were captured by No 2 Armoured Car Company at the end of the North African campaign. Two were returned to Cairo but the other two were kept and remained on strength until the late 1940s. Some considered them uncomfortable to drive as the driver was nearly lying down and they were awkward and time consuming to get out of, especially when a quick exit was needed. They were however, superior to any vehicle the Company had.

Other Armoured Cars

Other armoured cars were evaluated over the years but were not taken on or were unavailable. The AEC Mark I Armoured Car, Daimler Mark II Armoured Car, the Canadian-built Foxhound Armoured Car, the South African-built Marmon Herrington Mark IV and the United States-built Staghound I, were all attached in ones or twos to No 2 Armoured Car Company from 1942 up to 1948, but were never used in action.

One of the more unusual vehicles was the Citroen-Kegresse half-track, which was tested in Iraq during the late 1920s but was found to be unsatisfactory.

Tenders

For the RAF armoured car companies to perform their role effectively required tenders for use as wireless-telegraphy, radio-telegraphy or supply and fitters vehicles. The first supply tender was the standard RAF Crossley 4 x 2, which had been used during the First World War. The Rolls-Royce tender was, however, soon adapted as a W/T-R/T tender and supply tender and many soldiered on with No 1 Armoured Car Company until mid-1942. Heavy tenders were initially the Crossley 6 x 4, however, with the emergence of cheaper mass-produced commercial vehicles in the late 1920s and early 1930s, the RAF also purchased the Morris and later the Albion 6 x 4. In 1938, the Fordson 4 x 2 tenders arrived in 1938 and were used by the companies throughout the North African campaign.

During the 1920s and 1930s, the Crossley, Morris, Commer and Albion tenders were often fitted with a Lewis 0.303-inch mg mounted on a Scarff ring fitted to the cab roof.

The vehicle that proved of great utility was the Armed Ford 4 x 2 based on the Model T. These lightweight vehicles were useful in the operations in both the deserts and mountains and were used as fast moving forward scouts. The arrival in the early 1950s of the Land Rover 4 x 4 armed with a Bren LMG as the major operational vehicle for No 2 Squadron meant that they had a vehicle that could be used in a similar manner to the Armed Fords. In the Armed Fords we can see the early manifestations of the modern Land Rover-based WMIK reconnaissance and fire support vehicle.

Notes

1. Anon, *Armoured Fighting Vehicles of the RAF, the RAF Regiment and its Associated Overseas Forces* (RAF Regiment Museum Archives: Unpublished document, 1970) and Peters, R.J. "Armoured Cars of the RAF" *Military Modelling,* February-August 1972.
2. D. Fletcher, *The Rolls-Royce Armoured Car* (Oxford: Osprey Publishing 2012).
3. AIR 25/575B *Armoured Cars October 1923 - November 1924*. Correspondence: Wing Commander H. Primrose, OC Armoured Car Wing, to Air Headquarters Iraq, 14 August 1924.
4. *Ibid.*, Correspondence: Major W. Hill RA to OC No 5 Armoured Car Company, Mosul, 21 July 1924 *ff*.

Appendix 3

Establishments

Period	Unit	Vehicles
Iraq 1922-1925	Nos 3, 4, 5 and 6 ACC (three sections each)	3 Rolls-Royce armoured cars, 3 Lancia armoured trucks and 1 Armed Ford per section. Company HQ - 1 Crossley touring car, Triumph motorcycle, 2 Crossley 4 x 2 light tenders and 1 Leyland 3-ton heavy tender.
Palestine and Transjordan 1923-1925	No 2 ACC (three sections)	4 Rolls-Royce armoured cars and 2 Crossley 4 x 2 light tenders per section. The Company received one section of Lancias with the disbandment of No 1 Company, but these had disappeared by the mid-1920s and little mention is made of their use in Palestine.
Palestine 1930-1939	No 2 ACC (three and later four sections)	4 Rolls-Royce armoured cars, 2 Morris Armed tenders, 1 Morris W/T tender. There was often 1 Crossley, Morris or Albion 6 x 4 tender per section. The common operating unit was the half-section with 2 Rolls-Royce armoured cars, 1 Armed tender and 1 Rolls-Royce W/T tender.
Iraq 1930-1937	No 1 ACC (four sections)	3 Rolls-Royce armoured cars, 2 Armed Ford tenders, 1 Rolls-Royce W/T tender and 1 Morris, Crossley or Albion 6x4 heavy tender. Later in the decade the Armed Fords were replaced by the Morris and then Fordson 4 x 2 tenders.
Iraq 1938-1941	No 1 ACC (three sections at RAF Habbaniya and one section at RAF Shaibah)	6 Rolls-Royce armoured cars, 2 Fordson light tenders, 2 Fordson or Rolls-Royce W/T tenders and 1 Crossley and 1 Albion 6 x 4 heavy tender per section.
North Africa 1941-1943	No 1 ACC Detachment (HQ and two sections)	7 Rolls-Royce armoured cars, 3 Fordson light tenders, 2 Rolls-Royce W/T tenders per section. HQ Section – 2 Rolls-Royce armoured cars, 1 Rolls-Royce wireless tender and 1 Fordson tender. Humber Mark I Armoured Cars replaced Rolls-Royces at Alamein. No information on allocation per section.

Op *Compass*, Iraq and Syria 1941, Op *Crusader*, Gazala, Alamein and Tunisia 1942-1943	No 2 ACC (four sections)	4 Fordson armoured cars and 2-4 Fordson light tenders per section. Sometimes operated as a Half-Section of 2 Fordson armoured cars. In 1943, acquired jeep and 3-tonners. The number of cars varied depending on breakdowns and losses in combat.
Palestine and Jordan 1944-1948	No 2 ACC (four sections)	6 GMC Otters, 2 3-ton tenders, 1 15-cwt ME21 R/T tender and 1 5-cwt Jeep per section. By 1945, there were also 7 GMC Otters in the HQ Section.
Iraq and Jordan 1948-1952	No 2 ACS (three flights)	7 GMC Otters, 1 motorcycle, 2 3-tonners, 1 jeep and 1 water bowser per flight. 1 Diamond T recovery vehicle was on strength of the Squadron.
Iraq 1952-1953	No 2 ACS (three flights)	7 Humber Mark IIIA light reconnaissance cars and 7 Land Rovers, each with a mounted Bren LMG, in Nos 2 and 3 Flights respectively. 7 GMCs were retained on No 1 Flight until early 1953. Each flight also had 3 Bedford QLD 3-tonners, 1 water bowser, 1 petrol bowser, 1 motorcycle and 1 Land Rover. A Diamond T recovery vehicle was located at Squadron HQ.
Aden 1928-1939	Armoured Car Section, Aden	Initially 2 Rolls-Royce armoured cars but then 2 and later 4 Crossley six-wheeler armoured cars. 4 Alvis armoured cars were assigned for a short time before they were returned to the United Kingdom.
Aden 1940-1944	Armoured Car Section	4 Fordson armoured cars, 2 Dodge, Fordson or Chevrolet CMP 15-cwt tenders.
Aden 1944-1945	Armoured Car Section	3 and later 7 GMC Otters.
Aden 1945-1947	Armoured Car Section	5 Humber Mark IV armoured cars and 1 Daimler Mark II armoured car, 2 3-tonners, 1 Chevrolet 15-cwt, 1 petrol bowser and 1 water bowser.
Aden 1947-1951	No 4001 AC Flight	7 GMC Otters.
Canal Zone 1952	No 4001 AC Flight	7 Humber Mark IIIA light reconnaissance cars, 4 Land Rovers, 1 Standard Vanguard car and 1 Bedford QL.

Appendix 4

Badges and Battle Honours

No 1 Squadron RAF Regiment

Honours with the right to emblazonment:
HABBANIYA
IRAQ 1941
EGYPT & LIBYA 1941-1943
GULF 1991

Honours without the right to emblazonment:
KURDISTAN 1922-1923
KURDISTAN 1930-1931
PALESTINE 1936
IRAQ 2003

The Squadron motto 'ARKISH SURRISH' is in cuneiform writing, meaning 'SWIFTLY-SUDDENLY'. Cuneiform was developed by the Sumerians, who were the earliest known inhabitants of Southern Iraq from the 4th Century BC. Both words are found in the inscriptions of the Assyrian kings and the literal translation is 'SWIFT AND SUDDEN'.

The badge depicts an Assyrian chariot of the period of Ashurbanipal, King of Assyria from 668 to 626 BC. The chariot has four occupants, one driver and three warriors, armed with bows and shields. The original of this representation, although facing in the opposite direction, can be found in the Musée de Louvre in Paris on a broken Assyrian sculptured slab.

The original badge of No 1 Armoured Car Company RAF was issued by the College of Arms in 1939 and signed as approved by His Majesty King George VI. As for the badge of No 2 Squadron, the current No 1 Squadron badge differs from the No 1 Armoured Car Company only in the substitution of 'Squadron' for 'Armoured Car Company' and 'Royal Air Force Regiment' rather than 'Royal Air Force'.

No II Squadron RAF Regiment

Honours with the right to emblazonment:
EGYPT & LIBYA 1940-1943
IRAQ 1941
SYRIA 1941
EL ALAMEIN
NORTH AFRICA 1943

Honours without the right to emblazonment:
TRANSJORDAN 1924
PALESTINE 1936-1939
IRAQ 2003

The Squadron motto is 'NUNQUAM NON PARATUS' and translates to 'NEVER UNPREPARED'.
The Squadron badge depicts a flying wheel viewed end on and is based on the tyres fitted on the early Rolls-Royce. The original badge was approved by His Majesty King Edward VIII in October 1936.

No 3 Squadron RAF Regiment

Honours with the right to emblazonment
FRANCE & GERMANY 1944-1945

Honours without the right to emblazonment:
IRAQ 1923-1925

The Squadron motto is 'IN ARDUIS AUDAX' and translates to 'BOLD IN ADVERSITY'.
The Squadron badge depicts a scorpion with tail erect in front of an infantry bayonet. The scorpion alludes to the desert origins of No 3 Armoured Car Company and the bayonet to the current infantry (field) squadron role. France & Germany 1944-1945 relates to the Squadron's origins in 1947 as the renumbered No 2757 Armoured Car Squadron.

Appendix 5

Car Names

Names appeared on the cars soon after they were received in Iraq and Palestine. Cars in Palestine were named with two Rolls-Royces of No 2 Company christened *Eagle* and *Renown* and a Lancia of No 1 Company called *Sirius*. This may have been a tradition inherited from the Light Armoured Motor Batteries of the Tank Corps, who had in turn taken it from the RNAS armoured cars units.

In Iraq, the Companies had different naming themes, though most are not known. No records have been found for the naming of cars in No 3 Armoured Car Company. The names, HMACs *Conqueror, Drake, Harvester, Orion, Shark, Sulaimaniyah* and *Terror* (renamed from *Salmon*!) were used for the Rolls-Royces of No 4 Armoured Car Company, while the Lancias were named after the novels of Sir Water Scott e.g. *Ivanhoe, Kenilworth* and *Waverley*. Two more were however, called *Manston* and *Dido*. The former was a reference to the air station where the RAF armoured cars were established in the United Kingdom. Three Rolls-Royce wireless tenders were known as HMRCs *Relentless, Rapid* and *Pathfinder*. The Armed Fords were given names with the suffix 'ford', such as HMAFs *Henford, Sleaford, Stamford, Stoneford* and *Tugford*. This style was continued with the Morris six-wheeled tenders, two of which were called *Mortlake* and *Morwell*.

Number 5 Armoured Car Company had the Rolls-Royce armoured cars, HMACs *Buffalo, Bison* and *Condor* and No 6 Armoured Car Company, HMACs *Avenger, Busrah* and *Explorer* and a Lancia called *Canada*. The experimental Crossley six-wheeler sent in 1935 to Iraq for trials was christened *Enterprise*. Most of these names continued in the Sections of the Armoured Car Wing formed in 1927, although there may have been some renaming by incoming personnel in new drafts.

Despite the disbandment and reorganisation of the Companies and Wing the tradition of naming cars continued and No 1 Armoured Car Company still retained a naming system in 1939 and into 1942. Cars were routinely moved between sections; however, an example from this period is as follows:

No 1 Section
RRACs *Avenger, Bedouin, Bloodhound, Dhibban, Diana, Fox, Terror* and RRWT *Mercury*

No 2 Section
RRACs *Cheetah, Conqueror, Eagle, Hawk, Jackal, Orion, Virginia, Vulture* and RRWT *Electra*

No 3 Section
RRACs *Adder, Astra, Buffalo, Explorer, Intrepid, Lion, Victory* and RRWT *Pathfinder*

No 4 Section
RRACs *Cerberus, Cleopatra, Curlew, Jaguar, Jubilee, Relentless, Shark* and RRWT *Panther*

Other car names were used during the campaign in North Africa from October 1941 to February 1942, such as, *Ajax, Cossack, Lalliyah, Mosul* and *Norfan*. The use of HMAC ceased early on in the war and the cars were often referred to in the Operations Record Book as RRAC (Rolls-Royce armoured car). The cars still retained a three-digit War Office WO number. There are rare accounts of the Humber Mark I armoured cars being named e.g. *Gladiator, Iron Maiden* and *Whirlwind*, however the names were often not painted on the cars and few records remain.

Number 2 Armoured Car Company for most of its existence did not name their Rolls-Royces. There were named cars for a short period in 1923 e.g. *Eagle* and *Renown* and during the late 1920s and periods of the 1930s e.g. HMAC *Ambuscade, Despatch, Lion* and *Tiger*. Naming was not, however, as consistently applied as in No 1 Company. Two Lancias, possibly inherited from No 1 Armoured Car Company received the names of the First Sea Lords, *Wilson* and *Beatty* in Palestine in 1924.

The cars of No 2 Company were numbered with an 'A' and two digits by the late 1920s, but this changed later to three digits e.g. A115. The Rolls-Royces armoured bodies which were placed on Fordson chassis' from 1939 to 1940 retained the same numbers, these being from A100-110, 113-117, 123-127 and 144. Some of the cars were given nicknames by the crews with A100 known as *The Yellow Peril* and A117 as *Libyan Thunderbolt*. The Fordson tenders were numbered A190 to 203.

The Aden Section numbered the Crossley six-wheeler armoured cars as AC1 to AC4. The Fordsons were numbered sequentially from AC 10 and later RAF 301 to RAF 304; however, it is unclear if these are the same vehicles. The GMCs were identified with the last three digits of the RAF number on the front plate e.g. RAF 226; although from June to December 1944, the names *Corsair* (RAF 226), *Cavalier* (RAF 299) and *Chieftain* (RAF 300) were used. In 1945, the GMCs were all renumbered with the prefix 555 i.e. 555300. Five of the Humber Mark IV armoured cars received in 1946 were numbered as RAF 110921, 110922, 110923, 110924 and 110925 with three being listed in an operational report as *Able, Baker* and *Charlie*. This system was carried on with the replacement GMCs that arrived on No 4001 Flight in 1947. The names *Zebra, Able* (91822), *Baker* (91837), *Charlie* (91841), *Dog, Easy, Fox* and *George* appear in operational reports at this time. The names were based on the single letter painted in the middle of the driver's front vision plate.

Appendix 6

The RAF Armoured Cars Association

The Association first assembled in Derby at the Midland Hotel in April 1998, and was originally known as the RAF Armoured Car Companies Association. 'Mel' Melluish (No. 1 Armoured Car Company) was the organising and driving force and its first Secretary, and he grew the association to approximately 65 members, including Squadron Leader M.P. Casano MC.

With an ageing membership and rather than allowing it to fold up it was decided that from October 2002, John Rolph, whose father had served with No 1 Armoured Car Company from 1930 to 1933 and No 2 Armoured Car Company from 1933 to 1936, should become Secretary of the Association.

In remembrance of the RAF Armoured Cars, two trees and the Company badges were dedicated at the National Memorial Arboretum in the following years. After the death of 'Cass' Casano in August 2006, the Association arranged a memorial service at the National Memorial Arboretum, which was attended by Air Commodore Peter Drissell, the Commandant General of the RAF Regiment, Squadron Leader David Tait, OC II Squadron, and Wing Commander Martin Hooker (RAF Regt Retd), the Regimental Secretary. This led to a new lease of life for the Association with a close relationship developing with the RAF Regiment.

Also present at the memorial service were some ex-members of No 2 Armoured Car Squadron, and they began to attend Reunions of the Association from April 2007. To reflect the involvement of veterans from both the Companies and the Squadrons the Association then changed its name to the 'RAF Armoured Cars Association'.

The Association continues to hold bi-annual Reunions near Derby, at Morley Hayes, which is further enlivened by the attendance of serving members of the RAF Regiment who are able to report on the current day activities of Nos 1 and II Squadrons.

Bibliography

Commanders' Despatches

General Sir Claude Auchinleck GCIE, GB, CSI, DSO, OBE, ADC, Commander-in-Chief, The Middle East Forces, 'Operations in the Middle East from 1st November 1941 to 15th August 1942,' Supplement to *The London Gazette*, 1948.

Air Chief Marshal Sir Arthur Longmore, Air Operations in the Middle East from January 1st 1941 to May 3rd 1941, Supplement to *The London Gazette*, 1946.

Air Vice-Marshal R.E.C. Peirse, *Abridged Despatch - Disturbances in Palestine 19 April to 14 September 1936* (London: Air Ministry, 1937).

Air Vice-Marshal Sir J. M. Salmond, Despatches, 15 February to 30 April 1923, Supplement to *The London Gazette*, 11 June, 1924.

General Sir Archibald P. Wavell GCB CMG MC, Despatch on Operations in the Middle East, from 7th February, 1941 to 15th July 1941, Supplement to *The London Gazette*, 3 July 1946.

National Archives, Kew, UK
Air Ministry

AIR 1/2391/228/11/146 *An account by course students of service experiences*: F/Lt. G. Martyn, 1914-1922.

AIR 2/7221 *Aerodromes: use of armoured cars for aerodrome defence, 1940-1942.*

AIR 5/188 *Proposed assumption by RAF of military command of Palestine, January 1921-December 1923.*

AIR 5/189 *Transition of control in, and withdrawal of, troops from Iraq, January 1922-December 1923.*

AIR 5/477 *Memoranda on RAF scheme of control Iraq (Mesopotamia) 1921.*

AIR 5/838 *Monthly War Diary for No 3 Armoured Car Company, January 1923-December 1924.*

AIR 5/839 *Monthly War Diary for No 4 Armoured Car Company, January 1923-December 1924.*

AIR 5/840 *Monthly War Diary for No 5 Armoured Car Company, January 1923-December 1924.*

AIR 5/841 *Monthly War Diary for No 6 Armoured Car Company, January 1923-December 1924.*

AIR 5/1212 *Armoured Cars Policy: Palestine, Transjordan and Iraq, 1933-1942.*

AIR 5/1239 *HQ RAF Middle East: monthly summaries Vol. I, 1921-1924.*

AIR 5/1243 *Operations in Palestine, Vol. I, Chapter 1 to 14 1920-1930.*

AIR 5/1253 *Operations: Iraq, Chapters 1 to 13.*

AIR 5/1254 *Operations in Iraq: Chapter 1 to 14 January 1924 – December 1928.*

AIR 5/1287 *Iraq Command: monthly operational summaries, Vol. I January 1921-December 1923.*

AIR 5/1288 *Iraq Command: monthly operation summaries, Vol. II, January-December 1924.*

AIR 5/1290 *Iraq Command monthly operational summary, Vol. IV January-December 1926.*

AIR 5/1291 *Iraq Command: monthly operation summaries, Vol. V, 1927-1929.*

AIR 5/1292 *Iraq Command: Monthly Operational Summaries, Vol. VI 1930-1932.*

AIR 5/1293 *Iraq Command: monthly operation summaries, Vol. VII, 1933-1935.*

AIR 9/19 *Palestine and Transjordan 1921-1936.*

AIR 10/1367 *RAF Operations in the Middle East and India from 1920 to 1924.*

AIR 10/1839 *Operations carried out in the Southern Desert in connection with the Iraq-Najd Borders, November 1927-May 1928.*

AIR 10/1845 *Report on Operations in Southern Kurdistan against Shaikh Mahmud, October 1930-May 1931.*

AIR 20/2336/3 *British, Dominion and Allied prisoners-of-war in Germany and German occupied territories: alphabetical list. Section 1: RAF Airmen.*

AIR 20/5996 *Report on Palestine Riots 23 August 1929-11 September 1929.*

AIR 23/543 'Aerowing': Mosul operations September-November 1924.
AIR 23/544 Mosul Operations, February-August 1924.
AIR 23/562 Disturbances in Kirkuk, May-September 1924.
AIR 23/565 Operations and Intelligence: Kirkuk and Sulaimaniya, 4 June 1923.
AIR 23/624 Southern Desert operations: south-east area, November 1929-January 1931.
AIR 23/633 Disturbances in Palestine: weekly resumé of operations, August-November 1936.
AIR 23/710 Armoured Car Reconnaissance, April 1943-August 1944.
AIR 23/1179 RAF Operations during withdrawal from Gazala to El-Alamein: Report, January-December 1942.
AIR 23/1345 Western Desert Operations 1941-1942.
AIR 23/1782 Location plan for RAF units withdrawing from Cyrenaica 1942, January-December 1942.
AIR 23/5921 Coup D'Etat, April 1941: defence of RAF Station, Basrah 1941.
AIR 23/5982 Habbaniya: operations by No. 1 Armoured Car Company, 1941.
AIR 23/6200 RAF operations in the Western Desert and Eastern Mediterranean, 18 November 1941 to 19 May 1942.
AIR 23/6480 Withdrawal from Cyrenaica: report.
AIR 23/8350 Report on the evacuation of RAF from Palestine, Air Vice-Marshal W.L. Dawson, AOC Levant, October 1948.
AIR 24/1678 Headquarters British Forces Aden January to December 1946.
AIR 25/575B Armoured Cars October 1923-November 1924.
AIR 27/2592 No 6 Squadron: Summary of Events 1951-1955.
AIR 29/180 Air Ministry & Ministry of Defence Operations Record Books: Miscellaneous Units - Air Ministry Experiment Stations.
AIR 28/330 Operations Record Book, RAF Habbaniya 1937-1945.
AIR 28/661 Air Ministry & Ministry of Defence Operations Record Books RAF Stations: Ramleh April 1933-July 1942, October 1942-December 1943.
AIR 28/663 Air Ministry and Ministry of Defence: Operations Records Books, RAF Stations, Ramleh. Appendices May-July 1936.
AIR 28/1040 Habbaniya Appendices April-December 1946, January 1948-August 1950.
AIR 28/1270 RAF Station Sharjah, January 1951-December 1955.
AIR 29/50 No 1 Armoured Car Company, Habbaniya: before 1 April 1930 Armoured Car Wing, Hinaidi; from 3 October 1946 No 1 ACC incorporated in RAF Regiment, redesignated No 2701 Squadron.
AIR 29/51 1 Armoured Car Company, Habbaniya, Iraq; appendices only, mostly Movement Orders, includes three photographs of armoured cars May 1946; includes appendices for 4 Section, 1 ACC and 1 ACC Detachment Western Desert, May 1936-June 1943.
AIR 29/52 1 Armoured Car Company, Mosul, Iraq, February-August 1944.
AIR 29/54 2 Armoured Car Company, Heliopolis (Egypt); formed 7 April 1922. Includes detachment at Amman (Trans-Jordan); moved to Ramleh (Palestine) 12 March 1923; moved to Amman 1 May 1928; moved to Ramleh 28 August 1928 with detachments at Amman and Ma'an; later detachments at Jerusalem and Haifa.
AIR 29/55 Operations Record Book: No 2 Armoured Car Company January 1940-October 1946.
AIR 29/56 2 Armoured Car Company, appendices only; September 1923-July 1946.
AIR 29/57 Armoured Car Section, Aden, January 1928 to September 1946.
AIR 29/1414 Independent Armoured Car Flight (No 2701 Squadron RAF Aden)
AIR 29/1713 No. 1 Armoured Car Squadron Qastina, Ramleh, Sundern, Lubeck and Luneburg, March 1947 to December 1950.
AIR 29/1714 No 2 Armoured Car Squadron, Middle East, Transjordan and Iraq, February 1947-December 1950
AIR 29/1719 No 4001 Armoured Car Flight, Aden.
AIR 29/1728 No 21 LAA Squadron, prior to August 1949 known as No 52 (Rifle) Squadron, Amman and Habbaniya.
AIR 29/2226 Field Squadrons: No 2, with appendices, 1951-1953.

AIR 49/48 Middle East Command, AHQ Western Desert, Miscellaneous Reports July 1941-January 1944.

Foreign Office
FO 371/104276, 371/104278, 371/104279, 371/104284

Home Office
HO 144/1447/307522 Nationality and Naturalisation: Poublon, Albert Victor Edouard Marie (known as Albert Casano), from Belgium. Resident in Folkestone. Certificate 4,097 issued 18 June 1919.

Special Operations Executive
HS 9/1080/2 Report by Major G.R. Musgrave.

War Office
WO 169/220 11 Hussars (Prince Albert's Own) September 1939-December 1940.
WO 169/14974 and 18977 1/10 Baluch Regiment, December 1943 and January 1944.
WO 201/2099 Protection of operational landing grounds in forward areas, April 1942-January 1943.
WO 372/8/171926 Medal Card, F.H.W. Guard.
WO 372/14/204928 Medal Card, J.H.F. Newland.
WO 373/47 War Office and Ministry of Defence: Military Secretary's Department: Recommendations for Honours and Awards for Gallant and Distinguished Service (Army), Military Cross.

Air Ministry Weekly Orders
AMWO 48 *No 1 Armoured Car Company: Formation, 19 January 1922.*
AMWO 86 *No 1 Armoured Car Company: Administration, 26 January 1922.*
AMWO 288 *No 2 Armoured Car Company: Formation, 6 April 1922.*
AMWO 477 *Movement of No 1 Armoured Car Company to Palestine, 15 June 1922.*
AMWO 75 *Formation of RAF Units in Iraq, 1 February 1923.*
AMWO 55 *Reorganisation of Armoured Car Companies in Palestine, 24 January 1924.*
AMWO 767 *Reorganisation of Armoured Car Company in Palestine, 16 October 1924.*
AMWO 912 *Disbandment of Armoured Car Wing Headquarters, Iraq, 24 December 1924.*

RAF Museum, Hendon
AC85/6 *The Erk and his Armoured Cars* (Unpublished manuscript, n.d.).

Newspaper and Magazine Articles
'Airmen for Mespot,' *The Daily Echo*, Southampton, 14 September 1922.
'Armoured Cars for Mesopotamia,' *The Times*, 24 September 1920, p. 10.
'Crash in the Wilds,' *Evening Post*, Wellington, NZ, 23 January 1935, p. 10.
'Killed in Smash – NZ Airman' *Evening Post*, Wellington, NZ, 27 September 1935, p. 9.
'Obituary, Michael Casano,' *The Telegraph*, 26 September 2006.
'RAF Flying Accident,' *Flight*, July 29, 1926, p. 465.
'Service Aviation: Appointments,' *Flight*, 14 June 1945, p. 649.
'The Air Estimates,' *Flight*, 15 March 1934, p. 257.
The Egyptian Gazette, c. February 1942.
Busvine, R., 'They fought with the armour of Lawrence of Arabia,' *Chicago Times*? c. 1943.
Cooke, W.A., 'No 14 (Bomber) Squadron,' *Flight*, January 18 1934, p. 52.

Price, A., 'Desert Hornet's Nest', *Flying Review International,* 20, 1964.
Tindale, G., '50 Years On', *Centurion,* 1997, No 3, p. 26.

RAF Regiment Museum Archives
Anon, *Armoured Fighting Vehicles of the RAF, the RAF Regiment and its Associated Overseas Forces.* (Unpublished document, 1970).
Anon, *'The First 75 Years', A History of 1 Squadron RAF Regiment* (Unpublished document, 1996).
Anon, *A History of II Squadron RAF Regiment* (Unpublished document).
Basham, K., *No 1 Armoured Car Company RAF Habbaniya March 1939 to April 1942.*
Childs, L.A., *Taped interview,* n.d.
Constantine, H.A., File.
Cox, J.A.S., *Photographic Album and Diary.*
D'Albiac, Air Vice-Marshal John, *Report on Operations in Iraq.*
Godsave, G.E., *Fi Kull Makáan,* ed. K. Oliver (Unpublished manuscript, 1969).
Godsave, G.E., *Tales of the Tin Trams* (Unpublished manuscript).
Ground Defence Narrative, Chapter III.
Hawkins, D.W.H., Correspondence: Hawkins to Squadron Leader R.D. Lynch, No 3 Squadron RAF Regt, Aldergrove, 26 September 1996.
Helby RA, Lt.Col. T.E.H., *Notes on the Defence of Landing Grounds.*
Jones, H.B., Extract from '*Aden – to be carried in the hand of every Airmen on arrival in England*', RAF Regiment Museum Archives, n.d.
Life in an Armoured Car in the Desert. Magazine article (no source information).
Melluish, E., Correspondence: Letter to Squadron Leader S. Miller, OC No 1 Squadron, RAF Regiment, RAF St Mawgan, 16 November 2002, RAF Regiment Museum Archives.
Middleton, E., Correspondence, 24 August 1978.
Peters, R.J., 'Armoured Cars of the RAF,' *Military Modelling,* February-August 1972.
Walker, W.B., Correspondence: W.B. Walker, ex-No 2 Armoured Car Squadron, 1952-1954, 'Mystery of the Ashes' to No II Squadron, n.d. No II Squadron History Room, RAF Honington.
Yorke Moore, T.P., Papers.

London Gazette
London Gazette, 23 September, 1932.

Interviews, Eulogies and Diaries
Bayliss, B., *Interview and letter to author,* 2008, 2013.
Cox, R.C., *Correspondence with author,* 2008.
Drissell, Air Commodore P.J., *Excerpt from eulogy delivered by Air Cdre Peter J. Drissell, Commandant-General RAF Regiment, at the Memorial Service commemorating the life of Sqn Ldr Michael Peter Casano MC. Held at St Clement Danes, London, 26 November 2006.*
Fairweather, R., *Interview with the author* and comments to author, 2008, 2013.
Foulsham RAF Retd, Wing Commander W., *Interview with the author,* 2008.
Frith RAF Retd, Air Vice-Marshal E.L., *Interview with the author,* June 2007.
Hill, R., *Interview with the author,* 2008, 2013.
Hodge, A., *Interview with the author,* 2008, 2010.
Jordinson, J., *Interview with the author,* 2008.
King, L., *Interview with author,* 2008.
Lee RAF Retd, Wg Cdr P.D., *Interview with the author,* 2010.

Morris, F., *Interview with the author*, 2011.
Morte, V., *Interview with the author*, 2008.
Nixon, R.M., *Interview with the author*, 2011.
Petrie, D.A., *Reminiscences of Sgt D.A. Petrie, RAFVR, No 2 Armoured Car Company (January to May 1945) and Aden Section (May 1945 to September 1946)*.
Prentice, P., *A Story to Tell - Paddy Prentice (O'Brien) (Gold Coast, Qld: Unpublished Memoirs, 1986)*.
Skellon RAF (Retd), Wing Commander R.C., *Interview with the author*, 2010.
Spybey, E.C., *Correspondence: Cpl E.C. Spybey, No 1 Armoured Car Company to his brother Harry, 4 January 1944*.
Stone, R.J., *Trouble with the Akhwan Tribes in 1927* (Short manuscript written 22 March 1928).
Walker, W.B., *Interview with author*, 2008, 2013.

Imperial War Museum Sound and Document Archives

Eastmead, S.A., *Interview 4504* (IWM Sound Archive, 1979).
Edwards, W.H., *Interview 4824* (IWM Sound Archive, 1981).
Ford, E.L., *Interview 4614* (IWM Sound Archive, 1980).
Hetherington, L., *Interview 4838* (IWM Sound Archive, 1981).
Jones, W.O., *Document 12373, Letter 02/43/1, Private Papers of Wing Commander W.O. Jones, 2 February 1943* (IWM Document Archive).
Norman, C.P., *Imperial War Museum Interview 4629* (IWM Sound Archive, 1980).
Simmons, L.A., *Private Papers 7284* (IWM Document Archive, n.d.).
Wentworth, M.S., *Interview 4768* (IWM Sound Archive, 1980).

RAF Armoured Cars Association

Brandon, V., *Correspondence*.
Fenwick, H., *Reminiscences*, 1972.
Ferguson, R., *Interview with J. Rolph*, 2008
Hawkins, D.W.H., *Interview with J. Rolph*, 2008.
Lock, R., *Correspondence*, 2008.
Melluish, E., *Reminiscences*.
Morte, V., *Interview with J. Rolph*, 2008.
Skellon RAF (Retd), Wg Cdr R.C., *Interview with J. Rolph*, 2011.
Wyatt, P.K., *Diary, Armoured Car Section, Aden 1941*.

Journal Articles

Anglim, S., 'MI(R), G(R) and British Covert Operations, 1939–42', *Intelligence and National Security*, 20(2005), pp. 631-653.
Anon, 'Summary of the Report of the Palestine Royal Commission,' *American Jewish Yearbook*, 1937-1938, pp. 503-556.
Churchill, W., 'Speech to the House of Commons, 15 July 1941,' *Hansard, Vol. 373*, cc. 463-467.
Cochrane, R.A., 'The Work of the Royal Air Force at Aden,' *Journal of the Royal United Service Institute*, LXXVI (1931), 88-99.
Cox, J.L., 'A Splendid Training Ground: The Importance to the Royal Air Force of its Role in Iraq, 1919-32,' *Journal of Imperial and Commonwealth History*, 13 (1985), p. 157-184.
Fawzi el Qawukji, *Memoirs, 1948, Part I, Journal of Palestine Studies*, 1 (1972), pp. 27-58.
Gil-Har, Y., 'Delimitation Boundaries: Transjordan and Saudi Arabia,' *Middle Eastern Studies*, 28 (2000), pp. 374-384.

Godsave, G.E., 'Armoured Cars in Desert Warfare,' *Journal of the Royal United Service Institute*, LXX (1925), pp. 396-406.
Hughes, M., 'The Banality of Brutality: British Armed Forces and the Repression of the Arab Revolt in Palestine, 1936–39,' *English Historical Review* Vol. CXXIV, 507 (2009), pp. 313-354.
Omissi, D., 'Britain, the Assyrians and the Iraq Levies, 1919-1932,' *Journal of Imperial and Commonwealth History*, 17 (1989), pp. 301-322.
Omissi, D., 'Technology and Repression: Air Control in Palestine 1922-36,' *Journal of Strategic Studies*, 13 (1990), pp. 41-63.
Salmond, J., 'The Air Force in Iraq,' *Journal of the Royal United Service Institute*, LXX (1925), pp. 483-498.
Skoulding, F.A., 'With Z Unit in Somaliland', *RAF Quarterly*, 2 (1931), pp. 387-396.
Witherow, M.S., 'The RAF's Associated Overseas Ground Fighting Forces,' *Journal of the RAF Historical Society* 49 (2010), p. 134-150.

Books

Abu Nowar, M., *The History of the Hashemite Kingdom of Jordan, Vol. I* (Oxford: The Middle East Centre, 1989).
Abu Nowar, M., *The History of the Hashemite Kingdom of Jordan, Vol II* (Oxford: Ithaca Press, 1989).
Agar-Hamilton, J.A.L. and L C.F. Turner, *The Sidi Rezeg Battles 1941* (Cape Town: Oxford University Press, 1957).
Ahmed, R., *History of the Baloch Regiment, 1939-1956* (Uckfield, UK: Naval & Military Press, 2004).
Air Ministry, *The Royal Air Force Armoured Car Manual, Air Ministry Publication 1418* (London: Air Ministry, 1931).
Anon, *Paiforce: The Official Story of the Persia and Iraq Command 1941-1946* (London: HMSO, 1948).
Anon, *Historical Records of the Queen's Own Cameron Highlanders, 1932-1948, Vol. I* (Edinburgh/London: William Blackwood & Sons Ltd, 1952).
Anon, *Yeoman Yeoman: The Warwickshire Yeomanry, 1920-1956* (Birmingham: The Queen's Own Warwickshire and Worcestershire Yeomanry Regimental Association, 1971).
Barclay, C.N., *The History of the Cameronians (Scottish Rifles), Vol. III, 1933-1946* (London: Sifton Praed, 1948).
Bartlett, J., and J. Benson, *All the King's Enemies* (Boston, Lincolnshire: Richard Kay, 2000).
Blight, G., *The History of the Royal Berkshire Regiment (Princess Charlotte of Wales's) 1920-1947* (London: Staples Press, 1953).
Bolitho, H., *Angry Neighbours* (London: Arthur Barker, 1957).
Bolitho, H., *The Galloping Third: The Story of The 3rd The King's Own Hussars* (London: John Murray, 1963).
Bowyer, C., *RAF Operations 1918-1938* (London: William Kimber, 1988).
Boyle, A., *Trenchard: Man of Vision* (London: Collins, 1962).
Bright, J., *9th Queen's Lancers 1936-1945* (Aldershot: Gale & Polden, 1951).
Brown, J.A., *Eagles Strike: The Campaigns of the South African Air Force in Egypt, Cyrenaica, Libya, Tunisia, Tripolitania and Madagascar 1941-1943, Vol IV South African Forces World War II* (Purnell & Sons: Cape Town, 1974).
Brown, R.A., *Shark Squadron: The History of No 112 Squadron RFC RAF 1917-1975* (London: Crécy Books, 1994).
Browne, J.G., *The Iraq Levies 1915-1932* (London: Royal United Service Institute, 1932).
Carr, S.J., *You are not Sparrows* (London: Ian Allan, 1975).
Charters, D.A., *The British Army and Jewish Insurgency in Palestine, 1945-1947* (London: MacMillan, 1989).
Clarke, D., *The Eleventh at War* (London: Michael Joseph, 1952).

Clayton, A., *France, Soldiers and Africa* (London: Brassey's, 1988).
Collins, D.J.E., *The Royal Indian Navy 1939-1945* (India & Pakistan: Combined Services Historical Branch, 1964).
Connell, J., *Wavell. Scholar and Soldier* (London: Collins, 1964).
Cowper, J.M., *The King's Own. The Story of a Royal Regiment, Vol. III, 1914-1950* (Aldershot: Gale & Polden, 1957).
Cross, K. and V. Orange, *Straight and Level* (London: Grub Street, 1993).
Davis, T.B., *The Surrey and Sussex Yeomanry in the Second World War* (Ditchling, Hassocks [Sussex]: The Ditchling Press, 1980)
de Chair, S., *The Golden Carpet* (London: Faber & Faber, 1944).
Dudgeon, A.G., *Hidden Victory: The Battle of Habbaniya, May 1941* (Tempus Publishing: Stroud, Gloucestershire, 2000).
Fairbanks, A., *Action Stations Overseas* (Yeovil: Patrick Stephens, 1991).
Fieldhouse, D., *Western Imperialism in the Middle East 1914-1958* (Oxford: Oxford University Press, 2006).
Fletcher, D., *The Rolls-Royce Armoured Car* (Oxford: Osprey Publishing 2012).
Freyberg, P., *Freyberg, VC: Soldier of Two Nations* (London: Hodder & Stoughton, 1991).
Frost, J., *A Drop too Many* (London: Leo Cooper, 1994).
Geraghty, A., *March or Die* (London: Guild Publishing, 1986).
Glubb, J.B., *The Story of the Arab Legion* (London: Hodder & Stoughton, 1948).
Glubb, J.B., *War in the Desert: An RAF Frontier Campaign* (London: Hodder & Stoughton, 1956).
Glubb, J.B., *Arabian Adventures: Ten Years of Joyful Service* (London: Cassell, 1978).
Gore, D., *On Kentish Chalk: A Farming Family of the North Downs* (Newbury [Berks]: Published by the author, 2006).
Hamilton, A.M., *Road through Kurdistan*, 2nd Ed (London: Faber & Faber, 1958).
Harris, A., *Bomber Offensive* (New York: MacMillan, 1947).
Hetherington, J., *Air War against Germany and Italy 1939-1943* (Canberra: Australian War Memorial, 1954).
Hopwood, D., *Syria 1945-1986: Politics and Society* (London: Unwin Hyman, 1988).
Houle, A., M. Lavigne and A. Gagné, *Group Captain A.U. 'Bert' Houle DFC & bar* (Quebec: Lavigne Aviation Publ., 2000).
Jackson, W.G.F., et al., *The Mediterranean and Middle East, Vol VI, Part 2,* History of the Second World War (London: HMSO, 1987).
Jackson, P.M., and A.J. Jackson (eds.), *A Lot to Fight For: The War Diaries and Letters of Squadron Leader J.F. Jackson DFC* (Toowoomba: Church Archivist's Press, n.d. [c. 1996]).
Jarvis, C.S., *Arab Command* (Hutchinson & Co.: London, 1946).
Jefford, C.G., *The Flying Camels* (High Wycombe, Bucks.: Privately published by the author, 1995).
Klein, H., *Springboks in Armour* (Cape Town: Purnell & Sons, 1965).
Laffin, J., *Swifter than Eagles* (Edinburgh: William Blackwood & Sons, 1964).
Lax, M., *Alamein to the Alps. 454 Squadron RAAF 1941-1945* (Wanniassa [ACT]: Published by the author, 2006).
Lee, A.S.G., *Fly Past. Highlights from a Flyers Life* (London: Jarrolds, 1974).
Lee, D., *Flight from the Middle East* (London: HMSO, 1980).
Lee, D., *Wings in the Sun* (London: HMSO, 1989).
Leeson, F.M., *The Hornet Strikes: The History of No 213 Squadron RAF* (Tunbridge Wells: Air-Britain Publication, 1998).
Liddell Hart, B.H., *The Tanks: The History of the Royal Tank Regiment and its predecessors Heavy Branch Machine-Gun Corps, Tank Corps and Royal Tank Corps, 1914-1945, Vol. I* (London: Cassell, 1959).
Liddell Hart, B.H., *The Tanks: The History of the Royal Tank Regiment and its predecessors Heavy Branch Machine-Gun Corps, Tank Corps and Royal Tank Corps, 1914-1945, Vol. II* (London: Cassell, 1959).

Lindsay, O., *Once a Grenadier: The Grenadier Guards 1945-1995* (Barnsley, Yorks.: Pen & Sword, 1996).
Longmore, A., *From Sea to Sky: Memoirs 1910-1945* (London: Geoffrey Bles, 1946).
Lunt, J., *Imperial Sunset* (London: MacDonald, 1981).
Lunt, J., *The Arab Legion 1923-1957* (London: Constable, 1999).
Mackay, J.N., *History of the 7th Duke of Edinburgh's Own Gurkhas Rifles* (Edinburgh: William Blackwood & Sons, 1962).
Martin, L., *The Treaties of Peace 1919-1923, Vol. II* (New York: Carnegie Endowment for International Peace, 1924).
Martin, T., *The Essex Regiment, 1929-1950* (Brentwood, Essex: The Essex Regiment Association, 1952).
McCorquodale, D., B.L.B. Hutchings and A.D. Woozley, *History of the King's Dragoon Guards 1938-1945* (Glasgow: Printed for the Regiment by McCorquodale & Co., 1950).
Molony, C.J.C. et al., *The Mediterranean and Middle East, Vol. V,* History of the Second World War (London: HMSO, 1973).
Munro, J.M., *The Nairn Way* (New York: Delmar, 1980)
Murphy, W.E., *The Relief of Tobruk* New Zealand in the Second World War 1939-1945 (Wellington, NZ: War History Branch, Dept of Internal Affairs, 1961).
Oliver, K., *Through Adversity: The History of the RAF* Regiment (Rushden, Northants: Forces & Corporate Publishing, 1997).
Omissi, D., *Air Power and Colonial Control: The Royal Air Force 1919-1939* (Manchester: Manchester University Press, 1990).
Orange, V., *Coningham: A Biography of Air Marshal Sir Arthur Coningham* (Washington DC: Center for Air Force History, 1992).
Orange, V., and Lord Deramore, *Winged Promises: A History of No 14 Squadron RAF 1915-1945* (Fairford: RAF Benevolent Fund, 1998).
Orpen, N., *War in the Desert, Vol. III* South African Forces World War II (Cape Town: Purnell, 1971).
Owen, R., *The Desert Air Force* (London: Hutchinson, 1948).
Phillpott, I.M., *The Royal Air Force: An Encyclopaedia of the Inter-War Years, Vol. I* (Barnsley, Yorks.: Pen & Sword, 2005).
Pitt, B., 'O'Connor,' in *Churchill's Generals*, ed. J. Keegan (New York: Grove Weidenfeld, 1991).
Platt, J.R.I., *The Royal Wiltshire Yeomanry 1907-1967* (London: Garnstone Press, 1972).
Playfair, I.S.O., et al., *The Mediterranean and Middle East, Vol. I*, History of the Second World War (London: HMSO, 1954).
Playfair, I.S.O. et al., *The Mediterranean and Middle East, Vol. II,* History of the Second World War (London: HMSO, 1956).
Playfair I.S.O., et al., *The Mediterranean and Middle East, Vol. III,* History of the Second World War (London: HMSO, 1960).
Playfair, I.S.O., et al., *The Mediterranean and Middle East, Vol. IV*, History of the Second World War (HMSO: London, 1966).
Raleigh, W,. *The War in the Air, Vol. I* (The Clarendon Press: Oxford, 1922).
Robertson, B., *Wheels of the RAF* (Cambridge: Patrick Stephens, 1983).
Samson, C.R., *Fights and Flights* (London: Ernest Benn, 1930).
Saunders, H.St.G., *Per Ardua: The Rise of British Air Power 1911-1939* (London: Oxford University Press, 1944).
Secter J.J., and J.P. Secter, *Recollections: Narrative reflections on the life and times of John J. Secter* (Victoria [BC]: Privately published, 2001).
Shores, C., B. Cull and N. Malizia, *Malta: The Spitfire Year 1942* (London: Grub Street, 1991).
Shores, C., N. Franks and R. Guest, *Above the Trenches: a Complete Record of the Fighter Aces and Units of the British Empire Air Forces 1915-1920* (London: Grub Street, 1990).
Sluglett, P., *Britain in Iraq 1914-1932* (London: Ithaca Press, 1976).
Stevens, W.G., *Bardia to Enfidaville*, History of New Zealand in the Second World War 1939–1945 (Wellington, NZ: War History Branch, Dept. of Internal Affairs, 1962).

Stewart, N., *The Royal Navy and the Palestine Patrol* (London: Frank Cass, 2002).
Sueter, M., *The Evolution of the Tank* (London: Hutchinson & Co., 1937).
Tedder, A.W., *With Prejudice, The War Memoirs of Marshal of the Royal Air Force Lord Tedder* (London: Cassell, 1966).
Thompson, H.L., *New Zealanders with the Royal Air Force Vol. III* New Zealand in the Second World War 1939-1945 (Wellington, NZ: War History Branch, Dept of Internal Affairs, 1959).
Tripp, C., *A History of Iraq* (Cambridge: Cambridge University Press, 2000).
Tullett, J.S., *Nairn Bus to Baghdad* (Wellington: AH & AW Reed, 1968).
Vincent, J.-N., *Les Forces Françaises Libres en Afrique 1940-1943* (Château de Vincennes: Ministère de la Défense, État-major de l'armée de Terre, Service historique, 1983).
Vincent, S.F., *Flying Fever* (London: Jarrolds, 1972).
Watson, J., and L. Jones, *3 Squadron at War* (Carlingford [NSW]: Halstead Press for the DAF 3 Squadron Association, 1959).
Wilson, R.D., *With the 6th Airborne Division in Palestine 1945-1948* (Barnsley [S. Yorks.]: Pen & Sword, 2008).
Wyndham, H., *The Household Cavalry Regiment: The First Household Cavalry Regiment* (Aldershot: Gale & Polden, 1952).

Index

n indicates an entry within the notes

Abdullah ibn Al Hussein, Amir of Transjordan and King of Jordan (1882-1951), 27-31, 33, 37, 39, 44, 45n, 143, 147-149, 151, 157, 162n, 291, 468, 511n, 551, 556-558, 583
Abu Dhabi, 572-574, 581
Abu Ghar, 103-107, 109-111, 127n
Abu Ghuraib, 302, 304
Abu Kemal, 90, 318, 321
Abu Khuwaimah, 138
Abu Suwan, 149
Abu Teyah, 93-94
Abyssinia, 4, 208, 243, 274, 313, 336, 520, 523, 525, 549n
Acre, 200, 237, 331, 458, 465
Acroma, 376, 386, 389
Aden, 94n, 126n, 165, 192, 244, 453, 511n, 515-516, 518-522, 524, 530-537, 539, 541-545, 547-548, 549n-550n, 556-557, 565, 573, 586, 588, 591n, 594n, 597
Aden Colony, 515-516, 519, 532, 547
Aden Government Guards, 535, 539, 546
Aden Protectorate Levies (APL): 516, 520, 533, 535, 537, 539, 543-549n, 573, 583-584, 586-587, 593n-594n, **No 2 Wing**, 547, **No 4 Sqn**, 546, **No 10 Sqn**, 548
Aden Works Department, 536
Admiralty, xv-xvi, 1-2, 7, 85
Admiralty Compass Department, 85
Adwan, 31, 33, 37
Adwan, Sultan ibn, 31, 37
Aegean, 313, 318
Afghanistan, 597-598
Agedabia, 259-261, 263, 351, 353, 357, 359, 420, 423, 425
Ahwar, 533, 547
Ain Dibbs, 60
Ain Ghazal, 90
Ain Sinya, 223-224, 227
Ain Zala, 314, 466-467
Air-Land Rescue, 544-545
Air Ministry, London, 1-3, 6, 9, 25n, 49, 199, 201, 207n, 212, 230, 235, 457, 516, 536, 548
Air Training Corps, 486
Ajarmi, 31

Ajman, 100, 131, 136-140
Al Abtiyyah, 134
Al Aqsa Mosque, 557
Al Aquila, 583-584, 586
Al Barkat, 100
Al Bassa, 458, 460, 463, 465
Al Faluja, 229
Al Hafar, 122, 125, 129, 595
Al Hamra, 305
Al Haniyah, 107, 118
Al Harrat, 88
Al Khadimain, 302, 304
Al Majdal, 214, 229
Al Masana, 519
Al Milah, 544
Al Riquai, 122, 130, 139
Al Ukla, 546
Alam el Halfa, 406, 408
Alam el Hatshi, 248, 251
Alam el Samm, 250
Albania, 240
Aleppo, 329-331, 333n, 460, 479-480
Alexander, Gen H., later Fld Mshl Lord, 404, 414n, 435, 443, 446, 452
Alexandria, 243-245, 257, 313,

631

333n, 379, 399, 403, 405, 430, 459
Algeria, 244
Allen, Cpl A., 423
Allen, FS A., 494
Allenby, Gen Sir Edmund, 192
Allenby Bridge, 152-153, 239, 494, 506, 551
Alleyn's School, 95n
Allied Air Forces:
    North African Strategic Air Force, 446, **North African Tactical Air Force**, 451n, **North West African Tactical Air Force**, 451n
Alloway, Sqn Ldr H.V., 310n
Almaza, 450n
Altun Kupri, 47, 58, 60, 63, 83, 188
AM (Greek National Liberation Front)
Amarat, 128, 131
American Embassy, 275
Amery, L., 4, 10n
Amiris, 539, 541
Amiriya, 372, 381, 396, 400, 405-406, 458
Amison, Fg Off G.N., 242n
Amman, 14, 27-28, 33-36, 39-40, 44-45, 85-89, 131, 143, 148, 150-153, 156-157, 159, 163, 204-205, 500-502, 507, 552, 555-556
Amyan, 544
Anatolia, 52, 466
Anderson, AC, 18
Anderson, Capt, 296
Anderson, Fg Off, 351
Andrews, L., 234
Anglo-American Committee, 492
Anglo-Egyptian Treaty, 569
Anglo-Iranian Oil Company, 565
Anglo-Iraq Treaty, 269
Anglo-Jordan Treaty, 571
Anglo-Persian Oil Company, 25, 86
Anglo-Transjordan Treaty, 551
Ansab, 103, 139
Anstey, Flt Lt W.I., 279, 310n
Antelat, 259-260, 357-361, 363-366, 372, 375n, 396, 418, 423, 425, 453
Aqaba, 155, 157-159, 162n, 198, 509, 514n, 552, 556
Ar Rams, 581
Arab Higher National Committee, 208, 233
Arab League, 590
Arab Legion (Jeysh al Arabi): 30-31, 33, 35-37, 39, 43, 45, 45n-46n, 126n, 143, 145-147, 150-152, 155, 157-159, 161, 200, 291-294, 299, 301, 311n, 322-324, 326, 451n, 511n, 551-552, 556-557, 570-571, 573, 592n, **3rd Mechanised Regt**, 511n, **Desert Mechanised Regt**, 291, 311n, **Desert Patrol (Al Badia)**, 152, 155, 157, 161
Arab Liberation Army, 503, 514n
Arab Revolt, 27, 30, 162n

Arab Revolutionary Army, 227
Arabian American Oil Company, ARAMCO, 572
Arabian Sea, 24, 536
Arbet, 181
Arbil, 57-59, 90, 188-189, 274, 288, 315, 468
Ariosto, 364
Armenians, 47
Armin, Col-Gen J. von, 433-434, 438, 446
Armistice, 21, 47-48, 52, 58, 244, 288, 304, 308, 313, 331, 364, 375n, 555
Armistice Day, 205
Artuf, 196
As Sufran, 100
Ash Shaqq, 137
Ashcroft, Cpl T., 66, 69, 77n
Ashur, 56
Assyrians, 4, 47, 50, 52, 62, 64, 66-67, 75n, 185-186, 189, 191n, 270
Ataiba, 131, 137
Ataishan, Turki ibn, 572-573, 582-585, 588
Ataq, 539
Ataroth, 195-196
Atlas, 364
Atrash, Sultan, 144
Attfield, Plt Off A.V., 418, 450n, 472n
Auchinleck, Gen Sir Claude, 336, 342, 344, 353n, 376, 382, 394, 397, 399-400, 403-404
Ault, FS, 248, 267n
Australia, 4, 125n, 243, 265, 354n, 471, 532
Australian Army:
    Divisions:
        6th Aust, 245, 252, 256-257, **7th Aust**, 319, **9th Aust**, 266, 400, 414
    Brigades:
        21st Aust Inf, 320, **25th Aust Inf**, 320
    Regiments:
        6th Aust Divisional Cavalry, 354n, **2/1st Aust Anti-Tank**, 327
    Medical:
        Aust General Hospital, 333n
Austria, 239, 482
Auxiliaries (Auxiliary Division, Royal Irish Constabulary), 21, 126n
Avroman mountains, 174
Awa Barika, 179-182
Aziz, Mufti, 315
Azraq, 39, 88, 143-146, 150-151, 161, 206
Bab el Haoua, 460
Baghdad, 9, 20, 25, 46n, 47-50, 53, 55-56, 58-59, 61-62, 64-65, 69, 79-80, 84-87, 89-90, 93-94, 95n, 96, 98-100, 103, 107, 115-116, 118-119, 125n, 127n, 131-132, 134, 138-139, 163, 165-167, 175, 183, 185-188, 191n, 200,

205, 233, 269, 273, 275-278, 282-283, 286, 288-290, 293-294, 296, 298-299, 301-304, 306-309, 312n-313, 315, 320-321, 328, 467-469, 516, 563, 565, 574, 576
Baghdad Boils, 'Leishmaniasis', 119, 127n
Baghdad Gaol, 69
Baghdad Pact, 590
Baheira, 379, 393
Baheira Main, 401n
Baheira Satellite 1, 401n
Bahra Agreement, 107, 109
Bahrain, 552, 562, 576-577, 589, 592n, 596
Baiji, 56-57, 59-62, 274
Baillie, LAC, 252, 255
Bair, 147, 149-150, 155
Baird, Brig J.E.A., 592n
Balad Sinjar, 329
Balfour Declaration, 27, 192, 201
Balkans, 244, 265, 460
Ballard, Flt Lt M., 69, 106, 200
Banbury, Fg Off B.A.C., 516
Banda (Italian Somali Irregulars), 525-526, 528, 530
Bani Mirt, 179
Baqubah, 50
Barce, 257, 365
Barclays Bank, 506
Bardia, 252, 254-256, 266, 357
Bargal, 532
Barrett, Wg Cdr J.B., 588, 594n
Barzan, 109, 184, 473n
Barzani, Nerchevan Idris (1966-), 473n
Barzani, Sheikh Ahmed (1896-1969), 467, 472n
Basham, LAC K., 272, 278, 294
Bash-Bulaq, 181
Basra, 20, 25, 47-48, 52, 55, 86, 96, 98-100, 103, 106-107, 113, 119, 127n, 129, 131, 136, 165, 187, 269, 273-275, 277, 305-308, 467, 563, 566, 576-597
Basra Gaol, 98
Basra Group Boxing Championship, 103
Basra Group Cricket League Cup, 104
Batt, AC1, 592n
Battle of Britain, 143, 569
Bay of Biscay, 23, 450n
Bay of Kuwait, 140
Bayliss, B., 474, 486, 489-490, 500, 511
Baziyan, 59, 61, 69-70, 80, 178-179, 181
Baziyan Pass, 59, 61, 69-70, 80, 178
Beamish, Gp Capt G., 376, 392
Beauman, Brig A., 230
Bec du Canard, 329
Beda Fomm, 260-261, 266
Bedouin Control Board, 150
Beersheba, 192, 200, 240
Beg, Karim Fettah 82
Beg, Mahrut, 128, 131
Beihan, 539, 543

Beirut, 86, 89, 210, 320-321, 331, 333n, 479
Beit Hakerem, 491
Belandah, 358-359, 423, 425-426
Belgium, xv, 7, 268n
Belhamed, 393
Bell, Sgt, 286
Bellerby, Sqn Ldr P., 539-540
Benghazi, 244, 256-261, 265, 351, 354n, 357, 360-361, 363, 365, 367, 369, 379, 403, 418, 423, 425, 453, 455, 597
Beni Huchaim, 103
Beni Kaab, 578-579
Beni Sakhr, 31, 39-40, 43, 46n, 92, 147-149
Benina, 256, 358, 365, 453
Bennett, AC, 367
Bennett, Flt Lt L.V., 223-227, 233, 242n
Benstead, Fg Off F., 93
Berbera, 10n, 523-526, 529, 532
Berca 2, 453
Betham, Flt Lt B.J., 544-547
Bethlehem, 232, 234
Bevin, E., 493
Bidon, Gen, xv
Bir Ahmed, 523
Bir Dufan, 424, 430
Bir el Gubi, 377, 382
Bir el Khamsa, 342
Bir El Khireigat, 254
Bir Habata, 254, 342
Bir Hacheim, 256, 376, 382-383, 385-386, 401n-402n
Bir Lussuf, 105
Bir Maknuk, 533
Bir Megasid, 251
Bir Saadi, 257
Bir Shagrah, 103, 105-106
Bir Shebicha, 104-105
Bir Sheferzen, 254
Bir Soltane, 439
Bir Uazan, 401n
Bird, Sgt, 279
Birks, Col H.L., 267n
Black and Tans (Royal Irish Constabulary), 21, 194
Black Sea, 23
Blake, Flt Lt H.E., 380, 389, 412, 442
Blitzkrieg, 244
Blomberg, Maj A. von, 288
Blomberg, Fld Mshl W. von, 288
Boer War, 5
Bohotleh, 529
Bolitho, H., 153-154, 162n
Bologna, 354n
Bolshevik Revolution, xvi, 50
Bolsheviks, 126n
Bombay, 19
Booker, AC2, C.S., 35, 37, 45n
Booth, LAC T., 242n
Bordj Zoumit, 441
Borton, Gp Capt A., 9, 10n
Bosphorus, 23
Bowen, Fg Off H., 104
Boyle, Gp Capt J.D., 22
Brace, Flt Lt E.A., 541-542, 550n
Bradley, Wg Cdr C.R.S., 59

Brandon, LAC V., 164, 167-168, 184, 190n
Brawn, Lt-Col J.A., 269, 309-310n
Brett, AC W.H., 20, 24, 26n
Brighton Road, 145
Brisbane, 354n
British Army:
British Expeditionary Force, xv, 244
British Troops in Palestine, 208, 489
Cyrenaica Command, 265
GOC Iraq, 5-6, 9
Middle East Command, 290, 336, 404, 467
Persia and Iraq Command, 404, 467
Army Groups and Armies:
18th Army Gp, 435, 443, 446, **First**, 433, 446, 451n, **Eighth**, 336-337, 340, 342-346, 351-354n, 356-358, 360, 365, 372, 376, 381, 383, 385-386, 391-392, 394, 396-398, 400, 403-406, 408-409, 413-414, 418, 423, 425, 428, 430, 432, 434, 438-439, 442-443, 445-446, 451n, 453, 568, **Ninth**, 460, 478, 480, **Tenth**, 257, 260, 265, 466
Corps:
X, 397-398, 416, 439, 442, **XIII**, 255, 257, 265, 340, 343, 356-357, 359-360, 364, 366, 368, 372, 375n, 378, 382, 414, **XXX**, 340, 348, 378, 414
Divisions:
1st Cavalry, 245, 290, 311n, **1 (UK) Armd**, 595, **1st Armd**, 357, 374n, 378, 400, 414, 439, 442, **2nd Armd**, 264-266, **6th Armd**, 446, **7th Armd**, 245-246, 248, 250-252, 254-256, 258-261, 266, 267n, 340, 378, 382, 400, 414, 418, 423, 425, 428-430, 446, **6th Airborne**, 481-482, 486, 492, 502, **1st Inf**, 230, 232-233, 478, **5th Inf**, 320, 464, 466, **6th Inf**, 320, 331, **44th Inf**, 414, **50th (Northumbrian) Inf**, 378, 389, 397, 414, 438-439, 445, **51st Highland**, 414, 425, 434-435, **56th Inf**, 466
Brigades:
4th Cavalry, 290, 311n, 313, 321, 324, 327, 331, 334n, 353n, **2nd Armd**, 360, 374n, **4 (UK) Armd**, 596, **4th Armd**, 252, 254, 258-260, 267n, 340, 382, 392, 426, **7th Armd**, 252, 260, 459, 466, **8th Armd**, 438, 441-443, **9th Armd**, 414, **22nd Armd**, 357, 401n, **87th Armd**, 460, **1st Army Tank**, 340, **12th AA**, 408,

412-413, 416, **2nd Inf**, 492, **14th Inf**, 234, 237, **16th Inf**, 234, 237, 320, **22nd Guards**, 266, 340, 401n, **131st (Queen's) Lorried Inf**, 429, **150th Inf**, 383, **200th Guards**, 357, 360, 374n, 401n, **201st Guards**, 386, 401n, 446, Cairo, 199, **7th Motor**, 378, 382, **1st Para**, 493, **1st Support Gp**, 357, 360, 374n, **7th Support Gp**, 260, **Northern**, 214, 227, 229-230, **Southern**, 214, 227, 229
Forces:
Aden Striking Force, 549n, **Bedouforce**, 479-480, 512n, **Birksforce**, 254, **Calforce**, 408, **Combeforce**, 254-255, 259-260, **Findforce**, 508, **Force E**, 345-348, 351, 354n, **Habforce**, 290-292, 295, 308-309, 311n, 315, 318, 320-321, 326-329, 332, 336, **North Gp**, 507-508, **Oasis Gp**, 344-345, **Paiforce**, 467, **Scottforce**, 479, **Western Desert Force**, 245, 251-252, 255, 266, 335-336, 354n, 448
Royal Armoured Corps:
241n, **No 1 Sub-Depot, Abbassia, RAC**, 246-248
Armour and Cavalry:
Life Guards, 290, 327, 333n, **Royal Horse Guards (The Blues)**, 291, 332, 333n, **1st Household Cavalry Regt**, 290, 298-299, 301-304, 311n, 314-315, 318, 321-322, 324, 326, 328, 333n, **1st King's Dragoon Guards**, 260, 264-265, 354n, 438, **4th/7th Royal Dragoon Guards**, 508, **1st Royal Dragoons**, 319, 435, 558, **3rd Hussars**, 250, 479, 512n, **8th Hussars**, 227, 229, **9th Queen's Royal Lancers**, 194, **11th Hussars**, 229-231, 238, 243, 246, 248, 250-251, 254-264, 267n, 332, 354n, 446, 448, **12th Lancers**, 200, 229, 241n-242n, **17th/21st Lancers**, 508, **20th Hussars**, 26n
Tank Corps/Royal Tank Corps/ Royal Tank Regt:
9, 19-20, 26n, 48, 55, 95n, 211, 218, 241n, 457, **2nd RTR**, 254, **4th RTR**, 508, **6th Battalion RTC**, 211, 219, 241n, **7th RTR**, 251-252, **Armoured Car Companies, 1st**, 26n, **2nd**, 26n, **3rd**, 241n, **4th**, 26n, **5th**, 241n, **6th**, 26n, **Light Armd Motor Batteries**, 7, 47, **No 1 Tank Gp**, 10n

633

Yeomanry:
  Royal Wiltshire, 290, 311n, 318, 321, 323-324, 327, 334n, Warwickshire, 290, 311n, 321, 323-328
Artillery:
  Royal Horse Artillery, 260, 267n, **4th Regt RHA**, 254, 3rd Fd Regt, 329, 60th Fd Regt, 290, 311n, **237 Bty**, 291, 296, 144th Fd Regt, 479, 512n, **43 Bty Royal Fd Artillery**, 63, 73rd Anti-Tank Regt, 355n, **1st Independent Anti-Tank Tp**, 311n, 14th LAA Regt, 442, 16th LAA Regt, 417, 6 LAA Bty, 355n, 'X' Tp, 6 (Coleraine) LAA Bty, 355n
Engineers:
  2nd Fd Sqn, 311n, 322, **1st Airborne Sqn**, 508, 20th Fortress Coy, 535, Aden Fortress Coy, 519, Boring Section, 311n
Infantry Regiments and Battalions:
  Argyll and Sutherland Highlanders, 26n, **2nd Bedfordshire and Hertfordshire Regt**, 81, 2nd Black Watch, 237-238, Buffs, The East Kent Regt, 258, **2nd Cameronians (Scottish Rifles)**, 76n, 232, Coldstream Guards, 365, 486, **2nd Devonshire Regt**, 591n, **2nd Dorsetshire Regt**, 223-226, **1st Durham Light Infantry**, 591n, **1st Essex Regt**, 290-291, 298, 301-302, 304, 311n-312n, 326-328, 332, 334n, **Glider Pilot Regt**, 492, Hampshire Regt, 237, 6th Hampshire Regt, 267n, Irish Guards, 23, **1st King's Own Royal Regt**, 269, 275-276, 278-279, 282-284, 286-287, 293-294, 296, 298, 309, 310n, 314, **King's Royal Rifle Corps**, 436, **1st King's Royal Rifle Corps**, 250, 259, **14th London Regt**, 95n, **1st Loyal (North Lancashire) Regt**, 208, **2nd Manchester Regt**, 49, **1st Northamptonshire Regt**, 185, 9th Northumberland Fusiliers, 46n, Para Regt, 557, **1st (Guards) Para Bn**, 507, **1st Para Regt**, 513n, **2nd Para Regt**, 310n, **2nd Queen's Own Cameron Highlanders**, 208, 215, 216-217, 223, 229, **Rifle Brigade**, 259-260, **2nd Royal Berkshire Regt**, 210, **Royal Fusiliers**, 26n, **1st Royal Inniskilling Fusiliers**, 64-66, Royal Scots Fusiliers, 5, **1st Royal Scots Fusiliers**, 211, 221, **15th Royal Scots**, 126n, **2nd Royal Ulster Rifles**, 238, Royal Warwickshire Regt, 503, Queen's Own Royal West Kent Regt, 237, **2nd Queen's Own Royal West Kent Regt**, 77n, **1st Seaforth Highlanders**, 210-211, 227-228, 230, **1st South Wales Borderers**, 196, 198, **2nd West Yorkshire Regt**, 76n, **1st York and Lancaster Regt**, 228
Machine-Gun Corps, xvi, 26n
RAMC:
  8th Light Fd Ambulance, 311n, **40th Combined Fd Ambulance**, 76n, **166th Light Fd Ambulance**, 311n
RAOC, 240, 265
RASC:
  591n, **3rd Reserve MT Coy**, 311n, **14 Coy**, 208, **552 Coy**, 311n
Other Units:
  G(R) unit, 526, 528-529, 532, 549n, **Long Range Desert Gp**, 419, 438, **Military Mission 106**, 549n
British Broadcasting Corporation, BBC, 321, 345
British Cabinet, 5, 50, 230, 275
British Government, 1-3, 30, 48-49, 78, 100, 113-114, 128, 131, 137, 140, 146, 151, 157, 192, 194, 206, 234, 243, 277, 480, 492, 499, 516, 558, 571-573, 578
British Overseas Airways Corporation (BOAC), 10n, 269, 283, 288, 536
British Somaliland, 3, 354n, 522-523, 526, 532
Broadhurst, Air Chf Mshl Sir Harry, 441, 451n
Brooke, Sqn Ldr B., 586
Brooke-Popham, Air Chf Mshl Sir Robert, 134, 141n
Brown, Sqn Ldr E.J.B., 558, 565-566, 591n
Brown, Gp Capt L.O., 255, 265
Bruges, xv
Brunt, Flt Lt L., 595
Brussels, 73
Brussels Conservatoire of Music, 268n
Bu Amud, 358
Budoor, 100, 134
Buerat, 426, 429
Buisson, Cne C., 316
Bulhar, 525
Bundar Cassim, 530-531
Buq Buq, 251
Buraimi, 572, 577, 580, 582-588, 590, 594n
Burao, 529, 532
Burg el Arab, 406, 408-409
Burma Bund, 279, 296, 298
Burn, LAC F., 363-364, 375n
Burnett, Air Cdre C.S., 138-140, 141n
Busaiyah, 107, 109-114, 117-119, 124-125, 127n, 130-134, 139
Butch (Casano's Dog) 371, 375n, 422
Butler, Cpl D., 242n
Byrne, LAC, 565
Cairo, 11, 13, 28, 46n, 85, 243-244, 246-247, 250, 259, 264-266, 267n, 291, 331, 337, 340, 348, 357, 371-372, 375n, 380-381, 400, 403-404, 410, 428, 432, 457-458, 467, 480, 487, 536
Cairo Conference 1921, 4, 50, 74, 516
Cairo Conferences 1943, 456, 458
Calvert-Jones, Brig P.G., 415n
Cameron, Rt Hon D., 597
Camp Bastion, 597
Campbell, LAC, 263
Campbell, Maj-Gen 'Jock', 267n
Canal Turn, 276-277, 284, 288, 296
Canal Zone, 476, 500-501, 508, 554-555, 558, 569, 590
Cape Bon, 446, 448, 451n
Cape of Good Hope, 377
Carabinieri, 263
Carter, Gp Capt G.L., 383, 401n
Carter, LAC 'Doc', 430, 444
Carter, N., 383,
Casano, Albert, 268n
Casano, Sqn Ldr M.P., 240n, 242n, 246-248, 250, 258, 267n, 268n, 291, 293, 301-304, 319, 321-327, 332, 334n, 345-346, 349-350, 353, 357, 362, 365-368, 371, 375n, 380-383, 385, 389, 391, 394, 410-411, 416, 418-421, 423, 427-428, 431-432, 436-437, 447, 451n
Castel Benito, 430, 450n-451n
Caterpillar Club, 205
Catterick, 561-562, 596
Caucasus, 152, 336, 466
Cauldron, 385-386, 389, 402n, 405
Caunter, Brig J.A.L., 254, 267n
Central Arabia, 37-38, 146-147
Central Asia, 28, 152
Central Treaty Organisation (CENTO), 594n
Chad, 244, 438
Chahar Shakh, 179
Chamberlain, Rt Hon N., 239
Chambers, 'Harthur', 12, 425
Chamchamal, 61, 64, 66-70, 80-81, 84, 173-174, 179, 181
Champion de Crespigny, AVM H.V., 472n
Chan Bichuk, 81-82
Chanak Crisis, 23, 52
Chanak, 23-24, 52
Chapman, Capt, 68, 77n
Chatham, xvi, 267n
Chaulan, 258
Childs, Sqn Ldr L.A., 500, 504-505, 507, 510, 514n, 552, 554-556, 589
Chisholm, LAC, 492

634

Choartah, 80, 174
Churchill, Rt Hon Winston S., xv-xvi, xviin, 1-4, 10n, 27, 266, 278, 312n-313, 332, 335-336, 403-404, 452, 456-457, 478
Circassians, 28
Citrus House, 491, 493
Clark, Cpl, 224
Clark, Maj-Gen J.W.G., 290, 295, 301, 304, 315, 321
Clarke, Capt, 217
Clay, Cpl C.T., 361, 363-364, 375n
Cobden, Cpl, 162n
Collishaw, AVM R.M., 245, 261, 266, 267n, 337
Colonial Office, 3, 9, 37, 78, 147, 157
Columns:
  'A', 296, 298, **Azrakcol**, 144-146, **Buscol**, 114, 119, **Camcol**, 82, **Comcol**, 93-94, **Frontiercol**, 58-59, 76n, 'G', 296, 298, **Gocol**, 314-316, **Grimcol**, 82, **Kingcol**, 290-291, 293-296, 298, 301, 304, 308, 311n, 313, 320-321, **Koicol**, 58-61, 76n, **Kowcol**, 128, 'L', 296, 298, **Mercol**, 318, 326, **Muscol**, 529-530, 532, **Nucol**, 114-115, **Petticol**, 468, **Ranicol**, 53, 'S', 296, **Stracol**, 150, **Sulcol**, 70-71, **Supcol**, 114, 'V', 296, 298
Combe, Lt-Col J., 246, 260-261, 267n
Commonwealth Keep, 376
Commonwealth War Cemeteries: **Aleppo**, 333n, **El Alamein**, 355n, 375n, **Hinaidi (Ma'asker Al Raschid)**, 173, **Pietermaritzburg**, 311n, **Ramleh**, 206, 240, 333n, 513n
Coningham, Air Mshl Sir Arthur, 337, 343, 352, 353n-354n, 357, 363, 366, 368, 378-379, 382, 385, 391-393, 396-397, 400-401, 403-404, 409, 428, 438, 449, 450n
Constantine, Air Chf Mshl Sir Hugh, 188, 191n, 214, 216, 242n
Constantinople, 23, 26n
Cook, Cpl A., 242n
Cook, LAC S., 363-364, 375n
Cooke, Wg Cdr G.G., 107
Copeman, Sqn Ldr M.G.D., 14
Corbett, Maj-Gen T., 404
Cornwallis, Sir Kinahan, 304, 312n
Corry, Maj, 110
Cos, 591n
Coultate, Cpl, 351
Coupethite, LAC, 252
Courtney, A., 491
Courtney, Sgt, 242n
Cox, Lt-Col Sir Henry, 146, 162n
Cox, Cpl J., 21-25, 47, 55, 126n
Cox, Sir Percy, 58, 101
Cox, Flt Lt R., 418, 421

Cranley, Flt Lt P.G.J., 589
Crater, 515-516, 519, 521, 547
Crete, 250, 275, 288, 309, 313, 332, 335, 349, 359, 406, 409, 598
Criminal Investigation Department, Palestine, 491
Cromwell, LAC O., 166
Cronin, Fg Off D.J., 502
Cross, Gp Capt K.B.B., 343, 358, 363, 365, 401n
Cruikshank, Sqn Ldr J.W., 55, 62, 68, 70, 77n, 94n
Ctesiphon Arch, 167
Cunningham, Gen Sir Alan, 336, 342-344, 498, 508
Curran, Flt Lt G.P., 532-533
Currie, Sqn Ldr A.J., 14, 25n
Cyprus, 162n, 244, 313, 336, 494, 499, 551, 563, 590, 594n, 597
Cyrenaica, 245, 254-255, 257-258, 261, 264-266, 275, 313, 319, 332, 337, 345, 352-353, 356, 358, 364-365, 372, 376, 378, 403, 418, 423, 427, 453, 455
Cyrene, 363
Czechoslovakia, 240, 271
D'Albiac, AVM Sir John, 43, 46n, 269, 295, 312n
Daily Echo, The, 23
Daily Mail, The, xviin
Dakar, 320
Damascus, 27, 30, 86, 142, 162n, 210, 234, 288, 319-321, 327, 478
Damascus Gate, 496, 500
Dante, 530
Dar ad Daula, 544-545
Dar Dahukha, 534
Dardanelles, xvi, 23
Daror, 529
Darwen, Gp Capt J., 418-420, 441-443, 451n
Davies, FS A.H., 430-431, 458
Dawes, Wg Cdr R.A.A., 583, 593n
Dawson, LAC F., 239
Dawson, Air Chf Mshl Sir Walter, 474, 482, 504-505, 507-508, 511, 511n, 513n, 551
Dawson's Field, 551, 553
D-Day, 483, 513n, 591n
De Chair, Capt S., 291, 302-303, 321-322
De Gaulle, Gen Charles, 319-320, 331, 385, 477
De Guingand, Maj-Gen F., 441
De Verdilhac, Gen A., 331
Dead Sea, 238
Deag, Sqn Ldr J.S., 483
Deir ez Zor, 328-330, 479-480
Denmark, 514n
Dennehy, Fg Off W.D., 205
Dentz, Gen H., 318, 320, 331
Deraa, 320
Derby, 22
Derna, 256-258, 264, 266, 358, 363, 367, 455
Dhafeer, 100, 103, 134
Dhaid, 580
Dhala, 518, 532-533, 535, 539-541,
543, 546
Dhuwaibi, Sheikh Awad al, 46n
Diana, 184-185, 188, 281, 299, 468
Dickson, Col, 137-138
Dickson, Flt Lt C.N.C., 516, 519
Dill, Lt-Gen Sir John, 230, 233-234, 242n
Diwaniyah, 99, 307
Dixon, LAC G., 406
Diyala River, 59
Djauf, 157
Dobbie, Brig W., 199-200, 207n
Dobbin, Col-Cdt H.T., 65, 71, 75n-76n
Dobbs, H., 74, 77n
Dodecanese, 245, 313, 591n
Douglas, Gp Capt A.G., 248, 250, 257-258, 263, 266, 267n, 298, 302, 346, 349, 355n, 370, 380-381, 464, 468, 548
Douglas, Air Chief Marshal Sholto, 450n
Dover College, 258
Dowding, Air Chf Mshl Baron, 200, 207n
Drabble, Sgt, 380
Drayton, Cpl J., 242n
Dreamland, 21
Druze, 86, 89, 142-146, 227
Druze Revolt, 89
Drye, LAC, 494
Dukhan, 188
Dunkirk, xv-xvi, 244, 446
Dunkocok, 530
Dunn, Cpl, 255
Durban, 415n, 472n
Durell, AC M., 383
Durham University, 10n
Duweesh, 103, 106, 109, 113, 128, 134, 137, 139-140
Duweesh, Feisal el, 109
Dyer, 2Lt, 248
Eades, Flt Lt E.S., 586
EAM, 458
Early, Cpl, 25
East Africa, xvi, 7, 243-244, 252, 265, 275, 313, 335, 337
Eastchurch Gate, 276, 281
Eastern Aden Protectorate, 515
Edbrooke, LAC F.J.W., 191n
Eden, A., 319, 456-457
Edwards, Fg Off., 421, 472n
Edwards, LAC W., 19, 62
Egyptian Air Force, 514n
Egyptian Camel Corps, 30
Egyptian Group, 11, 13
Egyptian Red Cross, 503
El Adem, 256, 352, 358, 369, 372, 376, 379, 382-383, 389, 392-393, 421, 426
El Agheila, 261-265, 353, 356-357, 368, 418, 423, 425
El Alamein, 376, 398-403, 405-406, 408, 413, 416-419, 430, 432, 438-439, 445-446, 448, 449n, 456, 467, 470, 552
El Aouina, 448, 453
El Assa, 450n
El Auja, 219
El Beida, 327

635

El Daba, 245, 248, 396, 398, 406, 414, 416, 419, 449n
El Ezziat, 257
El Ghegab, 258
El Hamma, 438, 442
El Hamraiet, 429
El Hasseiat, 357, 359, 423, 425
El Qariataine, 327
El-Husseini, Haj Amin, Grand Mufti, 195, 234, 275
Ellington, MRAF Sir Edward 94n, 110, 127n, 128, 131, 141n
Elliot, Flt Lt G.A., 65-69, 77n, 84
Ellis, FS, 273
Enba, 251-252
Enfidaville, 443, 445-447
England, xv, 9, 21, 23, 47, 74n, 85, 154, 354n, 380, 385, 513n, 515, 540
English Channel, xv
EOKA, 597
Eritrea, 520, 523
Es Safa, 125, 141n
Es Salt, 29, 31, 552
Es Sceleidima, 259
Euphrates River, 48, 90, 98, 100-101, 103-104, 106, 113, 126n, 136, 184, 186, 233, 269, 272, 276-277, 279, 285, 294, 296, 298-299, 301, 321, 328-331, 479, 554
Euz Demir, 52-53, 58-59
Everett, Lt-Col E.N., 278, 287
Evetts, Brig J.F., 208, 210
Exchequer, 1, 78, 516
Exercises:
Bats' Ashes, 588, Beware, 569, Delay, 567, Hatta, 570, John, 464, Scylla, 464
Fad'an, 92-93
Fahad Ibn Zebn, 147
Fairweather, R., 558, 561, 571, 581, 585, 592n
Falluja, 186, 269, 276-277, 281-282, 284-288, 296, 298-299, 302, 304, 309, 563
Fao, 96
Farlington, 375n
Fathah, 59, 61, 63
Fawzi el Qawukji, 227, 233, 293, 299, 312n, 315, 318, 325-326, 514n
Fazan, Flt Lt T.W.C., 242n
Federal Regular Army of South Arabia, 548
Feisal I, King of Iraq (1885-1933), 27, 48, 63, 96, 100, 140, 142, 162n, 184
Feisal II, King of Iraq (1935-1958), 275, 468
Feisal, Amir (Saudi Arabia), later King of Saudi Arabia (1906-1975), 571
Fender, LAC E., 242n
Fenwick, WO H.380-383, 387, 391, 397-398, 400, 409, 411, 416, 419, 432, 436, 444, 462, 477
Fenwick, Flt Lt W.L., 90-91, 112, 122, 124
Ferguson, Lt-Col A., 301, 304

Ferguson, Cpl R., 430, 437, 444, 455
Fernihough, Flt Lt F., 14
Ferrey, Plt Off A.M., 500
Field, Cpl C., 242n
First Gulf War, The, 473n
First World War, The, (The Great War), xvi, 1, 4, 6, 9, 14, 23, 26n, 27, 30, 37, 47-48, 86, 126n, 143, 152, 162n, 164, 178, 192, 203, 213, 312n, 354n, 516, 549n
Folkestone, 258, 451n
Forbes, Sqn Ldr L.F., 147-148, 195, 198
Ford, Fg Off E.L. 'Henry', 305-307
Ford, Fg Off R.A. 'Henry', 109, 111-112, 119, 122, 154, 162n
Foreign Office, 147, 571, 578, 584
Former Republic of Yugoslavia, 597
Forster, 110
Fort el Grein, 419
Fort Maddalena, 340, 342, 356, 419
Foulsham, Wg Cdr W., 205, 207n, 232-233
Fowler, Gp Capt I., 157, 160
France, xv-xvi, 1, 4, 7, 27, 52, 75n, 142, 244-245, 265, 275, 313, 320, 331, 380, 415n, 463, 473n, 477, 487, 520, 598
Fraser, Maj-Gen W.A.K., 275, 306-307
Free French Air Force:
267n, No 2 French Fighter Flt, 247, 259
Free French Army:
Free French Division, 319-320, Colonne Volante, 436, 438, 'L' Force, 438, 1st Free French Bde, 378, 382-383, 385, 1st Bataillon d'Infanterie de Marine du Pacifique, 436
French Army, xv
French North Africa, 319, 433, 449n
Freyberg, Lt-Gen Sir Bernard, 438, 441-442
Frith, AVM E.L., 271, 282, 288, 314, 457, 464
Frost, Capt J.D., 271, 310n
Fry, Capt O., 66-67, 77n
Fuka, 266, 396, 406, 414, 416
Gabes, 438, 442, 444
Gaddafi, 597
Galilee, 200, 234, 238
Gallipoli, xvi
Gambut, 255-256, 344, 356, 358, 363, 368-369, 371-372, 379, 382-383, 385-386, 389, 391-394, 397, 401n, 415n, 418
Gambut Satellite 1, 2 and 3, 401n
Garbut, 'Lofty', 380, 411, 457
Gardo, 530
Gariboldi, Gen I., 264
Garoe, 530, 532
Garrod, Air Chf Mshl Sir Guy, 175, 178, 190n
Gasr el Arid, 369, 381-382, 394, 401n
Gaza, 192, 200, 214, 218-219, 221, 229, 502

Gazala, 257, 351, 354n, 359, 363, 366-369, 371-372, 376-379, 381-383, 385-386, 389, 393, 396, 400-401, 404-405, 418, 421, 472n
Gendarmerie, 143, 192, 194
George II, King of Greece, 458
George V, King, 184
George VI, King, 598
German Army: 240
Panzerarmee Afrika: 359, 374n, 381, 400, 403, 408, 418, 423
Army Group Afrika: 434
Deutsches Afrika Korps: 265-266, 332, 336, 339-340, 342, 351, 365, 367, 374n, 382-383, 385-386, 394, 397, 406, 419, 446, 592n
Divisions:
5th Light, 264, *7th Panzer*, 265, *10th Panzer*, 436, *15th Panzer*, 335-336, 374n, 381-382, 406, 435, *21st Panzer*, 342, 359, 374n, 382-383, 386, 389, 392, 394, 406, 435, *90th Light*, 354n, 374n, 382-383, 385-386, 398, 406, 435, 446, *164th*, 436
Brigades:
15th German Rifle, 382, *Ramcke*, 408
Groups:
Gen Crüewell's Gp, 382, *Marcks Gp*, 359
Recce Units:
3rd, 406, *33rd*, 406.
German-Italian Army, 332, 351, 353
Germany, xv, 21, 206, 236, 239, 240, 243, 244, 271, 275, 330, 364, 438, 477, 513n-514n, 522, 568, 592n, 595-597
Ghalidh shepherds, 112
Ghazi, King of Iraq (1912-1939), 273, 275, 310n
Ghemines, 259-261, 361
Ghent, xv
Ghet Museilim, 252
Ghot Abu Taheima, 255
Ghot Wahas, 251
Ghweza Pass, 71
Gibbs, Flt Lt G.E., 25n
Gibson, Flt Lt H.M., 508
Giovanni Berta, 257-258, 363
Glazebrook, AC1 C., 570
Glubb, Lt-Gen Sir John, 43, 46n, 96, 104, 106-107, 126n, 130-134, 136-139, 141n, 142, 151-152, 155-157, 291-293, 299, 304, 311n-312n, 451n
Goddard, Sqn Ldr R.V., 173
Godsave, Sqn Ldr G.E., 78, 85-89, 95n, 96, 114, 118-119, 133
Godwin-Austen, Lt-Gen, 356
Golat, 76n
Golat Pass, 63
Golden Square, 275

636

Goldschmidt Officers' Club, 497
Gooch, Maj R.E.S., 314-316, 327
Goodsal, AC, 331
Goodwin, AC, 494
Gordon, Gp Capt R., 10n, 30, 39, 46n
Goring, Flt Lt C.H., 23, 26n, 60-61, 105
Gort, Fld Mshl Lord, 471
Gos, 529
Gott, Lt-Gen W.H.E., 404
Graham, Capt A., 296, 298
Gray, Capt J.W.G., 456, 472n, 479, 511n-512n
Graziani, Mshl, 245, 254-255, 257-258, 264
Great Britain, xv, 1, 14, 47-48, 55, 63, 75n, 146, 162n, 240, 243-244, 266, 274, 471, 492, 555, 571, 590
Great Sand Sea, 346-347
Greater Zab River, 58
Greece, 250-251, 265, 272, 275, 332, 350, 356, 359, 409, 458, 460, 472n, 483
Greek Army:
52, 458-460, **1st Greek Brigade**, 459
Green, Cpl, 351
Greenfield, AC, 18
Gregory, Fg Off A.J., 409, 415n
Griffith, Cpl R.C., 370
Griffiths, Flt Lt S.W., 339, 363
Grimwood, Capt, 82-83
Grobba, Dr F., 275, 288, 315-316
Grobbelaar, Lt-Col, 346
Guard, Sqn Ldr F.H.W., 100, 107, 126n
Gulf of Aden, 523-524, 536
Gulf of Aqaba, 159
Gulf of Sirte, 257, 345, 348, 353, 418, 425, 448
Guweira, 238
Habban, 543
Habbaniya, Lake, 187, 191n, 269, 287, 293, 298
Hadhina Plateau, 543
Hadhrami Bedouin Legion, 511n
Hadi, Daham el, 91-92
Hadid, 36
Hadiqa, 129
Haditha, 308, 318, 328
Haganah, 481, 512n
Haidara, 539, 543
Haifa, 86-87, 163, 198-200, 208, 210-212, 214, 230-231, 237, 247, 259, 265, 271, 274, 277, 314, 320, 331, 481, 490, 494, 499, 506, 508-509, 514n
Haifa Court and Governorate, 200
Haining, 237
Hajar Mountains, 579
Hakkiari, 50, 62
Hakoura, 494
Halebja, 80, 174, 182-183
Halebja Plain, 174, 182-183
Halfaya, 254, 266, 335, 340, 357, 396, 418
Hamasa, 572, 583

Hamilton, A.M., 191n
Hammar Lake, 96
Hammonds Bund, 288, 296, 298, 301, 304
Haniyah Ridge, 105
Hankin-Turvin, Maj J.M., 573, 578-579, 583, 592n
Hanmer, Flt Lt H., 11
Harab, 100, 104
Harb, 46n
Hargeisa, 525-526, 528
Harim, 461
Harries, Sqn Ldr D., 55, 61
Harris, MRAF Sir Arthur, 208, 237, 240n
Harris, Fg Off H., 516
Harrison, 528
Harvatt, AC1, 45n
Hasan Daran Sane, 535
Hashemite Kingdom of Jordan, 14, 28, 551, 557, 571, 592n
Hassan, Mohammed ibn Abdulla (Mad Mullah), 3-4, 10n
Hassetche, 330
Hatey, Fg Off W.V., 549n
Hathorn Hill, Sir John, 515, 532, 549n
Hawkins, LAC D.W.H., 280, 306
Hawkins, Fg Off K., 493-494
Hawtrey, Wg Cdr J., 315
Hayes, Capt, 515
Haymes, Fg Off P.R.T., 562, 565, 592n
Haza, 546
Hazbub, 434-436, 439, 450n
Hebron, 192, 197, 199, 201, 217, 232-233, 240, 291
Hedjaz, 27, 37, 39, 45n, 101, 106, 109, 130, 142-143, 147, 150, 157-159, 161n
Hellard, Sqn Ldr D., 280-281, 296, 298-299, 304, 314, 470, 483
Hellings, Plt Off M.B.B., 592n
Hergla, 443-444, 447
Hesban, 31, 36
Hetherington, L., 201, 203-204
Hezil Suyu, river, 71
Hibberd, FS E.V., 207n
Higgins, Cpl, 431
Higgins, AVM Sir John F.A., 64, 71, 76n, 85, 104, 106
Higgins, Air Cdre T.C.R., 110, 114, 127n, 457, 472n
Hill, Air Chf Mshl Sir Roderic, 230, 233, 235, 237, 242n
Hill, Cpl R., 558, 560, 563, 589
Hillah branch, 98
Hitchin, AC, 494
Hithlain, Naif ibn, 140
Hitler, Adolf, 239-240, 244, 263, 271, 336
Hoare, Sir Samuel, 49
Hodge, FS A., 476, 478, 480, 483, 486, 490-491, 496-498, 502, 513n
Holl, LAC W., 325, 333n
Holt, Maj, 183
Holt, Capt V., 183
Home Front, The, xvi
Homs, 89, 321, 326-327, 331

Hong Kong, 356, 597
Hook of Holland, 561
Hopton, AC, 77n
Hordio, 531-532
Horrocks, Lt-Gen Sir Brian, 439, 441-442
Houle, Gp Capt A., 420
Hoyland, Sgt, 248
Hoyles, LAC, 250, 254
Hoyles, Sgt, 351
Hubbard, Wg Cdr T. O'B., 27, 45
Hubert, LAC F., 207n
Hughes, Col C.E., 197
Hughes, Sqn Ldr J., 595
Huraine, 327
Hurley, Flt Lt W., 148-149
Husan Muhammad Husan, 535
Hussein ibn Ali, King of the Hedjaz (1854-1931), 27, 106, 109, 157, 162n
Hussein ibn Talal, King of Jordan (1935-1999), 511n, 557, 591n-592n
Huwara, 227
Huweitat, 90, 92-93, 148-150, 155, 157
Hyde, Cpl, 493-494
Hithlain, Naif ibn, 137-140
Humaid, Ibn, 137
Ibrahim, Sheikh, 57
Ikhwan (Al-Ikhwan), 37-39, 43, 46n, 78, 85, 90, 96, 100-101, 103-104, 106-107, 109, 111-113, 117, 122, 124, 128-134, 136-141, 141n, 146-147, 149, 151, 158-159, 195, 472n, 596
Illah, Amir Abd al, 275
Illingworth, Sgt, 536-537
Imperial Airways, 95n, 204, 218, 580
Imshash, 150, 155
India, 4-6, 9, 10n, 48, 58, 75n, 85-86, 164-165, 243, 269, 274, 290, 308, 356, 457, 474, 522, 532, 558, 591n
Indian Army:
5, 75, 78, 143, 331, 345, 391-392, 402n, 455, 466, 468, 523, 549n, 558, 576, 593n, Indian Expeditionary Force, 47
Divisions:
31st Ind Armd, 478-479, **4th Ind**, 245, 251-252, 357, 365, 367, 436, 439, **5th Ind**, 403, **6th Ind**, 47, **10th Ind**, 275, 277-278, 305, 307-308, 321, 328, 330-331, 397, 403
Brigades:
3rd Ind Motor, 378, **5th Ind Inf**, 319-320, **9th Ind Inf**, 378, **11th Ind Inf**, 252, **20th Ind Inf**, 275, 295, 305, 307-308, 329, 331, 392-393, **21st Ind Inf**, 305, 307, 329-331, **29th Ind Inf**, 344, 351, 378
Cavalry:
13th Duke of Connaught's Own Lancers, 330, **17th**

637

Poona Horse, 466, Central India Horse, 354n, Bikaner Camel Corps, 523
Infantry Regiments and Battalions:
   1/2nd Bombay Pioneers, 77n, 1/2nd Punjab Regt, 523, 549n, 3/2nd Punjab Regt, 354n, 2/5th Mahratta Light Infantry, 522, 1/6th Rajputana Rifles, 392-393, 402n, 10th Baluch Regt, 591n, 1/10th Baluch Regt, 468, 2/11th Sikh Regt, 76n, 3/11th Sikh Regt, 307, 1/12th Frontier Force Regt, 329-330, 1/13th (Coke's Rifles) Frontier Force Rifles, 59, 4/13th Frontier Force Rifles, 330, 5/13th Frontier Force Rifles, 330, 14th Sikhs, 53, 76n, 3/15th Punjab Regt, 549n, 2/18th Royal Garhwal Rifles, 591n, 32nd Sikh Pioneers, 402n, 48th Pioneers, 402n, 2/4th Gurkha Rifles, 295-296, 314, 2/7th Gurkha Rifles, 305, 312n, 2/8th Gurkha Rifles, 329, 2/10th Gurkha Rifles, 307
Artillery:
   18 Mountain Bty, 549n, 113 (Dardoni) Pack Bty, 77n, 120 (Ambala) Pack Bty, 63, 76n
Other Units:
   Queen Victoria's Own Madras Sappers and Miners, 298, 63rd Coy QVO Madras Sappers and Miners, 76n, 7th Ind Mobile Veterinary Section, 76n, 116th Animal Transport Coy, 77n
Inglefield, Sqn Ldr L.G., 556, 558
Iqrit, 238
Iranian Government, 473n
Iraq Army:
   50, 57, 63-64, 70-71, 75n, 78, 80-84, 90, 94n, 98, 100, 104, 107, 110, 112, 114, 117, 119, 130-131, 136-137, 139, 173-174, 178-180, 182-186, 227, 275, 277-278, 282, 286, 288, 293, 298-299, 301-302, 304, 306, 309, 314-315, 467-468, 590
   Mosul Bde, 77n,
   3rd Cavalry Regt, 76n-77n
   Motor Machine-Gun Coy, 130, 134, 136
   1st Pack Bty, 77n
   1st Transport Coy, 77n
Iraq Levies:
   4-5, 50, 52, 59, 64-66, 70-71, 74-78, 80, 83, 84, 90, 94n, 99, 170, 173, 185-186, 189, 191n,194, 269-271, 278-279, 282-284, 286-287, 296, 298-299, 304, 309-310n, 466, 554, 565, 569-570

Assyrian Levies:
   70, 184-185, 298, 468
Cavalry Regiments:
   1st, 75n-77n, 2nd, 75n, 81, 3rd, 75n
Artillery:
   Levy Pack Bty, 75n-76n
Battalions:
   1st (Marsh Arab), 75n, 2nd (Assyrian), 64, 69, 70, 75n-77n, 3rd (Assyrian), 75n-77n, 4th (Kurdish), 75n-77n
Companies:
   No 1 (Assyrian), 191n, 296, No 2 (Assyrian), 191n, 296, 310n, No 3 (Assyrian), 191n, 310n, No 4 (Assyrian), 189, 191n, 286, 310n, No 5 (Arab), 189, No 5 (Assyrian), 191n, No 6 (Arab), 191n, No 7 (Arab), 191n, No 8 (Kurdish), 170, 189, 191n, 279, 310n
Iraq Minister of the Interior, 173
Iraq Petroleum Company, 231
Iraq Public Works Department, 191n
Iraq Revolt, 335
Iraq Revolution, 590
Iraqi Police, 70, 81, 90, 110, 139, 174, 291, 306, 469
Irbid, 29, 200
Iredame, 530
Ireland, 6, 21, 194, 597
Irgun Zvai Leumi, 480-481, 489, 493-494, 497-498, 500
Irish Free State, 9, 21, 126n
Irish uprising, 9
Irka, 534-535
Isfahan, 468
Isle of Grain, 21
Isle of Wight, 23
Israel, 480, 508, 510, 555-556
Israeli Air Force, 591n
Italian Army:
Armies:
   First Italian Army, 435, 446, *Tenth Army*, 260, 265
Corps:
   10th, 374n, 382, 20th, 374n, 382, 435, 21st, 435
Divisions:
   Ariete Armd, 263, 342, 354n, 359, 374n, 382-383, 406, *Bologna*, 374n, *Brescia*, 354n, 374n, *Folgore Para*, 408, *Littorio Armd*, 406, *Pavia*, 354n, 374n, *Sabratha*, 354n, 374n, *Savona*, 354n, *Trento Motorised*, 263, 354n, 374n, 383, 385, *Trieste Motorised*, 342, 354n, 374n, 382-383, 455, 561, *Young Fascist*, 420
Brigades:
   Colonial, 524
Italian East Africa, 252, 265, 275, 313, 337
Italian East African Empire, 523, 532

Italian Legation, 275
Italian Marine Commandos, 455
Italian Somaliland, 243, 522-523, 530, 532
Italo-Abyssinian crisis, 243, 520
Italy, 52, 236, 239-240, 243-246, 261, 264, 275, 364, 414, 451n, 455, 463, 483, 520, 522, 568, 576, 591n
Jabbari, Sayed Mohammed, 67
Jackson, Sqn Ldr J.F., 256
Jackson, Fg Off R., 122
Jaf, 83, 175-176, 179-180
Jaffa, 192, 197-199, 201-202, 204, 209, 212, 234
Jahrah, 107, 129, 139
Jalibah, 103-106, 307
Jalo, 345, 348, 351, 420-421
James, Flt Lt V., 484-485, 501, 508, 539, 542, 550n
Japanese Legation, 275
Jarabub, 344-349, 355n, 419
Jarishan, 118, 122, 136, 140-141
Jazzi, Ibn, 93
Jau Hadiya, 104
Jebel Akhdar, 244, 257-258, 365, 418
Jebel Akhdar War, 593n
Jebel Ali, 576-578
Jebel Chebiba, 439
Jebel Dhana, 583
Jebel Druze, 142-143, 155
Jebel Jihaf, 539, 543
Jebel Sanam, 96, 118, 307
Jebel Sinjar, 90
Jeddah conference, 114, 130
Jenin, 14, 39, 200, 210, 214, 219-222, 227-228, 234, 237
Jenkins, Flt Lt, 84
Jericho, 31, 152, 223, 380
Jerusalem, 14, 19, 27, 30, 87, 152, 192, 195-199, 201, 205, 208-212, 214-217, 223, 227, 229-230, 232-234, 237-238, 275, 471, 474, 481-483, 489-492, 494, 496-501, 503, 506-508, 511, 551, 557
Jewish Agency, 497
Jewish Immigration, 4, 192, 195, 209, 492
Jeysh al Arabi, 30
Jezireh ibn Omar, 58
Jidrain, 117
Jijiga, 525
Jisr Mejamie, 200, 221
Johnston, 'Johnnie', 407
Johnston, Plt Off J., 320, 349, 380
Jones, LAC, 541
Jones, Plt Off G.W., 191n
Jones, H.B., 515
Jones, Wg Cdr W.O., 242n, 332, 339, 358, 360-364, 375n, 453
Jope-Slade, Gp Capt R., 72, 77n
Jordan Service Medal (*Midalat al Kidmat al Urduni*), 592n
Jordan, River, 27, 152, 494, 506
Jordinson, J., 558, 561-562, 581
Juffa, 323-324, 326
Julaidah, 138

Juwareen shepherds, 122
Kaf, 39, 146
Kairouan, 443
Kandahar, 597
Kani Kawa, 71
Kaolos, 184
Karachi, 20, 273, 275
Karbala, 131, 163, 301
Kasr, 42
Kasserine Pass, 434
Kastal, 42
Katinakis, H., 268n
Keattch, LAC H., 173
Keeble, Sqn Ldr N., 163, 178-179, 181-183, 190n
Keenan, Flt Lt, 304, 418
Kendal, AC, 77n
Kennedy, Sqn Ldr C.G.E., 471n, 483-484, 500-501
Kenney, Sgt, 33-35, 37, 45n
Kenya, 523
Kerak, 29
Kermanshah, 467
Kerry, Obs Off L.T., 13, 25n, 65, 67-69
Kessack, LAC A., 363-364, 375n
Khabbour el Bid, 330
Khabur River, 71
Khalla, 535, 546
Khan Lubban, 217
Khanaqin, 178
Khasin River, 329
Khireigat, 254
Khor es Zubair, 331
Khor Umeira, 533
Khurmal, 174-175, 178
Kifri, 79, 83, 175-176, 179-180
King David Hotel, 230, 489
King Khalid Military City, 595
King, LAC L., 412, 415n, 417, 420, 429, 432, 436, 443, 452, 457, 461, 471
King's African Rifles, 3
Kingerban, 53, 57, 59, 62-63, 65, 69-70, 75n-76n, 179, 182
Kingham, Fg Off F., 92
Kingstone, Brig J.J., 290, 298, 301-302, 311n, 313, 321-322, 324, 327
Kinna, Wg Cdr T.J., 11-12, 19, 25n
Kirkbride, A., 33, 35, 37, 40, 45n, 151, 162n
Kirkuk, 50, 53, 57-59, 61-65, 68-71, 74, 75n-77n, 79-84, 92, 95n, 109, 128, 163, 173-174, 185, 188, 231, 269, 274, 276-277, 308, 314, 321, 466, 468-469, 566, 568
Kittles, LAC W., 197
Klopper, Gen, 394
Knightsbridge, 377, 383, 386-387, 389
Knox, Paddy, 419
Koenig, Gen M.P., 385
Koi Sanjak, 58-59
Kolundia, 195-196, 237, 482, 496, 499, 506-508, 511
Kosovo, 597
Ksar Rhilane, 438
Ksar Tarcine, 438

Kurdish Autonomous Zone, 473n
Kurdish Democratic Party, 473n
Kurdistan Regional Government, 473n
Kurdistan, 13, 47, 50, 53, 58, 63, 65, 73-74, 76n-77n, 79-80, 84, 96, 173, 175, 184, 188-189, 274, 402n, 467-468, 473n
Kurds, 4, 47, 50, 66-69, 71, 75n, 79-80, 82-83, 180, 189, 270, 315, 467-470, 473n
Kut Al Amara, 47
Kuwait, 58, 86, 96, 103, 107, 112, 114, 118, 128-130, 136-140, 307, 551, 557-558, 574, 583, 586, 595-597
Kuwait City, 130, 595
Kuwait Oil Company, 558
La Forte, Sqn Ldr R.W., 473n
Lace, FS, 327-328
Laferug, 525
Lahej, 516, 521, 534, 539-540, 544
Lami, Jasir ibn, 140
Lamsdorf, 375n
Landing Grounds:
  LG 3, 271, LG 5, 271, 310n, LG 07, 393, LG 39, 400, 408, LG 75, 394, 397, 417, LG 76, 393-394, 418, LG 90, 412, LG 91, 405-406, 459, LG 109, 342, LG 110, 339, 342, LG 121, 405, LG 122, 342-344, LG 123, 342-343, LG 124, 343, LG 125, 345-353, 357, 418, 420-421, 426, 449n, LG 128, 343, LG 'D', 89
Landing Ships, Tank:
  Evan Gibb, 576, 578,
  Humphrey Gale, 584,
  Reginald Kerr, 547, 556
Law, Rt Hon B., 49, 58
Lawn Sgt, 351, 380
Lawrence, T.E. (Lawrence of Arabia), 162n, 514n
Laz Daua, 530
League of Nations, 1, 28, 48, 73, 142, 146, 184-185, 208, 477, 480, 509, 520
Lebanon, 27, 208, 234, 244, 320, 477, 555, 571
Leclerc, Gen, 438
Lee, Wg Cdr P.D., 558, 565-567, 574, 576-580, 586, 591n-593n
Lee, AVM A.S.G., 90-91, 95n
Lee, Cpl, 18
Lee, Flt Lt J., 594n
Leete, 205
Levant, 313, 318, 471
Lewis, FS 248, 255-258, 263
Lewis, Cpl G., 66-69, 77n
Libya, 240, 243-246, 252, 254, 263, 265-266, 275, 318, 332, 335-336, 339, 344, 352, 356, 371, 405, 418, 465, 568, 596-597
Liddell Hart, B.H., 6, 26n
Lille, xv

Lindsay, Lt-Col G.M., 10n
Linklater, Lt, 224-225
Lishman, Cpl J., 325, 333n
Lister, LAC D.F., 363-364, 548
Little Aden, 532
Little Zab River, 83, 188
Lloyd, LAC, 240, 255
Lloyd George, Rt Hon D., 1, 23
Lochmei Heruth Israel, 480
Lock, R., 483-484, 499-500, 503, 510, 511n
Locke, Maj-Gen, 110
Lodar, 535, 539, 544
London, xv-xvi, 3, 21, 53, 73, 147, 155, 268n, 321, 430, 486, 549n, 570, 594n
London Gate, 276
London Road, 276
Longmore, Air Chf Mshl Sir Arthur, 99-100, 103, 125n, 243-247, 261, 336-337, 449
Low Countries, 244, 275
Lowe, AC2, 349
Lowe, Wg Cdr M., 278, 294
Lucas, Flt Lt, 351, 365, 371, 412, 417, 422
Ludlow-Hewitt, Air Chf Mshl Sir Edgar, 163, 173-175, 178, 182, 190n
Luftwaffe: 261, 263, 265, 281, 288, 294-295, 313-314, 339, 344, 348, 352-333, 354n, 358-360, 365, 369, 372, 379, 381, 385, 389, 393-394, 403, 406, 409, 416-417, 429, 435, 438-439, 442-443, 446, 448, 481, 591n, *Fliegerkorps X*, 263, *Fliegerführer Irak*, 314, 318
Lussuf, 105, 128, 131
Lydda, 200, 223, 333n, 481-482, 489-490, 505
Lynch, Sgt P., 242n
Ma'alla, 547
Ma'an, 149, 152-155, 157-159, 161, 198, 205, 233, 246, 509, 552, 571
Maaten Bagush, 245, 248, 266, 291, 337, 339-340, 347, 396-397
Macdonald, Maj, 584
MacEwen, Gp Capt N.D.K., 37, 43, 45
MacLean, Lt-Col R., 100
MacMichael, Sir Harold, 237
Madaba, 42
Mafidh, 539
Mafraq, 142, 148, 510, 551-552, 554-556, 562, 570-571, 591n
Magrath, Flt Lt, 31, 33
Mahmud Barzinji, Sheikh (1878-1956), 53, 58-59, 63-64, 67, 70-71, 73-74, 75n-76n, 80, 82-85, 164, 173-176, 178-184, 467
Maitland Wilson, Lt-Gen Sir Henry, 320, 331
Makina, 25, 55, 100, 105-106
Maknassy, 443
Maktila, 248, 250, 252

639

Malaya, 275, 356, 576, 591n, 597
Maldives, 597
Maleme, 313
Malta, 199, 230, 244, 252, 356, 376, 394, 406, 408, 418, 449, 499, 562, 591n, 597
Maltman, AC2 J., 370
Manchester, 430
Manser, Cpl, 493-494
Mansuri, 547
Marble Arch, 423, 425-428
Mareth, 434-435, 438-439, 442
Margate, 21-22
Margil, 305, 558
Marivan, 469
Markhiya, 583, 585
Marne, First Battle of the, xv
Marshall, LAC A.B., 589
Martuba, 367-369, 379, 407, 418, 422
Martyn, Fg Off G., 11, 13
Mashur, Ferhan al ibn, 138-139-140, 141n
Matmata Hills, 434-436, 438-439
Mazzaid, 148
McAngus, 524, 531
McGuire, Air Cdre A.B., 594n
McHaffie, FS D., 242n
McKendrick, Cpl, 224-225
McKenzie, Cpl, 529-530
McKeown, LAC, 351
McNair, D.E., 380
McWalters, Cpl, 325, 351
McWhinney, Plt Off G.A., 239, 242n
Meager, WO G.G., 242n
Mecca, 27, 106, 116, 157
Mechili, 257-258, 261, 266, 346, 352, 363, 365-368, 373, 422-423
Medenine, 434-436, 438-439, 442
Mediterranean Sea, 244, 248, 257, 313, 336, 356, 378, 381, 406, 443, 449n, 461, 471, 474, 490, 537
Meisari, 535, 538
Melluish, Cpl, 289, 359, 362, 374n
Mena, 456-457
Merdjayoun, 320
Merry, Maj E.J.H., 318, 542
Mersa Brega, 264, 359, 425
Mersa Matruh, 243-245, 256, 266, 337, 344, 347, 357, 393, 396-398, 417-418, 421
Merser-Bennett, Lt-Col, 457
Meshashida, 301
Mesopotamia, 1, 4-6, 9, 10n, 21, 23-24, 26n, 47, 50, 58, 74n
Mezze, 478
Mezzouna Road, 443
Middleton, AC, 17, 21
Miller, Fg Off, 497
Milner, Lord, 3
Mitchell, Air Chf Mshl Sir William, 518, 549n
Mitla Pass, 509
Montgomery, Fld Mshl Viscount, 406, 408-409, 414, 414n, 418, 434-435, 438-439, 441, 444-446
Moray, 375n
Morocco, 244
Morris, AC, 77n
Morris, Sqn Ldr A., 109
Morris, F., 485, 492, 512n-513n
Morte, LAC V., 335, 339, 346-347, 349-350, 358, 362, 366-367, 370, 374n, 387, 390-391, 396, 403, 406-407, 410, 448
Mortimore, Flt Lt C.A., 242n, 532
Moscrop, 525
Mosley, Flt Lt, 346, 349, 368, 380
Mosul, 9, 47-48, 50, 52-53, 55-59, 61-63, 71-73, 75n, 77n, 78, 83, 89-92, 94n-95n, 109, 131, 163, 166, 169, 172-173, 185-186, 189, 207n, 274, 288, 299, 301, 304, 308, 314-315, 318, 321, 328-330, 332, 354n, 466-470, 472n, 566, 568
Mount Carmel, 481
Mount Jeman, 540
Mount Tabilba, 425
Moyne, Lord, 480
Msus, 257, 259, 352-353, 355n, 356-361, 363, 365, 373, 374n, 418, 423, 425, 453
Muan, 178, 182
Mudawarra, 157
Muhammerah Treaty, 101
Mujarra, 287, 293-295, 569
Mukeiras, 539, 544
Mulholland, Sqn Ldr D., 63, 205, 207n, 221-222, 230, 233, 242n
Munich, 239
Munich Agreement, 240
Munich Crisis, 271
Muntifiq Division, 126n
Murch, Sqn Ldr P.F., 452-453, 455, 457-458, 463-465, 475, 483, 512n, 522, 524, 529, 532
Muscat, 572, 592n
Muscat, Sultan of, 572-573
Musemir, 519, 521, 543
Musgrave, Maj G.R., 529, 549n
Mussolini, Benito, 240, 244, 251, 263, 394, 427, 434, 520
Mustafa Barzani, Mullah (1903-1979), 467, 472n-473n
Mustapha Police Station, 500
Mutair, 100, 103-104, 106, 109, 112, 118, 120, 122-124, 126n, 128, 131, 133-134, 137, 139-140
NAAFI, 166, 168, 273, 397-398, 469, 490, 513n, 542
Nabeul, 448
Nablus, 195, 199-200, 208-212, 214, 216, 219-220, 222-223, 225, 227-228, 234-235, 482
Nahadain, 117
Nairn, G., 86
Nairn, N., 86
Nairn Transport Company, 86-87, 89, 163, 205, 293
Najaf, 105-106
Naples, 127n
Nasiriyah, 96, 126n-127n
National Service, 501, 558, 561, 568
Naur, 36
Naval 138ers, 12
Nazareth, 200, 212, 231, 234, 475, 506-507
Nazi Germany, 206
Nebi Musa, 201
Neffatia, 434, 436-437, 439, 448
Negev, 555
Nejed, 37, 39, 45n-46n, 55, 96, 100-101, 103-104, 106-107, 109, 112-114, 116, 118-120, 122, 124, 133, 136-137, 139-142, 146, 148-150, 157, 161n
Nelson, Lt-Col E.J.B., 507
New Zealand, 4, 86, 153, 191n, 205-206, 243, 265, 313, 354n, 427, 441, 443, 445-446
New Zealand Army:
2 NZ Expeditionary Force, 354n, NZ Corps, 438-439, 441, NZ Division, 245, 340, 344, 397, 400, 2nd NZ Division (renumbered from NZ Division in 1942), 414, 424-426, 430, 434-435, 438-439, 441, 445-446, 5th Bde Gp, 425, 6th Bde, 441, 6th Wellington Mounted Rifles, 205, Divisional Cavalry Regt, 354n, 429
Neutral Zone, 101, 103, 112, 117, 119, 134, 138
Newland, Sqn Ldr J.H.F., 380, 390-391, 398, 400, 402n, 412, 416, 422, 429, 436-437, 444, 453, 455
Nibeiwa, 248, 251-252
Nicholl, Wg Cdr H.R., 114
Nichols, Col, 312n
Nigeria, 10n
Nigerian Brigade, 525
Nile Delta, 248, 313, 396, 447, 452
Nile River, 248, 261, 313, 396, 405, 447, 452
Nineveh, 274
Nisab, 539
Nisibin Plain, 57, 63
Nixon, R.M., 562, 584, 587, 589, 594n
Nobat Dakim, 521, 546
Nofilia, 423, 425-429
Normandy, 456, 463
Norris, AC2, 349
Northern Ireland, 597
North-West Europe, 463, 483, 513n-514n, 568
North-West Frontier of India, 4, 457
Norton, Wg Cdr E., 81
Norway, 275, 380
Notchfall, 167, 296, 298
Notre Dame, 501
Nuhair, Sheikh Nahdi ibn, 46n
Nukhaib, 131, 554, 588, 594n
Nuqrat Sulman, 104-105, 116
O'Brien, Flt Lt G., 71
O'Connor, Maj-Gen R., 245, 251-252, 255-259, 261-262, 265-266, 356
O'Keefe, LAC, 485

640

O'Malley, Sqn Ldr V.D., 176-176, 179
Oil Pumping Stations:
   H1, 321, H2, 271, H3, 271, 291-293, 321-322, 327, 333n, H4, 291, 293, 295, 320-321, 326-327, K1, 274, K3, 274, 321, T1, 321, 323, T2, 321, 323, T3, 323-327
Old Suez Road, 11
Olliffe, Sgt H., 492
Olliff-Lee, Sqn Ldr J. St.C., 339, 359-360, 363, 404, 439, 441, 445, 452
Oman, 572, 592n, 597
Operations:
   Agatha, 487, *Appearance*, 523-524, 532, *Barbarossa*, 319, 336, *Battleaxe*, 333n, 336, 379, *Boxer*, 573, 580, 590, *Brevity*, 335, *Capri*, 435-436, *Chocolate*, 418, 426, *Compass*, 243, 250-252, 354n, *Crusader*, 335-337, 339-340, 342, 344, 346, 353, 356, 377-378, 408, *Desert Shield*, 596, *Diver*, 513n, *Dry Trek*, 509, *Duststorm*, 551, *Exporter*, 319, 336, 477, *Granby*, 595, *Herrick*, 597, *Lightfoot*, 408, *Overlord*, 456, *Provide Comfort 2*, 473n, *Pugilist*, 438, *Reviver*, 472n, *Sunburn*, 489, *Supercharge*, 414, 441, *Telic*, 597, *Tidal Wave*, 453, *Torch*, 449n, 451n, *Turpitude*, 460, 462, *Vulcan*, 446, *Warden*, 473n, 'X', 227, 229, *Zipper*, 576, 591n
Oran, 320
Oribi Military Hospital, 311n
Orkneys, 127n
Osborne, AC2, 66-67, 77n
Ostend, xv
Ottoman Empire, 1, 9, 27-28, 37, 47-48, 100, 192, 516
Overland Mail Convoy, 87
Owen, Flt Lt A.H., 220-221, 233, 331-332
Page, Sqn Ldr J.J.J., 247, 250, 258
Paget, Gen Sir Bernard, 460, 478
Paige, FS, 286
Pakistan, 590
Palestine Police, 194-195, 200-202, 210, 234, 482-483, 489-492, 496, 499-500, 508, 513n, 592n
Palestine Post, 227
Palestine Potash Company, 238
Palestine Royal Commission, 233-234
Palestine Works Department, 505
Palmach, 480
Palmyra, 89, 93, 318-319, 321-328, 332, 333n-334n, 353n, 479
Paris, xv
Park, Air Mshl Sir Keith, 468
Parker, Flt Lt, 380, 383, 402n, 417, 423, 450n

Patullo, Fg Off, 383
Payne, Sqn Ldr R.J., 307, 457, 470
Peake, Capt E.G., 30, 37, 39, 43-44, 46n, 143
Pearl Harbour, 356
Peart, FS E.C., 242n
Peck, Sqn Ldr A.H., 92-94, 109, 114
Pedrick, AC1 J., 429
Peirse, Air Chf Mshl Sir Richard, 208, 210-212, 219, 230, 241n
Pellew, Plt Off R.H.B., 418, 429-430
Pemberton-Pigott, Flt Lt B.E.K., 535
Penjwin, 84, 174, 183-184, 469
Perim, Island of, 533
Persia, 173-174, 243, 304, 315, 318, 404, 466, 468, 470, 472n, 557, 565
Persian Gulf, 48, 99, 131, 140, 244, 273, 551-552, 554, 557-558, 571, 576, 580, 584, 586, 592n-593n, 597
Petah Tiqvah, 209
Peter, King of Yugoslavia, 456
Petley, Plt Off E., 286, 311n
Petrie, Sgt D., 536-537, 540-542
Pettigrew, Lt-Col, 468
Philby, H.St.J., 37, 162n
Phillips, AC, 18
Pilsworth, Fg Off O.R., 331-332
Pinkham, LAC, 250
Piper, AC1, 45n
Pishder, 53, 58, 173, 182
Playfair, Gp Capt P.H.L., 147, 162n, 192, 195-196
Plevey, AC1 J., 173
Ploesti raids, 453, 455
Plumer, Fld Mshl Lord, 143, 194
Point 171, 377
Poland, 206, 240, 244, 275
Polish Army of the East, 466
Pollard, Sqn Ldr E.M., 94n
Pont du Fahs, 447
Popular Front for the Liberation of Palestine, 590n
Port Said, 24, 186, 205, 476, 487
Portal, MRAF Viscount, 401, 402n
Porter, AC, 77n
Portsmouth, xvi, 20, 552
Post & Telegraph Department, Palestine, 223
Poste Weygand, 323
Powell, LAC, 349
Prentice (née O'Brien), P., 470, 473n
Prentice, Flt Lt W.W., 412, 445, 455, 462, 470-471, 472n-473n
Price, Fg Off H.E.G., 482
Primrose, Air Cdre W.H., 20, 26n, 55, 63, 69-70, 72, 77n, 107
Pyne, Sqn Ldr B.F., 279, 287, 294-295, 329-331
Qala Shirwana, 175, 179
Qalqilya, 221-222, 227
Qamichliye, 315-316, 330, 467
Qara Anjir, 66-68, 81-82, 84
Qaraghan, 59
Qasaba, 372, 381
Qasom, 46n
Qasr al Kharanah, 88, 206, 338
Qassimi, 581

Qataba, 518
Qataba, Amir of, 541
Qatar, 583
Qattara Depression, 399
Qsiba, 321
Queen Alia International Airport, 46n
Queensland, 470
Quinnell, Air Cdre J., 173, 190n
Quiyara, 314, 466-467
Quteibi, 544
Quwair, 57-58, 63
Rabat, 539
Rabia, 251
Radcliffe, 436
RAF Armoured Car Manual, 85, 95n, 210
RAF Benevolent Fund, 205, 570
RAF Iraq Boxing Association, 167
RAF Iraq Hard-hitting Cup, 167
Ramadi, 85, 92-93, 186, 191n, 276-277, 286-289, 291, 293-295, 298-299, 301, 314, 318, 321, 333n
Ramallah, 195-196, 211, 217, 227, 482, 496, 508
Ramleh, town, 204, 210
Ramsay, LAC, 45n
Ramsgate, 21
Rania, 53, 58
Raqqa, 479
Ras al Khaymah, 581
Ras el Ain, 330, 499, 502
Ras en Naqb, 509
Ras Quseir, 534
Rashid Ali el Gailani, 186, 275, 277, 280, 288, 299, 304, 309, 312n, 315, 457, 467
Rawlinson, Gen, 5
Rayak, 319, 331
Rayat, 188-189
Red Sea, 24, 37, 155, 157, 244, 274, 377, 515, 523, 532, 536
Reed, AC, 77n
Rees, Lt, 296
Rees, Gp Capt L.W.B., 144
Refada, Hamid ibn, 157
Regia Aeronautica:
   245-247, 250-252, 254, 256, 261, 263, 266n, 314, 352, 379, 438, 446, 448, 522, 591n, *Arditi Distruttori Regia Aeronautica*, 471n
Reid, Brig D.W., 344, 346, 351, 354n
Retma 'Box', 382
Rhodes, Island of, 288
Richardson, Fg Off G., 65-66, 69
Richardson, Flt Lt S.F., 248, 254-255, 257-259, 264, 267n, 380, 476-477, 479
Riggs, LAC, 215
Rihani, El Mulasim Awal Abdullah Effendi, 33, 35
Ritchie, Maj-Gen N., 344, 356-357, 376, 385, 389, 391, 394, 397, 402n
Riyadh, 46n, 109, 137, 140, 584
Robbins, Cpl H., 242n
Roberts, Sqn Ldr E.J., 592n

641

Roberts, Gen Sir Ouvry, 278, 294, 296, 310n, 312n
Robertson, Fg Off W.L., 516
Robinson, AC1 K., 513n
Robson, Plt Off H.G., 508, 563
Rocky Point, 288
Rogers, LAC J., 173
Rolph, LAC A., 164, 184, 190n-191n, 204
Roman Empire, 28
Rommel, Fld Mshl E., 265-266, 275, 319, 335, 339-340, 342-345, 351-353, 357, 359, 365-366, 368, 374n, 376, 381-383, 385-386, 389, 392, 394, 397-398, 400-401, 402n, 403-404, 406, 414, 414n, 418, 425-426, 429, 433-436, 438, 445
Ronksley, Flt Lt F., 150
Roosevelt, F.D., 456
Rosher, Lt-Col J.B., 457
Ross, LAC, 224-226, 233
Ross, Sgt, 351, 367-368, 406-407
Rowalla tribe, 150-151
Rowanduz, 52, 58-59, 185, 188-189, 191n, 274, 315, 467-469, 473n
Royal Air Force:
  Branches:
    Balloon, 415n, **General Duties**, 458, 470, **Ground Defence**, 598, **Technical**, 95n
  Commands:
    Iraq, 49-50, 52-53, 58, 60, 63-64, 85, 96, 107, 109-110, 114, 132, 137-138, 141n, 167, 190n, 272, 467, 472n, **Mediterranean Air**, 449, 450n, **Middle East**, 236, 240, 245, 409, 449
  Air Headquarters:
    Air Defences Eastern Mediterranean, 457, **Cyprus**, 590, **Egypt**, 337, **Iraq**, 63, 70, 73, 92-93, 104, 133, 185, 191, 270, 276-277, 472n, 552, 574, **Levant**, 458, 464, 479, 480, 483, 494, 498-499, 501, 506-507, 512n, 590, **Palestine & Transjordan**, 458, **Western Desert**, 337, 339, 343, 356, 366, 374n, 376, 385, 391, 393-394, 397, 406, 408-409, 429, 444
  Other Headquarters:
    RAF Cyrenaica, 265-266, **RAF Northern Ireland**, 26n, **RAF Trans-Jordania/Transjordan/Transjordan and Palestine**, 14, 30, 37, 43, 45, 142, 192, 195, **Sulops**, 69
  Desert Air Force (Western Desert Air Force):
    337-339, 342-344, 352, 356-357, 360, 363, 368, 372-373, 375n, 378-379, 381, 385, 389, 392, 394, 396, 400-401, 403-406, 408-409, 412-413, 415n, 423-424, 429, 434-435, 438-439, 441-443, 446, 448-449, 451n, 552, 570, 592n
  Forces:
    'A Sqn', 173, **Akforce**, 114, 130, **Air Striking Force**, 221, **Force A (Russia)**, 126n, **Force A (Desert Air Force)**, 409, 415n, **Force B**, 409, 415n, **Frontier Force**, 76n-77n, **Habbaniya Air Striking Force**, 278-279, 281-284, 286-287, 296, **Mobile Striking Force**, 75n, **Mosul Field Force**, 61, **RAF Support Helicopter Force**, 595, **Souforce**, 157-160, **Whitforce**, 345-346, 348, 352, 355n, 418
  Groups:
    No 38, 597, **No 202**, 245, 250, 252, 255-257, 265, 267n, 337, **No 205**, 337, 354n, 360, 379, 396, **No 211**, 266, 357, 365, 378-379, 382, 385, 394, 397, 401n, 408-409, 412-413, 415n, 418, 423, 426, 431, 435, 441, 446, **No 212**, 406, 409, 415n, 453, **No 216**, 418, 426, **No 221**, 162n, **No 242**, 451n
  Wings:
    No 232, 415n, **No 233**, 378, 381, 394, 401n, 415n, **No 239**, 378, 386, 393-394, 398, 401n-402n, 415n, 423, 426, 430, 441-442, 450n, **No 243**, 378, 401n, 415n, 418-419, **No 244**, 394, 409, 415n, 418, 423, 426, 435, 450n, **No 258**, 339, 342, 346, 352-353, 356-357, 360, 363, 365, 367-368, 374n, **No 262**, 356, 374n, **No 270**, 354n, **No 285**, 415n, 450n, **Aerowing**, 72-73, **Mosul**, 58, **Palestine**, 14
  Squadrons:
    No 1, 59, 70-71, 75n, 80, 82-83, 94n, 99, 100, **No 6**, 59, 69, 71-72, 74n-77n, 80, 90-92, 94n, 150, 161, 201, 208, 211, 219, 221, 227, 229, 234, 265, 267n, 378, 386, 390, 402n, 413, 443, 512n, 551, 565, 570-571, 573-574, 577-578, 582, 584, 590, 592n-594n, **No 8**, 69, 75n, 94n, 99, 104, 126n, 516, 520, 530, 543-544, 547, 550n, 565, **No 11**, 333n, **No 12**, 520, **No 13**, 492, **No 14**, 14, 30-31, 40, 43, 45, 46n, 88, 142-145, 147-150, 152, 157-159, 161, 162n, 199, 208, 221, 227, 312n, **No 20**, 598, **No 26**, 598, **No 30**, 59, 64, 69, 71, 74n-75n, 83-84, 94n, 128, 131, 173, 179, 184-185, 266n, 272, **No 31**, 275, 283, **No 32**, 479, 482, 499, 506, 512n-513n, **No 33**, 221, 229, 267n, 345, 348, 351, 353, 357, 374n, 401n, **No 37**, 267n, 278, 283, 333n, 513n, 593n, **No 38**, 267n, 333n, 489, 513n, 593n, **No 41**, 520, **No 45**, 64, 69, 75n, 89, 94n-95n, 99, 126n, 266n, 267n, 333n, **No 47**, 12, **No 52**, 472n, **No 55**, 9, 55, 59, 63, 69, 72, 75n-76n, 92-93, 94n,107, 114, 116, 119, 122, 131, 138, 140, 175-176, 178, 189, 191n, 265, 266n, 267n, 272, 594n, **No 70**, 64, 69, 75n, 94n-95n, 110, 114, 140, 185, 189, 191n, 266n, 267n, 272, 278, 310n, 333n, **No 73**, 265, 267n, 351, 380, 401n, **No 78**, 494, **No 80**, 267n, 333n, 374n, **No 84**, 75n, 94n, 96, 99, 103, 105, 109-110, 114, 116-117, 126n, 128, 131, 133, 138, 187, 191n, 291, 319, 366, 555, **No 94**, 374n, **No 112**, 267n, 361, 366, 374n, 401n, **No 113**, 266n, 267n, 345, 348, 351, 494, **No 114**, 536, 539, **No 117**, 449n, **No 127**, 329, 333n, **No 148**, 333n, **No 202**, 190n, **No 203**, 191n, 283, 291, **No 208**, 251, 255, 259, 267n, 333n, 365, 379, 401n, 482, 489, 499, 506, 512n-513n, 555, 593n, **No 211**, 266, **No 213**, 401n, 418, 420, 512n, **No 216**, 11, 25n, 151, 157, 159, 161, 199, 267n, **No 223**, 401n, **No 229**, 374n, **No 238**, 401n, 418, 420, **No 244**, 270, 281, **No 250**, 374n, 401n, **No 252**, 449n, **No 252/272**, 333n, **No 260**, 374n, 401n, **No 261**, 472n, **No 272**, 374n, 449n, **No 274**, 267n, 401n, **No 620**, 512n, **No 621**, 512n, 536, **No 644**, 512n, **No 651**, 512n, **Rhodesian**, 466
  Air Ministry Experiment Stations (Radar):
    No 5, 481, **No 510**, 369, 415n, 425, 429-430, 435, 439, 445, 450n, **No 606**, 439, **No 608**, 415n, **No 609**, 415n, **No 610**, 415n, **'Jumbo'**, 406
  Maintenance Units:
    No 120, 465, 499, **No 127**, 469, **No 138**, 468-469, **No 142**, 465, **No 160**, 481, 489
  Medical:
    No 3 RAF Hospital, 499, **No 10 Medical Rehabilitation Unit**, 481, **Medical Receiving**

Station, 429, 439, Palestine General Hospital, 148, 195, 204, 224
MT Companies:
  No 51 MT Coy, 503
Other Units:
  No 1 Air Armament School, 272, No 2 (Ground) Armament School, 415n, No 3 (Middle East) Training School, 409, 467, No 3 Refuelling Party, 348, No 4 Service Flying Training School, 240n, 267n, 270-271, 278, 281-282, 309, No 22 Personnel Transit Centre, 450n, 485, No 40 Air Stores Park, 449n, No 74 OTU, 464, Aircraft Depot, Iraq, 191n, 269, Desert Rescue Organisation, 554, First Armoured Car Detachment, 20-23, 25, 52, Inland Water Transport, Iraq, 107, Iraq Communication Flight, 570, Middle East Aircraft Intelligence Unit, 447, 451n, Sector A Party, 413, 418, 425, 427-428, 430, 435-436, 438-439, 442, 444-445, 450n, Seedaseer Lines, 532, Singapore Lines, 543, 547, Stores Depot, Kidbrooke, 206, 'X' Flight, 333n, 'Z' Unit, 3, 10n, 46n
Royal Air Force Levies, Iraq: 185, 554-555
RAF Stations:
  Aboukir, 163, Abu Sueir, 267n, 271, 380, Akrotiri, 46n, Aldergrove, 597, Aleppo, 479, Amman, 14, 17, 30-31, 35, 39, 42-44, 46n, 88, 143, 145, 147, 150, 157, 195, 199-201, 205-206, 214, 233, 239, 265-266, 267n, 291, 338, 409, 453, 455, 458, 467, 475-478, 494, 500-502, 506, 508, 510, 513n, 547, 551-552, 554-556, 569-570, 591n-592n, Aqir, 481, 494, 494, 499-500, 503-506, 512n, Basra, 92, 107, 109, 112, 114-115, 118, 123, 125, 128-129, 133, 137-138, 163-164, 189, 191n, 279, 295, 298, 311n, 552, 590, Basra Air Station, 597, Cairo West, 405, 455-457, 467, Cardington, 13, 476, 560, Colerne, 597, Cranwell, 13, 258, 315, 484, Dhibban, 186-187, 189, 233, 284, 286, 288, 296, 298, Digby, 164, 172, 205, Eastchurch, 164, 172, 272, Ein Shemer, 487, 489-490, 492, 499, 505-506, El Adem, 355n, 596, El Hamra, 509, Fassberg, 513n, Felixstowe, 597, Gutersloh, 597, Habbaniya, 48, 186, 189, 191n, 258, 269-280, 283, 285-290, 293-296, 299, 304-305, 307-309, 311n-312n, 313-314, 318-319, 321, 332, 338-339, 354n, 363, 380, 455, 457-458, 466-467, 470-471, 472n, 483, 492, 552, 554-556, 562-563, 565-568, 570-571, 573, 579, 582-584, 586, 588-590, 598, Heliopolis, 11, 14, 17, 19, 410, 500, 536, Helwan, 247, 339, 371-372, 380, 404, 452-453, 455, Hinaidi, 49, 61-62, 64-65, 70, 78, 92, 94n-95n, 106, 109-110, 115, 118, 128, 140, 163-164, 166-168, 170, 173-174, 178, 182, 184-189, 200-201, 205, 233, 269, 276, Hiswa, 532, 536, Innsworth, 560, Jabir, 536, Kabrit, 492, Kenley, 127n, Khormaksar, 515-516, 518-519, 532, 536, 543, 545, 547, Kirton-in-Lindsey, 513n, Laarbruch, 595, 597, Luqa, 597, Lyneham, 562, Madley, 476, Manby, 415n, Manston, 20-23, 164, 166, 172, Nicosia, 590, Petah Tiqva, 482, Qastina, 481-482, 492, 499, 512n, 554, Ramat David, 475, 478-479, 481-483, 506, 512n, 514n, Ramleh, 147-148, 150, 152, 157, 161, 184, 195, 199-201, 204-205, 210, 213-214, 218, 221, 233, 238, 242n, 246, 250, 267n, 325, 372, 379-380, 458, 460, 463, 471, 475-476, 480-483, 487, 489-492, 499-503, 505-506, 508, St Mawgan, 597, Shaibah, 49, 75n, 78, 94n, 100, 103-105, 109-110, 112, 114, 118, 122, 127n, 128, 136, 140, 164, 187, 189, 191n, 270-271, 273-275, 278-279, 281, 283, 295, 304-305, 307-308, 310n, 331-332, 472n, 552, 558, 565, 569, 576, 586, 589-590, Sharjah, 552, 573-574, 577-578, 580-584, 586-587, 593n-594n, Skegness, 476, 487, Steamer Point, 518, 521, 532, 542, Sudbury, 486, Uxbridge, 13, 19-21, 164, 172, Wali Road, 542, Warton, 562, Weeton, 560, West Drayton, 476, West Kirby, 560-562, Wittering, 597, Wombleton, 486-487
Signals:
  No 2 Air Support Signals Unit, 507, Air HQ Levant Telecommunications Centre, 481, Codes and Cyphers, Unit Signals, 473n, Wireless Observer Unit, 413
Supply and Transport Columns:
  No 5, 415n, 423, 426, No 6, 415n, 422, No 10, 415n, 423, 426, 429-430, No 11, 415n
Women's Auxiliary Air Force, 470, 473n
Royal Air Force Regiment:
  127n, 268n, 413, 418, 423, 449, 449n, 450n-451n, 453, 457, 460, 463-465, 470-472, 473n, 474-75, 481-486, 492, 499-501, 506, 508-509, 512n, 513n-514n, 539, 542, 547-548, 554-555, 557-558, 560-561, 568, 570-571, 577, 579, 586, 591n-594n, 595-598
Wings:
  No 3, 598n, No 4, 598n, No 6, 598n, No 19, 499, 551, 557, No 20, 499, 547-548, No 33, 597, 598n, No 1320, 482
Squadrons:
  No 1, 355n, 470, 473n, 499, 514n, 597, 598n, No II, 486, 587, 589-590, 594n, 597, 598n, No 3, 597, 598n, No 4 Armd Car, 514n, 592n, 596, No 15, 598n, No 20, 598n, No 21 LAA, 555, 570, 591n, No 26, 598n, No 27, 598n, No 34, 598n, No 51, 598n, No 52 (Rifle), 499, 506, 514n, 555, 591n, No 53, 499, 501, No 58, 499, 598n, No 62 (Rifle), 499, 508-510, 547, 551-552, 588, 596, No 63 (Queen's Colour), 598n, No 65 (Rifle), 499, No 66, 499, 598, No 701, 513n, No 702, 513n, No 2701 Armd, 486, 492, 512n-513n, 550n, No 2702 Armd, 486, 512n-513n, No 2742 Armd Car, 482, 592n, No 2757 Armd Car, 592n, No 2771 (Rifle), 482, No 2777 Armd Car, 592n, No 2781 Armd Car, 592n, No 2804 Armd Car, 592n, No 2806 Armd Car, 592n, No 2812 LAA, 514n, No 2902 Fd, 472n, No 2908 (Rifle), 482, No 2908 Fd, 472n, No 2912, 471n, No 2916, 471n, No 2917, 471n, No 2918, 471n, No 2919, 471n, No 2924 Fd, 472n, No 2926, 471n, No 2927, 471n, No 2931, 450n, No 2932 LAA, 472n, No 2933, 471n, 'B', 418, 450n
RAF Regt Depots and Training Establishments:
  484, Belton Park, 486-487, Catterick, 561, 596, Dumfries, 407, 560, Folkingham, 513n,

Grantham, 457, Honington, 592n, **OCTU, Isle of Man,** 514n
RAF Regt Force Protection HQ, 592n
UK Defence CBRN, 598n
Royal Australian Air Force:
No 3 Sqn, 256-257, 265, 267n, 327, 333n, 374n, 401n, 426, **No 450 Sqn,** 401n, 426, **No 450/260 Sqn,** 333n
Royal Flying Corps, 2, 5, 13, 46n, 143, 354n
Royal Hellenic Air Force:
No 13 (Hellenic) Sqn, 459
Royal Indian Marine Ship *Patrick Stewart,* 140
Royal Indian Navy, 524
Royal Iraqi Air Force:
269, 276, 468, 470, 555, **No 1 Sqn,** 470, **Al Rashid Airbase,** 276, 282-283
Royal Irish Constabulary, 21, 126n
Royal Naval Air Service:
xv, 2, 7, 13-14, 17, 21, 25n, 77n, 178, 190n, **No 1 Wing,** 190n, No 5 Sqn, 77n, **Eastchurch (Mobile) Air Sqn,** xv, **Armoured Car Force,** xvi
Royal Navy:
xvi, 1, 25n, 128, 157, 159, 164, 199, 212, 214, 252, 256-257, 265, 274-275, 313, 335, 364, 507, 515, 520, 524, 531, 542, **3rd Cruiser Squadron,** 214
Fleet Air Arm:
199, 319, 333n, 396, 406, **No 803 Sqn,** 333n, **No 806/33 Sqn,** 333n
Royal Marines:
xv, 128, 199, 507, 555, **42 Commando,** 507, 555
Royal Navy Ships:
HMSs *Ark Royal,* 10n, *Barham,* 199, *Centurion,* 23, *Ceylon,* 582, *Cockchafer,* 275, *Courageous,* 199, *Crocus,* 128, *Emerald,* 128, *Euryalus,* 508, *Hastings,* 158, *Lupin,* 128, 130, 140, *Penzance,* 157, 159, *Phoebe,* 509, *Revenge,* 23, *Sussex,* 199, *Wild Goose,* 577, 592n-593n, *Wren,* 583, Submarine, *P-38,* 364
Royal Tournament, 570
Rukhaimiyah, 112, 119, 122, 125, 133, 139
Rumaithah, 98
Rumania, 453
Russia, xvi, 50, 126n, 319, 330, 336, 466, 468
Russian Army, 567
Rutbah, 85-87, 89, 93-94, 95n, 131, 205, 271, 274, 287, 291-293, 308, 320-321, 467
Ruweisat Ridge, 403
Ryan, Cpl, 361

Sab Biyar, 324
Sabah, Sheikh Abdullah III Al Salim Al, Amir of Kuwait (1895-1965), 558, 584, 591n
Sabah, Sheikh Ahmad Al Jaber Al, Sheikh of Kuwait (1885-1950), 112, 127n, 128, 136-138, 591n
Sabkha Matti, 584-585
Sabratha, 450n
Sadad, 327-328
Safwan, 96, 136, 307
Sagan, 375
Sahara, 244, 438
Salem, Sheikh Abdul ibn, 578-579, 582
Salmond, MRAF Sir John, 47, 49-50, 52-53, 57-58, 60-61, 63-64, 73, 75n, 99, 126n
Samah, 139
Samaria, 219, 241n
Samarra, 55, 299
Samawah, 98-100, 103-106, 114, 116, 126n, 589
Samson, Cdr C.R., xv, xviin
Sana'a, 516, 520
Sanders, Fg Off T.C., 206
Sandhurst, 267n, 591n
Sandiford, Flt Lt H., 172-173
Sar Qala, 179
Sarafand, 19, 195, 204-206, 210, 219, 221, 224, 238, 502, 505, 508
Sardinia, 409
Sarona, 492
Sarrail, Gen M.-P.-E.,162n
Sassoon, Sir Phillip, 191n
Saud, Abd al Aziz ibn, King of the Hedjaz, Sultan of the Nejed, and King of Saudi Arabia (1902-1953), 37, 45n, 100-101, 106-107, 109, 113-114, 128, 130-131, 137-141, 141n, 146-147, 157, 161n, 572
Saudi Arabia, 37, 39, 45n, 145-147, 149-150, 155, 157-158, 161n, 195, 474, 548, 571-572, 574, 583-584, 595-596
Saunders, Air Chf Mshl Sir Arthur, 580, 593n
Saunnu, 359-360, 365
Savile, Gp Capt W.A.B., 270
Saward, Flt Lt N., 92-93
Scandinavia, 244
Scholes, LAC J., 370
Scotland, 375n, 380
Sea of Galilee, 200
Seager, Maj B.W., 534-535, 539
Second World War, The, 26n, 28, 46n, 127n, 162n, 190n, 240, 473n, 477, 532, 539, 569, 588, 591n, 598
Secter, Fg Off J.J., 259, 320, 323-327, 333n
Semakh, 14, 194, 200
Senna, 469
Senussi, 347, 453, 471n
Ser Amadia, 58, 77n, 169-170, 468, 563

Serao, 83, 174, 183
Serdash, 59, 174
Seven Sisters, 380
Seychelles, 234
Shafai, 516
Sharjah, 552, 572,576, 577-579, 581, 583, 585, 586 -587, 589, 593n
Shaikhan, 175, 178
Shaka, 544
Shakhbut ibn Sultan al Nahyan, Sheikh, 572, 578, 581
Shakir ibn Zeid, Amir, 148-150, 152, 162n
Shakir ibn Zeid, Fld Mshl, 162n
Shallufa, 476
Shamiyah Desert, 119
Shammar, 46n, 87, 137
Shammar, Iraqi, 91
Shammar Syrian, 91, 107
Sharafat, 148, 156
Shatt el Arab, 24, 191n
Shebicha, 104-105, 117, 128, 130
Sheikh Othman, 516, 519-521, 536
Sheikh Said, 533
Shenton, Flt Lt R.F., 210, 221-222, 242n, 494
Shepheard's Hotel, 375n
Shergat, 56-57, 60, 63, 72, 90
Shilaiwah, 105-106
Shipwright, Flt Lt A., 187, 214
Shufflebottom, Sgt, 587
Shuqra, 533, 535, 544, 547
Shuqra, Sultan of, 535
Sibilla, 137
Sicilian Narrows, 443
Sicily, 263, 409, 443, 446, 576, 591n
Sidi Azeiz, 254, 393-394, 418
Sidi Azeiz Satellite, 401n
Sidi Barrani, 245, 248, 251-252, 264, 266, 267n, 291, 336-337, 339, 342, 394, 405, 418-419
Sidi Haneish, 266, 347, 380, 396, 417-418
Sidi Mahmoud, 257
Sidi Muftah, 382-383
Sidi Omar, 254, 266, 340, 342
Sidi Rezegh, 342, 344, 352, 383, 389, 392-393
Sidi Saleh, 259-260
Sierra Leone, 597
Sierra Leone Railways, 126n
Sigudan, 526
Silat adh Dhahr, 228
Silver Ghost, 6, 96
Simmons, LAC L.A., 115-117, 125, 128-129
Simpson, Flt Lt J.C., 557, 562
Simpson, Flt Lt S., 65, 69-70, 77n
Sin el Dhibban, 284, 286, 288, 296, 298
Sinai, 157, 219, 381, 509, 536
Sinbad, 118
Sinclair, 410
Singapore, 243, 356
Singer, Flt Lt N.C., 242n
Sirte, 429
Sirwan River, 175, 178, 180
Siwa Oasis, 344, 347, 420

644

Skellon, Wg Cdr R.C., 247, 259, 262-263, 267n, 327-328, 333n, 351, 353, 357, 365-368, 380, 382, 385, 389-393, 409, 412, 455
Slade, LAC G., 240
Slayter, Adm Sir William, 582, 593n
Slim, Fld Mshl Viscount, 155, 307-308, 312n, 328, 330
Smart, AVM H.G., 270, 277-278, 289, 295, 310n, 312n
Smiley, Lt D., 315
Smith, Lt-Col, 529
Smith, Lt-Gen A.F., 404
Smith, Sgt B.W., 351, 370, 380
Smith, Wg Cdr S., 107
Smith, Plt Off W.R.M., 418
Smuts Report, 2
Sofafi, 248, 251-252, 266, 396
Sollum, 251-252, 255-256, 266, 335, 340, 357, 391, 394, 396
Soluch, 260
Somalia, 10n
Somaliland Camel Corps, 3, 532
Sorel-Cameron, Lt-Col, 66, 82
Sorman, 450n
Sousse, 443, 445
South African Army:
  Divisions:
    1st SA, 340, 378, 389, 400, 414, **2nd SA**, 378
  Brigades:
    2nd SA Inf, 525
  Artillery:
    4 Bty, 2nd Fd Regt, 355n, '**F' Tp, 6 Fd Bty**, 355n
  Armoured Cars:
    3rd SA Recce Bn, 354n, **4th SA Armd Car Regt**, 354n, **6th SA Armd Car Regt**, 354n-355n, **7th SA Recce Bn**, 346, 348, 354n-355n
  Infantry:
    Natal Mounted Rifles, 525
South African Air Force:
  Wings:
    No 3, 354n, 356, 393, 401n, 415n, 450n, **No 7**, 415n, 436, 442
  Squadrons:
    No 2, 374n, 401n, **No 4**, 374n, 401n, **No 5**, 401n, **No 12**, 401n, **No 24**, 401n, **No 40**, 379
Southampton, 22, 273
South-East Asia Command, 591n
Southern Desert, 55, 78, 96, 100, 101, 103-104, 106, 126n, 128, 132-133, 136, 140, 151, 472n
Southern Desert Camel Corps, 119, 126n, 131, 134, 141n
Southern Nigeria Regt, 5
Soviet Union, 288, 474
Spearing, Fg Off E., 248, 250, 252, 254, 259, 263-264, 267n
Special Operations Executive, 26n, 526, 549n
Spilik Dagh, 59
Spybey, AC C., 269, 280, 282, 284, 290, 309, 361, 363, 372
St Clement Danes, 268n
St Cyr, 312n
St George's Church, 554
St George's Road, 501
Stafford, Lt-Col E., 150
Stalags:
  VIIIB, 375n, *Luft III*, 375n
Stalin, J., 456, 466
Standstill Agreement, 573, 585
Steamer Point, 516, 537
Stephenson, Flt Lt, 331
Stern Gang, 480
Stevenson, Flt Lt W.J.L., 255, 291, 320, 332, 334n, 339
Stewart, LAC, 258
Stilwell, Sqn Ldr C.H., 238
Stockdale, Flt Lt T.H., 242n, 441-443, 451n
Stone, Fg Off R.J., 109-112, 119, 122-124, 127n, 133, 141n
Stoneage convoy, 418
Straits of Gibraltar, 23
Strictland, Maj, 296
Suckling, Flt Lt, 429
Sudan, 243-244, 523
Suez, 415n
Suez Canal, 24, 243-244, 246, 313, 318, 381, 394, 403, 515, 520
Suez Crisis, 571
Suez Road, 11-12
Sugden, 214, 233
Sulaimaniya, 53, 58-61, 64, 69-71, 74, 78, 80, 82-84, 163, 173-175, 178-179, 181-185, 188, 469
Sulman, 104-105, 114, 116-117, 130-131, 134
Sultan, 429
Sultan of Oman's Armed Forces, 511n
Sultanate of Oman, 592n
Sundern, 514n, 592n
Sunter, AC, 77n
Suttaih Bridge, 287-288, 299
Suweilah, 31, 33-34
Swaddle, AC1, 519
Sweetlove, FS, 242n
Switzerland, 52, 364, 375n
Sykes-Picot Agreement, 142, 162n
Symes, Col G., 518
Syria, 19, 27, 30, 36, 47, 63, 78, 86, 89-91, 107, 142-143, 145-147, 150, 155, 187, 195, 208-210, 227, 234, 244, 266, 275, 277, 288, 299, 313, 315-316, 318-322, 324, 326, 328-332, 335-336, 359, 394, 397, 448, 460-461, 464, 466-467, 471, 477-480, 508, 511, 514n, 555
Syrian Campaign, 328, 331-332, 335
Syrian Orphanage, 500
Tainal, 179, 181
Taj Wajale, 525
Taji, 302
Takrouna, 443
Talal I ibn Abdullah, King of Jordan (1909-1972), 557
Talavera Barracks, 215-216

Tanjero River, 82
Tanjero Valley, 181
Tarhuna, 430
Tarif, 581, 583-586
Tasluja, 80, 179, 181
Tasluja Pass, 70-71, 80
Tatahouine, 436, 438-439
Tebaga Gap, 438, 441-442
Techimul Lakan, 67-68
Tedder, MRAF Lord, 336-337, 339, 343, 353n, 356, 366, 376, 378-379, 400-401, 402n, 404, 409, 449, 450n
Tegart, Sir Charles, 234
Teheran, 456, 467-469
Tel Abu Dahir, 63, 76n
Tel Afar, 77n, 314
Tel Alou, 330
Tel Aviv, 192, 197-198, 201, 204, 209, 212, 455, 481, 483, 490-493, 499-500, 503, 513n
Tel Awainat, 63, 76n, 314
Tel Hadi, 330
Tel Kotchek, 330, 467
Ten Year Rule, 1-2
Thomason, Cpl, 526
Thomsit, Fg Off F., 544
Thorley, Cpl W., 242n
Thornton, AVM H.N., 40, 43-45, 46n
Thwaites, Maj O., 587
Tiarks, Brig, 327
Tiberias, 200, 237
Tickler, Flt Lt H.H., 418, 439, 441, 445, 468-469
Tigris River, 48-49, 56, 59, 62-63, 90, 120, 123-124, 274, 277, 299, 466
Tikrit, 60
Times, The, 126n
Timsah, Lake, 500
Tindale, Plt Off G., 10n
Tinsley, AC, 410, 590
Tmimi, 256-257, 354n, 356, 368
Tobruk, 252, 254-257, 265-266, 335, 340, 342, 344-345, 351-352, 356, 358, 363, 372, 376-381, 383, 385-386, 389, 394, 403
Tocra, 365
Tomkins, WO, 286
Toogood, Flt Lt C., 141n
Toulon, 487
Townson, Flt Lt W., 522
Transjordan Frontier Force, 143-153, 157-159, 162n, 194-195, 200-201, 205, 208, 290, 311n
Treaty of Alliance and Mutual Support, 274
Treaty of Iraq, 185
Treaty of Lausanne, 52-53, 59, 63, 71, 76
Tregunna, Sgt, 273
Trenchard, MRAF Lord, 1-6, 9,10n, 24, 53, 516, 590
Trigh Capuzzo, 254-255, 394
Tripoli, 244, 261, 263-265, 274, 277, 356-357, 364, 376, 378, 403, 424-425, 429-430,

433-434
Tripolitania, 245, 261, 263-265, 356-357, 427, 438, 479
Troopships and Steam Ships: HMTs *Cheshire*, 514n, *Dorsetshire*, 165, *Mauretania*, 415n, *Nevasa*, 305, *Samaria*, 476, MV *Sofala*, 532, SSs *Beaconsfield*, 524, *Braemar Castle*, 22-24, *Cola*, 532, *Empire Mace*, 487, *Empire Test*, 561, *Ranpura*, 205, *Somersetshire*, 273, *Tuna*, 532, *Varela*, 25, 273, *Windsor Castle*, 542
Trucial Oman, 590
Trucial Oman Levies, 551, 572-573, 578, 581, 583-584, 586-588, 592n, 594n
Trucial States, 552, 557, 571-573, 579, 582-583, 590, 592n, 594n
Truman, H., President, 480, 492
Tulkarm, 209-211, 219-220, 234, 237
Tummar, 248, 251
Tuneib, 39-40, 42
Tunisia, 244, 416, 433-434, 442-443, 445, 451n, 452, 464, 479, 568
Turcomans, 47, 50, 75n
Turkey, 4, 7, 9, 23, 26n, 47-48, 50, 52-53, 58, 63, 71, 73, 75n, 89-90, 185, 244, 288, 315, 329-330, 460-462, 466, 473n, 516, 590
Turkish Army, 50, 52, 57-58, 312n
Turkish Petroleum Company, 83
Turner, Fg Off W.F., 583-584
Type '0.2' Compass, 85
Um el Jemal, 148
Umm el Amad, 39, 42
Umm Malef, 254
Umm Qasr, 96
Umm Raas, 136
Umm Rahal, 106
Unilever, 10n
United Kingdom, xvi, 2, 19, 25n, 46n, 83, 94n, 104, 107, 126n-127n, 132, 163, 186, 201, 205, 207n, 237, 239, 242n, 243, 251, 264-265, 272, 331, 335, 337, 364, 377, 380, 404, 415n, 449n, 455, 457, 463, 472n, 473n, 474, 480, 482, 484, 494, 513n, 516, 522, 532, 542, 548, 549n-550n, 556, 566, 569, 590, 591n, 597-598
United Nations, 499
United States of America, 337, 473n, 480, 492, 572
United States Air Force, 545
United States Army:
 2nd US Corps, 451n
United States Army Air Force: 455
 XII Air Support Command, 451n, 316th US Carrier Wing, 426, 57th US Fighter Gp, 415n, 442, 450n, 12th US Medium Bombardment Gp, 415n, 450n
Upcraft, LAC, 162n
Uqair Protocols, 101, 107, 133-134
Uqubbah, 116, 134
Ur, 100, 114, 116, 124-125, 130, 184
Ur Junction, 99, 103, 114, 116, 307-308
Union of Soviet Socialist Republics, 473n, 477, 508, 552
Vaux, Gp Capt H.M., 554, 591n
Vaux Trophy, 591n
VE Day, 469, 477
Vernon, Flt Lt, 301-302, 304, 321, 326
Vichy France, 275, 277, 288-289, 314-315, 318-320, 324-331, 448, 477, 479
Vichy French Air Force, 210, 324-325
Vichy French Army:
 1st Light Desert Coy, 323,
 2nd Light Desert Coy, 324,
 6th Regt, Foreign Legion, 318, 320, 323-324
Villiers, D., 431
Vincent, Col-Cdt B., 75n-76n
Vincent, Sqn Ldr F.J., 110, 114, 127n
Vincent, AVM S.F., 143, 145-146, 162n
Vologda Railway, 126n
Wadi Akarit, 442-443
Wadi al Batin, 103, 118, 122, 129, 131, 136, 138-139, 595
Wadi al Qaur, 578-582
Wadi Faregh, 359
Wadi Melussa, 93
Wadi Miyah, 93
Wadi Natrun, 396, 405-406, 412
Wadi Sirhan, 39, 43, 46n, 145-146
Wadi Tamet, 429
Wadi Tiban, 519
Wadi Zem Zem, 430
Wadi Zigzaou, 438-439
Wahhab, Mohammed ibn Abd al, 37, 46n
Wahhabis, 37-40, 42, 43-45, 46n, 157, 312n, 572
Walker, Flt Lt H., 150
Walker, W.B., 558, 568, 576, 579, 581, 583, 586, 588
War Office, 1-3, 5-6, 9, 24, 210, 230, 236, 548
Ward, Cpl, 77n
Ward, Flt Lt A., 82
Wardle, Flt Lt C., 65
Warrenger, AC, 492
Warsaw Pact, 597
Washington DC, 354n, 473n
Waters, Flt Lt R.C.J., 281, 299
Wauchope, Gen Sir Arthur, 205-206
Wavell, Gen Sir Archibald, 208, 234, 237, 242n, 243, 245-247, 250-251, 257, 261, 265, 275, 290, 308-309, 313, 318-319, 321, 332, 335-336, 353n, 356, 548
Webb, LAC, 349, 355n
Webb, Sgt C.H., 552
Weeks, Flt Lt, 418
Weir, Sir Michael, 578-579, 593n
Welham, Flt Lt, 250, 254, 264, 346, 351
Wentworth, Sgt M., 152, 164-165, 170-173, 232, 235, 277, 279, 286, 310n
West African Field Force, 126n
West, Lt-Col J., 402n
West, Fg Off N.A., 93
Westbrook, AC2, 45n
Western (Wailing) Wall, 195
Western Aden Protectorate, 515-516, 518, 533-534, 543-545, 548
Western Front, The, xvi, 7, 94, 126n, 354n
Western Hadhramaut, 534
Whistler, Sqn Ldr H.A., 114
Whitbourne, Cpl, 279
White Hart Road, 20
White, Flt Lt R.N.J., 217, 224, 242n, 248
Whitley, Gp Capt E., 345, 355n, 418
Whittle, Flt Lt G.G., 547
Wigglesworth, Flt Lt H., 145
Wigley, LAC, 325
Wilders Gap, 438-439
Williams, LAC L., 242n
Williams, Sgt, 380, 445
Williams, Fg Off O., 141n
Willock, AVM R.P., 23, 55, 57, 76n, 467
Wilson, Lt-Gen Sir Henry, 3, 5-6, 10n
Winch, Flt Lt J., 69
Winnipeg, 333n
Witherow, Air Cdre M.S., 594n
Wood, LAC, 325
Woodhouse, Sqn Ldr J., 137-138
Wormwood Scrubs, xviin
Wyatt, P.K., 524-526, 528-531
Yadude, 39-40, 42
Yahia, Imam, 516, 520
Yard-Buller, Maj, 143
Yatta, 232
Yawar, Aijal el, 91-92
Yaxley, Gp Capt R.G., 211, 220, 233, 242n, 449n
Yemen, 516, 518, 523, 538-539, 541, 543, 548
Yemen Light Infantry, 549n
Yezidis, 50
Yorke Moore, Flt Lt T.P., 17-18, 31, 33-35, 37, 45n, 500, 551
Yorkshire, 375n
Zaidi, 516, 518
Zakho, 58, 71-74, 90, 466
Zakho Pass, 61, 71-72, 77n
Zambia, 597
Zayyad, 100, 134
Zerqa, 143, 145, 148, 151, 194, 206, 492, 551
Zeylmans, Flt Lt G.N., 547, 550n
Zingibar, 544
Zionism, 4
Zionists, 192, 492
Ziza, 39-40, 42-44, 46n, 147, 312n
Zuara, 450n
Zubair, 96, 107, 109, 118, 304, 331
Zubeiya Pass, 149